ROUTLEDGE LIBRARY EDITIONS:
EARLY WESTERN RESPONSES
TO SOVIET RUSSIA

Volume 7

RUSSIA IN TRANSITION

RUSSIA IN TRANSITION

A Business Man's Appraisal

ELISHA M. FRIEDMAN

Routledge
Taylor & Francis Group
LONDON AND NEW YORK

First published in Great Britain in 1933 by George Allen & Unwin Ltd

This edition first published in 2018
by Routledge
2 Park Square, Milton Park, Abingdon, Oxon OX14 4RN

and by Routledge
711 Third Avenue, New York, NY 10017

Routledge is an imprint of the Taylor & Francis Group, an informa business

British Library Cataloguing in Publication Data
A catalogue record for this book is available from the British Library

ISBN: 978-1-138-04993-2 (Set)
ISBN: 978-1-315-11072-1 (Set) (ebk)
ISBN: 978-1-138-08547-3 (Volume 7) (hbk)
ISBN: 978-1-315-11129-2 (Volume 7) (ebk)

Publisher's Note
The publisher has gone to great lengths to ensure the quality of this reprint but points out that some imperfections in the original copies may be apparent.

Disclaimer
The publisher has made every effort to trace copyright holders and would welcome correspondence from those they have been unable to trace.

Russia in Transition

A Business Man's Appraisal

BY ELISHA M. FRIEDMAN

London
GEORGE ALLEN & UNWIN LTD
Museum Street

FIRST PUBLISHED IN GREAT BRITAIN IN 1933

PRINTED IN U. S. A. BY THE VAIL-BALLOU PRESS

TO

MY FRIEND

O. F. WEBER

Preface

In 1931 the Union of Socialist Soviet Republics finished what was termed "The Third and Decisive Year of the Five-Year Plan," which really decided nothing. Will the giant new plants work, or will they be "white elephants"? The plants are built but will they produce the goods? Large credits fall due—will they be paid? Consumers' good are very scant—will they be supplied? Hopes have been held out—will they be realized? These are the questions to which the Russian masses are calling for an answer. The present state of affairs cannot continue. The Soviet Union is evolving. Russia is in transition.

The social structure throughout the world is quaking. As we go to our daily tasks, the numbing effect of routine prevents us from realizing the very historic character of the days in which we are living. Perhaps it is impossible at close range to have a proper perspective on the overwhelming events of our time. Abbé Sieyès, the brilliant pamphleteer of the French Revolution, once gave terse expression to this lack of appreciation of the significance of the events of one's day. When he was asked: "What did you do during the Terror?" he answered: "I lived." A similar answer would be given by the overwhelming majority of the present generation concerning the world crisis.

In order to get a perspective on the Soviet régime it is necessary to look upon it, not as an event of the day, but as a development of history. And I asked myself, if I were living in 1789, would I not go to France to observe the revolution and its social consequences? It was such a viewpoint that aroused in me a keen desire to go to Russia and see with my own eyes the catastrophe, the terror, the waste, the miracle, and the travail in the emerging of the new order.

The Russian scene is as fascinating to the student as a three-ring circus to a child. In fact, the prime difficulty, as in life itself, is to limit one's field of observation in order to avoid confusion and distraction. The Soviet experiment draws on every aspect of one's technical training, business experience, and social and economic studies. It is of double value to the western world, positively in its high social idealism and aims, and negatively in its cruel and wasteful method and procedure. The visitor, on leaving the country, cannot help hoping that the western world will progress toward a happier social scheme with less injustice to the thinking classes and with less suffering of the masses. This is the challenge to constructive statesmanship and broad-minded business leadership in America and Europe.

I had long been greatly interested in the social upheaval in the U.S.S.R. In 1922, during a year of travel on business in Europe, I visited Helsingfors, Finland. Being only fourteen hours from Leningrad I called upon the American consul to inquire about a prospective trip to the Soviet Union. He replied: "We know of no such country." There were great difficulties in obtaining a permit to travel or visa. The spectral posters appealing for succor from famine and disease, then prevailing in Russia, which lined the walls of the Soviet consul's office relieved my disappointment. During several visits to Europe thereafter, I was able to follow Russian developments only at a distance. I finally visited Russia during part of July and August of 1930. My prime purpose was to study industry and management rather than the sociological or cultural aspects of the Soviet experiment.

Upon my return there were many inquiries by friends. Some asked for a memorandum on my trip. I began to write it and found that it grew in the process. Ultimately the report developed into the present volume.

The object of the book is to inform and to clarify. It aims to throw light on affairs in Russia rather than to reflect heat of prejudices concerning Russia. It attempts to appraise rather than commend, to judge rather than condemn. Most of the books on Russia are either propaganda by Soviet sympathizers or by the Soviet government itself or by interests antagonistic to the Soviets. That this book has not fallen into either error may be presumed from the criticism that the manuscript received from partisans on both sides.

The book advocates steps toward conditional recognition of Russia, that is, provided she pays her debts. One-tenth of the world's population is underconsuming in that country, and for lack of credit it is forcing exports, thus becoming doubly a potent factor in the world depression. There would seem to be neither economic justification nor legal sanction for the policy of our government in refusing to consider terms on which American recognition might be extended.

The book is primarily an independent and scientific study, and is without relation to my business activities. I have had no business interests involving Russian affairs. Neither am I of Russian extraction, nor have I any relatives or friends in Russia. I went to Russia with an open mind, though it obviously is impossible to eliminate the effects of a lifetime of so-called capitalist training and thinking. When I presented to the Soviet officials some of the criticisms cited in this book, the invariable answer was that I was suffering from a capitalist bias, and that I was thinking in terms of what they called "capitalist ideology." This was particularly the case in my discussions with the representatives of the State Bank on the question of what seemed by all clear signs to be outright inflation.

The bases for the material in this book were several scores of interviews with officials of the government in the several commissariats, with directors and officials of industry, agriculture, labor, transportation, and finance and in the State Bank, the Supreme Economic Council, and the State Planning Commission. In addition, I spoke in Russian, through an interpreter, and in other languages to Russian engineers and university professors, plant foremen, laborers, students, and private citizens. American and other foreign engineers and journalists were particularly valuable sources of information on a wide variety of subjects. Immigrants into Russia, a veritable gathering of the radical clans from the four corners of the earth, presented the view of the faithful who returned "home" to live in the land of their dreams. Emigrés from Russia, who left their fortunes and some of their relatives behind, presented the opposite point of view. Trade representatives of the Soviet government in New York, officials of the Amtorg Trading Corporation and of the Soviet Union Information Bureau in Washington, have been of help in furnishing translations of original documents and reports. Last, but not least, I have discussed the contents of this book with a few officials of our government. Obviously, these many names cannot be mentioned or the views quoted, generally speaking. However, in some specific cases, cited in the text, exception is made. I have also drawn occasionally on the writings of Messrs. William H. Chamberlin, Walter Duranty, and Louis Fischer and on conversations with them in Moscow and again with the last two in New York.

Through the courtesy of the Soviet official travel bureau, Intourist, every request I made was granted. There is a notion abroad that the Russians try to hide the unfavorable aspects and to display the favorable ones. But one can find no evidence to support such a view. The poor and inadequate clothing and food are noticeable everywhere. The large department store in Moscow with its great tiers of vacant shelves and empty upper floors roped off, the almost bare grocery stores, the queues, the lack of soap, towels, etc., the miles of cut lumber piled high awaiting loading on boats in the port of Leningrad, the junk and rubbish sold as merchandise in the open market place, the high prices prevailing, the torn and threadbare overcoat of Lenin displayed in the museum—nothing is hidden from the foreigner.

The newspapers, instead of concealing defects, advertise them for the purpose of denouncing bureaucracy and "impersonalism." Some of these revelations of failure are cited in the chapter on industry. When I challenged the figures on real wages presented by the representative of the Commissariat of Labor, an American sympathizer with the Soviets traveling with a group of economists tried to hush what he regarded as an embarrassing question. But the Soviet official replied boldly and frankly. When Charles E. Stuart, of Stuart, James & Cooke, American consulting engineers to the Soviet government, was asked to study the coal industry, Vice-Commissar V. I. Mezhlauk instructed him to be unsparing in his investigation. He was. He criticized the very fundamentals of management and policy, and expected to be discharged as a result. Instead the Commissar had 10,000 copies of his report printed immediately and circulated to all executives and foremen in the coal industry and related fields. When Walter Duranty asked the censor whether the contents of this adverse report could be cabled to America, permission was promptly granted.

Except for a new section of the Putilov Iron Works in Leningrad, factories were open for inspection. Statistics and accounts were made available unexpectedly. The Steel Trust presented the detailed income and balance sheet, as well as the operating statistics for the last month on record, with comparisons for the preceding month and the preceding year for the trust as a whole as well as for each of the several individual plants. What private corporation in our country would be so candid with strangers, or even with their stockholders? Only then did I realize what one American correspondent in Moscow stated, that he had less censorship in Moscow than he had in New York.

To round out the personal impressions obtained in Russia I followed the documents issued by the Soviet government, by the British government and by the International Labor Office in Geneva. The newspapers in Russia, which are government-owned and official, give full and frank statements of "self-criticism" and the reports of Workers' and Peasants' Committees on Inspection and the statistical data on industrial production. The newspapers are keen to ferret out faults in industry, fearless in the exposure of error, and severe in flaying mismanagement. They are valuable source material.

In general, Russian statistics seem correct, and they check with each other during successive years and with related figures. However, there are occasional exceptions. Besides, the form of statistical information sometimes changes so as to make comparisons invalid. Not least, several versions are sometimes presented so that, for example, the Five-Year Plan is presented with a normal, minimum, and maximum variant. Figures on national income differ in several parts of the official version of the Five-Year Plan.

There is some statistical inconsistency concerning the question of present and pre-war real wages and cost of living. Judging by the clothes and food of the people in the Soviet Union today it would seem that, regardless of statistics, the standards of living, in the cities at least, are below the pre-war level, taking into account the fact that supplies are now rationed and that sometimes even the amount allotted on a ration is really not available.

Obviously there are difficulties in attempting to depict a scene shifting as rapidly as that of Soviet Russia. In the interval between the writing of the first draft of the manuscript and the revising of the printer's proof, the future tense had to be replaced by the past tense in several cases, as in the return of private trade in agriculture and the restoration of "small-time industry." Prophecy had become history.

These difficulties are increased by the frequent reversals of policy, as for example the reabolition of private trade in the autumn of 1932, only a few months after it had been reintroduced. Such a violent *volte-face* is a reflection of deep-seated and fundamental instability. Powerful economic forces are in contest. And social theory and political credo waver continually. Heterodoxy becomes orthodoxy. Expediency becomes principle.

This book covers a wide range of the activities of Soviet Russia. Part III, dealing with the Five-Year Plan, industry, agriculture, labor, banking, and the budget, should appeal particularly to engineers, accountants, and business men. Parts I, II, and IV may be of some interest to the sociologist and the general reader. Part V deals with legal and political matters and international affairs. Because of the different fields covered, the style of presentation must necessarily vary. In the appraisal of aims, method, and results there is some repetition from a new perspective of matters treated in detail in other sections. For these repetitions the indulgence of the reader is requested. The conclusions as to results and forecasts are necessarily tentative and subject to the contingencies of such a vast experiment. The Postscript attempts to summarize the book, and the Analytical Table of Contents gives a survey of the entire field. The indexes should aid in the use of the extensive and varied material assembled in the book.

The study was not made at leisure or in scholarly halls, but under difficulty, beginning with the autumn of 1930 after business hours into the early morning, during week-ends, and vacations in 1931 and 1932. If there are few evidences of this pressure of work, it is because of the reading and criticism of the text by engineers, officials of the United States Government, officials of Soviet bureaus and organizations in Moscow, New York, and Washington, university teachers, research students, journalists, and bankers, to whom I am indebted. Some of them have first-hand knowledge of the Russian situation through long residence or tours of Russia, either for business or study, or have been following the Russian situation in connection with their work: Mr. Adolph A. Berle, Jr., of the Faculty of Law, Columbia University, and Mrs. Berle; Mr. B. V. Cohen; Mrs. Vera M. Dean, Head of the Russian Division of the Research Staff of the Foreign Policy Association; Mr. Lawrence Dennis, formerly of the United States Diplomatic Service, author of *Is Capitalism Doomed?* and writer on foreign affairs and economics; Mr. Louis Fischer, author of *The Soviets in World Affairs, Machines and Men in Russia,* etc., and Moscow correspondent of *The Nation;* Mr. L. R. Gottlieb and Dr. Harry Hollitscher, of New York; Dr. Lewis L. Lorwin, of the Brookings Institution, Washington, D. C., formerly Moscow correspondent of the Chicago *Daily News,* frequent visitor to Russia, writer and lecturer on Soviet affairs; Mr. Eugene Lyons, Moscow correspondent of the United Press; Mr. Lucius W. Mayer, mining engineer, member of the firm of Rogers, Mayer & Ball, who visited Russia with me in 1930; Mr. Stephen Paul of Hallgarten & Co., bankers, New York; Mr. James H. Pierce, member of Stuart, James & Cooke, coal engineers and consultants to the Soviet Government; Miss Inez Pollak of the staff of the *Encyclopedia of Social Sciences,* who was a member of a group of American economists studying Russian conditions in the summer of 1930; Mr. Paul Scheffer, author of *Seven Years in Soviet Russia,* and correspondent of the *Berliner Tageblatt,* formerly in Moscow, now in London; Mr. E. Tobenkin, formerly Moscow correspondent of the *Herald-Tribune* and author of a recent series of studies on Soviet Russia; Dr. H. Parker Willis, who visited Russia in 1928; and a few friends who prefer to remain anonymous but to whom my debt is no less, including a professor of modern history, a banker in Central Europe, and a vice-president of a New York trust company in charge of foreign credits.

In the section on recognition I am indebted to Professors Ernst Feilchenfeld and Phillip C. Jessup, of the departments of international law of Harvard and Columbia Universities, for the reading of the manuscript and for helpful comment and suggestions, and to Messrs. Wilber Stammler and Samuel M.

Koenigsberg, students at the Columbia Law School, for their kind aid with citations and legal references. To my brother, Dr. E. David Friedman, professor of neurology at University and Bellevue Hospital Medical College, who has stimulated my thought concerning the psychological approach to social and economic questions, I am indebted for suggestions relating to the chapter on "The Soviet Mind." Mr. Sam A. Lewisohn, chairman of the American Management Association, was kind enough to give me the benefit of his observations on a trip in Russia, taken with a group of American business men under the auspices of the American-Russian Chamber of Commerce.

Some of the Russian material was made available to me through my guide in Russia. Official documents were translated and references verified from original sources by economists in New York reading Russian and having divers views on the Soviets. But I alone am responsible for the conclusions and ideas expressed here. Indeed, representatives of the Soviet Government dissented vigorously from the opinions in some sections of the book. Needless to say, officials of our government do not subscribe to the views on recognition. I am again indebted to Mr. Otto Wilson of Washington, D. C., who painstakingly checked the statistics, prepared the manuscript for the printer, read the proofs, and compiled the index.

E. M. F.

165 Broadway, New York City
October 1, 1932

THE HISTORIC COURSE OF REVOLUTION

MANY evils, no doubt, were produced by the civil war. They were the price of our liberty. Has the acquisition been worth the sacrifice? . . . We deplore the outrages which accompany revolutions. But the more violent the outrages, the more we feel that a revolution was necessary. The violence of these outrages . . . will be proportioned to the oppression and degradation under which the people have been accustomed to live. . . .

Thus it was in our civil war. The heads of the church and state reaped only that which they had sown. The government had prohibited free discussion; it had done its best to keep the people unacquainted with their duties and their rights. The retribution was just and natural. If our rulers suffered from popular ignorance it was because they themselves had taken away the key of knowledge. If they were assailed with blind fury it was because they had exacted an equally blind submission.

It is the character of such revolutions that we always see the worst of them first. Till men have been some time free they know not how to use their freedom. The final and permanent fruits of liberty are wisdom, moderation, and mercy. Its immediate effects are often atrocious crimes, conflicting errors, skepticism on points the most clear, dogmatism on points the most mysterious. . . . It is just at this crisis that its enemies love to exhibit it. . . . If men are to wait for liberty till they become wise and good in slavery they may indeed wait forever.

There is only one cure for the evils which newly acquired freedom produces; and that cure is freedom. . . . The blaze of truth and liberty may at first dazzle nations which have become half-blind in the house of bondage. But let them gaze on, and they will soon be able to bear it. In a few years men learn to reason. The extreme violence of opinion subsides. Hostile theories correct each other. The scattered elements of truth cease to contend, and begin to coalesce. And at length a system of justice and order is educed out of the chaos.

—THOMAS B. MACAULAY, *Essay on Milton*,
describing the English Revolution of 1688.

Contents

PART FIVE: WANTED—AN AMERICAN POLICY TOWARD RUSSIA

APPENDIX

Analytical Table of Contents

NOTE: *The numbered references throughout the book refer to the notes at the end of the text (pages 583–599) and relate only to the sources from which the information is taken.*

PART FIVE: WANTED—AN AMERICAN POLICY TOWARD RUSSIA

PART ONE

POSTSCRIPT AND SUMMARY

Though the mills of God grind slowly
Yet they grind exceeding small.
—Friedrich von Logau, *Retribution.*

You can never turn over any old falsehood without
a terrible squirming and scattering of the horrid
little population that dwells under it.
—Oliver Wendell Holmes, *The Autocrat of the Breakfast Table.*

Time and arithmetic will do the rest.
—Justice Louis D. Brandeis, *Other People's Money.*

CHAPTER I

PERSPECTIVES

A. Point of View

Americans living in Russia for five or ten years develop strikingly contrasting views concerning the Soviet Union. They become either ardent believers or devastating skeptics. Apparently long residence is not helpful in developing dispassionate judgment. Three American correspondents, for example, have lived in Russia for a number of years. One is optimistic and believes that the experiment will succeed. Another is pessimistic and is willing to name the date of the breakdown. The third cautiously suspends judgment and cites a pro and con for every declaration. In fact, opinions on the Russian situation are based not on fact but on prejudice. A judgment on Russia reveals not merely a capacity for observation but also the emotional bias of the individual.

It is not strange that this should be so. The scene is very large. There is much to see. Time is required to digest impressions. Something tremendous is going on—one feels that everywhere. Judgment is distorted because of the strange contrasts and contradictions. Besides, from what point of view can one appraise the situation? To judge what is happening one must attempt to understand the conditions that generated the revolution. From the perspective of pre-war Russia, the scene is revealed in a new light.

To the business man Soviet Russia stands as a model of incompetence and inefficiency. To the social worker it is a thrilling experiment in social adjustment. To the laborer it is an attempt at rule by the hitherto disinherited. To some sentimentalists who sojourn there for a few days it seems a beautiful dream. To the sightseer it is a grand show. And to the tourist *de luxe* it is a damnable discomfort. But there are offsets. When the tourists of the *S.S. Carinthia* arrived in Moscow, the writer was warned that he would have to vacate his room at the Grand Hotel, and that there were no other facilities available. Fortunately the Quaker House had a wooden cot which was to be vacant for a few days, and thither he moved his belongings. In the morning when he saw his neighbor, Mr. Albert Rhys Williams, breakfasting on tea, black bread, and a slice of dried salamiwurst and asked if this was the usual breakfast menu, Mr. Williams replied: "When you are conquering a wilderness you do not expect Ritz Hotel fare. The Soviets are pioneering in a new world. The comforts of the old order cannot be expected."

The American tourist is particularly impressed in places by the worshipful admiration of the Russian masses for America, which saved them during the famine and which has great factories, and whose laborers drive their own cars to work. Once when a boatload of tourists arrived at Moscow, preempting most of the available automobiles of the city, several thousand Russians, to whom the Americans were a sight, congregated in the great square in front of the Grand Hotel to see the phenomenon and to admire—much in the manner of the giraffe in the circus which looked down curiously at the farmer with eighteen children who came to gaze at him.

The scope of this study will necessarily be limited. It will not deal with many phases of Russian life, though they are interesting, such as penology, medicine, social welfare, home life, social relations, law and justice, art, drama, music, and literature. The psychological, educational, and political aspects will be touched on only in so far as they are linked with the main topic, the economic aspects of Russia. This book will be an attempt to study those elements of Russian life, such as industrial efficiency, business administration, banking, accounting, and public finance, which may throw some light on the question whether the revolution can continue in its present phase.

B. Historic Background and Precedents

The communist dictatorship in Russia is the outgrowth of the despotism that preceded it. Revolutions occur where slow and gradual change and adjustment is checked. Resistance to new ideas and repression provoke revolt and sudden disturbance—witness Christianity, Mohammedanism, the Reformation, the French Revolution. History reveals social upheavals as the result of new liberating ideas which challenge a static régime. The Russian Revolution is an historic phenomenon. Just as the growth of a child does not progress at a uniform rate, so the growth of society is not uniform. Revolutions and crises are its growing pains. With the advance of democracy in western Europe and America it was inevitable that a despotic Tsarist régime which could not bend should break. Historic determinism made some overturn inevitable. The democratic régime of Kerensky and Milyukov was too weak to prevail in the post-war anarchy. Bolshevism resulted.

Bolshevism is Russian and not international. It is a development growing out of specific Russian conditions. For this reason its doctrines have not found root in other countries with different traditions. And also for this reason it is unlikely that the Bolshevik idea will gain a foothold in other countries as the new "heresy hunters" fear, despite the threats of Soviet propagandists.

Bolshevism is the outgrowth of over two hundred years of Russian oppression. It is a form of social behavior. It cannot therefore be transplanted to communities not subjected to the same repression. In the Moscow Museum of the Revolution there are records for the literate and pictures for the illiterate, describing the revolts in Russia of the past two hundred and fifty years. The uprising of Stenka Razin in the Volga Valley about 1670, the peasant revolt of Pugachev about a hundred years later, the attempt of the Dekabrists in 1825 under the influence of the French Revolution to establish a constitutional assembly and to free the serfs, the rise of liberal revolutionary hopes, the first Social Democratic protest gathering in St. Petersburg in 1876, the First Social Democratic Congress in Minsk in 1897, the Bloody Sunday of 1905, when a demonstration of unarmed workers, with their wives and children, gathered in front of the Winter Palace to petition the Tsar, was fired on by order of Grand Duke Vladimir and 1500 persons were killed or wounded—these are the antecedent crises which precipitated the revolution. The serfdom of the peasants until 1861 and the grinding taxes constitute the background for the passionate hatred of authority which the westerner senses in the electrical atmosphere of Russia. Admittedly, philosophic communism was a determining factor, with its elements of utopianism, rationalism, pacific anarchism, ethics, and the theory of the class war. But the mainspring of the revolution seems not to have been fundamental western democratic ideals, so much as hatred of the Tsarist régime and resentment toward the institutions supporting the old order, the Church, marriage as a sacrament, and private property. The suppression of minority peoples, the persecution of the labor unions, and the crushing of peasant uprisings stand as a background and furnish the key to an understanding of Soviet policies and popular doctrines.

A psychologist discovers several interesting phenomena concerning the

Russian mentality. Because the Soviet leaders publicly profess a sense of inferiority to the west they build great plants to outstrip the west. Because of the handicap in the race for industrialization the Soviet leaders plan for a hasty and forced development under the Five-Year Plan. A white heat of emotion pervades Russia with respect to the plan for industrialization and with respect to their communist ideals. Can such fervor persist? An incandescent lamp subjected to excessive voltage wears out the sooner. It is also a psychological law, that the intenser the emotion the briefer it is. Again, it is a generalization in psychology that no two emotions can occupy the center of consciousness simultaneously. The stronger drives out the weaker. The zeal for communism has been displaced by the zeal for industrialization. Cherished political ideals have been subordinated to the imperious demands of factory efficiency.

Many of the phenomena described by visiting foreigners are not Bolshevik but rather old Russian. The extensive spy system, the secret police and secret courts, and the political executions prevalent in Bolshevik Russia are the survivals of Tsardom. No people can liberate itself from its past so quickly. Social memories and inherited institutions cannot be wiped out in one generation. Russia has been accustomed to poverty. And under the Soviet régime the populace tolerates poverty as a present necessity, though the resources are rich and should provide abundance. Because government has been exercised by an hereditary autocracy in the past, Russia today consents to government by the new autocracy. The people have had no training or preparation for liberty or democracy. And therefore they do not understand or achieve either. The Russia of today is partly the product of Tsarist psychology. A new Russian character is being created. A new social heredity is being built up.

Richard Hakluyt (1553–1616), the English writer on travel, describes the subjugation of the masses in Russia under Czar Ivan the Terrible (1533–84). History seems to be repeating itself.

> But all this is done of all the people so willingly at the Emperour's commandement. . . . Nowe the Emperour having taken these goods into his hands, bestoweth them among his courtiers.[1]
>
> Men may say that these men are in wonderfull great awe, and obedience, that thus one must give and grant his goods which he hath bene scraping and scratching for all his life to be at his Prince's pleasure and commandement. . . .

In defense of wholesale slaughter by the Cheka, and subsequently by the Ogpu, Soviet spokesmen point out that from 1906 to 1913 over 3000 persons were shot by court martial during the premiership of Stolypin. Decision by bullets rather than by ballots seems an accepted political device of the Slav. The British had their bloodless revolution of 1688. In more recent times Germany cast out its rulers practically without violence. Even the volatile Spaniards effected a revolution in 1931 practically without bloodshed. The character of the revolution is not based entirely on a biological heredity but rather on environmental factors. Because the oppression in Russia was more severe than in Germany or Spain, the recoil was more violent.

"Will the Slav temperament make it possible for Russia to get down to business and develop able mechanics, plant managers, and business executives?" is the question asked by foreign engineers. It would seem that there is nothing psychologically or biologically lacking in the Russians to prevent them from doing so. Immigrant Russians have risen to high positions in plants in the United States. Furthermore, industrial Britain asked the same question concerning Germany in 1870, and the industrial world did so concerning Japan in 1900.

Soviet Russia is developing the mental traits of youth—enthusiasm, idealism, riotous imagination, tactlessness, even cruelty, impracticability, and frankness. This frankness goes to extreme lengths in the devastating "self-criticism" with which they point out their own weaknesses. The notion current abroad that the Russians are trying to hide their defects and show only the favorable aspects is not borne out by the experience of visitors in Russia. The Five-Year Plan provides an outlet for the abounding energy of a youthful nation.

Some of the psychological reactions are infantile; a child will attempt the impossible and then if it fails place the blame on some one else. This has been a characteristic reaction in Russia. Engineers are brought up on charges for failing to achieve what no mature mind would attempt. Again, there is a certain paranoid reaction toward the outside world. For example, after the visit of Premier Laval to Mr. Hoover, *Pravda* wrote:

> Everything indicates Hoover and Laval talked about the formation of a united front against the Soviet. Apparently French imperialism has received American permission to form an anti-Soviet bloc, with the backing and direction of the United States.[2]

Or, similarly, Karl Radek, a Soviet journalist, writing from Geneva, in February 1932, criticized Tardieu's plan for an international police force as a nucleus for a capitalist army against the Soviets.[3]

C. Soviet Aims

The Soviet aim is a mixture of communism and socialism. The Soviet zigzags in economic policy, the "strategic retreats" reflect the oscillations between these two philosophies. The distinction between them was neatly stated by J. Ramsay Macdonald:

> Communism presupposes a common store of wealth which is to be drawn on by the individual consumer, not in accordance with services rendered but in response to "a human right to sustenance." . . . The distributive philosophy of communism contains the difference between that system and socialism. "From all according to their ability; to each according to his needs" is a communist, not a socialist, formula. The socialist would insert "services" for "needs." They both agree about the common stock: they disagree regarding the nature of what should be the effective claim of the individual to share in it. Socialists think of distribution through the channels of personal income; communists think of distribution through the channels of human rights to live. Hence, socialism requires some medium of exchange, whether it is pounds sterling or labor notes; communism requires no such medium of exchange. . . . Socialism accepts the idea of income, subject to two safeguards. It must be adequate to afford a satisfactory standard of life and it must represent services given. . . . Communism only considers the sum total required by an individual to satisfy his wants.[4]

Macdonald points out other distinctions, as that "the idea of the state is essential to socialism." But Lenin predicted the disappearance of the state. Communism and socialism likewise differ on the abolition of private property and the need for class war.

The philosophy of the Soviets is utopianism. It is the product of dreamers in exile, Karl Marx, a German exile in England, and Vladimir Lenin, a Russian exile in Switzerland, with little experience in practical political affairs—closet philosophers. These men contrived forms of social organization which had never worked anywhere or even been tested. The leaders of Soviet Russia are doctrinaires. They are not motivated primarily by love for the masses. In fact their policy often indicates contempt for the masses. But they are passionately dedicated to a political doctrine. They would transform into a communist society a people a hundred years behind Europe in political education and industrial maturity. They would develop this primitive community into a late product of social evolution featuring community ownership and control and the abolition of private gain. To quote from the Declaration of Rights of the Third All-Russian Soviet Congress, held in Leningrad on January 23, 1918, the program is the ending of "exploitation of men by men, the entire abolition of the division of the people into classes, the suppression of exploiters, the establishment of a socialist society and the victory of socialism in all lands" (*Malaya Encyclopedia,* II: 791).

The Soviets' aims affect not merely political life. They are creating not merely a new form of government. They are trying to initiate an entirely new industrial régime. They are trying to socialize agriculture, to develop new social relations in the home. To transmit this heritage, they are developing a new education. To realize their ideals no method is regarded as too ruthless. Fanatically convinced that they have a mission and have found salvation for the world they would, like a militant church, proceed to spread their doctrine by the sword. The conversion of the world is the creed of the Soviets. The rest of the world calls it a war against civilization.

At the cost of great suffering to this generation the group in power has determined to establish a communist régime. Out of this several by-products result. In order to socialize agriculture it must be mechanized. Therefore tractor factories are established. Machinery for these factories must be imported. To pay for these imports of machinery, foreign credits are needed; these are obtained by merchandise exports. The western world calls it dumping and the ruining of foreign markets. Meantime the Russian people must dispense with even necessities of life.

The observer is led to inquire what should be the aim of the state. Should it be the welfare and happiness of its citizens? This fundamental question in politics has had two opposed answers. Under a liberal régime the state is the common servant, and the individual is supreme. "The government is the servant (of the citizens) rather than the master." [5] Under tyrannies and dictatorships, from ancient Greece to present-day Italy and Russia, the state is supreme and the individual is its servant. But the ruler usually regards himself as the symbol of the state. *"L'état, c'est moi,"* said Louis XIV. "Politics, that is I," says Mussolini in reply to the Vatican's protest on education.[6]

Greek history reveals the ebb and flow of the forces of democracy and oligarchy. In the political world there seems to be a long-term cycle or rhythm fluctuating between the rule of the many and the tyranny of the few. With the rise of the factory system, the oppression of the masses resulted in their struggle for control, and the curtailing of the power of the industrial leaders. The dictatorship of the Kremlin should be succeeded by the sovereignty of the people. Again, for a brief period in the Russian Revolution, the mob ruled, but now there is emerging a new order in which the goods and satisfactions of life bear some proportion to ability and productivity. Indeed the physical structure of society depends upon the distribution of mental attainments throughout society. The distribution, as given by one authority, is of interest:

DISTRIBUTION OF INTELLECTUAL CAPACITY [7]

Class	*Percentage*	
Genius and near genius	0.25	
Very superior	6.75	
Superior	13.00	
High average	30.00	50%
Low average	30.00	
Dull	13.00	
Border line	6.00	
Moron	0.75	
Imbecile	0.25	50%

Such inequality of mental endowment determines the character of society. Will the numerical minority of superior mentality be offset by an equal number of subnormals, or dominated by the larger number of lesser intelligence and ability? Yet another implication of this statistical array is that until eugenic measures are taken to diminish the inferior strains and to increase the superior, society should preserve even the lowest class above some minimum standard of existence. This apparently is the technique of the Soviet régime. Social insurance sets the minimum level of life high enough to prevent discontent and revolt, but there is no freedom of opportunity for the gifted dissenter. Recent trends in Soviet Russia show the conflict between the individual and the state.

Yet regardless of the answer to this political question, it would seem to be unjust to oppress the living generation for the benefit of one not yet born. As one of the American livestock experts, advising the Russian government, is reported to have stated to Stalin in the spring of 1932: "Pigs will die if they are not treated right. They are not like human beings, who can stand suffering and adjust themselves."

Can any ultimate benefits to later generations compensate for the tragedy and suffering that is actually borne by the present generation? The very ruthlessness of the Soviet method raises the question whether it is based on a desire to benefit the masses or rather at any cost to realize a doctrinaire concept of society.

All Russia is living in the future. A glorious life-to-be is promised to compensate for the drab life that is. The aims are heroic. A new political system, freedom of thought, the emancipation of the individual, a new industrial system, abolition of social classes, a more equitable division of the good things of the world, and an accelerated industrialism—here indeed are vast objectives!

To accomplish them how great are the difficulties—the human material a people largely illiterate, a cumbersome government machinery, a lack of industrial tradition, and an inadequate administrative machine both in government and in industry! But the assets are many—zeal of the leaders that partakes of a religious fervor, patience and stolidity of the people, capacity to suffer under a low standard of living, submission to poverty and willingness of large numbers to support the government in the experiment.

D. Soviet Principles

The Soviet revolution seeks not merely economic freedom but freedom in the several aspects of life. The struggle for freedom is part of an historic process. From the dawn of history mankind has attempted to distribute power and freedom. The landmarks of history indicate the steps in this process. The kings rebelled against the pope. The nobles fought to abridge the power of the king. The rise of representative government was a struggle by the middle classes to abridge the power of the nobles. The Soviets attempted to reach the final stage of this progress without passing through the intermediate evolution. They shifted the emphasis to the masses of the workers. The change was a leveling process, but it leveled down for the average, not up. The theory was to "take from each according to his means and to give to each according to his needs," but the needs are many and the means are few.

The Bolsheviki had an impelling idea, the Marxian doctrine, but there was neither guide nor compass in the uncharted seas. At first, principles of communism were put into operation. Land was nationalized. The banks were abolished. Money was no longer the legal instrument of exchange, and such currency as remained in circulation depreciated to an infinitesimal fraction of its former gold value. Securities were made state property. Price was regarded not as a part of the mechanism of distribution to satisfy the consumer's needs but rather as a source of profit and a cause of economic inequalities between men. Without a price system the state attempted to supply the needs of the community—necessities and luxuries, material and cultural.

As in the colony of Virginia in 1607 the doctrine was: "Only those that work shall eat." Foodstuffs were taken from the peasants by requisition. Distribution was obstructed. Trade disappeared. But this attempt to apply pure communist theory plunged the land into anarchy and ferment. Then came a series of compromises with capitalist ideas in order to restore a semblance of economic organization. The right of private property was recognized. Money was legally restored. Banks were reopened. Free markets were again tolerated. Even quotations for securities were revived. Requisitions were replaced by taxation, at first in kind and subsequently in money. The New Economic Policy was developed. This compromise was forced by terrible necessity. But the Soviet spokesmen said it was merely an intermediary stage of the revolution preparatory to the institution of the socialist state, or as Lenin said—a step back in order to jump farther.

Unlike the socialist governments of Europe the Soviets eliminated private property and substituted state industry for private industry. The numerous private stockholders were replaced by one stockholder, the state. This arrangement is somewhat similar to the participation of the Belgian government in the Congo industries or the British government in the Anglo-Persian Oil Co., except that in Russia the state is the exclusive stockholder rather than the principal one, just as the United States government is the sole stockholder in the Panama Canal properties and the sole owner of the post office.

The common motives that actuate individuals, such as the securing of the material rewards of effort, the desire to make profits and to transmit property to children—these motives have been repressed. The principle in operation is altruism, service to the community— "No one shall have any cake until every one has bread." These are the ideals of the great religious teachers of the past, but for the first time Lenin and his followers have tried to apply them as practical schemes of life. Both the American and French Revolutions sought freedom for the individual. The Russian Revolution sought freedom for a whole group or class, the proletariat. The revolutions in France and America, however, largely achieved the freedom of the individual and secured it by the Bill of Rights and the Declaration of the Rights of Man. But the Russian Revolution has emancipated neither the proletariat group nor the individuals in it. In fact the coercion of the individual is its dominant note. Living in political exile Lenin and Trotsky and their associates—journalists, propagandists, and agitators—attempted to develop a working model which should embody their ideals, and suddenly they found themselves in actual control of an entire country, nay, of a very world. And apparently it was easier to spin theories than to apply them. The Soviets could indulge in fantasies until they got down to concrete tasks in industry; then they had to readjust themselves to facts. In every government the radical opposition becomes conservative when it assumes power, as for example the Labor Party in Great Britain. It is easier to wreck an old house than to build a new one. The lack of men with constructive capacities is evident in the straits in which the Russian people find themselves today. What the country needs primarily is not doctrinaires but men of affairs. Speculations in economic theory and experience in inciting revolution are not adequate preparation for founding a state.

It remains to be proved whether the principle of communism will do for Russia what individual initiative did for America. Private initiative built a civilization out of a wilderness in America. Will the Soviet régime be as efficient for the production of a great economic surplus and will it be applied more wisely? Will it give scope to the genius? This is a question which only coming generations can answer.

E. Qualifying Conditions of the Experiment

The Soviet Union contains about one-sixth of the world's area, about one-tenth of the world's population, incalculable resources, and a climate varying from arctic to sub-tropical. In area it is about two and a half times as large as the United States and in population about 25 per cent greater. The very size of the Soviet Union makes it of tremendous economic and political significance to the rest of the world. The Soviet régime is the greatest social experiment in history.

That the effort is at all possible is due to several conditions. First, the country is self-supporting. The smaller industrial countries of western Europe would fail in a similar attempt. Again, the Russians are a patient, stolid people. Gazing into their impassive faces one realizes that it must have been terrific oppression that goaded this lethargic people into revolution, and it is the same patient quality which makes it possible to try such a vast and painful experiment. For a people which emerged from a decimating famine eight years ago the shortage of food, shoes, clothing, housing, and soap and towels seems not a sacrifice but a mild inconvenience. Think, if you can, of such an experiment in a Latin country like Italy or Spain.

F. Soviet Method

In exile Lenin worked out the technique of revolt. He studied the French Revolution as a specimen. It was not love of the common man but hatred of the existing régime that motivated him. The execution of his brother was avenged in the death of the Tsar. One finds none of the fine tolerance that characterized Lincoln during the darkest days of the Civil War. A fateful juncture toward the close of the World War made it possible with German help for Lenin's technique to be applied. The whole conception is a negative one of fighting an enemy—hence the prolific use of military terms, as "socialized sector of agriculture" and the "vegetable front" (referring to the faulty distribution of fresh vegetables in the big cities), and the abundant use of warlike slogans, flaming banners, and "shock troops," referring to a brigade of efficient workers.

The keynote of the Bolshevik revolution was the rejection of tradition. Whatever be the demerits of this policy, it has one virtue—a willingness to test new methods. One of the leading professors of industrial chemistry in the east frequently quotes the witticism: "If you want a difficult job done, give it to the 'damn fool' that doesn't know that it can't be done." The Russian ignorance of the things that cannot be done may really enable them to achieve results incredible to the western world. However, in some respects the rejection of experience in industry has been costly. Before the war Russia had little need of managerial ability or engineering talent; therefore, no executives developed who could assume great responsibility. This deficiency is probably the outstanding difficulty of the Soviets.

With the abundant labor supply it would have been wiser for the Soviets to rely less on machinery and more on man-power, or at least to use machinery calling for relatively little skill. Ignoring the fact that the worker and the machine must be co-ordinated, the Soviets now put very complicated machines into the hands of unskilled workers, with the result that expensive machines are damaged and production restricted.

Not only do they ignore the lack of training of the workers, but they overlook the time factor. Time is the essence of social change. A skyscraper could not be erected in a month, regardless of how many workers were employed. The greater the haste the greater the waste. The Russians think of social change in terms of years of a man's life rather than of generations of a nation's history. "The Five-Year Plan in Fifty" is probably a truer statement of the prospects than "The Five-Year Plan in Four." Again, in the management of industry there is a discrepancy between the enthusiasm and idealism of the leaders and the dullness and selfishness of the masses. Can millions of people be prodded toward fervid enthusiasm indefinitely? It will take a generation not only to train the Russian masses technically but to bring their social ideals up to the levels of their leaders.

However, the process of mass education is obvious to the foreign observer. In the railway stations and the trams there are no advertisements of individual articles, but in the factory locker rooms there are injunctions both by the printed word and by signs: "Brush Your Teeth," "Wash Your Hands," "Learn to Read," "Become Efficient at Your Work." In the public dining rooms the education of women is carried on by means of posters and banners: "Don't Be a Kitchen Slave," "Eat at the Factory Kitchens," "Leave Your Child at the Crèche and Help Build Soviet Industry," and many similar exhortations.

Again, in walking through the Hermitage Galleries in Leningrad, one daily sees workmen by the hundreds in small groups being taught by professional guides. It is quite a sensation to see poor ignorant women with head-shawls or unwashed peasants with burlap rags, substitutes for shoes, standing in front of a Rembrandt which they are earnestly trying to understand. This is indeed government for the people, even if not government of the people and by the people.

The regard for the old culture is evident in the restoration of the art in some of the old churches and the preservation of the museums, which have been maintained in excellent condition. The mining museum in Leningrad, attached to the School of Mines, contains a model mine, and a pre-war collection of rare and beautiful minerals and mining apparatus which vies with that of the Munich Industrial Museum.

In the matter of university education the laboring class is favored, and sons of the formerly educated class are discriminated against. The biological and social consequences are obvious; the leaders are being pulled down to the level of the masses. This accounts in part for the exile of Trotsky and members of the old intelligentsia. Stalin is closer to the masses, because he is one of them. He lacked the education, the international experience, and the outlook of the intellectuals that surrounded Lenin. Undoubtedly, discrimination against the educated classes will retard the progress of the Soviet Union.

However, ultimately a new class of leaders will arise out of the masses. As Woodrow Wilson said of Abraham Lincoln:

> There is nowhere in the land any home so remote, so humble, that it may not contain the power of mind and heart and conscience to which nations yield and history submits its processes. Nature pays no tribute to aristocracy, subscribes to no creed of caste, renders fealty to no monarch. It does not run after titles or seek by preference the high circles of society. It affects humble company as well as great. It pays no special tribute to universities or learned societies or conventional standards of greatness, but serenely chooses its own comrades, its own haunts, its own cradle even, and its own life of adventure and of training. This is the sacred mystery of democracy, that its richest fruits spring out of soils which no man has prepared and in circumstances amidst which they are the least experienced.[8]

As Proctor stated, "The approach of a great man was in no sort indicated by scintillations along the genealogical track." The Russian condition today is similar to that in Germany in the period of inflation. In 1922 the writer met one of the professors of economics at the University of Berlin, a man who had been wealthy and had an international reputation. In December he sat in his unheated library, with a beaver hat and a lap robe, writing. He said that he had not been to the opera since 1914 but the wagon-maker and his children down the street had a weekly subscription. But the professor did not despair, as a new culture would arise out of the masses and the broader base might afford a more stable structure and a higher pyramid.

New motives are called into play. Not profit for the individual nor stockholders' dividends, but social position is the reward for constructive work. Private acquisitiveness is suppressed and attempts are made to foster social acquisitiveness. On the economic side the technique of mass production is being developed. Foreign engineers are the technical advisers of the government. Production is planned ahead. With the state as the sole producer of all goods and with a patient population that is willing to do without necessities, it is possible for a single producer to plan production, whereas in a competitive capitalist society it is the prices paid by consumers that determine the volume and even the cost of production.

At the end of the period of pure communism and the anarchy that resulted, the Soviet régime had a choice of two policies. Either small-scale farms could have been encouraged, creating a conservative capitalistic peasantry like that of France (such a peasantry, constituting the greatest part of the population, would have hampered the development of communist doctrines), or there could be made an attempt to develop socialism broadly in agriculture and industry.

When Lenin saw the failure of his communist doctrine in practice, he developed the so-called New Economic Policy, the Nep. It was euphemistically called a strategic retreat. But this retreat from pure communism was to be merely temporary, for as Lenin said in defense: "We do not make peace with capitalism, but war on a new plane." Even state capitalism was to be merely a temporary phase in the development of socialism.

The French Revolution went from the extreme left to the extreme right, and never returned to the extreme left again. The Russian Revolution, however, zigzagged to the extreme left of "war communism," then to the right in the "New Economic Policy" and in peasant proprietorship, then back again to the left in the socialization of agriculture, then in the summer of 1932 back to the right a second time and in the autumn of the same year a third reversal to the left.

The Soviet method is not that of a consistent, carefully thought out, cautious, slow-moving policy. It is an erratic, blundering method of trial and error, involving a violent reversal of policy when the error proves to be too costly.

The method of the Five-Year Plan has resulted in debasing the standard of living. Reduced to its simplest terms, the Five-Year Plan means that the individual Russian makes sacrifices and his savings are invested by the state in new plants. If these investments result in wasteful experimentation and inefficiency, then the individual Russian is much in the same position as an American workman who starves himself and then buys stock at high prices which proves to be worthless. There is this difference: that in the western world the buying of worthless stock is a voluntary act, while in Soviet Russia it is imposed upon the masses from above. It is very much as if a chauffeur took control of an automobile and drove it where he pleased rather than where the owner of the car wished it to go. The Soviet leaders ignore the fundamental fact that they were not elected by the populace and that they have never subjected or been willing to subject their policies to a popular test.

The methods of the Soviet are bound to lead to a reaction, if history affords any analogy. The French Revolution moved from a moderate to an extreme left policy, and then reverted to a dictatorship, and eventually ended in a republican parliamentary government. Again, after the régime of Cromwell, the ideals of Puritanism were replaced by the luxury of the Restoration period. The present methods of Soviet Russia are generating their own reaction.

G. Soviet Results

It is difficult to speak of results of a gigantic social experiment after its operation for only fifteen years. Though Soviet officials protest otherwise, it is still an experiment; it is too early to appraise it. The results in Russia cannot be regarded as independent of conditions throughout the world. Powerful forces had been moving society everywhere at an accelerated pace in recent years. Universal suffrage and universal education tended toward universal minimum standards of satisfaction and of living. Minimum wages and social insurance went hand in hand with heavier taxation. The poor were being leveled up and the rich leveled down. These results were being gradually approached in western Europe by legal and parliamentary methods. America, and generally the younger countries, lagged behind. But these world forces found more extreme expression in Soviet Russia than in other countries because of its less stable structure. A high wind will have a greater effect on the sand and cement of a house in the process of rebuilding than on a completed structure. And in the former case it will also be more obvious in which direction the wind is blowing than in the latter. Soviet Russia is the world's social weather vane, its signal of social trends.

The results thus far have been intangible. There is an abundance of idealism but a shortage of material comforts. There are lots of hopes but a lack of satisfactions. There is great impatience but slow growth. There is much experimentation but little achievement. There is gross inefficiency but gradual learning. What a strange paradox! In the western world the quest for private profit is often disguised under the cloak of idealism; department stores and sellers of consumers' goods maintain the slogan of "service to the community." In Soviet Russia idealism is ridiculed by the Bolsheviks, who profess a crass materialism despite the distinctly spiritual character of their aims.

The Five-Year Plan, which is a detailed program of progress for the future, provides indeed, for increasing production. The Soviets had succeeded in increasing their plant capacity. In fact they have overproduction already in some kinds of raw materials. Will the Five-Year Plan work equally well when production must be curtailed, as in so-called capitalist countries? The Five-Year Plan has succeeded in increasing the output of some raw materials but it has failed with respect to the quality of the product and the cost of production. Nor has it succeeded in delivering enough consumers' goods for the masses.

When private strips of land were replaced by collective farms, output and efficiency increased. By the pressure of taxes on private farms and exemptions on collective farms the process of socialization of agriculture was accelerated. As a result, there is unlikely to arise the conservative peasantry that grew up in France following the distribution of the lands of the nobles and of the clergy after the French Revolution of 1789. Instead, Russia is developing an agricultural proletariat; the farms have become factories. Further success in this field may result in the obsolescence of wheat farms in some other countries with high costs of production. Russia has become a world laboratory in agriculture. On the other hand, though agricultural output in general increased in Russia, the increase was less than planned. As for live stock, this actually decreased, curtailing both the food supply and consumers' goods.[9]

In industry, the Soviets have succeeded in having foreigners build giant modern plants, but they have not yet succeeded in having these plants successfully operated by Russian managers and Russian labor. These large plants merely prove that foreigners can build plants anywhere, provided the funds and materials are furnished. If the Russian masses will further forego satisfactions, building of plants by foreigners can continue. The lack of a trained native managerial staff and of native skilled labor is the conspicuous lack of Russian industry. The Soviets ignore the fact that industrial management in mass production is an art that requires patient application and long experience. The Soviets' attitude is that of the novice, who, when asked if he could play the violin replied, "I do not know. I never tried." There is a lack of balance between various classes of production, such as producers' goods and consumers' goods. Industrial plants are being run not for the workers but for profit, though the profits go to the state. Neither in quality nor in cost can Russian industry compete abroad. Furthermore, the Soviets have failed to keep exports up to the planned level. The decline in commodity prices resulted in increased competition with foreign countries and in straining relations with them.

In the field of labor, the conspicuous success has been the decline of unemployment. But, as the Soviets themselves admit, there has been a decline in the standard of living, due to the shortage of food and to the lack of consumers' goods. Again, the productivity of labor is low, the personnel is inadequate and poorly trained. Though labor is available in great quantity, the quality is poor because industry has been drawing for its supply on the peasantry. The freedom of labor and the control of plants by workers has all but vanished. Industrialization requires efficiency and discipline. As a result, the labor ideals of communism have been subordinated. In some respects labor is being exploited, even more so than in capitalist countries. Yet in other respects labor occupies a preferred position in the social scale, particularly in reference to distribution of goods that are scarce.

The rural standard of living is probably above the pre-war level. This is indicated by the fact that crops in 1930 were larger than in 1913 and exports were smaller. Obviously more grain was consumed within the country. However, in the cities it is doubtful whether the standard of living is above the pre-war level. The peasants will not exchange farm products, because the cities have no goods to offer. The claim that the workers' standard in the city is above the pre-war level is correct only psychologically. The workers have a sense of ownership of the plant in which they work and a hope for a better future. Certainly the standard of living whether in America, China, or Russia depends upon productivity per man rather than on abundant resources. Capacity to consume depends upon capacity to produce. The mere existence of an abundant supply of raw materials within Russia does not of itself raise the standard of living. It did not, for generations before the revolution. The standard of living could rise in Russia if its raw materials, cheaply produced at home, could be exchanged for consumers' goods, of good quality and at low cost, produced abroad. In other words, the standard of living in Russia would probably be higher if instead of experimenting in industry and making poor products at high cost they would trade their raw materials, grain, ore, oil and manganese, for foreign consumers' goods of better quality and lower cost. The shortages of meat, clothing, and household goods on the farms have at times indicated lower rural standards of living.

Because there is no surplus, life has taken on a grim austerity. There are no night cafés such as one finds on the rest of the continent, where people gather of an evening to relax, listen to music, and sip beer. Because there is a shortage of consumers' goods, the Russian ration is meaningless. Of what value is the minimum ration for privileged workers if they do not obtain it?

In banking, the Soviets have done bold experimenting. They have a managed currency, that is, one that operates independently of gold. It works, however, only at home. The evils of inflation are offset by a complicated system of ration tickets for workers. Classes other than manual laborers bear the brunt of inflation—they suffer. There is rigid control of exchange at the border. Exchange rates are artificially fixed and even death penalties are imposed for smuggling or offering currency at the market rather than at fixed rates. Therefore, the world charges the Soviets with "dumping." If Russian banking affords any lesson to the western world, it is that when the whole world is an economic unit, a managed currency requires world management, not national management.

In the budget, a balance is sought by the Soviets, just as in capitalist countries. A sales tax is the chief source of income. The government attempts to make each industry and each activity self-supporting, as the United States Post Office is, theoretically at least. Despite the theory that private property was abolished, the Soviet government offers loans to its citizens. It encourages saving and attempts to acquire the social surplus for investment in plant. The income taxes are high, though the minimum taxable income on other than the favored class is not as low as in England, and the rates in the lower brackets are no severer than the rates in the lower brackets in Germany. The inheritance tax is confiscatory, although in exceptional circumstances the French inheritance tax, on the testator and legatee together, almost matches the Soviet inheritance tax. Apparently the Soviets work on the principle that the income tax should be moderate so as to give the individual a sense of power in accumulation of wealth, but that the estate should revert to the community at death. In America large foundations have been created by voluntary gifts; in Russia the state is the sole foundation and the community is the residuary legatee.

Soviet propagandists gleefully say that the capitalist system is suffering from overproduction and unemployment, whereas the Soviets have a great shortage of labor. But they overlook the fact that the capitalist world is suffering from an overproduction of goods, whereas the Soviet world is suffering from an underconsumption. The current underconsumption in Soviet Russia is probably relatively greater than in capitalist countries during the depths of a depression. Besides, Russia is now undergoing a tremendous construction boom such as occurred in the United States when excessive expansion and railroad building helped to bring on the protracted depression of the seventies and nineties. Will Russia be able to avoid the inevitable profound depression which will result when the army of workmen now engaged in building plants have completed their tasks?

The Soviet Republic represents state capitalism. Private property has been abolished in production and in distribution and largely even in consumption. Restaurants are owned by the state; apartment houses are either state-owned or owned co-operatively. The government owns not merely the railroads and the public utilities as in western Europe, but also the mines, the factories, the stores, the banks, the taxis, the hotels, etc. In fact the economic life is the state. The state, it is business; business, it is the state.

And because everybody's business is nobody's business there is less individual responsibility for public property. Peasants who carefully tended their live stock as personal property neglected it in the collectives. Ownership forces responsibility. At a meeting of the directors of an American life insurance company, a farmer in default was being discussed. One director said "If necessary, let him reduce his amortization. If he cannot pay any amortization, let him pay the interest. If he cannot pay any interest, let him pay the taxes. If he cannot pay the taxes, let him pay the maintenance. But by all means keep him on the farm." Human nature seems alike everywhere.

It is still too early to speak of results. Do fifteen years of struggling existence mean that the Soviet régime can survive in its present form? And even if it can survive, will it be able to produce goods efficiently? Will it be able to remove the want and the sacrifices that now seem inherent in the present method? The capitalist countries are suffering from lack of markets, but the Soviets are suffering from lack of goods. With discrimination against property, how can savings be encouraged? How can a social surplus be created except by the current method of underconsumption, through exporting abroad the food needed at home? Not the prices tendered by people in need of food and clothing but the decrees of the government decide what shall be consumed and what exchanged for machinery.

The Soviets have not yet proved their ability to provide adequately goods for the populace. Furthermore it is conjectural whether the planned production will avoid the evils of the western world, of booms and depressions.

In aspects other than economic, important distinctive reforms and benefits have been effected. Social insurance is general. Compulsory education has been introduced. Illiteracy has diminished. Technical education has been disseminated. The whole social structure has been overturned. The manual laborers have become the new aristocracy and the brain workers, including the "white-collar" workers and the intelligentsia, have become the new proletariat.

Just as the majority persecuted the minority, as Protestants in France or Catholics in Germany during religious wars, so the masses persecute the classes in Soviet Russia. The hatred of the "kulak" has displaced other hatreds, and therefore the Jews and other minorities are tolerated there. The Jews, who are universally the lightning rod for the nations' hatred, apparently cease to be such, when other more virulent hatreds arise. A similar phenomenon was manifest during the World War. When the Germans prayed "Gott strafe England," they forgot to hate their own Jews. With a sense of frustration in Germany, anti-Semitism increased there after the war. If the Soviet experiment fails, it is possible that the same sense of frustration may turn again upon the Jews, the traditional bearers of Europe's hatred, the scapegoats of a world slowly emerging from barbarism. The tolerance of minorities, religious, racial, political, cultural, or economic, is an index of the civilization of a community.

The class struggle continues with merely a change of emphasis. The underdogs are now the privileged. The laborer's children get preferential admission to the universities, while the children of intellectual lineage must wait for an available vacancy. Truly a dysgenic selection! When brain is subordinated to brawn, society seems upside down.

Education is widespread, but only in the utilitarian field. The faculty of the humanities was abolished in the University of Moscow, and the professor of philosophy, one of the leading scholars of Europe, is now said to be reading printer's proof of communist propaganda leaflets for $50 a month. The mass production of propaganda literature has resulted in the standardization of thought and the suppression of independent or minority thinking. A society can be stable only when there is a vigorous minority, whether it be a political or a social group.

The facilities for education are widespread. The Park for Culture and Rest in Moscow, a sort of a Coney Island, has a good book store at a prominent location. In the center of Moscow, the International Book Store draws from every cultural center of the world. The German Journal of Physical Chemistry jostles the Italian Bulletin of Mathematical Statistics, and so on throughout the geographical and scientific world.

To the credit of the Soviets be it said that they emancipated the minorities and fostered the several national cultures. Almost two hundred races with distinctive histories are living under the Soviet régime. Corresponding to the Declaration of the Rights of Man in the French Revolution, was the Declaration of the Rights of Peoples, published in November 1917, shortly after the Bolshevik overturn. It abolished all national privileges, declared the sovereignty of the numerous nationalities, and granted the right of self-determination, including the right to secede. As a result, there is no bilingual problem. The linguistic rights of minorities are generally recognized.

Yet the censorship seems a permanent feature of Russian society. The pre-war opposition to a liberal régime persists under Soviet rule. The autocracy of the Tsar has been exchanged for the autocracy of the Soviets. Can one say that this is essentially a masochistic trait of the Slavs as depicted in Russian literature?

Soldiering and "ca'canny" by the workers and lack of discipline are indicated in the unique Soviet labor code. It shows that the ideals of communism are beyond the masses of the people. The leaders are socially minded, but can one say that the peasants and workers are? The masses are still spiritually unprepared for the high ideals demanded by communist theory. The prophets are always ahead of the people, and as one maligned leader said some three thousand years ago, "Would that all the Lord's people were prophets and that the Lord would put His spirit upon them."

H. Effect on the Western World

If the Soviet government achieved nothing else, it set up a civilization which affords a foil and a contrast to the west. The Soviet régime has given us a new perspective on our own problems. Though the Russians are suffering, the west is getting the benefit of their failures and successes. From several countries of Europe and from the United States unemployed workers went to Soviet Russia; only a fraction stayed. This fact is perhaps a test of the comparative merits of the two systems in meeting the requirements of the common man. At the end of 1931, as a result of increasing unemployment throughout the world, several thousand workmen went to Russia, but in the spring of 1932, the Soviet government refused to admit any more, and many of the immigrants returned.

The policy of centralizing political and financial power has spread throughout the world, not only to Italy and Hungary, but even to Germany. The series of economic and political decrees concerning regulation of prices, wages, interest rates, and mortgages in Germany went into effect in 1931. Whether such increasing centralized control was a result of the Soviet régime or whether all countries of the world are being independently affected by the same forces it is too early to tell, but even in the United States financial power is being centralized in Washington. Our government has gone into the business of buying wheat and cotton, making loans to railroads, liquidating insolvent banks, and in other ways encroaching upon the field hitherto reserved to private capital. However, this is merely the extension of a process that has been going on for a generation. The policy of *laissez faire* is on the wane. Government bodies like the Interstate Commerce Commission, the several public utility commissions, the Federal Farm Board, the Federal

Trade Commission, funds for insurance against accident, old age, and recently, unemployment, graduated taxes on incomes and inheritances, are evidences of increasing governmental control in what had been regarded as private affairs.

However, the Russian principle of planning is not new. Germany had planned to develop her industries, such as dyes, chemicals, ship-building, electrical manufacturing, etc. for a generation before the war. Planning to increase production has been carried on by industrialists throughout the world. Increasing production, however, is not a difficult matter; it is always characteristic of periods of inflation and great prosperity. Planning to decrease production is difficult; this is a stage which Russia will eventually reach. When American producers attempt to plan by co-operating with their competitors to curtail production, the government has always been opposed.

It is true that capitalism represents freedom of the individual, but in so far as cartels, syndicates, or pools attempt a curtailment of production that freedom is abridged. Under the western system, private manufacturers surrender this freedom to the industry as a whole, if the government sanctions it. In Germany the government has not hesitated to give its sanction, but in America it was only the catastrophe in the copper and oil industries that removed the traditional antagonism of the government to such planning by industry and then only on a pretext of conservation of natural resources. In Russia it is the government itself which will ultimately decide that production must be curtailed according to a plan.

Undoubtedly the western world has something to learn from Russia. Planning on a national scale is a new social invention now being tested there. Russia is teaching the world national management. On the other hand, Russia can learn from the western world shop management and technical administration. Capitalism and communism are not two distinctive things. The western world is already partly socialized. The Soviet régime is moving increasingly toward capitalist methods, as in wage scales, savings banks, government loans, etc. The two are reciprocally interacting and influencing each other profoundly.

I. Communism vs. Capitalism

The Soviet régime is not communist. Nor is the western world capitalist. There is no sharp line of division. Denmark has had large co-operatives in production, consumption, banking, and credit for over a generation. Germany has had social insurance for over two generations. Great Britain, under the pressure of a mature industrial system, became socialized. The United States, lagging in the process of industrialization behind the older countries of Europe, has gradually introduced increasing social control. The prospects are that this trend in the western world will continue. Beginning at points far apart, the Soviet system and the western world are in competition. The so-called capitalist countries must become increasingly solicitous of the workers' welfare. Mass production involves specialization of labor, greater interdependence of the workers, and therefore requires greater socialization. Not only must capitalism become more humane, but communism must become more efficient. The question then will arise which of the two systems can deliver goods more effectively and which can keep the door of opportunity open for the individual? Can the efficiency of capitalism co-exist with the idealism of communism? In other words, is it easier for the Soviet régime, with its system of social ethics, to learn to become competent, or, say, for the relatively efficient New York City government to get rid of its grafters? In Moscow such grafters would be executed. Are scientific management and an ethical code necessarily incompatible? The old Tsarist régime was both incompetent and honeycombed with graft. The new régime is rid of graft and is merely incompetent. Can it also become as effective as western society? Will Moscow or New York be the first to achieve a social scheme which is both ethical and efficient?

J. A Forecast

As the sociologists have reiterated, progress is not inevitable in society. Progress is a reward for social effort. Civilizations have actually decayed in the past. Only sound, just, and rational policies will avoid the decay of future civilizations.

Once universal suffrage is granted, an ultimate socialized civilization becomes inevitable. The "have-nots" necessarily are more numerous than the "haves." Universal suffrage establishes the machinery to make effective the mass demand for a more equal distribution of wealth. Russia has distributed wealth equally so that nobody has anything. Can the western world make a better job of it? Can it maintain a system of material rewards sufficient to elicit the maximum of individual initiative, without suffering the evils of extreme maldistribution of wealth? The race is on between Russia and the western world. Will the Soviet régime debase the standard of living in the western world so that we shall all be having tea, black bread, and cabbage as our diet? Or will Russia develop an efficient régime of production so as to make possible greater consumption and a higher standard of living?

If the Soviet industrial program continues to call for privation and want on the part of the masses, the danger point of popular resentment may be reached. Under a two-party system, with a responsible government, the minority is always ready to replace the majority and to maintain a stable régime. But where there is but one party, and no trained minority ready to assume power, governments have collapsed. Under a scheme of universal education such as prevails in Russia, autocracy cannot long survive. The emergence of popular government in Russia is inevitable within a generation. If the present régime cannot within the next few years show that the sacrifices of the Russian people to build huge plants have not been in vain, a political readjustment is inevitable. There are possibilities that Russia, with the greatest area in the world, with the greatest power plant in the world, with the largest grain farms in the world, may also achieve the distinction of having the greatest economic crash in the world, and another political upheaval which will outdo the greatest of all time—the downfall of Tsardom. The policy of the Kremlin in the next few years is fraught with significance for Russia and for the world.

The future of Russia is contingent in large measure on the policy of the world. On her part, Russia has discarded the propaganda of world revolution. Trotsky, its supreme advocate, is in exile. If ever the moment was propitious for a world revolt, it is now, both in Germany and in China. But what has Russia done? It has remained passive. Dreams of world revolution have faded before the imperious demands of the Five-Year Plan. And Germany is making the industrial equipment for the Soviets. Furthermore, Russia has signed non-aggression pacts with all its important neighbors. And at Geneva the only advocates of genuine disarmament and world peace have been the Soviet spokesmen.

The world is an organic unit. When one nation is suffering, be it Germany or Russia, the world as a whole must suffer. And the restoration of Russia to economic life as a member of the family of nations should stimulate industry everywhere. The opening of our west created a boom for our industrial east, indeed for the whole country. Similarly, the economic building up of Russia should stimulate the manufacturing nations, indeed the world as a whole. A world conference on Russia, involving some reasonable settlement of debts, on a basis similar to that now likely to be offered to the other defaulting nations in Europe and South America, should precede any plan for full readmittance into the family of nations. That Russia is likely to accept any reasonable terms is obvious. With credit costs ranging around 30 per cent per annum as a burden on a total foreign trade of about one billion dollars, Russia is virtually paying interest on the total of her defaulted debt without receiving any benefit therefrom. A composition with her creditors would restore her credit, facilitate her foreign trade, and do much toward restoring world prosperity.

Two new factors have changed the status of Russia with respect to the other powers. First, three years ago Russia was the only important nation which had defaulted on her debt. Today she has plenty of company in other countries of Europe and Latin America. Three years ago Russia would have had to settle her defaulted debt on a high basis. The quotations on the world stock exchanges of the debts of the defaulted governments are so low that Russia today could probably settle easily on a comparable basis. Whenever the several powers in default scale down their debts in reorganization, Soviet Russia should be able to re-enter normal financial relations after a similar composition. Secondly, the Lausanne Conference marked a tremendous step forward. The hatred of Germany which had prevailed in France yielded to a spirit of practical co-operation. The attitude of war was replaced by an attitude of peace. A similar reversal of world sentiment toward Russia seems inevitable in time. Sentiment in America is gradually turning from a spirit of strong antagonism to one of understanding. A definitive settlement of the inter-allied debt should have as its sequel a world settlement of the Russian problem. It is conceivable that the two may become part of the same general settlement.

PART TWO

THE BACKGROUND

Communism in Colonial Massachusetts

THE experience that was had in this commone course and condition, tried sundrie years, and that amongst godly and sober men, may well evince the vanitie of the conceit of Platos and other ancients applauded by some of later times; that ye taking away of propertie and bringing in communitie into a commone wealth, would make them happy and florishing; as if they were wiser than god. For this communitie (so farr as it was) was found to breed much confusion & discontent, and retard much imployment that would have been to their benefite and comforte. For ye young men that were most able and fitte for labour & service did repine that they should spend their time and strength to work for other mens wives and children without any recompence. The strong, or man of parts, had no more in divission of victails and cloaths than he that was weake and not able to doe a quarter ye other could; this was thought an injustice. The aged and graver men to be ranked and equalized in labours, victails & cloaths with ye meaner & younger sort, thought it some indignitie & disrespect unto them. And for mens wives to be commanded to doe service for other men, as dresing their meate, washing their cloaths, etc. they deemed it a kind of slaverie, neither could many husbands well brooke it. Upon ye pointe all being to have alike and all to doe alike, they thought them selves in ye like condition and one as good as another; and so, if it did not cut of those relations that God hath set amongst men, yet it did at least much diminish and take of ye mutuall respects that should be preserved amongst them. And would have been worse if they had been men of another condition. Let none objecte this is men's corruption, and nothing to the course it selfe. I answer, seeing all men have this corruption in them, God in his wisdome saw another course fiter for them.

—Governor William Bradford, *History of Plimoth Plantation.*

CHAPTER II

AN HISTORICAL ANALOGY—THE FRENCH REVOLUTION

To understand the Russian Revolution one must look back to the precedents of history. To regard it as a totally new phenomenon makes diagnosis, prognosis, and therapy difficult. History offers the French Revolution as an analogy. Both revolutions illustrate the principle that repression evokes violence. Failure to adjust law and institutions to changing conditions leads to social strains, for social life is in a state of continuous flux and evolution. Social institutions, if slowly modified, can meet new conditions, but if they are rigid or static, elements of instability are introduced. Unchanging institutions become obsolete and are eventually replaced, often with violence.

A. The Impetus to Revolution

In comparing the French and Russian Revolutions, one is impressed with the fact that the human mind reacts similarly to similar conditions, in spite of differences in time. Centuries of oppression tend to culminate in violence. The *ancien régime* in France and the Tsarist régime in Russia persistently ignored the demands for readjustment of the political institutions to a changing order. In both cases the masses were treated as being without rights and without freedom. To quote Lowell on the French Revolution:

> So grew and gathered through the silent years
> The madness of a people wronged by wrong.
> There seemed no strength in the dumb toiler's tears,
> No strength in suffering; but the Past was strong.
> The brute despair of trampled centuries
> Leaped up with one hoarse yell and snapped its bands,
> Groped for its right with horny calloused hands
> And stared around for God with bloodshot eyes.

In both the French and the Russian Revolutions the motives were freedom and justice. Both revolutions were national in their beginning. In both cases there was an attempt to make the revolt international, to propagate the idea in other countries. Ultimately the French Revolution influenced all of Europe, and as a result the nations from Greece and Spain on the south to Scandinavia on the north remodeled their governmental forms.

The forces of history seem to reflect the continuous tendency to diffuse power.[1] Originally the king was all-powerful and the feudal vassals had no rights. The English barons in 1215 forced the king to grant the Magna Charta, thus reducing the power of the king in England and increasing the power of the nobles. In France the revolution in 1789 reduced the power of both king and nobles. The unprivileged classes, professional men, artisans, business men, the bourgeoisie as well as the peasantry acquired legal rights not hitherto enjoyed. Parliamentary government based on the representative principle received a great impetus. "Liberty slowly broadens down from class to class as the enfranchised sections of the nation tend to become the whole of the nation." [1a]

In 1917 in Russia the first revolt against the Tsarist régime seemed to be the extension of the democratic principles of the French Revolution to Russia. But after the overturn of the Kerensky régime and the introduction of the communist idea the revolution developed along totally new lines, for which there is no historic precedent.

B. Similarities

1. Prophets of Revolution. The French Revolution had its prophet in Rousseau. His book, *The Social Contract,* was its Bible. Its ideas became law.[2] Marx was the prophet of the Russian Revolution. His *Communist Manifesto* was its Bible. Its ideas are embodied in legislation and social organization. In Russia disputes are settled by references to Karl Marx, just as in the French Revolution Rousseau's very words were often the final arbiters of policy.

In both cases, an utterly unscientific notion was the basic doctrine. In his book Rousseau maintained: "Man is born free, yet everywhere do we find him in chains." His conception was that men originally were a happy lot of individuals in a state of nature, unfettered by legal or social restrictions, and eventually a society developed wherein individuals surrendered their rights to the community through a social contract. Such an idea sounded plausible in 1762, but anthropology has since shown that the most primitive state of mankind affords no indication of happy isolated individuals. Early society was organized in tribes or clans. Rousseau's approach was unscientific and doctrinaire. He constructed a theory to fit his wishes, namely that sovereignty rests in the community, that kings and officials simply represent this sovereignty, that the ultimate source of power rests in the individuals that compose the community. Sovereignty does not come down to the people from the king, ruling by divine right. Sovereignty rises from the people through their popularly elected representatives. The conclusions of Rousseau were sound; they were the end product of an historical evolution in the diffusion of sovereignty from king through nobles to the common people. His premises were wrong.

Similarly the Marxian approach is through the class struggle. This is a doctrinaire and not an historical approach. He oversimplified society. He divided it into two classes, the toilers and the exploiters. A living society cannot be thus simplified. The small capitalist may be a toiler. The artisan may be a rentier. And studies in history and sociology indicate the unscientific character of the Marxian conception.

Other parallels may be cited. The French Revolution produced Saint Just, who conceived a France on the lines of a Sparta. The individual was to live simply and serve the state. In Russia today the low standard of living has enforced this Spartan simplicity. The demands of the party compel service to the community.

2. Methods and Technique. In method the two revolutions have much in common. The technique of revolt was carefully worked out. The members of the Jacobin Club in Paris were skilled propagandists. Apparently spontaneous uprisings and demonstrations were carefully planned and instigated by its members. Lord Acton wrote: "The appalling thing in the French Revolution is not the tumult but the design. The managers remain studiously concealed and masked; but there is no doubt about their presence from the first." [3] The technique of the Russian Revolution was devised by Lenin and his associates during their exile. The technique of propaganda, of swaying the masses, is a highly developed and essential part of the Soviet program.

In both the French and the Russian Revolutions the peasants revolted. The landlords were driven out and the land was distributed. Abbé Siéyès estimated that 200,000 nobles and priests held a large part of the land and ruled the 25,000,000 in the *tiers état* in pre-revolutionary France. Similarly, in Tsarist Russia, about 200,000 landlords owned one-quarter of the land and dominated the destinies of over 100,000,000 peasants.

In both cases, the overturn is marked by an historic date. August 4, 1789, and October 25, 1917, are the two outstanding dates which mark the overturn of the old régimes. In both cases the long centuries of oppression developed an impatience with slow and constitutional change. The oppressors had to be overturned immediately. The Constituent Assembly justified speed in the words, "Only by attacking and overthrowing all the abuses at the same time can we hope to be freed from them. Slow reforms have always resulted in no reform."[4] This is the tempo of an oppressed people, upon achieving freedom. And it is true that when the world is in flux, quick changes can be accomplished. In a settled world change must necessarily be slow. After the World War the Treaty of Versailles effected changes which normally would have taken generations to accomplish by parliamentary means, and quickly created maladjustments which it will probably take generations of travail to undo.

3. THE COURSE OF EVENTS. Both revolutions started conservatively. Mirabeau tried to make of France a constitutional monarchy. He would retain the king but reform the government along the lines laid out in the Constituent Assembly. In Russia Milyukov and Kerensky tried to introduce a constitutional republic. In France the advocates of a constitutional monarchy were succeeded by the Girondists, who wished to introduce a republic along liberal and idealistic lines. Like the Milyukov group, they were the scholars—students of politics and of the law. The Girondists were succeeded by the more radical Jacobins, who drove the Girondists out of power and imprisoned them. In the Russian Revolution the Bolsheviks, the extreme lefts, drove the Mensheviks from power and imprisoned them. In France most of the leaders of the revolution were young men under forty; in 1917 most of the Bolsheviks were under forty. In the French Revolution personal violence was the test of loyalty to the revolution. Marat was an extremist like Lenin. Both made it their policy to avenge wrongs to the masses; "Death to the royalists" was the program of Marat. "Let the bourgeois die" was and is the policy of the Russian leaders.

In both revolutions the leaders came from obscurity and rose to meteoric heights, only to fall. They furnish the illustrations from the history of mankind for Goethe's theme of the song of the Fates in *Iphigenia auf Tauris:*

Es fürchte die Götter
Das Menschengeschlecht!

. . . .

Der fürchte sie doppelt
Den je sie erheben!

. . . .

Erhebet ein Zwist sich;
So stürzen die Gäste,
Geschmäht und geschändet
In nächtliche Tiefen
Und harren vergebens,
Im Finstern gebunden,
Gerechten Gerichtes.*

In France the procession of the fallen consisted of Mirabeau, Marat, Danton, Robespierre, and Barras. In Russia the list is not yet complete but it runs—Kerensky, Milyukov, Trotsky, Radek, Zinovyev, Kamenev, and more recently Rykov, Bukharin, and Tomsky. Who will replace Stalin depends upon the nature of the schism on policy and the skill of the antagonists in maneuvering. That the leaders of the Russian Revolution have not been killed as were the leaders of the French Revolution may be due to a greater humanity or perhaps to a prudent policy of not making martyrs around whom legends may be built and opposition crystallize. The rise and fall of leaders is an indication of the political instability characterizing the two revolutions.

In both the French and the Russian Revolutions, religion was under attack. It was regarded as the ally of the oppressing régime. In both cases the churches were persecuted, belief in God was attacked, atheism was fostered. In both cases the landholdings of the church were confiscated. In both cases the calendar week was changed, probably to confuse the day of religious rest with other days. The French Revolution had a ten-day week; the Russian Revolution a five-day week. In both cases the opposition was subjected to inquisitorial cruelties. In the French Revolution the Committee of Public Safety followed a policy of terrorism. The Revolutionary Tribunal was a

* Oh, fear the immortals,
Ye children of men!

. . .

Whom they have exalted
Let him fear them most!

. . .

If contest ariseth,
The guests are hurled headlong
Disgraced and dishonored
To gloomy abysses,
And fettered in darkness
Await with vain longing
A juster decree.
—Anna Swanwick, translator.

court in which any one suspected of being opposed to the Republic was tried summarily and sent to the guillotine. In Russia the night rides of the Cheka and its successor, the Ogpu, and the secret trials, unknown deaths, and cases of exile to distant regions furnish the modern counterpart.

C. Dissimilarities of the Two Revolutions

1. Differences in Aims. The aim of the French Revolution was the freedom of the individual. The doctrine of the natural rights of man was its guiding policy. It reflected the yearning of the individual. "Liberty, Equality, Fraternity," was the slogan. The Declaration of the Rights of Man was its program. On the other hand the Russian Revolution offered little to the individual. The Declaration of the Rights of the Peoples of Russia was its program. Racial groups, linguistic groups, and workers' groups, the sufferers under the old régime, were the agents and the beneficiaries of the uprising.

The chief concern of the Russian Revolution was the struggle of the working class. Its doctrine was not liberty and equality; its slogan was, originally at least, "to take from each according to his means and to give to each according to his needs." It is around these differing slogans that the discontent crystallized. Voltaire, forerunner of the French Revolution, fought for freedom of speech by the individual; he was opposed to a censorship by society. The Soviets achieved a censorship as rigorous as that of the Tsarist régime. Freedom of the group and repression of the individual make the Russian Revolution the antithesis of the French. The Bolshevik Revolution stated as its aim: "The dictatorship of the proletariat" and the rule of the working class.

The French Declaration of the Rights of Man dealt with the individual. "Men are born and remain free and equal in rights. . . . The free communication of ideas and opinions is one of the most precious rights of man. . . . No person shall be accused, arrested, or imprisoned except for specific offenses in accordance with legal procedure." This declaration was aimed against tyranny and autocracy. The Russian Revolution not only achieved no such freedom for the individual, it actually set up a tyranny as great as the one which the French Revolution destroyed. It was not a spontaneous uprising but rather a movement imposed by a strong and well-organized minority on a war-weary and politically apathetic country.

In Russia a similar declaration dealt with the rights of groups. The Declaration of the Rights of the Peoples of Russia, published November 15, 1917, establishes the following principles: "The equality and sovereignty of the peoples of Russia, the rights to free self-determination, including organization of a separate state . . . abolition of all national privileges and limitations, and free development of national minorities."[5] The Bolsheviks conceive individual liberty as a consequence of the final abolition of all classes and the ultimate disappearance of the state.

2. DIFFERENCES IN PRIVILEGED CLASSES. In the French Revolution political power was transferred to the masses; in the Russian Revolution power was transferred to the Communists, about two per cent of the population. The French Constitution provided for universal manhood suffrage. The Soviet scheme gives universal suffrage, but by devices of politics limits control of Soviet affairs to members of the Communist Party. In both revolutions the abolition of large estates created small peasant proprietors. These supported the revolution because they profited from its reforms. In France the small peasant proprietorship developed a conservative peasantry. The Communists, fearing this result in Russia, planned to socialize the peasantry. This policy aroused intense antagonism, which constitutes one of the difficult problems of the Soviet régime. Should the large collective farms and the state farms succeed, the Russian Revolution would have diverged from the historical pattern of the French Revolution. In the French Revolution the bourgeoisie, professional men, business men, and artisans, who had been without privileges, achieved a new status. The nobles and the clergy were abolished. But in the Russian Revolution the bourgeois also are persecuted. The privileged classes are the manual laborers. The "white-collar" workers and many former professional men, particularly lawyers, are the less privileged or even unprivileged.

3. DIFFERENCES IN METHOD. Karl Kautsky pointed out the differences in the progress of the two revolutions:

> The comparison can, however, be very misleading if it is made without sufficient attention being paid to the differences. . . . The Jacobins may be distinguished from the Bolsheviks . . . by the fact that they were a middle class, or lower middle class, and not a . . . party. . . . In 1792 and 1794, the circumstances under which the parties rose to power were quite different from those which helped the Bolsheviks into the saddle in 1917. It is true that there was war in both cases. In 1792, however, the war was the outcome of the revolution, while in 1917, on the contrary, the revolution was the outcome of the war. The terrorists of the great French Revolution attained power by the fact that they were the people who carried on the war most energetically and ruthlessly against the enemies who were pressing in on them from abroad.
>
> The terrorists of 1917, on the contrary, who dissolved the Constituent Assembly, attained power, not merely by furthering but by actually bringing about, most definitely and most ruthlessly, a capitulation to the enemies of their country.

> In the French Revolution, the Terror was the effect of the war, not of the revolution. It ceased as soon as the external pressure of the enemy countries came to an end. It lasted only two years. . . . (In Russia), however, it turned out quite differently. The Terror is not merely a war measure in the Bolshevik system; on the contrary, it has consistently dug itself in more and more firmly in the decade of peace since 1920. . . . If it is desired to make comparisons between the first French and the last Russian Revolutions, the Bolsheviks should be compared with the Bonapartists rather than with the Jacobins. . . .
>
> It may then happen that one of the revolutionary classes, or parties, obtains such a preponderance of power over all the others, that they are able to monopolize the fruits of the revolution and to relegate all the other revolutionaries *en masse* to the same state of powerlessness and paralysis which they all suffered before the revolution. By this process, the revolution is brought to nothing, as far as the great majority of the revolutionary classes are concerned. . . .
>
> And has not it (Bolshevism) deprived the workers and peasants little by little of all freedom of movement, after having outlawed, from the start, all intellectuals who were not in its camp? What has Stalin still to do in order to arrive at Bonapartism? Do people think that this will only come about when Stalin gets himself crowned Tsar? [6]

D. Attitude of Europe toward the Two Revolutions

Also in the attitude of the rest of the world, the course of the French Revolution affords an interesting pattern for the Russian Revolution. As in the case of the Russian Revolution the idealists of the world were at first greatly moved. For example, Shelley, writing of the revolution said: "Such a degree of unmingled good was expected as it was impossible to realize." [7] At first England sympathized with the French Revolution. The establishment of a constitutional monarchy and parliamentary government seemed a wise precedent. Fox had faith in the French cause. However, Burke predicted in his *Reflections on the French Revolution* that the revolt against authority would lead to excesses, and the September massacres, in which hirelings of the communes murdered over one thousand suspects in prison, justified his prediction. The whole world was horrified by this massacre, and the idealists who had faith in the revolution turned against it.

In the case of both revolutions the nobles left the country, became *emigrés*. From their foreign domiciles these emigrés tried to arouse the antagonism of Europe. They were regarded as the hated enemies of the new order. The anti-Soviet propaganda that emanates from Russian nobles in Berlin and Paris has its precedent in the anti-republican propaganda that emanated from the French emigrés.

Just as the Emperor of Austria and the King of Prussia tried to intervene in 1791 to enable the King of France "to establish with the most absolute freedom the foundations of a monarchical form of government," so the Allied Powers tried in Archangel to intervene against the Soviets. The important difference was that the Allied Powers intervened on behalf of the liberal régime of Kerensky as against the radical régime of Lenin. Admittedly, reactionaries behind Kolchak and Denikin, intervened for the old régime. In both cases, Allied intervention was intended to check "dangerous" ideas. This was followed by the revolutionists' attempt to spread the new idea. There were mutual hatred and mutual fear between the revolutionists and the rest of the world.

In both revolutions there was an attempt to force the new idea upon unwilling peoples. On December 15, 1792, the November Propaganda Decree was carried out. The French generals were to force freedom upon all the territories under French control and were to "treat as enemies the peoples who, refusing liberty and equality or renouncing them, may wish to preserve, recall, or treat with the Prince and the privileged castes." [8]

The revolutionists carried their propaganda into other countries. As a result the powers feared propaganda at home. There were expeditions in England after the French Revolution to hunt down radical elements. Today the communist propagandists are sought out in America and elsewhere. As the government feared the attempt to arouse radical elements against King George and the aristocracy, many pro-French societies which arose in the early days of the French Revolution came to be regarded as dangerous, such as the Revolutionary Society, the London Correspondence Society, etc. In America, many liberal societies are labeled "Reds." However, every important movement to extend wealth, power, or freedom to larger groups has met with opposition by the smaller group in control. Originally such movements are regarded as heresy and their leaders as radicals but as the minority grows, what were once radical ideas become accepted and respectable.

E. The Effects of the French Revolution

1. General Effects. It is premature to consider the effects of the Russian Revolution. The action is too recent. But the perspective of over a hundred years places the effects of the French Revolution in bold relief. The French Revolution destroyed the *ancien régime.* The new system which emerged, not only in France but in other countries, was socially a better one. Unlike the American Revolution of 1776, which was primarily political, the French Revolution affected almost every aspect of life—economic, political, legal, and religious. In this regard it is somewhat similar to the Russian Revolu-

tion. In both cases the lives, thoughts, and perspective of the people were profoundly affected.

The French Revolution had its repercussions, both immediate and remote, throughout the rest of Europe. It is very likely that the Russian Revolution will likewise have an effect throughout the modern world. In both cases there was a violent departure from tradition which made it possible to experiment along new lines. Some of the effects were short-lived: for instance, the French made a new calendar, abolished the old religious holidays, provided new civil holidays, and initiated a ten-day week. Russian calendar changes are somewhat similar, except that the Soviets did not start the Year 1 with the date of the revolution, nor did they rename the months. Like the French Revolution the Russian Revolution established new museums, new schools, and new systems of law. Both abolished the old aristocracy.

Of every great revolution it may be said that the old evil conditions are never wholly destroyed, and that the new desirable conditions are never wholly retained. This principle seems to have applied to the French Revolution; it probably will also apply to the Russian Revolution.

2. Liberalism and Reaction. The contrasting effects of the French Revolution may be seen in two countries. Prussia was directly exposed to the French Revolution; Russia was not. In 1780 Russia and Prussia had certain common characteristics. In both there were autocratic kings and privileged classes of nobles, who owned most of the land; suppressed classes of serfs; and between them were the bourgeoisie without significance and without power. For over two subsequent generations the same conditions continued to prevail in Russia, but Prussia moved toward a liberal monarchy. Admittedly, the French Revolution was not the sole factor; there were other influences as well. The backward countries of eastern Europe will probably feel the leveling effect of the Russian Revolution and reflect it in a generation or so in tolerance for minorities, universal education, etc.

While the French Revolution stimulated liberalism in the backward countries of Europe, it precipitated a reaction in liberal England and checked reforms already under way. Plans of the younger Pitt for the better government of India, abolition of the slave trade, concessions to Ireland, etc., were abandoned. An Alien Act was passed, placing foreigners under surveillance and permitting their deportation. Sympathetically, reactionary legislation likewise brought suffering to native Britons. This reversal is paralleled by the revulsion of political feeling produced by the Russian Revolution on the western world, where, among other effects, dictators and reactionaries came into power in Italy, Hungary, Poland, Spain, and Rumania.

The change in enlightened liberal opinion with respect to the revolutionary changes in France is well reflected in the attitude of the poet Wordsworth, who wrote, concerning the events of 1789:

> Bliss was it in that dawn to be alive
> But to be young was very heaven.

But as the revolution wore on and ran its bloody course, leading to the Napoleonic campaigns, first for propagating the republican idea but later for the building of a world empire, he wrote:

> Frenchmen had changed a war of self-defense
> For one of conquest, losing sight of all
> Which they had struggled for.

The effects of the Russian Revolution cannot yet be gauged. In many respects the Soviet régime is a form of reaction, for it has reverted to the worst phases of the Tsarist régime in Russia or even to the *ancien régime* of France. There are again unprivileged classes. A censorship prevails. Jobs are given chiefly to the faithful members of the privileged party. A political machine has been set up to seize power and hold it autocratically. The Sandwich Islander has a myth that the ghost of the man he kills enters his own body. Thus does the ghost of the old Tsarist régime seem to have entered into the Soviet body politic.

Before the French Revolution the heaviest direct tax, and one of the causes of the revolution, was the *gabelle* or salt tax. Under the Soviet régime one of the largest sources of income is the sales tax, which bears most heavily upon those least able to carry the burden. The *ancien régime* in France was an autocracy, and the modern Soviet régime is an autocracy. The nobles were the ruling class in France. The members of the Communist Party are the ruling class in Russia. The under-privileged class in France was the *tiers état;* the unprivileged class in Soviet Russia are the *lishentzy*—in both cases small merchants, artisans, lawyers, etc. However, in the case of Russia this is probably a temporary state. The effects on Europe will be more striking when Europe has less to fear from a succeeding moderate Russian government than it has from the present régime.

F. Soviet Prospects in the Light of History

It took France from 1789 to 1871, over eighty years, to establish a stable democratic government. The Soviet régime has existed now for fifteen years, and the government is not stable, but rests on force ruthlessly exercised. Nor is it democratic. Whether from the forces within, such as jealousy among the leaders for power, or whether by action from without, under pressure of the exiled Soviet leaders, some change is likely to occur. The French Revolution passed from a moderate through a radical stage, from a constitutional monarchy to an outright republic, and ultimately to a demand for economic equality. At this point arose a strong man, Napoleon, who translated the revolution to his own personal aggrandizement.

The Russian Revolution started as a constitutional republic under Kerensky, and was transformed into a communist régime by Lenin. Its failure led to a movement to the right, and the New Economic Policy was announced in the fourth year (March, 1921). The French Revolution was modified in its fifth year, and in its twelfth year it was in its Napoleonic stage. In its twelfth year, the Russian Revolution was in the Stalin stage; likewise a strong man had arisen. However, Stalin did not follow the historic pattern of swinging to the extreme right, but, after eliminating Trotsky, made a *volte face* toward the extreme left.

Will history repeat itself? Will the Russian Revolution move from autocracy to democracy, from force and terrorism to voluntary co-operation, and from social pressure to freedom of the individual? The abandonment of Lenin's New Economic Policy and the swing to the left by Stalin may have been due primarily to his desire to retain power. In the factional struggle within the Communist Party the Trotsky faction lost and its leader was deported to Turkey. Then to win Trotsky's followers Stalin out-Trotskied Trotsky by adopting an ultra-radical policy. The pressure of events in the summer of 1932 seems to be forcing another strategic retreat toward the right by the Soviets, despite their denials, or rather as proven by their denials. If state socialism in industry and agriculture does not relieve the want and poverty of the Russian people, such a retreat may be extended indefinitely. Then the historic pattern will again be realized, namely a reaction to the right following an extreme swing to the left.

In France the populace supported the terrorist régime not so much out of sympathy with its principles as out of fear of foreign invasion. In Soviet Russia the constant fear of foreign invasion aroused in the masses by the papers and the cinema may be a deliberate move by the leaders to frighten the people into supporting the Soviet régime. In France, the Jacobins maintained that they were saving the country; in Soviet Russia the Communists do likewise. In France as soon as the country was secure against attack there was a violent reaction against the terrorist régime; so probably in Soviet Russia, when the fear of foreign invasion is eliminated, the masses may turn from a régime of force to a more democratic state.

Parties and individuals held in power autocratically cannot remain there long after a revolution. Latent discontent crystallizes and ultimately removes them. This was true in France; it probably will be true in Russia. Revolution, like bodily illness, must work itself out in its natural course. Stable political form will be reached when the machinery of democratic succession is perfected. Under a free régime, spiritual life will be spontaneous. Campaigns against both superstition and corruption, masking as religion, were necessary and effective. The Church in both revolutions sided with injustice and oppression. However, after an absence of seven years God was again readmitted into France; in Russia there is already a recrudescence of religious forms. With freedom and tolerance, religious influences should again assert themselves.

CHAPTER III

THE SOVIET MIND

The Russian Revolution is too generally regarded as a political and economic phenomenon. It may also be approached as a study in human behavior and in human motives. The psychology of war explains the political policy. The love of power explains the emergence of strong men. The backwardness of Russia explains the feeling of inferiority which expresses itself in the desire to overtake and surpass the capitalist world. An analysis of some of the attitudes and behavior patterns may be of interest.

A. Revolution—The New Revelation

The characteristics of Russia in revolution are the characteristics of the young—great faith, great energy, great industry, fanaticism, intolerance, iconoclasm, erratic judgment. On the square facing the Grand Hotel in Moscow the tourist reads Lenin's epigram: "Every revolution is destructive and sweeps everything before it." This destructive, intolerant, dynamic attitude is characteristically Russian. The traits of the psychopathic Tsars have impressed themselves on the national character, and the revolution gave them free scope.

On the favorable side, the revolution has kindled a certain high idealism akin almost to religion—moral indignation, insistence upon social justice, and a passionate hatred of oppression, such as ran through the words of the Hebrew prophets. The idea of sacrifice on behalf of the community, the obligation to live a frugal, even ascetic life in order to promote the national aim, the appeal for participation in some grand social enterprise such as building the largest power works—all draw upon socially desirable traits. On the other hand, the Soviets maintain their control of the masses by preaching the doctrine of a benighted outer world. World propaganda either by word or by sword is flattering to the masses. They have a "mission." They have the same sense of superiority over the rest of the world that the missionary feels toward the heathen. The privileges enjoyed by the manual laborers over the professional classes and "white-collar" workers create a sense of exaltation.

Communism bears many of the marks of a religious movement. It calls for great faith, to live and to suffer as a believer. It calls for fanatic opposition to the unbelievers. It has its creeds and its dogmas. It offers salvation to the believer and threatens damnation to the rest of the world. Just as Christianity was spread by a militant church, as Mohammedanism was spread by the sword, so communism with its blind faith in its self-righteousness would spread its doctrine to an unwilling world even by violence. The Soviet propagandist has the zeal of a missionary.

Communism possesses other characteristics of a militant church. Communists are like other true believers, be they Christians or Mohammedans, who feel that all non-believers are doomed but that they ought to be saved, even against their wish, and who are confident that the elect bear the truth. And just as the theologians in early church history had bitter controversies over fine distinctions in doctrine, so the various schools of communists debate their differences with zeal and positiveness. The party is the established church. The "party line" is the analogue of the creed. The "left opportunists" and the "right opportunists" are analogous to dissenters, who must be punished. Just as Catholicism had its Inquisition, at which the accused were questioned as to their beliefs, so Bolshevism periodically has its *chistka,* or "cleansing" of persons whose orthodoxy is suspected. The informers under Catholicism were the prototypes of the Ogpu, the secret police of Bolshevism. In the Inquisition, the children of heretics bore the taint of their parents' heresy; and in Bolshevism the children of the bourgeois likewise carry the taint for a generation. The penalty for heresy in Catholicism was death or expulsion from the church or exile. In the case of Bolshevism the penalty is likewise death or expulsion from the party or exile.

Like formal religions, communism is a matter of perpetual promise for the future. The promise of a next world can never be verified. But communism promises more good in the existing world. To an extent it must therefore realize on its promises. Capitalism on the other hand makes few promises. It just performs, sometimes crudely. It is realistic. It is increasingly efficient. For this reason it has less of the spiritual appeal. It does not call for the enthusiasm of service, but it does furnish the material basis of life out of which realizable enthusiasm can grow.

The group of movements in Russia which are designed to impress adolescents and young people reflect the contagious appeal of communism. It releases energies and calls for the expenditure of more energy. The Soviets have the vigor of youth. Just as nascent or freshly generated oxygen is more potent in its chemical activity than ordinary oxygen, so every freshly generated social movement has unusual vigor. At the beginning Christianity and Mohammedanism were more idealistic and more vigorous. As time went on they settled into institutionalism. Fanaticism yielded to tolerance. Similarly the newly born nations of Europe had a great burst of forces, both constructive within their borders and destructive toward their minorities and their neighbors, before they were mellowed by time. The vigor and ruthlessness of the Soviet idea are characteristic of its newness.

B. The War Psychosis

In some respects the psychology of the Soviet régime is the psychology of war. Danger is discovered everywhere. If a machine breaks down, an engineer is accused of sabotage and punished. If internal affairs go wrong, the blame is placed on the small trader. If credits are not readily available, because the Russians have not paid their debts incurred before and during the war, the capitalist world is said to be plotting for their downfall. If the agricultural program does not move rapidly, the blame is laid on the kulaks and they are deprived of their property and exiled. And if the Five-Year Plan should miscarry, some individual or group will be blamed therefor. In the cinema-like mock trial of the Soviet engineers in 1931, in which self-confessed traitors were released on light sentence, the motive seemed to be the desire to reveal an international plot to attack the Soviets. Similar characteristics were displayed by the belligerent nations in the World War.

The atmosphere of Russia throughout is the atmosphere of war. The self-sacrifice, the heroism, the tremendous display of energy, the will to win, the social idealism, the brotherly feeling between the racial and religious elements of the population, as well as the cruelty and waste, which characterized the fighting nations in the World War, now also characterize Russia. There the very language is the language of war. For instance, in the Economic Survey of the State Bank of the U.S.S.R. (March 1930), somewhat similar to our Federal Reserve Bulletin, appear these curious words in an explanation of some credit changes: "If an economic process takes place that is not provided for in the Plan, then the Bank is in the position *to signal the breach in the sector of the planned front."* The terminology in daily use is that of war—"shock brigades," "socialized sector," "economic front," etc.

This war atmosphere is due in part to the fact that the Russians are naturally a stolid and an apathetic people. It requires continuous stimulus to stir them on. Propaganda assails them from sunrise to sunset. At five o'clock in the morning the loud-speaker opposite the Hotel de l'Europe in Leningrad starts going. At midnight the movie finishes the day's reiterations of the glory of the Soviets and the misery of the capitalist nations. Not merely in word but in deed is the military idea carried out. The young communists are formed into brigades on a military basis and dispatched like troops for service in mines, factories, railroads, or special projects. Just as in wartime in the belligerent countries, so in the Soviet régime the whole population is dominated by a single purpose, and all dissent is unwelcome. The individual counts for naught. The needs of the state are supreme. And therefore, with the Soviets presumably at war, coercion of the individual is accepted as a matter of course. If things went wrong in the World War, the answer was, *"C'est la guerre."* If things go wrong in Russia the answer is similarly, "After the Five-Year Plan all will be well." Life in Russia has been fifteen years of continual crises, similar to those suffered by the peoples of the warring countries.

Further psychological analysis suggests that the Russian population is suffering from a sort of social paranoia. They have delusions of persecution. Whenever an international conference is called on such matters as disarmament or reparations, the Russian press sees in it a cabal to destroy the Soviets. When the Eleventh Plenary Session of the Executive Committee of the Communist Internationale was held at Moscow in April 1931, *Pravda* printed a resolution concerning the preparations for war against the Soviet Union. The basis of the charge was that a committee for the relief of farmers was formed by Alexander Legge, who had been vice chairman of the War Industries Board in the United States. The French and Americans were said to have bought $500,000,000 worth of military supplies in anticipation of intervention.[1] Similarly, the *Red Star*, newspaper of the army, and other Moscow papers, stated that the Hoover Plan for a moratorium was preliminary to an offensive on the Soviet Union. The visits of Secretary Mellon and Secretary Stimson were to sound out the European powers concerning the formation of an international league against the Soviets.[2]

When the food is short, it is due to enemies within. If long queues of people must wait for food, the blame is laid to counter-revolutionary plots. If the currency depreciates, people who accumulate silver are shot. The paranoid subject sees enemies all around, and in Russia the enemies are sometimes the small peasants, sometimes the kulaks, and sometimes the inefficient engineers.

C. The Sense of Inferiority and Its Results

The Russian leaders have a keen sense of inferiority about their vast country. They feel that they are a hundred years behind the western world. In an address before the First Conference of the All-Union Communist Industrial Executives, Stalin amplified this point:

> Russia is from fifty to a hundred years behind the rest of the world in knowledge. It is our job as Bolsheviks to make up arrears in these ten years, because laggards always suffer. That is what happened in old Russia—she was always backward and paid for it dearly. . . . They (the capitalists) beat her because of backwardness—military, cultural, governmental, industrial, and agricultural backwardness. . . . And that is why we must make up arrears. As Lenin said, "We must die or catch up and surpass them." We must do that or they will smash us.[3]

In individuals this inferiority complex is often the mainspring of achievement and genius. In the Russian people it is indeed the mainspring of their gigantic efforts. Therefrom comes the tremendous urge for universal education and for technical training. Therefrom comes the Great Plan to enable them to accomplish in five years the tremendous industrialization that would normally take five decades. The continuous slogan is, "We must overtake and surpass the capitalist countries."

This sense of inferiority has also resulted in other great plans. Leningrad becomes the greatest lumber port of the world. Dnieprostroy becomes the greatest power plant, Magnitogorsk the greatest steel plant in the world. Gigant is to be the biggest farm in the world. The very magnitude of these undertakings is a reflection of the sense of inferiority of their founders. They *shall* prove to the world that they are not inferiors. This sense of inferiority likewise often betrays itself in loud assertions of superiority. To buttress the Soviets' longing to feel superior, they pity and denounce the capitalist world and try to convert it to their better doctrines. The cocky and blustering tone assumed by their representatives for years at international conferences likewise betrays a consciousness of inferiority. Such an attitude is not taken in negotiations between equals.

The suppressed working classes, who were regarded and who regarded themselves as the inferiors of society, were taught the doctrine of their superiority. They avidly swallowed the doctrine. Enjoying preferences as to food, shelter, and university education, laborers have acquired a sense of superiority which exalts them, and therefore they support the communists who foster it. Men usually think highly of those who agree with them. In a sense the message of communism is similar to that of Christianity, "Arise, ye disinherited." "Ye that are nothing shall become everything," is a phrase of the Internationale, but the Gospels likewise say, "The meek shall inherit the earth" and "The first shall be last and the last shall be first." In both, salvation is promised to those who believe.

D. Psychological Gains

The Soviet revolution was a great leveling process. The position of social inferiority under the Tsarist régime was removed. Freedom was achieved for the lowest class. Women were emancipated. Minority groups were treated as equals. This emancipation and freedom released a great deal of energy and creative power. The Russian waiter or porter is unlikely to accept a tip, particularly from a stranger. He feels the equal of the hotel guest—and the hotel guest waits submissively for his tea and bread. Again, the leveling process was a leveling down rather than up. All manner of display, therefore, is frowned upon. The well-dressed person attracts attention and social disapproval. The simple life is idealized. There is less servility in Russia than there is in the western world. There is less distortion of values as the result of the worship of wealth. Incompetents do not occupy places of responsibility because of their fathers' social position. There is no incentive to make money in order to display power. Social position is based on service to the community. The system of honors and decorations established by Napoleon was intended to place social distinction upon the basis of social service, and the Soviets offer similar rewards for contributions to the common good.

E. Psychological Losses

A sense of fraternity and of love is not obvious. Rather everywhere one sees signs of hatred. Class hatred is strong. The manual laborers are the preferred class. The "white-collar" workers are discriminated against. And each class hates the other. The observing foreigner has a strong sense of hatred in action. The motive of the revolution was hatred of the Tsarist régime. Stalin himself said: "My whole atmosphere was saturated with hatred of Tsarist oppression and I threw myself whole-heartedly into revolutionary work." [4] The psychoanalyst would say that the anti-father complex is manifest in the opposition to all social institutions, state, property, marriage, and religion. This hatred is now directed against the kulaks and other formerly well-situated classes. Beyond Russia it is directed against the capitalist world. Hatred is a dominant note in both domestic and foreign relations.

The people one meets are tense from over-activity. They also seem fatigued and tired from lack of food. Low spirits are in evidence as you see the Russians in their factories, in the street-cars, or even in the Park for Culture and Rest. There is little of the buoyancy or cheer of relaxation that one meets in the western world. It is difficult for the visitor to appraise this dullness or trace its roots. To some extent, it may be a Slavic trait which has always existed. To a larger extent it is more probably due to the present difficult conditions of living. The masses are not only subjected to lack of food, of clothing, and of shelter, but they work under high tension and live in a continuous state of suspense and expectancy. Something is always just about to happen. Secret accusations of sabotage directed against engineers or foremen, and an occasional "cleansing" of the party bring unexpected and unknown terrors to the superior man. Psychological conditions of this kind afford little background for humor or the lighter side of life for adults, although in the playgrounds and parks the children and care-free young people seem to have a very pleasant time.

F. The Thirst for Power

The struggle for wealth in a competitive capitalist state affords an outlet for the energies of men. But where money has no purchasing power and can be accumulated only in a limited way, the struggle for power finds expression not through the accumulation of wealth but directly in attaining political status. Stalin's own career may be taken as an example. It is reported that not over 20 per cent of the original Communist group who were active with Stalin and Trotsky in the 1917 revolution are still in power. Of the seven assistants of Lenin who engineered the Bolshevik Revolution and later composed the first Politbureau of the Communist Party, only Stalin remains in power. As Trotsky himself wrote:

> The first campaign against Trotskyism was opened in 1923, while Lenin was on his deathbed, and during the protracted illness of Trotsky. The second and more violent attack developed in 1924, shortly after the death of Lenin. The members of the old Politbureau, the body which actually governed the Soviet Republic, were Lenin, Trotsky, Zinovyev, Kamenev, Stalin, Rykov, and

> Tomsky, with Bukharin as alternate. In the present Politbureau only Stalin is left of the old staff, although all its members except Lenin are living. . . . The present staff with few exceptions are men of the new crowd. A majority of them took no part in the October Revolution. A very considerable number were in the camp of its open enemies. Those that did belong to the Bolshevist party before the October Revolution were of second or third magnitude. Such a combination is wholly according to the laws of history.[5]

Lenin is dead, Trotsky is in exile. Kamenev and Zinovyev are politically extinct. Bubnov is without influence and retains his office as Commissar of Education only through sufferance. Radek, Kamenev, and Zinovyev, who helped Stalin in his fight on Trotsky, had to repent their opposition and are today without prestige. Lunacharsky has been removed as Commissar of Education and has had to bow to Stalin's will. Chicherin resigned as Commissar of Foreign Affairs. Rykov, Tomsky and Bukharin, who were used by Stalin in his fight against Trotsky, were stripped of power because of their leanings toward the right. Then followed Uglanov, former Commissar of Labor, and Osinsky, member of the Supreme Economic Council. The lesser lights who have been shorn of power are legion.[6] Charles F. Murphy, the noted boss of Tammany Hall in New York, used no more clever or ruthless methods to retain his leadership. When the energies of men are confined, as under the Soviet régime, they find intense expression in the quest for and exercise of power.

G. The Social Heredity

The Russian workman inherits none of that tradition of skill and craftsmanship of the worker in the industrial countries of the west. He is still primitive in his reactions and unacquainted with machinery. On the main streets and squares of Moscow the tourist sees pedestrians jaywalking among buses, trolley cars, droshkes, and automobiles, utterly ignoring traffic, somewhat like peasants in country lanes. Therefore the busy broad streets of Moscow are lined off with ropes to keep pedestrians on the sidewalks. A lack of tradition of craftsmanship makes them forget to oil their machinery, so that depreciation is far more rapid than in the western industrial countries. The sense of efficiency is lacking. This is a slow growth of decades of industrialization and cannot be acquired in five years, no matter how energetic the methods.

Time means nothing to the good Russians. Groups of several hundred people may be seen everywhere waiting in long queues and sitting on the curbstone for the privilege of buying a few pieces of candy, some tobacco, potatoes, or meat, a national waste of time in a country where there is temporarily a great labor shortage.

Appointments are often one or two hours late. The schedules of breakfast, lunch, and dinner are two to four hours later than in the western world. It takes an hour for the hotel waiter to bring the simple *table d'hôte* breakfast of tea, black bread, and cheese. Amazed at the long delay the American tourist soon learns how to say, *"Skorayye pozhalysta!"* "Please hurry!" All in vain! The waiter keeps on with a reassuring *"Saychas,"* the idiom for "Immediately." But literally *"saychas"* means "this hour." This bit of etymology gives an insight into Russian notions of time. And when the tourist's patience is exhausted and he frets about upsetting a full day's appointments, the waiter murmurs blandly, *"Nichevó!"*—"It does not matter!"

The foreign engineers say that on arriving they chafe at the slow pace and the halting progress. But finally they give up the struggle and relax to the Russian tempo. Another example of Russian notions of time may be of interest. The Cunard liner *Carinthia,* bearing about 300 passengers, came to Leningrad on a cruise in the summer of 1930 while the writer was there. The port authorities and the government tourist agency had had several months' notice. The ship channel in the harbor had to be deepened to admit the liner. Yet, as one foreign engineer stated, the last bucketful of muck was dredged only when the *Carinthia* was actually nosing its way into the channel. Again, the simple pine board dining tables needed to accommodate the 300 tourists in the Grand Hotel in Moscow were hastily slapped together by a force of night workers who finished the job at 3 a.m. of the day of the arrival of the visitors in the city. With much effort and with little efficiency the Russians manage to keep just about one hop ahead of trouble. In view of such a lack of the notion of time the Soviet belief that a Five-Year Plan will work gigantic changes in a short time becomes comprehensible.

At the Stalingrad plant there are workmen who had never seen an electric light or any machine six months before they came to work there. The latest automatic conveyor belt was introduced for assembling tractors, but the men were unfamiliar with machines and did not know how to accommodate themselves to the traveling belt. The storerooms look like junk heaps, and alongside of a modern machine, one finds industrial processes handled in the crudest manual fashion.

The psychology of an industrial community is not yet apparent, not merely in factory efficiency, but in administrative routine. The cumbersome methods of merchandising look humorous to the westerner. The Russian has not yet developed the behavior pattern of the westerner which is necessary to carry out the ambitious industrial program.

H. Changing Human Nature

In this vast experiment new motives must be discovered, and new behavior patterns must be developed. Basic changes in attitude have already taken place. The engineer has replaced the priest, and from this fact flows a series of consequences. The emphasis is not on the good to come in the next world, to compensate for the suffering in this world, but rather on changing this world for the better. This program calls for a display of energy and zeal such as was not generally in evidence in old Russia. On the walls of the entrance to the Kremlin in Moscow, near the Grand Hotel, appear the words, "Religion is the opiate of the people." An attitude of resignation to the inevitable has been transformed into one of mastery of the possible. The ardor for revolution has been sublimated into zeal for technical and industrial development. The change of environment has changed the character of the people. The apathetic Slav is trying to become an energetic mechanic. The notion that the Russians were a group of mystics and mere dreamers is dispelled when one watches the mechanics and their foremen in the factories or observes the array of technical books and technical magazines in foreign languages to be seen at the International Book Store in Moscow.

The incentive to earn money in order to accumulate a reserve against the emergencies of life is reduced. The state provides insurance against accident, illness, old age, and unemployment. The state provides the reserve; therefore the individual does not need to do so. Furthermore, the accumulation of money is socially stigmatized. As a result, the energy that the westerner expends in getting on personally in the world is left unutilized. In the western world the factory manager is under pressure for dividends, but in Russia there is the pressure of the Trust and its directors, the "socialist competition," his social status, and the danger of demotion or perhaps even of being shot, if he fails.

New motives that have not been tried in capitalist societies are being tested in Russia. The enlargement of the social unit means substitution of a larger group for the family. The benefits of competition have been proved in the capitalist world, but the possibilities of co-operation have not been fully tested. Substitution of new motives is changing human behavior. Of course, to the rank and file of the Russian workers much of the idealism is meaningless. The laborer has a job which enables him to earn a living, and he is interested in it primarily for that reason. At the same time under the piece-work system the old incentives of reward for effort are still effective in Russia. As a result and in the interest of efficiency the Soviet has resorted to the devices of capitalism to stimulate production. As for the form of organization, communist Russia is really capitalist, though the profits go to the state.

The psychological qualities that make a revolution successful are not those that insure the success of an industrial régime. A revolution requires journalists and propagandists, men who can dream of a new order and who can move the masses to follow them, men of courage with a capacity for martyrdom, haters of injustice, men who cannot find their place in the existing scheme. For an industrial régime, engineers, managers, and administrators are needed. They are concerned rather with the prosaic things of life, with increasing the supply of goods and organizing men so that they will work together. One of the greatest changes in human behavior that will be required in Russia is the transformation of a generation of orators and idealists into managers and industrialists.

I. Psychological Reaction and Disillusionment

After a spree of exaltation, spiritual exhaustion often follows. For instance, the World War marked the high tide of sacrifice and social idealism. The end of the war was the beginning of the ebb tide. The contest in which the Fourteen Points were the objective degenerated into a series of small squabbles and bickerings for petty advantage. Similarly time is slowly deflating many of the Soviet ideas.

Many of the phenomena that are now observable are not necessarily reflections of Russian characteristics, but rather mark the transition stage following the revolt of a people against their former oppressors. The swing of history from radicalism to reaction is merely a reflection of the psychological fluctuations in the lives of peoples and nations. For example, the French in revolution revealed many of the traits that now characterize the Russians. Yet today France is one of the most conservative states of Europe.

Similarly Jefferson believed in revolutions and made no bones about saying so. "I hold," he wrote, "that a little revolution now and then is a good thing and is as necessary in the political world as storms in the physical. . . . It is a medicine necessary for the sound health of government." And again, referring to Shay's rebellion: "God forbid that we should ever be twenty years without such a rebellion." [7] Can one imagine McKinley or Taft, or even

Roosevelt or Wilson, holding or expressing such views one hundred years later?

Life is forcing changes. Every doctrine is being tested against reality. Readjustment is inevitable. When it comes, there may follow a period of disappointment and disillusionment. Russia is a country of the young. Its revolution was the work of young men. What will happen when these idealists grow older and acquire the psychological characteristics of maturity or old age?

For years before the revolution the leaders of the new order had the joy of hoping and believing. The longed-for new régime is now here. Will they also have the joy of realizing their dreams or will they have to readjust themselves to the realities of the world as it is?

Schiller's poem, *Resignation,* may furnish a clue to what is happening in Russia:

> Zwei Blumen blühen für den weisen Finder,
> Sie heissen Hoffnung und Genuss.
>
> Wer dieser Blumen eine brach, begehre
> Die andre Schwester nicht.
> Geniesse, wer nicht glauben kann. Die Lehre
> Ist ewig, wie die Welt. Wer glauben kann, entbehre!
> Die Weltgeschichte ist das Weltgericht.
>
> Du hast gehofft, dein Lohn ist abgetragen,
> Dein Glaube war dein zugewogenes Glück.*

---

* Two flowers, for all who rightly seek them, blow—
The Hope and the Fruition.
He who has plucked the one, resigned must see
The sister's forfeit bloom.
Let unbelief enjoy. Belief must be
All, to the chooser; the world's history
Is the world's judgment doom.

Thou hast had Hope—in thy belief thy prize,
Thy bliss was centered in it.
—Charles J. Hempel, translator.

PART THREE

THE PRESENT SCENE

The Three-Generation Plan

I must study politics and war. . . . My sons ought to study geography, natural history, mathematics, agriculture, commerce, and navigation, in order to give their children a right to study poetry, painting, and music.

—John Adams, *Letters to His Wife* (1780).

CHAPTER IV

THE FIVE-YEAR PLAN *

A. Origin and History of the Plan

1. Pre-War Plan and Growth. Soviet Russia took as its heritage the confiscated property of the old régime. It is not only using the old physical assets, the plants and palaces, but is even using the old ideas, for the idea of planning the economic life of the country goes back to a book published before the war, *The Future State,* by Ballod.[1] Though this work was not the basis of an actual program of development it was an academic presentation of a plan of directed economic life. Other such studies are cited in a Memorandum of the Bureau of Research on Russian Economic Conditions, University of Birmingham, England.†

* The best presentation of the Five-Year Plan in English is to be found in William H. Chamberlin's *The Soviet Planned Economic Order* (Boston: World Peace Foundation, 1931). Books issued by the Soviet Government on the Five-Year Plan include:

The Five-Year Plan of the Soviet Union, by G. T. Grinko, Vice Chairman of the State Planning Commission. New York: International Publishers. 1930.

The Soviet Union Looks Ahead, issued by The State Planning Commission. New York: Liveright. 1930.

Soviet Economic Development and American Business, by S. G. Bron, formerly chairman of the board, Amtorg Trading Corporation. New York: Liveright. 1930.

Other good presentations are to be found in the following:

Economic Handbook of the Soviet Union. New York: American-Russian Chamber of Commerce. 1931.

Piatiletka, Russia's Five-Year Plan, by Michael Farbman. New York: New Republic, Inc. 1931.

The Origins of Economic Planning, by Lewis L. Lorwin. Article in the "Survey Graphic," February, 1932.

† The Bureau of Research on Russian Economic Conditions, University of Birmingham, England, has made some excellent economic and statistical studies of Soviet Russia, probably the best in the English language. It is under the direction of Professor S. Konovalov, Professor in the University of Birmingham and Lecturer at the Universities of Oxford and London, and the members include Mr. A. M. Baykov, Russian Economic Service in Prague; Professor Jean Lescure, Professor of Social Economics at the Faculty of Law, University of Paris; Professor S. N. Prokopovich, Russian Economic Service and Slavonic Institute in Prague; Mr. E. M. Schenkman, formerly secretary of the Moscow Institute of Economic Research attached to the Commissariat of Finance; and Mr. S. P. Turin, Lecturer in Russian Economics at the London School of Slavonic and East European Studies. Dr. H. Frijda, Professor of Economics in the University of Amsterdam, President of the *Vereeniging tot Bestudeering van de Planhuishouding in de Sowjet-Unie,* Amsterdam, co-operates with the Bureau.

The Memorandum referred to above is Memorandum No. 1, *Remarks on the Five-Year Plan,* May, 1931 (See p. 10).

Before the revolution, creative ideas in technical matters were published by the Russian Technical Society in St. Petersburg. The Minutes of the Meetings (1907–1914), when V. I. Kovalevsky and L. I. Lutugin were at the head of this society, contained all the leading ideas for industrial reconstruction now included in the Five-Year Plan. These minutes deal with the *Volkhovstroi*, the *Dnieprostroi*, the Turkestan-Siberian Railway, the Volga-Don Canal, a main line for the long-distance transport of coal from the Donetz region, and many other schemes including the removal of some of the big factories and works from Petersburg and Moscow. It was senseless to transport raw material from the interior of the country to work it up in the Petersburg factories using foreign coal, and then to convey it back to the interior for distribution to the consumer.

The Soviets crystallized the general plan and energetically brought it to the practical stage.

In the Memorandum mentioned the Bureau quotes the following from the official Soviet publication, *The Five-Year Plan* (Second Edition, Vol. I, p. 74, Moscow, 1929): "The Soviet economists were aware when embarking on the Five-Year Plan that the country was 'undertaking an unprecedented experiment of gigantic construction through a rigid régime of economy and a denial of primary needs for the sake of achieving great historical aims.' "

The development of Russian industry had been so slight that growth starting from such low levels naturally was very rapid. According to Premier Molotov, in the thirteen years from 1900 to 1913 the growth of the national income of Russia averaged 2.6 per cent per annum.[2] But this growth was not concentrated along definite lines as in the Five-Year Plan, nor was the population rationed and made to dispense with many necessities of life.

The rate of increase in the five years before the war in a few of the important factors was as follows:[3]

Activity	*1908*	*1913*	*Growth*
Iron (in million poods)	175	283	1.6 times
Coal (in million poods)	1590	2213	1.4 times
Power (in million units)	200	1283	6.4 times
Workers in industry (thousands)	1765	2518	1.4 times

In other lines equally rapid growth in these five years was shown. For instance, the output doubled in the chemical industry, trebled in the rubber industry, and grew seven-fold in the agricultural machinery industry. In the decade 1898–1907, 15,000 miles of railway were built and even in the decade 1887–97, 9000 miles were built. But in the five years ending in 1930 only 2100 miles (3400 kilometers) were built.[4]

Even before the war there seemed to be a feeling that Russia's one-hundred-year handicap had to be overcome. As a result of the industrial stagnation of Russia, she had fallen far behind western Europe in her development. A veritable ferment of activity characterized the five years preceding the war. Foreign capital was attracted by the rich resources of the country, and one-third of the total investment in Russian industry was foreign. It was estimated to range between 1750 and 2000 million rubles.[5]

2. History of Planning. One of the cardinal doctrines of the Marxian system is the necessity for planning. Socialist society is characterized by a centralized and deliberate planning of the national economic life in contradistinction to the system of private or capitalist development of industry. Lenin was the genius back of the Soviets' ideas of a planned economy. Repeatedly in his addresses he developed the theme now emblazoned on banners throughout the factories of Moscow, "Socialism is Co-operation Plus Statistics." In 1920 he appointed a State Planning Commission for the purpose of working out a scheme of electrification. The commission was appointed in February and in December reported to the Eighth Congress of Soviets a plan for electrifying Russia in order to develop the country.

When the plan was finished, the commission turned its attention to the next undertaking and in 1923 it outlined the first draft of a five-year plan "for developing a metallurgical industry between 1923 and 1927." [6] The reason for the plan was that the output of metal had fallen to about 7 per cent of pre-war production and the authors were content to plan to raise it in five years to 21 per cent of pre-war production.

The capitalist countries really forced the development of the idea of the Five-Year Plan because they threw Soviet Russia back on its own resources. Originally, at the stage of lowest production, the leaders of Russia sought to secure foreign help through concessions, loans, and credits. The western world expected, as a result of the granting of foreign credits, that the Soviet system would adjust itself to capitalism. In 1924 the Soviets negotiated with the British Labor government for a loan to be guaranteed by the British government. This loan was to have marked the entry of the Soviets into active economic relations with the rest of the world. Such a reconstruction of Russia would have been along the lines usual in the development of young countries, rich in resources. However, the fall of the Labor government set at naught the effort to negotiate foreign loans. The belief that the re-establishment of industry in Soviet Russia was impossible without foreign loans was stated by Krassin at the Twelfth Congress of the Communist Party in the Spring of 1924. If the foreign capitalists had extended credits at this time, the Soviets would not have been forced to a policy of self-sufficiency. They would have imported considerably and industrialized only slowly. In other words, the Five-Year Plan was determined partly by the financial boycott of the capitalistic world, resulting from Soviet debt repudiation.

The Soviets were thus gradually thrown upon their own resources. Instead of having to find annually merely the interest on foreign loans and extending the process of development over a long period of years, the Russians had to find at home the entire principal amount of capital for the new investments. If the social surplus was to be reinvested in building up the country, the output would have to be very greatly increased or the consumption very greatly reduced. Russia was too inefficient greatly to increase the output. But the people were sufficiently patient and accustomed to deprivation so that their standard of living could be lowered, and it was on this basis that the economic reconstruction of Russia took place. A rise in this standard is, of course, the aim of the Five-Year Plan.

Actual planning of the entire economic life of the country began in 1925 when the State Planning Commission used "control figures" for the ensuing year. "Control figures" cover the plan for one year. They set the objectives in every element of the country's economic life, production in agriculture and in industry, power output, transportation, productive labor, cost of production, capital investment, banking figures, note circulation, budget receipts, retail prices, and cost of living. A series of future Five-Year Plans is now being projected by the State Planning Department.

3. Trotsky's Version.[7]

The Opposition demonstrated that the bureaucracy was underestimating the possibilities of industrialization and collectivization; that the economic work was being carried on empirically in a hand-to-mouth manner; that it was necessary to adopt a broader scale and a faster tempo. The Opposition demanded the abandonment of the one-year for the Five-Year Plan, and asserted that a yearly 20 per cent growth of industrial production presented nothing unattainable with a centralized leadership.

The Stalin bureaucracy accused the Opposition at that time of superindustrialism and utopianism. . . . Defense of a tortoise tempo in industry and mockery of the planning principle—such was the platform of the Stalin faction from 1923 to 1928. All the present members of the Politbureau without a single exception answered our demand for an increased tempo of industrialization with the stereotyped question: Where shall we get the means?

How far Stalin himself fell short of the scale of the present Five-Year Plan a year before its ratification may be seen in the mere fact that in April 1927, answering Trotsky—who was then President of the Dnieprostroy Commission—he declared at a meeting of the Central Executive Committee: "For us to build the Dnieprostroy [the electrical power plant on the Dnieper] would be just the same as to buy the mouzhik a gramophone instead of a cow." In the stenographic report of the Central Committee these words are inscribed as the most authentic opinion of Stalin.

Subsequent attempts to explain his struggle against industrialization with references to the "prematureness" of the proposals of the Opposition are meaningless, since it was not a question of a particular task of the moment, but of the general prospects of industry and the five-year program. . . .

With its usual short-sighted empiricism the Stalin bureaucracy, under the influence of successes, began in 1928 to increase uncritically the tempo of industrialization and collectivization. Here the rôles were exchanged. The Left Opposition came out with a warning that with too swift a pace, not tested out by previous experience, disproportions may arise between the cities and the country, and between the different branches of industry, creating dangerous crises. Moreover—and this was the chief argument of Opposition—a too-rapid investment of capital in industry would cut off excessively the share allotted to current consumption, and fail to guarantee the necessary rise of the standard of living of the people.

Here, too, the Stalin bureaucracy has been ultimately compelled to listen to the voice of the Opposition. Quite recently a separate Commissariat of Manufacturing Industries was formed out of the staff of the Supreme Council of National Economy. Its task is to take care of the current needs of the population. At the present stage this reform has a purely bureaucratic character, but its goal is clear: to create in the government mechanism certain guarantees that the daily needs of the masses will not be too much sacrificed to the interest of the heavy industries. Here, too, the Stalin faction, lacking perspective and creative force, is compelled to bless today what it was cursing yesterday.

B. Motives Underlying the Five-Year Plan

The foreigner in Russia is perplexed by the haste involved in the plan. Most Americans are inclined to ask, as did the late Professor Henry Rogers Seager, of Columbia University, at a dinner in Moscow given by the Soviet Travel Bureau to a group of American economists in July 1930, "Why hurry the job within five years? You have all eternity ahead of you." The answer given depends upon the point of view. Most Russians will say that the country has a one-hundred-year handicap to make up and a handicap runner in a race usually puts forth every energy to overcome his disadvantage. The doctrine blazoned in stores and factories is "to overtake and surpass the capitalist countries."

The cynical Russian in Moscow, however, says: "These people are trying to build up a socialist state and they have no proletariat, therefore their first task is to create a proletariat, and the quickest way of creating one is to industrialize rapidly." The communists, however, say that with the drift of the peasants to the cities, industrialization was necessary to prevent unemployment.

Russia must be transformed from an agricultural country with small peasant proprietors, the conservative backbone of a capitalist country like France, into a nation with an economic system where every individual is dependent upon the community. Therefore, the socialist organization of industry and agriculture is carried out under the impetus and enthusiasm of the great plan.

The Five-Year Plan is also an excuse to justify the privation resulting from the cumbersome methods of state capitalism. A population which would hardly put up with the sacrifices resulting from the Russian policies of debt repudiation and the consequent lack of credit willingly makes sacrifices in the hope that a new day is to dawn. Present sacrifices are made in the hope of future happiness. The golden age ahead is to provide the elements of existence which are the *sine qua non* of the standard of living in capitalist countries, adequate food, modest clothing, and more than the 54 square feet of floor space allotted per person in Moscow, and is to end the conscription of labor and the sweating imposed in the name of a workers' state.

The Five-Year Plan is also proclaimed as a military measure. With memories of Allied intervention still fresh in their minds, the Russians conceive of the plan as a great scheme of military defense. A resolution of the Fifth Congress of the Soviets held at Moscow, May 28, 1929, states: "In regard to the strengthening of the defensive capacity of the Soviet Union, the Congress commissions the government, in executing the Five-Year Plan, to take concrete measures guaranteeing the development of those branches of economic life which are inseparably connected with the defensive capacity of the country." War Commissar Voroshilov, in a tour through the industrial regions of the Soviet Union, encouraged the efficient workers and roundly scolded the negligent. In an address at the Kuznetzk steel plant he stated that "along with the other giants of Soviet industry your metallurgic plant will arm the international proletariat in the struggle for socialism. The vast rôle which these giants will play in business and in our national defense requires no demonstration. In the future, war will be mechanized to the utmost limit and its issues will depend mostly on the fortress of economy and on the question of who is richest in metals, chemicals, and electric power." [8]

The official Soviet newspaper, *Izvestia,* says: "The manufacture of tanks and that of tractors have many points in common; artillery, machine guns and rifles can be made in machinery factories. The metal industries should provide also for the production of armament and ammunition." [9] In this policy the Soviets may be justified as much as the other countries, who in peacetime manufacture cash registers and typewriters and in wartime, hand grenades—the Schneider-Creusot plant in France, the Krupp plant in Germany, the Vickers plant in England, the Skoda plants in Austria and Czechoslovakia, and the Bethlehem plant in the United States. The Russians have the fear complex so intensely, that the Putilov plant in Leningrad is guarded by soldiers. When the writer visited the plant he found that certain sections making armament were shut off from inspection.

This notion of defense has determined not merely the nature of the industries to be established but also their location. Just as the capital was moved from Leningrad to Moscow, to be out of range of the gunfire of a foreign fleet, so new industrial projects have been located far inland, to constitute a second line of defense in case of invasion. The location of industries in the Urals and in Siberia in isolated areas devoid of population is due partly but not solely to military considerations, as economies of transportation have also been a determining factor. For example, a group of iron and steel plants are located at Magnitogorsk where the iron is to be found, and also at the Kuznetzk Basin where the coal is located. This will avoid much movement of empty trains. The development of American steel mills was originally in the Pennsylvania region where coal is found. Cars bringing ore from the Lakes returned empty. More recently, steel mills were built near the Lake Superior region where the iron-ore beds are located. The returning cars and boats carry coal. Russia utilized the latest experience of the world.

The enemies of the Soviets see in the Five-Year Plan merely an instrument of aggression and world revolution. The Soviets are said to be planning a great industrial system which will first ruin the capitalist world by cut-throat competition and then, after precipitating a world revolution, follow it up with military support. This is probably a paranoid fear of the western world. Russia has enough domestic problems to keep her busy at home for a generation.

C. Aims of the Five-Year Plan

The aim of the Five-Year Plan is to create a new civilization along the latest model, embodying the latest technical achievements as well as a most radical social system. It is a purposeful plan. It aims to reconstruct the country along social lines, to eliminate the motive of profit and substitute service to the community, and to raise the economic and cultural level of the masses. It is the most direct approach to socialism, for 125,000,000 individual peasants must be converted into a co-operating proletariat. The Five-Year Plan aims to create a powerful industrial state. The underlying principle is economic nationalism, the protectionist theory of the self-sufficient state. A primitive country, rich in resources, is to be forced by a hothouse development, through the entire gamut of stages of industrial development, until it is economically independent of foreign countries. The Five-Year Plan does not attempt to co-ordinate production and consumption. In fact, in some of the raw materials there has been serious overproduction and in consumers' goods a great shortage. Such an interpretation of the Five-Year Plan developed in the western world, where there is an excess of productive capacity.

D. Program of the Five-Year Plan

Perhaps the general program of the Five-Year Plan can best be stated in terms of the resolution of the Fifth Congress of Soviets in Moscow on May 28, 1929, as follows:

> The Five-Year Plan proposed by the government, being a developed program of socialist reconstruction of economic life, corresponds with the general course of the Soviet power toward the industrialization of the Soviet Union, toward the socialist reconstruction of the village, toward the overcoming of capitalist elements and the consequent strengthening of socialist elements in the economic order of the country, and toward the raising of the defensive capacity of the Soviet Union.
>
> The Congress especially approves the broad program of outliving the backwardness of agriculture indicated by the Five-Year Plan. Only this can assure the many millions of poor and middle-class peasants access to the road of economic upswing, and socialist reconstruction of the individual peasant farm.[10]

In the words of Mr. G. M. Krzhizhanovsky, formerly President of the State Planning Commission, the aim of the Five-Year Plan is "such redistribution of the existing productive forces of society, including therein both the labor power and the material resources of the country, as would guarantee in the highest degree the output of these productive forces without crises at the quickest possible tempo for the purpose of achieving the maximum satisfaction of the current needs of the toilers, and for bringing them as quickly as possible to the complete reorganization of society on the bases of socialism and communism." [11]

A development which, by a natural course, took fifty years in the United States, Germany, and Japan, is to be forced into a period of five years or perhaps ten.

To achieve this end the iron and steel industry is basic. One of the officials of the Steel Trust in Moscow, Mr. Lauer, stated the case significantly to the writer. "China has a textile industry, but China is economically a colony of the capitalist world. She has no independent iron and steel industry." Therefore, the Soviets are concentrating on the heavy industries. Now they manufacture chiefly producers' goods. Consumers' goods are to be manufactured increasingly later. Although capital, energy, and materials are being diverted into heavy industry, the lighter industries are not entirely neglected and are to receive more attention in the years to come.

The inquiring investigator wonders how it is possible to lay down a program for a development five years ahead, when the foreign market is an unpredictable factor, and when fluctuations in foreign costs or foreign demand may upset the calculations. The reply given by one Soviet official, Mr. Sushkov of the Planning Division, is that the program is based on the predictable home demand. For many years the home market for producers' goods will be unlimited. The country needs buildings, capital goods, and machinery far in excess of the capacity of the plants producing raw materials. For many years exports will be insignificant and for this reason the Plan need not concern itself with foreign conditions and need merely consider domestic conditions. Nor need the program concern itself with foreign costs, because the Soviet will not be motivated, as are capitalist industries, by the principle of private profit, but by the principle of national service.

Under the capitalist system the accumulation of small funds saved by the individual is attracted through investment channels by bankers on the basis of bankers' opinion as to the feasibility of a given venture and its possibilities of profit to themselves and to the investors, which in turn depend on consumer demand. In the Soviet Union the investment of the national surplus is based on the national need as determined not by consumer demand but by the Planning Commission. The possibilities of profit for the individual in Russia lie in buying government bonds for industrialization.

In defense against charges that the Five-Year Plan contains inaccuracies the officials of the Soviet Union answer as follows:

> It cannot be expected, of course, that any economic plan will be 100 per cent completely carried out, with absolute precision and without deviations in any direction, especially when the plan is drawn for a considerable period ahead and embraces the entire economic life of such a big country as the Soviet Union, with all the complex interplay of the most varied economic factors. The object of the plans is not to predict, by means of detailed estimates, and with absolute precision, the course of economic developments in all particulars, but to determine the basic guiding lines and the general scope of the economic efforts to be exerted in the period under consideration.[12]

The Five-Year Plan merely outlines certain broad objectives which are to be modified as conditions change. In other words it is not a rigid and precise program. It is rather an ideal to which to aspire.

1. The Percentage of Increases. The Plan is most ambitious. Secular growth of industry in the United States is about 3 per cent per annum. Russia is satisfied with no such modest figure. The heavy industry in five years is to increase 3.02 times or 202 per cent, at an average rate of 40 per cent per annum. Light industry is to increase 2.04 times or 104 per cent, at an average rate of 21 per cent per annum. Agricultural production is to increase 1.55 times or 55 per cent, at an average rate of 10 per cent per annum. The national income is to increase 103 per cent or at the rate of 20 per cent per annum.

	NATIONAL INCOME IN PRE-WAR RUBLES		NATIONAL INCOME IN TERMS OF 1926–27 PRICES	
Fiscal Year	*Millions of Rubles*	*Per Cent of 1913*	*Per Cent Gain over Preceding Year*	*Millions of Rubles*
1913	14,025	100.0	——	——
1926	13,376	95.4	——	——
1927	14,780	105.4	10.5	——
1928	16,013	114.2	8.3	24,429
1929	17,972	128.1	12.2	27,031
1930	21,450	152.9	19.4	31,299
1931 (program)	29,500	210.3	37.5	——

It is estimated that the total population should increase 11.8 per cent in five years, or about 2.3 per cent per annum, and the number of wage earners 18.2 per cent, or 3.6 per cent per annum.[13] Basic capital invested in industry should grow from 9.6 billion rubles to 30.7 billion rubles, or 4.2 billions per annum.[14] Output per man should be increased 95 per cent or an average of about 19 per cent per annum. Costs are to be reduced 32 per cent or at the

ANNUAL DEVELOPMENTS UNDER THE FIVE-YEAR PLAN [15]

	Amounts in Millions of Rubles							Ratio of Each Year to Preceding Year, Per Cent					Ratio of 1932–33 to 1927–28
	1927–28	1928–29	1929–30	1930–31	1931–32	1932–33	For 5 Years	1928–29 to 1927–28	1929–30 to 1928–29	1930–31 to 1929–30	1931–32 to 1930–31	1932–33 to 1931–32	
I. Gross production of industry, at 1926–27 prices	18,312	21,164	25,009	29,643	35,584	43,196	154,596	115.6	118.2	118.5	120.0	121.4	236.0
Of which, industries covered by plan of the Supreme Council of National Economy	10,909	13,247	16,090	19,649	24,320	30,447	103,753	121.4	121.5	122.1	123.8	125.2	279.0
II. Gross production of agriculture, at 1926–27 prices	16,659	17,367	18,845	20,804	22,897	25,806	105,719	104.2	108.5	110.4	110.1	112.7	155.0
Of which, agriculture proper	14,526	15,038	16,304	18,054	19,935	22,630	91,961	103.5	108.4	110.7	110.4	113.5	155.8
III. National income (net production):													
(a) At 1926–27 prices	24,429	27,149	31,289	36,294	42,154	49,690	186,576	111.1	115.2	116.0	116.1	117.9	203.4
(b) At prices of respective years	24,681	27,385	30,884	34,829	38,749	43,270	175,117	111.0	112.8	112.8	111.3	111.7	175.3
IV. Capital investments (at prices of respective years)	8,052	10,192	13,080	16,061	18,354	20,717	78,404	126.6	128.3	122.8	114.3	112.9	257.3
Of which:													
(a) Basic capital	7,112	8,612	10,836	13,115	14,896	17,142	64,601	121.1	125.8	121.0	113.6	115.1	241.0
Including:													
1. Industry (including industrial housing)	1,672	2,091	2,845	3,451	3,796	4,170	16,353	125.1	136.1	121.3	110.0	109.9	249.4
Of which, industries regulated by the Supreme Council of National Economy	1,318	1,659	2,331	2,880	3,165	3,465	13,500	125.9	140.5	123.6	109.9	109.5	262.9
2. Electrification, not including factory power plants	284	332	453	656	757	861	3,059	116.9	136.4	144.8	115.4	113.7	303.2
3. Agriculture	3,084	3,664	4,173	4,720	5,079	5,516	23,152	118.8	113.9	113.1	107.6	108.6	178.8
4. Transportation	896	1,128	1,497	1,878	2,394	3,105	10,002	125.9	132.7	125.5	127.5	129.7	346.5
(b) Operating capital	940	1,580	2,244	2,946	3,458	3,575	13,803	168.1	142.0	131.3	117.4	103.4	380.3
V. Government budget, central and local, net expenditures	5,879	7,123	8,633	10,120	11,810	13,669	51,355	121.3	121.2	117.2	116.7	115.7	232.5
Of which:													
(a) General administration and defense	1,751	1,878	1,991	2,195	2,406	2,716	11,186	107.1	106.0	110.2	109.6	112.9	155.1
(b) Social welfare and cultural activities	1,238	1,450	1,769	2,167	2,566	2,994	10,946	117.1	122.0	122.5	118.4	116.7	241.8
(c) Financing of national economy	2,424	3,284	4,204	5,058	6,081	6,981	25,608	136.0	128.0	120.3	120.2	114.8	288.0
(d) All other	464	511	669	700	757	978	3,615	110.1	130.9	104.6	108.1	129.2	209.9

BASIC INDICATORS OF THE FIVE-YEAR PLAN OF NATIONAL ECONOMY AS COMPARED WITH 1913 AND WITH THE PRECEDING FIVE-YEAR PERIOD [16]

					Total for 5 Years		Ratio to 1913		
	1913	*1922–23*	*1927–28*	*1932–33*	*1923–24 to 1927–28*	*1928–29 to 1932–33*	*1922–23 Per cent*	*1927–28 Per cent*	*1932–33 Per cent*
I. Population:									
(a) Total number (millions)	139.7	133.3	151.3	169.2	143.8	162.0	95.4	108.3	121.1
Including:									
Urban	25.7	21.9	27.9	34.2	25.3	31.5	85.2	108.6	133.1
Rural	114.0	111.4	123.4	135.0	118.5	130.5	97.7	108.2	118.4
(b) Number of persons working for hire, total (thousands) ..	11,200.0	6,803.0	11,350.0	15,764.0	9,740.0	13,794.0	60.7	101.3	140.8
Of which, in census industry ..	2,900.0	1,706.0	3,072.0	4,080.0	2,550.0	3,626.0	58.8	105.9	140.7
II. Electrification:									
1. Capacity of primary motors in industrial plants (thousands of KW.)	960.0	......	2,550.0	6,200.0	......	......	....	265.6	645.8
2. Capacity of primary motors in public utility stations (thousands of KW.)	96.0	......	880.0	3,750.0	......	......	....	916.7	3,906.3
3. Output of electric energy (millions of KW.)	1,945.0	1,095.0	5,050.0	22,000.0	16,000.0	65,000.0	56.3	259.6	1,131.1
III. Agriculture:									
1. Planted area (millions of hectares)	116.7	80.0	115.6	142.0	105.0	129.0	70.4	101.7	124.9
Of which, planted to grain	102.7	70.0	97.2	112.0	84.0	104.0	68.2	94.8	109.2
Of which, planted to industrial crops	5.5	4.0	7.3	12.0	6.0	10.0	72.7	132.7	218.1
2. Live stock: bovine cattle or its equivalent (millions of heads):	85.0	65.0	85.0	114.0	77.0	......	76.8	100.0	134.1
Of which:									
(a) draft animals (millions of heads)	36.0	22.0	31.0	48.0	27.0	......	61.8	86.1	133.3
(b) breeding stock (millions of heads)	49.0	43.0	54.0	66.0	50.0	......	87.8	110.2	134.7
3. Production (physical volume):									
(a) Grain (millions of tons)	81.2	61.0	73.7	106.0	335.0	445.0	75.1	89.5	130.5
(b) Cotton (thousands of tons) .	744.0	28.0	719.0	1,907.0	2,369.0	6,857.0	3.7	96.6	256.4
(c) Flax fiber (thousands of tons)	454.0	306.0	292.0	621.0	1,501.0	2,210.0	67.4	63.8	136.8
(d) Sugar beet (millions of tons)	10.9	2.0	10.1	20.0	31.0	74.0	18.3	92.7	183.5
(e) Oil seeds (thousands of tons)	2,554.0	2,098.0	3,401.0	6,721.0	14,257.0	25,275.0	82.1	133.2	263.2
4. Production at pre-war prices (billions of rubles)	10.5	7.8	11.0	17.0	49.6	......	74.3	104.8	161.9
5. Marketable portion of grain production (millions of tons)	20.4	....	8.0	19.6	44.0	65.0	....	39.2	96.1
IV. Industry:									
1. Production, physical volume:									
A. Producers' goods									

BASIC INDICATORS OF THE FIVE-YEAR PLAN OF NATIONAL ECONOMY AS COMPARED WITH 1913 AND WITH THE PRECEDING FIVE-YEAR PERIOD—*Continued*

	1913	1922–23	1927–28	1932–33	Total for 5 Years: 1923–24 to 1927–28	Total for 5 Years: 1928–29 to 1932–33	Ratio to 1913: 1922–23 Per cent	Ratio to 1913: 1927–28 Per cent	Ratio to 1913: 1932–33 Per cent
(a) Coal (millions of tons) ..	28.9	11.0	35.4	75.0	125.0	279.0	38.1	122.5	259.5
(b) Petroleum (millions of tons)	9.3	5.0	11.6	22.0	44.0	86.0	53.8	124.7	236.6
(c) Peat (millions of tons) ..	1.6	3.0	6.9	16.0	24.0	57.0	187.5	431.3	1,000.0
(d) Iron ore (millions of tons)	9.2	....	5.7	19.0	17.0	64.0	4.3	62.0	206.5
(e) Pig iron (millions of tons)	4.2	....	3.3	10.0	10.0	33.0	7.1	78.6	238.1
(f) Steel ingots, open hearth (millions of tons)	4.2	....	4.0	10.4	13.0	35.0	11.9	95.2	247.6
(g) Rolled steel (millions of tons)	3.5	.5	3.2	8.0	10.0	27.0	14.3	91.4	228.6
(h) Agricultural machinery (millions of rubles at pre-war prices)	67.0	14.0	125.0	498.0	286.0	......	20.9	186.6	743.3
(i) Cement (millions of barrels)	12.3	1.0	11.9	41.0	37.0	135.0	8.1	96.7	333.3
(j) Bricks (millions of pieces)	2,144.0	213.0	1,785.0	9,300.0	5,178.0	29,750.0	9.9	83.3	433.8
(k) Superphosphates (thousands of tons)	55.0	5.0	150.0	3,400.0	379.0	7,291.0	9.1	272.7	6,181.8
(l) Sulphuric acid (thousands of tons)	150.0	35.0	208.0	1,450.0	674.0	3,801.0	23.3	138.7	966.7
B. Consumers' goods:									
(a) Cotton yarn (thousands of tons)	271.0	75.0	328.0	620.0	1,148.0	2,367.0	27.7	121.0	228.8
(b) Wool cloth (millions of meters)	95.0	22.0	97.0	270.0	328.0	849.0	23.2	102.1	284.2
(c) Linen cloth (millions of square meters)	......	93.0	165.0	500.0	728.0	1,537.0	....	....	....
(d) Sugar, granulated (thousands of tons)	1,290.0 *	211.0	1,340.0	2,600.0	4,124.0	9,640.0	16.4	103.9	201.6
(e) Salt (thousands of tons)	1,978.0	950.0	2,300.0	3,250.0	8,269.0	14,473.0	48.0	116.3	164.3
(f) Rubber shoes (millions of pairs)	28.0	10.0	37.0	75.0	113.0	274.0	35.7	132.1	267.9
2. Production of census industry, at pre-war prices (billions of rubles)	6.4	2.0	8.1	21.0	......	......	31.3	126.6	328.1
3. Real wages of industrial workers, including rent and other municipal services (per cent of 1913)	100.0	54.2	122.5	208.9	......	......	54.2	122.5	208.9
V. Transportation:									
1. Mileage in operation (thousands of km.)	59.0	71.0	77.0	90.0	75.0	82.0	120.3	130.5	152.5
2. Freight traffic (in millions of tons)	132.0	58.0	151.0	281.0	111.0	217.0	44.3	114.4	212.9
Of which:									
Grain	18.0	9.0	14.0	25.0	13.0	19.0	50.0	77.8	138.9
Coal	26.0	8.0	30.0	58.0	21.0	45.0	30.8	115.4	223.1
VI. National income (billions of rubles):									
At pre-war prices	14.0	7.0	15.0	30.0	63.0	115.0	50.0	107.1	214.3
At prices of respective years	......	7.0	25.0	43.0	......	175.0	....	....	....

* 1914 production.

NOTE: Figures in columns 6 and 7 referring to population, planted areas, number of live stock, and transportation are five-year averages.

STATISTICAL SURVEY [17]

Principal Indicators of Economic Development, 1913 and 1925 to 1931

	1913	*1925–26*	*1926–27*	*1927–28*	*1928–29*	*1929–30 (prelim-inary)*	*1931 (pro-gram)*
I. Population:							
Total on April 1 (millions)	140.0	144.5	147.9	151.3	154.8	158.4	......
Urban (millions)	25.8	25.3	26.7	27.9	29.0	30.2	......
Rural (millions)	114.2	119.2	121.2	123.4	125.8	128.2	......
II. Labor:							
Total number of persons working for hire, annual averages (thousands)	11,200.0	10,217.7	10,989.8	11,455.6	12,150.5	13,129.0	16,300.0
In census industry (thousands)	2,900.0	2,678.0	2,838.6	3,033.3	3,269.9	3,835.0	4,798.0
Index of monthly real wages for workers in large-scale industry (including municipal services)	100.0	106.9	119.1	132.7	138.0	151.1	......
III. National Income:							
Million pre-war rubles	14,025.0	13,376.0	14,780.0	16,013.0	17,972.0	21,450.0	29,500.0
IV. Industry:							
(a) Producers' goods—							
Production of power (millions of kilowatt-hours)	1,945.0	3,270.0	4,098.0	5,165.0	6,208.0	7,714.0	12,700.0
In regional power plants (millions of kilowatt-hours)	431.0	1,121.0	1,429.0	1,814.0	2,315.0	3,414.0	6,800.0
Coal (millions of metric tons)	28.9	25.4	32.1	35.4	40.6	46.7	83.6
Oil (millions of metric tons)	9.2	8.3	10.3	11.6	13.7	17.4	27.5
Peat (millions of metric tons)	1.55	4.26	5.90	6.45	7.45	7.0	14.0
Iron ore (millions of metric tons)	9.21	3.31	4.82	6.03	7.12	10.25	16.1
Pig iron (millions of metric tons)	4.22	2.20	2.96	3.28	4.02	4.97	8.0
Rolled steel (millions of metric tons)	3.51	2.25	2.74	3.37	3.88	4.48	6.7
Agricultural machinery (millions of rubles at pre-war prices)	67.0	75.50	99.67	131.81	187.75	290.28	......
Cement (millions of barrels)	12.3	8.5	9.7	11.9	14.4	19.4	35.0
Bricks (billions of pieces)	2.1	1.0	1.4	1.9	2.5	4.8	5.7
Superphosphates, 14 per cent standard (thousands of metric tons)	55.0	80.0	90.0	150.0	213.0	400.0	1,112.0
Sulphuric acid, 100 per cent (thousands of metric tons)	150.0	146.5	168.8	208.1	271.8	360.0	728.5
(b) Consumers' goods—							
Cotton cloth (millions of meters)	2,275.2	2,030.0	2,343.0	2,543.0	2,836.0	2,419.9	2,835.0
Cotton yarn (thousands of metric tons)	271.0	240.0	277.0	322.2	352.7	299.5	410.0
Woolen cloth (millions of meters)	95.0	64.8	85.4	99.4	118.1	131.9	125.0
Granulated sugar (thousands of metric tons)	1,290.0	1,063.0	870.0	1,340.0	1,280.0	836.0 †	2,527.0
Salt (thousands of metric tons)	1,978.0	1,537.0	2,061.0	2,365.0	2,670.0	3,330.0 *	4,517.0
Rubber footwear (millions of pairs)	27.9	25.1	29.6	36.3	42.2	42.7	42.5
Leather shoes (millions of pairs)	5.5	12.0	15.3	23.6	32.7	62.8	84.6
Matches (millions of cases)	3.76	4.03	4.25	5.5	7.0	9.1	12.3
Total output of census industry (billions of pre-war rubles)	6.39	6.02	6.88	8.43	10.24	13.45 *	......

	1913	*1925–26*	*1926–27*	*1927–28*	*1928–29*	*1929–30 (prelim-inary)*	*1931 (pro-gram)*
V. Transportation:							
Length of railway lines in operation (thousands of kilometers)	58.5	74.6	75.7	76.9	77.6	78.0	81.0
Railway freight operations (billions of ton.-kilometers)	65.7	68.9	81.7	88.2	106.7	138.0	186.4
Railway passenger operations (billions of passenger-kilometers)	25.2	23.4	22.1	23.6	29.5	46.8	68.0
Freight carried by railways (millions of metric tons)	132.4	116.7	135.9	150.6	176.5	234.9	330.0
Passengers carried by railways (millions)	184.8	262.7	254.2	280.8	343.2	510.2	720.0
Freight turnover on inland waterways (millions of metric tons)	48.2	33.4	35.2	39.9	50.2	64.0	116.1
Freight turnover of Soviet maritime ports (millions of metric tons)	44.0	16.6	18.9	19.5	25.0	47.2	68.5
Total freight carried by transport system (millions of metric tons)	224.6	166.7	190.0	210.0	251.7	346.1	514.6
VI. Finance: (in millions of rubles)							
Currency circulation (as of beginning of each year indicated)	2,359.0	1,142.9	1,343.1	1,628.3	1,970.8	2,642.2	4,302.0
Federal budget—							
Revenues	3,431.0	3,986.4	5,713.3	6,950.9	8,036.9	12,527.0	21,774.0
Expenditures	3,383.0	3,877.0	5,662.1	6,747.6	8,021.1	12,246.0	20,274.0
VII. Foreign Trade: (in millions of rubles)							
(a) Total turnover	2,894.1	1,433.0	1,483.2	1,723.3	1,713.9	2,071.0	......
Exports	1,520.1	676.6	770.5	777.8	877.6	1,002.3	......
Imports	1,374.0	756.4	712.7	945.5	836.3	1,068.7	......
(b) Soviet-American trade ‡	55.8	72.7	92.8	113.5	138.4	180.2	......
Exports (Soviet sales) ‡ (in millions of dollars)	26.5	24.1	21.1	22.3	30.7	31.0	......
Imports (Soviet purchases) ‡	29.3	48.6	71.7	91.2	107.7	149.2	......

	1913	*1925*	*1926*	*1927*	*1928*	*1929*	*1930*	*1931*
VIII. Agriculture:								
(a) Total sown area § (millions of hectares)	114.2	106.3	112.3	115.0	115.7	120.4	127.8	143.0
Grain crops (millions of hectares)	100.2	89.1	95.4	97.1	94.9	98.2	102.0	111.0
(b) Gross production—								
Grain (millions of centners) ¶	801.0	746.7	783.8	735.8	733.2	717.4	873.6	978.6
Cotton, unginned (millions of centners)	7.4	5.7	5.6	7.2	8.2	8.6	13.5	21.0
Flax (millions of centners)	4.5	3.6	3.1	2.8	3.2	3.6	4.3	5.7
Sugar beets (millions of centners)	109.0	90.7	63.7	104.1	101.4	62.5	151.7	214.4
Oil seeds (millions of centners)	25.5	34.8	27.5	33.2	33.9	30.1	31.2	52.0
Dairy products (millions of centners)	245.0	288.0	312.0	323.0	310.0	337.2	...	...
Eggs (billions)	9.0	8.5	9.6	10.5	10.5	10.2	6.5	10.6
(c) Live stock—in equivalent of million head of cattle	84.9	76.2	81.1	86.4	90.2	89.3	92.7 *	...
Working horses (in millions of head)	27.3	19.9	21.2	22.8	22.5	23.3	21.3	21.3
(d) Total production (billions of pre-war rubles)	10.2	10.3	11.1	11.0	11.2	11.5	13.1 *	...

* These figures represent the program, the data for actual results being not yet available.
† This represents the sugar produced from the beet crop of 1929, which was largely destroyed by plant pests; the sugar output from the beet crop of 1930 amounted to 1,750,000 metric tons.
‡ For years 1925–26 to 1929–30, inclusive, the figures given are those for Soviet sales and purchases made through the various Soviet trading organizations in the United States. For 1913 the U. S. Department of Commerce figures for exports and imports are used.
§ Cultivated area is shown as originally sown, exclusive of area of winter crops resown.
¶ One centner equals 1/10 metric ton or 220 pounds.

DEVELOPMENT OF SOVIET NATIONAL ECONOMY [17a]

Items		(*a*) *1931* (*Preliminary Results*)	(*b*) *1932* (*Control Figures or Program*)	(*c*) *Fiscal Yr. 1932–33* (*Original 5-Year Plan*)	*Per cent Increase* (+) *or Decrease* (−) (*b*) *as Compared with* (*c*)
I. FINANCE	*bill. rubles*				
National Income		57.8	49.2	43.3	+ 13.6
Capital Investments					
National economy	*socialized sec.*	16.1	21.1	12.5	+ 68.8
Industry		8.2	10.7	4.1	+161.0
Agriculture		3.6	4.4	——	——
Transportation, total		2.7	3.3	3.0	+ 10.0
II. ELECTRIFICATION					
Capacity	*mill. kw.*	4.1	5.6	5.5	+ 1.8
Output	*bill. kw.-hr.*	10.6	17.0	22.0	− 22.8
III. STATE LARGE-SCALE INDUSTRY					
Output	*bill. rubles, 1926–27 prices*	26.0	35.4	30.5	+ 16.0
A. Producers' Goods—					
Coal	*mill. tons*	58.6	90.0	75.0	+ 20.0
Oil	*mill. tons*	23.6	28.0	21.7	+ 28.0
Pig iron	*mill. tons*	4.9	9.0	10.0	− 10.0
Steel ingots	*mill. tons*	5.4	9.5	10.4	− 8.6
Copper	*thous. tons*	53.0	100.0	84.7	+ 19.0
Machine-building including:	*mill. rubles*	4,700	6,800	4,775	+ 43.0
Agricultural machy.	*mill. rubles*	750*	940	610	+ 54.1
Tractors	*units*	40,700	82,000	55,000	+ 49.1
Automobiles	*units*	23,400	73,000	130,000	− 43.7
Locomotives	*units*	918*	1,300	825	+ 57.5
B. Consumers' Goods—					
Cotton cloth	*mill. meters*	2,470.0*	3,061.0	4,700.0	− 34.9
Leather shoes	*mill. pairs*	77.0	91.5	80.0	+ 14.4
Canned goods	*mill. cans*	520.0*	1,000.0	650.0	+ 53.8
IV. TRANSPORTATION					
Railway freight carried	*mill. tons*	250.0	320.0	281.0	+ 13.8

DEVELOPMENT OF SOVIET NATIONAL ECONOMY—*Continued*

Items		(*a*) *1931* (*Preliminary Results*)	(*b*) *1932* (*Control Figures or Program*)	(*c*) *Fiscal Yr. 1932–33* (*Original 5-Year Plan*)	*Per cent Increase* (+) *or Decrease* (—) (*b*) *as Compared with* (*c*)
V. AGRICULTURE					
A. Sown area	*mill. hectares*	136.6	144.0	141.6	+ 1.7
State farms		9.6	14.0	4.4	+218.2
Collective farms		61.2	108.0	14.5	+645.0
Cotton		2.1	2.4	1.5	+ 60.0
Sugar-beets		1.5	1.7	1.1	+ 54.6
B. Collectivization	*% of total*				
No. of households		62%	75%	9.6%	+681.3
Sown area		45%	75%	10.2%	+635.3
C. Machine-Tractor Stations	*number*	1,400	3,100	——	——
VI. LABOR					
No. Wage Earners	*million*	18.7	21.0	15.8	+ 32.9
Total Wage Fund	*bill. rubles*	21.1	26.8	15.7	+ 70.7

* Program or estimate.

rate of about 6 per cent per annum. Wages are to rise 36 per cent or about 7 per cent per annum, and real wages or purchasing power should rise 52 per cent or at the rate of about 10 per cent per annum.†

In an address before the Sixth Congress of the Soviets in March, 1931, V. Molotov, Chairman of the Council of People's Commissars, stated that the third year was the decisive year of the Five-Year Plan. The "control figures," which revised upward the original figures, called for an increase in the national income of 39 per cent, an increase in industrial production of 45 per cent, a decrease in the cost of production of 10 per cent. In the third year 518 new industrial enterprises would be completed as against 323 in

† For further details see, *The Soviet Union Looks Ahead—The Five-Year Plan for Economic Reconstruction,* by the State Planning Commission of the U.S.S.R. New York, Liveright, 1930.

the entire four years preceding. At the prevailing rate of progress he predicted that the Five-Year Plan would be completed in four years in iron, steel, and cotton goods; in three years in anthracite coal, peat, cement, and sugar, and in 2½ years in copper mining, petroleum, shipbuilding, and manufacture of engines and machinery. The heavy industries would complete their Five-Year Plan on the average in three years and all industries in 3½ years.

The "control figures," showing percentages of increase of total production under the Five-Year Plan follow: [18]

Fiscal Year	*Original Estimate 1927 per cent*	*Revised Dec. 1927 per cent*	*Estimate Dec. 1928 per cent*	*Final Estimate per cent*
1928–29	16.3	18.1	21.9	21.4
1929–30	13.1	16.6	20.2	21.5
1930–31	13.7	17.6	21.8	22.1
1931–32	10.5	13.8	22.6	23.8
1932–33	10.5	12.8	22.6	25.2

The final estimates were based on a progressive scale because of the ease with which the first year's estimates were realized. The Plan figures for a few of the major industries for the final year of the Five-Year Plan follow:

TOTAL PRODUCTION IN 1932–33 [19]

		Original Estimates of Five-Year Plan	*Revised Estimates*	*Per cent Increase*
		in millions		
Coal	*tons*	75	130	73
Oil	*tons*	22	41	86
Coke	*tons*	12	20	66
Peat	*tons*	14	33	135
Pig Iron	*tons*	10	17	70
Steel	*tons*	10	20	100
Steel, rolled	*tons*	8	15	87
Copper	*pounds*	169	530	214
Cement	*barrels*	40	100	150
Bricks	*units*	6,000	26,000	333
Electro-technical industry	*rubles*	896	4,260	375
Electrical energy	*kw.-hrs.*	22,000	33,000	50
General machine building	*rubles*	2,100	6,000	185
Agricultural machinery	*rubles*	610	2,000	228
Shoes	*pairs*	80	190	137
		in thousands		
Tractors	*units*	53	150	183
Automobiles	*units*	105	200	90

It took until 1929 for the Soviet steel industry to attain the pre-war level of production. The official figures given to the writer by the Planning Department of the Steel Trust were as follows:—

OUTPUT OF STEEL INGOTS IN SOVIET RUSSIA

	Year	*Million Tons*
Pre-war	1913	4.24
	1914	3.96
War Years	1917	3.00
	1918	0.41
Post-war	1921	0.18
	1922	0.32
	1923	0.61
	1924	0.91
	1925	1.86
	1926	2.91
	1927	2.96
	1928	3.28
	1929	4.02
	1930	5.30
Estimated	1931	7.10
	1932	11.50
	1933	17.00

The project of the non-ferrous metal industries is shown in the accompanying table.

PROJECT OF NON-FERROUS METALS INDUSTRIES [20]

	Date of Completion (Actual or Scheduled)	*Ultimate Annual Capacity, Pure Metal metric tons*
COPPER		
Krasnoural copper smelting plant (Urals)		
First unit (Capacity for first year 5000 tons of ore daily)	1930	25,000 (first and second units)
Second unit	April 1930	
Kazmedstroy (Kazakstan Copper Trust)	August 1932	50,000
Sverdlovsk electrolytic copper plant (Urals, foundation laid May 25, 1930; cost 22 million rubles)	1932	100,000
Sverdlovsk copper rolling plant (Urals)	1932–33	150,000
Total copper		325,000

PROJECT OF NON-FERROUS METALS INDUSTRIES—*Continued*

	Date of Completion (Actual or Scheduled)	*Ultimate Annual Capacity, Pure Metal metric tons*
ZINC		
Ridder electrolytic zinc plant (Altai Mts., Kazakstan)		
First unit	1928	25,000 (First and Second unit)
Second unit	1932	
Konstantinovka zinc distillation plant (Near Kharkov. Completed year ahead of schedule; cost 14 million rubles)	October 1930	14,000
Kemerovo electrolytic zinc plant (Kuznetz Basin, Siberia)	End 1931	50,000
Cheliabinsk electrolytic zinc plant (Urals)	1931	20,000
Belovsky zinc plant (Siberia)	October 1930	12,000
Alagir electrolytic zinc plant (North Caucasus)	1932	10,000
Total zinc		131,000
LEAD		
Ridder lead plant (Altai Mts., Kazakstan)		
First unit	1928	25,000 (First and Second unit)
Second unit	1932	
Tetukhe lead plant (Far Eastern Region —British Concession)	October 1930	15,000
Alagir lead plant (North Caucasus)	1931	5,000
Chimkent lead plant (Turkestan)	1932	50,000
Nerchinsk lead plant (Far East)	1932	20,000
Total lead		115,000
NICKEL		
Ural nickel plant (at Ufaley)	1933	2,500
ALUMINUM		
Zvanka plant near Leningrad (Cost 30 million rubles)	Early 1931	5,000
Dniepropetrovsk plant (Ukraine)	End 1931	15,000
Total aluminum		20,000

Details of tractor production are given herewith:

FIVE-YEAR PLAN FOR MANUFACTURING TRACTORS [21]

(in thousands)

Names of Factories and Power of Tractors to Be Produced	1928–29	1929–30	1930–31	1931–32	1932–33	*Total for Five-Year Period*
Red Putilovets, 10 h.p.	3.0	10.0	20.0	20.0	20.0	73.0
Stalingrad, 15 h.p.	—	0.2	25.0	40.0	50.0	115.2
New Kharkov, 30 h.p.	—	—	1.5	30.0	50.0	81.5
Cheliabinsk, 50 h.p.	—	—	1.5	30.0	50.0	81.5
Dniepropetrovsk Cultivators, 10 h.p.	—	—	—	1.5	20.0	21.5
Kharkov Locomotive Wks. 50 to 75 h.p.	0.2	0.6	1.5	1.5	1.5	5.3
Total number of tractors produced	3.2	10.8	49.5	123.0	191.5	378.0
Total nominal 10-h.p. tractor units	4.0	13.3	77.0	329.0	522.5	945.8

This schedule of production was far from being realized. Further figures as to plans are shown in the section under "Results." (See p. 113.)

2. THE INVESTMENT. Mr. G. M. Krzhizhanovsky, formerly President of the State Planning Commission, stated: "The basic problem of the Five-Year Plan is to define the possible dimensions of capital investments for the ensuing five-year period, in general, and to give a concrete basis for operating programs of financing long-term construction projects, designed for the five-year period, in particular." [22]

The total capital investment, including expenditures in new construction and improvements, was first estimated at about 78 billion rubles. (As finally adopted, the State Plan called for an investment of 86 billion rubles.) But if the Plan is ultimately completed it will probably require 100 billion rubles.[23] The actual investment in the fiscal year 1928 amounted to 8.2 billion rubles and for the fiscal year 1933 should involve 27.7 billion rubles.[24] The magnitude of these figures reveals the daring scope of the Plan.

For comparison a few figures are given. Total investment in railroads in the United States over a period of more than fifty years amounts to about 20 billion dollars, equivalent to 40 billion rubles. The total investment in the public utility industry, chiefly in the past twenty years, amounts to about 10 billion dollars, or 20 billion rubles. This slow growth allowed for a period of comfortable living for the masses during the process of saving. To attempt an achievement as bold as the Five-Year Plan must therefore call for a great deal of self-denial and sacrifice on the part of the population.

3. THE AMBITIOUS SCALE. The actual program of the Five-Year Plan is staggering. Mr. Albert Kahn, president of Albert Kahn, Inc., of Detroit,

FIVE-YEAR DEVELOPMENT PROGRAM [25]

DISTRIBUTION OF BASIC CAPITAL IN THE SOVIET UNION

(Per Cent of Total)

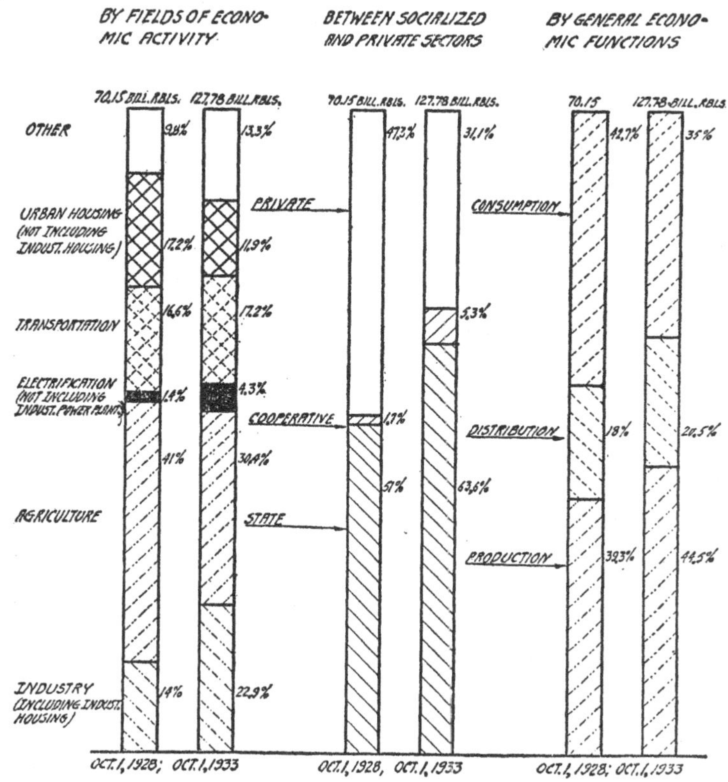

which has charge of the building of an automobile plant and other construction work for the Soviet Union, in an address to the Cleveland Engineering Society presented the usual American point of view.

> It is indeed difficult to understand the Russian psychology which dictates the erection of such huge establishments. We in this country would begin with a smaller lay-out, so arranged as to make expansion easily possible. We would

> organize a small operating crew, and enlarge it gradually and within a reasonable number of years build up a complete organization as large as necessary. Not so in Russia . . . where they say, "We haven't time to learn to run, we must fly." [26]

A similar view was given by Mr. Charles Stuart of Stuart, James & Cooke, consulting engineers to the Soviet Government on coal mines. (See p. 275.)

The Russians say with enthusiasm they will have the biggest electrical testing laboratory in Europe, the longest dam in the world, the greatest power works, the largest tractor factory. The foreigner is struck with critical wonder, but the communist is aglow with enthusiasm. The speed of construction matches that of highly industrialized America. The construction period is very brief, judged even by American standards. The machinery is most modern.

The schedule originally adopted for the Five-Year Plan had a low figure and was called the "minimum variant." It was then decided to increase the objective and a second plan called the "maximum variant" was proposed, and finally when in several industries the first year's objective was attained by a substantial margin the highest goal was set in the "Five-Year Plan in Four."

The ambitious schedule of the Five-Year Plan may be illustrated by citing one concrete instance. The production of tractors and agricultural machinery was formerly negligible in Russia whereas America in 1910 already produced 4000 tractors. Soviet Russia turned out only five tractors in the fiscal year 1924. Yet the Soviet officials now believe that the Soviet Union will surpass America in the production of agricultural machinery. How rapidly Soviet manufacture has grown is indicated by the value of total production of agricultural machinery. In 1913 it totaled 70 million rubles whereas that of the United States was three times as great, or 210 million rubles, as long ago as 1899. In 1929 the Russian production was equivalent to the 1922 production in the United States; in 1930 Russian production was equivalent to the 1927 American output, and in the fiscal year 1932 the Soviet Union production is estimated to exceed the 1928 production in the United States by 11 per cent. By 1933 Soviet Russia "will have firmly established its position as the first country in the world in the production of agricultural machinery." Again, the United States now turns out 25,000 combines per annum and the Soviet Union is planning two factories with an annual capacity of 25,000 combines each. Also, the two tractor factories in the Soviet Union have a capacity of 50,000 tractors per annum whereas the United States produced 74,000 tractors in 1921, about 167,000 in 1925, over 228,000 in 1929 and

202,000 in 1930. According to the Five-Year Plan the Soviets expect to surpass the United States in the production of tractors by 1933 and the production of agricultural machinery by 1932.[27]

4. THE SERIES OF PLANS. The Five-Year Plan is merely a section in the development of the socialist state. The five-year period is not a formula. Nor is it a period of wizardry. It merely indicates that one five-year section of a long-range plan has been accomplished and that a new five-year plan will follow. The informal plan of 1923, covering only a few industries, was completed in 1928. It had little publicity. The next Five-Year Plan is to end in 1932. Even if it is fully realized it will not raise the standard of living of the masses to that generally prevalent in the United States, in which the per capita production is seven or eight times as high as in the Soviet Union. The Five-Year Plan is merely a step in the direction of this goal, a device for stirring up popular enthusiasm for definite objectives. When these objectives are attained, there will be other plans to achieve new goals.

A new ten-year plan for the electrical development has been prepared. G. I. Lomov, Assistant Chairman of the Committee on the Five-Year Plan, in an address before the first All-Union Conference on planning scientific research, predicted that in the next ten years the Soviet Union would surpass the United States in electrification projects. Within the next five years Russia would also surpass the United States in other fields, producing 60 million tons of pig iron, 450 million tons of coal, 150 million tons of oil, and 60 million kilowatts of electrical energy.[28] His hopes seem too ambitious, in view of subsequent reductions of estimates. To achieve these goals an expansion of the institutions for scientific research is necessary. To prepare for the next Five-Year Plan covering the period 1934–38, a committee of eighteen industrial executives was formed with the head of the Planning Department, Mr. Gurevich, as president and with Mr. G. M. Krzhizhanovsky, former head of the State Planning Commission and compiler of the original Five-Year Plan, as associate.[29] On August 1, 1931, the preliminary figures for the second Five-Year Plan for agriculture were published. Under this plan the acreage would be doubled by the end of the second term to a total of almost 500 million acres. The yield per acre would likewise be doubled through the use of fertilizers and agricultural machinery. To end the acute shortage of meat and dairy products a second Five-Year Plan should have a census of 70 million hogs, 150 million sheep, and 500 million fowl, giving a per capita consumption of meat of 110 pounds per annum.[30] These figures compare with the Russian census in 1916 of 20 million hogs, and 111 million sheep, and with the United States figures for 1930 of more than 53 million hogs, more than 52 million sheep and lambs and about 470 million chickens.[31] In the United States the per capita meat consumption was 131.7 lbs. in 1930, 136.8 lbs. in 1929 and 149.7 lbs. in 1924, not including lard consumption, which was 13.8 lbs. in 1930.

E. Method of the Five-Year Plan

The method of work was outlined in the official Five-Year Plan, extracts from which give an idea as to the mode of procedure.

> The Fifteenth Congress of the All-Union Communist Party gave exhaustive political and economic directions for the construction of a Five-Year Plan of national economic life, proceeding from the general course toward the industrialization of the Soviet Union, toward the socialist reorganization of the village, toward the overcoming of the capitalist, and the consequent strengthening of socialist elements in the economic system of the country. . . . It has been the duty of the State Planning Commission of the Soviet Union and of the whole system of planning organizations to translate these general political and economic propositions and instructions into the language of concrete economic and technical-economic calculations, and to work them over into a plan of economic construction for the ensuing five-year period. The present report on the Five-Year Plan of national economic life is an attempt to solve this problem.[32]

The State Planning Commission is a centralized body which plans the growth of industries for each year and for a series of periods of five years, *pyatiletka*. Just as American crop estimates are made up from statistical data submitted by agents throughout the country, so statisticians throughout Russia furnish the figures. The goals are set for each individual plant. The figures are assembled by the Trust covering all its plants, and these are then submitted to the Supreme Economic Council. Each of the federal states of the Union has a planning commission to co-ordinate its plan with the Plan of the Soviet Union. The Gosplan, or State Planning Commission, then makes up figures for one year and five years. The Gosbank, or Central Bank, then checks the figures from the point of view of financial requirements. The Council of Labor and Defense ratifies the figures and acts as an arbitrator to reconcile differences.

In preparing the Five-Year Plan the commission realized that there might be a number of contingencies which would affect the results achieved. To provide for such contingencies the Plan was prepared with a number of variants. The official version of the variations follows:

About the two variations of the Plan: The State Planning Commission assumes the necessity of preparing the Five-Year National Economic Plan in two variants. The maximum variant reckons with:

(a) The absence of any serious crop failure during the course of the Five-Year Plan.

(b) Considerably broader economic ties with world economic life as a result of the existence of greater export resources within the country.

(c) A sharp upturn in the qualitative indices in economic development during the next two years (cost of production, harvest yield, etc.).

(d) A smaller relative weight of expenditures on defense in the general economic system.

The difference between them is calculated, approximately, at 20 per cent (a number of indices remaining identical), i. e., approximately, at a year's period of development. In other words, the maximum program, which under certain conditions we can accomplish within five years, under the less favorable conditions characteristic of the minimum variant will be stretched out, approximately, over six years. The framing of the Five-Year National Economic Plan in two variants, in view of all the difficulty of this matter, must assure greater maneuvering possibilities in the annual economic plans, and greater preparedness for the overcoming of those enormous difficulties which stand in the way of the achievement of the five-year program of economic construction.[33]

Because certain phases of the Five-Year Plan showed greater progress than the schedule called for, the Soviet officials decided to attempt to complete the Five-Year Plan in four years. The "control figures" were then set above the original estimates. Industrial production for the fiscal year 1930 was fixed at 32 per cent above the preceding year as against 21.5 per cent in the original estimate. As a result the actual industrial production achieved in the fiscal year 1930 exceeded the original estimate in the Five-Year Plan but did not quite attain the revised estimates of the "control figures." But even the "control figures" themselves were actually exceeded in agriculture, transportation and the All-Union budget.[34]

At the beginning of each year "control figures" are compiled based on the progress of the past year and providing the program for the next year. These annual figures are then broken up into monthly sub-totals for the industry and for each factory. The factory then applies the Plan to each department and, theoretically, to each workman. Separate plans in greater detail are also prepared quarterly for the several fields of economic activity and monthly for individual enterprises.[35]

The Supreme Council of National Economy covers industries only, but in addition to industries the Gosplan includes the railroads, electrical power production, agriculture and trade, domestic and foreign. The items covered are: requirements of raw materials, productivity of labor, idle time, production costs, financing (which is subject to the State Bank), and the expansion of industry (which is correlated with the budget).

The buying trusts and the selling trusts confer and attempt to avoid overproduction and accumulation of inventories: for example, the managers of the steel-rail mills adjust their output to the needs of the railroad administrators.

It is interesting to observe the apparatus which is used to carry out the Five-Year Plan. In the western world an industrial company issues instructions from the head through the various grade of officers to the rank and file, but in the Soviet Union the technique of execution involves an appeal to the masses. The Manifesto of the Central Committee of the All-Union Communist Party concerning the third year of the Five-Year Plan makes an appeal of which the following is part:

> (1) All forces of the party, Young Communist and economic organizations and of the trade unions to concentrate on the development of socialist competition and the shock-brigade movement.
>
> (2) Immediately to carry out measures which guarantee a decisive strengthening of labor discipline . . . in the matter of raising the productivity of labor and the factual realization of one-man management in economic administration.
>
> (3) To guarantee the development of the initiative of the engineers and technicians in production and technical questions.
>
> (4) In order to combat labor turnover in the plants, to carry out a system of measures guaranteeing the attachment of the workers to the factories by means of a corresponding development of proletarian public opinion. . . .
>
> (7) Decisive struggle against slackening the pace of work in connection with summer vacations.[36]

The resolutions of the Fifth Congress of the Soviet Union, May 28, 1929, read in part as follows:

> The Congress summons the many millions of poor and middle-class peasants decisively to support the plan of developing agriculture which has been indicated by the Communist Party and the Soviet power, and by powerful toiling co-operation to hasten the solution of the great problems of socialist reconstruction of the village. . . . The Congress turns to the broad masses of workers and peasants, to technical experts, to educational and medical workers, etc., with an appeal to help by their activity, initiative, and toiling discipline the accomplishment of these tasks which are set by the plan. . . . The Congress expresses its firm confidence that, notwithstanding the prophecies of enemies and the waverings of the timid, the toilers of the Soviet Union will overcome the difficulties which stand before them, and, after smashing the resistance of the hostile capitalist forces, will victoriously solve the great problems of socialist construction.

The idea that an industrial program should be carried out through a political party is foreign to the western mind but it is of the essence of the Russian method. The Communist Party is not a political party in the western sense. It is the agency of the Russian Government. There is no other party.

F. Difficulties of the Five-Year Plan

To the observer who has had experience in business and who therefore realizes the problems arising in planning not for five years but for one year, and not for a whole country but for one industry and sometimes even for one corporation, the difficulty of planning the industrial life of a nation seems staggering. The problems are numerous: Can the rate be maintained? Can the variables be controlled? Can labor, equipment, raw materials be held in harmonious relationship? Is it possible to determine costs five years from now? And where foreign trade is involved, a host of new complications enter.

Even in a country industrially advanced, politically stable, and enjoying an adequate supply of trained managers, such a task would be formidable. But with a country still in a primitive state, industrially backward, undeveloped, without adequate facilities for the manufacture of machinery, with labor untrained and supplies of raw materials not flowing smoothly owing to lack of credit, the difficulties multiply in geometric ratio.

Many Soviet economists and some foreign engineers maintain that Russia always has been and always will continue to be a country of abundant and cheap labor and that therefore it will be more economical to develop the resources through the utilization of cheap man-power than through mechanization and mass production.[37]

1. The Rate of Growth. A growth of 18 per cent per annum compared to about 3 to 4 per cent in the United States and 2.6 per cent in pre-war Russia, would in five years result in a growth of production of almost 2.5 times, in ten years almost 5.5 times and in twenty years almost 30 times. At this rate of growth Russia would in twenty years "overtake and surpass even the United States." Such an expansion assumes adequate supplies of raw materials, adequate managerial skill, adequately trained labor, and adequate financial facilities. The mere projection of this rate of growth suggests grave difficulties.

A technician at the Nizhni Novgorod Automobile Plant, himself a member of the Communist Party, stated that in spite of the Manifesto of the Central

Committee of the Communist Party urging the workmen to speed up the work, the rate of construction called for by the schedules could not be realized. As a result he was expelled from the Communist Party and branded as an "opportunist," a term of opprobrium in Soviet Russia.[38]

2. Control of Variables. The communists try to live by formula. To do so life must be simplified. Oversimplification leads to unreality. An attempt to estimate all the variables in industrial production is based on the assumption of a simple economy and many constants. But life is neither simple nor constant. All organic growth is complex and subject to many variables. In any industrial country of the western world industries rise and fall rapidly owing to some unexpected development. In the western world a change of style in shoes, the substitution of ties and pumps, has dislocated the leather industry. The introduction of simpler women's clothing has dislocated the textile industry. Unexpected changes in raw materials have taken place—rayon for example, now competes with cotton and silk and aluminum with agateware. Discovery of new raw materials, new processes, new machinery, new methods of production, new manufactured products, changes in consumers' habits and standards of living, and even the change of rate in growth of population have all profoundly affected economic life in the United States and in other countries. Scientific inventions in the fields of chemistry and electricity have changed industrial processes and consumers' habits. Such things the planners cannot forsee. Already an unexpected fall in commodity prices in the international markets has profoundly dislocated the Five-Year Plan. Soviet Russia assumes an unchanging world, a predictable future, in which to apply its plans.

These variables are the long-term factors, but even seasonally there are important variables which radically affect economic life. Weather conditions may favor or upset any plan. In 1924 the United States was in a depression. An abundant harvest in the United States and a drought in other grain-producing countries changed the situation in agriculture and industry within a few months. A fall in commodity prices harms producers and benefits consumers. A drastic decline in the price of wheat resulting in part from Russian exports has in turn greatly curtailed the value of these exports and has thus likewise curtailed the import of machinery, which was assumed as one of the constants in the Five-Year Plan. Again, the shortage of machinery resulted in the Soviet policy of exploiting existing machinery more fully by introducing three working shifts. The change affected other factors which were assumed to be constant. The supply of raw materials proved inadequate, the machines wore out more quickly through excessive use, and production was dislocated.

3. Shortage of Supplies, Skilled Labor, and Management. There are many other causes for failure of the plan to be realized fully. These are treated in detail in the sections on "Industry" and on "Labor," but some of them may be mentioned here. There is a shortage of raw materials and some of these raw materials—cotton, flax, sugar, leather and wool—are dependent upon unpredictable conditions. With the rapid increase of building construction there is a great shortage of manufactured materials—brick, mortar, glass, iron, and other metals. Production of some of these raw materials is, in turn, dependent upon the development of other plants. A production schedule designed under the Five-Year Plan may be upset because raw materials are not available or transportation is inadequate. Sometimes the supply of raw materials is upset by governmental policy. When the policy of enforced collectivization of cattle and live stock was put into effect, there resulted a shortage of meat, hides, bristles, brushes, leather and shoes. The state plan called for an increase but the state's policy resulted in a decrease in the supply.

One of the chief causes of delay has been the failure of the domestic industries to supply building materials such as lumber, iron, steel, and cement or to supply equipment. For a number of years it has been the case that the shell of a building would be finished and meanwhile equipment would be unavailable, or sometimes that machinery would be installed and there would be no electric power. Again, in order to protect themselves against the possible shortage of equipment some industries would over-order and have an excessive inventory whereas other plants would lack these machines or goods.[39]

When the trusts in charge of constructing the automobile plant attempted to order machinery and equipment from the several trusts, each one tried to prove that the order should be placed with some other trust. Sometimes a trust would accept an order on the ground that it required some imported equipment to fill the order and that since the government gave priority on appropriations for the automobile plant, this trust would thus be enabled to obtain additional appropriations.[40] Under the auspices of the newspaper *Za Industrializatsiu,* a conference was held in 1930 to inquire into the failure of the construction program of the "Giant Builders," the great industrial plants. A summary of the causes of the failure indicated the economic disorganization. The Director of the Kharkov Tractorstroy stated that the construction plans were delayed; that Russian equipment was undelivered; that the Supreme Economic Council made changes sometimes when work was already far advanced. The representative of the Magnitostroy stated that the size and capacity of the project was changed suddenly from 250,000 tons to 2,500,000 tons and that the time limit for construction was considerably shortened. No appropriation had been made either for shelter or for food for the workmen. As a result the labor turn-over was exceedingly high, about 66 per cent per month. The representative of the Stalingrad Tractor Plant explained why the operating plan of the plant was not realized. The receipt of equipment was delayed and it was incomplete when it did arrive. There was a lack of experienced foremen and workers. A select body of 230 skilled workmen were to have come from several other plants, but these plants sent on their drunkards and hooligans, half of whom had to be returned immediately. The 300 American workmen were not utilized because of the hostility shown by some of the Russians. Raw material, such as steel from the Red-October Plant, was inferior and parts for the assembly belt such as bolts, nuts, carburetors, magnetos and radiators were undelivered.[41]

In America even the largest automobile plants do not manufacture more than 60 per cent of their parts. The remaining 40 per cent is supplied by independent manufacturers. But in Russia these are lacking and therefore Soviet automobile production lags.[42] To discuss the difficulties of obtaining parts and accessories needed by the Nizhni Novgorod Automobile Plant a three-day conference was organized by Avtostroy, the organization constructing the automobile plant. A few of the specific difficulties are typical. The Moscow Glass Trust which was to supply the non-shatterable glass for automobiles sent two of its engineers abroad to study this process. Though the men had returned after a long stay abroad, no one knew where they were then working. The engineer sent abroad to study the making of attachments for automobile bodies spent much time and money but discontinued his investigation and went abroad again to study the manufacture of automobile chains, although such chains would not be used on the Nizhni Novgorod automobiles. The plant for making bolts and rivets for automobiles was started about two miles from the automobile plant and suddenly construction was stopped. The manufacturing cost of the imitation upholstering leather proved to be five times the cost in the United States.

These are a few of the so-called "miscalculations and disproportions" which have crept into the working of the Five-Year Plan.[43]

Again, a growing supply of skilled labor was assumed, but so many huge undertakings were begun simultaneously that a great shortage resulted. The Plan outran the available supply of skilled labor and the trade schools were utterly inadequate to increase it as rapidly as the Plan called for.

In the Donetz Basin, the output called for by the Plan was not realized, as the number of workers steadily declined because the co-operative stores were unable to supply the necessities of life.[44]

Furthermore, in the haste and resulting poor organization labor at times became less efficient even where it was numerically adequate (though the statistics indicate that production per man in 1930 was higher than in 1922). The speed of industry resulted in an excessive wear and tear on machinery. The ignorance of the workmen resulted in the mishandling of machines, so that they wore out more rapidly. As a result of inadequately trained labor, large turnover and poor equipment, the Stalingrad Tractor Plant performed only a small fraction of its schedule. More than 1000 workmen and more than 300 machines were kept idle. A group of American specialists had to be sent to organize the plant, and supervise and co-ordinate the various units. The disorganization in the new plants prevented the realization of the goals set for the third and critical year of the Five-Year Plan. For example, at Stalingrad, the plant was suffering from "infant diseases." Production was not organized. There was no firm administrative control. The "self-paying" basis of operation was fictitious. There was no centralized responsibility. As a result the production schedule was greatly behind.[45] Similarly, the Putilov works at Leningrad produced less than one-third of the scheduled number of tractors because the castings delivered were defective. Millions of man-hours of labor are wasted throughout the country owing to lack of co-ordination of supplies and equipment for the human element.[46]

Inefficient use of machinery and lack of industrial organization resulted in a very unsatisfactory performance of the Soviet United Building Industry, even though there was no lack of building materials and the number of workmen was 15 to 20 per cent in excess of the requirements.[47]

4. World-Wide Decline of Prices. The Plan called for a reduction in the cost of production, but the lack of adequate supplies, the breakdown of the equipment, the inadequacy and inefficiency of labor, not only prevented the planned reduction of costs but substantially increased some of them. As the price of manufactured goods rose, the peasants refused to sell their wheat or exchange it for such goods as were available. The equilibrium between agricultural and industrial prices was upset and this in turn upset the Plan. The fall in world prices as a result of the depression further set the balance

askew. The fall in prices was partly due to Russian exports. In other words, the stepping up of production under the Five-Year Plan itself helped to upset the Plan. According to Grinko, Commissar of Finance, the leading industries which have expanded most rapidly have actually profited least on operations. Goods have been exported at less than the cost of production in order to make possible the importation of foreign machinery. Lumber is reported to be sold at a price that hardly covers the cost of transportation.[48] The plan for reducing costs of production and selling prices has not been realized.

5. Foreign Trade. Another variable which it is impossible to estimate is the factor of foreign trade. If the Soviet Union were a closed industrial system and if the factors above mentioned, material, labor, and equipment, were under control then planning might be possible. However, as soon as the Soviets sell their products and buy machinery, they introduce new and uncontrollable variables. To gauge world demand for Russian products is impossible, not only five years but even five months ahead. What is the world demand for coal, manganese ore, flax, wheat, lumber, etc. at the present price? At a price 10 per cent lower? Or 10 per cent higher? Soviet officials and economists, like Mr. Sushkov in the State Planning Department and Professor Katzenellenbaum of the University of Moscow, told the writer that price is not an important factor, that exports are limited by the home surplus and the foreign demand is not important, that overproduction for the domestic market is impossible under the Soviet system of planned economics. But they did admit that overproduction in foreign trade is possible.

6. "Miscalculations and Disproportions." The failure of a plant at some point is ascribed to "miscalculations and disproportions." For example in the canning industry, plants were built without a survey of available fish or vegetables to be canned. The Central Consumers' Co-operatives, the Centrosoyuz, built a large model cannery near Stalingrad, but when it was completed it was found that the territory may not have the necessary produce to supply the cannery. Again, the United Fishing Industries built a cannery at Astrakhan for canning a fish, the *cyrpinus vimba,* but no test was made to determine whether this type of fish could be successfully canned.[49] A terracotta plant costing 2½ million rubles was built in the Tula District. When the plant was finished, it was found that there was no available supply of raw materials in the district and as a result the engineers in charge were accused of economic counter-revolution and sabotage and of choosing the wrong site deliberately.[50]

The Soviet officials themselves recognize the failure to realize the Five-

Year Plan. The Manifesto of the Central Committee of the All-Union Communist Party concerning the third year of the Plan specifically cites the causes for this failure.

> The most important causes of the non-fulfillment of the productive tasks of industry, especially in its basic branches, are . . . insufficient use of existing equipment, low number of additional shifts, lack of energy in overcoming the shortages within an undertaking, frequent stoppage of equipment as a result of the failure to organize and adjust material and technical supply, the numerous accidents from criminal neglect and poor technical control, the absence of systematic work for rationalization and the extremely unsatisfactory character of planning within the factories.[51]

A major example of poor planning is revealed in the placing of the "Ural-Kuzbass Kombinat," the unit of iron and steel production, in a locality which requires the hauling of iron ore from the Ural Mountains and coal from the Kuznetzk Basin over tremendous distances. There are only three cases in the world where the distances are so great. The cost of carrying a ton of coal from mine to plant is estimated at 15.18 rubles ($7.59), whereas in the United States the cost of carrying iron ore from the ore beds to Lake Superior by rail and then by water to Lake Erie ports ranges between $1.14 and $1.66 per ton. Production costs for iron and steel will manifestly be above the world level, and even though the plant is intended in part to serve national defense its location obviously represents a gross "miscalculation and disproportion."[52]

The difficulties are obvious and efforts to carry out the Plan have brought a whole series of maladjustments. The Plan is based on too simplified a conception. It involves world economics. It looks too far ahead. The country's industrial activities have been continually interrupted.

The even front expected under the Plan has already been broken. Quantitatively some heavy industries are far ahead of the Plan, others are far behind. Production of consumers' goods is generally behind.

When the Plan breaks down, the difficulty is not traced to its source, the impossibility of carrying out such a gigantic task. Instead, the blame is laid on the enemies within and without the country. In reply to charges of incompetence and waste, Soviet spokesmen point to the waste of the capitalist system. They speak of speculative construction of railroads and factories followed by bankruptcies and reorganizations, to the helter-skelter construction of competitive plants based on desire for private profit and in disregard of national need, to the waste of competitive advertising and other faults of the competitive system.

G. Burdens Imposed by the Five-Year Plan

1. Curtailed Consumers' Industries. The Five-Year Plan was designed to increase greatly the production of raw materials, and to a relatively less extent that of consumers' goods. Not merely were comforts of life to be dispensed with, but consumption was to be reduced to the point of sacrifice, in order to make possible increased plant capacity. The great expansion in kilowatt capacity is slight comfort to the underfed and underclothed man in the street. The Five-Year Plan will absorb about 45 per cent of the national income for the purchase of machinery for industry. As the estimates were raised 105 per cent in the chemical industry, and 100 per cent in electric-power production, they were curtailed 22 per cent in textile manufacturing, 28 per cent in garment manufacturing, and 19 per cent in foodstuffs.[53]

As quoted by the Bureau of Research on Russian Economic Conditions, "the financing of the Plan amounts to 'putting a steel hoop around consumption' (*Planovoe Khozyaistvo,* 1929, III, p. 283. Planned Economy, official publication).

"The extent to which consumption has contracted is shown in the fact that goods for personal consumption formed 28.5 per cent of the foreign imports in 1913; in 1925–26 the percentage was 20.3 per cent; in 1929–30 only 8.9 per cent." [53a]

In the determination of allocations and in the distribution of the burden, the masses have no voice. These matters are imposed from above. Realizing the sacrifices involved in the Five-Year Plan, Commissar Valerian Kuybyshev, in an address before the All-Union Congress of Technical Engineering Societies, stated that in 1932 light industries would be developed to a greater extent in order to raise the standards of living of the masses. The general aim is that after the first Five-Year Plan there will be greater emphasis on the light industries, possibly because the heavy industries will have already been adequately expanded.[54]

2. Shortage of Consumers' Goods. As a result of the diversion of capital from light to heavy industry there is a great shortage of consumers' goods, estimated by responsible officials at 300 million rubles annually. The vast industrial expansion has greatly increased the number of factory workers, drawing them from the land, where they could produce not only their requirements in food but also, in part, clothing and tools, to the city, where they make producers' rather than consumers' goods. And the more rapidly the process of industrialization goes on the greater the vacuum thus created.

Before the war home industry supplied more than 50 per cent of the country's consumers' goods. When Soviet statistics report a large increase in manufacture of consumers' goods over pre-war figures, the comparison applies only to that part of the goods made in factories and so reported by the census. Actually the combined production of home and factory is less than before the war.[55] Moreover, the drive against private business has diminished the output of handicraft workers, just as the campaign against the kulak checked the agricultural output.

When the endurance of the masses reached the breaking-point, the government reversed its policy of persecution of the "remnants of capitalism," and reduced its tax on home industry (*kustarnye promysly*), or business carried on by people working alone or in groups.

To a certain extent poor distribution also accounts for the shortage of consumers' goods. Attempts have been made to distribute food and clothing for the workers through the factories where they are employed. In this way the government can insure better control of labor and also prevent the non-privileged classes from obtaining merchandise.

The shortage of consumers' goods brings many subsidiary difficulties in its train. For example, shoes are very expensive, and the demand for shoe-repair service is very great. According to official Soviet sources, the workshop of the co-operative has had as many as 71,000 pairs of shoes awaiting repair. The daily output is about 1500 pairs and the demand is for more than 2500 pairs. The high cost of hosiery creates a great demand for mending, but the Leningrad Clothing and Knitting Union requires three months to mend a pair of socks. Either the pace of industrialization will have to slacken, or the population will have to put up for several years with this shortage of consumers' goods.

In capitalist countries crises are often due to overproduction of goods and falling prices. In Soviet Russia the crisis is due to a lack of consumers' goods and rising prices.

3. Lowered Standard of Living. The visitor standing on the street corner in Moscow is impressed by the variety of clothing of the passersby. Every type of garment is worn; in addition to Russian blouses, one sees men wearing shirts, bathing-suit tops, sweaters, coats without underwear, and occasionally nothing above the waist and attracting no attention. In the factory kitchens, the bill of fare reflects the exchange of food for machinery. Cakes are made without butter, oranges are unobtainable, sugar is scarce. The workers understand why—like the foreman in a Leningrad factory, who said, patting an American machine about which he was quite enthusiastic: "It cost $12,000.

Think how many loaves of bread that would buy!" To conserve coal, the Moscow Soviet authorities postponed the heating of homes, offices, and factories for an additional fortnight beyond the usual date. Because of the sacrifices it involved, the speeding up of the Plan has been greeted with great enthusiasm. It meant that there was one year less to endure and that half the trial was over.

4. Increased Pressure. In November 1930, the Russian papers printed an official manifesto warning against the failure to realize the third-year program. A supreme effort to overcome the lag was decreed. The manifesto called for an increase in the productivity of labor, a tightening of labor discipline, the boycotting of workers who left their jobs, etc., and made a strong appeal to the public to ward off the threat to the Five-Year Plan.

How long it will be possible for a people making such great sacrifices to increase their effort, time alone can tell. The Plan has increased the quantity of output but created an offsetting disorganization of life. The discontent and even dismay have more than once had their effect on party leaders whose consequent advocacy of a relaxation of the pressure of the Plan has caused their downfall. Premier A. I. Rykov, chairman of the Council of People's Commissars, favored slowing down the Plan, and was joined in his opposition by M. Tomsky, Chairman of the Trade Unions Congress and N. Bukharin, Editor of *Pravda,* members of the Supreme Economic Council and therefore in a position to have access to the facts. All three opposed the high speed of socialization of agriculture and industrial construction, but were forced to recant their views publicly in phrasing reminiscent of the recantation of Galileo under pressure of the Pope. (See p. 402.) Despite the recantation, all three were compelled to resign their important posts. A similar "right" opposition, though one less influential or well-known, was led by Sirtzov, ex-premier of the Russian Republic and Lominadze, an influential communist in Trans-Caucasia. This group likewise opposed the extension of industrial production and believed rather in intensive development, improving the quality of the product, strengthening the organization, and checking the decline in the workers' standards of living. They opposed as detrimental rather than beneficial some of the particularly communistic devices in industry such as socialist competition, "shock brigades," committees on inspection, and the like.[56]

Although Stalin replaced Rykov with one of his subordinates, Molotov, as head of the Council of Commissars, it is probable that the speed of the Plan will be reduced. Stalin's policy has always been to resist an important change, to dismiss its advocate, and then subsequently to adopt it *in toto.*

The pressure on the people may cause a slackening of the pace of industrialization. Such reversal of policy is not unusual in Russia. Pressure and force resulted in the collectivization of 90 per cent of the farms in some districts, and then when the policy was relaxed collectivization dropped there to 11 per cent. Similarly, industrialization may be made to proceed at a slackened pace under the plea of a strategic retreat.

H. Results Achieved and Failures

1. Plan vs. Achievement. It is too early to appraise the results of the Five-Year Plan. Before it was launched, the production of important items in Russia compared to pre-war figures as follows: [56]

Item		*1913*	*1928*
Pig iron	*million metric tons*	4.2	3.3
Iron ore	*million metric tons*	9.2	6.0
Coal	*million metric tons*	28.9	35.4
Oil	*million metric tons*	9.2	11.6
Bricks	*billions*	2.1	1.9

In consumers' goods the growth had been relatively small. In several other important fields there had been an actual decline.

The first two years' operation of the Plan showed some statistical progress. In the first fiscal year, ended September 1929, the increase in industrial production was said to be about 24.3 per cent or 3 per cent higher than the Plan required. For the second fiscal year, ended September 1930, industrial production was reported to have increased 24.6 per cent over the previous year.[57] This was 3.1 per cent over the original plan, but about 7 per cent less than the rate of increase scheduled by the "control figures" for that year. Figures showing detailed accomplishments, furnished by the State Planning Commission and presented by V. Molotov, chairman of the Council of People's Commissars, at the Sixth Congress of Soviets, Moscow, March 8, 1931, were as follows:

FULFILLMENT OF FIVE-YEAR PLAN, 1928–29, 1929–30 [58]

Items		*Contemplated for 2 Years*	*Fulfilled in 2 Years*	*Percentage of Fulfillment*
National income	*billion rubles*	58.3	59.5	102
National budget	*billion rubles*	17.0	21.0	124
Capital investments in basic public enterprises, at current prices	*billion rubles*	12.7	13.8	109

FULFILLMENT OF FIVE-YEAR PLAN, 1928–29, 1929–30—*Continued*

Items		*Contemplated for 2 Years*	*Fulfilled in 2 Years*	*Percentage of Fulfillment*
Aggregate output of planned industries (including food products), in prices of 1926–27	*billion rubles*	29.3	30.5	104
Area under crops	*million hectares*	239.0	245.8	103
Production of marketable grain	*million bushels*	221.2	267.3	121
Turnover of freight	*million tons*	350.9	409.2	117
Unified financial plan	*billion rubles*	24.8	32.5	131
Coal production	*million tons*	87.7	84.2	96
Petroleum production	*million tons*	28.0	30.6	109
Agricultural machinery	*million rubles*	472.0	515.0	109
Tractors	*machines*	8,000.0	12,600.0	157
Sown area of collective farms	*million hectares*	20.0*	43.0	—

* This figure, 20 million hectares, was planned for the area to be sown by the collective farms by the end of the Five-Year Plan period, i. e., 1933.

Molotov further stated that in the field of electrification the plan for the past two years had been completely fulfilled. In production costs, however, the reduction was only 11.4 per cent as against 14.5 per cent set by the Plan.

The president of the State Planning Commission, Mr. V. V. Kuybyshev, gives the following estimates for a few of the important fields for the two years of the Five-Year Plan, ended October 1, 1930: [59]

		Estimate	*Actual*	*% Excess over Plan*
Oil	*million tons*	28.0	30.6	9.3
Steel	*million tons*	9.9	10.3	4.0
Electrical machinery	*million rubles*	588	786	33.8

These figures are rather startling. But it must borne in mind that Russia begins at a very primitive state, and the increases, though seemingly large in percentage, really are small in actual figures. Moreover, it is a natural law that early growth is relatively faster. It holds for social as well as biological growth.†

† According to Moscow despatches to New York papers [59a] the results for the first eight months of 1932 were unfavorable. Apparently the difficulties increased at an accelerating rate.

The Plan, however, did not succeed in realizing reduction of costs for the fiscal year 1929–30. Instead of the projected average decrease of 7 per cent, the actual decrease was only 4.2 per cent. Furthermore, a part of the decreased manufacturing cost was due to the relaxing of the requirements for amortization. The introduction of a seven-hour day in the fiscal year 1929 also prevented the planned reduction in costs. Such reduction as was accomplished was due partly to the introduction of modern equipment and the better organization of production. In the first half of 1930, the planned reduction in manufacturing costs was also not realized.

Item		*Program* For Year	*Program* Jan.-Aug.	*Results* Jan.-Aug.	*Results* Per Cent Plan Realized
			in millions		
Coal	*tons*	85.0	56.7	42.0	74
Pig iron	*tons*	9.5	6.3	4.0	63
Steel	*tons*	8.8	5.9	3.7	63
Rolled steel	*tons*	7.6	5.1	2.8	55
Copper	*pounds*	200.0	133.4	70.0	52

Other important items failed of their goal, oil production by 25 per cent, freight car loadings by 30 per cent, building construction by 50 per cent. The lag was accelerated in July and August when the figures for coal, pig iron and steel declined below the April levels by 20 to 40 per cent. On September 1 the state grain collections were almost 50 per cent below the corresponding figures of the preceding year. New sowings for autumn were 40 per cent lower. The figures apparently were rapidly getting worse.

In August production must have declined sharply for the percentage of the Plan realized for seven months were better, as follows:

Item	*Per Cent Realized*
Coal	81
Pig iron	79
Oil	78
Heavy machinery	90

The failure to realize the Plan was even greater in the food industries, according to the monthly *Pishchevaya Promyshlenost* (Food Industry) for September 1932. Production not only fell short of the Five-Year Plan, but declined so greatly in July and August 1932 as to reduce the results in the eight months of 1932 to 6 per cent below the corresponding period of 1931, as against an actual gain, though slight, in the first six months of 1932. The greatest decline in production for the eight months was in granulated sugar, meat, salt and fish.

PRODUCTION JAN.-AUG. 1932

Item	*Percentage Decline under 1931*	*Percentage of Plan Realized*
Granulated sugar	56.9	45.8
Meat	41.7	62.9
Salt	23.7	53.1
Fish	9.3	64.7
Canning	2.5	53.6
Butter	2.0	98.0

The question now is whether the Five-Year Plan will be declared completed. The government has advertised the Plan so greatly and even promised fulfillment in four years, that it

PER CENT DECREASE OF MANUFACTURING COSTS

	Industries of National Importance	
	Planned	*Accomplished*
Heavy Industries	11.9	16.6
Light Industries	9.5	3.3
All Industries	10.5	5.1

The following industries have fallen below the average estimate for decrease in manufacturing cost:

	Planned	*Accomplished*
Iron and steel	11.0	2.7
Mineral and raw materials	12.5	0.2
Asbestos	8.0	2.8
Lumber and wood-working	12.4	3.5
Wood distillation	17.3	2.0
Linen	10.5	2.4
Matches	13.6	3.3
Distilling	7.9	1.7
Brewing	11.0	3.7

Other unfavorable factors were the continuous lowering of the quality of the raw materials, delay in starting operations in the newly constructed plants, break-downs in both old and new plants, delay in increasing the productivity of labor, and failure to realize efficiency in production, i. e., utilize American methods of scientific management.[60] A public recognition of the partial failure of the second year of the Plan is indicated in the manifesto of the Central Committee of the All-Union Communist Party:

> To All Party, Economic, Trade-Union, and Young Communist Organizations: The growth of industrial production by 27 per cent indicates a sharp decline from the increase of 32 per cent which was prescribed by the Plan. The Plan was left unfulfilled not only in light industry, where this was caused to a certain extent during the present year by the lack of raw material, but also to a consid-

cannot well admit failure on the eve of preparation for the Second Five-Year Plan. Instead it will probably seek to offset the failures in the basic industries by successes in other directions.

The decline in 1932 of the heavy industry is so great that it is likely that the year 1933 will be devoted merely to making up the lag of 1932, so that new projects are not likely to be begun in 1933. Heavy machinery contracted for will probably continue to be imported. However, since the great "giants" are not successes, further import of heavy machinery is very likely to be either greatly curtailed or almost eliminated. It is even possible that a year's breathing space between the first and second Five-Year Plans may be made. In other words, the Five-Year Plan in Four will be changed back to the Five-Year Plan in Five. Events are justifying the program of the former Premier Rykov, who had been a persistent advocate of a more moderate tempo. Since the original pace cannot be maintained, he may become a more important figure as the plan slackens down.

erable extent in heavy industry, a fact which is especially important. The visible slackening of the work of industry during the last months created a direct threat of failure to carry out the annual production program, which was accepted by the party and the Soviet power. Instead of Bolshevik rates of development, one observes in many branches of industry recently a disgraceful reduction of tempo and an opportunist tendency to drift with the tide.

The course of capital construction is also clearly unsatisfactory. Less than half of the plan of capital construction was fulfilled during the first three quarters.

Especially disgraceful is the lagging behind of capital building in the chemical and coke and gas industries, in the steel, machinery and the agricultural implement industry. These developments in capital building threaten the pace which has been undertaken and the fulfillment of the Five-Year Plan in four years.[61]

Huge investments have been made in various fields. In the five years 1924–1928 over 26 billion rubles were invested in various enterprises. The Turkestan-Siberian Railroad, about 900 miles long, took 100 million dollars. The hydroelectric plant on the Dnieper required about 110 million dollars. Large sums were spent on the agricultural machinery plants in Stalingrad and Rostov and on the pipe lines from Baku to Batum. During the two fiscal years 1928–29 and 1929–30, 280 new industrial establishments started operations. The automobile factory at Nizhni-Novgorod with an estimated output of 140,000 cars per annum was completed January 1, 1932.

2. General Progress. In spite of the many obvious defects, the first Five-Year Plan did develop the heavy industries, and thus laid the basis for mass production of producers' goods, consumers' goods, and foods. It converted agricultural operations from a small scale to the largest scale in the world and at the same time ownership was converted from individual peasant proprietorship into the socialistic form, collective farms and state farms.[62]

The highest schedule for the whole plan adopted in the winter of 1929–30 has not been attained, according to *Pravda,* but in some industries the 1933 schedule of the original minimum plan has already been exceeded, as indicated in the following Soviet figures: [63]

		Original Estimates for 1933 Production	*Projected Output—1931*
Coal	*million tons*	75.0	83.6
Oil	*million tons*	21.7	27.5
Cement	*million tons*	41.0	35.0
Pig iron	*million tons*	10.0	8.0
Industrial machinery	*million rubles*	2059	2483
Agricultural machinery	*million rubles*	610	760
Electrical machinery	*million rubles*	896	1145

The growth was less rapid in the light industries partly because of the lack of raw materials. There was a shortage of raw materials in the textile, food, fat, and other industries. The growth of industry put a great strain on the railroads.

The Amtorg Trading Corporation compiled comparisons of the growth of industrial production, using as a basis the fiscal year 1921–22. This year represented the lowest point of production and therefore on such a base the annual increase showed up as exceedingly rapid and very greatly above that of countries whose output had not shown a similar fall after the war. The output at that low point was about one-fifth of the last pre-war year and the pre-war level was not attained until five years later. Even taking these facts into account, however, the increase was still very much above the average for other countries:

	Annual Gain	*% of 1921–22*	*% of 1913*
1921–22	....	100	21.8
1922–23	45.8	145.8	30.0
1923–24	30.8	190.7	39.6
1924–25	63.0	310.9	62.5
1925–26	42.7	443.8	89.2
1926–27	17.2	520.1	104.5
1927–28	22.5	637.1	131.1
1928–29	23.7	788.1	162.5
1929–30	24.2	978.8	201.9

The output for some of the important heavy industries shows a still more substantial percentage of growth due to the fact that capital, labor, and energy concentrated on them: [64]

		Fiscal Year 1913		*Fiscal Year 1925–26*		*Fiscal Year 1929–30*	
		millions	*Relative per cent*	*millions*	*Relative per cent*	*millions*	*Relative per cent*
Electrical Energy	*kilowatts*	1,945.0	100	3,240.0	166	8,000.0	412
Coal	*tons*	28.9	100	25.4	87	45.7	158
Oil	*tons*	9.3	100	8.5	92	17.1	184
Pig Iron	*tons*	4.2	100	2.2	52	5.0	119
Rolled Steel	*tons*	3.5	100	2.2	63	4.5	129
Cement	*barrels*	12.3	100	8.5	69	24.0	195

The rate of growth of the Soviet Union in comparison with western countries was indicated in an address of V. Kuybyshev.[65] The Soviet Union surpassed England in 1929 in the production of pig iron; France in 1928 in the production of steel. The output of coal in little Belgium at one time substantially exceeded the output of the Soviet Union. The 1931 Soviet program called for a coal requirement three times as great as that of Belgium and in excess of that of France. In connection with a loan flotation the point was made that the Soviet Union had attained a place second to America in the output of agricultural machinery and of oil.[66] In 1900 the Russian petroleum industry led the world, but in 1921 it produced only one-tenth as much as the United States. In 1929 the Soviet production of steel was 9 per cent of that of the United States; output of coal and electric power about 6 per cent; ton-miles freight, about 14 per cent and railway mileage about 20 per cent.[67]

The wide divergence between the calculations of Soviet officials and expert investigators outside of Russia is illustrated by the following comparison given in a memorandum of the Bureau of Research on Russian Economic Conditions:[67a]

In a speech to the Central Executive Committee, January 4, 1931, Molotov, the President of the Council of Commissars said:

> It is interesting to compare this figure (38.3 per cent) with the statistics on national income for the pre-revolutionary period. It will be found that between 1900 and 1913, i. e. during a period of thirteen years, the total growth in the national income of Tsarist Russia amounted to 39 per cent or an average increase of 2.6 per cent per annum. Therefore the percentage increase in national income which in Tsarist Russia was the result of thirteen years' development is in our time achieved in one year.

M. Molotov based this pronouncement on the imaginary *Gosplan* increase of 38.3 per cent for 1931, and on the real pre-war average annual increase of 2.6 per cent. As a matter of fact, this figure for 1900–1913 to which M. Molotov refers was worked out by Professor S. N. Prokopovich (*Opyt Ischislenya Narodnago Dokhoda 50 gub. Evr. Rossii v 1900–1913,* edited by S. N. Prokopovich, Moscow, 1918, pp. 67–69) whose recent calculations for the year 1931 assess the real increase in that year at a figure substantially lower than 2.6 per cent.

A summary of the growth of the Soviet Union in the ten years since the New Economic Policy was introduced by Lenin, ending in the spring of 1931, was presented by V. Molotov, chairman of the Council of People's Commissars, at the Sixth Congress of Soviets, March 8, 1931.[68] The national income in this decade had increased four times and the production of census industry twelve and one-half times; the seeded area one and one-half times; the turnover of trade five and one-half times and the railroad freight tonnage six times. The share of production of private industry in the total of industry subject to census had decreased from 36 per cent to 5 per cent, in retail trade from 75 per cent to 5.5 per cent and in agriculture the seeded area had decreased from 99 per cent to 67 per cent. Greatest progress had been made in the socialization of trade and least progress in the socialization of agriculture. The rate of industrialization of the country was indicated in the increase of industrial workers from 2.4 million to 6.4 million. The average monthly wage of the worker in the census industries had risen from 14 rubles to 80.4 rubles. The productivity of the worker had increased five times. However, statistical comparisons of 1931 with 1921 are unfair because the year 1921 was marked by almost complete paralysis of industry and trade. It was a period of "war communism" and economic anarchy. Production had declined to a small fraction of the pre-war level. The increase is great only compared to 1921, but not 1913. The rise was not due to planning. Most of it occurred before the Five-Year Plan went into effect. During the decade 1931–41 a similar relative growth is highly unlikely. The accompanying chart shows that the pre-war level of production was not attained again until the fiscal year 1926–27.

3. Specific Achievements. The results are to be measured not by general estimates so much as by specific accomplishment and failures. The record in some of the important fields follows.

a. Products of Farm and Forest. *i. Farm Products.* The annual increase in income over the preceding year of the agricultural population beginning with the fiscal year 1928 was 9.8 per cent, 17.8 per cent, and 21.9 per cent. This increase refers to money receipts alone and does not include the intangibles of the socialist economy. This increase was due partly to the rise in prices for farm products and partly to increased earnings from home industry and private trading.[69] By the fiscal year 1930 the grain problem seemed solved, through technical and socialist reconstruction in agriculture. About 22 per cent of all peasant farms were collectivized, and together with the state farms yielded 34 per cent of the total grain production and 60 per cent of the marketable surplus.[70] By 1932 the passive resistance of the peasants, the stealing of the state crops, and the refusal of the peasants to plant and harvest indicated that the problem of agriculture remained unsolved.

ii. Forest Products. In forest resources the Soviet Union leads the world, having about 902 million hectares (1 hectare = 2.47 acres) and about 30 per cent of the world's total forest area. The construction program of the Five-Year Plan has created a great demand for timber and therefore, although the total value of the timber production is several times the pre-war total, exports have not grown proportionately. In 1930, however, Russia became an important exporter of timber. The value of Soviet exports rose from $70,000,-

GROSS PRODUCTION OF THE SOVIET UNION [71]

(In Billions of Rubles at Pre-War Prices)

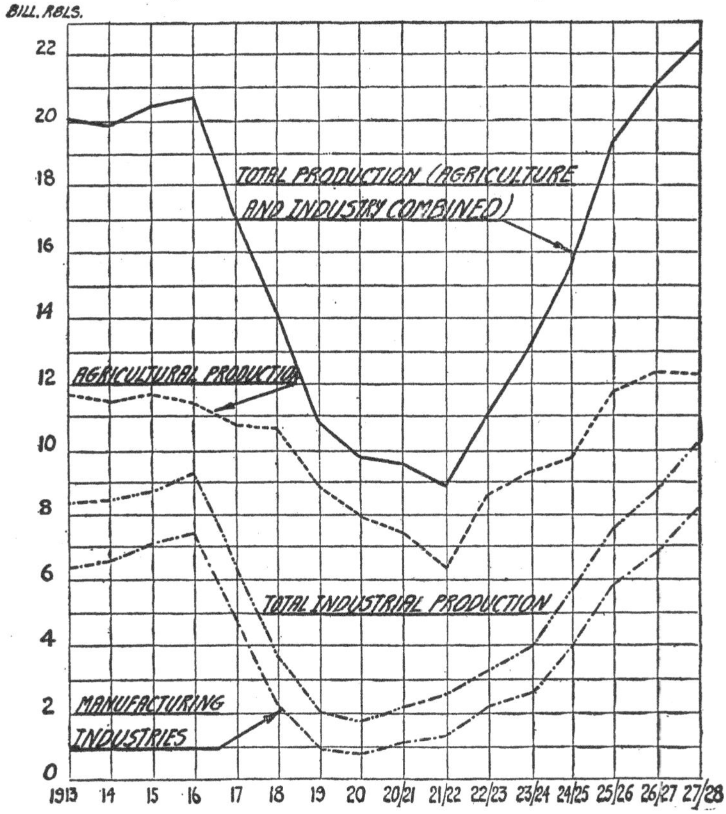

000 in 1929 to $91,000,000 in 1930, whereas exports of the United States declined from $139,000,000 to $123,000,000 in the same time. Timber exports of the United States in 1930 were 10.5 million cubic meters and of the Soviet Union 12.0 million cubic meters,[72] less than the pre-war amounts.

For 1932 the Soviet timber export is planned to be three times as great as that of the United States. Little of this timber goes to the United States, averaging but 1 to 3 per cent of the American timber imported from 1927 to

1930 and less than one-eighth of 1 per cent of the total American consumption. The depletion of native American spruce has required the importation of foreign spruce for the paper industry, and spruce is the only kind of Soviet timber now imported by the United States.

iii. Foods. In addition to the export of grain, butter, eggs, and other raw foods, the Soviet Union is planning to produce and export prepared foods. A cannery, the largest in Europe, with an annual capacity of 90 million cans, is being built in the Northern Caucasus on an American plan.

b. Raw Materials. *i. Coal.* The coal reserves of the Soviet Union are estimated at 556 billion tons. However, owing to the inadequate geological survey and inadequate transportation facilities these resources have not been exploited. For example, the Asiatic part of the Soviet Union, containing over 84 per cent of its known coal reserves, produced only one-seventh of its annual output. The output of coal rose greatly owing both to the development of old beds and the exploitation of new ones.

OUTPUT OF COAL BY REGIONS [73]

(in million metric tons)

Region	*1913*	*1929–30*	*Original 5-year Plan 1932–33*	*Revised Plan 1932–33*
Donetz	25.3	35.8	50.0	75.0
Moscow	0.3	1.7	4.0	10.0
Ural	1.2	2.3	6.0	11.0
Kuznetzk	0.8	4.6	6.0	27.0
Others	1.3	2.3	9.0	7.0
Total	28.9	46.7	75.0	130.0

A comparison of the entire actual output for typical years with "optimum" figures of the Plan follows:

ACTUAL COAL OUTPUT AND "OPTIMUM" FIGURES OF 5-YEAR PLAN [74]

(in thousands of metric tons)

Year	*Actual Output*	*5-Year Plan "Optimum"*
1913	28,900	....
1918	13,000	....
1921	8,500	....
1922	9,000	....
1923 *	10,600	....
1928 *	35,400	35,400
1929 *	40,600	41,100

ACTUAL COAL OUTPUT AND "OPTIMUM" FIGURES OF 5-YEAR PLAN—*Continued*

(*in thousands of metric tons*)

Year	*Actual Output*	*5-Year Plan "Optimum"*
1930 *	46,500	46,600
1931	57,600	53,000
Program		
1932	....	63,000
1933	....	75,000 †
		120,000 ‡

* Fiscal year ending September 30. † Original plan. ‡ Revised plan.

ii. Peat. The peat reserves of the Soviet Union are three-fourths of the total for the entire world. Less than 500,000 acres of all bogs have been prospected out of a total of over 72 million acres having a probable content of over 500 million tons.§ The rise of the production of peat is shown herewith.[75]

Year	*Output in thousand metric tons*
1913	1,550
1926 *	4,260
1930 * (preliminary)	7,000
1931 (program)	14,000

* Fiscal year.

iii. Petroleum. The known petroleum reserves of the Soviet Union are estimated at about 35 billion barrels. This does not include areas in Siberia and Central Asia which have not been fully prospected and which probably contain additional reserves. The output of petroleum has grown very rapidly:

PETROLEUM PRODUCTION AND TRADE [76]

(*in thousands of metric tons* *)

Year	*Output of Crude Oil*	*Output of Refined Oil*	*Exports of Oil Products*
1913	9,234.9	5,702.4	947.7
1926 †	8,322.6	5,876.0	1,473.8
1930 †	17,405.6	14,836.0	4,554.9
1931	23,100.0	....	....
1933 (original 5-yr. Plan)	21,700.0	....	....
1933 (revised Plan)	46,000.0	40,000.0	....

* One ton figured at approximately 6.5 barrels. † Fiscal year ending September 30.

§ I. M. Gubkin, Soviet geologist, estimated 63 billion tons for European Russia (March, 1932).

The Soviets with an output of about 150 million barrels in 1931 have now attained second place among oil-producers of the world, being preceded only by the United States and exceeding Venezuela, whose outputs in 1930 were 896.6 million barrels and 141.7 million barrels, respectively. Because oil production can be rapidly increased, the production and exportation of oil is likely to be one of the Soviet's most important sources of national income and of foreign exchange.

The increased output of oil is one of the striking results of the Five-Year Plan. The goal at the end of the five years was attained in two and one-half years. The original plan for the fiscal year 1933 called for 21.7 million tons, as contrasted with 11.5 million tons output in 1928, but the five-year objective was reached in half the time. This was due not merely to the exploitation of existing pools but to the discovery of new pools. Oil has been found near Sachi on the shores of the Black Sea, in the Emba District, in Georgia, in the Ural region near Perm, in Turkmenistan (on the eastern shores of the Caspian Sea), and in Sakhalin Island. Furthermore, the Grozny oil field was extended 50 miles to the southeast and bituminous shale was found in Transcaucasia of a thickness of 40 meters over an area of 200 square kilometers (77 square miles).[77]

Great as the actual increase over 1913 has been, however, the percentage of increase in 1930 over 1913 was far less than in any other important oil-producing country except Mexico:

WORLD PRODUCTION OF PETROLEUM [78]

million barrels *

	1913	*1929*	*1930*
United States	248.0	1,006.6	896.6
Venezuela	.0	138.9	141.7
Persia	1.8	42.5	43.5
Roumania	13.5	33.6	40.0
Mexico	25.7	44.7	39.5
Dutch East Indies	11.2	36.1	37.1
Colombia	.0	20.3	20.3
Peru	2.1	12.5	12.4
Russia, including Sakhalin	63.0	98.1	130.0

* Conversion rate, 1 ton = 7 barrels of 42 gallons.

iv. Iron and Steel. The known iron-ore reserves of the Soviet Union had been figured at about 3 billion metric tons until the Kursk beds were discovered six years ago with an estimated reserve of 20 billion to 40 billion tons of ore. The estimate of pig-iron production for the last year of the Five-Year Plan was originally 10 million tons, then 15 million and still later 17 million tons. If the last figure is reached, the Soviet Union will lead Europe and will be second only to America in the production of pig iron. The 1913 output was not attained again until 1929 in steel and until 1930 in pig iron, but the production for the last year of the Five-Year Plan is planned to exceed greatly the pre-war production. It is very unlikely to do so.

ACTUAL AND PLANNED PRODUCTION OF PIG IRON, ROLLED IRON, AND STEEL [79]

in thousands of metric tons

	Pig Iron		Rolled Iron and Steel	
Calendar Year	*Actual*	*5-Year Plan Optimum*	*Actual*	*5-Year Plan Optimum*
1913	4,220	....	3,509	....
1918	515	....	357	....
1921	116	....	224	....
1922	188	....	250	....
1923 *	300	....	457	....
1928 *	3,282	3,300	3,370	3,200
1929 *	4,020	4,100	3,880	3,600
1930 *	5,091	5,000	5,000	4,000
1931	4,900	6,200	4,100	4,900
Program				
1932	....	7,800	....	6,100
1933	....	10,000 † } 17,000 ‡ }	....	8,000

* Fiscal year ending September 30. † Original plan. ‡ Revised plan.

v. Manganese. The total known reserves of manganese in the Soviet Union are estimated at about 220 million tons. The largest deposits are in Georgia and the next largest in the Ukraine. Before the war Russia produced 54 per cent of the world's output of manganese ore. The percentage fell to 4.4 per cent in 1923 and rose to about 40 per cent in 1928.

OUTPUT OF MANGANESE ORE IN RUSSIA [80]

Year	*Thousand metric tons*
1913	1,240.0
1923–24	493.6
1929–30	1,561.0

The first large Soviet plant for the making of ferro-manganese was begun in November, 1930, at Zestaphony. The estimated output is about 40 thousand tons of ferro-manganese as compared with an average production in the United States of about 300 thousand tons.

vi. Non-ferrous Metals. The pre-war production of copper, zinc, and lead was insignificant. Although Russia has reputed reserves of nickel, tin, and aluminum, there was no production of these metals before the war. Only 2 per cent of the lead and 55 per cent of the copper used in Russia were produced there. The growth of the production of the non-ferrous metals is shown herewith:

PRODUCTION OF NON-FERROUS METALS IN RUSSIA [81]

in metric tons

Fiscal Year	*Copper*	*Zinc*	*Lead*
1913 *	29,000	2,947 †	1,321
1923	2,710	187 †	190
1925	12,578	1,493	644
1930	46,064	4,894	11,442
1931 (program)	150,000	30,000	26,870

* For territory now within the U.S.S.R. † Zinc concentrates.

The demand for non-ferrous metals increased very greatly owing to the increased requirements of the electrical industry, the manufacture of agricultural and automotive machinery, the chemical industry, and transportation. The program for 1931 called for an investment in the production of non-ferrous metals of almost 300 million rubles and for the five-year period almost one billion rubles, of which 100 million rubles were to be used for prospecting and exploitation. Of the metals not produced at all before the war there are now being produced in small quantities mercury, tin, tungsten, and molybdenum, and two large aluminum plants are under construction. The production of magnesium, nickel, and antimony were provided for in the Five-Year Plan. The production planned for the fiscal year 1932, the last year of the Five-Year Plan, follows: [81]

	Thousand metric tons
Copper	195
Zinc	148
Lead	116
Aluminum	20
Nickel	2.5
Magnesium	1.0
Antimony	1.0
Tin	1.0
Mercury	0.6

In spite of the increased domestic production, a considerable quantity of these metals had to be imported. In the fiscal year 1930 domestic production provided 60 per cent of the copper, 18 per cent of the lead, and 16 per cent of the zinc.[82]

vii. Chemicals. Before the war the chemical industry lagged behind industry in general. Dyes, fertilizers, and pharmaceuticals were all imported. But the chemical industry has grown rapidly.[83]

Fiscal Year	*Output in million rubles*
1923	177
1927	507
1928	627 *
1929	834 *
1930	1,294 *

* At 1927 prices.

viii. Building Materials. The rapid rate of construction of plants and residences required a great increase in building materials. The so-called "industrial giants" required also the building of new communities, including homes, hospitals, and workers' clubs. As a result the output of building materials rose far above the pre-war level.

OUTPUT OF BUILDING MATERIALS IN RUSSIA [83]

Fiscal Year	*Cement (million barrels)*	*Bricks (billions)*	*Glass (thousand metric tons)*
1913	12.3	2.1	385
1928	11.9	1.9	320
1930	19.4	4.8	434
1931 (program)	35.0	5.7	. . .
1933 (original 5-Year Plan)	41.0	9.3	800

One of the problems which should cause grave concern to the Soviet officials is the prospect of declining demand for building materials as the construction program slackens. The farther production is pushed above the average normal demand for building materials the greater will be the stagnation in these industries as the building program approaches completion.

c. Heavy Industries. The results in the heavy industries approximated to the Five-Year Plan more closely than did the production in the light industries.

i. Machinery Manufacture. The machine-manufacturing industry was greatly stimulated by the general program of industrialization. Old plants are being expanded and many new plants are being built. Yet the demand for several types of machinery will be inadequately covered and it will still have to be imported to a very considerable extent. For example domestic manufacture provides only 75 per cent of the demand for locomotives, 70 per cent for oil-field equipment, 65 per cent for coal-mine equipment, 40 per cent for chemical equipment. These types of machinery constitute important items of the Soviet import trade. The growth of the machine-manufacturing industry is seen in the following table:

MACHINERY OUTPUT IN RUSSIA [84]

Type of Machine		*Fiscal Years* 1912	1930	1931 *
Locomotives	*number*	13	599	1,000
Freight cars	*number*	13,000	23,600	51,150
Trolley cars	*number*	170	552	905
Diesel engines	*h.p. capacity*	35,000	116,000	224,000
Steam turbines	*kilowatt capacity*	5,900	200,000	600,000
Boilers	*thousand sq. meters*	28	144	300
Metal-working machine tools	*million rubles*	2.5	20	45
Textile machinery	*million rubles*	6.5	37.5	73

* Program.

In addition a large variety of new kinds of machinery is being manufactured in Russia which had been unknown before. Such manufacture is being expanded rapidly. The percentage of the new types of machine to the total machinery has risen rapidly.

NEW TYPES OF MACHINERY PRODUCED [84]

Year	*Million rubles*	*Percentage of All Machines Produced*
1927–28	41	7
1928–29	80	10
1929–30	225	20
1930–31	532 *	. .

* Exclusive of automobiles and tractors.

The increase of production of selected types of new machinery has been as follows:

PRODUCTION NEW TYPES OF MACHINERY IN RUSSIA [84]

in million rubles

Type	*Fiscal Years* 1928	1931 †
Coal cutters	0.1	5.0
Chemical apparatus	3.0 *	40.0
Equipment for oil industry	6.8 *	51.0
Steam and water turbines	2.0	20.0
Road-building machinery	0.6	30.0

* 1928–29. † Program.

Total production of machinery for the fiscal year 1931, exclusive of agricultural machinery, was expected to reach 2.5 billion rubles, or an amount equal to the output scheduled for the fifth year of the Plan. In other words, the Five-Year Plan for the machinery building industry was to be accomplished in three years.[85]

The largest machine works in Soviet Russia is being erected at Kramatorsky. This is another in the series of giant undertakings. According to the plan, this plant will cover eight square kilometers, will contain 2500 machines, employ 17,000 workmen and 2000 engineers, and will manufacture equipment for steel mills, cranes, motors, etc. But as in the case of other new plants, construction is being delayed through inadequate planning and lack of discipline.[86]

ii. Agricultural Machinery. Before the war agricultural machinery made in Russia consisted only of the simplest types of tools and equipment, which were used on small farms. The development of large collective farms and the large state grain factories greatly increased the demand for agricultural machinery.

OUTPUT OF AGRICULTURAL MACHINERY IN RUSSIA [87]

Fiscal Year	*Total million rubles*	*Percentage Tractor-drawn*
1913	67	—
1930	313	24
1931 (program)	760	67
1933 (original 5-Year Plan)	610	—

During the fiscal year 1930 the output of agricultural machinery was almost five times the pre-war output. For 1931 the output was expected to exceed the original estimate for the fifth year of the Five-Year Plan. Even if it had done so, the Soviet Union would still have had to import agricultural machinery extensively, chiefly from the United States. But actual results were much below expectations. In the country's newest and largest agricultural-machinery plant 1931 production was 45 per cent below schedule.[88]

iii. Tractors and Automobiles. One of the most important of the new industries is the manufacture of automobiles and tractors. At the beginning of 1929 the Soviet Union had altogether only about 27 thousand automobiles and 32 thousand tractors, mostly imported.

OUTPUT OF TRACTORS AND AUTOMOBILES IN RUSSIA *

Year	*Tractors*	*Automobiles*
1928	1,279	800
1929	3,267	1,063
1930	9,337	4,425
1931 (program)	56,000	34,000
1933 (revised plan)	175,000	250,000

* The tractor and automobile industry showed an increase in output and improvement in the percentage of the plan realized.

"The tractor plants controlled by the United Automotive and Tractor Industry (Vato), turned out 21,018 tractors during the first six months of 1932, as against 5724 tractors produced during the corresponding period of 1931. The Stalingrad Tractor Plant turned out 13,515 tractors and the Kharkov plant, 7493 tractors, compared to the quota for the year 1932 of 40,000 and 30,000 respectively.

"The total Soviet output of automobiles during the first half of this year was 9127 passenger cars and trucks, which compares favorably with 7769 machines turned out during the corresponding period of 1931, and 2448 during the first six months of 1930. The quota under the Plan was 34,000 for the year 1931.

"The automotive and tractor industry, in spite of difficulties has shown great progress. Nearly all machines turned out during 1932 were made of parts manufactured in Soviet plants, whereas during the second half of 1931, 83 per cent of the production in the Nizhni Novgorod plant consisted of assembling American made parts." [88a]

In spite of the improvement in production, the quotas are far from being attained. The Nizhni Novgorod plant was scheduled for an annual production of 144,000 cars, but the average output up to September 1932 was at the rate of about 47 cars a day or 16,000 a year, or about 11 per cent of the schedule. However, even these figures are probably high because the Soviet statistician counts uncompleted cars. For example, *Pravda* reported that 600 motor trucks were standing in the yards at Nizhni Novgorod incompletely assembled for lack of parts. The Kharkov Tractor Plant reported 65 tractors produced per day early in August, but none of the tractors had any radiators.[88b]

To provide for the increased requirements, plants for the manufacture of automobiles and tractors are being constructed or rebuilt in various parts of the Soviet Union. As noted below nine additional automobile assembly plants were to be constructed within three years. In spite of the rapid growth of Soviet manufacture, there will still be a demand for foreign machines as well as for parts to service both the imported and the domestic machines.

CONSTRUCTION OF NEW PLANTS (n) AND ALTERATIONS OF OLD PLANTS (o) [89]

AUTOMOBILES:	*Location*	*Date of Completion*	*Planned Annual Output*
Nizhni Novgorod (n)	Nizhni Novgorod Region	1931	140,000
AMO (o)	Moscow	In partial operation	50,000
Yaroslavl (o)	Ivanovo Industrial Region	....	20,000
TRACTORS:			
Stalingrad (n)	Lower Volga Region	1932	50,000
Kharkov (n)	Ukraine	1932	50,000
Cheliabinsk (n)	Ural Region	1932	40,000
"Red Putilov" Tractor Dept. (o)	Leningrad	In operation	35,000

iv. Electric Power. As noted above, the original scheme for economic planning involved much electrification. The State Commission for Electrification was formed by Lenin in 1920. This plan called for 30 new power plants, with a total capacity of 1.5 million kilowatts, in about 15 years, providing a total capacity for the country (including pre-war plants) of 1.75 million kilowatts. However, by 1933 the program should cover 76 plants with a total capacity of over 7.6 million kilowatts.

CAPACITY OF POWER PLANTS AND OUTPUT OF ELECTRIC CURRENT [90]

Fiscal Year	*Capacity of Power Plant * thousand kilowatts*	*Output of Electric Current million kilowatt hours*
1913	1,210	1,945
1925	1,364	2,274
1928	1,874	5,165
1930	2,885	7,714
1933 (orig. 5-Year plan)	5,500	22,000
1933 (revised figures)	7,700	26,000

* At end of year indicated.

On the Dnieper River the second largest hydroelectric power plant in the world, to be exceeded only by the Boulder Dam Plant, has been built, with a capacity of 750,000 horsepower (558,000 kilowatts). It was begun in 1927 and was formally completed May 1, 1932. Its opening was dramatic. The thousands of workers who had spent five years building the plant watched with intent interest the machinery beginning to whir.

The plant should serve 70,000 square miles and a population of 16 million, including the Donetz Coal Basin and the new metal works now being built. The total project cost 220 million rubles. It is located in the midst of an area rich in agricultural and mining resources and having many industries. Furthermore, other large industries dependent upon abundant and cheap electricity are to be established, such as the manufacture of ferromanganese, aluminum, fertilizer, nitrates and other chemicals, and steel. The plant was erected with Colonel Hugh Cooper, who built the Mississippi Power Company's dam at Keokuk, Iowa, the Muscle Shoals plant, and other important projects as consultant. The turbines of 84,000 horsepower each are the largest in the world and exceed the Niagara turbines, whose capacity is 75,000 horsepower. The power output per annum will be more than 2.5 billion kilowatt hours.[91]

Even after the plant is completed the number of kilowatt hours per capita in the Soviet Union will be relatively small, only 165 as contrasted with 3000 in Norway, 2000 in Canada, and 1000 in the United States. Furthermore, in spite of the huge increase projected under the Five-Year Plan, even the revised figures or maximum projected for 1933 of 26.0 billion kilowatt hours compares with 30 billion kilowatt hours in Germany in 1930 and 113 billion kilowatt hours in the United States. Apparently a further development is necessary before Russia reaches the stage of industrialization of other economically advanced countries.

v. Electrical Equipment. As a result of the huge increase in the output of electric power, the manufacture of electrical equipment has increased very greatly.

OUTPUT OF ELECTRO-TECHNICAL INDUSTRY IN RUSSIA [92]

Fiscal Year	*Million rubles*
1913	45.1
1922	9.4
1928	170.0
1930	488.0
1931 (program)	1,145.0
1933 (original 5-Year Plan)	896.0

One of the principal plants, the Electrozavod in Moscow, "the giant of the electro-technical industry," increased its production very rapidly. Its output in the fiscal year 1928 was 9.4 million rubles. In 1929 the output trebled, and in 1930 the output more than doubled again, reaching almost 60 million rubles. The rate of production scheduled for the last year of the Five-Year Plan was reached in March 1931. In other words, Electrozavod finished the Five-Year Plan in two and one-half years.[93] The "Sevkabl," or cable factory, likewise finished its Five-Year Plan in two and one-half years. The fifth year of the Plan called for a production valued at 55 million rubles, but during the first quarter of 1931 this annual rate was exceeded.[94]

The industry making rubber used in insulation also completed the Five-Year Plan in two and one-half years. "Kauchuk," the Moscow rubber factory, in the year ending April 1931, had produced an output valued at almost 43 million rubles as compared with 43.2 million rubles set in the Plan for the fifth year.[94]

4. Labor. A Soviet spokesman maintains (though the statistics cannot be verified and seem too favorable), that in the fiscal year 1927 real wages were about 15 per cent higher than 1913; that at the end of the fiscal year 1929 real wages were 33 per cent higher than 1913, and that in addition the workman had many social benefits such as insurance against illness, accident, unemployment, and old age, facilities for recreation and education, and an annual holiday, making real wages 67 per cent higher.* That real wages did not increase quite so rapidly is implied in Soviet official organs like *Pravda,* which said, October 2, 1930:

> Actual prosperity of workmen's families, however, depends now not so much on slight changes in real wages as on the number of bread-winners. Money wages of industrial workingmen increased considerably above the estimates of the plan during the fiscal year 1930–31 and therefore real wages have also somewhat increased. But owing to the shortage of labor more members of the same family are working for wages and are increasing the family income.

The number of workers in the larger factories had increased in 1929 by 236,000 and in 1930 by 566,000.[95] Between 1922 and 1930 the productivity per man increased four times over, and daily wages 3.6 times. The seven-hour day was introduced and benefited more than 500,000 by the end of 1929 and more than one million by the end of 1930. It was planned to put 89 per cent of the workers on the seven-hour day by the close of 1931 and 100 per cent by the close of 1932, besides establishing the five-day week in 1931 for 93 per cent of all industrial workers. The hours were shortened without lower-

* See also Stalin's Report to the Executive Committee of the Communist Party at the Sixteenth Congress, 1930.

ing the wage level. There is said to be little involuntary unemployment now except among the dispossessed classes formerly property-owners.

In the fiscal year 1928 the income of the urban population rose 13.6 per cent; in 1929, 16.1 per cent; and in 1930, 27.3 per cent over the preceding year. These figures are substantially in excess of the Plan. To show the diminishing place of private economy, Soviet statistics indicate that beginning with the fiscal year 1928, the income of the small artisans and traders in the cities declined in three successive years 0.2 per cent, 20.3 per cent, and 15.7 per cent from the preceding year. The so-called capitalistic elements showed an even more striking decline in income, amounting for the same three years to 19.3 per cent, 33.4 per cent, and 40.5 per cent.[96]

5. Exports. Because of the success in increasing the output of lumber, oil, and manganese, the Soviets exported heavily. The world's markets became panic-stricken and ascribed the exports not to the need for obtaining credit abroad but rather to the desire to sell goods below cost in order to precipitate a world revolution. It was the large exports of Soviet Russia that first called attention to the growing achievements of the Plan and raised the fear of a great menace in the future.

I. Quotas Unrealized

In several industries production lagged behind, as, for example, in construction work and in the output of coke, chemicals, and chemical machinery.

1. Capital Construction. The capital construction program for the first quarter of 1931 was realized only to the extent of 50 per cent, and in some districts to a considerably smaller extent as, for example, in the Leningrad region, 34 per cent, in Nizhni Novgorod, 39 per cent, and in the Ural region, 30 per cent.[97] By April 1, 1931, the value of the construction at the Nizhni Automobile Plant should have amounted to 118 million rubles but it was actually only about 33 million rubles, or 29 per cent of the Plan.[98] For the Soviet Union as a whole the capital construction program for the year 1930 was realized only 83 per cent. The poorest result was shown for new construction projects which were carried out only 66 per cent, whereas capital repairs were carried out 100 per cent. As a writer in *Pravda* remarks, the tendency of the construction industry was to develop along the lines of least resistance. According to the Central Statistical Bureau capital construction for the first half of the fiscal year 1930 was completed only about 30 per cent and in some industries the results were considerably worse. Construction

was very low in some industries, as in the non-ferrous metallurgy 15 per cent, and in the chemical industry 13 per cent of the Plan. Construction of plants for automobiles, tractors, and building materials,[99] and construction in the great steel centers at Magnitogorsk and Kuznetzk were likewise far behind, the latter realizing the plan only 52 per cent in the first quarter of 1931 and only 28 per cent in April 1931.[100]

2. HEAVY INDUSTRY. Several of the heavy industries also fell far behind, such as the production of basic metals and coal. The output of large-scale industries in the fiscal year 1930 fell short of the planned increase by about 7 per cent. In addition, the quality of the goods was decidedly inferior.[101] For the calendar year 1931 steel production was reported to be about 5,400,000 tons; pig iron 4,900,000 tons; and coal 57,600,000 tons against quotas of 9,500,000 tons of steel; 9,000,000 tons of pig iron; and 77,000,000 tons of coal.[102]

a. Tractors. The United Agricultural Machinery Industry failed to achieve its quota by a large margin. During the "shock" quarter, October to December 1930, the plan was realized only 65 per cent; during the first quarter of 1931 only 58 per cent; and during May 1931 only 47 per cent.[103] As noted above, production for the full year 1931 in the largest farm-machinery plant was only 45 per cent of the quota.

At Stalingrad the record was still worse. Instead of an output of 1500 tractors per month, only 526, or 35 per cent of the quota, were produced in February 1931, and of these 55 had no carburetors. The quota of motors for agricultural combines was realized only to the extent of 30 per cent.[104] However, by December 1931 the output rose to 2725 and by April 1932 to 2991 machines.

Because of the failure to realize the plan a special commission was appointed to investigate the conditions at the Stalingrad Tractor Plant and to report to the Supreme Economic Council. The report stated in summary that a better lay-out of buildings or equipment was not to be found anywhere in Europe or America. Yet the output of the plant was only 20 per cent of the plan in the "shock" quarter. Failure in spite of adequate machinery and equipment was ascribed to mismanagement and lack of co-ordination.[105] It is interesting to note that old-established plants were far more successful, indicating that as a major policy it would be better to expand old plants rather than build giants in totally new territories.

b. Machinery. The Red Sormovo Plant manufacturing transport machinery and equipment filled only 69 per cent of its program for the fiscal year

1929. In some departments the percentage realized was far lower—54 per cent in the output of Diesel engines, 52 per cent in oil-drilling equipment, and 64 per cent in boilers.[106] Not much progress was made for a year later. The output for the first quarter of 1931 was only 66 per cent of the Plan.[107]

3. LIGHT INDUSTRY. The output of the light industries fell far below that of the heavy industries. In the fiscal year 1930 the light industries fell 10 per cent behind the Plan. Accumulating the deficits on the percentages realized, it would be necessary for the output in the fourth year to be increased 113 per cent over the third year in order to realize the Five-Year Plan in full. This obviously is impossible. The causes of the lagging of the light industries is due partly to unfavorable crop conditions, lack of raw material, withholding from the market by the peasants of the products of home industry, and the favoring of heavy industry by the government.[108]

> For the first six months of 1932, the production plans of Soviet light industry was carried out only to the extent of 41.8 per cent. It must be remembered that one cannot overcome excessive spoilage of manufactured products by various "campaigns," "storm-attacks," and other such methods. Only steady effort and persistent struggle will bring about an improvement of workmanship. Inspection departments are not well organized and their work is not always regarded seriously. One frequently finds inspection departments engaged in checking up on finished goods rather than on work in process. Production costs in light industry, instead of showing a reduction, have increased about 5.2 per cent.[108a]

4. HIGH COSTS OF PRODUCTION. Not only did many industries fail to realize their quotas of output, but the estimated reduction of costs was not realized. For the first half of the fiscal year 1930 the average manufacturing costs for all industries decreased less than 5 per cent instead of 11 per cent as planned.[109] For the whole year 1930, the costs of production declined only 7 per cent.[110] Furthermore, the productivity of labor failed to rise in accordance with the Plan, increasing only 10 per cent instead of 25 per cent as planned. The failure to lower costs was due to inadequate labor productivity, waste of raw and finished material, and inefficient expansion of output.[111] In some industries the costs not only failed to go down as planned but they actually increased. For example, in July 1930, the mining cost in the Donetz Coal Basin rose 7.4 per cent; in the Moscow district 23 per cent; and in the Ural district 26 per cent.[112] The steel mills of "Stal" reduced production costs during the special quarter by 0.43 per cent instead of 6.1 per cent and other steel mills, including the largest plants of the steel trust, actually increased costs by 7 to 9 per cent.[113] Construction costs did not decline to the extent planned—in the fiscal year 1929 only 8 per cent as

against 15 per cent planned and in the fiscal year 1930 only 5 per cent against 14 per cent planned.[111] Costs of producing machines are extremely high. For instance, the cost of a tractor produced at Stalingrad is 4000 rubles (about $2000), which is far higher than the prices in the United States or Germany. The reason given by the Soviet officials themselves is that the factory has over 15,000 surplus workmen and that instead of turning out 150 tractors daily, the average output is only 23 tractors. These facts help to explain the failure to realize the costs set in the Plan.[114]

The case of the Stalingrad factory is not unique. The total number of workingmen in the Soviet industries increased in the spring of 1930 over the preceding half year by about 11.8 per cent instead of 4.7 per cent as planned; in the metal industries by 20.2 per cent instead of 8.6 per cent as planned, and in the coal industry by 14.5 per cent as against 8.4 per cent planned. As a result of the increase in the number of workers, productivity of labor declined, and nominal wages rose only 5.6 per cent, instead of 9.1 per cent over the preceding year.[115] The output per worker in "census" industry increased 45.8 per cent from 1927 to 1930 and 9.0 per cent in 1930.

But in 1931 it actually decreased 8.9 per cent instead of increasing 22.6 per cent as planned. The cost of production for 1931 should have decreased by 10.5 per cent but actually increased by 2.0 per cent or according to other data by 3.7 per cent. The cause was the reduced productivity of labor, the increase in food prices, in the wages fund and the budget index.[115a]

5. Deterioration of Quality. Not only was the Plan unrealized with respect to quantity, but far more so with respect to quality of workmanship. This was true not only of finished goods but even of some semi-finished products and raw materials such as coal, coke, ores, and metals. The poor quality of the raw materials caused great waste, which in turn raised production costs. For example, in the "shock" quarter, the percentage of rejected iron at the Dzerzhinsky plant, making open-hearth iron, rose from an average of 14.1 per cent, in the fiscal year ending September 1930, to 20.8 per cent in October 1930. At the Rykov plant the percentage of spoiled material rose from 12.7 per cent to 25.5 per cent; and at the Tomsky plant, from 6.9 per cent to 27.3 per cent for the same period.[116]

The Bureau of Research on Russian Economic Conditions, University of Birmingham, says:

> The quality of production continued to decline throughout 1931. This deterioration in quality in large-scale industry is estimated at 30 per cent, which may be

regarded as a safe minimum for the years 1930 and 1931 (*vide* also Memorandum No. 3, pp. 5, 15, 16).[116a]

6. Rate of Increase. In spite of the increase in industrial investments in 1930 and the increase in the number of workingmen coming from the farms and cities, the rate of increase in production has not been maintained according to the Plan. The reasons were, possibly, the reduction of hours of labor in certain industries, shortage of consumers' goods, and perhaps the growing complications of rapidly expanding industries. The annual increase of between 20 and 25 per cent is unlikely to be continued. Yet it could be greatly reduced and still be substantially higher than the rate of growth of most capitalist countries.

J. The Second Five-Year Plan

The second Five-Year Plan came to the notice of the world in the spring of 1932. Its outstanding factors are: curtailing the development of industries making raw materials and machinery and stimulating industries making goods for the consumer. For example, in the production of pig iron, the first Five-Year Plan, as published in November 1930, called for 17 million tons, a figure which was reduced at the end of the first Five-Year Plan in 1932 to 9 million tons, and for the end of the second Five-Year Plan, in 1937, set at only 22 million tons. The second Five-Year Plan conforms to the proposals of the "right opposition," whose spokesmen, Rykov, Bukharin, and Tomsky, had to recant. Writers sympathetic to the Soviets state that if this policy had been adopted in 1928 the giant plants devoted to steel, coal, automobiles, tractors, and machinery, would not have been built, nor would agriculture have been socialized successfully. Furthermore, the development of consumers'-goods industries requires as a foundation the creation of producers'-goods industries. Besides, in 1928 there was a long enough interval before the world crisis became serious during which such heavy construction was possible. In 1932 a Five-Year Plan for heavy industries would have been impossible.[117]

The general economic development is divided into three periods: (1) restoration up to 1928; (2) construction of heavy industries and agriculture in the first five years 1928 to 1932; (3) the satisfaction of the consumer in the second five years 1933 to 1937. A summary of the second Five-Year Plan was presented in the official press.[118] The aim of the second Five-Year Plan is made a piece of Soviet propaganda:

a. To complete the liquidation of the capitalistic elements of the population;
b. To do away with the factors making for class distinction and exploitation of the people;
c. To eliminate from the minds of the people the survivals of capitalism;
d. To transform the entire working population into the builders of a classless, socialistic society.

But specifically, the program is stated to be:

a. To provide the population with consumers' goods;
b. To increase the output of food two to three times.

In specific fields the program of the second Five-Year Plan is as follows: Machinery for agriculture, industry, transportation and consumption should be increased between three and three and one-half times. Electric power production should increase from 17 billion kilowatt hours in 1932 to 100 billion in 1937. The coal output should rise from 90 million to 250 million tons. Production of oil should increase two and one-half to three times. The output of pig iron should exceed 22 million tons. In the non-ferrous metals—copper, lead, zinc, aluminum, etc.—the output should equal the domestic consumption, making imports unnecessary. In transportation, the railroad mileage is to increase by 30,000 kilometers (about 19,000 miles), a number of railroads are to be electrified, and the entire system is to be equipped with automatic couplers and an automatic signal system. Locomotives and freight cars are to be increased in size and efficiency. Construction of highways and automobile roads is to increase at a greater rate than that of any other type of transportation. In agriculture, the collective-farm developments are to be continued. State farms should be extended so as to cover all types of agriculture, not merely the raising of grains. Live-stock breeding should be the chief aim of the agricultural plan. In addition, the output of grain is to reach 130 million tons. The output of cotton and flax is to be doubled. The output of sugar beets is to be tripled. In the consumers' goods industries, the consumption of the masses is to be increased threefold. The output of cotton cloth is to rise from 3 billion meters in 1932 to 7 billion in 1937, the output of linen from 180 million meters to 1200 million meters. The per capita consumption of electric power is to exceed that of any other European country by 1937. The recent growth in Russia has been as follows:

Year	*Kilowatt Hours per capita*
1913	14.4
1926	22.0
1932	103.0

For comparison, the per capita consumption before the depression was as follows:

United States	942
Germany	480
England	330
France	319

K. Appraisal and Forecast

The Five-Year Plan is a mechanistic conception. But life is organic. It grows not by formula but as a result of innumerable forces which influence it in varying degrees. Growth involves the time factor. Economic life involves the development of relationships between the consumers, the ultimate basis of economic society, the manufacturers of consumers' goods, the producers of raw materials, etc. These inter-relationships cannot be predicted precisely five years ahead.

The Soviet officials themselves realized the academic character of the approach. At the opening of the Planning Academy, Kuibyshev, the chairman of the *Gosplan,* delivered an address in the course of which he raised very interesting questions:

> Have we at our disposal, plans prepared with adequate technical and economic knowledge and worked out not only for individual industries but also covering whole districts and regions? To this question, our candid reply is that, for the time being, we have no such reliable and carefully probed plans. . . . Our plans, if I may say so, suffer too much from a "statistico-arithmetical" bias and lack clear technical ideas. The experience gained in preparing the plans for 1931 shows that the technical element in our planning must be strengthened. So far we have approached our problems mainly as arithmeticians. This is strikingly demonstrated by our indices. The planned-economy experts must be able "to face reality, they must consider facts and adjust plans to realities and material possibilities." [118a]

It becomes more and more apparent that the reserves of technical and economic knowledge at the command of the Soviet Government are quite insufficient to cope with the enormous task of planning out and directing the economic life of 160 million people occupying a sixth of the globe. This difficulty now begins to be understood at Moscow.[118b]

Planning in a nation's economic life is not essentially a communist idea. The old imperial régime of Germany planned the future growth of the country in many respects, encouraging the building of a merchant marine and the expansion of key industries such as the manufacture of dyes, chemicals, optical goods, fine electrical machinery, etc. The economic development of America was planned in part by industrialists and by the government. The tariff developed infant industries. But the idea of developing the entire industry of a country according to a preconceived plan is a novel conception. It is an interesting experiment. The gathering of money from one industry to be spent on another is a bold and large conception hitherto carried out only in war time when costs of production were ignored and inflationary profits so stimulated production as to cause deep depression later. The directing of labor and materials, the granting of priority in transportation, the denial of many essentials of life to the population—these are daring measures which can be applied in peace time only to a submissive and willing people accustomed for centuries to the imposition of the will of the government, inured to hardship, and schooled in want.

That the Plan has had some measure of success is undeniable. Granting even that the several lines of production have developed very unevenly, and recognizing all the burdens it imposed and the failures it suffered, the stark fact stands out that a primitive country, with limited outside financial aid, achieved remarkable progress in its agricultural and industrial development. It is a tribute to the organizers of the psychic and material resources of a nation, and an example unequaled in history of a nation's will in action in times other than war. The principle of planning is a significant and probably a permanent factor of the life of Soviet Russia.

The attempt to manipulate social forces is indeed an ideal worth striving for. But are we wise enough to do it successfully? Concluding a keen and scholarly study of the business cycle, Wesley C. Mitchell, one of the world's leading authorities on that subject, confesses that we know too little about business activity to be able to guide and direct it. "The defects in the system of guiding economic activity and the bewildering complexity of the task itself allow the processes of economic life to fall into those recurrent disorders which constitute crises and depressions. To recognize this fact is but the beginning of wisdom."[119] Elsewhere he says that, "we still know too little of the relationships between the economic forces at work to be able to mold them." And a physician who does not understand the pathology of the organism may create more ills than he can cure.

The attempt of Russia to accomplish so much in five years was bound to lead to mistakes. Some of them have proved to be very costly. "The more haste the less speed," is true for a nation as well as for an individual. How different is the policy of the successful manufacturing companies! The chemical or electrical firms that develop new processes in the laboratory first erect a small experimental plant in which the process is perfected commercially, but on a small scale. The plant is then operated for a long period so as to give an accurate test of the processes, of the costs and of the marketability of the product. Similarly, in mines an experimental reduction plant or smelter is built to test the method of winning the metal. Small plants mean small mistakes and facility in making changes. This is the usual method of industrial managers. The Russians disregard all this experience and proceed immediately into uncharted ground to operate on a huge scale, where every error is magnified a thousandfold and where every major correction or change or retreat becomes a fearful burden.

Has the Five-Year Plan actually worked in Russia? Generally speaking, the quotas are being realized. But there is no evenness of success, and no way of assuring it. Incalculable factors constantly affect the result, both for good and for ill. On the one hand, new oil discoveries sent production far ahead of the Plan. On the other, when 58,000 coal workers in the Donetz Basin left their jobs, they dropped production not only below the Plan figures for the quarter but below that of the corresponding quarter of the year before. The very fact that some industries have gone ahead and some have fallen behind indicates the academic nature of the Five-Year Plan. It is impossible to keep a nation's economic progress moving like a military parade. As to the benefits to the working class it is undoubtedly true that because of inadequate rations real wages have fallen at least below the level of wages called for by the Plan.

Even where there has been spectacular success the unexpected advances have tended to dislocate the Plan almost as much as unexpected failure. "Five years of proletarian Russian oil in two and a half is exactly like capitalistic wildcatting in Oklahoma. Does not five years of Soviet petroleum in two and a half years come dangerously close to the capitalist vice of planless overproduction?" [120] Or as stated by the Bureau of Research on Russian Economic Conditions:

> The actual results of the year 1931 differ so largely from the planned estimates that they lead us to regard the economic order now existing in Russia not as a system of planned economy, but as a state monopoly unavoidably bound to tolerate within itself the existence of uncontrollable elemental forces.[120a]

The Soviet leaders say that the Five-Year Plan is a success, that Russia is booming, whereas the western world is in depression. But the western world is in depression because it has been producing too much goods and is struggling to find a market for them. If the Five-Year Plan is a success, it is because there is no such problem of finding markets; but on the contrary the Russian people are underconsuming. The capitalist countries have been growing slowly while the population was rising in its standard of living; Russia is growing rapidly while both its urban and its industrial population lower their standard of living.

Furthermore, whatever success the Five-Year Plan has achieved is attributable partly to foreign engineering genius. The achievement of Colonel Cooper at the Keokuk power station is repeated at Dnieprostroy. Stuart, James & Cooke, coal engineers, merely applied their American experience to the Donetz and Kuznetzk Basins. Kahn's work in building automobile plants in Detroit is repeated at the several sites of Russian plants. The success of John Calder at the Remington Typewriter Company is duplicated at the Stalingrad plant. And so with many others—although of course it must always be remembered that the great attempt would be impossible without the daring conceptions of Soviet leaders and the patience and willingness of the Russian people to be the guinea-pigs in the experiment.

Because of the haste with which the plants are built, there will be need for considerable reorganization. Poorly located plants will have to be abandoned, much of the equipment will be idle, because the growth has not been an integrated one. Some industries will produce raw materials far in excess of the demand for them.

After the current Five-Year Plan is finished, a new Five-Year Plan is provided for, with a new set of goals. The second Plan may simply be a recognition of the obvious—five years is an inadequate time in which to build up a nation's industries. And if the task is to be done in a series of five-year plans, then the pace may be reduced, and suffering mitigated. Perhaps this is Stalin's intent, just as it was Rykov's proposal.

The Five-Year Plan in Fifty would be a more practical slogan than "The Five-Year Plan in Four." Germany, starting with a highly literate people and a well-organized social life, needed about forty years to catch up to England, the leading industrial country of Europe. Japan, without any violent political change, required fifty years to attain an important rank. Is it likely that Russia will require much less? Even though she is richer in material resources, the intangible elements, technical education and industrial tradition, require much time to develop. To quote a statesman of 2650 years ago, who became so great that he is now known as a prophet, Isaiah: "Who hath heard such a thing? Is a land born in one day?" The fact that many of his ideas are regarded as new social discoveries in Russia today should make the Kremlin ponder this query.

CHAPTER V

AGRICULTURE

A. Aims

1. Socialism in Agriculture. In extending socialism to industry the state merely confiscated property belonging to an individual, a family, or a number of stockholders, and then operated the plant, using the same technique, but the laborer for the former private employer remained as laborer for the state. In agriculture the problem was more difficult. It involved a more basic change. The land could not be taken from the peasants as the factories were taken away from the industrialists. The revolution was successful, in fact, because it permitted the great mass of peasants to appropriate the land, although theoretically the land always belonged to the Soviet state.

During the régime of Kerensky, the Mensheviks had planned to redistribute the land, under legal and constitutional restrictions, after consideration and vote by the representative assembly. The Bolsheviks decided to turn over the land to the peasants immediately, but to retain the title in the state. This policy brought the peasants to the support of the Bolshevik revolution. The retention of the title by the state was disregarded by the peasantry. If the Bolsheviks had proceeded to take the land from the peasants it would probably have provoked a new revolution. The Soviet policy was therefore first to drive out the rich peasant, and then by inducements and pressure to bring the poor peasants into collective farms and try to develop the state lands as huge farms with socialization of labor. The aim of this policy of collectivization was that "our united means of production and our common organized labor may be used for the purpose of forming a large collective economic entity and in this manner insure a complete and effective victory over the kulak, over all exploiters and enemies of the workers, over poverty and ignorance, over the backwardness of individual economic entities, and create a high labor output and marketable surplus by collective means."

Socialism was thus extended to agriculture. The Soviet leaders realized that it was impossible on the one hand to run industry on a socialized basis with a modern industrial technique, and on the other hand to leave agriculture on the basis of private property with primitive methods. To permit agriculture to remain on that basis would be to threaten the success of the socialization of industry.

The mere subdivision of the land does not in itself make for socialism. Because the French peasantry, with its small holdings arising from the distribution of land of the nobles after the French Revolution, is today the most conservative element in the French State, the communists decided on the policy of the socialization of agriculture as well as of industry.

2. Pre-War Experience. The experience of the peasant before the war may throw some light on the present situation. At the time of the agricultural reform in 1861, the emancipated serfs were not given the property as individuals. The land was turned over to the commune, which allocated a particular plot of ground for cultivation by each peasant. Title did not vest in the peasant, and he could not sell his share of the land of the commune. Nor had he the unconditional right to leave the commune. Certain elements of serfdom remained. The discontent of the peasants resulted in the uprisings of 1905. As a result the Stolypin agricultural-reform act of 1906 was introduced, freeing the peasant from the land and making it his private property. He could sell it and he could leave it.

Not merely did his social status change, but agricultural technique was improved. In the five years before the war there was a five-fold increase in the use of agricultural machinery, and a four-fold increase in the use of fertilizers. The introduction of private property resulted in the sale in the seven years before the war of over one million small farms, while the holdings of the richer peasants increased in size.

Before the revolution 88 per cent of the peasant families owned less than two-fifths of the land, the holdings often divided up wastefully in narrow strips.[1] Agricultural technique was primitive. The standard of living was low. Russia's pre-eminence as an exporter of farm products, in fact, was based on the low standard of living of the peasants.

In a Congress of Peasant Deputies several months before the Bolshevik uprising, Lenin stated that large state farms, operated with labor-saving machinery, would increase the output and raise the standard of living of the peasants. This idea was new to a peasantry that had been accustomed to almost the diametrically opposite conception.

B. Reasons for Collectives

The current tendency to collectivization of agriculture and the creation of the large farm has moved almost as inevitably as a Greek drama. Collectivization is a final link in a chain of events. The state tried to requisition the grain of the peasant, who resisted and refused to grow more than he needed. The Soviets thereupon decided to eliminate private operation of farms, first, to increase the productivity of the land, second, to break down the capitalist character of the ownership, and third, to make it possible to plan production in agriculture as in industry.

1. Requisitions and Grain Levies. Until 1921 the communist policy called for corn levies, the situation, as Lenin put it, being one "in which every pood of grain over and above what was indispensable to the peasant farmer must be taken over by the state." But in 1921 this levy was replaced by a tax in kind. The principle was reversed, and the state, instead of taking over the peasant's surplus, permitted him to keep all the surplus in excess of a fixed tax in kind. This change was part of the New Economic Policy. At the same time the peasant was permitted to sell his goods in the open market and freely and legally to exchange his wares for merchandise. The tax in kind was based on a quota set for each district. The levy was payable either in grain or in cash at five times the value of the grain. If the peasant was short of his quota his stock or other property were sold by the tax authorities to pay the levy.

2. The Peasant Capitalist. The peasants had been won over to the Soviet régime because they received land, and now their strong sense of ownership, in turn, hampered the Soviet tax policy. In all countries the small peasant is conservative. He regards his produce as a reward for his toil. And when the Soviet grain levy or even the tax in kind was imposed, the peasant refused to grow any surplus. He felt that he was being exploited for the benefit of labor in the town. Or in terms of the current *bon mot,* "In the olden days the nobles owned the land but the peasants enjoyed the fruits, but today the peasants own the land but others enjoy the fruits." As a result, agricultural production declined very greatly below the pre-war level. The farmer refused to produce as an altruist.

The News of the Revolutionary Committee, published by the strikers in the Kronstadt uprising in 1921, reflected the resentment of the peasants at the socialization of the land. One issue reads as follows: "The communists . . . selected the best pieces of land and . . . weigh still more heavily on the poor peasants than did the former land owners. . . . A new communist serfdom arose. The peasant in the Soviet farm became a slave, and the worker in the factories a day laborer. The working intelligentsia disappeared." [2]

Policies which ignore human instincts often work out in a manner contrary to their aims. In France, during the war, when the price of wheat was fixed and the price of other grains remained free, the peasants found it cheaper to feed wheat to their cattle and sell the other grains for profit. And so in Russia the peasant thought it was to his advantage to raise only enough for his own needs and pay no taxes rather than raise a surplus and turn it over to the state.

While the output of the farms rose continually up to 1929, the marketable output available for consumption in the cities increased but slightly, and exports actually declined. Most of the marketable surplus had come from the large estates, which had been divided up. Furthermore, the peasants themselves consumed more locally. As a result, in a country primarily agricultural there was a shortage of vegetables, eggs, milk, and butter. Although before the war about 40 per cent of the exports from Russia was grain, that commodity came to constitute in the twenties only an insignificant fraction of the total exports. The small capitalists, the peasants, were not producing as much as the larger estates of the old régime.

The Soviet authorities were in a dilemma. They could not well afford to let production continue at the existing low level and dispense with the export of grains, which were essential to obtain credits abroad. If they should abandon their principles and encourage production by utilizing private incentives, the efficient would produce much, increase their land holdings, and with hired help develop large privately owned farms on the basis of private profit. But capitalist agriculture would then constitute a constant threat to socialized industry. The other alternative was to socialize agriculture, either by way of collective farms or by state farms. It was this course that the Soviets adopted.

3. Need of the Five-Year Plan for Increased Output. The innumerable small holdings constituted the bulk of the farm lands of the country. Their surplus output was insignificant. They barely supported themselves. It has been estimated, in fact, that the standard of life was so low that an increase of output of at least 25 per cent was essential merely to feed the population properly. Furthermore, the returned Russian prisoners-of-war, who had observed the higher standards of western Europe, aspired to new and better ways of living.

Increased output was also necessary to keep the population on the land, for it had been flowing constantly into the cities and for some time had been aggravating the unemployment problem. Such increase could be obtained through the application of scientific management to agriculture, but this was impossible under the system of small holdings. It would be possible, however, if they were aggregated into large farms. The desirable greater use of machinery could also not be applied on small strips of land. Finally, a capitalist basis of agriculture interfered with the Five-Year Plan. The production of millions of independent peasants could not be planned—it depended on such uncertain factors as the farmer's choice of cereals according to his own needs and wishes, and the relative selling prices of different crops. But a planned agricultural output was all-important, since the amount of such output determined the cost of living of the industrial worker, which was a vital part of the Five-Year Plan.

C. Collective Farms

Collective farms and state farms seemed to offer a solution to these troublesome problems.

1. Pressure to Collectivize. By every conceivable device the peasants were influenced to join the collectives. The methods involved both punishment and reward. The rich peasants, or kulaks, were persecuted, even with armed force, and the drive on them removed the incentive for the small farmer to become a kulak. Other peasants operating privately were denied the use of water for irrigation, the use of electricity, and other privileges, and were threatened with boycotts and with deprivation of voting rights. Even a peasant who was not a kulak might be threatened with "dekulakization"—that is, he might be driven from his home, and his lands and sometimes even his personal property confiscated. Cases were reported where peasants had their clothes taken off their persons in the streets.

As a result of such measures, a considerable opposition arose among the peasants to the *kolkhozy,* or collective farms. In some cases, instead of organizing the collective farm as an artel, in which only the land was collectivized, they were forced to form a commune, in which even the personal property was collectivized. The wealthy peasants said that after the government had despoiled the kulaks, it would despoil the *seredniaks,* or middle-class peasants. As a matter of fact, in some districts where the kulaks had anticipated the new policy and had sold their farms voluntarily, the local communist leaders proceeded to "dekulakize" the middle-class peasant in order to prove they were not neglecting to function.

In some cases collectivization was merely a paper achievement. For instance, in the Leningrad province a collective was organized by administrative order. Forty-eight villages were united into a great collective farm, called "The Ways of Lenin." The procedure was as follows: First, all the property in the district was registered by the local superintendent of the fire department, presumably in order to furnish the State Fire Insurance Company with the necessary data. On the following day, the people were notified that all property registered was to be surrendered to a collective. As a result, great numbers of peasants withdrew from membership whereupon the collective farm broke down. Not a single plow or a single farm horse was taken from the individual peasant and used collectively.

Again, in the Riazan Province, the agents of the government refused to permit the peasants to organize artels, the mild form of collectives, but insisted on setting up communes. Those who refused to enter the communes could not buy from the consumers' co-operatives. As a result, the membership rose to 72 per cent of the total available peasants. If any peasant advocated the organization of an artel instead of a commune, he was subject to fines and discriminatory measures.[3]

Membership in the collectives was often theoretically voluntary but actually forced. Instead of asking the peasants whether they wished to join collective farms, the agents of the government asked merely that those who did not wish to join collective farms should say so. Such a refusal was in some cases made a cause for arrest—in one case 108 peasants of the poor and middle classes were so arrested. In other cases, dissenting peasants were deprived of the right to buy necessities.

In some cases collectivization of the whole district was decided by a small minority of the peasants. In the Bolashov District, complete collectivization of a village of 407 peasant households was voted upon at a meeting which only fifty peasants attended. Twenty-seven of them voted against it, but it was introduced as if it had been approved by a majority of the peasants concerned.

At another meeting where the peasants had expressed opinions against collectivization, the state agents asked for a show of hands on the question, "Who is against Soviet rule?" Since no one was willing to go on record as an opponent of the Soviet régime, the agents regarded the vote as a unanimous resolution to organize a collective farm.[4]

In the case of farm laborers, threats to confiscate their property and to deprive them of voting rights, were futile. They had no property, and they could not be deprived of voting rights because of their very obvious proletarian origin. A variety of other measures was adopted, however, to force them into collective farms.[5] The officials in charge of the work generally ignored their wishes and proceeded on information obtained from the local units of the Communist Party. The result was bureaucratic inefficiency and the need for increased pressure.[6]

2. Inducements to Collectivize. On the other hand, inducements to socialize were held out to the peasants. Those joining collectives enjoyed lower tax rates and in some cases even exemption from taxes for a specific period, the use of agricultural machinery, abundant credit at low rates, and the services of trained experts in various fields. In addition, the best land was given to the collectives, and peasants who wished to operate individually faced the prospect of having to use poor and barren land. The collectives also had preferences in the distribution of seed and in the allotment of consumers' goods and, even though goods and food were scarce in the cities, the collective farms were favored.

To accomplish the mechanization of agriculture the Soviet government proposed to extend credits of more than one billion rubles to the collectives in 1931. In addition, the State Bank was to grant large credits to finance planting and harvesting. Further, about 200 million rubles were to be used to purchase 120,000 more tractors, and another 500 million rubles for 1000 central garages and machine shops to house them. This policy would make it possible to bring under mechanized agriculture about 45 million acres, compared with 10 million actually mechanized in 1930. This step was intended to overcome the decline in production resulting from the elimination of the efficient rich peasants.[7]

At the Sixth All-Union Congress of the Soviets, held in Moscow, March 8, 1931, resolutions were passed outlining the program of increased government aid to agricultural collectives who were to be supplied as follows:

1. In 1931, 120,000 additional tractors.
2. In the next two years 1040 additional machine and tractor stations.
3. Agricultural machinery and implements that year were to be almost $400,000,000 as against about $200,000,000 supplied the year before.
4. Seven thousand trucks and light automobiles.
5. About two and a half million tons of fertilizer and $20,000,000 worth of supplies for combating pests.
6. More than 2,000,000 tons of improved and selected seed.

7. More than half a billion dollars was to be advanced to the collectives and machine and tractor stations in long-term loans and about $180,000,000 advances were to be paid out to collectives for contracted crops.[8]

According to this resolution, collectivization would be completed at the end of the fifth year of the Plan. The resolution also provided that the artel was to be retained as the basic form of the collectives for the time being.

As a further inducement to the peasant to join collective farms, the entire agricultural tax schedule was based on the principle of lightening the burden on the collectives and increasing the burden on the individual peasant. Under the law of February 23, 1930, known as the New Single Agricultural Tax, the purpose was stated in a decree of the Central Executive Committee and the Council of the People's Commissars:

> The progress of the collectivization of agriculture, which already takes in a considerable portion of the peasant households of the country, the transition to the complete collectivization of whole districts and regions, and the resulting problem of liquidating the kulaks as a class in the regions of complete collectivization necessitate the revision of the single agricultural tax law in order to assure the greatest assistance for the development of large-scale collective farming. . . .
>
> The new law provides that the tax rate for collective farms shall not increase as the income of the farm grows, in contradistinction to the progressive rate for individual peasants, particularly in order to stimulate animal husbandry and to develop industrial crops.

The tax rate on collective farms is generally lower, and there is no supertax which rises with the size of the income and the size of the farm as in the case of the individual holder. Furthermore, the tax-exempt minimum is higher for the collective farm than for the individual. The rates of the tax and the tax-exempt minimum are also fixed so as to favor those co-operatives which keep books of account.

Reduction of or exemption from taxes is also used to stimulate the plowing up of virgin or abandoned land, the practice of crop rotation, and the growth of industrial crops such as cotton, flax, hemp, sugar beets, soya beans, and castor beans.[9]

Additional advantages extended to the collective farms included further exemption or reduction of taxes, cancellation of indebtedness, and remission of fines. The decree of the Central Executive Committee of the All-Union Communist Party of April 2, 1930 proposed to the Council of People's Commissars and the Central Executive Committee of the Soviet Union that the following advantages be conferred on the collective farms:

To free from tax liability for two years all the socialized working animals in the collective farms (horses, oxen, etc.); also cows, pigs, chickens, and sheep, both those collectively owned by the collective farm and those in the individual possession of its members.

To establish for socialized gardens and garden collective farms a 50 per cent reduction from the rates of garden income established for the given region. Land which is newly planted in socialized gardens and garden collective farms is to be free from the agricultural tax for two years. . . .

For the purpose of improving the material position of the collective farms:

To cancel for collective farm members indebtedness in connection with the land arrangement which was in effect before they entered the collective farm.

To cancel all fines and court sentences connected with the non-fulfillment of agricultural obligations, non-payments, etc., imposed upon peasants entering the collective farms before April 1, 1930.

To free the collective farms from the payment of debts on the confiscated kulak property which has passed into the possession of the collective farms.[10]

3. Forms of Collectivization. The agricultural collective, or *kolkhoz,* exists in three forms. The principal distinction between them is the extent of the collective ownership. In the mildest form, the land is cultivated in common, but the farm animals and other property are held privately. Such a collective is called a comradeship (*tovarishchestvo*). The next stage is the artel. In this form, not only is the land collectivized but also those animals employed in work, such as horses and mules, and other animals raised for the sale of milk, meat, or wool. In the extreme form of kolkhoz, the commune, all property is collectivized; even the homes, the private gardens, and the poultry are collectively owned. The members live in a community house and dine in a community dining room, and the children are cared for in a community nursery. Practically all needs are provided for, and there is little need for wages. The communes are favored by the tax system.*

Changes were made in the statutes concerning collective farms in the spring of 1930. In the comradeship, or the association for joint tilling of the land, the working live stock, seeds, forage, and breeding stock were to be socialized, and 25 per cent of the socialized property was to be segregated into a so-called undivided fund. In the artel, the houses as well as the live stock were to be socialized, and the undivided fund was to be 50 per cent of the socialized property. In the commune, all the property of the mem-

* A good description of the agricultural scheme may be had in *Economic Life of Soviet Russia,* by Calvin Hoover, pp. 90 *et seq.* The several books of Maurice Hindus are devoted largely to the agricultural phase of Russian life.

bers was to be socialized and turned into the undivided fund, and, in addition, all home life, particularly cooking and feeding, was to be socialized.[11]

In the Lower Volga Province, the Executive Committee introduced rules concerning the undivided fund. The membership of the collective was divided into four groups: (1) Farm hands and poor peasants who had no taxable income; (2) poor peasants whose income was so small as to be tax exempt; (3) peasants who paid the single agricultural tax, but whose income was too small to be subject to the surtax; (4) peasants whose income was subject both to the tax and the surtax. The first group put into the undivided fund 25 per cent of the shares of the investment which they received, the second group put in 30 per cent, the third group 50 per cent, and the fourth group 80 per cent.

The distinctive feature of the undivided fund was that a member withdrawing cannot recover his part of it. The entrance fees ranged from two to fifteen rubles, depending on the group. In addition to the entrance fees, members had to pay in an investment share. This was ten rubles for the first group, 30 rubles for the second, 60 rubles for the third, and 120 rubles for the fourth. In the district of the German Republic on the Volga, socialization of the property of members of collective farms was on a different basis. If the value of a farm inventory was over 300 rubles, 20 per cent of the socialized property was put into the undivided fund. The percentages rose to 30 per cent for an inventory of 600 rubles and 80 per cent for an inventory of 1200 rubles. In other words, what would be considered a small farm, with an inventory of $600, would be subject to an 80 per cent property tax to be put into an undivided fund which could not be withdrawn by the peasant. Such measures did not stimulate voluntary participation in collectives.[11]

The collectives vary in the manner in which products of labor are distributed. In the commune, distribution is on the basis, not of service, but of need. The larger the family the greater the allowance. In the artel the income is distributed on the basis of the amount and quality of labor. To induce the peasants to turn in all their property a fixed percentage of the total production is to be set aside to compensate those members who have contributed property. The work is done in organized teams as in a factory. Plowing, sowing, and reaping, and care of machinery, are organized as in factories, under foremen. And there is a collective barn, from which the total produce is distributed to the workers.

4. Wage Systems. In March 1930, a law was passed adopting payment by piece work and by task, and in March 1931, the All-Union Congress rec-

ommended the enforcement of this plan in the interest of efficiency. The fact that there was much shirking in some artels where equal pay was given to all the members led to enforcement of the piece-work system. In the most efficient artels payment was based on the nature and amount of work done. And if there was not enough work for all the members, payment was nevertheless based on the amount of work distributed.

In the early part of 1931 piece work was introduced into more than 85,000 collectives. The principle of equal pay for all labor was abandoned. It was found that though the industrious applied themselves to the community's interest, the shirkers received the same compensation. The incentive for initiative and effort was restored. Superior intelligence brought greater rewards.

Originally, all members of a collective were compelled to turn in their cattle and machinery and the proceeds of the harvest were to be equally divided. But the results were unsatisfactory and under the revised procedure the member was rewarded in proportion to his investment. As in other fields a compromise was made with capitalist principles.

Commissar of Agriculture Yakovlev, addressing the Sixth Congress of Soviets, meeting in Moscow March 8 to 17, 1931, pointed out the disadvantages of the principle of payment on the basis of need rather than on the basis of service. In his opinion, the principle should be: "He who does more and better work shall receive more, and he who does not work shall receive nothing." He said further that in order to bring out the advantages of the collective form it was necessary to distribute the income on the basis of labor performed rather than on the basis of equal distribution. This result could best be accomplished through a system of piece work, which provided an incentive for every member.

Yakovlev cited examples where collectives changed from equal pay to piece work, and in every case the output per worker increased greatly, twice or even threefold.[12]

In accordance with this opinion of Yakovlev, the Sixth Congress of Soviets endorsed the piece-work system, and the People's Commissariat of Agriculture issued a decree (April 24, 1931) putting it into effect. The decree reads:

> Work in agricultural artels is to be done according to the piece-work system. The administration of each collective will work out forms of each kind of work and the payment for each type of work in terms of working days. The reckoning must be based on the degree of difficulty of performing the definite type of work, the amount of experience and skill required for its performance,

the quality of the work done and its importance to the collective. The estimates worked out by the administration are to be presented for final action to the general assembly of collective members.

The distribution of the income of the artels among their members is to be made not on an equal basis, but in strict accordance with the number of working days to each member's credit. . . .

Collective members having large families will receive, through action taken by the administration and general assembly of collective members, special assistance either from a fund created for those who are unable to work or through guaranteeing to the working members of such families, in the distribution of work, a sufficient amount to enable them to provide for the non-working members of their families.[13]

Apparently the piece-work system worked so well that a few months later, July 13, the Peoples' Commissariat of Agriculture decreed that thereafter payment should be made only on the basis of quantity and quality of work performed. The object was to stimulate the interest of the peasants and to increase production. The piece-work system had been in effect in a number of collective farms, but under the new decree it became mandatory throughout the Soviet Union.

To extend the piece-work system in the payment of labor on collective and state farms, a decree was issued on July 6, 1932. It provided in addition a scale of bonuses to be paid in money and in crops for those exceeding the quotas and penalties for those falling behind the quotas. The decree includes the following items:

1. Labor must be organized on efficient lines and paid liberal wages on a piece-work basis.
2. Payment must be made in kind as well as in money, and peasants are to have the right to sell their grain on the open market.
3. Those collective farms that show the highest efficiency shall be permitted to keep a higher percentage of their produce for themselves.

In connection with this decree, signed by Stalin for the Central Executive Committee of the party and Molotov for the Counsel of People's Commissars, it was stated, "Four-fifths of the entire spring-sown area is now cultivated by collective and state farms. The Soviet Union is based on a new socialistic foundation and destroys the bourgeois theory that the Soviet Union is turning back to capitalism."

5. Model Articles of Association for an Artel. A general idea of the conditions to which peasants are subject on entering an artel is to be had in the articles of association. A model form of such agreement follows:[14]

ARTICLES OF ASSOCIATION

I. Purposes and Objects

1. We, poor peasants (*bedniaki*) and middle peasants (*seredniaki*) of the village of ——— in the district of ——— in the area of ———, of our own free will, unite in an agricultural artel so that our united means of production and our common organized labor may be used for the purpose of forming a large collective economic entity. . . .

II. Land

2. All boundaries separating the arable holdings of the members of the artel are to be removed. . . .

3. No land can be withdrawn from the pool by a member leaving the artel. Those leaving the artel can only obtain land from the free lands of the state.

III. Means of Production

4. The following are communized: All draft animals, agricultural implements, all other livestock, all seed reserves, fodder in such quantities as is necessary for the feeding of the common livestock, farm buildings necessary for the running of the artel farm, and all agricultural plants. Living quarters of the members of the artel are not communized. . . .

In the case of a holding having a number of cows, one cow is left for the individual use of the member of the artel, and the remainder are communized. Productive livestock is in all cases communized. . . .

In areas where there is no small livestock farming, pigs and sheep are not communized. Poultry is not communized.

Apart from the small live stock and poultry left to individual ownership, collective farms organize small stock and poultry enterprises.

IV. Activities of the Artel

5. The management and members of the artel undertake the following obligations:

(a) To increase the amount of land under cultivation by making use of all the land available. . . .

(b) To make full use of all motive power, all implements, all tractors, all machines, seeds, and other means of production. . . .

(c) To arrange for the proper use and upkeep of all livestock and implements. . . .

(d) To improve pasture and arable land and take the agricultural measures necessary for the increase of the yield. . . .

(h) To raise the cultural and political level of members of the artel.

(i) To improve the living conditions of the members of the artel, especially of the women and children.

V. Membership

7. Any worker, upon reaching the age of 16, can become a member of the artel. . . .

Peasant families who, before entering a collective group, slaughter or sell their livestock, get rid of their implements, or with ill intent dispose of their seed, are not admitted.

VI. Resources of the Artel

8. Each person entering the artel must deposit an entrance fee of from 2 per cent to 10 per cent of the value of all property. . . .

The entrance fee for agricultural laborers shall not exceed five rubles. . . .

9. From the value of the communized property of a member of the artel, from 25 per cent to 50 per cent is credited to the reserve fund of the artel in such a way that the wealthier peasant households pay a higher rate of contribution to the reserve fund. The balance of the value of the property is reckoned as the share of the member of the artel. . . .

11. Out of the income of the artel at the end of the economic year provision is made for the expenses of running the artel, for the support of persons who are unfit for work, for the reserve and other communal funds.

VII. Organization and Payment of Labor

12. All the work in the artel is carried out by the personal labor of its members. . . .

The hire of temporary labor is allowed only in exceptional cases. . . .

14. . . . Standards of output and costing schedules shall be laid down, records shall be kept of the quality and quantity of work, and payment by piece and task work shall be adopted.

15. . . . In the course of the economic year advances (in kind or money) shall be made to the members of the artel for food and other necessities, but not more than 50 per cent of the amount due to them for their work. . . .

16. The artel gives assistance to those members who are unable to work and to those who are temporarily incapacitated.

6. Extent of Collectivization. The program of collectivization was pursued with much vigor, but without adequate preparation. As a result by the spring of 1930 almost 50 per cent of all the peasant families were collectivized. But because there was inadequate preparation, lack of machines, seed, animals, and experts, the number of members then declined. After the extreme urge to collectivize, the peasants were allowed to withdraw and as a result the percentage of farmers collectivized dropped from a maximum of about 57 per cent to a later minimum of about 30 to 40 per cent for the country as a whole. In certain sections, where collectivization was achieved under pressure, the percentage of farms collectivized reached in some cases a maximum of almost 90 per cent, and subsequently in the same region when the pressure was relaxed it fell to 5 per cent. In the Moscow area it rose to 76 per cent and declined to about 12 per cent. Even these figures are in excess of the Five-Year Plan, which provided that collectives include 10.3 per

cent of the total arable land by 1933. But in spite of withdrawals it is expected that percentages will be increased.

The campaign to collectivize farming began in the spring of 1929, and affected at first about 10 per cent of the peasant holdings. But the results were so encouraging that they led to an urgent drive. The harvest for 1930, for the first time since the revolution, yielded a larger crop than in 1913. As a result, in the spring of 1931 the rate of voluntary collectivization was higher than during the period of forced collectivization in the spring of 1930.[15]

The growth of the movement for collectivization has been exceedingly rapid, as shown in the following table: [16]

	Number of Collectivized Households (In thousands)	*Per cent of Total Number of Households*
October 1, 1927	286	1.1
October 1, 1928	595	2.3
October 1, 1929	2,131	8.1
October 1, 1930	5,565	22.2
March 1, 1931	8,830	35.3
March 10, 1931	9,337	37.5
June 20, 1931	13,499	54.7

The period of greatest enrollment coincided generally with the annual meeting of the collectives, when results were published concerning yields and profits. In many localities the income per household in 1930 was more than twice as great for the collectives as for the individual peasant, and for the entire Soviet Union it was estimated to be one and a half times as great. The economic advantage of collective farming over individual farming is more effective than pressure or threats in stimulating the growth of the movement.[17]

The number of peasant households collectivized increased sixty-one times, the harvested area increased eighty-one times, and the output of grain increased more than eighty-six times in 1931 compared to 1927. The Plan has been exceeded by over 160 per cent in the area harvested. The tendency was toward an increased size of collective farm. In 1928 the average area was only 40 hectares, but in 1930 it was 460 hectares (one hectare equals 2.47 acres). In 1930 the average area of the grain collective farm was 1300 hectares and in 1931 more than 3000 hectares.

PROGRESS OF COLLECTIVIZATION, 1927–31 [18]

	1927	*1928*	*1929*	*1930*	*1931*	*1932–33 (Original 5-Year Plan)*
Number of collective farms *	14,832	33,258	57,003	82,276	217,800 †	......
Relative percentages	100	224	384	555		
Number of peasant households collectivized *	194,700	416,700	1,002,700	6,150,000	13,560,000	......
Relative percentages	100	224	514	3160		
Percentage of total peasant households collectivized	0.8	1.7	3.9	23.6	55.1	9.6
Sown area *thousand hectares*	749	1390	4190	34,820	80,600	14,500
Relative percentages	100	186	559	4649	10,761	1935
Sown area *per cent of total*	0.7	1.2	3.6	28.5	58.7	10.2
Gross output of grain *thousand tons*	490	910	2710	25,260	42,290	11,950
Relative percentages	100	185	552	5200	8650	2440
Gross output of grain *per cent of total*	...	1.2	3.8	28.9	43.2	......
Marketable output of grain *thousand tons*	200	360	1270	10,000	......	4960
Relative percentages	100	180	635	5000		2480

* As of June 1 of each year. † As of July 1.

At the June 1931 session of the Communist Party, Commissar Yakovlev said that in districts producing grain, cotton, and sugar beets, more than 50 per cent of the farms in number and 50 to 60 per cent in area were organized into collectives. These districts were expected to be completely collectivized by the spring of 1932, thus exceeding the program of collectivization set by the Sixth All-Union Soviet Congress.

The state farms sowed an area in 1931 twice as large as in 1930. The area controlled by the State Grain Trust, the Industrial Crop Trust, and the Animal Husbandry Trust totaled over 8.0 million hectares in the spring of 1931 compared with 3.2 million hectares in 1930. As a result of the development of state farms and the organization of collective farms, "the Soviet Union has become a country of the largest-scale agriculture in the world," according to Yakovlev.[19]

The actual results have exceeded the Five-Year Plan for agriculture as shown herewith:

DISTRIBUTION OF HARVESTED AREA [20]

Year	*Total Area (In million hectares)*	Per Cent of Total Area in— *State Farms*	*Collective Farms*	*Individual Peasant and Misc. Holdings*
1928	112.96	1.5	1.2	97.3
1929	118.03	1.9	3.5	94.6
1930	127.77	3.1	30.0	66.9
1931 (Program)	140.42	6.4	43.1	50.5
1933 (Original 5-Year Plan)	141.60	3.1	10.2	86.7

The degree of collectivization is far from uniform over the country. It ranges from about 14 to 16 per cent of the total number of households in the districts of Moscow and Leningrad to over 70 per cent in the Steppe districts and the North Caucasus and in Crimea. Up to March 1931 the following results had been achieved:

COLLECTIVIZATION BY SECTIONS [21]

District	*Percentage of Households Collectivized*
R.S.F.S.R.	
Northern	15.8
Leningrad	16.1
Moscow	13.7
Nizhni Novgorod	17.8
Ural	44.5
Middle Volga	47.4
Lower Volga	67.1

COLLECTIVIZATION BY SECTIONS—*Continued*

District	Percentage of Households Collectivized
North Caucasus	77.1
Daghestan	11.7
Crimean	73.1
Kazak	42.1
Eastern Siberian	24.8
Far Eastern	28.3
Yakut	14.4
Ukrainian	48.5
Steppe Districts	70.0
White Russian	18.7
Transcaucasian	
Azerbaidzhan	25.7
Georgia	28.0
Armenia	18.2
Central Asia	
Uzbekistan	52.2
Tadzhikistan	24.5
Total for U.S.S.R.	37.5

7. REDUCED TEMPO. After a very large percentage of all farm lands had been collectivized under pressure in the first six months, and millions of peasants enrolled in the collectives, the situation grew critical and got out of hand. Apparently the growth had been too rapid. The peasants expressed their resentment by rising against the government agents, and thus put the government in a tight corner. A reversal was inevitable.

Under a parliamentary régime, the government would have had to resign. How could an autocratic and irresponsible government reverse itself and still maintain its dominating position? Stalin did so by a very clever device. He actually scolded his agents and denounced the very things that the peasants resented. The peasants, as powerless as under the Tsar, accepted the relief that Stalin offered almost with devotion and reverence.

a. "Dizziness from Success." Stalin's classic speech was entitled "Dizziness from Success" (*Golovokruzhenie Ot Uspekhov*) and printed in all the Soviet newspapers March 2, 1930. A few of the more important points were as follows:

> The collectives cannot be organized by force. That would be stupid and reactionary. The collective movement must depend on the active support of the basic masses of the peasantry. . . .

One of the most important prerequisites for a vigorous collective movement is that it should be voluntary and adapted to the diverse conditions of the different parts of the U.S.S.R. . . .

Conditions have not yet ripened for the agricultural commune, in which not only production but also distribution is socialized, to become the predominant form.

The basic form of the collective movement, its predominant form at the present moment, the form on which we must now concentrate, is the agricultural artel. In the agricultural artel the basic means of production, mainly in the cultivation of grain, are socialized; labor, use of land, machinery, and other equipment, working stock and farm buildings. However, small gardens and orchards, homes, a certain portion of the cows, smaller live-stock, poultry and so on, are not socialized. The artel is the basic link of the collective movement because it is the most expedient form for the solution of the grain problem. . . .

In a number of districts in the U.S.S.R., where the struggle for existence of the collectives is far from being ended, and where the artels have not yet become strongly established, attempts are being made to jump through the artel form, and leap right into the agricultural commune. The artel has not yet been established, but they are already "socializing" homes, small livestock, poultry; in these cases "socialization" degenerates into arbitrary, bureaucratic decree-making, because the conditions making such socialization necessary do not exist. It might be supposed that the grain problem was already solved in the collectives, that it represented a stage already passed, that the main task at the present moment was not the solution of the grain problem, but that of livestock and poultry. . . . To provoke the peasant-collectivist by socializing his home, all his cows, all his small livestock and his poultry, even before the artel form of collective has become firmly established—isn't it clear enough that such a "policy" can be useful and advantageous only to our enemies? [22]

b. Resolutions to Moderate Tempo. Within two weeks after Stalin's address, the Central Committee of the Communist Party ordered a reversal of tactics and a repudiation of the policy which had aroused the peasants. Following are excerpts from its decree:

The principle of voluntariness in building up the collective farms is violated. In a number of regions voluntariness is replaced by compulsion to enter the collective farms under the threat of expropriation, deprivation of electoral rights, etc. . . .

It is forgotten that our basic agricultural problem is not the "chicken" or the "cucumber" problem, but the grain problem. It is forgotten that the basic link of the collective farm movement at the present moment is not the commune, but the agricultural artel. . . . Consequently, we must not permit a frivolous jumping from the artel form to the commune. . . .

The Central Committee makes it obligatory for party organizations:

1. To stop the practice, observed in a number of places, of forced methods of collectivization, and simultaneously carry on further persistent work for attracting the peasantry into the collective farms on a voluntary basis and strengthening the existing collective farms. . . .

3. Not to permit the transfer of agricultural artels to the constitution of

agricultural communes without the confirmation of district collective farm unions or district executive committees, and to stop the forced socialization of dwellings, small cattle, birds, and unmarketable milk cattle.

4. To examine the lists of persons who have been expropriated and deprived of electoral rights and to correct without delay the mistakes which were committed in this field. . . .

6. To forbid the closing of markets, to re-establish bazaars and to refrain from checking the sale by peasants, including members of collective farms, of their products on the market.

7. Decisively to stop the practice of closing churches administratively, with a fictitious justification of a voluntary desire on the part of the population. . . . To hold guilty persons to strictest responsibility for mocking the religious feelings of peasant men and women.[23]

c. Results of Reversal of Policy. As a result of the reversal of policy, the number of farms in the collectives declined more rapidly in one month than it had risen in many months preceding. For example, in the province of the Lower Volga the collectivization was merely a paper affair and after the government's pronouncement, many collectives immediately fell apart. Of the 973,000 farms in the province of the Lower Volga, the percentage collectivized was as follows: October 1, 1929, 17.0 per cent; December 1, 1929, 62.0 per cent; March 1, 1930, 68.9 per cent; April 1, 1930, 53.9 per cent.[24]

8. TRADING BY PEASANTS REAPPEARS. A decree, signed on May 7, 1932, jointly as usual by Stalin and Molotov, introduced a basic change in the collection of grain and in private trading. Under the old system, the collectives and peasants were permitted to keep enough grain for food, feed, and seed, and turned the balance over to the state at fixed prices. Under the new system, the state buys a smaller fixed amount from the collective farms and the peasants at the fixed price, but in return allows the entire surplus to be disposed of on the open market. The percentage collected by the state is reduced by about 20 per cent, which part may be sold on the open market. It is hoped that such freedom of trade will stimulate production, furnish more food to the cities, increase industrial output, and in return, furnish goods to the peasants. Furthermore, the state collected such large percentages of the total last year that some collectives did not have enough grain left for food and seed. Under the new decree, it is likely that exports of Russian grain will diminish, at first, as the government will have less to sell. Eventually, however, the increased output as the result of the stimulation of private initiative may result in increased crops. The state farms, of course, are not affected by the decree.

To encourage private sale, the government will exempt the resulting profits from the agricultural tax of the state and communities. Another new decree, dated May 21, 1932, applies also to the sale of chickens, eggs, dairy products, vegetables, fruits, and other farm commodities, as well as bread and meat. It is expected that the shortage which has been acute for some time will thus be relieved. Under the decree the individual peasants must sell at the open-market prices so as to compete with the speculators and illegal traders, but the collectives must charge the average price of the state stores. To stimulate such private trade, the state bank has instructed all its branches to make loans to collectives to finance private trading. In addition, some cities have made appropriations to build additional and attractive markets, including restaurants, and quarters for peasants coming to town.

The peasants, who, until lately, had been heavily taxed and almost outlawed in their trade, were skeptical of this reversal of policy. To overcome this skepticism, the President of the Soviet Union, M. I. Kalinin, on June 3, 1932, issued a statement in the official press, urging the co-operatives, the local governments, and the political parties to encourage such trade, but he vigorously resented the implication that there was any return to private capitalism. The press issued a barrage of propaganda to meet the charge of some members of the Communist Party, who were regarded as being "infected" with a petty-bourgeois conception of socialism and had objected to the introduction of cost accounting and the elimination of equal wages, and had been advocating the abolition of money, prefering barter, or direct exchange, and the centralized distribution of goods.

In defense of the new policy, the authority of Lenin was invoked. Lenin held that the Soviet state should be based "on a combination of the stimulus of individual gain with the general interest of the proletarian dictatorship." Therefore he advocated piece work in industry and on the farms, and the right to sell agricultural produce in the open market under competition. "Since live stock and poultry represent the unsocialized part of the property of members of the collective farms, the permission to trade in meat, poultry, and dairy produce will stimulate the expansion of this property." By decree of June 11, 1932, the government drastically reduced the amount of fruit and vegetables which the peasants had to deliver to the state buying organizations, thus automatically increasing the amount available for private sale.[25]

9. Result—Rationing Ends. The effect of the several decrees giving the collectives and the peasants the right to sell privately was to transfer the government's burden of feeding the cities to the private markets. Rationing and the restrictions on the purchase of food were largely ended and the number of

items on the ration list was reduced. Any buyer who had the cash but no ration ticket could buy milk, eggs, cheese, and tea, candy, soup, cigarettes, knitted goods, and canned food, except canned meat. Yet in this free trade prices were still high and supplies small. For example, cauliflower sold at 3.5 rubles ($1.75) and apples at 2.5 rubles ($1.25) per piece.[26]

D. State Farms

1. Growth. Almost immediately after the revolution some state farms were organized, but they were few and small. In 1928 the first of the large state farms devoted to grains were established. Others were subsequently established for the growing of sugar beets and of cotton and for the breeding of cattle and of sheep. These farms were then combined into trusts. The area rose from 4 million hectares to over 40 million hectares in 1930. Recent growth of the grain farms has been very rapid, as follows: [27]

Year	*Number of State Farms*	*Million Hectares Sown*	*Yield in Million Tons*
1930	131	1.0	0.9
1931	200	4.5	4.4

At the Sixth Congress of the Soviets in Moscow, beginning March 8, 1931, Commissar Yakolev reported that the area under state farms was then three times as great as in 1930, and the marketable output would likewise be three times the value, or about 600 million rubles.[28]

He further reported on the plan and the achievement on the state farms. In 1928, the government planned to create a chain of state farms, *sovhozy,* which within four years would produce about 16.5 million metric tons of grain for the markets. But by 1930 the Zernotrest, the Grain Trust, had organized 143 state farms with a seeded area of over four million acres, producing 11.8 million metric tons of grain. These figures, he said, should increase six fold by 1933.[29]

2. Operation. There are several large farms. The largest in the world, Gigant, has an area of more than 170,000 hectares, or about 420,000 acres. It has 3500 employees and a total population of more than 17,000. Its several hundred agricultural machines cost more than 7,000,000 rubles, and the buildings more than 16,000,000 rubles. Such farms are really great grain factories.

The laborers work eight hours a day, with extra rates for overtime. During the harvest period, additional seasonal workers are hired and the work is done in two or even three shifts. The workers on the state farms are employed about nine months in the field. During two months the machinery, equipment, and buildings are repaired and reconditioned, and the remaining month is a vacation period.

There are other farms somewhat smaller. The average size of the state farms in 1930 was slightly under 60,000 hectares. Each branch of agriculture will probably have an optimum size of unit, which is as yet unfixed.

3. Difficulties. The Soviet authorities are not unaware of the difficulties in the operation of these farms. At the Sixth Congress, Yakovlev pointed out some of these difficulties. Machinery was misused; the organization of work at harvest time was poor; the technical problems of agriculture were not understood. To meet them the government issued a decree making deliberate injury to machinery a criminal offense. Workers who were careless with machines were to be held strictly accountable. To fix responsibility on one workman, and to insure good care of the tractors, each workman was assigned to a particular tractor, and the various machines had a permanent station. The poor organization of work at the harvest was due to the fact that the state farms had been established very rapidly, and much new machinery introduced which was formerly unknown. Prior to 1925, combines were unknown, but in 1931 thousands of them were used at harvest time. Their successful use involves the co-ordination of the various kinds of agricultural labor.

The grain farms, and in particular the live-stock farms, required a technically trained staff which was not available. However, short-term training courses were given to more than 25,000 students, and almost 20,000 were given practical instructions on the cattle farms. New agricultural schools were opened for training specialists in live stock.

4. Value and Benefits. The average yield per hectare on state farms is about 19 per cent higher than on the farms of the individual peasant, and cost of production is much lower. This is due to the greater application of machinery and power. The state farms also are of considerable aid to the collective farms. In 1930, their machines plowed and sowed more than 700,000 hectares for the collective farms and for the poor peasants. In addition, hundreds of thousands of workers were trained on the state farms for work on the collective farms. By the organization of labor and by a progressive agricultural technique, the state farms have induced the peasants to turn to collectivization.

According to Mr. Yakovlev, the state farms are analogous to the state industries, but the collective farms are voluntary organizations of peasants working on lands belonging to the state and leased to them for cultivation. He denied that the state intended ultimately to absorb the collective farms.[30]

By 1933 the Five-Year Plan calls for over 14.5 million hectares (35.8 million acres) of collective farms, to produce about 4.35 million tons (150 million bushels) of grain in 1932–33 and 5.43 million tons (about 190 million bushels) in 1933–34.[31] But instead of waiting until 1933 the total area planted by collectives in 1931 was about 150 million acres,[32] and in 1930 over one-half of the marketable grain came from the "socialized sector," that is, the state and collective farms.[33]

E. Immediate Results of Collectivization

1. Difficulties and Evils. Hasty collectivization was followed by many difficulties. When the collective was organized, the peasants had to contribute heavily toward its capital. Often, after having paid the entrance fee and bought a share in the investment, members would find that additional funds had to be paid, such as an advance on a tractor, advances for seed, grain, etc. The members had to pay almost daily, but on the other hand they were not permitted to sell any produce in order to obtain an income. The results were deplorable.

Furthermore, the collectivized live stock was neglected, and cows, horses, hogs, and poultry died for lack of care. In some cases members of the collective farm refused to care for their own former live stock, which had become common property, and the management was even obliged to hire outside labor for this work.[34]

Because of the haste in collectivization and the lack of skill of farm hands, many collectives organized chiefly with farm hands faced serious problems. A collective farm in the Yaroslavl District, made up entirely of farm hands, had even no bread. In another district, Samara, the farm hands were in a serious condition. They had living quarters, the home of a former rich peasant, but had nothing to eat. In a farm in the Middle Volga Province, farm hands were allotted a monthly ration of flour, for which they were unable to pay. In some cases the farm hands who joined collectives were obliged to beg.[35]

2. Elimination of the Kulak. Among the immediate effects of collectivization was the elimination of the rich peasant, the kulak. A kulak is a peasant who on the average owned 10 acres or more and had a few horses and cows. Many kulaks started with practically nothing when the land was redis-

tributed, but by dint of initiative and energy managed to increase their holdings of land and then hired as laborers the peasants who had sold their bit of land. Any peasant who thus raised himself above the average was a kulak, and therefore subject to discrimination. Naturally, the energetic and able peasants opposed collectivization. Their principle was the motto of William Tell, "Der Starke ist am mächtigsten allein." *

Because the kulaks were opposed to the government policy of requisitioning of grain and other social policies, and because they encouraged the middle-class peasants in opposing the government, a policy of extermination of the kulak was announced by the government in December 1929. Millions of peasants, rich in the Soviet Union but poor by western standards, were to be "liquidated." The "liquidation" consisted of confiscating their property and removing them to another part of the country. The official decree against the kulaks was issued by the Council of People's Commissars and the Central Executive Committee on February 1, 1930.

Local officials, either through zeal or venality or sadism, carried on the work of liquidation as if it were wholesale theft or pillage. It was an opportunity for the local Soviet official to even old scores with envied or hated neighbors. After an individual was labeled a kulak, it became a public duty to despoil him.

In April 1931, a new war on the kulaks was undertaken. Every kulak had to be registered with the police and had to obtain a permit in order to move. Kulaks were denied any occupation other than manual labor. Although most of them were assigned to the Arctic Zone for work in lumber camps and road construction, some pretended not to be kulaks and obtained good positions. By a sort of modern Inquisition they were ferreted out for registration and observation. They had to carry their badge of shame, as was the case with religious minorities in the Middle Ages.[36]

The result of the elimination of the able peasant was a sharp decline in the agricultural output. The efficient farmer with a capacity for farm management, producing a high yield per acre, was replaced by the less competent farmer, who either did not know how to increase his output or had no energy to do so. The Soviets found that ruining an efficient peasant did not necessarily make an inefficient peasant succeed. Individual initiative was penalized, and the social consequences were inevitable. Now the government had the problem of overcoming these consequences and the remedy tried

---

* "The strong man needs no help."

was the policy of collectivization. With the richer and more efficient peasant eliminated, the poor and inefficient peasant had to be made efficient.

Instead of waiting to prove to the peasant the superiority of collective methods in lessening hours of labor, increasing output, and raising standards of living, the government resorted to force to obtain results. Collectives were formed very rapidly, but there were not enough machines, teaching experts, and facilities to take care of them. And the attempt to include the treasured personal effects of the peasant, the poultry and small live stock, aroused deep opposition.

3. Decline of Live Stock and Prohibition of Slaughter. The Soviet issued a decree forbidding the peasants to slaughter their live stock when they joined a collective, but it was not effective in preventing this slaughter, not only by prospective members of collectives but also by other peasants.[37] For a few months toward the close of 1929, assassinations and murders were reported at the rate of 40 per day, committed either by the peasants or by government officials in reprisal.

Furthermore, in deep resentment the peasants consumed their live stock, as mentioned above. The result was a shortage not merely in meat, fats, milk, butter, and eggs, but also in the by-products, hides and bristles. The shortage of shoes and the shortage of toothbrushes were in part a result of this policy. According to Commissar G. F. Grinko, the losses were tabulated as follows:

LIVE STOCK SLAUGHTERED IN 1929–31 [38]
(in millions)

	1929	*1930*	*1931*
Large-horned cattle, total	67.2	51.8	58.8
On state farms	0.2	0.4	3.5
On collective farms	0.4	3.5	8.5
In individual possession	66.6	47.9	46.8
Pigs, total	20.5	11.7	20.2
On state farms	.1	.2	.9
On collective farms	.1	.4	3.3
In individual possession	20.3	11.1	16.0
Sheep, total	132.7	89.2	102.6
On state farms	1.2	3.6	4.8
On collective farms	.6	2.5	6.0
In individual possession	130.9	83.1	91.8

As one writer aptly put it, for a few months the peasant gorged himself with meat and then went on a vegetarian diet. In a violent protest against the government, many peasants killed even their horses in order to hamper the government policy. The resulting shortage of horses led to the decree that individual peasants must place their draft horses at the disposal of the collective farms on a hire basis. The cities' food supply was curtailed and an acute shortage resulted. At a meeting of the Communist Party in the summer of 1930 official admission was made that the country lost one-half of its pigs, one-third of its sheep and goats, almost one-third of its cattle, and from 60 to 75 per cent of its poultry. Rykov stated that this forcible collectivization cost the country as much as the civil war and the intervention combined. Since the propertyless and the propertied peasants were to share alike, the program induced them to enter the collectives with as little property as possible. "We are going in stripped," they said.

The standard of living set by the Five-Year Plan was thus made unattainable. The shortage was intensified by the fact that the wholesale slaughter was merely the culmination of a policy which previously had penalized the breeding of large herds of cattle, since any peasant who bred cattle to maturity became a kulak and was punished, while the peasant who consumed his cattle remained poor and was favored. With the assets of the country so diminished live stock had to be actually imported, thus curtailing imports of needed machinery and retarding the industrialization program. The work of restoring the lost herds, partly through imports, presented the paradoxical spectacle of agricultural but communist Russia bringing in thousands of breeding animals from industrial but capitalist Germany to make good the ravages of reckless political experimentation. Soviet authorities believe that it will take years to replace the slaughtered herds, and that the program will further hamper Soviet credit.

To remedy the evil resulting from the slaughter, a new decree was issued on November 1, 1930, by the Central Executive Committee and the Council of People's Commissars. Under this decree, the state farms, the collective farms, the individual peasants, and the stockyards in villages and in cities were forbidden for one year to kill calves, lambs, and young pigs up to a specified age limit. The slaughter of stock by the United Meat Trust was regulated by special rules. Violators of the law must pay ten times the value of the slaughtered animal. If the offenders were kulaks they might have their entire herds confiscated, and be prosecuted in the criminal courts, imprisoned for two years, and deported from the district.[39]

4. Permission to Slaughter and Sell Privately. On March 26, 1932, the

central committee of the Communist Party issued an order prohibiting the forced collectivization of cattle.[40] The order was not only opposed to the forced requisition of cattle and live stock, but further, it aimed to encourage every collective farmer privately to own his cows and poultry. The collective farms were to increase their live stock not by requisition of private property but by purchase and by breeding. The order warned against changing from the mild form of co-operative, the artel, to the communal or extreme type. The object was to encourage individual production of pigs, sheep, and goats in order to increase the food supply. Furthermore, by a decree of May 10, 1932, signed jointly by Stalin and Molotov, the government cut in half its requisitions of meat at low fixed prices and permitted sale by the individual peasant for profit. On June 18, 1932, the government lifted the ban on the slaughter of live stock. The object here again was to increase live-stock breeding through the stimulus of profit to the peasant. The effect of the new measures soon became evident in the urban centers. Furthermore, in the interest of more efficient operation and control, the size of the socialized live-stock farms was reduced.

As usual the Soviet spokesmen denied that the move was a return to a "neo-Nep," or to a new economic policy encouraging large private enterprises for profit.

5. Result—Stealing Crops and De-collectivization. Because of the newly granted right to sell privately and the inability of the Kremlin to deliver consumers' goods to the collective farms, individual peasants began to leave the collectives. In the movement of food to the towns and of merchandise to the farms there was a leak in the system of state distribution which provided an incentive to theft and an opportunity for speculative profits. The policy of private trade apparently had unfavorable repercussions. Individual peasants at night would cut off the ears of grain or "barber" the crop. The evil became so extensive that the extreme penalty, death by shooting, reserved for anti-social crimes was imposed. Further, a penalty was imposed of 10 years' imprisonment for inducing a peasant to leave a collective farm. A decree was also promulgated that traders and speculators who attempted to profiteer at the expense of workers and peasants would be confined in concentration camps up to 10 years. To prevent the peasants leaving the collectives, it was decreed that they could not regain the land which they had contributed but would receive state land at a considerable distance from the collective farm.[40a]

6. Private Selling Re-abolished. As a result of the above evils, a new decree

was issued by the Council of Labor and Finance, rescinding the decree of the early summer which permitted peasants to sell their own produce directly to the consumer.[40b]

The government gave as its reason for such rescission that the privilege was used for speculative purposes. Furthermore, as a result of the food shortage, a second decree was issued to the effect that the meat collections "would have the force of tax obligations" and that non-delivery would be punished by a fine. "Collections" became virtually requisitions. Every peasant would be required from October 1, 1932 to January 1, 1934 to deliver to the government a certain percentage of his meat output at fixed prices. This decree prevented peasants from taking advantage of the preceding decree authorizing them to sell the surplus production in private markets.

These decrees may lead to the food-tax policy of the period of "war communism" which failed then because of the shortage of consumers' goods and the weakness of the distributing system.

7. Effect on the Industrial Plan. An adequate food supply is essential for the success of the Five-Year Plan. Industrial labor is now underfed, and its efficiency is therefore lowered. If the collectives succeed in increasing the country's agricultural output, the Five-Year Plan will be facilitated. If they fail the program of industrialization will be seriously hampered.

F. Long-Range Results of the Agricultural Program

1. Increased Crops and Increased Exports. For the territory of the present Soviet Union, the gross yield of grain in 1930 exceeded the pre-war level for the first time. The sown area was 2.4 per cent greater and the yield was 9.1 per cent greater. The area sown to industrial crops greatly exceeded the 1913 figure, in cotton by 123 per cent and in sugar beets by 78 per cent. However, the increase of output was less, being only 82 per cent in cotton and only 40 per cent in sugar beets.

Because of the growth of the state and collective farms, the marketable surplus increased greatly. In 1928 the state and collective farms produced only 2 per cent of the gross output and 3 per cent of the marketable surplus, and in 1930 about 25 per cent of the gross output and about 50 per cent of the marketable surplus.[41]

By increasing the output of wheat on the collective and state farms, Russia may again attain her pre-war position as a great exporter of wheat. In the five (fiscal) years before the war her exports averaged about 165,000,000 bushels annually, as compared with 107,000,000 bushels for the United States, 94,000,000 bushels for Canada, 85,000,000 bushels for Argentina, and 50,000,000 bushels for Australia. In the fiscal year 1929 Russian exports were nil, in 1930 they were about 92,000,000 bushels, and in 1931 they were about 91,700,000 bushels. This amount represents a large part of the wheat which the United States Farm Board had to buy in order to maintain the price. But no legislation or attempts to peg the price on the part of the United States will offset the future potential price decline caused by the flood of wheat which will issue from the Russian fields. In 1930 Russia produced about 700,000,000 bushels of wheat and in 1931 estimated at 1,097,000,000 bushels, which compares with 809,000,000 bushels and 851,000,000 bushels for the United States. (See accompanying table.) Because wheat forms a ready means of obtaining credits abroad Russia will probably continue her export policy. Since sunshine and rainfall produce as good grain on the Russian steppes as on American prairies the quality of Russian wheat, unlike that of her manufactures, is up to the world standard and world markets readily accept it.

Russia is now trying merely to regain her pre-war status as a wheat exporter, and in the attempt to do so she will probably reduce prices further. But when they fall below a certain point it will doubtless be more profitable to turn her attention to other crops which will yield a larger net return.

WORLD WHEAT PRODUCTION [42]

(in millions of bushels)

	Average 1909–13	1928–29	1929–30	1930–31
Canada	197	567	305	398
United States	690	915	809	851
Argentina	147	349	163	239
Australia	90	160	126	205
Danube Basin	330	369	303	334
Russia	759	795	703	1,097
Export Countries	2,213	3,155	2,409	3,124
All other	1,587	1,616	1,792	1,708
Total World *	3,800	4,771	4,201	4,832
Carry-Over	200 †	418	591	554
World Supply of Wheat	4,000	5,189	4,792	5,386

* Excluding China. † Rough estimate.

INTERNATIONAL TRADE IN WHEAT

(in millions of bushels)

(Year ended June 30)

Exports

(Official reports)

	Average 1910–14 Actual	Average 1910–14 Per Cent	1929 Actual	1929 Per Cent	1930 Actual	1930 Per Cent	Shipments (Trade reports) 1931 10 Mos. Actual	Shipments (Trade reports) 1931 10 Mos. Per Cent
Canada	94	15.3	423	44.3	184	29.6	219	34.9
U. S.	107	17.4	164	17.2	153	24.6	109	17.4
Argentina	85	13.7	227	23.8	161	25.9	84	13.4
Australia	50	8.1	108	11.3	62	10.0	115	18.3
Dan. Basin *	115	18.7	33	3.5	55	8.9	13 †	2.1
Russia	165	26.8	0	0.0	6 ‡	1.0	87	13.9
	616	100.0	955	100.0	621	100.0	627	100.0

* Hungary, Jugoslavia, Roumania, and Bulgaria. † Black Sea shipments only.
‡ In disagreement with other authorities.

2. Government Independence of the Small Peasant. As the collectivization of the farms continues and the output increases, the standard of living should rise. It should become unnecessary to limit consumption in the towns by means of ration cards. As the collective and state farms succeed, the peasant's power to dictate government policy is curtailed. The government will thus have more than one string to its bow, and can depend upon the "grain factories" to supply the food requirements of the population.

According to Yakovlev [43] although the peasants in the collectives constituted only 30 per cent of the number engaged in private farming, the area sown by them was 62 per cent. In 1930, the first year of their large-scale operations, the collectives sold three and a half times as much grain to the government as did the kulaks in the fiscal year 1927, and one and a half times as much as the landlords before the war. In the spring of 1930, 6,000,000 peasants organized in collectives sowed 81,000,000 acres, or 13½ acres per peasant, whereas the 20,000,000 individual peasants sowed only 130,000,000 acres, or 6½ per peasant.[44] Thus direct government control over production swiftly increases.

In an address to the Economic Conference of Industrial Managers, June 23, 1931, Stalin said:

> We have overcome the bread difficulties, so much so that we are now exporting grain in quantities unprecedented during the whole existence of Soviet rule. Even the blind can now see that upon the front of *Kolkhoz* and *Sovkhoz* construction we have been definitely victorious, having attained tremendous successes.

But apparently the conclusion that Russia has solved her agricultural problem is premature. The peasant rebelled in the only way that was left to him—by passive resistance. He resented the fact that the government had taken too much of his grain in its collection program and had not furnished him with the necessary household goods and clothing. He thereupon became apathetic and hostile to the efforts of the government to stimulate an increase of sowing. In fact the official newspaper, *Pravda,* reported numerous cases of crops left unharvested. The harvest of 1932 lagged considerably behind that of 1931 at the corresponding dates. Furthermore the fall sowings for the 1933 crop also lagged. Up to September 15 fall grain sowings totaled 44 million acres, or 45 per cent of the Plan, as against 57 million acres in the preceding year. Collections up to September 15 were 26 per cent of the Plan as against 48 per cent for the corresponding date of 1931.[44a]

As a result of a careful study of the agricultural situation, the Bureau of Research on Russian Economic Conditions at the University of Birmingham concludes:

> Soviet collectivization of peasant households in the chief grain-growing regions has failed so far to solve the grain problem. In the *kolhoz* farms the conditions of live-stock husbandry are far from satisfactory. Bread cards have not been abolished and bread, if bought without cards, is expensive.[44b]

3. Rise of the Standard of Living. The Russian peasant had a very low standard of living. He was inefficient and unsanitary. The collective and state farms are modern, and, as planned, embody the best practice of large-scale American farming. They are more efficient in the use of the land and machinery. In one collective of 1600 families or about 8000 persons in the Northern Caucasus, the results were reported for two years, the first year of private operation and the second year of collective operation, as follows, according to *Izvestia,* of July 29, 1931:

	Acreage	*Yield per Acre tons*	*Value thousand rubles*
Private operation	25,000	0.40	500
Collective operation	35,000	0.75	950

After paying the usual expenses and interest and also providing for sinking fund, social insurance, and expansion there was left a profit of 375,000 rubles for distribution. Each family in the collective is said to have received a substantially larger return. The poorest families had a net return equivalent to that of the "middle" peasants, while the "middle" peasants received an additional allowance for their contributions of capital and utensils, and a bonus varying with the quality and quantity of work. But the discrepancy between the poor peasant and the middle-class peasant now is less than formerly.

Commissar Yakolev's report to the Sixth Congress of Soviets in March 1931, stated that peasants who joined collectives in 1930 increased their income at least one and a half times. The reasons were the use of agricultural machinery, too expensive for the individual farmer, the elimination of fences, which increased the acreage per peasant, and the distribution of selected seed by the government.[45]

The land holdings of the poor peasantry were doubled in size. As their production was increased, their living conditions rose. The peasants themselves consumed more of their products, in wheat, rye, meat, eggs, and dairy products, than before the war. The consumption of meat in 1929 was double the pre-war level for the peasant population. The middle and poor peasants in 1929 consumed 90 per cent of their production of grain, which amounted to six-sevenths of the total crop.

In many other ways living standards are raised. Nurseries for the children provide superior hygiene and education. Mechanical advantages, such as running water, electric light, and other modern farm conveniences are lifting a most backward peasantry to levels prevailing in western Europe and the United States. Compulsory elementary education and other advantages of community life are developed. And not least, by precise accounting methods not only is the status of the collective as a whole revealed, but likewise (and for the first time) the financial status of the several members.

4. Mechanization of Farms. State farms and collective farms require machinery. At present the state farms are only 3 per cent of the total area, but as they grow the need for tractors and agricultural machinery will increase.

The total value of agricultural machinery in use in the Soviet Union in the fiscal year 1927 amounted to about 1.0 billion rubles, about 1.4 billion rubles in 1929, and 1.7 billion rubles in 1930. Yet in 1930 the Soviet Union had only one tractor for every three thousand acres sown, whereas the United States in 1928 had one for every four hundred thirty acres sown.[46]

In 1929 the total area under cultivation in the Soviet Union was about four-fifths that of the United States. The average yield per acre of wheat was only 10¼ bushels in the Soviet Union for the two preceding years as compared with 14½ bushels in the United States.[47] One reason for the smaller output was the smaller number of tractors in use. The use of fertilizer was only one-tenth as great in 1929.

The growing demand for farm machinery involves the building of factories, the making of steel, the mining of coal and ore, the development of water power, etc.

The agricultural program thus involves an industrial program. The two are interdependent. As Yakovlev pointed out large-scale and mechanized farming requires development of an agricultural-machinery industry. The Sixth Congress of Soviets therefore ratified the program to expand the manufacture of harvesting machinery.

Under a system of less rapid development Russia could for years export her agricultural products to the industrial nations and in return import manufactured goods and later machinery for industrialization. But with the protectionist philosophy that dominates Soviet Russia she wishes to be independent of foreign industry as promptly as possible.

As pointed out above, the Soviet program depends upon intelligent care of machinery. The misuse of farm machinery is one of the chief problems confronting the managers of the state and collective farms. One returned American instructor on tractors and combines at a state experimental farm in Verblud, Russia, says:

> I can't begin to tell how the Russians mistreat their machinery. Our harvest, which started on July 1 and should have lasted only forty days was not finished when I left the farm on September 22. It was absolutely impossible to keep a piece of machinery running for any length of time. Combines that will run from twelve to fifteen years in the United States do very well if they last through the second season there. Tractors good for ten years' hard work here will last through three seasons there. For example, I had twenty tractors this year that were in their third season. They were worked in the field about 1000 hours and were in the shops undergoing repairs over 900 hours. I think the biggest reason they wear out so much machinery is the utter indifference of the average Russian worker. He does not care whether it runs or not.[48]

Recognizing the seriousness of the misuse of machinery the Central Executive Committee decreed that the criminal code of the Soviet Union be extended to include punishment for the spoiling and breaking of tractors and agricultural machinery belonging to state farms, to collective farms, or to tractor stations. The penalty is forced labor up to six months if the breakage is a result of criminal negligence, and up to three years if the offense is repeated continuously or results in heavy loss. On the other hand, in order to encourage careful handling of tractors, premiums are paid at the end of each year to the mechanic whose tractors are in the best condition, have had the largest output, and were most economically operated.[49]

5. An Agricultural Proletariat. The result of the agricultural reform is the transformation of Russia's individual peasants, potential small capitalists, into an army of agricultural workers. The rich peasant disappears, and all peasants become employees of the state, or workers on co-operative farms. This is the trend of the development.

Though the motive of their overlords is different, the peasants are as powerless to resist their new rulers as they were the old. True, under the Tsar's régime, they suffered to benefit the landlord, while under the Soviets the intention is ultimately to benefit the peasants themselves. In this policy, however, they have no voice, but are subject to coercion and force.

G. Agricultural Prospects

1. Effect on Russia. If, as a result of the introduction of the state farms and collectives, Russia can feed her population, the small peasant will disappear. The peasant, who is a strong individualist, will ultimately become the socialized employee of the state farm or the socialized member of a collective. This will mean a most portentous development of the Soviet régime. The state farms will develop rapidly and are likely to succeed. They represent the extension of state capitalism into the field of agriculture. This is Lenin's contribution to the theories of communism—the attack on the agrarian problem by collectivization. Politically this eliminates the peasant as a small capitalist. Economically it increases output and lowers costs. However, the ultimate success of collective farming is yet to be established.

Increased efficiency on the state and collective farms will result in the same technological unemployment which has been troubling the western world. What solution will develop in Soviet Russia? Within three or four years it is expected that the state farms will include about 30 million acres,[50] which will be operated with 120,000 farm machines. On this basis 1,200,000 workers would be enough to cultivate the entire arable area of Russia, which now carries 26 million families and a population of about 100 millions. Thus an enormous amount of labor will be released. This may result in part in the reduction of working hours, or it may result in a development of related agricultural industries for the preparation of food and the utilization of the by-products of agriculture, such as hides and leather, as well as the development of underlying mechanical industries.

The release of vast numbers of agricultural laborers may also stimulate industry. This has been the case in the United States for several decades as our farms have become mechanized. The whole economic aspect of Russia may change as a result of the program of efficient agricultural production.

2. Effect on the World. If Russia succeeds with its state and collective farms, the results may throw much light, for the rest of the world, on the relative value of the large and the small farm as to efficiency and costs. The competition of private, collective, and state farms may reveal their relative efficiency in production and their relative value as furnishing a satisfactory way of life. Perhaps it may even offer a solution to the agricultural problem now troubling the world, and reveal under what varying conditions agricultural products can be raised profitably even at the present low prices.

CHAPTER VI

LABOR

The observer of Russian life is struck by the contrast between economic phenomena in Russia and in the western world. In its labor aspects particularly the economic problem affords a contrast. New motives are utilized. The standards of living and of labor are different. The cost of living seems painfully high, and in spite of Soviet statistics real wages seem lower than in other parts of industrialized Europe. In scientific management, particularly, the whole-hearted co-operation of the workers and the unions is remarkable. The cost of production, nevertheless, is high. Labor is undisciplined and irregular in working habits. The ideal of industrial democracy contrasts with efficiency. Freedom and authority conflict, here as elsewhere. The workman is not so likely to strike against his employer because his employer is the state. Yet, notwithstanding the ideal of a classless state, labor under certain conditions is exploited as nowhere else.

A. Motives and Incentives

The motives and incentives in Russia are in some aspects quite different from those of the western world, and in others very similar.

1. New Motives. Some workers tell visitors that they feel like the owners of the plants and for this reason part of the management. For a time they did not co-operate with the old bourgeois engineers, whom they suspected of treason to the working-class state. They respond to social incentives instead of the motive of individual gain. For example, at the Putilov works in Leningrad there is a team of four lathe workers—women, strong, stolid, and apparently efficient. They have a sign above the machines, "Kommuna, Putilov"

Note: An extensive study of the labor problem in Soviet Russia is contained in *The Soviet Worker*, by Joseph Freeman. (New York: Liveright, 1932.)

(communal team). Regardless of the fluctuations of their wages, they pool their earnings and share equally. This arrangement is unknown in the western world. In the electrical factory in Moscow great banners in the courtyards and in the plants bear the legend, "Collective work leads to our aim," which is communism.

In order to secure efficiency, all the social pressure of public opinion is invoked. As the visitor enters the Putilov works, he sees a great bulletin board with the various departments listed. The efficient ones are listed as "reds"; the inefficient as "blacks." Again in each department of the several factories that one visits, the efficient workers are likewise listed on the "red" side of the board and the inefficient on the "black" side. The work called for under the Five-Year Plan is distributed to the various departments. The department that exceeds its schedule of production is listed as "red," the deficient department as "black." Each workman has a production quota, proportioned to the output expected of the entire plant, and is judged by his quantitative output.

If work is particularly poor, it is exposed to public gaze similar to the Puritans' stocks and pillory, with the names of the workers producing the defective parts. The rewards and punishments seem almost like those for schoolchildren. Appeal is made to the individual on behalf of the socialist state. In the electrical factory "Electrozavod," which the writer visited, he saw cartoons of all sorts aiming to promote efficiency. There were cartoons of the lazy man holding up the Five-Year Plan, the stupid man spoiling material, the drunkard who was a general nuisance, and a cartoon of idlers and malingerers, with the motto, "Kick out the idlers." In one department of the Putilov Iron Works, Leningrad, where there were no posters, the writer asked an old worker why there were none. He smiled a knowing smile and said: "Old stuff—that is for the young, we know all that."

In addition to combating anti-social conduct, great banners in the various factories urge the individual to constructive effort. One blazons the message: "Work seven hours, study one hour." Another reads: "When going on a seven-hour day make the Five-Year Plan in three," and another: "Work to win the factory banner." Then again at the entrance to various factories there are numerous appeals for subscriptions to the government loan—"Subscribe to the Five-Year-Plan-in-Four Loan," or "Subscribe to the government loan for collectivization" (of the farms). Although subscriptions are theoretically voluntary, strong social pressure is brought to bear. And here again the departments are listed as "red," if oversubscribed, and as "black," if undersubscribed, and the workmen in the plants are similarly classified.

Rewards and honors are conferred for distinctive service. These include various decorations such as the Order of Lenin, and privileges, such as additional vacations or travel tours. Engineers or technicians who distinguish themselves are sent abroad to study and observe. Furthermore, the incentive of social approval is used to elicit the best efforts of individuals or of shop groups. Photographs appear in the papers and magazines of groups of workmen who have made particularly good records. In the Park of Culture and Rest at Moscow there is a street like the Siegesallee in Berlin, with a row of likenesses of men who have done outstanding jobs in the factories.

Honors are evidenced by medals, but in addition they confer upon the holder a reduction in taxes, and important privileges such as passes on the railroads during vacations and the right to enter street cars at the front. These rewards are directed toward developing and utilizing individualist motives as distinguished from the social motives which are the backbone of the Soviet scheme. At first, in appealing to social motives so insistently, the leaders neglected individualist motives, and production declined. It was the French Revolution that illustrated the value of a system of honorary orders. Probably because of his military training and perspective, Napoleon established the Legion of Honor, with its various grades for service to the community.

The stress on co-operation leads to neglect of the element of individual competition in the factories, banks, and other businesses. Instead, the incentive of "socialist competition" is applied. In the State Bank, for instance, one group of bookkeepers is pitted against another group on postings. In the shops one department is pitted against another making the same goods, or two departments operating in sequence set the pace for each other by manufacturing the goods at the same rate so as to avoid damming up the flow of goods in process.

In addition to the individual prizes, the social idea of the Soviets found expression in collective prizes. The Eighth Trade Union Congress in December 1928 favored the creation of a new form of remuneration, the collective bonus, and in October 1929 the Council of the People's Commissars decreed that it be established. It was designed to stimulate groups of workers to effect an increase of output, a decrease in cost of production through the lower requirements of raw material or fuel, an improvement in quality, etc. These special "funds for the encouragement of social competition" were derived from reserves created out of savings resulting from suggestions and equivalent to 40 per cent of such savings.[1]

The results of these prizes are announced periodically. For example *Signal,* the newspaper of the railways, announced prizes equivalent to over $600,000 to be awarded to the best railway repair shops, to be used for improving living conditions, such as providing new community centers or clubs and excursions. A small amount, however, about $20,000, was reserved for distribution to individuals.[2]

That these incentives are successful is the testimony of the technical manager of the Electrical Trust, Mr. Clark, the son of an Englishman who for almost thirty years worked under the so-called capitalist system, in Russia, part of the time in the Riga plant of the German General Electric Company, the A.E.G. In answer to skeptical queries, he stated that he had worked under both systems, and he knew the new incentives did produce results.

2. Old Motives. On the other hand, in the various factories one finds appeals to the old motives, as exemplified on the one hand in piece rates, bonuses and prizes, and on the other in such penalties as demotion and punishment. Fear and force are still applied.

The state owns, controls, and operates practically everything—mines, factories, railroads, hotels, and restaurants, educational and recreational facilities. The great masses of people are employees. They work for what they may earn. The status of the employee is the same as under the capitalist régime. He seeks advancement, extra reward for extra effort, and a bonus when profits are large. The incentive of the laborer in Soviet Russia is similar to that in capitalist Germany. Recognizing this fact, the trusts have stimulated increased output by offering a premium to the individual for efficient work. Individuals who exceed their allotted quota are rewarded by bonuses or an extra holiday. Workers making suggestions which will increase efficiency receive prizes. Not only is there a premium or bonus for increasing output, but there is a penalty for inefficiency.

Base rates or normal rates of wages are set both by the management and the workers' committees, the latter being permitted to advise, but not to decide. Apparently the motives for increasing output are much alike under a socialist as under a capitalist scheme. Mr. Ivanov, vice-commissar of the Department of Labor, stated that wages are based preponderantly on piece work, in order to stimulate production, and that workers participate in the profits resulting from increased efficiency.

Furthermore, what the sympathetic observer sees as social idealism may be regarded by the cynic as group selfishness. The worker is asked to be efficient in order to destroy capitalism and exalt the power of the Soviets.

"Every percentage of decrease in cost of production will give the Soviets power;" reads one banner, and another: "Efficiency is the weapon in the hands of the Soviet in their fight against capitalism."

In addition to these old motives, primitive measures such as attended the beginning of the industrial era are used, including force, threats, and scolding. Motives dominating the management and the engineers are fear of imprisonment, and even of exile or death, if mistakes occur in their plants. Such cruelty of policy may be a heritage from the Tsarist régime. While foreigners may introduce modern machinery within five years, it will take much more than five years to introduce the spirit of free and spontaneous co-operation which characterizes the western factory enjoying progressive management and intelligent labor leadership. The fear motive checks initiative and the assumption of responsibility, and many able men because of such a handicap prefer to take minor positions.

B. Supply of Labor

1. Increase of Industrial Workers. Unemployment in the cities originally resulted from the movement of peasants from the land in the hope of improving their standard of living. Stalin stressed this flow of labor in his address before the Conference of Industrial Engineers in Moscow in June 1931. As a result of this movement the number of unemployed rose rapidly to a peak in January 1929, but declined to practically nil in the autumn of 1930. As given by various Soviet publications the number of unemployed between 1925 and 1930 was as follows:

NUMBER OF UNEMPLOYED IN RUSSIA

Date	*Number*
January 1, 1925	848,000
January 1, 1927	1,353,000
October 1, 1928	1,374,000
January 1, 1929	1,516,000
August 1, 1929	1,264,000
February 1, 1930	1,168,000
May 1, 1930	936,600
August 1, 1930	607,000
October 1, 1930	None

At present there is obviously no unemployment problem in Russia. But when the tremendous construction program is finished, unemployment will probably return again, if the experience of western nations is a guide.

Not only is there no unemployment, but the expansion of industry brought a labor shortage, which the introduction of the continuous working week and the multiple shift was intended to relieve. The Soviets now have the problem of obtaining a suitable supply of trained labor. For example, in the iron and steel plants only 20 per cent of the workers in 1930 were employed there before the war. The rest are former peasants and the new generation of workers.

The number of workers engaged in production work rose rapidly as follows:[3]

1923	6,736,000
1924	7,330,000
1925	8,256,000
1926	9,808,000
1927	10,313,000
1928	11,456,000
1929	12,150,000
1930	13,684,000
1931	16,200,000 (program)

The number of workers in the heavy industry rose from 2,365,000 in 1927 to 4,240,000 in 1931.[4]

As a result of the heavy migration to the cities, living conditions became difficult. A shortage of food and of housing developed and the flow of peasants into industry was thus checked. This reversal of flow was well described by Stalin in an address to the Economic Conference of Industrial Managers in Moscow, January 23, 1931:

> To secure labor power for our industrial enterprises, no particular effort in the sense of endeavoring to attract and recruit workers to the factories was formerly necessary. This was due to the fact that there was unemployment, the village was breaking up into rich and poor, there was poverty and the fear of hunger which drove people from the villages into the towns. . . . The peasant was driven by the fear of hunger, by unemployment, by the fact that the village was a step-mother to him, and he was glad to flee from her anywhere, even into the devil's embrace, if only to secure work. . . . However, we have supplied the village with scores of thousands of tractors and agricultural implements; we have smashed the kulak, have organized the collective farms and enabled the peasants to live and labor under human conditions. Now the village can no longer be described as a step-mother to the peasant; the peasant begins to settle in the village, rather than "flee to the town," so that there is no natural stream of man power.

As this shortage of labor increased, the Soviet government offered special privileges to induce the individual peasant to leave his small holding and go into industry, particularly to those industries that required difficult and onerous labor. The Central Executive Committee and the Council of the People's Commissars issued a decree which offered concessions to peasants who would work in lumbering, fishing, transportation, industrial construction, and on the state farms. These concessions include exemption from various taxes, including the agricultural tax, giving the families that leave the farm privileges now enjoyed by industrial workers, and in addition the right to return to the farm after the industrial contract is fulfilled without losing any farm privileges.[5] This decree was issued primarily because of the need for labor for 518 new factories in 1931.

2. WOMEN IN INDUSTRY. Women are to be found everywhere in industry, even performing heavy manual labor in machine shops and iron and steel plants. In Moscow one can see them late at night, huddled in shawls, at street railway junctions throwing the hand-switch for trolley cars. While this wide employment of women is due in part to the doctrine of equality of women with men, it received its great impetus from the labor shortage.[6] In December, 1930 the Council of People's Commissars issued a decree concerning the employment of women in industry and on state and co-operative farms:

> In order to satisfy the labor demands of rapidly developing industry and other branches of national economy, and in order to attract more and more women into active socialist construction, it is essential to develop the employment of women in all branches of the national economy.
>
> Past experience of the employment of women in the industrial life of the country fully demonstrates the possibility and propriety of an extensive employment of women even in those branches of national economy in which women have hitherto not worked at all or only in negligible numbers.
>
> In the interest of a more effective introduction of women into industry, the Council of People's Commissars of the R.S.F.S.R. decides . . . to approve in principle the drawing up, by the People's Commissariat of Labor of the R.S.F.S.R., of lists of occupations in metallurgical, electro-technical, chemical, mining, paper, leather, sewing, and textile industries, and lists of posts in state and co-operative administrations, in which women are to be exclusively or chiefly employed.

U. Larin, who developed the five-day week, outlined a plan to increase the number of women in industry.[7] His plan consisted chiefly in eliminating the household duties of women. He would recruit 800,000 women, now doing household work at the large industrial centers. In order to do this it would be necessary to establish community nurseries, kindergartens, community kitchens, and laundries so that the home could be mechanized and operated along industrial lines with specialization of labor. The displaced unmarried women workers could then be moved to the outlying construction centers.

To increase the number of women on the collective farms, the Central Executive Committee decreed that schools be opened in agricultural districts to teach women to operate farm machinery and to handle the administrative work of the farms.[8] The results of the enlistment of women workers in agriculture seemed successful. On some state farms the per capita area plowed by women was higher than that of the men.[9] As a result of the campaign to impress women into production work, almost 3,000,000 women were enlisted by 1930 and the plan called for an additional 1,500,000 women in 1931. At the electric-power project on the Dnieper over 2000 women are doing manual labor, and the women members of the "shock brigade" out-did the male brigade in completing their jobs. Women are engaged in a great variety of occupations including not only office work, but also work as municipal police, operators and conductors of street cars, and bosses and workers at the machines in factories.[10] In the light industries 50 per cent of the working force is composed of women and in the heavy industry about 17 per cent.

Even members of the *lischentzy,* the declassed traders and small merchants, have been admitted to the factories, to become members of the privileged class. Housemaids leave domestic service to enter factories and join the proletariat, the élite of Russia.

3. Reduction of Turnover. The effective labor supply is reduced by the turnover. To lessen this turnover, the Central Executive Committee and the Council of People's Commissars issued a decree on December 15, 1930, reorganizing the labor exchanges. The Commissariat for Labor was to determine what persons were eligible to register for employment at the exchanges, and persons registered who refused without good and valid reason to work at the trade assigned to them by the labor office were removed from the list for six months. However, preference in assignment of work must be given to those closest to the working class.[11] (The question of the supply of labor is also treated in the section on forced or drafted labor, p 227.)

4. Quality of Labor. The Russian workers have important qualifications as well as deficiencies. Physically they are strong, have great endurance, and are hard workers. True, the Russian worker never has been very energetic. And now he must exert himself to the utmost under the new régime. The routine requirement of mass production is a powerful incentive to steady and continuous activity, although, undoubtedly, Russian labor is bearing a great burden due to the incompetence and lack of experience of the manage-

ment. The worker must by overexertion compensate for the deficiencies of the foreman and the superintendent.

In some factories, for instance in the electrical factories, the workers are quite literate. On the other hand, the new industrial workers coming from the land are primitive. Some of them had never seen an electric light before coming to the city and are utterly without the tradition and feel for machinery. It is difficult to recondition them psychologically to the new environment; they will not discard their old ways. One peasant mechanic is said to have kicked and beaten his tractor as he used to kick his horse because it would not work. The government has issued an order subjecting to severe penalties, ranging from six weeks' forced labor to three years' imprisonment, all mechanics guilty of "wanton cruelty" to agricultural machinery.[12] An American engineer in from the field tells a story illustrating socialist competition at work. Twenty-four new tractors had just been delivered at one of the state farms, and the energetic and enthusiastic communist peasants raced the tractors full speed to the farms and broke nearly one-third of them. Schools for training workers in industry are intended to relieve the shortage of engineers and skilled workers.

Lacking a feel for machinery, the laborers mishandle delicate parts. One observer reports that during the construction of the Dnieper Dam the use of the locomotive crane was introduced. The Soviet workers had no idea of its lifting capacity, and for the first few months one-half the cranes were kept busy lifting up the other half which had fallen over because of overloading. However, after a period of learning, the workers developed more accurate judgment as to loading capacity. Again, at Stalingrad, to see how the machine worked and hear the noise a carpenter dropped a 10-ton automatic hammer on the block and cracked the hammer head in two, resulting in a loss of weeks of work for the shop. The Russian workmen are acquiring the mechanical feel but are taking their lessons on some very expensive machinery,[13] much like a novice learning to play on a Stradivarius.

As a result machines which would last ten years in America wear out in Soviet Russia in two years. This depreciation rate is an important element in raising cost of production which the Russians do not seem to figure. Furthermore, several foreign engineers report that the Russian workman is not inclined to lend himself to the discipline of monotonous routine factory work. He is impetuous rather than steady. He sometimes becomes lazy and will not co-operate as will men who have been accustomed to teamwork at their jobs. Then again, he will undertake a new task energetically, but as his enthusiasm wanes he will not follow it through. As a result, the output of the Russian worker, according to the engineers in charge, sometimes is as low as one-fourth that of the western workman. Since real wages must depend on the productivity of the worker, Soviet discussion about high real wages in Russia seem like statistical metaphysics.

5. Education of Labor. The Central Institute of Labor has worked out a series of courses to educate the laborers. After the manner of Antioch College in Ohio, workers are taught the theory of their work and then are sent back to the factory. They are paid while studying. The technical colleges are generally under the supervision of the related trusts. Each factory has a school for apprentices. For example there is a trade school adjoining the electrical works, where students receive special training to fit them better for their work. There are special advanced classes for skilled workers seeking advancement, somewhat like the classes in our technical evening high schools. These factory schools are open evenings and the workman may use his fifth day, the day of rest, for study.

In addition to the factory schools, trade schools, and the higher technical institutions or engineering schools, there are so-called worker faculties or special schools for preparing factory workers for college like the American labor schools at Katonah, New York, and Bryn Mawr, Pennsylvania. The rapid rise in the number of institutions for the technical training of workers is shown herewith: [14]

	1928	*1929*	*1930*	*1931* *
General technical and higher schools for adults	41	48	317	565
Factory schools	95	100	220	800
Technical institutes	160	181	212	590
Colleges and universities	189	194	217	285

* Program.

In addition to the technical and specialized education, the factories also have facilities for teaching the illiterate adults. The object is to enable them to read factory instructions and to understand the Soviet message. The prevalence of illiteracy is indicated in the abundance of picture posters. At the exit of one of the divisions of the Electrozavod factory in Moscow there is a battery of faucets and above them are pictures for the illiterate, and printed suggestions for the literate, of workmen washing off the grime after the day's work. As a part of the scheme of general education, the foreign languages, English, French, and German, are taught.

C. Hours of Labor

1. Working Day. The average length of the working day in the Soviet Union has been gradually reduced far below the pre-war average, which was nine to twelve hours. According to various Russian authorities, in the years 1913–14 the day averaged 9 hours 54 minutes; in 1924 about 7 hours 37 minutes, in 1927 about 7 hours 18 minutes, and in 1929 about 7 hours 22 minutes.

By the end of 1930 about 45 per cent of the workers in all industry were on a seven-hour basis and 77 per cent of the workers in the heavy industries. According to the Plan [15] over 92 per cent of all the workers in the industries under the Supreme Economic Council were to be put on a seven-hour basis.[16] In the spring of 1932 over 83 per cent of the workers were included.

Soviet statistics supply the following figures: [16a]

Year	*Working Days per Annum*	*Working Hours per Day*
1913	257.4	9.87
1919	183.0	8.30
1921	219.5	8.50
1927	262.1	7.47
1929	263.0	7.37

On the state farms the hours of labor were as follows: [17]

Season	*Hours per Day*	
	Permanent Workers	*Seasonal Workers*
Winter	8.2	8.3
Spring	8.5	8.9
Summer	8.8	9.2
Autumn	8.4	8.8

The hours of forestry workers were still longer. In the spring of 1929 the average length of the working day in the forests was eleven hours 18 minutes. The work was interrupted by breaks which averaged about one hour 18 minutes but this reduction in actual working hours was offset by a loss of 2 hours per day in going to and from the place of work.[18]

Minors under 18 may not work more than six hours nor work in dangerous occupations, as in chemical factories, mines, etc. Workers in X-ray plants are limited to four hours. After the day's work is over, however, most workers have supposedly voluntary tasks assigned to them, such as inspecting state stores. In the summer of 1930 the harbor of Leningrad was filled up with miles of lumber piled thirty feet high. Our guide, a young factory worker, told us he had volunteered to work after hours for three or four hours a day to help move the lumber out of the port, work that is done by machine, in any modern port. Some workers donate their fifth day, the day of rest, to such volunteer work. The existing labor code thus represents the ideal, not the actual practice.

2. WORKING WEEK. The change to the five-day week and the subsequent six-day week is discussed in the chapter on "Industry" (see p. 260). The official decree of the Council of the People's Commissars of September 24, 1929, stated that in every undertaking which was to adopt the continuous working week, except building construction and seasonal work, a five-day working week was to be introduced, consisting of four days of work and one day of rest.[19] Under this arrangement every employee received an uninterrupted weekly rest period of not less than 42 hours.

On September 24, 1929, five revolutionary holidays per annum were decreed: January 22, the anniversary of V. I. Lenin, and of January 9, 1905, of the old calendar; May 1 and May 2, the anniversary of the International; November 7 and 8, the anniversary of the October Revolution. Additional holidays were later added as follows: January 1, New Year's Day; March 12, the anniversary of the overthrow of the Tsarist régime; March 18, the anniversary of the Paris Commune. It is most unusual for any people to celebrate the holiday of another. Apparently national lines are ignored in Russia in an effort to establish the international fellowship of labor.[20]

Under the five-day week there were 72 days of rest per annum, and with the additional holidays the total working time was practically the equivalent of our working week, or five and a half days out of seven. The six-day week was introduced to overcome the shortage of labor. It consisted of five days of work and one day of rest and resulted in an increase of one working day per month or twelve per annum.

D. NOMINAL OR MONEY WAGES

This section on nominal wages will deal with the various systems of payment and the spread between skilled and unskilled wages, and with the subject of how the equalization of wages and its unfavorable effects on production was replaced by considerable differentiation of wages. The trend of nominal wages will be shown in piece work as well as in the supplementary compensation or social wage.

1. Systems of Payment. a. Time Work. Although piece rates were used in industry before the war, the trade unions preferred hourly wages. The presumption was that piece rates were intended to drive labor. This pre-war tradition was effective after the revolution. As a result time rates were generally applied. Consequently, the output of labor declined.

b. Piece Work and Bonuses. Within three months after the Bolshevik revolution, the workers themselves, realizing that it was to the advantage of the industrious worker to have piece rates, asked for their restoration. By a special decree of January 7, 1918, piece work was reintroduced into the metal industry in the Petrograd Province. In June 1918, it was reintroduced in the Moscow District and, in September 1918, among the dock workers on the Neva River at Leningrad. It was also reintroduced in the locomotive works. The effect was to increase the output.[21]

The trend toward piece work increased as a result of the demands of the workers. In the middle of 1918 in Petrograd only 20 per cent of the workers were on a piece-work basis. On May 19, 1919, the Union of Metal Workers adopted a resolution reproaching the government for delaying the reintroduction of piece rates, and asserting that "wages should be fixed according to the principle of the value and the productivity of the worker." They insisted on the necessity in the interest of increased productivity of applying piece rates wherever possible, and of supplementing these rates by a system of special bonuses.[22] At a meeting of the Central Executive Committee, March 4, 1919, the president of the Supreme Economic Council showed that as a result of the great decline in output a system of piece work had been reintroduced and that output had increased 30 per cent.[23] At the Second Congress of Trade Unions held in 1919, after a report by the Commissariat of Labor, a resolution was passed recognizing the need for "adopting a system of remuneration which would stimulate workers to vie with each other in increasing output, a system of piece work and bonuses, with fixed standards of output and with higher remuneration and shorter hours as a reward for an output in excess of the standard." [24] Since 1919 piece work has been officially recognized and was to be applied wherever possible. To reduce labor costs and to increase output it was necessary to revise the system of wage rates.[25] The development of piece work in Russian industry is shown in the following table: [26]

Fiscal Year	*Percentage of Piece Work to Total Work*
1923	40.6
1924	44.3
1925	52.5
1926	58.8
1927	61.2
1928	61.6

The foreign press apparently discovered only in 1930 and 1931 that the Soviet Union was introducing piece work. As a matter of fact, by that time it had been in effect for more than a decade.

c. Maximum Wage Limits and "Soldiering." Under the original system of piece rates the total wage was limited. According to *Trud,* the official organ of the trade unions, this limitation led the workers to limit their output, since if they did not, wages might be reduced and the worker would receive no wage at all for the additional output that he might produce. Apparently the Soviet worker thinks in terms of his own expenditure of effort just as does the worker under the capitalist system. The latter prefers his own good to the employer's profit and the Soviet worker prefers his own good to the common good. In both systems there is "soldiering" or "ca' canny," and in both there is likely to be resentment by the less competent worker when the superior worker exceeds his quota. As a result a resolution of the Central Committee of the Communist Party, August 15, 1924, demanded "the suppression of the limits to the additional remuneration for piece work and the periodical revision of the quotas or output and the scale of piece rates in accordance with the improvements in the technique of industrial organization and other measures which would lead to an increase in output."[27] Apparently this resolution contradicts the view given below by Mr. Clark, Technical Director of the Electrical Trust, that workers whose output rises far above the average ask that their wage be reduced.

d. Unlimited Maximum and Bonuses. The principle of unlimited piece rates with additional bonuses, as a means of increasing productivity, was introduced by the Sixth Trade Union Congress, meeting in November 1924, and on December 30, 1924, the Supreme Economic Council, the General Council of Trade Unions, and the Labor Commissariat issued an order to the effect that "a system of unlimited piece rates should be introduced . . .

in order to stimulate productivity. For laborers working on time rates a system of bonuses should be introduced in order to increase output." [28]

2. SPREAD BETWEEN SKILLED AND UNSKILLED LABOR. The conflict between the desire to equalize wages in the interest of communist theory and to differentiate wages in the interest of increasing output resulted in a zigzag policy.

a. Differentiation of Wage Scales. Originally during the period of "war communism," it was intended to pay equal wages regardless of the skill of the workers. Payment was to be based not on productivity but on need. The principle of equality was carried so far as to assume that needs were equal. The system broke down, for production was too low to maintain the social machine. With the introduction of the New Economic Policy under Lenin, the principle of equality of wages was abandoned and wages were again differentiated in accordance with the workers' skill and productivity. The establishment of piece rates was a step in that direction and the establishment of basic rates varying with the degree of skill was another step.

When differentiation of wage scales was first adopted, the maximum spread between the wages of low grades of labor and the highest grade of labor was less than it was later on. The first series of gradations contained seventeen classes. Taking the wages of the first grade, the common laborer, as 1, the wage of the ninth grade or manual worker was equivalent to 2.7, and the wage of the seventeenth grade, the highly skilled worker, was equivalent to 5. The several industries also introduced varying schedules as follows: [29]

Wage Group	*Unskilled Labor*	*Manual Workers*	*Highly Skilled Workers*
Chemical	1	4	7
Metal	1	3	8
Textile	1	4	9
Petroleum	1	3½	10

b. Standardization of the Grades. Because of these varying classifications, the trade unions attempted to establish a uniform scale for all industries. A new standard scale was recommended, namely: unskilled labor, 1; manual labor, 3.5; highly skilled labor, 8.[30] Difficulties arose between the various classes of workers. The manual workers were opposed to having as many as seventeen grades in the scale. Again to satisfy the highly skilled specialists whose work entitled them to compensation above the maximum scale, a special supplementary remuneration was provided by a Specialist Fund which is a fixed percentage of the total wage provided for in the Plan.[31]

c. Variations Too Extreme. The standardization of the wage scale resulted in an excessively wide spread. The skilled workers were greatly favored as against the unskilled workers. M. Tomsky, chairman of the General Council of Trade Unions, in an address to the Seventh Trade Union Congress, stated that under Soviet leadership and under the dictatorship of the proletariat, the difference in wages of the skilled worker and the unskilled is greater than in western Europe.[32] The actual average wage for nine trade unions showed a still higher spread than the standard scale, thus increasing still further the discrimination against the lowest or unskilled workers: [33]

Grade of Worker	*Theoretical Scale*	*Actual Scale*	*Actual Average Monthly Wages in Rubles*
1	1.0	1.0	25.20
4	1.8	2.2	56.50
9	3.5	4.7	118.74

In other words in the ninth grade the workers received 4.7 times the lowest grade instead of the theoretical figure of 3.5 times.

d. Reduction of the Spread. To eliminate complaints of the unskilled workers, the spread in favor of the skilled workers was reduced. The ratio of the wage of an average grade of adult skilled worker compared with that of the average grade of an unskilled worker as follows: [34]

Industry	*1924*	*1926*	*1927*	*1928*
Average for all	1.47	1.45	1.38	1.38
Mining	1.54	1.55	1.48	1.24
Chemical	1.53	1.44	1.40	1.27
Woodworking	1.61	1.43	1.22	1.35

Not only was the ratio for skilled workers reduced with respect to unskilled workers but from 1924 to 1928 the trend was downward.

As a result of reducing the discrepancies, the actual wages paid tended to become equalized and to rise. Actual monthly wages from 1924 to 1929 almost doubled in rubles, the average rising from about 41 to 77 rubles. In 1924 only 17 per cent of the workers received more than 60 rubles per month, whereas in 1929 more than 64 per cent did.[35]

	1924	*1926*	*1928*	*1929*
Average monthly earnings in rubles	41.21	58.64	74.79	77.51
	Per cent	*Per cent*	*Per cent*	*Per cent*
Workers receiving—				
Less than 20 rubles	18.5	4.9	0.6	11.0
From 20 to 40 rubles	40.9	25.9	13.5	...
From 40 to 60 rubles	23.6	29.8	26.3	24.7
Total to 60 rubles	83.0	60.6	40.4	35.7
From 60 to 80 rubles	9.7	18.1	23.7	23.9
From 80 to 100 rubles	4.1	10.0	14.8	16.5
From 100 to 150 rubles	2.5	8.6	15.4	17.5
Over 150 rubles	0.7	2.7	5.7	6.4
Total above 60 rubles	17.0	39.4	59.6	64.3
Grand totals	100.0	100.0	100.0	100.0

The trend in wages is an interesting illustration of the larger trend of the Russian development. It shifted from the communist theory of equal wages to the practical program of differentiating wages according to output and skill, and resulted in a discrimination in favor of highly skilled workers, greater even than that in the western world. The final result was the reduction of the discrepancy and the adoption of a more moderate scale. This zigzag is symbolic of the course of the general economic trend.

3. NOMINAL WAGES BY INDUSTRIES AND BY YEARS. The trend of nominal wages in the Soviet Union has been upward.[36]

Fiscal Year	*Average Monthly Wage (in rubles)*
1927	60.38
1928	66.90
1929	73.35
1930	76.22

Wages in the several classes of labor for the fiscal year 1930 and 1931 (estimated) are shown herewith:[37]

	Average Monthly Earnings for 1930 (Actual) Rubles	*Percentage of 1927–28*	*Average Monthly Earnings for 1931 (Control Figures) Rubles*	*Percentage of 1927–28*
Industrial	84.2	123	87.2	127
Educational	74.0	135	81.8	149
Total non-agricultural	78.9	124	83.9	132
Agricultural	41.3	162	51.4	202
Total proletariat	73.5	129	78.7	129

The increase in wages exceeded the percentage fixed in the Plan. The monthly earnings for 24 working days for the coal mining, iron and steel, metal and engineering, chemical, textile and paper industries was on the average 77.74 rubles per month. Owing to the difference in the availability of food and the cost of living the average monthly earnings in Moscow were 95.65 rubles but in the Ural District only 62.04 rubles.[38]

In the third quarter of 1929 the average monthly earnings for permanent agricultural workers for a day averaging about 8½ hours were as follows: [39]

Agricultural trust	38.5 rubles
State farms	75.7 rubles
Sugar trust	42.3 rubles
Total agriculture	42.4 rubles

Forest workers averaging 11.3 hours per day in the second quarter of 1929, earned 42.0 rubles per month for workers on foot and 62.2 rubles per month for mounted workers.

4. Supplementary Compensation and Socialized Wage. a. Nature and Amount. To the nominal wages in rubles must be added the socialized wage, i. e., the value of lower rents, socialized restaurants, expenditures on education for workers and their children, sanitary and health resorts for workers, the reduction in working hours. Literacy in the Soviet Union has been raised to about 63 per cent as compared with 33 per cent in Tsarist Russia. In addition to these advantages there are other actual benefits such as insurance against accidents, sickness, maternity, disability, and old age, and free vacations with pay varying from two to four weeks.

In the Soviet Union the entire insurance fund is borne by the industry and not by the workers. The cost of social insurance amounted to 16 per cent of the average wages during the last several years.

According to the Supreme Economic Council these supplementary allowances amount to about one-third of the average wage of the industrial worker. Therefore, in determining the actual nominal wage the Soviet statisticians add 33 per cent to the actual payments.[40] However, before the war there were also some supplementary allowances which amounted on the average to about 8 per cent of the wages of the individual workers.[41]

b. Offsetting Deductions. Some supplementary allowances, such as expenditures on vocational schools and shop committees, do not add to the wages of the individual workmen. Then, too, as pointed out by Stalin,[42] though the worker pays much less in rent than do the workers in capitalist countries, his allotment of space is very small. Just as in the purchase of food, clothing, and other consumers' goods, the prices may be low but the amount available is very limited, so also in housing. One could set off against the socialized wage the sacrifices of Soviet workers in dispensing with what workers in other countries regard as minimum necessities.

As a more direct and serious offset against the socialized wage is the fact that workers are subject to various substantial taxes. For example, the General Council of Trade Unions deducts about 9 per cent per month for various taxes and contributions.[43] Finally, and not least, from all workers' wages there is a deduction for the purchase of government bonds. This is theoretically voluntary, but, as noted above, actually social pressure is brought to bear to compel subscription. In addition there are membership fees and deductions of various sorts.

5. Opinion of Soviet Officials. It is reported that the industries making consumers' goods enjoyed the largest increases in wages. In the industries making producers' goods and on the railroads the rise has not been as great. At the Putilov works the foreman in the metal-turning division stated that skilled workers earned 50 rubles before the war and are now earning 150 rubles. The Assistant Commissar of Transportation, Mr. Spundi, stated to the writer that a locomotive engineer received a fixed compensation of 129 rubles per month, and in addition a bonus for saving fuel and increasing his train mileage. A good engineer on a passenger train would earn 225 rubles per month, on a freight train about 200 rubles. The maximum is about 250 rubles. The fireman received 125 rubles per month. Day laborers averaged about 3.4 rubles per day in 1930 compared with 2.8 rubles in 1928. The pre-war levels were much lower.

Mr. Ruhman, commercial director of the Electrical Trust, gave the writer the following comparisons for his factory: Before the war the average wage was 35 rubles per month for a day of ten to twelve hours, and for a six-day week.

Today for the same work the wage is 182 to 190 rubles for a month with one day's rest in five, and a seven-hour day. This comparison seems too favorable. The pre-war wage did not include social insurance or vacations, and present levels include both. Furthermore, at present 10 per cent of the profits of the trust at the end of the year are allotted to the trade unions for housing and welfare work. In addition there are bonuses to individuals and to factories when production runs above the allotted quota.

The maximum wages that any member of the Communist Party might receive were originally 300 rubles per month though additional payment was made for articles contributed to the press. This maximum applied to Joseph Stalin, Premier Molotov, the head of the State Bank, and all other Communist officials. However, the privileges granted might reach the equivalent of many times as much. These salaries were increased in the summer of 1932.

E. Social Welfare

1. Labor Standards. Labor standards have risen as a result of the revolution. Almost immediately after the first revolution in March 1917, the workers' organizations urged the adoption of a minimum wage. Early in 1918 one of the first acts of the Soviet government was the establishment of a compulsory minimum wage. The minimum wage varies for the several districts and is dependent upon the cost of living, climatic and other specific local conditions, and the industrial importance of the district. The minimum wages were set at first at seven to ten rubles a month, but the actual wages paid have risen so that the lowest grade of labor is now paid more than the upper limit of the minimum-wage schedule.[44]

In 1929 the minimum rates for selected occupations according to the wage district varied as follows: [45]

Group	*Rubles per Month*
Agricultural engineers	104–127
Veterinarians	98–122
Physicians	98–122
School teachers	48–100
Dentists, pharmacists, etc.	44– 59
Police	39– 80

Child welfare has advanced. Sanitary standards have been raised in the factories. Labor legislation is adequate. Women are protected. According to the Labor Code women and minors under 18 may not be employed at night without the authorization of the Labor Commissariat and the Council of Trade Unions. In dangerous occupations the workers receive special attentions helpful to the maintenance of health. On the other hand, in the machine shop of the Putilov works at Leningrad the wash basins have signs all about them, "This water is infected with typhoid germs, do not drink it." The desire to maintain high labor standards is checked by the inefficient social organization.

The problem of unemployment was met by the creation of relief work, and the payment of unemployment relief. Unemployment benefits range from three to eighteen rubles per month and in addition to these allowances some services are free to the unemployed such as rent, light, water, transportation, and other municipal services.[46]

2. Recreation. Welfare work in Soviet Russia is similar to that of the large American companies which furnish gratis to employees housing, lighting, and recreational facilities. The workers in Russia have recreation centers, so-called "parks for culture and rest." These include theatres, crêches and nurseries, workers' clubs, athletic fields, etc. There are no dance halls. Life in Russia is Spartan in its simplicity and Puritanical in its outlook. Workers' Clubs, which have replaced the old saloon, are the center of social activity. Sick workmen are granted a rest at a convalescent home, usually the former residence of a nobleman. Workmen in good health receive two weeks' vacation with pay, and miners one month. Summer excursion schedules are announced on the factory bulletin boards. Esperanto and literary circles meet at the factory clubs. Several plants post a plant newspaper, a sort of house organ, on the bulletin board, with cartoons for the illiterate workers. "Self-criticism" is free to a very surprising extent, and the lampooning of the management is noticeable in the factory sheets everywhere. The monthly calendar, or schedule of important events in the factory, is posted both for the engineers and for the laborers.

3. Education. Before the revolution the school expenditure per pupil amounted to eight to ten rubles per annum. The appropriations gradually rose until in the fiscal year 1931 the expenditures amounted to about 68 rubles per pupil per annum. The appropriations for the entire educational system before the war amounted to 381 million rubles, as against 3600 million rubles in 1931. The rapid growth of education is indicated herewith:

EDUCATION AND CULTURAL DEVELOPMENT, FISCAL YEARS 1928–1931 [47]

	1928	*1929*	*1930* *	*1931* †
NUMBER OF STUDENTS:		(*in thousands*)		
Pre-school institutions	....	754	2,071	4,843
Elementary schools (4 years up)	9,748	10,138	11,790	14,220
Schools for over-age pupils	....	90	149	3,122

* Preliminary. † Program.

In the fiscal year 1930 almost 12 million children, or 90 per cent of the total, attended the elementary school as against about 7 million, or 50 per cent of the total, before the war. Until 1930 compulsory attendance for children applied in the cities, and after that year it became universal. By October 1930, about 24,000 new schools were opened for about 1,500,000 children between the ages of 11 and 15. In 1931 more than 3,000,000 children were taught in special schools for retarded pupils. As a result of the vigorous campaign for general education illiteracy decreased rapidly. In 1920 about 61.7 per cent of the male population was literate and in 1926 about 65.4 per cent. Similarly in the female population literacy rose from 33.6 per cent in 1920 to 36.7 per cent in 1926. In 1926 about 57 per cent of the total population could read and write and by 1930 about 62 per cent. The plan is to "liquidate illiteracy" of all adults under 45 before the end of 1932. The rapid growth of schools for illiterates is shown herewith: [48]

	1928	*1929*	*1930*	*1931* *
NUMBER OF STUDENTS:		(*in thousands*)		
Schools for illiterates	1,322	2,700	7,500	13,192
Schools for semi-illiterates	....	1,186	6,970	11,868

* Program.

The rise in literacy was accompanied by a rapid rise in the circulation of newspapers which rose from 2.5 millions in 1913 to more than 22 millions in 1930. There are more than 630 newspapers for the Union of Soviet Republics and the various regions in each republic. The growth of education and of the means of communicating ideas, including the spread of propaganda, is shown herewith: [49]

	1928	*1929*	*1930* *	*1931* †
		(*in thousands*)		
Newspapers (copies)	8,250	12,521	22,330	27,000
Books and magazines, in thousand folios of 16 printed pages each	1,850	2,400	2,500	4,500
Radios, receiving units	348	671	2,600	5,130

* Preliminary. † Program.

4. Social Insurance and Public Health. An important contribution of the Bolshevik régime is the wide extension of insurance to the great emergencies of life, illness, accident, disability, unemployment, and death, and to old age. This, of course, is not essentially a communist notion. Social insurance has been developing since 1883 in Germany, upon whose experience the Russian legislation is based. Section 176 of the Labor Act of Soviet Russia states:

> The social-insurance system comprises: (a) medical insurance; (b) benefits in case of temporary loss of working capacity (illness, injury, quarantine, pregnancy, confinement, care of a sick member of the family); (c) supplementary grants (nursing of infants, medical requisites, burial); (d) unemployment benefit; (e) invalidity or permanent disability benefit; (f) grants to survivors in case of death or disappearance of head of the family.

In case of unemployment, the monthly allowance is 12 to 30 rubles. The unemployed are chiefly young people who are just entering industry, unskilled peasants who enter the cities for work, and employees discharged for purposes of economy. Maternity insurance is granted, including both pre-natal and post-natal care and full pay for 12 to 16 weeks. The mother is entitled to a rest of one half hour every 3 to 4 hours for nursing her child in the nursery attached to the factory.

Because of better public sanitation public health has improved greatly compared with the pre-war level. The death rate declined from 28.3 per thousand in 1913 to 20.9 per thousand in 1926, a decline of 7.4 per thousand in 13 years as against a decline of only 4.0 per thousand in the 25 years 1888–1913. In Moscow the improvement was still more notable. The death rate declined from 23.1 per thousand in 1913 to 13.4 per thousand in 1926, and the infant mortality declined from 27 per cent in 1913 to 12 per cent in 1929.[50]

F. Standards of Living and Cost of Living

1. Comparison with Pre-War Standards. It is difficult to measure present against pre-war standards of living (especially for one like the writer who had not visited Russia before the war), largely because of the system of rationing consumers' goods. But according to such authorities as the statistician of the State Bank, for example, the standard of living is definitely higher. At the World Grain Conference in London in May 1931, it was shown in a paper presented by the International Institute of Agriculture (Document No. 1) that while Russia's population in the five years 1925–29 had increased about 14 per cent as compared with the five pre-war years 1909–13, the domestic demand for wheat had increased about 30 per cent and for rye more

than 20 per cent.[51] Also, while the manufacture of consumers' goods is said to have increased, the demand has increased more rapidly and as a result there is a general shortage.

The pre-war standard was very low. Russia was exporting to the limit of her capacity—more than the country's condition warranted, in the opinion of both Russian and foreign economists. Vishnegradsky, predecessor of Count Witte as Minister of Finance, is reported to have said: "We *shall* export, even though we have insufficient food for ourselves." While this remark applied to the late eighties, it was true for the whole period up to the war. The agricultural output in 1913 was only $24.17 per capita, of which 12 per cent was exported, leaving a domestic consumption of about $21 per capita.[52]

The impartial observer is strikingly impressed with the incomparably low standard observable in the streets, stores, and homes. Yet the standard varies for the several elements of the population. Native Russians will say confidentially that the peasants and the workers have a lower standard of living than before the war. The intelligentsia, the merchants, traders, office workers, teachers, lawyers, and the "white-collar" group generally, are very much worse off than before the war. Some of them are living on the ragged edge of existence. The present generation made great sacrifices during the World War, again in the revolution, and again during the period of war communism. And now comes a final prolonged sacrifice during the period of Soviet experimentation.

As against the shortage of the necessities of life, the worker has the advantage of shorter hours of labor, annual holidays, recreation facilities and clubs, insurance against emergencies, and the several other items of socialized wages. These are the gains of the revolution.

An American government official, born in Russia and a close student of the present Russian situation, states in a private letter to the author that—

> . . . There is not enough information about the pre-war standard of living of the Russian workingman to enable one to judge whether any improvement has taken place. Because of intangible factors one cannot place much faith in a comparison of present and pre-war conditions based on Russian statistics. Money values cannot be used as a basis, since under the Russian system of rationing supplies, money does not always mean purchasing power. Neither can one take commodities as a basis because the official rations for various classes of the population in the Soviet Union implies that the goods rationed are to be found in the co-operative stores or government stores. This is not always the case, and therefore in estimating the standard of living of the Russian workman one must take into account the continual shifting percentage of the supplies that must be purchased in the open market at much higher prices than those fixed for the

rationed amount. A comparison of the housing conditions would be impossible in view of the lack of statistics on the subject. The real gain by Russian labor in raising its standard of living is to be found primarily in the political status of the workingman and the assurance that any improvement resulting from a higher productivity or from other economic progress will be enjoyed by labor first of all. Such a gain is largely psychological rather than statistical, but it is undoubtedly a factor of considerable importance in the sentiment of the Russian masses.

2. Geographical Differences in Cost. The cost of distribution of merchandise is a problem in Russia, as in other countries. Here particularly inefficient methods of distribution result in a great fluctuation in commodity prices, as well as in wide ranges of prices for similar wares. In the Central Caucasus, where 10 eggs cost 2 rubles, and a small roast chicken 2.5 rubles, there is an abundance of meats, sausage, bacon, and fresh fruits, and one observer actually reports a surviving pre-war "free-lunch" counter, where with a glass of vodka costing one ruble one may eat one's fill of a list of *hors d'œuvres*. In the larger cities vodka is not too plentiful, and food is never given away.[53]

3. Price Indexes and Some Price Lists. The Central Statistical Office of the Commissariat of Labor has been keeping index numbers of the cost of living since the beginning of 1917 but the method of calculating them has been frequently changed. The first index number was based on 16 articles of food and on prices prevailing in 97 towns. The cost-of-living index was obtained by dividing the market price of these 16 articles in any specific period by the cost of the same articles in the same district in 1913. The cost-of-living budget was revised in 1922 by the addition of articles other than foodstuffs. The index was then based on 15 items of food and 9 non-food items. In 1923 the basis was again revised and a new index was established on January 1, 1924. In 1926 the index was revised once more because up to the end of 1925 accommodation and municipal services were free or at low prices, whereas during and after 1926 rents and these municipal services rose. Again, as the standard of living rose, new items of expenditure had to be included and therefore the relative importance of the old constituents changed. For example, the percentage of food fell from 52.8 per cent of the former budget to 44.5 per cent in the revised budget. Again different prices prevailed in private trade, co-operative shops, and state stores. It was necessary to equate the percentage of the purchases in each of the three systems of distribution. To private trade was allotted 42.7 per cent, co-operative trade 47.6 per cent, and state trade 9.7 per cent of the total purchases. As a result there were in 1926 three index numbers of the cost of living, one based on private trade, one

on socialized trade, and a weighted index number including both. In addition each of these indexes was divided into two parts, one representing chiefly food items and the other including rent, municipal services, newspapers, amusement, etc. In October 1928, the Central Labor Statistical Office once more revised the method of calculating the cost-of-living index number, based on the percentage of private trade in the total of the consumers' purchases, which varied from about 11.5 per cent in the Moscow and Leningrad Districts to about 25 per cent to 27 per cent in Kharkov and the Donetz Basin.

In view of this complicated system of figuring index numbers and the continuous change in the basis of calculation, it is obviously difficult to use official statistics in comparing the cost of living in the Soviet Union today with pre-war figures or with those of other countries.

An attempt at finding order among these numerous index numbers is made by Zagorsky: [54]

AVERAGE INDEX NUMBERS FOR THE WORKER'S BUDGET IN THE U.S.S.R.

Based on prices in chervonetz rubles

1913 = 100

	Fiscal Years			
	1926	*1927*	*1928*	*1929*
Index (incomplete)	218.5 *	215.7 *	209.7 *	227.6 *
Index (complete)	202.6 †	203.3 †	201.7 ‡	219.8 ‡

* For 33 commodities. † For 40 commodities. ‡ For 39 commodities.

The index of wholesale prices computed by the State Bank shows that in the spring of 1930 the level was 1.819 times the level of 1913.[55]

The index of wholesale prices showed that the maladjustment between agricultural and industrial prices was eliminated between 1924 and 1929. Taking 1913 prices as 1000, the index of agricultural products rose substantially while the index of industrial products declined.

WHOLESALE PRICE INDEX FIGURES OF THE STATE PLANNING COMMISSION

1913 = 1000

Fiscal Year	*Agricultural Products*	*Industrial Products*	*General Index*	*Ratio of Industrial to Agricultural Index*
1924	1,342	2,157	1,702	1.61
1925	1,669	1,924	1,792	1.15
1926	1,713	2,009	1,856	1.17
1927	1,566	1,967	1,755	1.26
1928	1,567	1,877	1,715	1.19
1929	1,650	1,874	1,773	1.14

Similarly the retail index showed a rise in agricultural and a decline in industrial products: [56]

RETAIL PRICE INDEX FIGURES

Fiscal Year	*Agricultural Products*	*Industrial Products*	*General Index*	*Ratio of Industrial to Agricultural Index*
1925	1.87	2.28	2.02	1.22
1926	2.10	2.40	2.20	1.14
1927	1.97	2.11	2.03	1.07
1928	2.17	2.17	2.17	1.00
1929	2.29	2.17	2.17	0.92

As a result of measures to expand the state and co-operative stores and to drive the private traders out of business the index of retail trade rose as follows: [57]

ALL-UNION RETAIL PRICE INDEX OF CENTRAL STATISTICAL OFFICE

1913 = 100

Fiscal Year	*Total Trade*	*State and Co-operative Trade*	*Private Trade*
1926	210	202	224
1927	201	191	226
1928	197	184	244
1929	210	192	308

It is interesting to note how the index of retail commodity prices indicated the items of which there was a shortage. These showed a terrific rise in price in the free or private trade, which is a true index of actual demand. The accompanying table gives examples.

During the first half of the fiscal year 1930, the private sector of trade was 14.8 per cent of the total trade and the socialized sector 85.2 per cent but in the second half the private sector fell to about 6.6 per cent of the total. The price shows some very significant figures. Articles that were in great demand sold in private trade at a price several times as high as in the state stores. Apparently the government ration was inadequate. For instance vegetable oils were 7.7 times as high in price in the private stores as in the state stores; sugar 3 times; salt 2.1 times; meat, milk, and eggs about 2.5 times. Raw materials, which were not in great demand, sold in the private stores at levels relatively lower than consumers' goods. For instance, chemicals, silicate products, and lumber sold in the private stores at only about 1.5 times the prices in the state stores. Similarly in comparison with the prices in the preceding year, the rise in private trade was greatest for consumers' goods such as vegetable oils, which rose nearly 150 per cent, and lowest in producers' goods such as silicate products, which rose only about 12 per cent.[59]

RETAIL PRICE INDEXES MAY 1, 1930 [58]
1913 = 100

Commodities	(a) *In State and Co-operative Trade*	(b) *In Private Trade*	(c) *Ratio (b) to (a)*	(d) *Per cent Changes in Price from May 1, 1929* *State and Co-operative Trade* *Per cent*	(e) *Private Trade* *Per cent*
Total index	203	491	2.42	+ 0.5	+ 47.4
Index for industrial products	204	406	1.99	+ 1.5	+ 42.5
Index for agricultural products	201	670	3.34	− 2.0	+ 56.2
1. Textiles	189	540	2.86	− 4.9	+ 59.2
2. Silicate products	190	290	1.55	− 1.6	+ 12.5
3. Chemicals	168	272	1.64	− 1.6	+ 26.5
4. Kerosene	106	156	1.47	+ 0.5	+ 25.0
5. Tobacco	239	292	1.24	+21.2	+ 48.9
6. Sugar	196	590	3.01	− 2.7	+ 98.6
7. Salt	140	288	2.06	− 4.2	+ 20.8
8. Vegetable oils	156	1202	7.70	− 5.9	+146.5
9. Lumber and firewood	230	373	1.62	+ 0.9	+ 28.6
10. Meat and meat products	226	571	2.51	+13.2	+ 85.4
11. Milk products and eggs	247	607	2.47	+ 4.4	+ 80.5

In a dinner party at Moscow in the summer of 1930 there were a number of American shoppers, and some of the open-market prices they brought in were as follows:

MOSCOW RETAIL PRICES, 1930

Article	*Unit*	*Cost in rubles*	*Equivalent in dollars*
Coffee	*pound*	10.0	$5.00
Chocolate	*four ounces*	8.0	4.00
Meat	*pound*	6.0	3.00
Bread	*pound*	0.06	0.03
Apples	*each*	0.25	0.12½
Cotton socks	*one pair*	5.50	2.75
Eggs	*10*	2.40	1.20

Other open-market prices were equally high. Taking the ruble at par, about two to the dollar, butter in the open market costs the equivalent of $5 to $6 per pound. Oranges cost $1.50 each if obtainable at all, four small pears $1.50, cauliflower $1.50, chicken $5.00, small peaches 30 cents each, shoes $60 a pair. One observer reports, however, that comparisons in foreign currency are erroneous and that prices are not as high as they seem. He stood in front of a store window in Moscow where women's sweaters were on display at 64 rubles each, the equivalent of $32.00 (with the ruble at par), but really worth not more than $3.00 abroad. But in order that the price in Russia equal the foreign price, the ruble would have to sell at 10 per cent of its par value, or 5 cents.[60]

According to a Moscow despatch to the *New York Times* the shortage in food and the inflation of the currency, brought about a raise in prices by government decree for the second time in 1932 on September 1. The rise affected chiefly the products that were available in the stores for Americans and other foreigners and not for Russians. As shown elsewhere (see page 339) sour cream and meat were raised 50 per cent, cheese about 125 per cent, and eggs 250 per cent. In addition rations to foreigners were reduced 50 per cent. Vegetables and fruits were available in the open market as a result of the decree permitting peasants to sell privately and prices in the open market were frequently lower than in the government stores. However, though bread and fish were still available the average Russian was not much affected. He eats little besides vegetables as he cannot afford to pay for meat, eggs and dairy products.

4. Specific Shortages. The paradox that strikes even the casual observer in Moscow is that everybody is busy, that the stores are empty and there is little to eat or wear, whereas in other countries one finds unemployment, business depression, and a glut of merchandise. In the Soviet Union there is a shortage of food, shortage of clothes, and shortage of housing. The very air is rationed. As a result of the rapid increase in the population of Moscow, the floor space allotted per person has declined to about 6 square meters or 65 square feet from the original allotment of 12 square meters. In less crowded Leningrad the limit is 9 square meters, or 100 square feet. Several people occupy the same room. Sanitation is bad and privacy impossible. However, efforts are being made to remedy these conditions.

Yet it is possible to live, stoically, under such conditions. An elderly professional man, whom the author visited in his one-room home, smiled as his wife called the table their dining room, the desk their living room, the book shelf their library, the cot their bedroom, the oil-stove their kitchen and the sink their bathroom. A university professor proudly showed the author his second room,—a sign of privilege and power.

Fuel is scarce and is rationed. As a result the minimum legal temperature for homes has been reduced from the equivalent of 55 degrees Fahrenheit to 48 degrees, and the date when the legal minimum temperature becomes effective has been postponed for one month. The severe cold of Russia makes this reduction a serious sacrifice.

Food is scarce in the greatest agricultural country in the world. There is a serious shortage of milk, butter, eggs, and meat. Since the Five-Year Plan went into effect, food has been exported abroad and rationed at home. The worker is entitled to a monthly allowance of a quarter of a pound of butter and 5 eggs. Chocolate and cigarettes are scarce. Soap, towels, and toilet paper are obtainable only with great difficulty. The allowance of black bread is ample. Food in excess of the amount rationed may be obtained at the state and co-operative stores at higher prices, but even there the supplies are scant. In the free market, additional quantities may be obtained but at prohibitive prices.

A peculiar shortage developed in the summer of 1931. Tableware ran short in the public eating places, owing to the opening of numerous new dining halls. Knives, forks, spoons, plates and glasses were each short more than a million pieces.

Clothing is exceedingly scarce. This was the outstanding impression of the writer at the very border when entering Russia. One of the crew on the "Pullman" train walked about the platform not in a uniform but in a torn, sleeveless undershirt, a threadbare pair of trousers, and a worn-out pair of shoes. He spoke German poorly and his first inquiry, as he eyed me, concerned the prices of several articles of my clothing. He thereupon gave the cost in rubles of similar articles, equivalent to three or four times American prices, taking the ruble at par. "Then," he remarked stolidly, "even at these prices we can't get any."

On any street in Moscow one sees a motley array of attire, in both men's and women's garments. The best-dressed persons in Russia are the specialists or officials whose work takes them abroad occasionally and who get clothes there at reasonable prices and without a rationed limit. The great department store in Moscow, Mostorg, is practically bare of merchandise. Instead of goods the windows contain busts of Lenin or placards carrying revolutionary propaganda. The only departments that are well stocked are those of woodenware, toys, and trinkets made of domestic raw materials. Old jewels and antiques are still to be had. The empty shelves are in keeping with the underfed and underclothed crowds that pass by them. In this department store of Moscow in 1930 the upper floors were roped off and the lower floors had great tiers of empty shelving. One of the standing jokes is that this store needs only one employee to run it. He stands at the door and tells the customers there is no merchandise within. There must be a shortage of several years of merchandise both in the homes and in the shops.

Clothing and shoes are worn out. Before leaving Moscow the writer was asked by refined and cultured Russians, whom he met, for his beret, shoes, towels, soap, and toilet articles. When the *S.S. Carinthia* arrived in the summer of 1930 the Soviet official made a grand display at the Grand Hotel of soap, chocolate, biscuits and other goods of which there was a shortage. The people of Moscow heard of the good news and cleaned out the supply in a few hours. Relatives of resident Russians sometimes leave behind a good part of their clothes, which are more desirable than cash. An American woman, working in Moscow, felt faint and sent out for some spirits of ammonia. Her Russian assistant returned, after several hours, and reported that none was to be had. These shortages are very obvious, despite statistics of increased production of consumers' goods. The Soviets themselves admit the adverse effect on industry of the current shortages. The output of light industries in the fiscal year 1931 was to have been 20 per cent above the previous year, but only 37 per cent of the planned output was produced in the first five months.[61]

The dearth of consumers' goods is ascribed by Soviet officials to the rising demand of the peasants for a better standard of living. For example, Mr. E. Y. Kadik, vice-president of the All-Russian Textile Syndicate,[62] said that the production of factory-made shoes in 1930 amounted to 63 million pairs compared with 29 million pairs in 1929 and 5.5 million in 1913. Before the war there was said to be no shortage of shoes largely because peasants generally wore wooden or straw sandals, but now that they are beginning to demand factory-made shoes and boots, while the demand from the workers is also increasing, there is a great shortage. The point Mr. Kadik overlooks is that before the war factory-made shoes indeed amounted to only 5.5 million pairs but great numbers of peasants in some communities made shoes by hand for local consumption. This type of industry has been driven out of existence by the attack on private artisans and private trade and part of the shortage in consumers' goods is ascribed to this policy. The 1930 rate of factory production of shoes would allow one pair per capita every 2½ years—a good index of the shortage.

In view of the low standard of living, the shortage of taxicabs is not surprising. For the tourist, it is a positive inconvenience. Parked taxicabs are not to be seen. If for any reason a taxicab stops and a passenger alights, persons will rush from all directions to engage it, in striking contrast with Paris and New York where the taxicabs hail the passersby. Tourists wishing to engage a taxicab, or hotel guests desiring taxicabs to meet trains, enter reservations twenty-four hours in advance.

Other consumers' services are difficult to obtain. To curtail private telegraphing, the toll rates have been increased from seven kopeks to ten kopeks and messages limited to 25 words. Telegraph offices throughout the country have been choked with messages and at Stalingrad alone at one time more than two thousand outgoing messages accumulated. In Moscow there were once ten thousand complaints at the Central Post Office about the failure to deliver magazines and newspapers. Domestic letter rates have been increased from 10 to 15 kopeks. Parcel-post rates have been increased and parcel-post weight limits have been reduced.[63]

Repair services are woefully inadequate. In the workrooms of the Leningrad Leather Co-operative in 1930 there were 71,000 pairs of shoes waiting for repair and the additional repair jobs were coming in at the rate of 2500 pairs per day, although the capacity of the shops was limited to 1500 pairs per day. So great was the congestion that customers had to stand in line all day in order merely to leave shoes to be repaired. It took three or four months to get the work done. Similarly at the Leningrad Clothing and Knitting Union it required three months to have a pair of socks darned and one month to get a coat or pair of trousers repaired.[64]

With the approaching completion of the "Five-Year Plan in Four," it is clear that the Russian standard of living has not only not "overtaken and surpassed" the capitalist countries, but has decidedly lagged behind. Living conditions in 1932 were not better but worse than in 1928. The supply of clothing was inadequate. Consumers' goods were unavailable. The meager promise of the Five-Year Plan of four eggs a month to the farmer and seven eggs a month to the city worker was not realized. Housing was not improved. An American correspondent counted 18 peasants sleeping under the scaffolding of his hotel in September, 1932.

Food conditions were the worst since the famine of 1921. Not only were milk, butter and eggs unavailable but meat, gruel and potatoes as well. The only rationed articles still to be had at the coöperative stores were black bread, herring, sunflower-seed oil, sugar and tea. There was a definite shortage of food in the cities and in the country it was even worse, as the peasants had to trade their food products for household goods. They lacked the most elementary working needs, such as pails, hinges, and buckles, and therefore had to deprive themselves of food so that it could be used as a medium of exchange. In Grozny, for example, peasants paid one ruble for 5 nails of 4-inch length and 10 rubles for a small flour sieve.[64a]

5. Low Rations. Only members of trade unions and their families are entitled to ration cards. Rations are highest for the manual laborer, less for the "white-collar" worker. Until August 1932 the "declassed" were not entitled to any ration cards—they must trust to luck and a good purse to obtain the minimum necessities of life. Workers in factories are entitled to buy cigarettes at the factory, and the shortage of cigarettes results in long queues of waiting workers who ought to be at their machines. Cigars are unobtainable in Russia—the cigars which the writer had with him on his visit worked wonders with slow waiters, porters, etc., who had not smoked any in years.

The quality of the food served is very poor. The writer ate at factory kitchens in Moscow and Leningrad and at a public eating place near the Hermitage, a vaudeville theater in Moscow. The food beggars description. A western worker would not touch it. But the people have no alternative. There is no other food. At the big hotels, the Grand or Savoy at Moscow and the Hotel de l'Europe in Leningrad, the food is good but the quality and variety are inferior to those of hotels of similar rank in other capitals of Europe.

To obviate the shortage in so far as it is due to poor distribution, the state factories are used as "closed distributing centers" where food, textiles, etc., are sold to employees.

The monthly budget (1929) for the worker theoretically contained the following items:[65]

Commodity	*Quantity*	*Commodity*	*Quantity*
Flour and meal (rye, wheat, buckwheat), *kilos*	11.5	Moleskin, *metres*	0.33
Bread (rye, wheat), *kilos*	8.6	Woolen cloth, *metres*	0.23
Vegetables (fresh, dried, canned), *kilos*	15.2	Ironware, *articles*	1.7
Meat (beef, mutton), *kilos*	5.0	Glass, *articles*	1.6
Melted butter, *kilos*	0.2	Petroleum, *litres*	0.5
Whole milk, *litres*	7.6	Ordinary soap, *kilos*	0.6
		Cigarettes, *packets of 25*	2.16
		Matches, *boxes*	1.5

Commodity	Quantity	Commodity	Quantity
Fresh eggs, *number*	10.6	Firewood, *cubic metres*	0.22
Vegetable oils, *kilos*	0.3	Rent, *square metres*	5.3
Salt herrings, *kilos*	1.0	Electricity, *hectowatt hours*	1.1
Sugar, *kilos*	1.5	Water, *hectolitres*	5.6
Salt, *kilos*	0.7	Newspapers, *copies*	3.6
Tea, *kilos*	0.04	Notepaper, *sheets*	12.0
Shoes, *pairs*	0.12	Cinema, *tickets*	0.8
Calico, *metres*	3.84		

The 1929 budget below shows changes from budgets of previous years. The following items were changed:[66]

Commodity	*1922–23*	*1923–24*	*1928–29*
Decreases:			
Potatoes, *kilos*	16.0	15.2	10.5
Cabbage, *kilos*	3.6	3.2	2.7
Increases:			
Meat, *kilos*	3.0	3.1	5.0
Eggs, *number*	6.0	3.0	10.6
Salt herrings, *kilos*	0.8	1.2	1.0
Soap, *kilos*	0.3	0.4	0.6

In April 1930, the schedule of food rations was as follows:[67]

Commodity	*Kilos per Month*		*Relative Figures*	
	Manual Laborers	*Other Laborers*	*Manual*	*Other*
Bread	24.00	12.00	100	50
Meat	4.40	2.20	100	50
Sugar	1.50	1.20	100	80
Tea	.025	.025	100	100
Butter	.30	.30	100	100
Herring	1.20	.80	100	66

During 1930, according to another authority, the rations allowed in Moscow to manual laborers holding food booklets were as follows (1 kilogram = 2.2 pounds):

Commodity	*Kilos per Month*
Bread	26.13
Meat	6.00
Macaroni	6.00
Grits	18.00
Sugar	1.50
Tea	0.05
Butter	0.40
Eggs, *number*	5 per month

Consumers other than manual laborers could obtain only one pound of bread per day and a quarter of a pound of meat per day. Children as well as manual laborers received five eggs per month, but eggs were not available at all to ordinary consumers. Milk was reserved for children under twelve years of age, and the limit was one-half liter per day at the fixed price of 24 kopeks per liter (about 12 cents per quart). Subsequently the sale of milk at fixed prices in government or co-operative stores ceased, and it was available on the open market at prices that ranged from 60 kopeks to 1.50 rubles per liter (about 30 to 75 cents per quart).

Among the fruits and vegetables the only regular and dependable supply was that of cabbage and potatoes. Others were not generally available. The average Russian family was short of milk, dairy products, and fats but did have an adequate supply of herring, potatoes, cabbage, bread, and grits or *kasha*. There were ten or twelve meatless days every month.[68] In the opinion of Chamberlin, a close and accurate observer, the workers' standard of living under the food restrictions was hardly equal to the standard which prevailed from 1925 to 1927, when free private trade in food was permitted and before the Five-Year Plan went into operation.

As a matter of comparison there is given herewith the average quantity of food consumed by the adult male in the United States.[69] It is not intended to compare the quantity and variety with that of the Soviet Union worker. The list is furnished merely to indicate the diversity of food and the quantity available as a measure of what the Soviet standard actually is. The measurements have been converted into kilograms per month so as to be comparable.

Article	*Kilos per Month*
Meats: including, beef, fresh steak, roast, stew, and other fresh beef; beef, salt, corned, dried; veal; pork, fresh and salt; bacon; pork, salt, ham and shoulder; pork, salt, side, dry; pork, salt, side, pickled; mutton chops, roast mutton; stewed mutton and other mutton; poultry, including hens and other poultry; sausage, liver, kidney and other meat, not canned; beef, including canned; pork, canned; ham cooked; tongue cooked and other cooked meats	4.45
Seafood: including fresh and salt fish, canned salmon and other canned fish, oysters, and other seafood	0.57
Milk and Other Products: including milk skimmed and not skimmed, evaporated or condensed, buttermilk, ice cream, cheese, both ordinary American and others	5.90
Cream and Butter	0.77
Fats: including oleo and other butter substitutes, vegetable, cooking and table oils, lard, and other fats	0.85

Article	Kilos per Month
Eggs . . . . . . (each)	18.42
Grain Products: including wheat, rye, and other flour, corn meal, hominy grits, cornstarch; breakfast foods including wheat, corn, oats, and others	5.00
Bread: including wheat, rye, and other breads, rolls and buns, crackers, cakes, and cookies	5.52
Macaroni, spaghetti, noodles and rice	0.60
Pies, tapioca, sago, sugar, molasses, sirup, honey, candy, and chocolate	2.27
Fruits, Fresh: including apples, peaches, bananas, lemons, oranges, grapes, berries, watermelon, canteloupe, and other fresh fruits	1.22
Fruits, Canned: including peaches, pineapple and others, jellies, preserves, marmalades, and peanut butter	0.20
Fruits, Dried: including apples, prunes, raisins, peaches, and other dried fruits	0.27
Vegetables, Fresh: including Irish potatoes, sweets and yams, cabbage, spinach and kale, peas; string beans, tomatoes, onions, corn, lettuce, celery, beets, turnips, sauerkraut, asparagus, and other vegetables	12.96
Vegetables, Dried: including beans, peas, and others	0.42
Vegetables, Canned: including baked beans, peas, corn, tomatoes, asparagus, and others; gelatin and canned soup	0.57
Tea, coffee, coffee substitutes, cocoa, nut and other foods	0.69

Toward the autumn of 1932, food became increasingly scarce.[69a] Foreign newspaper correspondents were put on a ration for the first time. Foreign specialists had their rations cut in half, with butter practically omitted. The new ration was as follows:

Item	*Quantity per Month kilos*	*Price rubles per kilo*
Meat	7	3
Fish	3	1.10
Flour	2	0.90
Butter	1	5.0
Sugar	3	0.95
Sausage	3	6.0
Cheese	3	3.50
Bread	24	0.43

Previously bread had not been rationed. The only foreigners exempt from such restrictions thus far have been the diplomats.

A comparison of the housing facilities of the worker in the United States and in the Soviet Union is likewise of interest as presenting a measure for the Russian standard. For typical cities the average number of rooms per family in the United States is 5.0. The average minimum for families with incomes under $900 is 4.2 and the average maximum for families with incomes over $2500 is 5.9 rooms. For apartment dwellers the minimum average is 3.7 rooms for families with incomes under $900 and 6.0 rooms for families with incomes over $2500, or a total average of 4.5 rooms.[70]

6. Causes. The decline in the standard of living is due to the policy of industrial expansion of the country and the consequent curtailing of the comforts of the individual. Production of consumers' goods does not keep pace with the development of heavy industry. The first of the five years of the plan for expansion of industry and agriculture was also the first year when food became scarce and rationing began. At first only some, but later all the articles mentioned above became scarce. The food shortage was due partly to the attempt to enforce the collectivization of peasants' live stock and the wholesale slaughter described above, and partly to a lack of warehouse and cold storage facilities, resulting in spoiling of much food, and partly to the export of food.

One cause for the shortage in goods was inadequate railroad and distributing facilities. Another was the rapid growth of the cities. There were fewer producers of home-made goods and more consumers. Still another was the attempt to speed up production, resulting in poor quality and thus further intensifying the shortage.

The people need clothing, but the state produces pig iron and manganese and buys machinery. They need shoes, but it produces lumber for export. The people need meat, but the state produces superphosphates. Then a basic question in political theory arises: "What should be the aim of government? Is it the life, liberty, and the pursuit of happiness of the people or aggrandizement of the state?"

7. Privileged Buyers. Prices vary with one's social status. Only the privileged are allowed to buy goods at the low fixed prices in state stores. In Moscow 60 per cent of the population, including the soldiers, rank as workers, 30 per cent are employees, including office workers in the government bureaus, and 10 per cent are the declassés, including priests and persons living on income sent from abroad. Food is sold at fixed prices on a card system. The workers get first preference, government employees second preference, and if there is anything left the other groups may buy.

Some of the declassés buy occasionally through a friendly worker or peasant. The workers are entitled to double rations of bread and meat, and trade-union members get tickets for amusement places at half rates. But the food ration is so low that even the workers must buy some goods in addition, either at the co-operatives' price, which is slightly higher, or in the open market, which is highest of all.

The laborer receiving a wage of 200 rubles a month cannot afford meat or butter if he cannot buy them in the co-operatives. Though it is equivalent at par to about $100, 50 rubles of this salary has a value of about $25, if devoted to rent and rationed food at co-operative stores. The remaining 150 rubles has a value of about $5.

TYPICAL RELATIVE PRICES, AUTUMN, 1932 [70a]

Item (*per pound*)	*Co-operative Stores* *rubles*	*Open Market* *rubles*
Sugar	1.40	....
Meat	1.46	16.00
Butter	1.80	13.00
Potatoes	.66	1.00
Gruel	.30	....
Black bread	.06	2.00

On January 14, 1932, the consumer classes were reduced from six to three: (1) Factory workers, including engineers, technicians, and school teachers; (2) office workers; (3) children under fourteen, regardless of social origin. Members of class 2 receive only half as much as members of class 1. Children receive larger rations of milk, butter, cereals, etc., than do adults.

The factories reduce cost by eliminating distribution costs. For example at the factory kitchen of the electrical factory, in 1930 food could be bought apparently below cost. A plate of soup and gruel cost 23 kopeks (11 cents). A *table d'hôte* lunch of cabbage soup, leg of chicken, plenty of cabbage, bread and tea cost 45 kopeks (22 cents). A glass of tea cost 3 kopeks (1½ cents). But the food was of very poor quality, and the dishes and utensils judged by western standards were filthy.

8. Queues, the Cost of Waiting for Rations. The cost-of-living figures do not include the cost of waiting. This is an intangible overhead which adds greatly to living costs.

Under a régime of free prices, when goods become scarce, prices rise but nobody waits in queues. Under a régime of price control, as in Russia when goods become scarce, prices do not rise. But everybody needs the goods, and therefore in distributing them they must be pro-rated. Price as a regulator of production and consumption is ignored in the Soviet Union. An American engineer who was supervising a night excavating job in Moscow told the writer that he came home at two o'clock one morning and found lines formed before the butcher shops that were to open at nine o'clock that morning. The time spent sitting on the curbstone from two until nine o'clock in the morning waiting to get a few scraps of meat is an overhead expense which must be added to the fixed low prices quoted for meat.

On almost every street in Moscow one sees hundreds of people waiting in line for sugar, tobacco, meat, candy, groceries, etc. Some two to three hundred people will be standing for hours on end in front of stores or merchandise booths. The pressure on the transportation system is so great that people will wait in line 24 hours for a ticket. For transportation for a two weeks' vacation people will stand in line at intervals for several days. An estimated minimum of one million man-hours per day and perhaps as high as five million man-hours per day are wasted. Here is a waste that could be applied to productive purposes and constitutes an added item of living cost. In view of the labor shortage this waste is serious indeed.

9. State Stores, Higher Prices, without Rationing. As a remedy for the shortages, new state stores were opened at which goods were sold freely but at high prices. The Soviet Union was thus following the precedent of the other countries of Europe shortly after the World War. For example, in Germany, Finland, and other countries, rents after the war were fixed at low levels by the state. As a result there was a shortage of space, and the state reserved the right to curtail the amount of space available to the old tenants. Congestion of housing resulted, and there was no building. Gradually the restrictions were lifted, at first on rents in new buildings that were built as an investment. As a result these buildings were completely and promptly rented as soon as constructed. Gradually other restrictions were released until the law of supply and demand relieved the congestion. The Soviet Union seems to be following the same historic trend with respect to commodities.

On May 12, 1931, a decree was signed by Premier Molotov and Joseph Stalin abolishing the state's limit on all consumers' goods except food. The objects of the change were manifold. First, it was intended to displace private trade by state trade and have the large profits accruing to private trade go to the state. Again, from the point of view of banking and of currency inflation, it was the intention to bring some of the rubles back from hoards into circulation by having the state sell goods at high prices. Again, high prices on consumers' goods were intended to stimulate the light industries which had fallen behind relative to the heavy industries. Finally, the release of consumers' goods would lessen the sacrifices that the public had to make on behalf of the Five-Year Plan.[71]

The opening of these state stores to sell goods at high prices without any limit was also ascribed in part to the sharp increase in nominal wages. Piece rates and bonuses had increased the buying power of the workers, which in turn created an increased demand for merchandise. The new state stores were intended to supply this demand. For the average workers who did not receive bonuses or extra compensation, there were "closed distribution centers" at the factories, which sold merchandise against ration cards and at fixed low prices.[72]

10. PRIVATE TRADE FREED, RATIONING ABANDONED, RISING PRICES AND WAGES. Shortly after the issuing of the decree lifting the restrictions on private trade by peasants, in the summer of 1932, described in the chapter on "Agriculture," farmers flocked into the cities and offered food for sale. The industrial workers came in large numbers to buy. Prices were only slightly higher than in the stores, still selling the fixed rations.

In some cases, despite the lifting of the restrictions, the goods were not available. For example, owing to the diversion of sugar to the Russian troops in the Far East, and the need for using sugar in the manufacture of industrial alcohol for war materials, a great shortage of sugar resulted. Therefore, although candy was removed from the rationed list, it was practically unobtainable.[73]

In line with the general policy of extending private trade, the government decreed on July 24, 1932, that the artisans' co-operative associations would be free to buy raw materials independently of the state supply organizations and to sell the resulting finished goods at a profit. It was intended that the free price and the resulting profit would stimulate the production of consumers' goods. As a result of free private trade and rising prices, wages fell out of line with the price level. The question of increasing the salary of members of the Communist Party in the government service 200 per cent was then settled, raising the maximum from 300 rubles to 900 rubles per month. This is in line with the growing trend of paying industrial salaries in proportion to ability and skill. The low salaries made it necessary for government officials to engage in outside remunerative activities, which diminished their effectiveness. Furthermore, workers began to demand increases of wages, which would involve increasing government expenditures, new paper issues, and further depreciation in the purchasing power of the ruble.

11. INTERNATIONAL COMPARISONS. Because rations are limited and prices vary for the different social classes, it is difficult to compare the cost of living in Russia with that of other countries. An estimate based on the cost of allotted

rations would be incorrect because the consumer must also buy in the free market for his actual needs. But even using the minimum prices applying to the fixed rations, the cost of living in Russia in June 1927 was 221 per cent of the pre-war cost (1914 = 100), according to Chamberlin,[74] as compared with 173 per cent for the United States, 168 per cent for the United Kingdom, and 148 per cent for Germany. But in these countries there was a free market, an abundant supply, and a uniform price for all.

Because the ruble does not move freely in international exchange, its purchasing power in international markets cannot be compared with other currencies, whether on a gold basis or on a fluctuating basis, which have a daily free public quotation at which buying and selling can be done both within and without that particular country. The ruble had (1930) a purchasing power in the "black bourses," where smuggled rubles were sold, as in Berlin and Constantinople, of between 8 to 12 to the dollar or about 12 to 8 cents thus making invalid all comparisons based on the parity of the ruble, about 50 cents.

The Bureau of Research on Russian Economic Conditions, University of Birmingham, after a scholarly study concludes that—

> However great the economic privileges enjoyed in the U.S.S.R. by industrial workers as compared to other classes of the population, their standard of living is still substantially lower than that of workers in Western Europe and America.
>
> Thus, despite the privileged position occupied by workers in the U.S.S.R., and despite the fact that workers in capitalist countries are not supposed to command a similar position, the standard of material well-being attained by the former does not compare favorably with that enjoyed by the latter.[74a]

G. Real Wages

Though money wages have risen greatly above the pre-war level, yet in Russia it is difficult to figure real wages because there is no free market for consumers' goods. It would be necessary to figure what percentage of the consumer's needs is allotted to him under the rationing plan at a low price, and then to average this amount with the additional quantity that must be purchased in the free market at a considerably higher price before obtaining an average cost of the amount of goods necessary to maintain the pre-war standard of living.

Furthermore, the determination of real wages is more difficult in Soviet Russia than in countries where trade is free. Even though two workers may have identical wages, the purchasing power of those wages will depend upon many factors peculiar and unique to Russia. One laborer may work in a factory which has a well-supplied co-operative store, or in a town which is in an agricultural area, and therefore has adequate food at reasonable prices. Similarly, the facilities of restaurants, adequate housing, etc. make the purchasing power of the ruble vary greatly. Therefore, the statistics on real wages given below are offered with reserve.[75]

No such exact figures are available for real wages as for nominal wages. However, questions directed to the authorities in the Commissariat of Labor and in the labor sections of the various trusts and trade unions do reveal approximate figures. According to the State Planning Commission, real wages reached the pre-war level, on the basis of the pre-war standard-of-living index, in the year 1926–27. However, according to an American observer who had been living in Russia for five years, real wages in 1930 had declined about 25 per cent from their 1926–27 peak level, for during the earlier period the New Economic Policy was in effect and cheap consumers' goods were available unrationed, while at present the ration of food and clothing is less than the pre-war standard, and money wages are inadequate to buy the full amount needed to maintain pre-war standards of living. The open market prices are generally high and beyond the reach of the average laborer.

Several actual estimates as to real wages were made to a group of visiting economists in 1930. Mr. Ivanov, Vice-Commissar of Labor, estimated that real wages are now 139 per cent of the pre-war level, and that welfare and insurance features are equivalent to an additional 28 per cent, making a total of 167 per cent of the pre-war level. Mr. Amazov of the Railroad Workers' Union, estimated on the same basis that the real wages, including workers' compensation and other benefits, were equivalent to 162 per cent of the pre-war level.

The Labor Commissariat apparently accepts the calculation that real wages were 70 per cent higher in 1931 than before the war. It is likewise true that from the low point of chaos in 1921, wages rose until 1928, when the Five-Year Plan went into operation. The uncertain question is whether from 1928 to 1932 real wages rose in view of the great demands which the heavy industries made upon the national income, thereby curtailing both the quantity and the quality of goods available to the consumer, a phenomenon noticeable to those students of Russia who returned to the country annually after 1927. Professor Katzenellenbaum of the University of Moscow, author of the plan for the organization of the State Bank and a trained economist, in a discussion with the writer estimated that in general nominal wages were about four times as high as the pre-war wages, confirming the estimate of Mr. Ruhman, director of the Electrical Trust. With prices approximately twice the pre-war level, he thought that the real wage, or purchasing power of the nominal wage, was twice as high as before the war. These may be partisan estimates, and are difficult to check.

A critic of the Soviet régime makes the following comment on real wages: The pre-war level was a very low standard, in fact so low that labor was engaged in a continuous series of strikes against employers. The present employer is the state, and strikes are now out of the question. Real wages in Russia before the war were among the lowest in Europe, yet in the rest of Europe real wages are now above the pre-war level. As for the salaries of office workers, teachers, postal clerks, etc., even the pre-war level in Russia has not yet been attained.

1. Present and Pre-War Levels. a. Two Indexes, Discrepancies and Explanation. Because of the variations in the cost-of-living indexes indicated above, the several indexes of real wages do not tally closely. But in general it is known that after the war real wages fell to very low levels. At the lowest level, during the period of communism from 1918 to 1920, they were about one-third of the pre-war wages. The abandonment of communism and the introduction of the New Economic Policy raised productivity and real wages. By the fiscal year 1927 real wages exceeded the pre-war level. Two sets of estimates, by Soviet authorities, for workers in large-scale state industry are of interest. (See p. 207.)

These two lists show a discrepancy of more than 11 per cent for the fiscal years 1925, 1926, and 1927. This is a very large variation and it is therefore difficult for an outsider to draw reliable and accurate conclusions from these statistics.

The indexes for the fiscal years 1925 to 1929 are not strictly comparable because the basis was changed three times. In fact Zagorsky in his *Wages and Conditions of Labor in the U.S.S.R.* (prepared for the International Labor Office of the League of Nations) admits that this comparison of real wages based on cost-of-living indexes results in many difficulties due to the frequent changes in the composition of the index numbers and the method of compiling them. However, the Soviet statisticians generally say that by 1930 the real wages of the individual had risen to 1.33 times the pre-war level. According to Stalin, including social insurance and the socialized portion of the wage, real wages increased to 1.67 times the pre-war level.[76] Soviet statistics show but a very slight increase in real wages during 1931.[77]

b. Evidence of Decline in Real Wages. A keen analysis by the Bureau of

AVERAGE REAL MONTHLY WAGES OF WORKERS IN LARGE-SCALE STATE INDUSTRY [78]
(Based on pre-war rubles)

	A		B	
Fiscal Year	*Rubles*	*Index Numbers*	*Rubles*	*Index Numbers*
1913	30.49	100	25.00	100
1914	29.65	96.9	—	—
1915	28.67	93.6	—	—
1916	28.06	91.8	—	—
1917	22.38	73.4	—	—
1918	13.20	43.3	—	—
1919	10.64	34.9	—	—
1920	10.40	34.1	—	—
1921	10.15	33.3	—	—
1922	12.50	41.0	—	—
1923	15.88	49.2	—	—
1924	20.75	67.1	—	—
1925	25.18	82.6	23.38	93.5
1926	28.57	93.7	26.67	106.7
1927	32.14	105.4	29.70	119.1
1928	—	—	33.16	132.5
1929	—	—	33.36	133.4

Research on Russian Economic Conditions, University of Birmingham, leads the Bureau to the conclusion that real wages have declined in 1931:

It is to be regretted that in a time when shortage of supplies is felt all over Russia, the Soviet Government should be content to publish calculations on the level of wages in the chervonetz denomination alone and that it should disregard entirely the changes in the purchasing power of the ruble.

Socialists have always affirmed that the real wages and not the nominal wages are of consequence to the workers. Lenin and other prominent Russian communists have stressed this point repeatedly. Yet for the last two years, at the conferences of the Central Executive Committee, at the sessions of the Soviets, at the meetings of the Communist Party and even at the Congresses of the Trade Unions, no participant has ever referred to the subject of real wages, to the cost-of-living (budget) index, nor even to the index of wholesale prices.

These indices were used by L. Eventov, Member of the State Planning Commission (*Gosplan*) in the paper which he read at the Twenty-ninth Session of the International Statistical Institute held at Tokio in September, 1930. Having given the indices of nominal and real wages, Eventov points out that "so far, we have referred to individual wages paid to individual workers. But the worker in the U.S.S.R. enjoys a great and constantly increasing measure of collective remuneration, including a system of social insurance effected entirely at the expense of industrial undertakings. He also receives certain benefits by way of educational provisions and improvements in the general conditions of life which are likewise provided by industrial undertakings, etc. If we take into account this form of remuneration, which in industry amounts to 20 per cent of the money wage as against 8 to 9 per cent in pre-war times, the dynamics of real wages in the U.S.S.R. would display a still greater rise above the pre-war level." (L: Eventov, *Zarabotnaya plata v S.S.S.R. i v kapitalisticheskykh stranakh. Planovole Khozyaistvo,* 1930, IX, pp. 143–144.)

The indices were also reproduced by S. O. Zargorsky in his work on wages in the U.S.S.R., published by the International Labor Office in Geneva. (S. Zagorsky, *Les Salaries et la reglementation des conditions du travail dans l'U.R.S.S., Geneve,* 1930, p. 193.)

In the Control figures compiled annually by the *Gosplan* for the coming year, the figures on wages in chervonetz rubles agree with those given by this Bureau. The conversion of these wages into commodity rubles as given in the Control figures for 1925–26 to 1927–28, are also in agreement with our figures. But in the Control figures for 1928–29 we come across a sudden change—an upward leap in the indices of real wages for which no explanation is given in the text. . . .

It is obvious that in 1928 the State Planning Commission made some change in the method of calculating real wages, with the result that their level (as expressed in index figures) was given a "surplus increase" of 13 to 14 per cent. These exaggerated *Gosplan* indices were accepted and used by statisticians, and thus contributed to a misrepresentation of the situation. . . .

Among the various new economic factors introduced by the Soviet economic system, was the institution of compulsory capital accumulation, a peculiar characteristic of monopoly unknown in the competitive capitalist order. But the outcome of compulsory accumulation was that, from 1928 onwards, the expansion of wages was slowed down and then stopped altogether:

COURSE OF REAL WAGES

Fiscal Year	*1913 Rubles*	*Index*	*Adjusted Index* *
1913	24.3	100.0	100.0
1923	11.5	47.3	46.5
1924	16.8	69.1	67.9
1925	20.7	85.1	83.5
1926	23.5	96.7	94.7
1927	26.3	108.4	104.9
1928	27.0	111.1	106.6
1929	28.1	115.6	104.1
1930	27.8	114.4	100.8

* Real wages index after deductions on account of deterioration in quality of consumers' goods and virtually forced subscriptions to loans.

The real wage figure for 1930 was taken from *Planovoe Khozyaistvo.* (1930, VII–VIII. pp. 41–42).

In previous years the rates of growth of money wages and real wages were always available. The cost-of-living (budget) index is also no longer published in the Soviet Press. From Molotov's and Kuybyshev's speeches, no information can be gathered as to the movement of real wages, but both speakers express satisfaction at the 17 per cent increase of money wages in 1931. If, however, the index of prices increased in 1931 by 50 per cent (and the budget index increased even more) a 17 per cent increase of money wages means a decrease in real wages of more than 30 per cent. Some of the causes which determine the decrease in real wages are the rapid growth of industry, which attracts large masses of unskilled and poorly paid labor from the villages. The mere fact of the increase in the number of workers renders it difficult for them to retain their privileged position regarding the distribution of the national income. The level of wages tend to fall as economic considerations supplant revolutionary and political policies. . . . To stem the increase of money wages in the second half of 1931 the Supreme Economic Council issued a decree, November 29, 1931 forbidding wages to be increased when leading to a rise in the cost of production . . . under penalty of fines and in case of intentional transgression those guilty will be arraigned for a penal offence.[78a]

c. Variation in Wage Scale. The above figures for real wages in the large-scale industries by no means represent the whole actual situation. The fact is that real wages in 1929 varied very greatly among the several industries as compared with the pre-war level, ranging from 0.81 times to 2.01 times. The variations are related to the changes in demand for goods resulting from the revolution and from the Five-Year Plan. Since there is a great shortage in consumers' goods, such as food, clothing, and paper, wages in these industries showed the largest increase above the pre-war level. In 1913, wages in the consumers' goods industries was below the average and now they are greatly above it. In the field of producers' goods, the increase over pre-war wages was much less. Before the war the highest wages were paid in the iron and steel industry while in recent times the highest wages have been paid in the printing industry.[79]

d. Shortage of Consumers' Goods and Decline of Purchasing Power. Soviet statistics of real wages do not show the actual situation. Owing to the emphasis on the heavy industries, a shortage of consumers' goods, clothing, shoes, etc. developed in 1925. Owing to the inability of the Soviets to produce enough consumers' goods for the peasants, they refused to part with their grain and as a result bread became scarce in 1928 and in some towns was available only on presentation of a bread card. Other agricultural products, such as meat, butter, eggs, and other foods, became scarce in 1929, and these could also be obtained only on presentation of food tickets. Then rationing of bread became almost universal. In 1930 a shortage of candies and cigarettes developed, and any visitor to Moscow at that time could see at every turn scores of people waiting in long queues for hours at a time for a few pieces of candy. The small booths at which cigarettes were sold were also always decorated with long queues. For other goods also prices had gone up in the free markets and the goods were rationed in the controlled markets. This represented a genuine decline in real wages which is not shown in the statistics or in the theoretical cost-of-living budgets.

In the coal fields of the Donetz Basin unskilled workers were receiving 75 to 100 rubles a month, while food cost a minimum of 70 to 120 rubles a month, according to *Za Industrializatsiu*. At the prevailing open-market prices for bread, a worker receiving 150 rubles per month would have just enough to buy 3 pounds of bread per day. Taking the exchange value of the ruble on the "Black Bourse" as equivalent to about 3 cents, in August 1932, 2 rubles a pound would be equivalent to about 6 cents, which is approximately the price in New York City. Of course, such inflation as exists in Soviet Russia indicates that industrial expansion has been taking place at the expense of the workers' wages. Little wonder that 25,000 miners came and went within two months or that the daily output declined from 186,000 tons in March to 85,000 tons in August, 1932.[79a]

Tourists who visited Russia regularly year after year and were strongly sympathetic to the Soviet régime expressed their great regret at the disappearance of foodstuffs and consumers' goods, at the high prices and the decline in quality, since private trade was restricted. It might be much simpler and more candid if the Soviets did not try to make the statistics show an improvement in real wages for the years 1925 to 1929, when as a matter of fact real wages probably declined for the reasons stated. A frank admission that the Soviet Union is attempting a huge and unique task in industrializing the country and that the people must make sacrifices, perhaps only temporarily to pay for this policy, would seem to be preferable.

H. Wage Comparisons with Other Countries

1. International Comparisons, Present and Pre-War. Soviet spokesmen maintain that real wages in the Soviet Union in the spring of 1928 were higher than in Prague, Vienna, Rome, or Warsaw. They use the figures of the International Labor Office as of the spring of 1928 in comparison with the pre-war figures. (See p. 211.)

According to this table real wages in Russia rose to 1.6 times the 1905–09 level, in contrast to British real wages, which stayed the same, French real wages which showed a decline, and German real wages which showed a very modest rise. Furthermore, in the spring of 1928, real wages in Russia were higher than those in several European capitals.

REAL WAGES IN EUROPE [80]

	Pre-War 1905–1909	*Spring 1928*
England	100	100
Germany	63	71
France	65	56
Russia	34	52
Prague	—	47
Vienna	—	45
Rome	—	43
Warsaw	—	40

On the basis of compilations by the *International Labor Review*,[81] which give the hourly wages for several cities expressed in the several local currencies, the Soviet spokesmen conclude that "the money wage of all Soviet workers, including the provincial backward districts, is greater than even the average wage of the skilled workers in the largest cities of Austria, Poland, Italy, and Yugoslavia, and greater than the wages of the unskilled workers in these four countries, as well as Spain." Moreover, the average wage in the large cities of the Soviet Union is about 25 per cent greater than the average for the entire country.

STANDARD HOURLY WAGES OF ADULT MALE BUILDING WORKERS IN JULY 1930 [82]

Country and City	*Bricklayers and Masons* *Cents*	*Building Laborers* *Cents*
Sweden, Stockholm	85.0	53.3
Sweden, Malmo	51.5	38.1
Great Britain, London	41.0	29.0
Germany, Berlin	36.7	30.2
Austria, Vienna	23.6	18.2
Spain, Barcelona	29.0	19.3
Italy, Turin	20.0	15.0
Poland, Warsaw	21.4	13.6
Yugoslavia, Belgrade	15.2	11.3
Soviet Union, Moscow *	31.4 †	
Soviet Union, Leningrad	32.4 †	
Soviet Union, average hourly wage of all workers in large-scale industry (skilled and unskilled), exclusive of any payments in kind (social insurance, etc.) ‡	24.5	

* Statistical Survey (in Russian) April, 1930; hourly wage computed from daily average wage in January, 1930, on the basis of an average work-day of seven hours.

† Masons only.

‡ Figures for U.S.S.R. based on computation given in text.

In the Soviet Union payments to the social-insurance fund are made by the enterprise itself whereas in European countries part of the fund is paid by the workers out of their wages.[83]

2. Soviet Errors in Statistics. This comparison of Soviet wages, real or nominal, with those of other countries and with pre-war wages is misleading because the figures are not really comparable. The *International Labor Review* gives the wages in the currencies of the countries, and the Soviet statisticians converted the several currencies, including the Russian, into dollars at par. But the ruble is neither quoted nor accepted at par anywhere in the whole world except in the Soviet Union. The Soviet officials themselves admitted the depreciation of the ruble in settling a rate of exchange with the Japanese on a fishing concession. In the markets of Constantinople and Berlin the ruble was quoted at from eight to twelve cents, in the summer of 1930. If Soviet wages are converted into dollars on such a basis then it would be obvious that Soviet wages are far below the pre-war wages in Russia and below the wages prevailing today in other European countries. Because the Soviet ruble is not freely quoted in the international markets, whereas the currencies of the other countries are, the comparisons are invalid and the statistics inaccurate. Again, the buying power of the ruble is only a fraction of its par value. The currency has been inflated but wages have not risen proportionately. For this reason sufficient consumers' goods are not available and they must be rationed. Also money alone does not constitute purchasing power but it requires in addition a legal right to buy freely, which is restricted to certain classes. Again, the social wages included in the Soviet figures are also supplied in the other countries compared above, such as insurance of all kinds, working tools, etc. On the other hand, the other countries do not deduct from workers' wages forced loans, contributions, and other items to which practically all workers in the Soviet Union are subjected.

Comparison of pre-war and present costs of living and real wages is the source of much difference of opinion among the observers of the Soviet Union. The opinions are based not so much on facts as on the sympathies of the observer. However, after checking all the available statistics in this field one can only conclude that there are not enough data at present to prove the Soviet contention. Such statistics as those above cannot deceive the impartial economist. Nor can the Soviets assert that the standard of living for the workingman is higher in the Soviet Union than in Vienna, Barcelona, Turin, and Warsaw, because the observing traveler can see with his own eyes that the people in these cities are better dressed and enjoy a greater variety of food and can have it in unrationed amounts. The appearance of the shops and stores and their inventories show how inaccurate are the Soviet statistics on real wages. The writer happened to be in Vienna and Barcelona in 1929 and in Warsaw and Berlin in 1930 and could see from even superficial observation that in food, housing, and clothing the living standards of the people were higher than those of the workingmen of Moscow and Leningrad, whom he saw in the summer of 1930. Besides, as stated above, the much lower productivity of the Russian in itself implies lower real wages, just as the American worker's highest productivity makes possible highest real wages. The introduction of the element of currency hides this simple fact and complicates the statistics. Nor can these statistics deceive those Russians who were adults before the war and who know what the standard of living of the workingman was then and is now.

The profound relationship of productivity of the worker to his wages is indicated in Memorandum No. 6, (July 1932, pages 13, 14) *Wages of Industrial Workers in the U.S.S.R.*, prepared by the Bureau of Research on Russian Economic Conditions of the University of Birmingham:

> In capitalist countries growth of wages is primarily brought about by increase in labor productivity, irrespective of whether such increase is due to improvement in machinery and equipment, to better organization, or to the additional skill and energy of the workers. So close indeed is interdependence between wages and productivity that the level of wages is even regarded by some as reflecting the productivity of labor.
>
> In his work on the movement of wages in 1913–1922,[83a] Strumilin pointed out that the problem of rising wages was not only a problem of distribution but also of production, and that a solution could not be found by approaching it from the angle of social service based exclusively on principles of equality and justice, but that the wages policy should aim at attaining maximum efficiency and productivity.
>
> For all the efforts of the Communist Party and of the economic departments of the Soviet Government, i. e., the Commissariat of Labor and the Trade Unions, to regulate arbitrarily the level and distribution of wages, they proved in the end powerless to alter the mutual dependence of economic forces which are no less operative in the U.S.S.R. than in western Europe, America and the colonial countries. The War, the October Revolution, communist theory and the dictatorship of the Proletariat affected wages not so much directly as indirectly through the changes wrought in industrial conditions. What decisively influenced wages was the effect of their close, almost functional dependence on the productivity of labor. Any injury caused to large-scale industry and its productive power was immediately reflected in the level and distribution of wages. On the whole, the dependence of wage levels on the productivity of labor during the years of Revolution and of the Dictatorship of the Proletariat proved to be

one of those stable social-economic phenomena on which the communist ideology, the revolutionary storm and the non-economic pressure from the authorities, had but a limited and passing effect.

It is true that workers have shorter hours, enjoy vacations with pay, and have the benefit and security of social insurance. Yet, taking these into account it is still unfortunate that the Soviets stultify themselves by their claims. The Soviet workingman has advanced not in material comforts but in psychological values. He feels himself an owner and co-operator in industry. He hopes that eventually the plan of industrializing the country will give him and his fellow workers greater comforts. But that he does not have these comforts today is beyond question. The workingman of today is making great sacrifices. He is discounting present good for future happiness. It would seem to the objective outsider that the Soviet Union would be wiser to admit that real wages in Moscow are lower than in the European cities mentioned and to justify it on the ground that present privations will mean a higher standard of living in the future, rather than to pretend that the government can accomplish both mass industrialization of the country and the maintenance of a high standard of living for the workers at the same time.

I. Factory Discipline

After the revolution, when the workers felt emancipated, labor discipline broke down. The results were exceedingly unfavorable to industry. Consequently the authorities, at first with gentle recommendations and later with drastic regulations, set about correcting the abuses, but they are still very widespread.

1. Breaches of Discipline. The discipline of the workers is often exceedingly lax. They leave the job without permission. They get drunk during working hours and dawdle or even sleep on the job. Either through incompetence or indifference they break or neglect machinery. Insubordination to the technical or managerial staff has been common. These obvious and universal breaches of discipline are exposed in the numerous satirical cartoons and the appealing mottoes on the factory walls.

The usual infractions of discipline found in capitalist countries, such as shamming illness, absenteeism, and soldiering, are also present in Russia, but in addition the Soviet Union has developed some serious breaches of discipline which are unique, arising from the feeling of the workers that they own the plants. For example, workingmen will argue with engineers about technical instructions, and dispute with and even assault their superiors, and will malinger and forge illness certificates to collect social insurance. A few typical examples are quoted from the official reports and the comments of the Committees of Peasants' and Workers' Inspection revealed in the government press. According to Mr. Tolstopiatov, formerly Vice-Commissar for Labor, lax discipline assumes various forms, such as drunkenness, lateness, absence, theft, and deliberate lowering of production, as well as sleeping during working hours and assaulting the engineering or administrative staff.[84] Again, in a report to the Trade Union Congress in December 1928, M. Tomsky, chairman of the General Council of Trade Unions, added to these instances the attempt by workers to destroy tools or plants so as to stop production and thus receive pay without working; disobedience, insult, injury, and even attempted murder of their superiors; and not least, the increasing number of fires and explosions which occur either through the negligence of the workers or sometimes through their criminal intent.

At the Putilov Iron Works in Leningrad 120,000 man-days were lost through unjustified absenteeism in one month, June 1928. A large number of workers who were in good health were reported as sick.[85]

Again at the Stalingrad Tractor Plant, according to reports, discipline was very poor. Production foremen did not know how many of their workers were on the job on any given day. Sometimes the timekeeper's rolls showed more workingmen present than were actually in the factory so that "ghosts were mysteriously operating in the plant."[86] At the Nizhni Novgorod Automobile Plant, time lost for smoking and rest was very great. "Whenever one visits the construction, one finds the machines standing idle and the attendants scattered around, smoking and lounging, despite the fact that signs are posted everywhere, 'Dismissal for Smoking'."[87] At the Red Sormovo machine-building plant the workmen spent only 40 per cent of their time in actual production. Generally several thousand workmen waited at the gates to leave before the closing whistle blew. An investigating committee found that not only the workmen but even the engineers were found asleep.[88] At the new textile mill, Melange-Kombinat, more than 20 per cent of the goods were spoiled by oil stains because, when the looms were repaired, machinists would handle the material with dirty hands and put their tools on clean, newly woven cloth. The women weavers used the freshly made woven goods as table cloths at lunch time. The foremen feared to penalize the workmen for spoiling the goods because then they would smuggle the soiled goods to another department in order to shift the responsibility. Absenteeism rose from month to month.[89]

The discipline on the railroads is likewise very poor. The chief inspector of the People's Commissariat for Transport in an official report told of lax discipline on the Samara-Zlatoust Railroad, as a result of which in one month 38 locomotives froze and 34 trains were stranded. The breakdown of locomotives during operation increased from 14 in October 1929 to 122 in December. At the Amba Station on this railroad fifteen locomotive engineers were successively assigned to take a train out on a run. Of these twelve were found intoxicated and three did not report. Sixteen engineers had to be called to find one to start the train.

2. Causes of Poor Discipline. Because a workman cannot be as readily discharged as in western countries, penalizing the undisciplined is difficult, and much of the disciplinary value of discharge as a last resort is lost. Again, the Russian worker, still green from the farm, has not yet developed the characteristics of an industrial worker. The doctrine that the disinherited will inherit the earth has not been helpful to labor discipline. Since the proletariat is supreme under the Bolshevik doctrine, the disciplining of the new élite was difficult.

3. Remedies for Lax Discipline. The remedies tried for lax discipline have included appeals to the workers, centralization of authority, and a series of penalties ranging from deductions from wages to imprisonment at forced labor.

a. Appeals to the Workers. At the Stalingrad Tractor Plant in 1930 there were bulletin boards bearing appeals to the workers "to liquidate the disorderliness and irresponsibility" and to abolish dirt in the foundry because it increased the number of spoiled castings. Shock brigades at Stalingrad issued challenges to the workers at the Red Putilovetz Tractor Plant to reduce the percentage of damaged goods.[90] By an order of the Central Executive Committee of the Communist Party, the management "must constantly remind the workers that all measures to improve discipline . . . are intended to improve the position of the working class and to strengthen the dictatorship of the proletariat."[91]

b. Centralization of Authority. The separation of responsibility and authority resulted in lax discipline and regulations were accordingly issued to centralize authority. The Supreme Economic Council promulgated regulations to define the powers and rights of the managing staff in state enterprises.[92] These regulations "clearly re-established the principle of personal and authoritative management rather than the 'collegiate' methods instituted at the beginning of the Communist revolution. The manager is the sole head of the undertaking. His permission is required for every operation. He may on his own responsibility impose disciplinary punishment on the workers, salaried employees and the technical staff."

The managers must also dismiss any officials who are too lenient toward workers guilty of a breach of factory discipline. A more severe order was issued concerning factory discipline by the Central Committee of the Communist Party. According to this order the manager of an enterprise alone will be responsible for the execution of the plan of production and of the budget. He alone can give orders with regard to production. Officials, employees, and workers must obey the manager's orders regardless of the position they occupy in the Communist Party or in the trade unions. The decision of the director with reference to hiring and firing workers cannot be changed "merely because the trade union workers' council does not agree." These bodies merely can refer their differences of opinion to the higher authorities.

In June 1931, a decree of the Central Executive Committee was issued holding every government employee responsible for property used in his work, including the clothing worn and the machines used. Under this decree any governmental body may order a worker from one job to another and, if the worker refuses to go, he will be charged with violating the labor code.[93]

c. Deductions from Wages. Wage penalties, originally rather mild, increased in severity. On August 27, 1929, the Commissar for Labor issued regulations on penalties for lax discipline. The management was given the right to reprimand the worker and, within the limits of the collective agreement, could deduct the cost of material damaged by him. Deductions from wages for work of inferior quality were also ordered. The management could refuse to admit an intoxicated worker and be relieved of paying wages during absence for such cause. If workers were voluntarily idle or unjustifiably absent, the management could deduct pay for the time lost. These penalties seem mild in comparison with those that came later.[94]

d. Dismissal. According to the regulations of July 19, 1927, a worker could be reprimanded and dismissed for a number of offenses such as absence or departure without leave; refusal to do the work for which he was hired or to work overtime; idling and preventing others from working; breaches of regulations concerning safety and involving risks of accident; loss of tools or theft of tools; excessive use of material and drunkenness or gambling. A mere recital of this list of offenses indicates the problems of discipline that had to be met. A worker might also be dismissed if he forged or gave away a pass, an order for work, or a medical certificate, forged signatures in the employment books, feigned illness, exaggerated his illness, inflicted wounds upon himself so as to become incapable of working, or threatened or insulted his superiors. If he assaulted them, he might be turned over to the courts.[95]

e. Imprisonment or Forced Labor. As the milder penalties did not produce adequate results, more severe penalties were imposed. According to a decree of the Central Executive Committee and the Council of People's Commissars of November 23, 1929,[96] the systematic or mass production of inferior goods and the failure to observe standards was made a matter of criminal responsibility, and as a penalty it was decreed that workers guilty of the first of these offenses should be deprived of liberty for a maximum period of five years, and of the second for a maximum of two years, or be set to forced labor for a maximum period of one year. Furthermore, the Supreme Court issued an order to the local judicial officials in the Soviet Union that after May 22, 1931, carelessness would "be regarded as a crime and would carry the penalty of imprisonment or exile." The local factory courts had acquitted such offenders on the plea of "accident," but under the new court ruling proof of intention to damage machinery or set a fire would not be necessary. Carelessness alone would be a crime and the offenders would be tried under criminal statutes.[97]

J. High Labor Turnover

1. Facts. In several factories visited, the directors and foremen stated that the workmen might and did leave the job freely and seek other work. Involuntary unemployment has ceased, but the rapid shifting from job to job has made labor inefficient. At one time in the summer of 1930 complaint was made that the labor turnover rose as high as 200 per cent annually. The government statisticians estimated that in 1930 the total turnover for the country was as high as 40 per cent.

The labor turnover varied with the nature of the work. It was less on municipal works, somewhat higher in industrial enterprises, and exceedingly high on new construction work in isolated regions. In the Moscow municipal undertakings the labor turnover in the fiscal year 1930 was as follows:

Quarter	*Labor Turnover Per cent per annum*
1	36.5
2	41.9
3	42.3
4	47.9

In his address before the Conference of Industrial Executives on June 23, 1931, Joseph Stalin said: "The turnover in a number of plants is not disappearing but is increasing. You will find very few enterprises where the labor turnover has not been 30 to 40 per cent during the half or even quarter of the year," or at an annual rate of from 60 to 80 per cent, or even 120 to 160 per cent.[98]

The turnover was particularly extensive in the heavy industries. For example, in the Red Putilovetz works in 1929 it exceeded 30 per cent and in 1931 it was running at the rate of 46 per cent. In the same periods it rose from 28 to 40 per cent in the Leningrad Metal-Working Plant. In the Ural District the labor turnover in the coal mines was 137 per cent per annum and in the metallurgical industry 176 per cent per annum. In the iron and steel industry in one quarter of 1931 it reached 50 per cent or at the rate of 200 per cent per annum. In the textile industry it was so high as to threaten the production program, and in the coal industry the turnover was even higher.[99]

At the hydro-electric development on the Dnieper, three thousand men left suddenly one night without notice.[100]

The "industrial giants" during construction suffered from a labor turnover more than the old established industries in the big cities. In the construction projects it ranged in 1930 from about 300 per cent per annum up to almost 1700 per cent, as shown in the following table:

LABOR TURNOVER IN CONSTRUCTION PROJECTS[101]

Construction Project	*Period*	*Hired*	*Quit*	*Per cent*	*Annual Rate Per cent*
Magnitostroy	April 1 to August 1	25,538	17,153	67	201
	August 1 to August 31	4,526	3,869	86	1032
	September 1 to September 25	4,700	1,106	23	330
Coke ovens at Magnetic Mountain	August 1 to August 31	845	210	25	300

LABOR TURNOVER IN CONSTRUCTION PROJECTS—*Continued*

Construction Project	*Period*	*Hired*	*Quit*	*Per cent*	*Annual Rate Per cent*
Siberian agricultural-combine plant	August 1 to September 20	1,400	650	46	322
Nizhni Novgorod Transstroy (Transportation construction trust)	August 1 to August 31	3,780	2,907	77	924
	September 1 to September 25	1,880	1,250	67	965
Cheliabinsk tractor plant	September 1 to September 20	7,857	6,395	82	1470
Bobrik chemical and fertilizer plant	September 1 to September 20	7,863	7,342	94	1690

High turnover continued in 1932. In the iron and steel section of Southern Russia 571,000 men were hired and 583,000 men quit in the first six months of 1932. In the coal industry, 9000 men quit in July and 30,000 men in the first half of 1932. As a result, the output in July per miner was 36.2 tons against 43.7 in July 1931.[101a]

In April 1931, at the Thirteenth Building Trust, which erected the Nizhni Novgorod Automobile Plant, 2486 men were hired and 1902 quit. The turnover in that month was thus 76 per cent or at the annual rate of 912 per cent.

2. CAUSES OF HIGH LABOR TURNOVER. The migration from place to place of workingmen, both individually and in groups, may be ascribed chiefly to the variations in working conditions and in the rates of wages, and to the availability and price of food.

a. Differences in the Standards of Living. For example in the Donetz Basin, the inefficient distribution of food supplies was reported as the cause of the high labor turnover. With an abundant crop of vegetables in the Ukraine, there was a great shortage in the Donetz Basin, where even rotten cabbage was sold and tomatoes cost about fifty cents a pound. The difficulty was in the distribution. While the Donetz Basin received less than 50 per cent of the amount of food called for by the Plan, other districts received more than 600 per cent of their requirements.[102]

Poor housing accommodations are another cause. At Magnitostroy the number of workers and members of their families exceeded 25,000 with only

2022 rooms available, and of these about 1100 were merely plain rooms in barracks. The approximate allotment was four square yards per man, a space, say of three feet by twelve feet.[103]

At the Nizhni Novgorod construction the high turnover was ascribed not only to poor living quarters but also to inadequate distribution of food and of consumers' goods.[104] In the Ural District the high turnover was ascribed to the same causes, lack of facilities for taking care of the newly hired workers, poor housing, and lack of necessities of life. The co-operative stores were inefficient and the workers had to wait days and weeks for goods to be provided by the store.[105] In the Urals the lack of schools and educational facilities was given as a factor in the migration of the workers.

b. Wage Differences. In the Urals, labor migrated also because of the difference in the pay offered for the same work by the several enterprises. Stalin pointed out this factor in his address to the Conference of Industrial Managers on June 23, 1931:

> Wherein lies the cause of this labor turnover? In the incorrect organization of wages, in an incorrect wage-scale system, in a "leftist" equalization of wages. In a number of enterprises our wage scales are so arranged that the difference between skilled and unskilled labor, between hard and easy labor, has practically disappeared. The result of equalizing wages is that the unskilled worker shows no interest in becoming skilled, and is thus deprived of prospects of promotion. Hence, he considers himself merely a visitor at the factory, who is working just long enough to "save up" a little and then go to some other place "in search of luck." This equalization of wages leads the skilled worker to travel from enterprise to enterprise in order to find finally a place where skilled labor is properly valued. Hence the "universal" shifting from enterprise to enterprise, the high turnover of labor.[106]

Apparently not merely the difference in wage scales of various plants but also the lack of a reasonably uniform scale of wages for the same degree of skill in the various plants makes workers migrate.

The competition for labor and the poor selection of men are also factors. Agents hiring workers often promise inducements that cannot be realized. Again, migrating from job to job enables the worker to accumulate some clothes. For example, at the Magnitostroy many new workers came for jobs, received new clothes and boots, and then disappeared.[107]

The numerous investigating commissions studying the problem of labor turnover reported that division of authority made it difficult to attack the problem. It was regarded by the factory managers as a problem of the trade unions, but the trade unions asserted that it was a problem for the managers of each individual factory.[108]

3. Remedy for High Labor Turnover. The problem of labor discipline has been worrying the Soviet leaders. On March 6, 1929, at the request of the Supreme Economic Council, an order was issued to tighten discipline. On July 2, 1929, another more stringent decree was issued. In August 1930, a series of mild measures was proposed to strengthen discipline. Wages were to be made more uniform to prevent workers from leaving in search of higher wages. Again, staying at one job was to be rewarded. Living conditions were to be improved, and commodity prices were to be kept low. To check high labor turnover, the stimulus of socialist competition was to be used, and prizes given for men, shops, and industries with the best record. By December 1930 the migrating worker was subject to loss of civil rights and to prosecution. By June 1932 luring workmen away by plant managers was regarded as criminal.

a. Differences in Wage Scales. To check the shifting of labor, it was decided to equalize the wage scales for the same degree of skill, to impose a penalty on the roving worker, and to give an inducement for workers to "stay put." Stalin attacked the problem of shifting labor:

> To secure workers is not the whole problem. In order to provide our enterprises with labor power it is necessary to attach the workers to the enterprises and to create a more or less permanent staff for each enterprise. It is hardly necessary to prove that without a permanent staff of workers who have to some extent mastered the technique of production and have become accustomed to the new machines it is impossible to make progress.
>
> In order to do away with this evil [high turnover] it is necessary to abolish equality of wages and the old wage scales. In order to do away with this evil it is necessary to organize a system of wage scales which would take into account the difference between skilled labor and unskilled labor, between hard labor and easy labor. We cannot tolerate a situation where the skilled metal worker should receive the same wages as the floor sweeper. We cannot tolerate a situation where a locomotive engineer should get only the same wages as a copyist. Marx and Lenin say that the difference between skilled labor and unskilled labor will exist even under socialism, even after the destruction of classes, that only under communism must this difference disappear, hence that wages even under socialism must be paid according to work performed and not according to need. But our "equalizers" among the industrial directors and trade unionists do not agree with this and assume that this difference has already disappeared under our Soviet system. Who is right, Marx and Lenin or the "equalizers"? We must suppose that in this Marx and Lenin are right. But this means then that the people who are building up the wage system on the "principle" of equalization without taking into account the difference between skilled and unskilled labor are breaking with Marxism, are breaking with Leninism. . . .
>
> To attach them [workers] to an enterprise, to a department, means to stabilize the entire staff of workers. It also means to strike at the root of the labor turnover.

> But how can they be attached to the enterprises? This can be done only by promoting them, by increasing their wages, by establishing wage scales which would properly compensate the skill of the worker. And what does it mean to promote these workers and to raise their wage level? It means, in addition to everything else, opening up prospects of promotion to the unskilled workers and the creation of an incentive for advancing into the ranks of skilled labor. . . . But in order to create skilled workers it is necessary to provide incentives and opportunities for the untrained workers to move upward.[109]

b. Rewards for Staying at Jobs. To accomplish this result bonuses and premiums were offered to workers for continuous employment at the same plant. According to a decree of the Central Executive Committee and the Council of People's Commissars: "All workers employed directly in the mining, metal, chemical, textile, and building-materials industries, in railroad, water, and automobile transportation, and on large construction projects, and who shall have worked in the same enterprise for two successive years after November 1, 1930, will be allowed an additional three days' vacation a year or its equivalent in wages." [110]

Other measures were promotion to higher positions in the trades and the granting of premiums in the shape of better homes, leave of absences, better supply of rationed goods, educational facilities for the children, etc. In some cases workingmen voluntarily pledged themselves to stay at the same factory until the end of the Five-Year Plan. The making of such pledges was to be encouraged by the management but force was not to be used.

c. Penalties for Roving. In addition to bonuses for staying, workers were also subjected to a penalty for roving. Slackers and floaters were deprived of the right to work for a period of six months.[111] According to a decree of the Central Executive Committee and the Council of People's Commissars: "Persons who maliciously interfere with production and who leave their work in a socialized enterprise without good cause will not be assigned to work in industry or transportation for a period of six months from the date of application for work at a labor office." [112]

d. Severer Restrictions. Eventually more rigid measures were introduced. A decree of the Central Executive Committee was issued [113] on December 15, 1930, prohibiting the switching of jobs without consent of the authorities. Wages were to be made uniform throughout the country for the same class of work. Workers who deserted their jobs were not to obtain employment for a period of six months, and unemployed workers who refused jobs offered were to be stricken from the privileged list for a specified period, or even expelled from the union, with loss of valuable civil rights and privileges for themselves and their families. Such workers would be deprived of ration tickets for food and clothing. Technical men who quit their jobs might be prosecuted. Again, the Commissar of Labor, jointly with the trade unions, was to have the right to transfer workers without their consent to industries requiring them, such as coal mines. Workers who refused to comply with such orders were not to be re-employed through the official labor exchanges.

e. *Injunctions on Managers.* Furthermore, not only are workers penalized for roving, but plant managers are prohibited from inducing employees to leave one plant for another. According to a decree of June 8, 1932, such action is regarded as criminal. Workers, particularly engineers and other professional workers, had been lured to new jobs by promises of higher wages, better living conditions, etc. Under the new decree, such switching of jobs was subject to the approval of both the new and the old employer.

K. Union Agreements and Strikes

The trade union is open to all workers. The unions are controlled by the Communist Party, and have a membership of more than 11 million. There are 23 separate trade unions united in the All-Union Central Council of Trade Unions, which is made up of representatives of the several trade-union committees. The central committee of each union contributes about ten per cent of its income to the Central Council and applies the remainder to educational and social work among its members. The members contribute two per cent of their monthly salaries.

Representatives of the union and of the management of an industry draft annually a collective agreement fixing the scale of wages, living conditions, and working standards. Collective agreements generally cover the entire industry. A trust covering the entire country will have a single agreement with all its employees. The Soviet government itself enters into agreements with its employees, as for instance in the railroad administration and the post office. The approval of the trade union is required for the appointment of a new manager by the trust.

Labor agreements run for one year. Differences between the workers and the management are arbitrated by the representatives of their respective groups. In case of disagreement appeal is made to a higher committee and, if no decision is then reached, the matter goes ultimately to the Commissar of Labor for final settlement. The workers have the right to strike, but strikes are rare because of loyalty to the Communist Party. Disloyalty would be dangerous. Strikes are discouraged by the state, and efforts made to secure peaceful settlement.

The nationalization of the trade unions has not been an unmitigated benefit to the workers. In capitalist countries trade unions are independent bodies, but in Soviet Russia they are allied with the Communist Party and with the Soviet government, and therefore they generally favor the state rather than the workers. Tomsky fought for the principle that the trade union should be free to retain its bargaining powers. He lost the fight and his office, too.

The trade unions were deprived of their powers with regard to labor legislation by the Circular of June 3, 1922, issued by the Commissariat for Labor and the General Council of Trade Unions, whereby trade unions shall not have the right to issue orders concerning the application of the labor code. However, every decree or government order which concerns labor may be issued only with the approval of the Central Council of Trade Unions. The trade unions do take part in the drafting of all labor legislation and supervise its application. The trade unions also look after factory inspection.[114]

L. The Exploitation of Labor

The theory of the Soviets was that, if the incentive to private profit could be removed, the demands of labor would be met and the exploitation of labor would cease. Further, a more even distribution of wealth would remove the tendency of the workman to resort to sabotage, and "ca' canny." The pressure of the desire for profits under a capitalist scheme was regarded as the chief incentive by managers to curtail wages and to reduce expenses. But in Soviet Russia, though private ownership has been eliminated, labor is exploited, nevertheless.

1. Piece Work and the Speeding Up of Production. As in the capitalist countries, piece work is used to speed up production. Here there is a compromise between the theoretical ideal of equal wages for all and practical considerations of higher wages for more output. Using the incentive of the Five-Year Plan and the need to hasten the industrial development of the country, the state exploits the individual workman. Instead of being masters of industry, as was promised at the beginning of the revolution, the workers in Soviet Russia, like the workers in capitalist countries, sell their labor, though in the one case the sale is to an individual employer and in the other case to the state.

The theory of equality of wages was abandoned early. The efficient worker was being penalized. The incompetent worker was being subsidized. Under the Soviet régime today the range of wages between the lowest and the highest is a very wide one. In fact as shown above some workers earn six or more times the wages of the lowest group. Labor is compelled to conform to the system of the conveyor belt which the Soviets formerly condemned as degrading man to the level of the machine. The Soviet has adopted Ford methods and in some respects has gone further. Output is increased by overtime payment, and managers will not hesitate to cut wages in order to show profits for their trust.

2. Abandoning Labor Standards. Under the guise of working for an ideal, the worker is sweated. Hours of labor are prolonged, wages are reduced, and labor standards are lowered. As the Five-Year Plan proceeds on an ever-widening scale, the shortage of workmen increases. Although the eight-hour day had originally been reduced to seven hours in many industries, yet, under the urge to complete the Plan, a ten-hour day has been reintroduced in many plants. Again, under the pressure of circumstances the Supreme Economic Council in the middle of 1929 found it necessary to reduce piece rates and to speed up production. To lower costs certain trusts reduced wages automatically without prejudice to a further reduction if the output rises.[115]

In order to reduce the cost of production to the level planned for, industrial managers have proposed to change the standards of output and piece rates so as to reduce wages basing their action on the principle of the General Council of Trade Unions that any saving in wages might be applied to reducing the cost of production.[116] Apparently the problem of the industrial manager in Soviet Russia is very similar to that of the industrial manager in the western world.

Mr. Tomsky, former President of the Trade Union Council, called attention to the fact that in some cases directors of plants economized at the expense of the workers, in order to show profits at the end of the year. The fact that profits went to the state instead of a private individual seems to have produced no very different results than those of the western world. The conflict still remains: How shall the surplus be divided between wages and profits? Labor standards are lowered, because some directors regard labor protection as an unproductive expense. As shown in the earlier part of this chapter, the Soviet labor code set up high standards. But under the pressure of necessity decrees have been promulgated which offset many gains and even resulted in clear losses to the workers in the standards of labor, as the latter sections of the chapter demonstrate.

As a result of the wholesale quitting of workers in the coal industry mentioned above, the coal administration violated an important clause of the Labor Code and enrolled women as coal miners.[116a]

3. Forced Labor. As a result of the pressure of the Five-Year Plan workers of various grades may be shifted from place to place or from job to job without their consent as cited above. Far from controlling industry, the workers in the Soviet Union often cannot even control the disposition of their own labor.

a. Forms of Drafted Labor. Drafted labor has taken on three forms, namely, that of self-imposed obligation, that involving indentured workers (i. e., workers "drafted" through the offering of some special inducement), and that of labor drafted by statute and without any inducement.

i. Self-Imposed Obligation. According to a decree of the Central Executive Committee and the Council of the People's Commissars, dated February 13, 1930, a village may be called upon to impose a task upon itself. A general meeting of the village is then held to ratify or reject the proposal. Kulaks, priests, and other "class enemies" may not attend the meeting and one-fourth of the total register of voters constitutes a quorum. If more than one-half do not raise their hands in objection the task is regarded as voluntary, and the obligation then becomes mandatory. Individuals or groups which resist the performance of such obligation are subject to imprisonment, confiscation of possessions, and even banishment from the district. In carrying out the task (for example, the cutting and shipping of a certain amount of lumber), the village soviet is authorized by law to assign work to individual farmers who are not members of a collective farm and to impose fines on those who refuse to carry out the assignment. The amount of the fine must not exceed five times the value of the work assigned and, if it should not be paid, the property of the offender may be sold at auction and the live stock becomes subject to confiscation by the village soviet. Of the amount of the fines so collected 25 per cent is to be used for creating a reserve for the co-operatives and for collectivizing the poor peasants.[117]

ii. Indentured Workers. To stimulate the output of lumber it was planned to have the collective farms and the timber co-operative cartels supply approximately one million individual laborers to cut and float lumber for the timber industry. The Commissariat of Labor ordered each collective farm to assign a certain number of workers to a specified lumber camp. In cases where peasants had not joined collective farms, they were to be drafted by special recruiting agents, organized into groups, and sent to some particular camp.[118] As an inducement the drafted workers and their families retain privileges in the collective.

iii. Statutory Draft. On September 14, 1930, the Council of Labor and Defense ordered that "extraordinary committees of sixes" be sent to the timber region to enforce the fulfillment of the lumber program, and to stimulate transportation of timber to ports. They were authorized to introduce compulsory service wherever necessary. Able-bodied men were to be drafted for compulsory labor, with pay, to haul and float the timber.[119] Rewards for exceeding a standard and penalties for failing to attain the standard were provided.

b. Labor-Draft Decrees. On October 9, 1930, the Commissar of Labor, Mr. Tsikhon, issued decrees.[120] All unemployed persons may be drafted. State labor exchanges must put the unemployed immediately to work. Insurance bureaus must discontinue payment of unemployment benefits. All unemployed must accept not only work in their own calling but also unskilled labor. No worker might refuse to accept the work assigned to him except in case of illness. Labor may be commandeered for state purposes. Workers living in Moscow may be required to live elsewhere unless they have a valid reason for remaining. Workers leaving their jobs are regarded as deserters and government agencies are forbidden to give them new work except manual labor. Engineers and technicians may be transferred to another location at the wish of the government and without their consent. Unemployed workers must accept any job offered anywhere or lose their status. Workers are put in the class of soldiers. The purpose of these far-reaching decrees was to strengthen discipline and to promote the execution of the Five-Year Plan.

On October 20, 1930, the Central Committee of the Communist Party ordered that skilled workmen employed in the unimportant branches of industry might be removed at the order of the Commissariat of Labor and sent to important industries such as coal mining, iron and steel manufacture, and large construction enterprises.[121] Managers of enterprises were to be held responsible if they prevented these employees from being transferred from their organizations. The managers were also to be held responsible for failure to use skilled labor fully and for inducing men to desert their jobs at other plants.

A decree of the Central Executive Committee of the People's Commissars dated December 15, 1930, provided for labor contracts for periods not exceeding three years whereby the Commissariat for Labor might transfer skilled workers to other branches or to other localities where their special training would be better utilized. Such transferred workers were to be guaranteed that their old living quarters would be kept for them until they returned and that at the new job they would have housing accommodations, educational facilities for their children, and other privileges.[122] Engineers and technicians might be transferred at the wish of the government.

In a decree dated January 16, 1931, Commissar of Labor Tsikhon ordered a mobilization of all railroad workers.[123] All government departments and trusts must make a list of employees having experience in railroad work and must dismiss them with two weeks' salary. The employees listed must appear at the nearest labor exchange for work on the railroads. Employers and workers who might try to evade the decree were made subject to criminal prosecution. The object of this mobilization was to facilitate the distribution of seed, fertilizer, and farm machinery for the sowing of the following spring.

c. Instances of Forced Labor. A similar situation of forced labor prevails in the lumber camps and mines. Wherever work is difficult and labor is short, either on account of the cold or the hardship, conscription is resorted to. It is estimated that several hundred thousand laborers, some guilty of political offenses, have been drafted by government order. Forced labor has been employed particularly in work in the forests, on the grain farms, in coal mines, and on river transports.

i. Forestry. The official instructions concerning forced labor in forestry are contained in instructions of the Commissariat of Agriculture, June 1, 1929.[124] These instructions deal with forced labor of timber workers without detention under guard. The Commissariat of Agriculture instructed all organizations to explore the possibilities of using for work in the forests persons sentenced to forced labor. Generally forced labor is used on work where no skill is required. The quotas for output are prescribed and, if the person sentenced completes the quota, he may be released before the end of the day. By decree of the Central Executive Committee, *Tsik,* and the Council of People's Commissars, February 13, 1930,[125] the Central Executive Committees of the several republics were authorized to institute compulsory paid labor in the preparation and haulage of timber.

ii. Grain Transport. According to a decree of June 5, 1929,[126] compulsory cartage for the transportation of grain is authorized, against payment, from the first of July to the 15th of September to either railway or steamship terminals. This decree was intended to include the work of loading and unloading cargoes of grain as well as transporting it.[127]

iii. Coal Mining. When the coal industry fell behind, the Central Administrative Board of the Collective Farms issued an order that the collective farms must send twenty thousand members to work in the coal industry. As an inducement, the families of peasants working in the coal mines retained the same right to their share of the next grain crop as did the families of the peasants who remained on the farms.[128] It is interesting to note that, whereas in the western world labor flows as a result of a movement of wages and as a result of the choice of the laborer, in Soviet Russia it moves primarily as a result of government orders.

iv. River Transport. According to a decree issued by the Commissariat of Labor, all workers who had experience on ocean or river craft in the last ten years were ordered to return to such work.[129] Enterprises which had such workers on their payrolls were ordered to dismiss them within five days. The officers and technical men with experience on water transportation were to report and be assigned to new posts, by the Commissariat of Water Transportation.

v. General Labor. According to the Labor Code of Soviet Russia: "In exceptional cases, such as fighting the elements or lack of workers to carry out the most important state work, all citizens may be called upon for work in the form of compulsory labor service in accordance with special decision of the Council of People's Commissars or of their authorized agents."[130]

Soviet Russia, attempting to pioneer along new lines of social freedom, has really gone back two centuries and restored to some extent the status of indentured servants. These in the western world originally had freedom and voluntarily bartered it away for a period of years. In the western world the laborer today has freedom of contract. It is a real right. He can always refuse employment. He may suffer as a result, but the alternative is always his.

vi. Convict Labor. As shown by official documents, courts have been instructed in imposing punishments to make offenders available for timber cutting and hauling. (The subject of the use of convict labor is fully discussed in a publication of the Bureau of Research on Russian Economic Conditions, University of Birmingham[130a] which cites official rules concerning wages of convict labor and official statistics of convict and other forms of compulsory labor.)

M. Industrial Democracy vs. Efficiency

According to an American observer sympathetic with the Soviet régime, labor has an opportunity for participating in the management. Workmen have a consultative voice in the management, in the establishment of wage levels, and in the setting up of labor standards, and are represented in arbitrations and in disputes. This self-expression of labor is a safety valve against discontent. Mr. Clark, technical director of the Electrical Trust, a Russian of German and British descent, made the observation that under a capitalistic system the manager of a plant directs and the workers follow, whereas in the Soviet Union the workmen are permitted to co-operate and there is democratic control of industry.

1. Self-Expression of Labor. In any given industry the workingmen are represented on the board by the general director. In addition there are assistant directors in charge of wage scales and of workers' suggestions. The workers are also represented by workers' committees in the preparation of annual wage agreements. There is also a conflict committee, or arbitration committee, to adjust difficulties. This factory committee is chosen semi-annually. It may suggest changes in operating methods and in conditions of work, and recommend candidates for factory managers, including the "Red" director, the representative of the Communist Party. In addition, Mr. Eshba of the Amtorg in Moscow, states that workers' committees confer after working hours on methods of increasing the output and improving the quality. These suggestions are submitted to the management and, if approved, bring bonuses and prizes to the individuals and to factory sections. The workers not only carry out plans prepared by the directors, but are permitted to suggest details in the execution of these plans in their particular shops. This procedure generates a sense of workers' control in industry. Technical directors of several factories stated quite independently that suggestions for increasing efficiency, concerning management, methods of work, and wages, came from the workers by the thousands.

2. Administrative Difficulties. In Russia, as in capitalist countries, the conflict between industrial democracy and factory efficiency has arisen. The problem of factory administration and management has not been solved by the substitution of a single employer, the state, for numberless competing private employers. This is not solely an economic problem. It springs neither from private profit nor from distribution of the surplus. Even though there is theoretically no conflict between labor and capital, yet there is a labor

problem, primarily a problem of administration—how to secure maximum production. There is still the need for reconciling the demands of the workmen for high wages and the demands of the employer, the Soviet state, for profits or the surplus over wages. The pressure of efficiency is working toward the reduction of endless talk and innumerable committee meetings. Gradually the Soviet state is veering toward the centralization of authority and responsibility, and the curtailing of the original wide power and participation of labor in the management.

3. Centralization of Authority.[131] The trend in industrial management is like that in other departments of Russian life. The freedom resulting from the revolution developed a desire to seek new bases of social organization. Experimentation was universal. But these experiments finally resulted in the resurgence of the old tested methods of an historically evolving world, which happens to be capitalistic. Many existing institutions of the western world are the result of competition, struggle, and the survival of the fittest institutions. A series of compromises between new Russian experiments and the old western methods resulted in the gradual and virtually complete restoration of these practical working methods in industry.

The originally extensive participation of workers in management resulted in inefficiency. Therefore the Soviet leaders decided to give the factory managers increasing authority. In fact concentration of authority and responsibility was inevitable. Industrial democracy has decreased, but the motivating influence has not been the desire to increase the private profits of the individual employer but to insure the success of the Soviet system. Such a reason for the introduction of centralized authority has been accepted by the laboring classes. The foreign engineers, representatives of the capitalist system, have less success in this regard than the representatives of the Soviet régime, who can rigidly enforce authority and sometimes autocratic power in a way that the foreign technical managers cannot. A Soviet manager can drive Soviet workmen harder than a "capitalist" engineer. In line with this policy the Central Committee issued an order that Soviet factory managers must be obeyed by all workers, that authority must be centralized in all factories, and that workers' committees must not interfere with the exercise of the managerial functions of the "Red" director. They may still make suggestions, but the decision rests with the manager. His increased powers, as in capitalist countries, include the right to "hire and fire" the engineering and administrative staff except the foreign specialists. He also has the right to hire, dismiss, or transfer manual laborers.

This right, however, is not unrestricted. In hiring men the management enters an application at the nearest labor exchange, whose list gives priority to members of the Red army, then to members of the Communist Party, then to labor-union men in good standing, and last to the "declassed." The Red director does not have great discretion in selecting applicants. In case of discharge the worker may appeal to a committee of workmen, then to an arbitrater, then to the Commissar of Labor.

The trade union officials are consulted, but they have no power to countermand the orders of the manager. They may, however, appeal from his decisions to the constituted authorities.

CHAPTER VII

INDUSTRY

The Soviet Union is attempting to hasten the development of industry. The favorable conditions are extensive natural resources and an abundant supply of common labor. According to the statistical subdivision of the Central Executive Committee the total area of the Soviet Union is 21,236,100 square kilometers (8,200,000 square miles), and the official figures for population on January 1, 1931, were 161,006,200.[1] The deficiencies are lack of skilled labor and of a trained personnel and shortage of capital. The incentive to production, as in capitalist countries, is profit, though not to individuals but to state.

A. Raw Materials

Apparently the geological survey of the territory now in the Soviet Union has not revealed the natural riches fully. One of the directors of the steel trust stated that they "stumbled" over Magnitogorsk. Russia controls about 38 per cent of the world's petroleum resources. Its forests of over two billion acres constitute the largest timber stand in the world and almost 27 per cent of the world's total. Almost 80 per cent of the world's peat is to be found there. In addition there are unestimated quantities of coal, iron ore, manganese, potash, asbestos, zinc, lead, and other important raw materials. Despite these resources Russia counted for little as an industrial factor before the war; but they constitute the basis for the development of Soviet industry.

Before the war explorations for mineral resources were limited, the appropriations in 1913 amounting to only $100,000. Under the Soviet régime the budget for geological survey was expanded rapidly from $4,000,000 in 1928 to $20,000,000 in 1930. As a result many important discoveries were made.[2] During the fiscal year 1929 more than 1300 surveying parties worked on topographical, geological, and mining exploration.[3]

Although the success of the industrialization program depends so largely on the possession of adequate mineral resources, especially those of iron ore, the extent of these resources is still very uncertain.

On the basis of *The Five-Year Plan* (see third edition, Moscow, 1930), the reports of the Commission on Power Resources, the reports of the Soviet Academy of Sciences, and *The Wealth of the Soviet Union,* Isaac Don Levine concludes that the Soviet coal reserves are inadequate, too scattered, and too far removed from the industrial centers.[4] The Donetz Basin in the Ukraine has three-quarters of one per cent of the world supply and is the main source of coal for European Russia. The United States, with an area twice that of European Russia and with about the same population, has about 48 per cent of the world's coal deposits. But seven-eighths of Russia's coal reserves are in Siberia, an area two and one-half times as great as that of the United States and with about one-tenth the population. The United States has more than fifty times the coal reserves of European Russia and seven times the reserves of the whole of Russia. The total coal resources of all of Russia are less than those of the State of Wyoming, which is 1/82 as large.

According to the official *Wealth of the Soviet Union* [5] the iron-ore resources of the Soviet Union rank in size below those of the United States, France, England, or Sweden. Including deposits in both European and Asiatic Russia deposits in the ground amount to 1836 million tons of ore, with an iron content of 774 million tons. Half of this amount is "visible and probable" reserve, the other half "possible" reserve. This compares with United States deposits of nearly ten billion tons of unmined ore.

Professor A. Archangelsky, at the meeting of the Soviet Academy of Science in Moscow in June, 1931, said that, considering its vast area, including the Urals, the European part of the Soviet Union was relatively poor in iron ore. At this meeting another authority, Mr. A. E. Fersman, returning from a geological survey in Siberia, said that "the supplies of minerals are insignificant compared to the enormous scale of construction work in Siberia. The proven iron-ore deposits per capita are 4 tons in Siberia, 100 tons in England, and 390 tons in Sweden. Similarly, Professor V. L. Tukholka in the official report "The Wealth of the Soviet Union" states that in the actual size of iron-ore deposits the Soviet Union is surpassed by the United States, France, England, and Sweden, and on a per capita basis also by Germany, Spain, Norway, Greece, and Luxembourg. With reference to the inadequate supply of iron ore for a particular iron and steel plant, Professor K. I. Bogdanovich, in his book *Iron in Russia,* published by the Soviet Academy of Science, says that the ore reserves available for the use of the Magnitogorsk Steel Works are as follows:

	Million Tons
Visible	15
Probable	44
Total	59
Total, including possible	93

In the entire Urals the iron-ore reserves are as follows: Visible and probable, 135 million tons; total, including possible, 360 million tons. But most of the ore is low-grade and of limited exploitability.

As shown on page 89 Magnitogorsk was originally designed on a modest scale. However, it was so greatly enlarged subsequently that the above supply of ore would be fully depleted in less than ten years. If no new ore reserves are discovered in the meantime the cost will have to be amortized rapidly, greatly increasing the cost per ton, and the useless plant would stand as a monument to the planlessness of the Five-Year Plan.[4]

In nonferrous metals the known resources are small. The widespread impression that the country is rich in copper is not borne out by definite information. Prof. A. D. Breiterman, termed the leading Soviet authority on copper, states that the total reserves of copper ore in the Urals can be fixed at about 600,000 tons, less than half the amount smelted in the United States in twelve to fifteen months. Known deposits of other nonferrous metals, nickel, aluminum, tin, etc., are also said to be small.

This lack of adequate proven reserves was confirmed again in the official publication *Planovoe Khozyaiztvo* (*Planned Economy*) for May 1932. The mineral reserves were classified into four categories in the order of determinability. The conclusion of this survey is that the mineral requirements of the Second Five-Year Plan (1933–1937) exceed the proven reserves in the cases of oil, coal, copper, lead, zinc and iron ore, and other materials. The problem is therefore to block out further the probable ore reserves and to increase exploration surveys. However in vein mines throughout the world the reserves are usually not blocked out for five years ahead. Indeed it is only in a unique type of mine like the porphyry coppers, consisting of fairly uniformly disseminated ore, that the length, breadth, and thickness of the ore bed can be blocked out and the output and life thus estimated. Unforeseen developments often are favorable in the field of geology. The United States Geological Survey predicted in 1918 exhaustion of our oil reserves in twenty years, but the country has been glutted almost continuously since. The Rand mines in South Africa and the Dome mines in Canada have exceeded the predictions of output and ore reserves made by conservative engineers. New processes of extraction have lengthened the life of the Miami copper mines. Tailings of big copper mines like Utah, discarded under old methods, have proved "good pay" under modern methods. The Soviet Union may have "prospector's luck." On September 1, 1932, according to the Amtorg Trading Corporation, Soviet geologists reported the discovery of a new field of copper ore of 500 million tons in the Southern Urals in the Vashkir area, near an existing group of copper mines. The metal content is estimated at 2 per cent, or 10 million tons of copper. If this report is confirmed, this deposit would rank with that of the great copper mines of the world, "Utah Copper" in North America, "Chile Copper" in South America, and "Katanga Copper" in Africa.

However, the Soviet procedure is certainly open to criticism. The Five-Year Plan is based not on the known or proven reserves but on the probable or even the possible reserves. To that extent the gamble is increased. There is always the risk that the reserves may not be available. On the other hand the large appropriations for geological survey and the statistical probabilities relating to the distribution of natural resources in Soviet Russia, spreading over one-tenth of the world's area, favor the extension of the known reserves and the discovery of new sources. Soviet leaders have proven to be gamblers on a colossal scale, in geological, as in agricultural, industrial, political, and social affairs. However, minerals cannot be conjured forth by the ballyhoo which has been so signally successful in the Soviet Union in mobilizing public sentiment, and in inducing a large, lethargic mass of mankind to quicken its thought and action.

Nevertheless, this potential shortage of raw materials remains but a minor threat to the Five-Year Plan. To the extent that the Plan fails it will be due not to a lack of natural resources, as some writers predict, but rather to the magnitude of the task, the short time allotted to realize the goals, the difficulties in organization and management, the fatigue or passive resistance of undernourished workers and disaffected peasants.

B. Capital Requirements

The industrialization of a young country requires a large investment of capital. The United States, Canada, Mexico, Argentina, Brazil, Australia, South Africa, all developed over a period of decades by means of capital furnished by investors of the older countries. Before the war Russia was a field for investment by foreigners, who had put 2000 million rubles into industry or about one-third of the total invested therein. In addition, another 2000 million rubles were invested in public utilities by foreigners, chiefly France, Great Britain, Germany, and Belgium.[6] Most of this investment was in the form of machinery and equipment, of which over two-thirds was imported.

Because of the repudiation of the Tsarist external debt, Soviet Russia has little credit. Investors will not sink further capital in Russia, and her credit abroad is limited practically to the value of her exports. The repudiation of the debt has limited the supply of capital available, and therefore the Soviets must "dump," must make maximum use of existing machinery and equipment. If and when foreign capital again becomes available to Russia, it should no longer be necessary for her to force exports on foreign countries. Nor should it be necessary to speed up machinery, or depress living standards of her people.*

C. Machinery

Much of the capital assets of the country are a heritage from the old industrial corporations. But because of the lack of credit and abundance of unskilled and half-trained labor, some machines were run 24 hours a day, 360 days a year. Production was increased, but the lack of care of the machinery also increased the rate of depreciation. Machinery was undermaintained, and until 1923 there was said to be no provision for depreciation. Therefore maintenance and depreciation charges will have to remain high for a considerable time, and will reduce the bookkeeping profits of the government. Foreign engineers in charge of operation of tractors or employed at various factories in Russia say that machines that should have a life of seven to ten years must be discarded after two years' operation.

In the tractor division of the Putilov works there is a large variety of American machines—in fact the array looks like an exhibition of American machinery. Ten or fifteen American states are represented. One of the workmen, leading us through the plant, regarded the machines almost with affection, and put them through some stunts for us. It was evident that he looked upon them as a collection of grand toys.

* Commenting on this subject two Washington economists point out that old Russia also forced exports of wheat to meet interest payments, and that during recent years Soviet exports have averaged about one-half of those under the Tsar. Soviet coal, pulpwood, lumber, and manganese command exceptionally high prices.

D. Labor

The labor aspects of industry are summarized from the preceding chapter. As the Five-Year Plan develops on an ever-widening scale the shortage of labor grows more acute. Sites may be selected, materials may be bought, but trained workmen must be available. It was expected that in 1931 the Five-Year Plan would call for an additional 500,000 skilled workmen, or about one-third the total number of skilled workers then in industry. The supply of labor is a key difficulty of the Five-Year Plan.

Not only is there a shortage of trained men, but the efficiency of labor tends to decline with the increasing scale of industry. The introduction of a double shift resulted in a dilution of the quality of labor. Unskilled workers were brigaded with skilled workers. The quantity of the output was increased but the quality was lowered. Furthermore, constant change or shift in labor or management tended to diminish efficiency. Other factors which tended to impair the productivity of the workers were the lowered vitality resulting from insufficient food and lowered standards of living. Decreased efficiency was also due to a lack of knowledge of machinery, and to the fact that maintenance and repairs were inadequate. The workmen were careless and accidents increased substantially in recent years. The Soviet officials may have to recruit foreign skilled labor to run their factories, just as they have brought in foreign engineers and technical experts to help build them.

E. Management

1. The Organization of Industry. Most of the large-scale industries are nationalized and are organized into trusts. Each trust embraces all the factories in an industry. The trust supervises the production, distribution, and financing of the industry. A few of the important trusts are as follows:

Name	*Abbreviated Russian Name*
United Agricultural Machinery Industry	Soyuzselmash
United Alcohol Industry	Centrospirit
United Automobile and Tractor Industry	Vato
United Aviation Industry	Vao
United Chemical Industry	Vsekhimprom
United Coal Industry	Soyuzugol
United Construction Industry	Soyuzstroy
United Electrical Industry	Veo
United Fur Industry	Vps
United Heavy-Machinery Industry	Vomt

Name	*Abbreviated Russian Name*
United Metal-Products Industry	Metizoobedineniye
United Nonferrous Metal Industry	Tsvetmetzoloto
United Non-Metallic Minerals Industry	Vopni
United Oil Industry	Soyuzneft
United Steel Industry	Stal

The president, vice-president, and directors of the trust are appointed by the Supreme Economic Council. Though the Council exercises broad supervision over the trust's activities, the board of directors is actually responsible. It includes a "Red" director, a technical director, a factory director, a commercial director, and a general director. All except the "Red" director must have had experience in the industry. Each factory manager is responsible for the operations in his plant. He is appointed by the directors with the advice of the labor union in the industry.

After the October Revolution the workers had maximum latitude in managing their factories. A committee elected by the workers in each industry actually had charge of the management. But the results were so poor that the management was concentrated in the hands of the Supreme Economic Council. Most of the large-scale industries are now nationalized and are under the control of the Supreme Economic Council. The smaller industries are generally in the co-operative system and several are in the control of foreign concessionaires. The very small industries, i. e., handicrafts and home industries, are scattered among the small artisans, who are sometimes organized into industrial co-operatives, or artels.[7]

This extreme centralization, however, has interfered with efficiency. It has involved red tape and bureaucratic methods. The "Red" directors in the factories are communists, former propagandists for the revolution, and former political exiles. The managers are responsible for the profits of their plants, and like managers of plants in the western world, they must reduce costs, even at the expense of wages and labor standards.

2. Lack of Experience. Aside from being former political prisoners, most "Red" directors have few qualifications for their place. Many of them have little general education. Most have no technical education. Nor have they as a rule any actual experience in industry. Their inexperience in management is one of the gravest industrial problems of the Soviets. To translate it into terms of our own experience, what sort of manager would our average politician be in a large plant of the General Electric Company or the Bethlehem Steel Company? In private corporations the character of the management is

the first test of the soundness of a corporation. And so in Russia the first test of the soundness of the state's industry is the character of the management.

The shortage of merchandise is due to the lack of competent managers as much as to the lack of goods. Perishable foods rot in the freight yards, while the adjoining city is suffering a shortage. Railroad cars are stalled on sidings and used as warehouses, resulting in transportation jams. If Russia cannot find enough technical skill to manage the existing plants and transportation system where will she find the engineers, technicians, and managers to run the larger economic system now being developed?

Stalin, in an address to officials in industrial plants [8] admitted such a deficiency in Russian industry. He said, "We have the will, but have we the proper management for our industry? Too often communist executives lack the mastery of technique which is essential to factory management. . . . For this reason sabotage by the 'class enemy' engineers was possible. . . . The communist executives lacked technical knowledge." Because time must elapse before experience can be gained, it would seem reasonable to expect that in the interim the management of industry will be inefficient.

3. LACK OF ENGINEERS. There is an actual shortage of trained men. The Soviet experiment presupposes abundance of technical skill. In industrialized countries, engineers, draftsmen, and highly skilled labor constitute over ten per cent of the employees, but in Soviet Russia only two per cent.

For the completion of the Five-Year Plan Russia will need 175,000 engineers and 260,000 technicians, a total of 435,000 trained men. The present supply consists of 24,000 native engineers, about 27,000 engineering assistants, and about 50,000 technicians, a total of about 100,000. Furthermore, the "shock brigades," or trained workers, and the "flying squads," or units which travel from factory to factory to speed up production and to investigate defects, are quite inadequate, being only a small proportion of the total number required.

Not only is there a shortage of engineers but those that are available are inadequately trained. In a census of 270 factories only 9 per cent of the managers had university training, only 16 per cent had high school training, and 72 per cent never progressed beyond the elementary school. Further, the technicians and managers do not stay put; the turnover is said to be as high as 30 per cent per annum.

The demand for specialists is likewise greatly in excess of the supply. The percentage to which the demand has been filled in a few of the leading classifications follows: [9]

Classification	High Grade Per cent	Medium Grade Per cent
Agricultural experts	3.4	0.2
Mining experts	25.6	4.8
Construction engineers	22.2	6.2
Chemists	33.6	4.2
Metallurgists	—	5.8
Heating experts	28.7	1.0
Electricians	46.7	14.2
Textile experts	14.8	3.9
Economists	9.1	0.5

The fact that the demand for experts of medium grade is so poorly filled is due to the fact that the available men have been pushed into posts which require higher qualifications.

Of the total number of specialists in the Soviet Union only 38.4 per cent have had a university education, only 22.5 per cent have had a high school education and 39.1 per cent have had no formal education but only practical experience. Some industries particularly are lacking in technically trained experts. For example, 65.9 per cent of the technical men in transportation work lack university or secondary education. In the other industries this proportion is 55 per cent.

In view of the campaign against the so-called pre-war engineers, who were trained under the old régime and who were formerly the technical backbone of industry, it is very significant that the percentage of specialists originating among workingmen is relatively small and the percentage from the old middle and upper classes is the majority. A classification of the specialists made by the Commissariat for Labor on May 1, 1930, is shown herewith:

Grade	Workingmen Origin Per cent	Peasant Origin Per cent	Middle-class Origin Per cent	All Others Per cent	Total Per cent
Total specialists	24.3	26.1	39.4	10.2	100
Specialists with university training	11.4	20.5	52.9	15.2	100
Specialists with secondary education	22.7	27.3	41.1	8.9	100
Men with special training only	31.7	31.0	30.8	6.5	100
Men with only practical experience	47.8	30.5	16.8	4.9	100

The Soviet government press constantly discusses the question of "proletarizing the governing apparatus" in industry, in collective agricultural farms (*kolk-*

hozy), in state-agricultural farms (*sovkhozy*), in transport and in trading organizations. (*Planned Supply of Specialists in the U.S.S.R., Gosplan,* Moscow, 1930, p. 28.) The outcome of this tendency was shown as early as 1929, when 43.7 per cent of the important posts requiring the highest technical qualifications, and 59.7 per cent of those requiring only a secondary technical education, were occupied by persons without specialised technical education. At the beginning of the economic year 1929–30 there were in the U.S.S.R. 120,000 qualified civil engineers and technicians and 170,000 so-called "practical" workers. The number of new specialists needed for the execution of the Five-Year Plan is calculated at 1,212,000.[8a]

The higher the qualification of the specialist, the lower is the percentage of workingman origin. More than two-thirds of the specialists with university training come from social strata other than the proletariat. Furthermore, the specialist of peasant origin usually comes from the kulak element in the villages.

What is more significant is that only 13.3 per cent of all the experts are members of the Communist Party. The older the class of specialists, the smaller the percentage of communist members. For example:

Length of Experience	*Communists per cent*
13 years	6.0
10 to 13 years	8.9
6 to 9 years	13.2
5 years or less	20.4

In view of these statistics, the Soviet officials realize that the discrepancy between the demand for specialists and the supply, the inadequate training of the existent personnel, the small percentage of party members makes a satisfactory system of technical education the supreme industrial problem of the day.[9]

4. Training of Russian Engineers. The training of additional engineers represents the attempt to solve this difficulty. The Soviets are now using the old engineers that directed the plants before the revolution. In addition they are training new engineers, the first class of Soviet engineers having graduated in 1927. Brief and hurried courses are given. The four-year curriculum is reduced to two years, and the schools work on two shifts. This wholesale training is not the equivalent of the slower and more thorough training in the western world, and at best the technical schools will be unable to turn out more than one-third of the engineers required by the Plan.

In order to increase the number of technicians and foremen, evening schools for workingmen on a wide scale will be necessary. In fact, the whole army of labor must be raised to a higher technical level. Soviet leaders are aware of the wide gap between the efficient modern equipment of the new plants and the low order of technical skill of the workers who are to operate the machines.[10]

As a result of the forced speed of education, the Russian engineers, though well versed in theory, are unfamiliar with actual practice. Foreign engineers testify that the present Russian engineering school graduate has a superiority complex and will not mingle with the working staff. Too often they will also not co-operate with American engineers. Their point of view is different. Russian engineers will stay in the office all day whereas American engineers will spend most of their time on the construction site.[11] One of the foreign engineers assisting in the construction of a rayon plant near Moscow told the writer that in America an engineer starting a plant would work all day in the boiling room despite its heat and steam to show the laborers how to perform the operations. He did so in Russia to the astonishment of both the laborers and the Soviet technicians.

Lacking the experience the Russian engineer is unable to show the workman how to operate or repair a machine. Lacking a tradition of many years he has not the mechanical "feel." And for this reason Russia for a considerable time must require the aid and advice of trained foreigners.

In 1929 eleven engineering schools were established and twenty more were under construction. The schools are controlled by the trusts in the several industries. Students are paid while they are studying and obtain practical experience in the plant. Upon graduation they are expected to work for the trust in whose school they were trained. Russian engineers are also sent abroad. According to one of the officials of the Gosplan there are more than one thousand Russian engineers in America. One hundred are at the Ford plant, considerable numbers are in the oil fields, in tractor factories, and in industrial construction work. According to one of the directors of the Electrical Trust there are twenty-five Russian engineers at the Berlin works of the Allgemeine Elektricitäts Gesellschaft, fifteen at the Schenectady plant of the General Electric Company, and about ten at the Vickers plant in London.

5. Attitude toward Bourgeois Engineers. The engineers of the old régime are being replaced by the new Soviet engineers. The old engineers, who

operated the plants before the war, were also stockholders and were accused by the Soviet officials of maintaining contact with the former owners, and at the behest of the latter of hampering the development of the works beyond the pre-war levels and turning out poor quality of work. In some cases it was charged that they received salaries from their former employers. Because these old engineers were suspected of sabotage, preference was given to engineers who come from the families of manual laborers.

a. Conciliation of Bourgeois Engineers. The policy of suspicion and antagonism to the old engineers proved costly and in a vigorous address Stalin outlined the error of the old way and made suggestions for a new attitude toward technical men.[12]

Among these comrades there are quite a few non-party members. But this should not serve as a barrier to their quick promotion to leading positions. On the contrary, these very non-party comrades should be surrounded with particular attention. They should be promoted to managerial positions so that they may become convinced that the party knows how to value capable and talented workers. Some comrades think that only party comrades should be advanced to the leading positions in factories and mills. On the basis of this they very often shove aside capable non-party comrades with initiative and promote party members to the leading posts although the latter are less capable and show less initiative. Needless to say, nothing could be more foolish and reactionary than such a policy.

By such a policy it is possible only to discredit the party and to repel the non-party workers from our party. It is not at all our policy to transform our party into an exclusive caste. Our policy is to promote between the party and non-party workers an atmosphere of mutual trust.

The question of the attitude of the old bourgeois industrial and technical intelligentsia arises now in a new way. Now that the intelligentsia has turned to the side of the Soviets our attitude should be to attract and assist the technical intelligentsia. It would be stupid and irrational to consider every specialist and engineer of the old school as an uncaptured criminal and wrecker. The anti-specialist psychology has always been considered by us as a pernicious and shameful mania.

We have definite signs of change in a certain section of the intelligentsia formerly sympathizing with the damaging activities against the Soviet Government. The fact that not only this section of the old intelligentsia, but even a definite, a considerable section of the actual damagers of yesterday have started to work in a number of shops and factories side by side with the working class—this attests incontrovertibly the fact that the change has already commenced among the old technical intelligentsia. It follows from this that we must change our policy with regard to the old technical intelligentsia accordingly.

During the height of the damaging activities our attitude toward the old technical intelligentsia was expressed mainly in a policy of suppression. But now, when the intelligentsia is turning toward the Soviet Government, our attitude toward them must be expressed mainly in a policy of attracting them to us and concern for them.

Our task is to change the attitude toward the engineering and technical forces of the old school, to accord them the utmost attention and solicitude, to draw them more boldly into work.

Carrying out the intent of this address, Y. E. Rudzutak, member of the Political Bureau and close friend of Stalin, addressed the Society of Technical Engineers on the same subject. He said that although the foundations of socialist industrialization were already laid and its form and scheme had taken shape, it was all inadequate without competent persons in charge. In defense of the new Soviet policy of conciliating the old engineers he referred to Lenin's reply concerning a question about high wages for exceptional service. Lenin said: "This is justified if the job to be done would cost more without such high pay." Mr. Rudzutak said further,

We must not look back at sabotage and treachery, that is past, but at the problems of new construction in the future. All those who work for the Socialist state are comrades, including those who have joined the working class in that work as well as those born in it. Henceforth the Communist Party and the working class will make no difference in rights. It is how a man acts that counts. Yesterday is forgotten. A man is for us or against us.[13]

Once the attitude toward the "white-collar" class might almost have been summed up in the phrase, "When anything goes wrong blame it on the nearest specialist." Mr. V. V. Kuybyshev, another member of the Political Bureau and President of the State Planning Commission, speaking to the Steel Construction Section of the Society of Technical Engineers took the same attitude as Mr. Rudzutak.

b. Reasons for Reversal of Attitude. According to William B. Grady, American mining engineer who was employed in Soviet Russia for eighteen months and who has been antagonistic to the Soviet régime, the change of front was not voluntary but was forced. He said that the causes were the lack of funds to secure the services of foreign engineers, the failure of the Soviet engineers to co-operate with the foreigners, and the dissatisfaction that resulted therefrom. Furthermore, Stalin may believe that the Soviet is so firmly established that it is unnecessary to resort to the "stocks and pillory" for bourgeois "saboteurs" to keep up the morale of the Russian people. Then, the attitude of the outside world may be a factor. The counter-revolutionary plot of November 1930, with its loud speakers and theatrical display was regarded as a "plant" and treated as a joke in foreign countries.

Furthermore, the world-wide protest against the execution of famous scientists may have influenced this reversal of policy.[14]

Perhaps the real reason was the impasse which resulted when the giant plants were completed and the technical skill to operate them found to be either inadequate or unavailable. Although the Stalingrad Tractor Plant has been completed for a long time, it is not operating satisfactorily, either as to quantity, quality, or cost of production. The increased demand for skilled managers and engineers required that the policy of political persecution of old engineers cease. The Russian experience illustrated the ruthless discipline of stern reality. Oratory may be successful in making propaganda but in running machines both oratory and propaganda are useless. You cannot persuade a machine. You must conform to it. This requires technique.

c. Results of the New Policy. The results of the change of attitude of the government toward the old bourgeois engineers soon became apparent. At a trial of sixty-seven persons accused of sabotage at the Moscow Railroad freight station, ten were acquitted, including two high executives, and light sentences were imposed on the others, while heavy penalties were inflicted on thirty-three workers for negligence and misconduct. Furthermore, the *Railroad Gazette* demanded an investigation and punishment of the persons responsible for putting on trial an engineer in the Volga region. Again, under a decree of the Central Executive Committee five engineers were granted amnesty for having "repented of their former sins and shown their repentance by a year's conscientious work" at the aviation factory. These five engineers were restored to full rights and received prizes up to 10,000 rubles.[15]

As a further step for conciliating bourgeois engineers President Kalinin and Premier Molotov signed a decree placing engineers and specialists on the same plane as the highest category of proletarian workers with respect to food, living quarters, vacations, education for the children, and other privileges and rights.[16] The official *Za Industrializatsiu* has discussed the question of the extent to which engineers should take the initiative and risk in meeting a new situation rather than following red-tape and waiting for instructions from an office that may not know as much about the problem as the engineer on the job.[17] The Central Technical Engineering Institute likewise proposed to give greater freedom to the engineers and to form a committee jointly with representatives of the Supreme Economic Council to decide the question of how much risk an engineer may take in an unusual situation which requires initiative and prompt action.[18]

6. Penalties vs. Initiative. Except for the amount of the compensation the incentives which motivate the Russian manager are similar to the incentives in other countries. Success leads to promotion. However, in Russia failure, incompetence, and certainly mismanagement are subject to severe penalties.

The following is an illustration of the new policy of holding managers individually responsible for mismanagement and visiting drastic punishment upon them for failure:

> Twenty-seven men, mostly Communists, were arrested and ordered to stand trial for disorganizing the food supply. All were discharged from their jobs and those who were Communists were expelled from the party—a severe measure of punishment in a country where Communists are the highest members of society. All of them held high positions, either directors or assistant directors of trusts such as the coffee, tobacco, canning, and textile trusts. Before the court these men will be held responsible for such acts as shipping perishable goods without packing so that they spoiled en route.
>
> Some of the charges were: A load of pastry goods was dumped into a freight car helter-skelter without wrapping or boxes. A shipment of 25,000,000 cans of canned goods was loaded in cars loosely with the result that many were broken through bouncing about. One man was blamed for holding 190,000 boxes of tobacco in a warehouse for a long period without shipping. A trust was indicted for holding back 25,000,000 rubles' worth of perfumery articles. In another case a shipment of sugar was packed in ripped sacks and dispatched in leaky cars.[18a]

To change a backward country like Russia into a highly developed industrial power is a huge task. Even in the more slowly developing western world factory problems crop up continuously which can be solved only through much research and study. In Soviet Russia, when difficulties arise, the problem is not regarded objectively, but some one must be blamed and usually it is the manager. If the error is mild he may be transferred, but if serious, he may be tried and exiled or even shot. A cool and competent manager may also be replaced by an ardent communist with less skill.

The Russian engineer consequently fears to take responsibility, and to avoid it many a good man prefers to take second place. This is particularly true since the schedule of salaries gives no material incentive for the assumption of responsibility. Furthermore, the initiative of engineers is often restricted by the obstruction of "Red" directors who are appointed through political "pull," and who exercise their power without knowledge or understanding of the technique of the industry

7. Foreign Technical Aid. It has been traditional in Russia to rely on foreigners. As far back as the days of Peter the Great and Catherine II, artisans,

shipbuilders, and philosophers were brought from foreign countries. Importation of foreign talent may have been due either to an historical sense of inferiority of the Russian to the more cultured western European or else to a complete absence of chauvinism, the existence of an international point of view, and a desire to obtain the highest skill regardless of nationality.

Before the war Russian industrial plants which were partly owned by foreigners were largely manned by foreign engineers, foreign managers, and foreign technicians. There were relatively few Russians in this field. One of the directors of the Electrical Trust stated that the Riga plant of the German A.E.G. employed about 2200 men before the war and most of the higher-grade men were foreigners. The same applied to the Siemens-Schuckert plant in Leningrad. Recently there were in Russia about 1000 American engineers, 2500 Germans, and perhaps another 1000 engineers from the several countries of Europe. The importation of foreign technical men is an attempt to offset the lack of native skill and the attempt to benefit by the traditions of craftsmanship of the older and more slowly growing countries.

The total number of foreign specialists employed by the Soviet Government in 1929–30 averaged 2950 and in 1930–31, 4140.

The total expenditure on foreign labor and technical assistance amounted to 18 million rubles in 1929–30, and to 38 million rubles in 1930–31. According to M. Yanovsky, of the Commissariat of Finance, it was planned to spend 150 million rubles on technical assistance during the whole five-year period. Lately, the Soviet Government made every effort to induce foreign and more particularly the German specialists, to accept a reduction of salary, and payment exclusively in Soviet rubles. But the foreign specialists insisted on the strict fulfilment of their contracts.[18b]

There are three types of technical assistance by foreigners to the Soviet Union: (a) Special contracts for specific jobs; (b) employment of foreign experts; and (c) technical aid by foreign firms receiving orders from the Soviets. The amounts spent for this purpose rose rapidly, particularly after the adoption of the Five-Year Plan, as follows:

Year	*Amount in Million Rubles*
1923–26	1.8
1927	2.3
1928	4.7
1929	8.7

An appeal was made to Soviet workmen and engineers to supervise the work of the "foreign technical assistance" which is purchased at such high prices and to see that it was well utilized.[19]

The Soviets lean strongly toward America for technical advice, because Russian and American conditions are so similar. Both countries are rich in natural resources, both constitute large free-trade areas with populations well over 100 millions, and neither has political designs against the other. America has advanced far along the road that Russia wishes to travel, namely the mechanization of industry, the emancipation of the worker from heavy physical toil, the high productivity per man, and the resulting increase in the consuming capacity of the worker. For this reason the Soviets are looking toward American corporations and American engineers to realize the Five-Year Plan. They are offering American engineers salaries far in excess of the maximum wages paid to Soviet engineers, and in addition give them numerous privileges and advantages.

The Russian engineering schools have not yet succeeded in turning out a sufficient number of trained men. Even though the courses in some of the schools were cut down to as little as six months, and the students worked day and night in order to finish their training, the number of graduates was found to be inadequate for the jobs. As a result the Soviet government planned to import approximately 13,000 additional foreigners, in order to keep up with the Five-Year Plan. These were to include about 3000 engineers, 3000 foremen, and 7000 skilled laborers.[20] About 5000 were to be Americans. This is a large number in view of the fact that more than 4000 foreign experts were already under contract with the Soviet government and 2000 additional were employed by the 124 foreign corporations which have contracts for technical aid to the Soviets. The depression forced the Soviets to curtail this program.

The foreign experts are being used to build the plants and to operate them until native personnel can replace these experts. The work of the American engineers in Russia today is analogous to the work of the American engineers, when the gold mines of South Africa and Australia were opened to which they brought the experience of the gold fields of California and Alaska. Similarly the African copper mines were developed by American engineers who were familiar with the great porphyry mines, with disseminated ores like those of the Utah Copper Company, for example. In both cases the Americans were subsequently replaced by British and Belgian engineers. The success of the Five-Year Plan depends in good part on the ability of the Soviets to retain foreign engineers and foreign workers.

a. Benefits. The utilization of foreign technical assistance has benefited the Soviet Union greatly. For example, the Stalingrad Tractor Plant was constructed at a speed which was theretofore unknown in Russia. The Russians cite numerous advantages of American technical assistance in the construction of this plant. The co-operation of American firms made it possible to complete the work in a record time. The technological processes were improved by the application of American standards for machining, and of new methods in heat treating and in assembling. The preparation of the plans in the United States gave the Russian engineers who were to operate the plant an opportunity to study identical processes in American factories. As a result of American co-operation, the floor area of the machine shop was decreased 20 per cent, the number of machines was diminished 25 per cent, and the capacity per machine was increased 28 per cent. In the forge shop the American engineers introduced changes so that floor space decreased 43 per cent, the number of workmen decreased 53 per cent, the output per workman increased 250 per cent, and the output per square meter of floor area was increased 100 per cent over the original Soviet plans. Again, the American advisory engineers stepped in to fill the gap due to the shortage of Soviet engineers. They applied American methods of carrying on construction work during the winter. They introduced new methods for assembling and erecting metal structures which speeded up the construction work, particularly through the use of construction machinery. The American system of parallel construction, instead of the Soviet method of construction in sequence, was introduced. In the opinion of the Russians, the "utilization of foreign technical assistance in the construction of the Stalingrad Tractor Plant was considered very satisfactory." [21]

An interesting appreciation of American efforts by the Soviet Union is contained in a letter by G. L. Pyatakov, Vice-Commissar of Heavy Industry, to Messrs. Stuart, James & Cooke, consulting coal engineers, who had been assisting for six years in the development of the Soviet coal industry. The American engineers were credited with the "removal of many difficulties in the development of the coal industry and with the speeding up of coal production which in turn had a favorable effect on the steel industry." [22]

b. Difficulties. Foreign engineers complained that their Russian co-workers were reluctant to take up modern methods.[23] In the construction of the automobile plant at Nizhni many of the young Soviet technicians engaged in construction work were merely apprentices, but they regarded themselves as skilled experts. As a result, Soviet straw bosses and administrators attempted to teach their American advisers and obstructed the American engineers who were imported to introduce their own methods of work. "Even the most insignificant suggestion of an American usually undergoes severe criticisms. In some instances such discussions last from two days to two months. Every student who is working at the construction offers his 'counter-suggestion.' This is called 'wholesome criticism.' The Americans patiently explained that the methods suggested by the Soviet technicians were abandoned in America 25 years ago and stated the reasons. At one time an American expert had only one pupil left and he was the superintendent of the Avtostroy construction department. All the others, two hundred or more, wanted to be his teachers. To curse Americans has become good form." [24]

At the Stalingrad Tractor Plant there was an interesting example of the difficulty encountered by the American engineers in securing the co-operation of their Russian associates.[25] Over 300 American mechanics worked at the plant, as instructors and supervisors. Their function was to start the various machines and tools going, to organize production, and to teach American methods to the Russian workers. Some of the Russian engineers and even the workingmen were antagonistic and did not believe the presence of Americans was at all necessary. As a result of the hobbling of the American engineers, the plant suffered great losses. In the assembly shop four very expensive tool machines were put out of commission. A new milling machine arrived and instead of asking for the American engineer in charge, the Soviet workmen proceeded to assemble the machine by their own methods, namely, by the use of crowbars and sledge hammers, and the machine was put out of commission for months. In the power plant the general superintendent was an American engineer but the Soviet director, who had no technical education or experience, sidetracked him and as a result the plant suffered a number of breakdowns and operated very irregularly. In the tool room the secretary of the local "cell" of the Communist Party publicly declared, "We made the revolution ourselves and we will be able to organize production ourselves," and he refused to work with the Americans. In the opinion of the Soviet investigating committee "such underestimating of American experience is decidedly harmful." [25]

At Magnitogorsk, which will be the largest metallurgical plant in Europe, a similar attitude of noncooperation with Americans has prevailed. Mr. John Calder gave such satisfactory service in erecting the plants at Stalingrad and Cheliabinsk that he was appointed chief engineer of the steel construction plant at Magnitogorsk. The chief Russian engineer opposed Calder and had to be discharged. His successor also opposed Calder, who complained, "The whole job is at sixes and sevens, and everything is in a muddle. People are moved without my instructions. Superintendents act on their own initiative without consulting me. Not only old engineers but even the youngest think they have nothing to learn from us." Once a student-worker actually said to him one day, "And what do you know about geodesy?" [26]

The Austin Company of Cleveland had a contract to construct the automobile plant costing 40 million rubles near Nizhni Novgorod. The plant was to produce 140,000 cars and trucks per annum. In addition there was to be a model industrial community. The Soviet manager in charge of construction, Tsarevsky, blamed the delay in part on friction between the American and Soviet engineers although other factors entered such as a shortage of materials, lack of skilled labor, inefficient supervision, and bureaucratic methods. Tsarevsky said that the Americans did not understand the difficulties in Russia, that in America "it was sufficient to press buttons to get what they wanted. That is good in the United States. It is a place full of buttons. In the Soviet Union there are no buttons." George Bryant, vice-president of the Austin Company, replied: "An American fails to respond to the Socialist theory of placing important party members in charge of important construction projects." [27]

c. Remedies Proposed. At the suggestion of Mr. Charles E. Stuart of the engineering firm of Stuart, James & Cooke of New York, consulting engineers for coal-mining companies, two mixed commissions of Americans and Russians were formed, one to reorganize the coal industry and the other to handle the relations between the Soviet executives and the foreign technical advisers. Stuart, James & Cooke were to furnish ten American specialists to form a semi-permanent committee along with the executives and technicians of the Executive Council to act as a supervisory board to the coal department. The second commission was to consist of seven Americans and seven Russians with three additional Russians, one representing the Communist Party, one economist, and one expert on the fuel requirements of the Soviet Union.[28] By means such as this it is hoped that the noncooperative attitude of the Soviet engineers may be overcome.

d. Suspension. The Soviet government also decided, in the interests of economy, to suspend temporarily, but not to abandon, the full advisory engineering services. Several of the important firms withdrew their field staffs and maintained one or two representatives in Moscow in a consulting capacity and as a nucleus for future expansion. As a result of the financial strain, the Soviet government took advantage of a clause in its standard contract with foreign engineers which gave it the right to break the contract in case of *force majeure*. They offered Soviet rubles in payment of salary instead of foreign money. The low purchasing power of the Soviet ruble, however, made it impossible for the foreign engineers to satisfy their requirements. As a result, most of them left. One American firm, Albert Kahn, Inc., severed its relation as consultant in the building industry, which ran from May 1929 to March 1932. Since Soviet rubles have no exchange value outside of Russia, such payment was impractical. However, this firm stated that the separation was friendly and that there was hope of resumption at some future time.[29]

F. Foreign Contracts

1. American Corporation Contracts. In addition to the employment of American engineers the Soviet government has made contracts for technical aid with numerous American corporations. A few of the better known companies and the nature of their aid are: [30]

Hugh L. Cooper & Company, New York City, consulting engineers on the construction of the Dnieper River hydroelectric power plant in the Ukraine.

Stuart, James & Cooke, Inc., New York City, technical assistance to the coal industry, in the planning, equipping, and rationalizing of the coal industry.

Du Pont de Nemours & Company, Wilmington, Delaware, technical assistance in erecting fertilizer plants.

Electric Autolite Company, Toledo, Ohio, technical assistance to United Electrical Industries in production of electrical equipment for automobiles and tractors.

Ford Motor Company, Dearborn, Michigan, technical assistance in the construction and operation of the Nizhni Novgorod automobile factory.

Freyn Engineering Company, Chicago, Illinois, consulting engineers for the Gipromez (State Institute for the Designing of Steel Mills) for plants in various parts of the country.

International General Electric Company, New York City, technical assistance in Soviet electrical industry and exchange of patents with the state electrotechnical trust.

Albert Kahn, Inc., Detroit, Michigan, designing of buildings for the Stalingrad tractor factory; also contract for general consultation services to the Supreme Economic Council as architect on industrial construction.

Koppers Construction Company, Pittsburgh, Pennsylvania, building of coke and by-product plants.

Lockwood, Greene & Company, New York City, technical assistance in the reorganization and reconstruction of existing textile mills and in the design and construction of new plants.

Arthur G. McKee & Company, Cleveland, Ohio, technical assistance to

Magnitostroy (Bureau of Construction of the Magnitogorsk Steel Mill) in the construction of the Magnitogorsk mill in the Urals.

Newport News Shipbuilding & Drydock Company, technical assistance in the construction of turbines.

Radio Corporation of America, New York City, exchange of patents and technical information with the Soviet Weak-Current Trust.

Southwestern Engineering Corporation, Los Angeles, California, assistance to the United Nonferrous Metals Industries in the design, construction, and operation of concentration plants.

Sperry Gyroscope Company, Brooklyn, New York, technical assistance in the manufacture of marine instruments.

Timken Detroit Axle Company, Detroit, Michigan, technical assistance to the United Automobile and Tractor Industry in the production of axles.

Westvaco Chlorine Products Company, Inc., Charleston, West Virginia, aid in the production of chlorine for United Chemical Industries of U.S.S.R.

Hugh L. Cooper & Co. and Stuart, James & Cooke, were the first two American firms engaged for Russian work. The latter had thirteen contracts, the largest engagement of any foreign firm.

2. MAGNITOGORSK STEEL PLANT. One of the most interesting contracts is that of Arthur G. McKee & Co., of Cleveland, who are building the Magnitogorsk plant. This is to consist of eight furnaces, with an output of 2,500,000 tons per annum, and the job is to be completed by October 1932. This project is larger than any other industrial construction in the world. It is more than a large construction undertaking. The capacity of each of the eight blast furnaces will be as great as that of all the blast furnaces of entire European plants. The inventory of railroad equipment will be as much as that of many small railroads. The reservoir for water storage has a dam one kilometer (0.621 mile) long and seven meters (23 feet) high. The electric power plant will have a capacity of 236,000 kilowatts, as much as a power plant for a good-sized American city. A technical college, one of the largest in Soviet Russia, will be connected with the plant.[31]

This plant compares in size with the Gary plant in the United States, which has a slightly larger annual production but which required more than ten years to build. The Magnitogorsk plant is to have a capacity of 4,000,000 tons eventually.

The cost of construction, 800,000,000 rubles or about $400,000,000, would be equivalent to an investment of $160 per ton of annual output. This figure is relatively high, considerably higher than the capitalization per ton of important American companies. This high cost of the Russian plant may be a reflection of the depreciation of the ruble. The McKee authorities believe that actual production costs in the new plant will be 25 to 40 per cent less than the costs in the old Russian plants. Yet its influence in the international market will probably be slight, because of the higher production costs and other reasons. Rails are figured to cost $28 per ton in the new plant as compared with $55 per ton in the old plants, and structural steel shapes about $39 as compared with $55. Freight costs from the Urals will probably restrict the area of competition with the steel-producing plants of western Europe.

3. FOREIGN CONCESSIONS. At first the Soviet Union attempted to attract foreign capital and foreign skill by means of concessions. This would have had the advantage of relieving the government of all the technical and financial problems involved in building up the industries. The government could have shared in the profits and have had a provision whereby, after a specified period of time, it would have the right to take over the plants on some equitable basis of cost or replacement value plus some profit.

Although many large concessions were talked of, such as the oil concessions offered to W. Vanderlip and to Sinclair, only two large concessions were actually started. W. A. Harriman of New York obtained the manganese concession in the Chiatouri District. The Lena Goldfields, a British corporation, obtained a concession in the gold, lead, zinc, and copper mines in the Urals and Siberia, but this was merely a confirmation of the pre-war title held by this British company. The concessions were signed in 1925. The former was terminated in 1928 and the latter in 1930. The former was amicably settled through the issuance of Soviet government bonds. The latter ended in a law-suit which was adjudicated in the British law courts. The total output of industries operating under concession is insignificant. Because of the inability to induce foreign capital and foreign skill to operate in the Soviet Union and because the Soviet government wished to retain direct control the concession idea was abandoned in favor of the plan of importing foreign skill and of making contracts with individuals or foreign corporations.

4. CONTRACTS WITH INDIVIDUALS. To increase their control and become less dependent upon foreign companies, the Soviet government favors the policy of making contracts not with corporations but with individuals.[32] The advantage is lower cost per expert and greater degree of control. On the other hand the advantages of the corporate contract include continuity of relationship, some warranty of quality, and the assumption of responsibility by the corporation for completing and servicing jobs. Furthermore, the foreign corporation has the responsibility of selecting adequately trained engineers. The Soviet government may be a less qualified judge of the

competence of an expert, in fact, the unemployed foreign engineers whom they might hire would probably be less competent than the skilled men furnished by the corporations. Of course, when they try to hire, as individuals, the engineers sent by corporations having contracts with the Soviets, as they have done, they avoid this error of judgment but arouse mistrust as to their business ethics.

5. Comments and Recommendations of Foreign Engineers. In discussing the problems of Russian industry with a large number of foreign engineers living at the Grand and Savoy hotels in Moscow, the writer received a good perspective on the problems involved and the difference of approach of the American technician and the Russian plant director. A few of the important comments follow:

a. Russia affords the greatest opportunity in history for standardization of products, mass consumption, scientific management, and mass production at low cost.

b. A new economic society is being built late in industrial history, and it can therefore embody in all its plants the latest successful devices that have evolved in other countries.

c. The great defect of Soviet Russia is lack of skill in organization and management of large plants. This is a matter of growth and tradition. Such knowledge cannot be bought; it cannot be installed on short notice.

d. Introduction of large-scale machinery implies organization and also the assimilation of man-power to the machinery.

e. Innumerable reports are requested and received on which no action is taken.

f. Changes in plans and new proposals are made continuously, even after the job is begun.

g. Men in charge lack authority and responsibility and are frequently changed. Local problems, instead of being settled on the spot by subordinate officials willing to take responsibility, are referred back to some distant official in a central office who is unfamiliar with the problem and whose decisions are delayed.

h. Fear of punishment deters plant managers from taking necessary prompt action. Inactivity is sometimes a greater vice than error. Unwillingness to assume responsibility is worse than making a mistake.

i. In general, the foreign engineers approach a problem without political prejudice and are interested, in the spirit of the craftsman, in doing a good job under new and difficult conditions. They are zealous, industrious, and in no small measure responsible for much of the industrial progress made in Russia.

j. Russian technical men are inadequately trained, and are critical of the foreigners who come to help them. Many have a good theoretical background, but are utterly lacking in practical experience.

k. American engineers stay on the job. Russian engineers sit in their offices. American engineers, having practical experience, go into the plant and teach the workmen; Russian engineers do not have enough practical experience to do so. Besides, the American engineer is more democratic in his relations with the manual laborer. The Russian engineer, despite the term "comrade" feels superior to the laborer.

l. The Russian engineers are addicted to innumerable conferences; the foreigners as a rule dislike much talk. The Russian managers as a rule are overwhelmed by details and routine; the foreign engineer as a rule delegates routine and tries to keep free for the larger tasks.

m. The foreign engineers prefer to make relatively small expenditures in expanding existing plants and in increasing their output; the Russians prefer to conceive large schemes and new ventures. The foreign engineer is matter-of-fact; the Russian gets romantic and imaginative.

G. Scientific Management or Rationalization

Because of the lack of capital for the importation of machinery, the idea of scientific management is looked on with special favor. Not merely the government but the trade unions also sponsor a policy of increasing the output per machine. In fact, one of the reasons for the introduction of the 24-hour day and the uninterrupted working year was to utilize machinery more fully. The idea of scientific management, or rationalization, as it is called in Europe, pervades the Five-Year Plan. The Supreme Council of National Economy has a Department of Rationalization. Similarly, the trade-union organization has a section on rationalization.

1. Methods. Each factory has a rationalization committee, which fixes the production quotas for each shop and for each man. In the Electrical Trust, for instance, there is a special department containing about sixty engineers who devote their entire time to this purpose. Similarly, in the Steel Trust each plant has its "rationalization bureau." Workers' suggestions come in by the thousands. Mr. Clark of the Electrical Trust stated that in a specific fight against waste they received seventeen hundred suggestions. These were examined by workers' committees, and those approved were passed on to the division of scientific management in the factory. If a suggestion was actually adopted a prize was paid to the originator. As a result of these numerous suggestions the efficiency of labor was increased. If a chairman of such a workers' committee is successful, he is promoted as efficiency assistant to the manager of the plant.

In the fiscal year 1930 more than 8000 suggestions were offered to the plant management of the "Electrozavod," the electrical-equipment manufacturing plant at Moscow. The saving through the adoption of these suggestions in 1930 amounted to more than 1.5 million rubles. Eighty per cent of the proposals came from the workingmen, five per cent from the office staff, and fifteen per cent from the engineers and technical men. The average saving per suggestion amounted to 435 rubles per worker, 1500 rubles per office man, and 4500 rubles per engineer.[33]

2. Establishment of Wage Rates. A basic wage rate is set for a normal output, the quota being fixed by the management with the advice of the workers' committees, who confer after hours. Stop-watch studies are continuously made for the purpose of shortening processes or increasing output. A "conflict committee" or "arbitration board" decides what is a fair wage rate, when a new method of work is devised. An unparalleled experience of the writer was the testimony of the officials of the Steel Trust and of the Electrical Trust that workmen ask for a reduction in wages when a new method of operation produces too high a wage. Mr. Clark of the Electrical Trust happened to have on his desk a metal part for making which a worker devised a short cut. His piece rate was not lowered, and when his total wages rose to an unusual height, he felt disloyal to his co-workers and asked for a reduction of 40 per cent in his rate. In Mr. Clark's service of more than twenty years before the revolution both as a worker and as manager at the Riga plant of the A.E.G., he had never had an experience of this sort. He said that under the capitalist system labor and capital tried to exploit each other. Under the Soviet system the workers and the state co-operate for a common end, and the new social standards discredit any attempt at exploitation by either labor or capital.

a. Piece Work and Bonuses. For a number of years the tendency was to increase compensation in accordance with output. According to the decrees of the Supreme Economic Council it was desirable to keep the piece workers interested in increasing their output and therefore the trade unions and the industrial managers were instructed not to introduce too great an equality between piece rates and time rates in the fiscal year 1930.[34] Furthermore, in order to stimulate the workers to improve their skill, the wages of skilled and unskilled were set so as not to be too nearly alike. In the wage agreements for the fiscal year 1930 greater remuneration was therefore granted to skilled workers and to piece workers.[35]

The pressure to graduate earnings in accordance with skill and efficiency increased. All during the spring of 1931 public opinion was being led by the three Moscow dailies away from the principle of equalization of wages of skilled and unskilled workmen and of old workers and new workers. "The time has come to introduce piece work and bonus systems in all production processes so that maximum efficiency may be achieved and the percentage of spoiled goods be reduced to a minimum."[36] This general policy was crystallized in Stalin's much quoted address to the Economic Conference of Industrial Managers in June, 1931, in which he deplored the results of "leveling" wage scales. (See p. 221.)

b. Errors in Rate Making. In the zeal for setting rates that would induce increasing output, the rate setters were so inexperienced that tremendous discrepancies resulted. In one case a workingman earned on piece rates 62 rubles a day and another 111 rubles a day.[37] Again, workingmen of the same degree of skill were paid different rates for the same work in the several departments of the same factory. For example, in the Baltic Factory at Leningrad crane operators received wages that varied from 65 kopeks up to 1 ruble 21 kopeks (32.5 cents to 60.5 cents) per hour, depending only on the department. Locksmiths of the same degree of skill earned 57 kopeks per hour in one department and 1.25 rubles per hour in another department. As a result of high piece rates workingmen preferred to hold their jobs on piece rates rather than accept promotion to a foremanship where the earnings were limited, or after accepting a promotion they would ask to be transferred back to their position as workers. Sometimes men who were just above the grade of common workman received as much pay as the foreman of ten years' experience. This disorganized shop management and tended to impair discipline.

3. Trade-Union Attitude. In Russia, because of the difference in organization and aim in industry, there is no opposition to scientific management by either workers or trade unions. In fact the trade unions, actively further scientific management. In the electrical industry, for example, stop-watch studies were made at the behest of the unions and of the workers' committees. The resulting profits go not to any individuals but to the state. If the output is increased substantially, wages do not increase proportionately but the increase is limited to 20 per cent of the savings effected by the new method.

4. The Five-Day Week. a. Theory. The introduction of the five-day week was a phase of the movement for increasing efficiency. Each workman had one day's rest in five, but the plants worked continuously all year except on five holidays commemorating the revolution. The advantage was an increase in the output of the plant without adding to the hours of labor of the workers. This advantage was offset in part by the interference with the routine of the plant. Conferences were difficult because some member or other of the management would be absent. One man would be very busy on his fourth day in anticipation of his fifth day of rest, and he would be

very busy on his first day because the plant had kept on working, and the routine required him to make up the lost time. Unless it was known on what days of the month an official had his fifth day off his business relations were likely to be upset. To lessen these difficulties, important officials were limited to the second or fourth day for resting. Again, a holiday could not be enjoyed if four-fifths of one's friends were at work. Several of the foreign engineers at the factories in Moscow and Leningrad did not take their fifth day off because most of their fellow-engineers were at work and there was no spirit of rest and play. On the other hand, the cultural and recreational facilities were not overtaxed. The museums were well attended every day of the week. There were no days of peak loads and of idleness in the museums and recreational grounds. And if industry suffered somewhat from the inefficiency of the five-day week, culture and recreation benefited.

b. Practice. After considerable experience with the five-day week the managers of industry began to realize its difficulties. Work was disorganized. Large groups of skilled workmen failed to appear on certain days and it was difficult to check idle absentees. Since there was no universal or fixed day of rest workingmen frequently changed their particular day off without the approval of the management. Production schedules broke down as a result. Practical engineers in charge of plants began to discuss the re-establishment of the normal production week with one day off, uniform for everybody. Such a move would eliminate the irregular absentees, and the idleness of expensive machinery which carried a high overhead. Furthermore, and most important, the uniform production week would make it possible to distribute the skilled workers more evenly. It would make it possible to assign a particular worker to a particular machine and keep him responsible for its production and its good condition and would thus eliminate the fault of irresponsibility, or as the Russians call it, "impersonalism." It would simplify control of personnel and payment of piece rates. The maintenance gangs could use the uniform day of rest to overhaul and repair the machinery and thus to prevent its rapid deterioration. Such were the actual conclusions of the engineers in charge of the "Selmash," the agricultural machinery plant at Rostov.[38]

c. Stalin's Views. The death blow to the five-day week was given by Stalin in the address to the Industrial Managers.[39] Realizing the practical effects of the five-day or non-stop week, Stalin abandoned theory and took his cue from the plant managers. He reversed his attitude completely and vigorously denounced the continuous working week and the faults which it generated.

As a matter of political strategy, however, he stated that the abandonment would be only temporary and that ultimately the five-day week, with its defects eliminated, might be restored.

> Under the present large scale of production, with the new gigantic industrial enterprises, irresponsibility has become a foe of industry, endangering all our production and achievements in organizing industrial enterprises.
>
> How was it possible for this irresponsibility to establish itself in a number of enterprises? It crept into our enterprises as an illegitimate companion of the continuous work week. . . . The point is that many of our enterprises went over to continuous production too hastily, without preparing the necessary conditions, without properly organizing the shifts, so that they should compare more or less favorably in skill, without establishing the responsibility of each worker for a given task. As a result of this the continuous work week, left to take its natural course, has led to irresponsibility. . . .
>
> It is no wonder that the workers say "We would increase the productivity of labor and would improve the situation but who would give us credit if no one is responsible for anything?" . . .
>
> Or where conditions are not conducive to such an experiment, we must throw out entirely the "paper" continuous work week, and adopt temporarily a six-day week with one rest day, as was done recently in the Stalingrad Tractor Plant, and then prepare the ground for the return later to a real continuous work week, to a continuous work week without irresponsibility. . . .
>
> The question is, who needs such a continuous work week? Who would be prepared to place the interests of maintaining this continuous work week, perverted or on paper, above the interests of a proper organization of labor, above the interests of increased productivity of labor, of a real continuous work week, of our socialized industry? Is it not clear that the quicker we bury this continuous work week on paper, the sooner we will attain the organization of a real continuous work week?

d. Abandonment of the Five-Day Week. By a decree of the Council of the People's Commissars dated November 23, 1931, the five-day "uninterrupted working week was abandoned. The six-day week with a full day of rest uniform for everybody was substituted. The new week went into effect in December, 1931, and applied to all business and office work, except that connected with the cultural or life needs of the population such as co-operative stores, dining rooms, transportation. Shifting from the five-day to the six-day week meant a loss of one day in every thirty to the workers. To offset this loss the working hours per day were reduced. The official decree came after the six-day week had been restored in the important industrial centers.

5. Automatic Devices. In several factories one sees a curious combination of old-fashioned manual labor and the most up-to-date mechanical devices. In the Moscow electrical factory, for instance, there is a traveling crane, fitted with an electro-magnet which picks up transformers weighing many

tons and carries them several hundred yards to the other end of the factory. In the same shop a worker can be seen filing by hand the rough edges left by an automatic punch. Again, automatic hand trucks, operated by electricity, scoot up and down the electrical plant, but at the railroad siding one sees men pushing a loaded freight car out of the factory by hand, work that could be done more efficiently by any one of a number of devices.

In following a job through a process the observer is impressed with the great discrepancy in efficient handling. One stage will be handled by automatic machinery, quickly and at a low labor cost. The next stage will be handled laboriously by the most primitive methods. The saving of time and labor in one process is offset by waste in the subsequent stages. In some plants, where a continuous process seems almost inevitable, one finds much hand work, with the consequent damming of the flow of goods through the plant.

6. Lack of an Efficient Spirit. But the question of efficient production is not merely one of machinery but rather one of a tradition of efficiency. A foreign railroad engineer who had crossed the country on the Trans-Siberian Railroad during the war and again in 1930 told the writer in Moscow of the abandonment of the automatic coal-handling machinery erected during the war to speed coal to industrial plants. The workmen went back to shoveling coal by hand because that was the way they had been doing it for years, and they would have nothing to do with this "crazy contraption" of the foreigners. Again, when a foreign engineer gave an oil-can to each of a group of Russian workmen with instructions to lubricate some newly assembled tractors he found them later with jobs not done and all huddled around one machine which had been taken apart out of curiosity.

In walking through the various plants the writer was impressed by the general disorder. In some shops the inventory of merchandise was in utter disarray so that it looked almost like a junk heap. This was not merely the isolated observation of the writer. It is the general testimony of American visitors with experience in management or in factories and with an industrial background. In a talk before the All-Union Western Chamber of Commerce in Moscow an engineer representing an automobile company gave some impressions of Soviet factories he had visited:

> The indifferent attitude of factory managers toward the untidiness of their factories is most startling. Factory floors and yards are strewn with all kinds of materials, and are extremely dirty. To get to their jobs the workmen must wade through a sea of mud. If all the raw materials and scrap scattered about in fac-

tories were assembled it would constitute an adequate supply for several weeks' operation.[40]

This lack of experience in management is revealed not only in the inventory of raw materials and finished goods, but also in a lack of records concerning inventories, in interruptions of the flow of work, and in such an excessive supply of labor as to interfere with production rather than to facilitate it. The erection of tremendous plants has revealed in a most striking way the great need for competent industrial management. It calls for a high degree of executive power, which can be developed only over a long period of time and which is entitled to a compensation far higher than the scale of Russian wages provides.

In the case of those raw materials in whose manufacture nature does the work, such as coal, oil, grain, timber, and perhaps certain manufactured raw materials, Russia may be a factor in world production. But in the making of machine products her problems in training labor in the efficient handling of machinery, and in developing a class of foremen and superintendents, plant managers and industrial executives will take more than a year or even five to solve and therefore her position in world markets for locomotives, automobiles, tractors, etc., is likely to be negligible for a long time to come.

In an investigation by the Moscow paper *Za Industrializatsiu,* John Calder stated at Stalmost, the new steel center: "There is no organized program, no proper assortment of materials, which lie everywhere in heaps, and no system of management. If anything goes wrong the engineers, instead of doing something, just draw up a protocol." The representative of the paper stated that though materials and men were abundant, neither were utilized at the right place or at the right time. The blame was laid on the higher executives who were ignorant in the technique of management and of the scientific organization of work.[41]

Stalingrad presented a concrete picture of the lack of an efficient organization. According to the records at the plant 20 per cent of the workmen shifted every month from one department to another. In other words in less than six months the entire personnel was turned over. Still worse, even, within the same department workingmen would shift from machine to machine instead of going to an appointed place at the conveyor at a particular time under the supervision of a job setter or foreman. Again, at the Stalingrad plant instead of utilizing the Soviet holidays, May 1 and 2, for repairing equipment, which was in bad condition, the management ordered that routine work be done to prepare a sufficient number of parts to turn out a certain number of tractors on the day following. The plant was so disorganized that members of the executive staff had not slept more than a few hours a night for months because of their herculean efforts to overcome the difficulties in plant operation.[42] As Harrington Emerson, the American efficiency engineer, said in an address to a group of industrialists, some years ago, "Effort is not efficiency, nor is strenuous work scientific management."

The lack of an efficient spirit or a technique of management was revealed at a conference of labor correspondents of the Moscow newspapers who were studying the operation of the Stalingrad plant. There was no co-ordination between the departments or between the workers in the departments.[43] A summary of the ills of management was presented in their appeal to the representatives of the Communist Party, the trade unions, and the management, calling for efforts to put all departments on a profitable basis, to organize piece work, to introduce centralized control giving executives authority over workmen, to fight mercilessly against low labor discipline and spoiling of work, to eliminate labor turn-over, to plan rationally the processes of work, and to struggle for lower costs, for better quality, and for greater economy of raw material and fuel.[44]

7. Poor Planning and Inadequate Routing. One of the essentials of scientific management, as practiced in Amercia, is the principle of the flow of work, i. e.: that raw material shall be routed so that at various points it meets the job requiring it. This calls for skill in organization. In Soviet Russia serious waste results from the failure to apply this principle. At one of the textile factories visited the workers had to go home because the raw material expected was not delivered on time, and while they were waiting they would receive doles. There seems to be a continuous shortage of raw materials. Plans are made for construction work, but no plan is made for having cement, brick, and mortar delivered at the right time and the right place. Sometimes important construction work is delayed because some machine or important part is held up in delivery, and labor must remain idle.

A typical case is that of the Second Watch Factory. A watch, instead of being routed through a logical sequence of operations, sometimes reverses its tracks, resulting in an increased cost of production and poorer quality. For example, some parts are machined after hardening, resulting in greater cost and greater breakage, amounting in some cases to 70 to 75 per cent of the parts produced. Then to insure an adequate supply of parts the plant produces 100 spare parts in order to have 25 that will pass inspection. Again, at "Geophysics," a plant manufacturing precision instruments, orders are marked with four or five degrees of urgency, which interfere with the orderly flow of production throughout the plant.[45]

Because of the lack of efficient routing, inadequate use is made of the skilled and highly paid foreign engineers.[46] Construction work by the firm of Albert Kahn, Inc., was delayed because the "designing trust" lacked competent help, and the expensive American experts had to do the work of cheap native draftsmen. Then the "construction trust" failed to carry out the instructions of the "designing trust," and instead of drafting plans for the entire plant as a unit adhered to the old Russian system of planning each section separately.

Scientific management is the finished product of a long-established and well-regulated industrial system, and cannot be grafted on to a primitive and rapidly developing industrial system. The inefficiency that characterizes Soviet Russia today results in low productivity per capita, so that even if better distribution of goods among the masses were achieved there would be less to distribute.

8. Typical Situations. The difficulties of management are admitted by the Soviet officials and are exposed frankly and mercilessly in the Soviet campaigns of self-criticism. A few typical situations at the leading new giant plants are given herewith.

a. Stalingrad Tractor Plant.[47] This is the first large plant in the Soviet Union to be constructed for mass production of machinery along American lines. Many other plants will be built along similar lines. It is therefore of interest to see how the Stalingrad plant illustrates the Russian approach to the problem of management. The Russians themselves admit "mass production methods have not been learned as yet." "The flow of 4000 parts which go to make a tractor will be continuous only when all machines in the factory, in the foundry, in the forge shop, in the tool rooms, and in the stock rooms are co-ordinated so that suitable parts meet at the assembly belt. If any one of the many thousand factors are overlooked by the management continuous production is impossible. The Stalingrad plant lacks such a system of co-operation and therefore there is no continuous production. The conveyor implies a continuous flow of parts but it stands still for a longer time than it moves. Various reasons are given for the interruption. Sometimes parts are spoiled; sometimes machine tools are broken; sometimes compressed air is lacking. One day the Stalingrad factory found itself without water, though it is situated right on the Volga, because the water pumps stopped working owing to a breakdown of the power plant. Less than a third of the plant is being used. Whatever production there is, costs nerve-racking work, constant speeding up where there is a shortage, and mad rushing of some sections of the plant while others are forced to be idle."

The cause is a lack of plans for the organization of production and lack of discipline. The Soviets admit the lack of both planning and control. The management does not know on one day how many tractors are ready for assembly the next day. Generally the first assembling shift does not produce a single tractor because the lack of an important part is discovered in the morning and there are no reserve inventories of such parts. Then follows a frantic struggle during the day and the conveyor belt starts to move at evening and assembling goes on during the night. There is no planning. The foreman races about searching for missing parts. Periodically accumulated heaps must be inventoried to find out how many parts are available. An illustration of how "trifles" interrupt production is the so-called "rag problem." For lack of plain wiping rags which cost a few cents the Stalingrad plant wasted thousands of dollars. One milling machine costing $27,000 was spoiled because there were no rags to wipe off the metal shavings which accumulated in the oil lubricating the machine.[47]

The routing of parts is inadequate. At one time the conveyor stopped because of a lack of bolts. At another spokes for the tractor wheels were missing. The staff rushed around searching for spokes and found great quantities of them in the forging department, the manager of which had forgotten to send them to the assembling shop.[48]

The records, which are an essential part of factory administration, are poorly kept. On one occasion the principal cause of the failure of output of the Stalingrad plant was the irregular supply of steel, iron, and coke. The keeper of the store room had neglected to give attention to the rapidly waning supply. As a result the foundry was shut down and the machining of the cast-iron parts ceased. Then high-grade steel was lacking so that the forging department had to shut down.[49] In a well-run European or American plant there is generally a perpetual inventory with well-kept records, and when the inventory clerk finds that the reserves are being depleted to the danger line he notifies the management.

Routing of important equipment is neglected. "Owing to the inefficiency of Soviet trade representatives abroad, American equipment ordered for Stalingrad was delivered to other factories and now search is being made all over the country for the strayed machines."[50] Poor routing within the country also obstructs the continuous flow of work. Two thousand fan belts ordered from the rubber factory "Kauchuk" remained undelivered for four months and all inquiries by the Stalingrad management remained unanswered.[51]

The Soviet critics score the management of the Stalingrad plant on several counts. The management does not give detailed instructions to the foremen, who in turn do not teach the workmen. As a result equipment is damaged, tools are spoiled, and the output is inferior. Valuable materials are not properly stored. The tool room and repair shop are ordered to manufacture tractor parts. There is no system of records for labor material and supplies. The various departments are not organized on a cost-accounting basis. There is lack of piece rates for the various processes.[52] Again, management suffers from the inadequate training of the workers. More than 75 per cent of the workmen and more than 80 per cent of the engineers are young and have no practical experience. Not only the workmen but even the foremen are "technically illiterate." The high turnover of labor and its inefficient utilization have upset the Plan, both in finance and production.[53]

At the request of the newspaper *Za Industrializatsiu,* John Becker, an American engineer at the plant, wrote an article on "How Not to Start a Plant," reciting some outstanding causes of mismanagement. The article concludes, "The foregoing is sufficient to explain why not a single tractor has stood up in an actual test; after 70 hours of work they 'open at the seams.' "[54]

b. Magnitogorsk Steel Plant. The Magnitogorsk project, which is about five times as great as the Dnieprostroy electric project, is regarded by the Soviets as the key of the Five-Year Plan. The Council of People's Commissars issued a decree ordering all agencies to lend assistance to the Magnitogorsk project; yet it took a longer time to transport excavators from the port of Leningrad to Magnitogorsk than it did to bring them from New York to Leningrad. Three or four years after the project was first designed for a capacity of 650 thousand tons of pig iron per annum, a plant four times as great, about the size of the United States Steel plant at Gary, Indiana, was decided upon. This was done with little preparation. As a result, machines have been idle a good part of the time while demurrage charges piled up in the railroad yards.[55]

c. Rostov Agricultural Machinery Plant. The "Selmash" agricultural machinery plant at Rostov shows similarly a lack of technique of mass production. For instance after parts are manufactured by modern machinery they are sent to work benches to be finished off by hand. The production curve fluctuates from peak production down to zero almost daily due to the lack of inventory of parts. The conveyor stands idle until the missing parts are made. Because of the lack of a running inventory of parts Saturday afternoons are set aside, and a hundred or more communists, special selected "towing" parties, sort out and pile up the inventory. The work is futile because the factory continuously dumps new parts into the yard. These dumps are scattered near the various departments and the contents are unknown. When the assembling of parts is interrupted "excavation" parties go to the several piles to seek the missing items. The managers, instead of supervising, rush around hunting for parts. The shortage of parts, instead of being anticipated, generally remains unknown until it is actually discovered at the assembly belt.

Then again breakdowns of machines are frequent. The causes are the lack of centralized responsibility, the failure to assign workmen to a definite machine, and the lack of adequate maintenance. As a result, production is discontinued on "special breakdown days" during which necessary repairs are made. Naturally, the so-called continuous production week ceases to exist. The plant has its day of rest; but it comes not regularly, as in the western world, but sporadically when the machines can no longer work.[56]

d. Nizhni Novgorod Automobile Plant. The construction of the Nizhni Novgorod plant was begun on May 1, 1930. After the plant was under way it was discovered that many of the elements that go into the making of an automobile were not available in the Soviet Union. To manufacture the 140 thousand automobiles per year would require that many industries in the Soviet Union be created and others revolutionized. Primarily there was a lack of high-grade steel needed for the manufacture of an automobile. About 200,000 tons of high-grade steel were needed and its domestic manufacture was a difficult industrial problem; some therefore had to be imported. Then, besides, cork, fiber, celluloid, paint, and a host of other materials were necessary and there were no facilities to produce them in adequate volume. Again, the electrical equipment for an automobile would have to be imported because there is no industry in Russia making it. The problem of manufacturing speedometers, shatter-proof glass, Bendix drives, spark plugs, electric bulbs, etc., presented difficulties. "In America it is only necessary to whistle to have hundreds of salesmen come to your door who will be ready to offer any product at any time, but in Soviet Russia the demand of the automobile industry for an annual supply of millions of electric bulbs, a million cushion springs, hundreds of thousands of square meters of glass of a grade never before manufactured in Russia, and special steel unknown to Russian metallurgists, is a special problem which should have been solved before." [57]

In other words the United Automobile and Tractor Industries "are going to offer the people of Soviet Russia an automobile without tires and seats, without windows, without carburetors, and without starters. It will be an automobile in which the ignition will come from the fiery zeal of its creators, and the frightened eyes of its chauffeur will serve as headlights." [57]

The breakdown was ascribed to numerous causes. The large-scale production called for the operation of hundreds of conveyors. However, there were actually operating only two. The others stood idle for lack of parts. Instead of carrying red-hot castings on conveyors, they were carried in hand-litters. In the spring-manufacturing department, the conveyor was out of order, and the workmen carried on their backs "up to 60 tons a day of spring leaves that go to the furnaces for tempering." Because the conveyors did not work, great stacks of parts accumulated between machine tools. The trucks used for conveying parts did not operate because the "plants have no floors and the yards are not paved. The entire area of the plant looks as if it had suffered from a recent earthquake or bombardment."

> The yards are cut by ditches and the earth is piled up here and there, and there are great gaping holes elsewhere. The inspection department is lax. Horns and headlights which were condemned were subsequently put into use. Work in the assembly shop is inaccurate. Assembled machines are left uncared for and out in the open.[58]

The plant was completed on January 1, 1932, and began working. Owing to mismanagement and poor labor discipline, the plant shut down on April 3, 1932. By the autumn of 1932 it was turning out 40 cars per day.

After the automobile plant at Nizhni Novgorod was completed, a new crop of difficulties arose. In April 1932, when the program called for the completion of 1075 cars over a given time there were produced only 301 motors, 143 front axles, and only two rear axles. The difficulty is primarily in the management.[59]

> The technical equipment in the shops of the automobile plant is sufficient even to exceed the production program. Nevertheless, the plant must be shut down due to poor management. The plant has no unified control. Instead of business managers, the plant was run by local members of the Communist Party. An "anti-specialist" attitude and a baiting of the administrative and technical personnel prevailed at the plant. There is no clear division of functions among the

numerous assistant directors and there is no clear-cut supervision of production.

The troubles were not due entirely to internal conditions in the plant. The material supplied was unsatisfactory. For example, one steel plant (Zlatoust) shipped 200 tons of steel for the making of automobile springs. This shipment was unsatisfactory, as some of the steel was cracked and uneven and the shapes were inaccurate, by as much as 7 per cent. It was so brittle that it crumbled easily under the pressure of the foot. Automobile springs cannot be made from such material.[60]

One plant made only 150 types of bolts and rivets instead of the necessary 450 types. Other accessory plants failed to turn out a single ignition lock, horn, or wiring set, and what accessories were supplied were of unsatisfactory quality. Steering wheels, gears, and speedometers are turned out in insufficient quantities. The automobile production at the Nizhni Novgorod plant depends upon the successful operation of about 35 accessory plants that produce more than 1000 parts. When the Nizhni Novgorod plant shut down on April 3, 1932, it was expected that it would resume operations again on April 15. However, even in the middle of June 1932, "the plant did not succeed in organizing a continuous flow of parts. Over 300 machines turned out in April and May were stored in the yards, waiting for some part or other. For example, some automobiles came off the assembly conveyors with mudguards on one side only." Accessory plants are delinquent in supplying the necessary parts. "Therefore, it was decided to suspend further automobile production at the plant and to limit its operations to the production of motors for combine harvesters." [61]

e. Electric Power Plants. The newly built electric power plants are inefficient in their operations. Owing to the delay in the construction of transmission lines and substations, they cannot operate at full capacity. For instance, at "Ivgres," the electric power plant in the Ivanovo Province, the plant suffered from incomplete installation, improper handling of equipment, frequent breakdown, incompetence of personnel, and excessive moisture of the peat. As a result, the cost of power produced per kilowatt-hour rose 71 per cent, from 4.3 kopeks, as planned, to 7.4 kopeks. Owing to the incomplete utilization of the equipment, the charge for maintenance, depreciation, etc., rose about 60 per cent.[62]

The chief difficulty seems to be the lack of trained personnel for the operation of the plants, the lack of spare parts, and the absence of repair shops. As a result, at the power plants at Stalingrad and elsewhere, repairs are made only when the machinery is at the point of breaking down.[63]

f. The "Giant Plants" Don't Work! The innumerable difficulties cited above, which were experienced during the process of building the "giant plants," forecast the difficulties that would be experienced in the operation of these plants. In the second quarter of 1932, official reports indicated that the great plants were idle. The giants were sick. For example, the Saratov combine plant produced less than one-half its quota. The Communard produced one-fourth its quota, and the Rostov plant produced nothing of its quota of 1100 machines. At the Rostov plant, the largest agricultural machinery plant in Europe, the conveyor belt stood still. Of the 1700 combines needed for the 1932 harvest, only 124 were fully assembled. The Stalin truck plant, formerly called Amo, in Moscow, had dropped in production to less than 50 per cent of its recent performance. At Kharkov, production dropped 30 per cent. At the Molotov automobile plant at Nizhni Novgorod, despite the Communist Party edict that the plant must start regular production on April 15, 1932, there had been no mass production by the late summer. At the Cheliabinsk tractor plant in the Urals, not a single machine had been turned out up to the summer of 1932, except experimental machines, although the plan called for an annual output of 40,000 large tractors of the caterpillar type.[64]

9. Remedies. To remedy the number of appalling difficulties of mass production in the Soviet Union it was decided to reduce the number of investigations, to help the backward plants catch up by "towing by shock brigades" and to restore the small (*kustar*) industries.

a. Reduce Investigations. The numerous investigating committees and inspecting commissions obstructed production in industry. There was a veritable epidemic of them. At a commune, a co-operative farm in the Lower Volga, several investigating committees appeared in one month. It happened at the harvest season and urgent seasonal work was delayed. No copies of the reports were left behind and the work was duplicated. Hours were wasted in preparing accounts and statistical data. "The workers on this farm were very indignant and suggested that all 'brother inspectors' should agree between themselves to get together, but having finished the investigation should not bother the workers again." The Sugar Trust was investigated 94 times in twelve months. The Zlatoust plant was investigated by 30 commissions in the first quarter of 1930. As a result the R.K.I., the People's Commissar of Workmen's and Peasants' Inspection, issued an order forbidding the directors of industrial plants to permit any investigation without its approval.[65]

b. "Towing" by "Shock Brigades." In the western world, if a plant falls behind, a firm of efficiency engineers will survey it and attempt to straighten out the difficulties. But in Russia if a plant is backward other plants in various parts of the country will voluntarily and without solicitation ship towing crews to help the factories catch up to their schedules or straighten out their difficulties. For example, when the Stalingrad Tractor Plant got into a jam, the newspapers reported the difficulties. Thereupon zealots in plants at Leningrad and Kharkov decided to send picked workers "to show their Stalingrad brothers what is what." Other backward plants have like experiences. For example, the large metallurgic unit, the Ural Kombinat, finds it will need about 1½ million laborers within a year. The Central Executive Committee of the People's Commissars issues a decree about the need for getting a suitable labor supply. Thereupon the newspapers appeal to the factories to send their best "shock troops" to storm the Ural citadel.[66]

c. Management by Government Fiat. When difficulties become threatening, the government issues orders and decrees, in order to improve the management. A few typical examples follow. Because the steel industry was failing in its production, the Supreme Economic Council issued a decree reorganizing the labor management. The decree cited that the conditions were extremely unsatisfactory, plans for production and construction remained unexecuted, economic and technical control was lacking, machinery breakdowns were increasing, and the shortage of skilled labor was growing. Therefore the decree provided for the immediate reorganization of factory management on the basis of a single control, of a budget, and of the extension of the piece-work system.[67] Again, because of the difficulties of the coal industry in the Donetz Basin a joint decree was issued by the Communist Party and the Council of People's Commissars and by the Supreme Economic Council, ordering a revolution in methods and organization in the Donetz Basin coal mines within ten days. The mines must produce 56 million tons of coal in the year, considerably more than the current production. To attain these results the decree required mechanization of the plants and improvement of the living conditions of the workers and the development of "social competition and shock brigades," as well as general and technical education. This decree put into effect the suggestions of Mr. Charles E. Stuart, member of Stuart, James & Cooke, American coal engineers and consultants to the Soviet Union, appointed by the Supreme Economic Council to report on the difficulties of the coal industry and on the methods of increasing the output. He worked with the Vice Commissar of the Industrial Council, V. I. Mezhlauk. Mr. Stuart's report recommended that piece work be introduced, bonuses paid for good work, and the workers made responsible. Also 50 per cent of the mines were to be mechanized by the end of the year and were to attain an output which would be charted for them. Living conditions of the workers were to be improved in order to reduce the turnover of labor, food lines were to be eliminated, fuel and water promptly delivered, and efficiency in management fostered by the Communist Party, the local trade unions, the local soviets, and the communist youth clubs, which were to cultivate friendly relations with the old engineering personnel. Finally, fifteen new mines were to be brought into production. This last order was contrary to the suggestions of Mr. Stuart, who thought that it would be simpler to increase the production of the old mines than to open new ones.[68]

The Supreme Economic Council ordered the following measures at the Stalingrad Tractor Plant: Introduction of cost accounting in all departments, clearing up of all scrap and waste, unconditional obedience to the management, closing of the plant to all inspection committees, and abandonment of the continuous week or five-day week. This latter order was also applied to the Kharkov and the Nizhni Novgorod plants.[69]

Other examples of substitution of factory management by government decree and by official threat in place of technical intelligence and factory experience follow. On April 25, 1932, a decree of the Central Executive Committee of the Communist Party publicly reprimanded four high officials of the steel construction trust, Stalmost, for failure to fulfill the program. They were warned also that if the difficulties were not promptly remedied, disciplinary measures would be taken against them. The stoppage of operations at Nizhni Novgorod and the practical cessation of operations of the plants at Amo, Stalingrad, and Kharkov, the obstacles in the construction of the new machinery-building plant and the sudden decline of coal production, and the chronic confusion of the transportation system constituted the basis for such unusual disciplinary measures.[70]

Similarly, when the operations at the Stalingrad auto-truck plant declined to zero on some days and to 30 to 50 per cent capacity on others, owing to the irregular delivery of material, the president of the Supreme Economic Council, G. K. Ordzhonikidze, threatened with severe punishment the director of each enterprise responsible for the failure to ship the necessary materials by a specified date.[71]

d. Restoration of Small Industry. In the plans of large production, the Soviets overlooked the importance of the home crafts and industry of the peasants, (*kustarnye promysly*). Some authorities say that more than 50 per cent of the consumers' goods before the war were produced under these conditions. As noted in an earlier chapter, when the statisticians cite the much larger factory production of consumers' goods at present than before the war, they overlook the fact that the pre-war output of the home industries was not included in the census figures. The campaign against the small producers and traders, as a result of which the stores throughout the country are almost empty, began in 1928 and by measures of taxation and other local restrictions they were almost destroyed. To revive them, the Soviet government reduced taxation on home production by one-third and actually stimulated such production by governmental aid. Though this may seem like a reversal of industrial socialization, it is but another step of revising communist doctrines to fit the realities of life.[72]

e. Recommendations of American Engineers. The American engineers in Russia have been sincerely interested in the program of industrialization and have done much to help, both in doing concrete jobs and in making helpful criticisms. For example, an American engineer who has inspected a score or more of factories in Moscow, Leningrad, and Nizhni Novgorod, gives as his criticisms that the plants are dirty, inventory is disorderly, and labor discipline is poor. He thinks the cause of these difficulties is the idea of the Soviet engineers that their industrial progress depends on the introduction of modern methods of mass production. He thinks that they are foolish to attempt to introduce efficiency by the mere introduction of a conveyor system or the mere imitation of American efficiency experts. He believes instead that it would be preferable to utilize more fully the existing machinery, and to extend existing plants rather than to build modern giant plants.[73]

American engineers working at Stalingrad organized the "Society of Technical Assistants to the Soviet Union" to help remove the difficulties experienced by the Soviets in mass production.[74]

Mr. Charles E. Stuart likewise criticizes "the temperament which prefers gigantic new construction with big capital expenditures to simple, inexpensive measures of rationalization in existing mines which would give millions of additional tons of coal much more quickly and cheaply."[75] His report is of interest from several other aspects. The Russian output per man in the coal mine is about one-fifth that of the American worker. This conforms to the foreign estimate that the productivity of the Russian worker in general is rarely higher than one-third that of the American. The report criticizes and makes specific criticisms. "In three years there was more variation of the projects submitted by us here than in our twenty-seven years' experience in the United States." The Russian manager fears to assume responsibility. There is a preference for talk over action. Interminable conferences are held that rarely decide anything. Insistence on negligible details often delays action on major projects. Russians frequently lack practical experience. The turnover of the personnel is incessant. These difficulties are due to a lack of organization, fear of responsibility, unwillingness to take the initiative, ignorance, and mistrust. To remedy them Mr. Stuart suggests that before asking a foreign engineer to prepare a project the Russians should first decide on what they want and not change it later. The foreign consulting engineer should have access to the highest officials rather than waste time combating bureaucratic inertia and the hostility of minor officials. Conferences should be reduced to a minimum. Subordinates should be given greater authority on the ground that honest mistakes are preferable to bureaucratic inaction.[76]

H. High Cost of Prcduction

Costs of manufacturing are high. For example, at the Nizhni Novgorod automobile plant, the best factory, the "Labor Banner" factory, produces a carburetor for 55 rubles, whereas in America the cost is equivalent to 9 rubles, according to estimates. At the "Labor Banner" co-operatives, spark plugs and tool kits cost six to fifteen times as much as the equivalent cost in the United States.[77] However, in making these estimates Russians take the ruble at par. The reported high cost of Soviet production may be due, in good part, to the depreciation of the ruble.

The various items mentioned heretofore which make for inefficiency contribute heavily to high costs, such as excess of raw material in some factories while others are short; unnecessary machines in some plants, idle machines in others, and overworked machines in still others; the Russian engineer's sense of superiority over manual workers which often prevents instruction of the worker through actual demonstration; interruption of the flow of materials because of lack of foreign credit, inadequate transportation, or lack of co-ordination in and out of the plants—these are but a few examples of the loose workings of the economic machinery of Russia which add immeasurably to the final cost of the finished manufactured article.

1. Breakdown of Machinery. Because of the shortage of credit for the importation of machinery, the existing machinery must be fully used, and continuous use, such as the five-day week and the 24-hour day involve,

results in heavy depreciation, inadequate inspection, and frequent breakdown. These three elements result in increased cost. The items of maintenance, repair, and depreciation are certainly higher than they would be if Russia had abundant credit and did not force the pace of industrialization. "In order to make a good showing, the management of numerous Soviet factories deferred the necessary maintenance and repairs." This led to an increased number of very serious breakdowns and to very high production costs.[78]

At the Stalingrad Tractor Plant, for example, the breakdowns of machine tools were frequent. On every one of the 1100 machines in the machine-assembly department of the plant repairs were required for not less than two breakdowns a month. The chief mechanic at the plant was always behind. A vicious circle resulted from the lack of management. In order to meet the quota of output, the management had ordered the repair shops to machine those tractor parts of which there was a shortage, and then the regular machines did not get needed repairs and therefore did not turn out tractor parts because the machine repair shops were busy making tractor parts rather than repairing machines. Furthermore, the repairing of tractors was poorly done. Shops were inadequately equipped. There was a shortage of lathes. The available machine tools were frequently worn out. Laboratories for testing equipment were lacking. Labor discipline was lax. As a result the actual cost of repair work exceeded the estimates by several hundred per cent. Tractors were even sent out poorly repaired and broke down again soon thereafter.[79]

2. SHORTAGE OF SKILLED LABOR. Because of the great shortage of skilled labor industrial costs are high. Labor is inefficient, as in boom times in all countries. If a laborer is reprimanded for incompetence, he needs but to go to the nearest factory to find another job. In fact, the trusts compete with each other for labor, with all the resulting evils common in the western world. The shortage of trained labor results in an independent attitude on the part of the workers and a very high turnover. Inefficiency, lack of discipline, and turnover not only prevent the reduction of costs but decidedly increase them.

That the securing of an adequate supply of labor has been the outstanding problem was well illustrated at the Stalingrad Tractor Plant. Handling of the labor personnel was inadequate. Until recently the plant administration did not know how large the personnel of various departments was, where it came from, or who the workmen were. It was not the original intention that the Stalingrad plant should develop its own staff but that a sufficient number of skilled workmen and specialists would be shifted from other plants. This transfer was ineffective. An order for a transfer of 7000 skilled workmen to Stalingrad resulted in the arrival of less than 2000. An order to transfer another 1000 workmen brought only 142. Efforts of the Young Communist League to obtain a thousand resulted in 216 and a second drive to transfer 1500 men brought only 137. Not only was there a shortage of labor but such labor as was available was young and unskilled, 60 per cent ranging from 17 to 24 years. Of about 5200 men more than 45 per cent had had less than six months' factory experience and about 80 per cent less than one year's. When production was started the plant managers recruited plowmen from the villages and nomads from the steppes and set them to work running expensive machine tools.[80]

3. Productivity of Labor. The low productivity of labor in Russia as compared with that in western countries has already been commented upon, but in view of the great bearing it has on the high cost of production it will be worth while to give a number of further instances.

The low productivity of Russian labor is admitted in the official version of the Five-Year Plan: [81]

> According to our calculations the productivity of our agricultural labor is approximately five times lower than that of our industrial labor. In the United States agriculture is twice as productive as in the Soviet Union; industry three and one-half times as productive. The productivity of a miner in the United States is six times that of one in the Soviet Union.[81]

One foreign engineer, sympathetic with the Soviet régime, stated that one workman in his country was equal to four Russians. The president of the Economic Council, Mr. V. V. Kuybyshev, cites examples of comparatively low output.[82] In blast-furnace work the annual output per worker in the United States is 3330 tons, in Russia 330 tons. In the textile industry the number of workers per thousand spindles is three in the United States against eight in Russia. Yugoff gives the relative productivity in Russia as 9 units as against 26 in France, 65 in Germany, and 80 in Great Britain, and states that wages form a higher percentage of total cost of production than in the United States, the percentage being 26 in 1927 as against 17 in the United States.[82]

In the coal report of Mr. C. E. Stuart mentioned above he said: "The Russian miner, who produces less than half as much coal as the German and English miner, and less than one-fifth as much as the American, is not inferior to any other miner in strength, energy, and industry. What is lacking is adequate co-ordination of men and equipment to the conditions of each mine and adequate co-ordination of the mining industry as a whole, both internally and in its relation with other industries." There was no shortage of labor in the Donetz mine but a great shortage of proper labor organization.[83]

The Secretary of the International Ladies' Garment Workers' Union investigated production methods and working conditions of the garment industry in the Soviet Union. Before the war he had been a Russian revolutionist and therefore his judgment should be favorable to the Soviets. Yet he says:

> In the largest garment factory in Russia, the Bolshevichka in Leningrad, there are 4000 women employed. They are organized along American lines of specialized production and assembly. The work in the Soviet shops is very intense, yet production seems to be quite low. This factory, according to figures furnished on the premises, turns out 6000 coats a day, or about a garment and a half per worker. In the United States with such an equipment the output would be at least nine garments per worker. In the Kharkov factory, the Tiniakovka, the output is three garments per day per worker, or far behind American standards. The blame for this slackness cannot be placed upon the workers. They hustle because they are all piece workers and have an interest in speeding up the work and seem to have an earnest desire to aid in the progress of the Five-Year Plan. The fault seems to rest with the management.[84]

It is true that the productivity of the Russian worker has shown signs of increasing. According to one authority the daily output per worker in all industry has increased as follows in terms of pre-war rubles:[85]

Fiscal year	*Output Rubles*
1925	7.55
1926	8.42
1927	9.45
1928	10.75
1929	12.50

Nevertheless, the standard of output compared with other countries is still unfavorable.

According to a foreign engineer, then a neighbor of the writer in the Grand Hotel in Moscow, this difference in productivity of the Russian workman is due not to a lack of innate capacity so much as a lack of co-ordination of work, and also to certain naïve characteristics of the Russian workman. In his country, he said, when a workman received a special assignment he would proceed to do it alone. In Russia, if a man had a job to do his fellow-workmen would assemble to discuss, comment, and advise. He told of one instance when he had ordered a workman to repair a roof, and on coming back later to watch progress he had found four workmen sitting on the roof talking.

Another American, a mining engineer in charge of a large project in Russia, who had had experience in handling gangs of workers in Mexico and Ecuador, including Indians and Negroes, stated to the writer that the Russian workingman was far above these in intelligence. He has a keen mind and learns quickly. His chief difficulty is to submit to discipline. Russian workers will talk together but they will not co-ordinate their work as an American group of workers will. An agricultural laborer is accustomed to working independently of others, and when he enters the industrial field he does not readily submit to shop discipline.

That Russian labor is inefficient is admitted.[86] According to the statistical department of the Supreme Economic Council the number of employed in 1929 increased 13.6 per cent as against a planned increase of 4.7 per cent. Yet the industrial program for the year was carried out only 95 per cent. The reason was not a shortage of labor but inefficiency of labor. Although the productivity of labor increased over the preceding year, in the fiscal year 1928 by 10.1 per cent and in the fiscal year 1929 by 16 per cent, yet in the fiscal year 1930, it actually declined 12.5 per cent.[87]

With labor fully employed the sole method of increasing production is the increased productivity per workingman. According to the Five-Year Plan, it should be 16 rubles per day but it has actually averaged less than 10 rubles. To the extent that wages were based on day rates the cost of construction rose at the Nizhni Novgorod automobile plant.[88] The low productivity of labor is due partly to poor planning, to poor routing and to poor management. For example, a special commission investigating the "Electrosila" plant at Leningrad, manufacturing electrical machinery, found that there was no synchronization and that the conveyors were used not as a means of assembly of machines but as a means of transportation of goods from one part of the plant to another.[89]

Other specific causes of faulty management are cited in the Soviet Press. In the Melange-Kombinat, the new textile mill at Ivanovo-Voznesensk, 450 looms were kept idle for ten hours because there was no filling yarn at the machines, although the spinning department in the same plant had a large stock of it on hand. Women weavers in groups of 15 to 25 assembled in the rest-rooms to discuss world politics for four and five hours at a time and forgot production work. As a result the productivity of the plant was about 40 per cent of expectations.[90] At the Red Sormovo plant, which manufactures machinery and equipment, boring machines remained idle about 60 per cent of the time and a drill press ran at 50 per cent of capacity.[91] At the Stalingrad Tractor Plant, during the "shock quarter," when extra effort was made to increase output, idle hours on the machines totaled almost 300,000, more than 40 per cent due to breakdown of machine tools. No one felt responsible for organizing production. The industrial training of the workmen at the plant was neglected. The 276 American experts at the Stalingrad plant were not utilized. When parts were lacking, more than 400 partly completed tractors were set out in the yard to rust for several weeks.[92] In field work in agriculture the productivity of labor is reduced owing to mechanical defects and lack of organization. For instance, at the Zaviazinsky tractor station the tractors remained idle from 30 per cent to 40 per cent of the time during the busy spring season.[93]

4. Subnormal Standards of Living. Inadequate feeding and clothing of the Russian workman is having its effect on productivity of labor and labor costs. An American workman has a heavy breakfast, including plenty of fats, fruits, and even meat. The Russian workman in Moscow, for instance, breakfasts on bread and tea. There is little or no milk, butter, eggs, fresh fruits, or fresh vegetables in the cities. These subnormal standards of living cause inefficiency, errors, and waste, and doubtless increase the number of accidents. Since 1927 accidents have increased 20 per cent, and although their growth is ascribed by a Soviet official to the influx of unskilled workers, malnutrition appears to be a contributing factor of importance. A foreign engineer with intimate knowledge of Soviet conditions stated that Russian engineers tire very easily, and seem to lack the stamina to maintain the same physical pace as foreign engineers. It is a question how long the people can maintain a chronic condition of under-nourishment. It seems to be a race between their growing weakness and the completion of the government's sweeping industrial plans.

5. Losses and Waste. Toward the end of 1929 the State Planning Commission organized a special committee to prevent waste and to investigate the utilization of raw materials and semi-finished goods. At a conference of Soviet factory managers some striking examples of waste were revealed. At the Red Putilovetz works in Leningrad about 47 per cent of the metal used was wasted and at the Rostov railroad shops 40 per cent of the copper in the foundry was wasted. In the Voronezh railroad shops, 36 per cent of the

copper and 26 per cent of the steel were wasted. In building construction 25 to 30 per cent more material was used than was actually needed.[94] At the Melange-Kombinat, the largest textile mill in the Soviet Union, cotton was strewn all over the floor and wasted in large quantities.[95] In this factory the waste is appallingly high.

> Workmen as a rule handle raw materials very carelessly. In the weaving department, for example, 80 per cent of the trash which is burned consists of good cotton. During the first six months, nearly 6000 spools were broken. Spools are used for footballs not only by the workmen, but even by foremen and their assistants.

At the Stalingrad plant, metal and fuel consumption was twice what it should have been and the cost of production had risen accordingly.[96]

In addition to the waste of raw materials there is a waste of capital. According to G. K. Ordzhonikidze, chairman of the Supreme Economic Council, the capital spent on building workers' cities in connection with large industrial enterprises was high in proportion to the enterprise itself. For example, of the total expenditure for the Kharkov Tractor Plant, of 58 million rubles, almost 18 million rubles were spent on workers' quarters.[97] Andreyev, chairman of the Workers' and Peasants' Inspection, listed capital idle or tied up in unfinished plants on January 1, 1931, as about 3.6 billion rubles, and waste of material in railway shops as from 60 to 75 per cent. Inventories are often excessive. For example, at the Stalingrad tractor works about 2.8 million rubles of material was in storage in 1931.[98]

I. Quality of Production

The success of the Five-Year Plan is usually tested by the quantity of output. But fully as important is the quality, especially of shop materials, where defective workmanship, for example in castings, interferes with production.

1. The Facts. Even before the war, Russians did not occupy an important place in the foreign market, because the quality of product was inferior. The quality of goods made since the revolution is even poorer than before the war. And more recently there has been further deterioration of quality. A few concrete cases cited frankly by the Russians themselves in the spirit of self-criticism are given.

> The experience of the Soviet factory for the manufacture of electrical equipment, the "Electrozavod," has given an illustration of poor workmanship in various factories which supply it with materials. During the first five months of 1930 this factory received materials of a total value of 1,361,000 rubles, of

which 21.2 per cent were found defective and sent back. Certain shipments consisted entirely of defective goods.

These defects indicate that the daily technical supervision over the production processes is inadequate. Thus, for instance, 1141 kilograms of strip copper supplied to the Electrozavod by the "Red Vyborozhetz" could not be used at all, because it was entirely too hard and was not sufficiently polished. The tungsten acid supplied by the Mining and Chemical Trust contained molybdenum. Another factory called "Rare Elements" sent a shipment of molybdate of ammonium, 75.9 per cent of which was unusable because it contained nickel and other matter. Of the calcium carbide delivered by the Kalinin factory 63.71 per cent did not correspond to the technical specifications on account of improper granulation. The cast-iron taps delivered by the Mostorg broke while being secured to the pipes. More than 70 per cent of the winding material delivered to the Electrozavod by the factories "Sevkabel" and "Mokz" could not be used for various reasons, mostly on account of poor insulation.[99]

The steel for the Stalingrad Tractor Plant was to be supplied by the "Red October" Steel Plant located nearby and by another steel plant in the Urals. These plants were not equipped to provide goods of sufficiently high quality. As a result of the dispute between the Stalingrad plant and the "Red October" works, a commission was appointed which concluded that the quality of the steel was inferior.[100] At the Stalingrad plant the number of spoiled castings was 2½ times that of good castings because of the inability of the plant to handle the technical processes involved.[101] Again, the assembling of tractors at the Stalingrad plant was handicapped because of the poor quality of the copper and bronze fittings made in the Leningrad factory "Znamia Truda." The threads failed to fit, the fittings leaked, and 80 per cent of the parts had to be junked.[102]

Because the raw material was poor the finished tractors could not stand up under use. A machine tractor station in Azerbaidzhan received thirty-two tractors from the Stalingrad plant. When they were assembled many defects were revealed. Their rims did not fit; the radiator pipes of thirty tractors leaked at two to seven places. Other difficulties too numerous to mention were found. After running in neutral for a short time the tractors began to backfire because the porcelain of the sparkplugs burst.[103] Similarly the tractors of the Red Putilovetz plant proved inferior in quality. Of a shipment of thirty sent to the Volokolam tractor station one was sent back within four days for an overhauling, and eleven others which could not even start to work were left out in the fields. But the loss from tractors which failed completely was less than from the others which must be stopped every two or three hours for repairs.[104] These criticisms were not confined to the tractor stations. From all over the Soviet Union came sworn complaints of difficulties, such as leaking radiators, poorly cast cylinder heads, loose bearings, broken valve springs, unsatisfactory threading on sparkplugs, etc.[105]

The "Electrozavod" factory at Moscow finished its Five-Year Plan in 2½ years as to quantity but the quality of the electric-light bulbs was so poor that complaints were universal that the bulbs burned out very rapidly and the screw caps fell off.[106]

The quality of consumers' goods is low and they wear out quickly—hence the high consumption per capita.

> The outstanding problem is the quality standard in Soviet footwear, which on the whole is still very unsatisfactory. Instead of the anticipated improvement, quality standards in a number of factories have even become worse. Thus, for instance, the shoe factories of the Leningrad Leather Trust show the following percentage of "non-grade" (very inferior) shoes; March, 17.7 per cent; April, 18.1 per cent; and May, 22.3 per cent. The low grade of shoes made by the standard process in the factory "Skorokhod" in March was 14.3 per cent of the total output; in April, 23.1 per cent; and in May, 31.7 per cent. In another factory the proportion of low-grade shoes in the total output increased in the period from March to May from 42.9 per cent to 55 per cent. Similar figures are reported for the factories of the Moscow Leather Trust and in various other localities of Central Russia and the Ukraine.[106]

The Melange-Kombinat at Ivanovo-Voznesenk is a huge textile mill as important in its field as the Stalingrad plant or the Magnitogorsk steel plant. About 70 million rubles, one-tenth of the entire capital investment of the Five-Year Plan for the textile industry, was appropriated for this mill. Its capacity is 18,000 workmen, 400,000 spindles, 4500 looms, and 5 huge dyeing establishments. The quantity provided for was very large but the quality of goods produced was very poor. During the first six months the estimate for damaged goods was 31 per cent, but it actually turned out to be 72 per cent. In some months the damaged goods in the weaving department ran over 90 per cent.[107]

The newspapers have carried complaints continuously from the public, concerning the quality of the output of various industries. For example, the men's clothing factory "turned out trousers with legs of different sizes."[108] The Kharkov Locomotive Works turned out tractors that did not move. The "Precision Mechanics Trust" manufactured calculating machines of which about 50 per cent produced the wrong results in the calculations and as a result buyers "no longer discard individual calculating machines but turn down an entire series because they know that all the machines in that series are defective."[108]

2. Causes of Poor Quality. The low grade of goods produced was ascribable to several causes. The raw material, such as pig iron and leather, is often poor. Again, the rapid growth of industry under the Five-Year Plan called for more labor than was available, and the drafting of rough labor for work requiring considerable skill inevitably led to poor workmanship. According to the Russians themselves—

> The new textile mill *Melange-Kombinat* at Ivanovo-Voznesenk has very few experienced textile workmen. Of the total 2388 textile workmen employed there are only 47 per cent of men with two years of experience in textile production, 23 per cent with five years of experience, and only 2 per cent with twenty-five years of experience. Nearly one-third of the workmen employed there are a farming type. About 1300 of the workmen are young men who have never before been employed in industry.[109]

Furthermore, continuous supervision by trained inspectors is lacking, and because machinery is not maintained in good repair, the quality of the work naturally suffers.

In other ways the demand of the Five-Year Plan for increased output and for lower costs also resulted in a poorer quality of workmanship. In some Soviet factories the percentage of spoiled output ran as high as 40 to 60 per cent. If the Soviet accounting made proper charges for defective work, the cost of the remainder of good work naturally should rise. For example, the production of the quota in one of the Soviet glass factories was realized by speeding up the machines. But certain departments of the factory were not equipped for the larger volume and therefore almost five million lamp chimneys were not annealed in the process. In the textile and shoe industries production is increased by eliminating certain operations thus damaging the product. The largest shoe factory in Russia, "Skorokhod," has turned out such defective merchandise that, according to affidavits by the consumers' co-operatives, it is usual for a case containing forty pairs of shoes to have about ten pairs completely defective and ten pairs seconds or thirds. Another cause for low standards of quality is the payment of the inspectors on a piece-work basis. To remedy this difficulty the plan was contemplated of making the inspection department responsible not to the local factory management but to the central office of the trust.[110]

3. Results. The result of poor workmanship has been to increase the shortage. Poor quality of wearing apparel means really a decrease in the real wages of the workers. In industry and in transportation defective materials and parts lead to increased expense and uncertain operation. For example, in the

Stalingrad tractor factory the quality of the steel delivered for a while was too poor to be used in stamping, and the additional treatment which it required delayed production schedules.

The need for a higher quality of consumers' goods becomes an important political matter. Although the quality is poor "the comrades will devour anything and take what they can get." [111] The economic effect is to decrease the real wages of the workers.

4. Remedies. The Russian papers are filled with complaints and criticisms concerning defective materials. Shock brigades of "workers' and peasants'" inspectors frequently roam from plant to plant to inspect the merchandise produced. Within the factory workers producing very defective goods are listed as in a classroom and their poor workmanship displayed for public disparagement. Similarly, workmen producing high quality of work are singled out for various forms of public approval. Originally commissions were set up to receive criticisms concerning the quality of goods. But none of these measures has been effective in attaining the standards of quality of competing imported goods.

J. Accounting System

One of the revelations to the foreigner visiting Russia is the absolute freedom with which business matters are discussed. What the capitalist world considers as trade secrets, to be withheld from competitors and strangers, are in Russia as much a matter of public concern as the census figures in the United States. When the writer asked one of the officials of the Steel Trust if he might see its income account and balance sheet, great tomes were brought forward covering the whole industry and numerous individual plants. Not only was no effort made to hide the facts, but full and frank explanation was made in answer to all inquiries as to discrepancies of costs as between several plants or at different times for the same plants. Statistics are kept monthly, per plant, per man, and per ton of output. These figures are also compiled so as to show percentage of the plan achieved and percentage of the previous month's record.

In the Electrical Trust plant somewhat similar statistics are kept, showing in addition the waste of raw material per man, percentage of idle machines, percentage of time wasted in waiting, earnings per hour, per man, and per department, as well as the percentage of the Plan realized. These figures are compiled per machine, per man, per section, and per plant, both in comparison with the preceding period and as a percentage of the quota set under the Five-Year Plan. Record is kept of suggestions for efficiency made per worker and per plant. The figures are very often also recorded on a large blackboard in the shop, exposed for public commendation or disapproval.

The methods of office work seem rather crude. Walking through the factories and offices one sees few adding machines but instead the type of abacus used by Chinese laundrymen in the United States and also to teach elementary school children to count. This device is common in the East and is an interesting reminder of the link in the habits of Russia and China. The Soviet filing systems and office devices do not seem to have advanced to the point where they can handle the technique of large-scale production effectively.

The aim of the cost-accounting system is to reduce the cost of production. Accountants and industrialists coming to Russia frequently express doubts as to the adequacy of their charges, and in reply to a question the officials of the several trusts almost uniformly state that interest on investment is charged against the plant by the State Bank and deducted from the profits. The charge of a fixed percentage for capital invested is similar to the charge made in capitalist countries. Again, depreciation and amortization charges are as heavy in Soviet Russia as in the western countries. Steel buildings are amortized at the rate of 2.5 per cent per annum, wooden buildings at the rate of 5 per cent, machinery at 10 per cent, and tools and equipment are written off at 33 to 50 per cent per annum. The accounting records are very detailed and conform in principle to the accounting systems of the United States, Great Britain, or Germany.

1. Income Accounts. A typical income account of the pig-iron plants of the Steel Trust is given herewith to show major items. Many detail items actually recorded are omitted from this schedule:

MAJOR ITEMS IN PROFIT AND LOSS ACCOUNT OF PIG-IRON PLANTS

Chief materials:

- Iron ore
- Manganese ore
- Slag of Martin furnace
- Slag of other furnaces
- Metals
- Pig-iron scrap (four items)
- Limestone

Fuel

- Coke and coal

Recovery items:

- Scrap
- Gas of furnaces
- Slag
- Flue dust
- Carbon monoxide

MAJOR ITEMS IN PROFIT AND LOSS ACCOUNT OF PIG-IRON PLANTS—*Continued*

Wages:
 Direct wages
 Overhead wages

Other shop expense:
 Steam
 Electricity
 Blowers and motors
 Turbines

Water
Employees' expenses
Cleaning of gases
Repairs
Transportation and loading
Labor protection
Idle time
Other wages
Amortization (classified under several items)
Other shop expense
General expense
Output as percentage of Plan

The books of account of this trust are carried in as great detail as the writer has ever seen in factories of America and abroad, and the officials are well versed in the theory and practice of accounting. It is interesting that, although suitable charges are made for depreciation, amortization, and interest, no charge is made for rent.

The importance of accurate accounting becomes apparent as large-scale production increases. Good management requires accurate cost accounting. In his address to the Economic Council of industrial managers in June, 1931, Stalin said:

> The principles of cost accounting were neglected in a number of our enterprises, where the conceptions of "régime of economy," "curtailment of non-productive expenses," "rationalization of production," have gone out of fashion. They expect that the State Bank will "advance them the necessary sums anyway." Production costs therefore began to rise. They were given the tasks of reducing costs by 10 per cent and actually they are raising them. What does curtailment of costs mean? Each one per cent reduction in costs means an accumulation of 150 to 200 million rubles in industry. Our task is to introduce and strengthen the principles of cost accounting.[112]

Accurate accounting explains the achievement of the Electrozavod, manufacturing electrical equipment at Moscow. This plant completed its Five-Year Plan in two and a half years. The chief reason given was the introduction of a single control, and the full authority given to executives in their departments beginning October 1, 1929. Each department head had complete charge and "maximum autonomy," and each department had to pay its own way under a cost-accounting system, *khozrastchot*.[113]

2. DISTRIBUTION OF INDUSTRIAL PROFITS. Of the total profits of industry, 6 per cent go to the State Bank as the equivalent of an interest charge, 40 per cent go to the state budget, 10 to 20 per cent to welfare work, a certain percentage is set aside for supplementary amortization and depreciation reserves, and

the balance is applied to expansion of the industry. A record of distribution of the profits, in million rubles, is shown herewith: [114]

	1923–4	*1924–5*	*1925–6*	*1926–7*	*1927–8*	*Total*	*Per cent*
Profits of industry	160	456	633	647	743	2639	100
Receipts of Treasury	126	185	283	445	391	1430	54

Accurate cost accounting becomes increasingly important because of the manner of the distribution of the profits of industry. Of the net profits in 1929–30 of state industrial enterprises operating on the principle of economic accounting, 11 per cent went to a fund for improving living conditions of the workers and 20 per cent to income tax, and the remainder was applied to the surplus and to strengthening the capital.[115]

K. Capitalistic Aspects

The directors of the various trusts in Russia attempt to stress the unique character of their production. They say that in the capitalist world, industrialists make individual guesses, but that in Soviet Russia a nation-wide unified plan is made, as a result of which it should be possible to avoid depressions. However, the industrial processes of the Soviets are shot through with capitalist technique and methods as shown throughout this book. The Soviets have made a series of compromises with their original communist principles and have now practically returned to the capitalist method from which they departed to develop a new system.

Though the technique is veering toward western methods in the recognition of individual effort, there has been no yielding on the fundamental principle of state ownership and state control of industry. The adoption of capitalistic methods does not imply the adoption of capitalistic aims. Rather the successful technique of the western world has been grafted onto Soviet theories, but modified to meet emergencies or new conditions. Even though piece work has been extended, cost accounting applied to each plant, the old engineers conciliated, and responsibility for management centralized and fixed, yet the adoption of these measures does not mean a departure from Soviet principles. The promulgation of the New Economic Policy by Lenin and the new policies outlined by Stalin were necessary and urgent adjustments in order to adapt their communist theories to the realities of life.

L. Remedies

1. Decentralization. What are the remedies for the industrial troubles in Russia? Plants have been built whose demands are vastly in excess of the supply of engineers or even of skilled labor. The desire for mere size has displaced the vital question as to quality of workmanship and efficiency in production and in distribution of merchandise. Stalin perceived the difficulty of finding business ability of sufficiently high order to manage the huge concentrations of enterprise and therefore, in his oft-quoted address before the Economic Conference of Industrial Engineers in June 1931, he outlined a remedy:

> It is essential that our present unwieldy industrial combinations, sometimes including from 100 to 200 enterprises, should be broken up at once into several smaller combinations. Obviously, the head of such a combination, having to do with a hundred or more factories, cannot really know these factories, their possibilities, and their work. Obviously, not knowing the factories, he is in no position to manage them. Therefore, in order to make it possible for the heads of the industrial combinations really to study and direct the factories, they must be relieved of excess factories, the combinations must be broken up, and the center brought nearer to the factories. To think that it is possible to manage industry by sitting in an office far from the factory is quite wrong. To direct a factory, more frequent and vital contact with the workers is necessary.
>
> For this it is essential that our industrial concerns should pass from collegium to individual management. As matters stand now, ten to fifteen people sit on the collegiums writing papers and carrying on discussions. To continue to manage industry in this way is not possible. It is time now for us to put a stop to paper "leadership" and get down to real businesslike Bolshevist work. Let the chairman and a few assistants remain at the head of the combinations. This will be quite enough to manage the work. The best thing for the other members of the collegium would be to go down into the shops and factories. This would be more useful both for themselves and for the industry.
>
> It would be a good deal better if our industrial leaders, instead of indulging in speech-making and soothsaying, should betake themselves to a mine or to a factory, say, for a month or two, study all the details of labor organization, and really do away with "impersonalism" [irresponsible management].
>
> For this it is essential, further, that our directors should manage their enterprises not "in general," not "in the air," but concretely, practically, that they should approach each question not from the point of view of generalities, but in a strictly businesslike manner, that they should not limit themselves to paper pronouncements or general phrases and slogans, but enter into the technical aspects of the matter, go into details—because only out of small things can great things be built.[116]

In spite of his lack of business experience Stalin seems to have had some capable critic diagnose the difficulty of excessive centralization.

2. Highly Paid Executives. Soviet officials realize something is wrong with their industrial organization. They realize also that it must be revamped, but they do not have a clear idea as to how to proceed. Therefore, they are looking for supermen, heads of industry with skill and efficient organizations at their command. To obtain their services the Soviets are willing to make a compromise with the principle of service for altruistic reasons and to pay important executives big salaries, using as a justification the reply of Lenin, quoted above, about the high-priced executive being cheapest after all.

3. Foreign Aid. According to foreign engineers who have lived and worked in Russia, the Russians do not as yet have a practical bent. Russian administration means low efficiency. And for some time to come the plants will have to be directed and staffed with foreign talent, trained and experienced in the western world.

How this foreign talent is to be obtained is not yet clear. Shall it be along the lines of aid by individual high-priced American executives with experience in running large American industries, and imported by the Soviet régime to operate Russian factories, or shall the Soviets send some of their ablest Russian industrial managers to America to perfect themselves in the technique of mass production? Or, as another alternative, shall the corporations with whom the Soviet Union now has contracts, like the International General Electric, supply the management along with the machinery, to remain until the Soviet factories run smoothly? Whether it would be possible to induce American corporations to take the risk of leasing or taking charge of the new giant plants is a question. There are too many political uncertainties to justify any long-term investment of capital. As for American firms starting new plants in the Soviet Union, that is unlikely. The old American plants now confiscated, such as those of the American Radiator Company, the International Harvester Company, the Singer Sewing Machine Company, are reminders of possible future confiscation by some new political régime. Yet the Soviets would undoubtedly make faster progress in the long run if they would make it profitable for some successful foreign companies to run the Russian plants for a time sufficient to train a Russian staff for each one. No price would be too great to pay, if after a number of years a smoothly running and efficient industrial organization could be turned back to the Soviet Union. Such a plan is not inconsistent with the principles of state ownership and operation on which the Soviet experiment is based. To transfer these huge plants erected out of state funds over to private capital indefinitely is out of the question for the Kremlin.

CHAPTER VIII

TRANSPORTATION

Transportation is vital to Russia because of her vast area. The Soviet program of industrialization has accentuated the need for railway facilities. Indeed, transportation is the Achilles' heel of the Five-Year Plan, because it involves the centralization of manufacture in the new great centers of industry to which raw materials must be brought, and in turn the redistribution of finished goods to the vast hinterland of consumers.

The business of transportation is in the charge of a separate Commissariat, which is organized into four departments dealing with railways, inland waterways, ocean shipping, and motor transportation on highways.

Although the Soviets succeeded in reconstructing track and structures and rolling stock destroyed during the war and the revolution, yet they have failed thus far in providing adequate railway facilities required by the huge construction program of the Five-Year Plan.[1]

A. Progress of Construction

As the result of war and revolution the railway system suffered destruction of one-quarter of the railway mileage, almost 8000 bridges, and a large amount of rolling stock. A reconstruction program was begun in 1921 and fairly good progress was made until 1925. The mileage in that year was almost 30 per cent above the pre-war mileage although there was no Five-Year Plan to stimulate construction. On the other hand, during the four years preceding the initiation of the Five-Year Plan the total mileage remained constant. In the three years 1929 to 1931 the railway mileage increased about 12 per cent. New construction was as follows: 1929, 1000 miles; 1930, 950 miles; 1931, 1980 miles. In addition, in 1931 about 2150 miles were double-tracked; construction was begun on 6200 miles and operations begun on 3000 miles.

New construction has exceeded the original goal set in the Five-Year Plan but is considerably below the higher figures in the revised plan. The first Plan called for a mileage of 55,900 miles by 1933.

The outstanding project in new construction by the Soviet Union has been the completion of the Turkestan-Siberian Railway connecting Siberia with Kazakstan and Central Asia.[2] This road was begun in 1927 and finished May 1, 1930. Its length is about 897 miles and its cost approximately $100,000,000. It is intended primarily to develop cotton-growing in Central Asia to supply Soviet textile mills, and it has already aided in increasing the area planted to cotton, and cotton production. The road is also intended to help in the development of other rich natural resources of Kazakstan and to supply Central Asia with grain and lumber from Siberia.

Since 1924 expenditure on new construction and new equipment (not including expenditure on the Turkestan-Siberian line) has been as follows:

NEW CONSTRUCTION AND NEW EQUIPMENT OF RAILWAYS [3]
(in million rubles)

	Equipment	*Lines*	*Total*
1924	54	1	55
1925	70	17	87
1926	166	27	193
1928	325	65	390
1927	190	37	227
1929	415	128	543
1930	—	277	—
1931	—	425	—

The importance to the Five-Year Plan of adequate transportation is indicated in the increase of capital investments in railways in the two years prior to 1932:

CAPITAL INVESTMENTS IN RAILWAYS [4]

Fiscal Year	*Total* *Million rubles*	*Share Allotted for New Construction* *Million rubles*
1928	757	—
1929	942	175
1930	1,551	310
1931 (program)	2,146	476

The following table shows the total railway mileage in recent years as compared with pre-war mileage:

RAILWAY MILEAGE IN RUSSIA [5]

Year	*Miles*
1913	36,119
1917	39,520
1925	46,202
1928	47,716
1929	47,841
1930 (preliminary)	48,438
1931 (program)	50,301
1932 (original 5-Year Plan)	55,890

The Soviet Union will require a considerable extension of its railway mileage in order that its transportation facilities may be adequate to the new program of industrialization. For example the United States, with an area less than two-thirds that of the Soviet Union, has about five times the railway mileage. For each 100 square miles of territory the United States has 9.2 miles of railroads as against 0.63 miles for the Soviet Union. On the basis of population the United States has 21.5 miles per 10,000 inhabitants as against 3.2 miles for the Soviet Union.

B. Railway Operation

Despite the inadequate facilities railway traffic increased tremendously. In the period of industrial stagnation accompanying "war communism," freight traffic declined to 25 per cent of the pre-war level. From this low point in 1921 traffic in 1928 overtook the pre-war level and in 1930 was about 78 per cent greater. By 1932 the freight traffic had reached some 250 per cent of the pre-war level.[6] Passenger traffic rose even more.

Traffic density increased greatly. Though the mileage in 1929 had increased only 32 per cent above the pre-war level and the number of locomotives only 4.5 per cent, freight traffic had increased 62.5 per cent, so that in that year the density of freight traffic equalled that in the United States and in 1930 exceeded it. For the Soviet Union the traffic density was 1,738,000 ton-miles per mile of road as against 1,608,000 ton-miles for the United States. The other European countries were substantially exceeded, corresponding figures for England being 887,500 and for Germany 1,133,000. In 1931 this growth in the Soviet Union still continued. The tremendous growth in passenger traffic was partly a response to the generally greater freedom of travel and partly to the huge turnover of migratory labor.

Freight traffic on the railroads in 1932 declined far below the planned quota. For example, oil loadings (as a percentage of the quota) declined from 94 per cent in May to 84 per cent in June and 77 per cent in July. According to Mr. Lomov, Commissar of Heavy Industry, coal loadings were very considerably below the Plan, as follows:

Destination	*Daily Carloadings*	
	Planned	*Executed*
Moscow	403	250
Leningrad	376	228

On the other hand passenger traffic, which is non-productive, rose by leaps and bounds. The number of passengers in 1932 was statistically 30 per cent above 1931 but the workers and peasants migrated from place to place and often jammed the trains without buying tickets.[6a]

The growth of railway operations is shown herewith:

RAILWAY OPERATIONS, 1913 AND FISCAL YEARS 1926–31 [7]

	1913	*1926*	*1927*	*1928*	*1929*	*1930 (preliminary)*	*1931 (program)*	*1933 (original 5-Year Plan)*
Length of railway lines in operation *thousand miles*	36.3	46.3	47.0	47.8	48.2	48.4	50.3	55.9
Railway freight operations *billion ton-miles*	40.8	42.8	50.7	54.8	66.3	85.7	115.8	101.0
Railway passenger operations *billion passenger miles*	15.6	14.5	13.7	14.7	18.3	29.1	42.2	22.0
Freight carried by railways *million metric tons*	132.4	116.7	135.9	150.6	176.5	234.9	330.0	281.0
Passengers carried by railways *millions*	184.8	262.7	254.2	280.8	343.2	510.2	720.0	455.0

C. Condition of Equipment

The huge increase in traffic was not attended by any increase in the number of locomotives and cars. As a result the equipment is in poor condition and a large percentage of it is in disrepair. In 1921, the year of lowest production and greatest economic disorganization, about 62 per cent of the locomotives, 50 per cent of the passenger cars, and 33 per cent of the freight cars were either out of commission or in need of repair. This condition has been improving ever since.

The production of new equipment did not come up to the quota set in the Plan. For example, against a quota of 1300 locomotives for 1932, only 554 were completed in the first half-year and of the 50,000 freight cars for 1932 only 6100 freight cars and 500 passenger cars were completed in the first half-year. In this period freight-car construction actually declined 25 per cent under the 1931 level, even though thousands of freight cars are idle awaiting repairs.[7a]

RAILWAY ROLLING STOCK [8]

	Locomotives		*Trucks*	
Fiscal Year	*Total*	*In Need of Repair*	*Total*	*In Need of Repair*
1913	20,320	3,414	500,000	40,000
1923	19,525	11,363	403,000	129,000
1924	20,208	10,908	435,000	135,000
1925	20,275	10,556	445,000	116,000
1926	20,456	9,225	449,000	72,000
1927	18,531	7,215	456,000	59,000
1928	17,574	5,632	472,000	35,000
1929	17,815	4,450	485,000	33,000

Passenger cars numbered 27,811 in 1927; 25,785 in 1928; and 27,798 in 1929.

D. Financial Statistics

Until 1923 the railways operated at a loss. Thereafter a steadily growing profit became an important source of revenue. (See table, page 297.)

In the budget for 1932 revenue from railways is 2937.5 million rubles and expenditures 2487 million rubles, or 10.7 per cent and 9 per cent, respectively, of the total budget. Of the total expenditures planned for the national economy about 12.5 per cent were to be devoted to railway transportation.[9]

E. Difficulties

Transportation is the weakest feature of the Five-Year Plan. The Plan did not provide for an increase in railway facilities to correspond to the increase in production. Grand railroad schemes in remote parts of the country were being carried out, but the railroads in active use were neither extended nor maintained adequately. The result was heavy congestion, delayed deliveries, tying up of equipment, demurrage charges, delays and uncertainty in delivery and in travel. Commodities were congested at some points and short in others. Equipment ran down. Accidents increased. The construction of the large industrial plants was delayed. Drastic orders and decrees from

FINANCIAL OPERATIONS OF RAILWAYS [10]

Fiscal Year	*Operating Revenue* *Million rubles*	*Operating Expenditure* *Million rubles*	*Net Operating Profit* *Million rubles*
1925	928.8	785.2	143.6
1926	1,271.7	1,093.9	177.8
1927	1,491.8	1,264.0	227.8
1928	1,729.8	1,374.8	355.0
1929	1,830.0	1,359.1	470.9
1930	2,967.4	1,618.3	1,349.1
1931 *	4,591.4	2,284.7	2,306.7

* Actual revenue was 700 million rubles less.

the Kremlin were vainly issued to remedy the situation. The official report of the State Planning Commission states:

> The means of transportation have become a serious obstacle to the development of the socialist economy of our country. At the mines there are large quantities of ore lying about; the surface is covered with dumps of coal that cannot be moved; agricultural produce, especially grain, lies at railroad stations in the open; manufactured goods are accumulated at factories; oil cannot be transported in needed quantities; lumber is piled up; building materials are awaiting shipment, etc.[11]

The effects of freight congestion were numerous. Because of delay in delivering manufactures to the peasants, the state grain collections fell behind. As a result the money stayed in the agricultural districts instead of returning to the towns, and a currency shortage arose there. Congestion in transportation was blamed for the delay in delivering lumber for factory construction and the lumber trust in turn complained of a labor turnover because of the failure to deliver food and clothing to its workers.[12] A year later similar complaints persisted. Although the Donetz coal field attained a record production of 119,000 tons per day, the railroad sidings at the pit heads were crowded with thousands of loaded cars while the industrial centers were short of fuel. Again, while the mine workers were living in tents and dug-outs, standard housing units for the mine workers were sidetracked awaiting shipment.[12]

The tremendous increase in passenger traffic further taxed the railway facilities. In taking the night train from Moscow to Leningrad the writer had to wait three hours for an overdue train coming up from the Crimea. The station was filled with people with large luggage mattresses and household goods. As each train pulled in, there was a mad rush and one had to dodge trunks and furniture which these physically powerful people carried about like toys. Tickets were difficult to get. Vacationists must wait days and nights in railroad queues. It has become a current witticism that when one of the queue is asked: "Where are you going to spend your vacation?" he shall answer "In the ticket line." The schedules are often late. Passengers will seriously ask for information: "What time does the nine o'clock train leave?" The trains are crowded. Boarding and leaving some trains is almost as difficult as in the New York subways. Because of the undermaintenance of equipment and overcrowding, accidents are more frequent than in other countries.

1. Causes of Transport Difficulties. The great construction program involves the moving of iron, lumber, and cement, in addition to the ordinary run of traffic. Russian railroads are suffering from the congestion that attends any building boom. During the Florida land boom the Seaboard Airline Railroad and the Atlantic Coastline Railroad suffered a similar terrific congestion. But in the Soviet Union neither mileage nor equipment were increased to meet the increased demands. The Commissar of Railways, in a report made in May 1931, presented the situation: "The technical condition of railroad transportation is terrible. The condition of the roadbed is bad. . . . There are large numbers of rotten ties. . . . The rails are light and worn out. . . . The locomotives and cars are antiquated, inadequate, and of low capacity." [13]

Even on the new Turkestan-Siberian Railway, the heralded achievement in Soviet construction, rails were laid on ties without ballast. Freight cars and locomotives which had been condemned as unfit for further use in Germany were pressed into service in Russia.[14]

In addition there is a lack of efficient railway management. The ability of former executives is often badly missed. The Soviet régime exiled the engineer who built the Trans-Siberian Railroad. The government attempted to recall him from Paris and he asked as a condition that it should restore to him his beautiful home in Leningrad, which is now in a neglected and ramshackle condition and is being used as a vacation hotel for workers. His request was refused.

A new generation of railroad managers has not yet been developed. The present management is distinctly inefficient. Mr. Gill of the Baltimore & Ohio, who acted as adviser to the Soviet Government, stated in January 1932 that the Russian railway workers were about one-seventh as efficient as the American. While the writer was in Moscow there was a vegetable shortage while hundreds of cars of vegetables were rotting in the railroad yards. The newspapers announced the discovery and declared a new war on the "vegetable front." "Freight cars are kept from six to seven days on sidings in Moscow even though loading and unloading goes on 24 hours a day. The factories in the Ukraine keep cars on sidings five to six times as long as the time allotted." [15] The Commissariat of Transport reported that in the Leningrad yards almost 3000 cars of grain and merchandise waited to be unloaded and in Moscow many thousand cars of potatoes.

Railroad labor discipline is poor. Drunkenness is common, causing accidents and delaying operations. On the Turkestan-Siberian Railway 88 per cent of the accidents were due to the railroad employees.[16] Part of the inefficiency of labor is due to the inadequate wages. The differential between the pay of skilled and unskilled labor on the railways was cited as the chief cause of the defective service. The difficulties of management are intensified by the tremendous length of the hauls in Russia. Iron and ore and coal are about 2000 miles apart instead of 400 miles as in the United States.

The percentage of defective locomotives is still high, varying from 24 to 33 per cent, as against the maximum provided in the Plan of 16 to 19 per cent (and as against 6 to 10 per cent in the United States). Only 46 per cent of the number of freight cars planned for were received by the Soviet railroads in 1931. The strengthening of the railroads is an important element in executing the Five-Year Plan.[17]

Railroad transportation faces another difficulty inherent in the lack of industrial development of the country. The equipment manufacturers do not supply a sufficient number of locomotives, cars, or spare parts. In the third quarter of 1931 only half the equipment planned for was delivered. The chief difficulty is lack of co-ordination between the makers of parts. Many engines are almost completed, but for lack of some vital part cannot be put into operation. These incomplete locomotives accumulate and stand idle, representing a great economic waste.[18]

2. Remedies. The American railroad men in the Special Railroad Commission

studying Soviet transportation problems in the summer of 1930 suggested that several remedies be put into effect. These recommendations are all technical, such as use of automatic couplers and air brakes, automatic signalling systems, modern systems of train dispatching, and reduction of grades. Their program of reconstruction involves use of larger locomotives and cars and longer trains.

The management of the Soviet railroads was reorganized in 1931. Bureaucratic methods were eliminated, the wage system was reorganized, piece work was extended, and other strong measures put into effect. These were designed "to eliminate irresponsibility, by attaching definite workers to definite locomotives, speeding up repairs, increasing wages by bonuses and piece work, strengthening discipline, and introducing strict methods of cost accounting." [19]

3. Looting of Freight. Thieves looted the railway trains. The incentive was either hunger or desire for large profits in selling food at high prices in the open market. Official statistics reported over 40,000 cases of theft, involving over 3 million pounds of merchandise and food. The Soviets blamed the kulak, the equivalent in the Bolshevik ideology of the devil in medieval theology. To check such offences they were classified as anti-social or political, which are punishable by death, which hitherto had been reserved for counter-revolutionary acts. In addition, an increased number of guards were assigned to railroads and river transports.[19a]

F. Motor Transportation

In developing a network of transportation Russia has an advantage. Instead of building and then scrapping its short-line railroads Russia can build up a system of motor highways which can be used as feed lines to a few trunk-line railroads. Each would serve in a distinctive and non-competing capacity, and would constitute an efficient and low-cost transportation system.

At the beginning of 1930 there were only 17,400 motor cars and 6340 motorcycles in the entire Soviet Union, or an average of one motor car to about 8000 people as against one to 124 in Great Britain and one to 4.5 in the United States. In each hundred square miles there are 1078 motor cars in Great Britain, 739 in the United States and 2.5 in the Soviet Union.

Realizing the importance of motor transportation both as a feeder to the trunk-line railroads and as independent transportation units for local traffic, the Soviet leaders have planned for mass production of automobiles along American lines. According to the revised version of the Five-Year Plan, the Soviet Union is to produce 250,000 automobiles by 1933 both in the new and old plants. The largest automobile factory is in Nizhni Novgorod, built by Americans, with a capacity of 150,000 cars per annum.

The difficulty in this program seems to be that there are only about 25,000 miles of automobile roads in the country. A program of expanding automobile production and motor transport would require a very great increase in the mileage of motor highways. In 1926 there were about 1300 motor cars operating over 265 routes and covering about 9000 miles. Under the Five-Year Plan about 5 billion rubles will be spent on road construction.

CONSTRUCTION OF NEW ROADS [20]

Fiscal Year	*Appropriations Million rubles*	*Roads to Be Built Thousand kilometers*
1929	161.7	—
1930	421.5	21.0
1931	1,060.2	72.1
1932	1,517.6	101.0
1933	2,107.4	156.9
Total	5,268.4	351.0

However, most of these will be dirt or gravel roads unsuitable for motor traffic.

G. Water Transportation

The system of navigable inland waterways of the Soviet Union is the largest in the world, amounting to over 55,000 miles compared with 29,000 miles in the United States. The potential mileage is four times the actual, and the Five-Year Plan calls for an increase of about ten per cent by 1933. In this sphere of transportation, however, the difficulty is not lack of routes but lack of equipment. The congestion in the railroads has increased water transport as shown in the table on page 302.

As a result of the war and of the revolution, over 60 per cent of the river fleet was destroyed and, as the table shows, the pre-war level of tonnage moved on inland waterways was not reached until 1929.

Similarly, a large part of the fleet of ocean-going vessels was destroyed during the war and post-war period and much of the remainder became

FREIGHT TURNOVER ON INLAND WATERWAYS [21]

Fiscal Year	Thousand metric tons
1913	48,162
1924	19,627
1925	24,671
1926	33,438
1927	35,200
1928	39,900
1929	50,200
1930	64,000
1931	116,100
1932–33 (original 5-Year Plan)	77,500
1933 (revised plan)	263,000

obsolete by 1923, when the fleet was again developed. According to the Five-Year Plan the total ocean-going tonnage will be several times the pre-war level.

MERCHANT FLEET OF RUSSIA [22]

Fiscal Year	Number of Vessels	Freight Capacity thousand metric tons
1913	974	495
1926	198	214
1927	185	207
1928	178	260
1929	182	270
1930 (preliminary)	390	495
1932–33 (original 5-Year Plan)	—	1,250
1932–33 (revised plan)	—	2,763

H. Air Transportation

The vast area of Soviet Russia and the lack of other adequate transportation facilities together with the low cost of opening new air lanes of traffic has stimulated greatly the development of an air service. Both in the mileage and the volume of traffic the air service grew rapidly.

By the end of 1932, 247 additional aerodromes were to be opened, including 78 for the landing of sea planes. The Moscow aerodrome, covering about 5600 acres, was nearing completion in 1932 and the program for 1933 called for the departure of 100 planes daily. The total air lines in actual

AIRLINE SERVICES IN RUSSIA [23]

Year	*Length of Lines Miles*	*Passengers Carried*	*Mail and Freight Carried Kilos*
1922	745	276	13,750
1923	1,000	1,433	27,885
1924	2,732	2,618	48,309
1925	3,095	3,398	76,789
1926	4,097	4,035	84,561
1927	4,361	7,079	170,381
1928	7,434	8,996	228,661
1929	11,390	8,619	147,511
1930	16,146	11,257	307,000
1931 *program*	33,520	51,650	1,560,000

operation in 1932 amounted to about 36,000 miles, the largest of any country in Europe and exceeded only by the United States. About 10,000 miles of main lines will be lighted for night flying.

In 1932, forty-seven new air routes were to be opened, including the Moscow-Vladivostok route totaling almost 5000 miles, bringing Vladivostok to within a week of London, or less if night flying is included. Airplanes are also being used extensively for survey work in exploring the resources of the country.

CHAPTER IX

TRADE—FOREIGN AND DOMESTIC

A. Foreign Trade

1. Relation to the Five-Year Plan. The nature and volume of Soviet foreign trade has been determined by the program of industrialization. The ambitious scope of the Five-Year Plan required primarily that machinery and construction goods be imported from abroad. These now constitute the bulk of Russian imports. On the other hand, since Russia lacks credit as a means of paying for these imports, she has had to export large quantities of the few materials which were produced in abundance, namely grains, petroleum, timber, manganese, and other raw materials.

2. Machinery of Foreign Trade. Foreign trade is a government monopoly and is under the supervision of the Commissariat of Foreign Trade. This body plans the volume of imports and exports so as to achieve a balance without relying to any great extent on invisible items, such as credits, immigrant remittances, etc. Therefore, tariffs are incidental. Goods are either admitted or embargoed. The determining factor is the requirement of the Five-Year Plan. The actual operations are conducted through special organizations covering each field of import or export trade. Each commodity has its own trading organization as *Exportkhleb* or Grain Export, *Exportles* or Lumber Export, *Rudoexport* or Ore Export, etc., and *Selkhozimport,* Agricultural Machinery Import, *Metaloimport* or Metal Import. In the principal foreign markets the Soviet government is represented by special organizations, like the Amtorg Trading Company in New York. Foreign trade is financed through the State Bank, which clears credits and debits between the import and export organizations and in turn between them and the trusts and co-operatives which supply the exports or use the imports.

3. Import Trade. a. Trade Control. Imports into Soviet Russia, unlike other

countries, do not reflect the desires or needs of the population. Goods do not move freely but are subject to a rigid control. The volume of goods to be imported annually is determined in advance depending upon the requirements of the Five-Year Plan. The total value of imports is limited to the total value of exports, except in so far as credits can be arranged. Obviously, economic conditions prevailing in other countries upset such calculations. The sharp decline in the price of raw materials, constituting the bulk of Russian exports, has upset the plan for importing machinery, the price of which did not decline so much relatively.

b. Volume and Nature. Under the Five-Year Plan the total volume of imports was to amount to about 6180 million rubles of which 78 per cent represented producers' goods, 15 per cent consumers' goods, and 7 per cent miscellaneous goods. As a result of the rigid system of control, the lack of credit, and political and trade restrictions in other countries, the volume of imports in 1930 of 1068 million rubles had not yet reached the pre-war level of 1140 million rubles, the average of 1909 to 1913. However, imports did rise in recent years, the 1925 value having been only 719 million rubles.

In the fiscal year 1930 about 42 per cent of the total imports consisted of industrial and agricultural machinery and automotive equipment. Metals and metal products were 18 per cent of the total. About 8 per cent were foodstuffs and 15 per cent were textiles or textile raw materials.

IMPORTS INTO SOVIET RUSSIA

(in million rubles)

Imports	*1929*	*1930*
Food products	68.0	86.5
Animal and animal products	57.4	45.7
Metals and metal products	115.1	190.8
Industrial, agricultural, and automotive equipment	214.5	438.4
Paper and paper products	16.5	16.1
Textile raw materials and textile products	255.9	158.6
Miscellaneous	108.6	132.3
Total	836.0	1,068.4

c. Trade with the United States. The Russians have preferred to trade with the United States, if for no other reason, because the similarities of climate, topography, and the vast distances make American machinery and plants more suitable than those of other countries. For this reason, the Russians have been willing to pay higher prices and to accept shorter term credits on American goods. From 1923 to 1931 American exports to the Soviet Union amounted to over $600,000,000, and United States imports from the Soviet Union amounted to less than $125,000,000, making a total trade of over $730,000,000, and a balance of exports from the United States of over $480,000,000. In the year 1931 alone the excess of exports from the United States amounted to over $90,000,000 and constituted 27 per cent of the United States excess of exports. The average exports during the eight years 1924–31 amounted to about $75,000,000 compared with average annual exports to Tsarist Russia of less than $25,000,000 in the years 1910 to 1914. In 1931 the Soviet Union was the seventh largest export market of the United States, whereas in 1929 it was seventeenth, and in 1922 it was twentieth in importance.

UNITED STATES TRADE

(in million dollars)

Year	*Exports to Soviet Union*	*Imports from Soviet Union*	*Total Trade*	*Excess of U. S. Exports*
1923	4.5	1.4	5.9	3.1
1924	42.1	8.1	50.2	34.0
1925	68.9	13.1	82.0	55.8
1926	49.9	14.1	64.0	35.8
1927	64.9	12.8	77.7	52.1
1928	74.0	14.0	88.0	60.0
1929	85.0	22.5	107.5	62.5
1930	114.3	24.3	138.6	90.0
1931 (preliminary)	103.7	13.1	116.8	90.6
	607.3	123.4	730.7	483.9

However, due to lack of credit facilities, the exports of the United States to Soviet Russia during the first six months of the year were only $5,500,000 in 1932 as against $40,600,000 in 1931. On the other hand, countries like Germany, which granted credits to Russia, increased their sales.

4. Export Trade and Trade Balance. Exports are regulated with the intention of providing means of payment for imports. Under the Five-Year Plan, exports should be somewhat higher than imports to provide a margin of safety and adequate credits. For the entire five-year period exports should amount to about 7000 million rubles. Exports also are still far below the prewar level. In 1929, exports totaled about 878 million rubles and, in 1930, 1002 million rubles compared with an average of 1521 million rubles in the years 1909 to 1913. Of this total about 60 per cent consisted of industrial products and about 40 per cent of agricultural products.

EXPORTS FROM SOVIET RUSSIA [1]

million rubles

Exports	*1929*	*1930*
Agricultural:		
Products of the soil	83.0	195.0
Animal products	138.3	98.0
Furs and fish products	124.8	100.5
Total agricultural	346.1	393.5
Industrial:		
Lumber and lumber products	138.5	180.1
Manufactured food products	79.9	71.7
Products of mining industry	176.9	206.2
Miscellaneous	135.8	150.4
Total industrial	531.1	608.4
Grand total	877.2	1,001.9

Imports and exports of Soviet Russia for the seven years 1925–31 are given by the Bureau of Research on Russian Economic Conditions, University of Birmingham, England, as follows, the revised figures being the result of the Bureau's own studies:

TRADE RETURNS OF SOVIET RUSSIA [1a]

million rubles

	Official Customs Returns			*Revised Figures*
Fiscal Year	*Imports*	*Exports*	*Balance*	*Balance*
1925	724	559	− 165	− 194
1926	756	677	− 79	− 106
1927	714	780	+ 66	+ 21
1928	946	778	− 168	− 203
1929	836	878	+ 42	+ 4
1930	1068	1002	− 66	− 103
1931	1044	890	− 154	− 208
Total	6088	5564	− 524	− 789

The Bureau also gives a summary of the balance of trade, showing not only the balance of movements of merchandise, but all incomings and outgoings, directly and indirectly connected with the foreign trade of the country, with the exception of all interest charges in so far as these are not included in the invoice price:

SUMMARY OF BALANCE OF TRADE

million rubles

Fiscal Year	*Official Customs Returns*	*Revised Figures*	*Fiscal Year*	*Official Customs Returns*	*Revised Figures*
1925	— 208	— 237	1929	+ 22	— 16
1926	— 78	— 105	1930	— 159	— 196
1927	+ 24	— 21	1931	— 142	— 196
1928	— 88	— 123			
			Total	— 629	— 894

5. International Balance. The Soviet Union has few invisible credits, such as interest on foreign investments, banking fees, immigrant remittances, insurance receipts, etc. Tourist expenditures constitute a rapidly growing item and are helping to pay for the import of machinery. Freight charges still constitute a small item. Only between 8 and 12 per cent of the total trade is carried in Russian bottoms. The growth of the shipbuilding industry should increase this revenue. In the fiscal year 1929 the Soviet government actually paid 120 million rubles to foreign shipping companies.

A summary of the balance of payments of the U.S.S.R. during the seven fiscal years 1925–31, prepared by the Bureau of Research on Russian Economic Conditions, follows:

SUMMARY OF BALANCE OF PAYMENTS OF THE U.S.S.R.[1b]

million rubles

Expenditures	*1924–1925*	*1925–1926*	*1926–1927*	*1927–1928*	*1928–1929*	*1929–1930*	*1930–1931*
I. Foreign Trade							
1. Merchandise imports	724	756	714	946	836	1,068	1,044
2. Imports of precious metals	46	9	15	—	3	1	—
3. Contraband imports	27	30	35	29	35	35	35
4. Commercial parcels imports	3	9	2	—	—	6	6
5. Brokerage commission, etc.	11	12	14	14	16	18	16
6. Overhead and administrative expenses	30	23	30	35	42	50	50
Total	841	839	810	1,024	932	1,178	1,151
II. Capital Movements							
1. Increase of currency reserves in the U.S.S.R. and abroad	—	—	33	—	27	—	—
2. Interest on commercial credits contracted abroad	6	9	13	17	25	30	35
Total	6	9	46	17	52	30	35

SUMMARY OF BALANCE OF PAYMENTS OF THE U.S.S.R.—*Continued*

millions of rubles

Expenditures	1924–1925	1925–1926	1926–1927	1927–1928	1928–1929	1929–1930	1930–1931
III. Foreign Labor and Technical Assistance	3	5	5	10	15	18	38
IV. Non-Commercial Transactions	8	26	25	21	6	25	30
Grand Total	858	879	886	1,072	1,005	1,251	1,254
Incomes							
I. Foreign Trade							
1. Merchandise exports (revised figures)	530	650	735	743	840	965	836
2. Exports of precious metals	70	81	49	155	70	9	110
3. Contraband exports	4	3	5	3	6	8	9
Total	604	734	789	901	916	982	955
II. Capital Movements							
1. Increase of short-term indebtedness abroad in comparison with the previous year	69	62	41	120	45	210	230
2. Decrease in currency reserves abroad in comparison with the previous year	62	15	—	—	—	—	—
3. Interest on short-term credits and deposits abroad	7	5	5	6	6	5	4
4. Profits, dividends and miscellaneous	8	7	5	6	6	5	6
Total	146	89	51	132	57	220	240
III. Non-Commercial Transactions Currency remittances, tourist expenditure, and other expenses of foreigners in the U.S.S.R.	43	43	43	35	32	43	55
IV. Items not accounted for under the above headings	65	13	3	4	—	6	4
Grand Total	858	879	886	1,072	1,005	1,251	1,254

6. "Dumping." a. Soviet Selling Not "Dumping." "Dumping," as understood in international trade, constitutes the sale of an excess of merchandise

at prices under those prevailing in the home market, sometimes for the purpose of ruining foreign competitors. However, the object of Soviet exports is to provide credits for imports. Furthermore, there has not yet been any evidence that the Soviets were selling goods abroad at prices less than those prevailing within the Soviet Union. Nor has it been proven that they have been selling abroad at less than the cost of production. The complaints of foreign countries have been due chiefly to the inflation of the Russian ruble. Its purchasing power at home is greater than abroad, due chiefly to the system of rationing and fixed prices for privileged buyers. A similar inflation facilitated exports from other European countries when they were off the gold basis. The charge of "dumping"' is discussed elsewhere. Litvinov pointed out at the Geneva Conference in 1931 that the world depression is most profound in those industries in which Russia is a good customer such as machinery and producers' goods, and that Russia sought the highest price, as did any merchants offering their wares.

b. Cause of "Dumping." The inflation of the ruble was the principal factor in establishing the low prices which brought the charge of "dumping." Wages paid in inflated rubles resulted in underpaying the Russia worker, such as was also the case in France and Germany during the period of inflation and as is now the case in England. The refusal of the western world to extend adequate credit to the Soviets necessitated the forced export of a few of the Russian commodities produced in abundance. If credit were available, such forced exports should cease. Despite such forced selling, however, the total exports of Russia in its principal commodities were still below the pre-war level. For example, Russia is now exporting less wheat than she did in 1913.

c. The Prospect. As the Soviets become able to supply their needs out of home manufactures, exports should diminish. Furthermore, the desire of the Soviet government to raise the standard of living of the workers should lead to a rise in the purchasing power of wages and to the consumption at home of goods now shipped abroad. Despite the assertions of the "Red-hunters" throughout the world, the Five-Year Plan has not proved a danger to the manufacturing countries. The demands of the home market in Russia are vast, and are growing more rapidly with the growth of literacy and the rise in the standard of living. It will be many years before the home demand will be satisfied sufficiently to make possible any exports of manufactures. Besides, the quality of merchandise produced in Russia is so very inferior to that of the western world as to make competition out of the question for a long time. The only reason for Russia's heavy exports has been the lack of credit. Goods that should have been consumed at home were shipped abroad. The bulk of these goods were not the handiwork of man but the products of nature, such as grain, manganese, timber, oil, furs. Furthermore, for a long time the Russian economic system will require an excess of imports and the problem will be to find the credits.

In foreign countries the attitude toward Russian dumping depends upon whether the country is a producer or a consumer of these goods. Consuming countries are glad to admit necessary imports at low prices. Producing countries have attempted to embargo low-priced Russian products or to raise their import duty. Finland and Italy have opposing interests concerning Russian lumber. The Ottawa Conference in the summer of 1932 revealed the deep and almost irreconcilable difference of attitude toward Soviet Russia of Great Britain and her dominions. The latter urged an embargo against Soviet Russia, which is in about the same stage of economic development as themselves and whose products are in competition with theirs. The British stated that a severance of trade relations between Great Britain and Russia would throw to Germany and the United States trade which had gone to British manufacturers. On the other hand, the British felt that over and above the question of imperial preference was the larger necessity of bringing back "the Russian market into a system of world economy as an essential factor in world rehabilitation. Britain must follow such a policy, regardless of the obstacles which Russia herself places in the way of realizing such aims."[2] At the Imperial Trade Conference at Ottawa, however, Great Britain concluded to bar the sale of Russian, or other, goods in the United Kingdom at less than world prices.

7. TRADE CREDITS. Russia's commercial and other debt to foreign countries in recent years is given by the Bureau of Research on Russian Economic Conditions, University of Birmingham, as follows:

SOVIET FOREIGN INDEBTEDNESS [2a]

Year Ending Oct. 1	*Acceptances, Bank Credits, and Other Commercial Debt*	*Contingent Liabilities*	*Total*
		million rubles	
1924	78.2	78.0	156.2
1925	147.2	65.0	212.2
1926	209.2	96.0	305.2

SOVIET FOREIGN INDEBTEDNESS—*Continued*

Year Ending Oct. 1	*Acceptances, Bank Credits, and Other Commercial Debt*	*Contingent Liabilities*	*Total*
		million rubles	
1927	251.0	140.0	391.0
1928	370.0	115.0	485.0
1929	415.0	299.0	615.0
1930	625.0	249.0	865.0
1931	855.0	350.0	1205.0

In 1931, the Bureau points out, Soviet Russia's real debt increased by 230 million rubles, or, if contingent liabilities, are included, by 340 million rubles. Her whole indebtedness increased two and a half times since the introduction of the Five-Year Plan, and on October 1, 1931, her real debt equaled the value of exports for 1930–31 and, if contingent liabilities be included, exceeded it by nearly 50 per cent.

a. Credits by Countries. In the early part of 1932, the short-term debt of the Soviets to foreign countries was as follows:

Country	*Millions of Dollars*
Germany	250
United States	60
England	60
Poland	30
Austria	15
Italy	17
Japan	15
Norway	5
Other countries	25
Total	477

The principal creditor was Germany. German exports to Russia were stimulated by the need for keeping the German workmen employed. In other words, the prospective loss on Russian business was offset by the saving on the dole to the German idle. As early as October 1925, the German Government arranged to guarantee its exporters to the Soviet Government 60 per cent of the amount of their sales up to a total of 250 million marks. The first guarantee of the German Government was financed, up to 70 per cent, by American, British and Dutch banks. In addition to this direct guarantee of the German Government, insurance of between 50 per cent and 75 per cent of general export credits made up almost as large a sum. After the Soviet had liquidated its first German credits, the guarantee was restored in 1930 to the same limit, viz., 250 million marks. Under these guarantees, Soviet orders totaled about 534 millions of dollars. In April 1931, probably under the pressure of the need for business, the German Government agreed to guarantee Russian credits by its exporters up to 75 per cent, up to a total of 400 million marks and the Federal States up to a total of 300 million marks. However, the Germans attempted to reduce the time limit from a maximum of 48 months to about 21 months. The Russians agreed to pay 2 per cent above the Reichsbank rate and to remit 20 per cent at the time of placing the order.[3]

A member of the Russian trade delegation in Germany stated that German exporters were adding 30 per cent to the Russian quotations, which did not seem an excessive surcharge to him. It is reported that Soviet indebtedness to Germany totals about 250 millions of dollars,* of which 65 per cent was due before July 1, 1933, and that the German manufacturers will accept nothing but cash on new orders. A new Soviet-German trade agreement of June 15, 1932, took the place of the agreement of April 14, 1931, under the terms of which Soviet orders in Germany in 1931 totaled 920 million marks, approximately $230,000,000. The longest credit under the 1931 agreement was 33 months and under the new agreement 29 months, although provisions are made for longer credits in special transactions. Again, the interest paid is to be 2 per cent above the Reichsbank rate, but never more than 10 per cent nor less than 7 per cent per annum. The credits extended by Germany have stimulated her exports to Russia, which rose in the first quarter of 1932 by 40 per cent, although the imports from Soviet Russia declined 13 per cent in the same period. According to the *Berliner Tageblatt* of

* The Bureau of Economic Research on Russian Economic Conditions of the University of Birmingham (England), in its Memorandum No. 4 on The Balance of Payments and The Foreign Debt of the U.S.S.R. (February, 1932, p. 23) gives the Soviet commercial debt in Germany at the end of the fiscal year 1931 viz:—

	million marks
Credit of the Golddiskontbank	20
Rediscount credits of the Reichsbank	50
Original credits of Ifago (Industriefinanzierung, A. G. Ost)	150
Additional credit of Ifago	45
Short-term credits extended by German banks	50
Capital invested by the suppliers themselves	200
Foreign credits	195
Total	890

June 17, 1932, the activity of the metallurgical plants in Germany improved, owing to Soviet orders and deliveries could be distributed in such a way as to provide employment until the end of the summer.[4] On July 29, 1932, a group of private German bankers arranged with the Reichsbank that Russian bills maturing within 20 months could be discounted with the Reichsbank up to 150 million marks.[5]

Dr. H. Schacht, the former President of the Reichsbank, in a lecture at Düsseldorf, stated that the nine hundred million marks of German long-term credits granted to Russia were frozen and that they could be liquidated only through the import of foodstuff and raw material, which would hurt competing German agriculture and industry. The credits were granted to provide employment in Germany, but by granting them, German industry involved itself in a crisis more serious than that which it had attempted to avoid. If the Five-Year Plan fails, the Russian Soviet government will be forced to stop payment. In the opinion of Dr. Schacht, the plan must fail, because a plant which can pay for itself only ten years after it is built cannot be financed on short-term credits.[6]

The second largest Russian credits outstanding are in favor of manufacturers in the United States, and totaled about $60,000,000. At the beginning of 1932 they were $40,000,000 and they have since been reduced. To provide means of payment, oil, platinum, and precious metals were shipped to the United States. The American credits are not guaranteed by the American Government.

Great Britain guaranteed the equivalent of $60,000,000 of Soviet credits, granted by British exporters. British exporters have also extended about $12,000,000 of additional credit. Finally, Russia buys some British goods for cash. Russian trade with Great Britain was hurt by the decline in the pound sterling, which had the effect, first, of causing an outright loss in depreciation of Russian sterling deposits, and secondly, of lowering the gold value of Russian sales to Great Britain, which are far in excess of Russian purchases in Great Britain.

With respect to the English handling of these credits the Bureau of Research on Russian Economic Conditions says:

> In addition to interest charges which are often higher than the usual rate, the London banks and brokers cover the risk connected with the transaction by charging large commissions. If the part of the commission exceeding the usual rate is regarded as an extra-premium, and the advance is calculated on an annual basis, it shows that this form of financing costs the Soviet Union approximately 20 to 22 per cent per annum, including ordinary interest charges. On the "black

bourse" for Soviet bills, the average rate varies from 16 to 35 per cent per annum.
The total amount of English capital invested in the financing of Russian foreign trade on October 1, 1931, is assessed at 45 million pounds, which can be considered as an underestimate rather than an overestimate.[6a]

Italy likewise signed a credit arrangement with the Soviet Union, under which exporters were guaranteed up to 75 per cent of their shipments. The total was at first about $18,000,000, and more recently almost $50,000,000. This guarantee stimulated Italian exports. The term ran as high as 54 months.

Other governments likewise guaranteed exports to the Soviet Union, Japan up to 65 per cent, Austria 60 per cent for ten years, and Latvia 75 per cent up to 13 months.

b. Will Russia Default? In the last seven years the net import balance of Soviet Russia was $450,000,000 and in the last two years $200,000,000. According to a study made by the British Government, the Russian import surplus since 1921 aggregated 1175 million rubles and her short-term debt from 1924 to 1931 rose to 855 million rubles. There are no indications that Soviet Russia could develop a surplus of exports within the reasonably near future, and therefore the British Government decided to limit its guarantees of Russian credits to a maximum of 12 months.[7] This has recently been increased to 18 months.

With reference to Germany, Russia cannot pay in goods her short-term debt to German exporters, owing to the efforts of the German Government to protect agriculture and industry by tariffs and to the new decrees restricting the import of wines, furs, etc. In fact, during the second half of 1931, German imports from the Soviet Union declined about 30 per cent. The Soviet Union will, therefore, be unable to repay German credits out of her exports to Germany, unless a new trade agreement is arranged, which would greatly increase Germany's imports from Russia of grain, pulp, timber, dairy products, coal, iron ore, and petroleum products, and unless the Soviets receive the preferential trade treatment which they have been bargaining for. A German-Soviet tariff agreement signed in 1932 lowers tariffs on many Soviet commodities.

Owing to the restricted commercial relations with other countries, Russia has few invisible credits in the way of shipping services, foreign investments, and expenditures of tourists or foreign residents.

Of course Russia could curtail her imports substantially, but to do so would jeopardize the prosecution of the Five-Year Plan. A check on the prosecution of the Plan would cause the present discontent over the lack of consumers' goods to become vocal, as it has hitherto been borne patiently in the expectation of results to be achieved on the successful completion of the Plan. Perhaps the recent action lifting the restrictions on sales of food by peasants and removing the ration on food and consumers' goods, may be the forerunner of a let-up of the Plan. The world-wide depression is ultimately having its effect on important Russian policies, such as industrialization and socialization of small industry and of distribution. A curtailing of the Five-Year Plan would shake the faith of the Russian masses in their leaders, so that the lack of foreign credits and the resultant need for curtailing imports may force a new orientation of Russian policy.

A summary of the position of the U.S.S.R. on international money markets, both before and since the war and the revolution, is given by the Bureau of Research on Russian Economic Conditions, University of Birmingham, as follows:

> According to the estimate of the credit department of the Ministry of Finance, in the three pre-war years for which figures are available, short-term indebtedness amounted to 558 million rubles. Soviet Russia's short-term debts abroad, which we qualify as real or effective, have reached 158 per cent of the short-term indebtedness of pre-revolutionary times, and if contingent liabilities are also taken, 221 per cent. The increase of short-term indebtedness partially replaced the long-term capital market which was no longer accessible to Russia after the revolution. While restoration of national production was chiefly due to mobilization of internal capital resources, the part played by foreign capital, more particularly in the decisive years of the Five-Year Plan, should not be overlooked. During this period, financial support was forthcoming from abroad to an increasing extent, and in the last two years foreign indebtedness, as was shown above, more than doubled and imports from foreign countries greatly increased in importance, and in some branches of economic life became essential to further the Soviet program of industrialization. Taking into account the fact that Soviet Russia's imports and exports are considerably below pre-war level, and that the security normally considered requisite by financiers and industrialists is not forthcoming, there is little justification for the assertion that the U.S.S.R. is the victim of an economic or financial blockade.
>
> Since the revolution the composition of the short-term creditors of Russia has changed. Before the war, 36 per cent of all short-term credits were contributed by industrial and commercial concerns, and 64 per cent by foreign banks; in 1931, 80 per cent of all credits were contributed by industrial firms and only 20 per cent by banks and banking houses. Though these figures show that foreign banks are disinclined to invest money directly in the U.S.S.R., they are, to all intents and purposes, carrying the whole burden of Soviet Russia's foreign debt, for inasmuch as they discount Soviet bills drawn by industrial firms, they are, as a matter of fact, supplying the capital necessary for her purchases abroad and for the production and delivery of commodities which she exports, simultaneously shifting the risks arising from such transactions to governments and firms.

While before the war Russia's foreign commercial debt consisted of shares and debentures up to 80 per cent and was widely distributed amongst the numerous classes of well-to-do people in England, France, Germany, Holland, Belgium and to a lesser extent in the United States, the foreign debt of Soviet Russia is concentrated in the hands of a limited number of banks and industrial and commercial concerns in Europe and America. The financing of the U.S.S.R. is therefore mainly a business of big finance and foreign governments. These governments assumed a responsibility not altogether devoid of political character when they guaranteed up to 50 per cent on the average, and in certain countries up to 70 per cent of the total debt of the U.S.S.R.

Owing to its short-term structure, the international indebtedness of the U.S.S.R. contains elements of uncertainty and instability. Soviet Russia has to pay off yearly roughly two-thirds of her outstanding debt. For this purpose the money forthcoming from exports is insufficient, and hence the contraction of new short-term debts is necessary. In other words, the financial account of the U.S.S.R. abroad can only be made good on the assumption that new loans will not be refused for the purpose of meeting the old ones. Should such a refusal take place and coincide with a serious drop in Soviet exports (a failure of crops for instance), a dangerous situation would arise. But as creditors seem satisfied so far with the present *modus vivendi,* there is no reason to expect that new credits will be refused to the U.S.S.R. We think, however, that both in the interest of the world and of the Russian people it should be realised that a lasting solution of the difficulties lies not in external security of government guarantees combined with high rates of interest, but in the creation in Russia of such conditions of life as would in themselves offer security.[7a]

Of course, Russia is very much like any private debtor who falls behind in his payments and who is kept going merely by the renewal and prolongation of his credits. However, the dismal forecasts made of a collapse of Russian credit and of the inevitability of a moratorium, as soon as Russia is prevented from "kiting" credits, may prove false prophecy. By dint of skillful political handling and prodigal expenditure of energy, the Soviet régime has squirmed out of many a tight corner in the past, and the gloomy predictions of a collapse of Russian credit, though based on logic and statistics, ignore the intangibles. Thus far, no foreigners have suffered any loss on commercial credits to the Soviets, nor have the Soviets threatened to declare a moratorium, so common in Eastern Europe.

B. Domestic Trade

1. Socialization of Internal Trade. When the Kerensky régime came into power, the country was extremely demoralized. The war had exhausted it. Production and trade were shattered. The new government attempted to regulate trade, particularly through establishment of a state monopoly of grain and flour, but conditions were too chaotic for its effective organiza-

tion. After the October Revolution of 1917 the state took over entirely the distribution of foodstuffs and all other commodities, and the free movement of goods ceased. In the spring of 1921, when the New Economic Policy was inaugurated, free exchange was reintroduced although the state continued to exercise close control. The swing to the left under Stalin has more and more crowded out the "Nepmen," or private traders, and the ultimate goal appears to be their complete extinction.[8]

2. Organization of Trade. Domestic trade is carried on primarily through three agencies: (1) state trading organizations, (2) co-operatives, and (3) private traders. In the fiscal years 1929 and 1930, the share of each in the total turnover in internal trade was as follows: [9]

DOMESTIC TRADE OF SOVIET RUSSIA

	1929 Per cent	*1930* Per cent
State trade	30.1	30.0
Co-operative trade	63.3	66.7
Total socialized trade	93.4	96.7
Private trade	6.6	3.3
Grand total, all trade	100.0	100.0
Million rubles	49,716	62,632

According to estimates covering the five years of the Plan, by the fiscal year 1933 the total turnover was to amount to 57,855 million rubles with the co-operatives handling 59 per cent, state agencies about 38 per cent, and private trade only 3 per cent.[10] By 1930 this percentage of socialized trade was reached and the total volume was exceeded.

a. Work of the Co-operatives. Co-operatives were not devised by the Soviet régime. Even before the war, co-operatives embraced millions of members and carried on a large share of the nation's trading. However, they have been incorporated into the Soviet system and were encouraged by the government. They may be classified into three divisions: (1) consumers' co-operatives, (2) agricultural co-operatives, and (3) home industries.

Membership in the consumers' co-operatives was expected to reach 70 millions in 1931, with a trade turnover of about 15 billion rubles.[11] They represent the principal organization of the socialized sector of Soviet domestic trade. This sector handled 99 per cent of the country's wholesale trade in 1930 and more than 89 per cent of retail trade. There are three general types: (a) the workers' and urban consumers' co-operatives, (b) the agricultural consumers' co-operatives, and (c) the transport and army co-operatives.

These co-operatives perform the general function of distributing the products of the country. They purchase from the state trusts, from private producers, and from foreign countries and supply consumers with manufactured goods. Through their thousands of locals they collect and distribute the agricultural produce of the country. They likewise own and operate factories, bakeries, canneries, flour mills, fisheries, etc., to supply the needs of their members.[12]

Agricultural co-operatives include numerous types of organizations. Some are concerned with several branches of farm production, such as truck gardening, potato-growing, sheep-raising, etc. There are also credit co-operatives, sales co-operatives, and handicraft and consumers' co-operatives in the agricultural system.

3. Difficulties. These do not always work efficiently, according to the Soviet press.

> The principal defect in the present-day co-operatives is bureaucracy, which handicaps the turnover of merchandise and creates an artificial shortage of goods while the wholesale warehouses are filled with such goods. For example, only recently long lines were seen in front of most of the Moscow co-operatives waiting to buy kerosene, while there was a supply on hand sufficient for one and a half months. Large stocks of goods are often stored in the cellars of co-operative stores while their windows remain empty. Goods are distributed at a very low rate, often being sent where not needed.[11]

In the Shakhta District of the Donetz Coal Basin—

> more than 100,000 coal miners live . . . yet no attention is paid to the problems of supplying these workmen with food products and other articles for personal consumption usually distributed through co-operative stores. On the whole, the co-operative system . . . is often unable to cover the demand of the market, and forces the consumers to resort to purchasing from private merchants. In the face of this, however, one co-operative in Piatigorsk managed to put through such "ingenious" business transactions as the wholesaling of over three tons of bacon and more than eight tons of sugar at twice the legal price. . . . In another district co-operative (in Central Russia) there are also a good many troubles. Wastes of various products due to numerous contingencies, such as leakage or drying of products, pile up and heavily tax the consumers. . . . At present a kerosene shortage is observed in the city of Vladimir. The population of that city, who use kerosene as lamp oil, stand in lines kilometers long to receive their ration of two liters.[13]

Other similar difficulties are treated in the section on "Labor Turnover." One can only wonder whether an efficient capitalist distributing organization like Sears Roebuck or the Great Atlantic & Pacific Tea Company, which delivers a good quality of merchandise promptly and at very small margin of profit may not serve society better, except for the psychological sense of ownership by the consumers.

4. Restoration of Private Trade. As indicated in the section on "Labor," the artisan class was freed from the restrictions of having to buy their raw materials from the state and sell their finished products to the state. According to government decree issued jointly by the *Tsik,* or the Central Executive Committee of the Communist Party, and the *Sovnarkom,* or the Council of People's Commissars, on July 24, 1932, co-operatives of artisans were given the right to produce and sell for a private profit. They were no longer compelled to sell to the government at fixed prices, but were free to buy their raw materials and sell their finished goods in the open competitive market. Not only would the government not interfere with these groups of artisans, but officials were ordered to encourage the artisans to increase their output in order to serve the nation. The object was to increase the supply of such homely articles as shoes, clothing, tinware, household goods. Because the large factories, with their centralization of buying, manufacturing, and distribution, failed to furnish the necessary goods, the Soviets returned again to the individual tailor and cobbler and smith. These artisans had been driven out of existence at the abandonment of the Nep and the beginning of the Five-Year Plan. The decentralization of small manufacturing is expected to furnish flexibility and increase the output of goods because of increased profit. These collective groups of workmen are to be helped by the banks.

As a result of the stimulus to private trading by the peasants and artisans, new markets arose rapidly throughout Soviet Russia. It became easier to buy necessities which hitherto had either not been available at all, even to the privileged classes, or could be had only in limited quantities in the co-operative stores. At first prices on these private, free markets were higher than in the "closed" shops of the government, but the increasing supplies brought out by the prospective profit reduced prices considerably and forced a downward tendency. The resulting decline in price in some commodities was as follows:

Item	*Old Price rubles*	*New Price rubles*
Milk *quart*	2.0	0.90
Potatoes *kilogram*	1.0	0.40
Butter *pound*	12.0	8.00
Eggs *per 10*	6.0	3.50

As a result of the enthusiasm both of the peasant sellers and the urban buyers, there was not enough market space to carry on business, and peasants had to sell their produce on the sidewalk.[14] In the early fall of 1932, however, supplies fell off and the food crisis again became acute.

As part of the same general trend toward relaxing restrictions, the so-called "declassed" elements were permitted to join the consumers' co-operatives, which entitled them to buy food and clothing at minimum prices. A decree of May 22, 1932 thus liberated five per cent of the population, including former owners of estates, merchants, clergymen, and some of the professional classes. However, they may buy goods only after the other classes of this theoretically "classless society," have been satisfied. Nor do they have the right to receive ration cards entitling them to buy commodities of which there is a shortage, such as bread, meat, butter, and sugar.

There was much discussion in Moscow as to whether this series of decrees liberating trade and restoring the principle of private profit was not a return to capitalism and whether the Soviet Government was not seeking relief from the difficulties of communism in the freedom of individualism. Of course the Soviet officials, by circuitous logic, tried to prove that these were merely temporary measures, that a socialist régime could appropriate the devices of capitalism, that there were now no middlemen but only direct trade between producer and consumer, and that the artisans could not hire workers to exploit.

The restoration of private trade stimulated wholesale stealing. As mentioned above (see chapter on Transportation) huge quantities of food en route from the peasants to the cities and of consumers' goods en route to the farms were stolen in transit and sold at a large profit in private trade which had recently been made legitimate. The restoration of private trade developed a crop of middlemen and speculators who acted as "fences" for the thieves. Apparently with the vanishing of fear and waning of idealism the old Adam cropped out in Russian economic life. The newspapers and the authorities admitted that theft and dishonesty were creeping throughout the social structure, not merely in the form of theft of freight in transit, but also of embezzlement from co-operatives and from the trusts. As a result of this wave of crime thousands of arrests were made throughout the country, unequaled since the winter of 1929–30, the period of forced collectivization. Decrees were issued against stealing "socialized property," including government supplies, the property of co-operatives; and standing crops of the collective farms. In addition, the possession of foreign currency or silver was deemed to be a result of trade operations. Therefore Russians who received funds from abroad were suspected and often arrested until they "contributed" the *valuta* to the government. As a result of these arrests and the difficulties thrown about the private trader, the decree restoring private trade was not very effective. Besides, the reversal of policy was regarded with skepticism and suspicion by the beneficiaries themselves. The government scheme of socialized distribution broke down on the one hand and on the other a system of distribution through private trade could not be reconstituted by fiat. Private trade is impossible without private traders.[14a]

5. Private Trade before the War. In attempting to centralize the production and distribution of consumers' goods and to socialize trade, the Soviet authorities overlooked the importance of the artisan and small tradesman in the rural communities. The great shortage of consumers' goods brought this fact home very forcibly. In the Peasant House in Moscow are samples of a great variety of clothing, household goods, and farm implements, made by individual artisans on the farms. In the opinion of some authorities, more than a half of the requirements of the Russian consumers before the war were produced by the small individual producer, alone or with a few workers. The program of eliminating the kulak, the artisan, and the private trader resulted in a shortage of the necessities of life. This shortage became so acute in February 1932, according to Mr. Duranty, that the workers in the small cities appealed to the peasants on the local collective farms to sell them foodstuffs. This tendency probably was a forerunner of the Soviet decree legalizing such trade. The permit to the individual to sell his produce for a profit is expected to be a temporary measure until the socialized agencies of production and distribution shall again function smoothly. However, other capitalist devices, originally adopted temporarily, became silently frozen in the social structure, and are now accepted as orthodox socialism.

CHAPTER X

BANKING

A. Nationalization of Banks and Abolition of Money

During the period of war-communism Russian economic life was in chaos. The banks were abolished and money and securities in custody were nationalized. Money ceased to be an instrument of exchange. The state attempted to feed, clothe, and house the population gratis. The government intentionally followed a policy of inflation in order to make money valueless and to "liquidate" it as the foundation of capitalism.

Since money was no longer a means of payment the decree of February 3, 1921, abolished taxation. The anarchy that resulted from these policies gradually led to a return to the universally accepted technique of economic life. Money was again legally recognized as a medium of exchange. The argument of the young theorists that there was no need for it was denied by G. T. Grinko, Commissar for Finance:[1]

> We cannot minimize the importance of money in a socialist state. Such sentiments are against the interests of socialist construction in its present stage. Money is still the great organizer for the accumulation of wealth for the country, a powerful lever for the development of socialistic construction.

Banks were reopened, but under government ownership and management, and a semblance of order was restored. As noted above, however, money's purchasing power is still limited, since a buyer must have not merely money but the right to buy. In many cases this right is restricted to the privileged classes such as workers or peasants.

B. Organization of New Banking System[2]

In November, 1921, the "Gosbank," or State Bank, was created. Originally it was intended to be the sole banking institution, but as new needs arose banks of various types were created to extend long-term and short-term credit to agriculture, industry, and trade under the auspices of the government and co-operative or private agencies.

1. ORGANIZATION AND FUNCTIONS OF THE STATE BANK. The State Bank is the central bank of the Soviet Union and is intended "to regulate the currency circulation and to provide short-term credits for industry, agriculture, commerce, transport, and other branches of the national economy." Its funds come from its capital, reserves, and surplus; from deposits of the Soviet government, of government and private businesses, and of individuals; and from the issue of notes. The bank is managed by a board of directors of seven members, who are nominated by the council. The council in turn has forty members and its chairman is the Commissar for Finance. Other members of the council include the Chairman of the Board of the bank, representatives of the several member republics of the Soviet Union, and twelve experts in currency and credit. The council meets at least twice a year, but it merely indicates broad lines of policy.[3]

From the beginning, the State Bank has been the sole bank of issue. The issue of notes is subject to the control of a board. In November 1922, a new unit of currency, the chervonetz, was first issued by the bank. These bank notes continue in circulation and are issued in various denominations. They must be secured to the extent of at least 25 per cent by precious metals and foreign currencies, and the remainder must be secured by marketable goods or short-term bills. However, they are not convertible into gold. Following their introduction chervonetz notes were exchangeable for the old war ruble notes but there was never any legally fixed ratio between the two currencies and ultimately the old notes became worthless.

During 1923–24 two paper currencies existed side by side, the chervonetz issued by the State Bank and the Soviet ruble notes issued by the Treasury. There was also no fixed ratio between these two kinds of currencies and the Treasury notes fluctuated greatly in relation to the chervonetz. In February 1924, the currency was unified by decree. A stable currency, reckoned in gold rubles, was introduced for use in trade and industry, the issue being limited to 50 per cent of the amount of the chervonetz notes of the State Bank. The stability of this new issue was obtained by thus limiting the volume, and by the action of the State Bank in agreeing to accept the notes at a fixed rate of exchange for chervonetz notes.

In 1928 the limit of Treasury issues was raised to 75 per cent of the chervonetz notes outstanding and in 1930 to 100 per cent. The law requires that the State Bank notes and the Treasury notes shall be accepted at par but neither can be exchanged for gold or foreign currency.

The Bank agreed to accept Treasury notes and gold ruble notes in a free exchange at the rate of one chervonetz for ten gold ruble notes. These ruble notes issued by the Treasury were similar to the currency notes issued by the Treasury in Great Britain during and shortly after the war in that both were fiat currency, as distinguished from the Bank of England notes. In 1925 the function of issuing gold ruble notes was transferred from the Treasury to the State Bank, again following the example of England when the currency note account of the government was merged with the bank-note account of the Bank of England.

Stabilization of the currency was an important factor in restoring stability of commodity prices, wages, and economic life in general. Once again communism had made a compromise and had introduced capitalist methods.

Besides being the sole bank of issue the State Bank is the fiscal agent of the Treasury and the chief commercial bank in extending short-term credits to industry and trade. As in the Bank of England the issue department and the banking department are separate. The Bank may lend money to the Commissar of Finance on short-term loans secured by precious metals up to 50 per cent.

The depositors of the State Bank are chiefly the trusts. Private companies and private individuals who were the chief customers of the former commercial banks play an insignificant part, although the State Bank performs the same service for industry as did the former commercial banks.

The State Bank handles the short-term operations and discounts as distinguished from the long-term or investment operations of the Long-Term Credit Bank. The Soviet State Bank functions like the Bank of England or the Bank of France, which may receive private deposits, and unlike the Federal Reserve Banks, which receive deposits only of member banks but not of corporations or of individuals.

In its discount policy the State Bank originally followed a policy of high rates, ranging as high as 2 per cent per month. In July 1923, the rate was reduced to 8 per cent per annum. The discount rate of the State Bank does not, as in capitalist countries, perform the function of regulating the supply of and demand for capital. The Soviet State Bank differs from the private banks in the western world in other regards. The state allocates its funds to the various trusts in accordance with the Plan. When the demands are great, it prorates the supply of credit, but does not discriminate between borrowers by raising its rate to one as against another. In conjunction with the State Planning Commission the State Bank plans its credit distribution for the ensuing month or quarter in accordance with the seasonal demands of trade or the growing demands of a developing industry.

The central bank of issue is really a commercial bank. It serves chiefly state institutions and the state trusts. Private borrowers are not desired and they rely on "bootleg" credit for their needs. Furthermore, private traders are reluctant to deposit considerable amounts of funds in state banks because it would attract attention. Savings are thereby discouraged. The State Bank carries almost 80 per cent of the total loans and discounts of the country. Most of the deposits are public deposits derived from state industries, state transport, state trade, trade unions, etc., the accounts of private clients constituting about three per cent of the total deposits. Loans and discounts naturally are allotted to these groups in proportion to the deposits.

2. Long-Term Credit Bank for Industry and Electrification. The Long-Term Credit Bank (Prombank) functions in the Soviet Union much as the investment banker does in the western world, extending long-term credits up to thirty years. It provides capital for industry and for electrical enterprises, both new and old. In the western world the investment banker collects funds from thousands of small holders, but in the Soviet Union the Long-Term Credit Bank obtains its funds from several sources, such as the long-term deposits of the government's industrial trusts which must set aside 12½ per cent of their annual profits for this purpose; the long-term deposits of the Commissariat for Finance provided in the budget for financing industry; the reserves for depreciation of industry fixed by the Supreme Economic Council and kept on deposit with the bank; bonds issued to the public, the special fund of the bank consisting of 40 per cent of its net profits and 10 per cent of the net profits of all government-owned enterprises; and finally the capital of the bank, which is increased by contributions from the several industrial undertakings.[4] The nearest approach to the Bank for Long-Term Credits would be our Federal Farm Loan Banks. These, however, do not loan directly to the farmers but to their co-operative loan associations, and obtain funds from private investors, not the state.

3. Bank for Foreign Trade.[4] The Bank for Foreign Trade succeeded the Russian Commercial Bank in 1924. It is controlled by the Commissariat for Trade, which owns its stock, together with the Commissariat for Finance and the State Bank. The Bank for Foreign Trade finances the exports of raw materials such as timber and petroleum, foods such as the grains and

dairy products, and products of industry. It also fosters the establishment of Soviet banks abroad such as the Bank for Russian Trade at London, the Banque Commercial pour l'Europe du Nord at Paris, the Guarantie und Credit Bank für den Osten at Berlin, the Svenska Ekonomie Aktiebolaget at Stockholm, the Nordiske Kredit Aktieselskab at Copenhagen, the Russo-Persian Bank at Teheran.

4. MUNICIPAL BANKS. These banks finance local and municipal undertakings. Their funds come from local deposits and from the allocations of the central and local governments. The Moscow Municipal Bank was established in January 1923, to finance local trade and industry, residential construction and other city needs. Its loans and discounts increased from 271 million rubles on October 1, 1927, to 460 million rubles on July 1, 1929.[4]

The Central Municipal and Housing Bank was established in March 1925. Its operations include long-term financing of municipal works and building co-operatives but it also finances individuals in the construction and repair of homes. It operates throughout the Soviet Union and receives its capital from the special tax on housing, from the contributions to the Workers' Welfare Fund, and from the profits of the government trading organizations.

5. AGRICULTURAL BANKS. There is a Central Agricultural Bank for the Soviet Union and also agricultural banks of the several member republics. The Central Agricultural Bank was established in July 1924 to finance the development of the land, the purchase of agricultural machinery, live stock, etc., and the sale of produce. It operates through the agricultural credit associations and the credit co-operatives which are the local units.[4]

6. ALL-UNION CO-OPERATIVE BANK. This bank was established in February 1922 to advance short-term credit to co-operative organizations which are its stockholders. The bank also advances long-term loans from a fund to which the affiliated co-operative societies appropriate 10 per cent of their net profits.[4]

7. SAVINGS BANKS. There is also a series of savings banks under the control and direction of the Commissariat for Finance. These banks receive deposits in small amounts. In the largest cities the savings banks are independent institutions but in the towns and country they are attached to agencies of the State Bank, to post offices, railway stations, factories, and village libraries, etc. To encourage saving, interest on deposits is exempt from the income tax, and the deposits themselves are exempt from inheritance tax. Demand deposits are credited with interest at the rate of eight per cent for individuals and six per cent for institutions. Time deposits receive one per cent more. In addition the savings banks issue savings certificates of five and ten rubles.

Interest is compounded and the value of the certificates is doubled at the end of six years. Other aspects of the savings banks are treated in the section on the Budget.[4] (See p. 378.)

Banks belonging to the state received their working capital from the state budget, which is the means for diverting the profits from one industry into another.

C. Balance Sheet of the State Bank

The balance sheet of the State Bank is similar to that of the Bank of England. As noted above there are two departments, the note-issue department and the banking department. The former carries its account in chervontzy, which are equivalent to 10 rubles, the latter in terms of rubles.

The statement of the Banking Department of December 1, 1931, is shown herewith:

BALANCE SHEET OF THE STATE BANK OF THE U.S.S.R.[5]

December 1, 1931

(in thousand rubles)

Assets		*Liabilities*	
Cash	163,226	Capital	400,000
Precious metals and foreign currencies	693,553	Reserve fund	176,280
Debtors	9,239,842	Notes in circulation	2,673,213 *
Special loans on Treasury account	53,503	Currency note account of Commissariat for Finance	2,452,464
Sundry assets	688,360	Government securities	151,954
		Treasury monies for allocation of loans	87,349
		Deposit and current accounts (including funds of Treasury)	2,235,755
		Offices, branches, and agencies	775,611
		Profit balance	711,145
		Sundry liabilities	1,174,713
Total	10,838,484	Total	10,838,484

* The total volume of currency in circulation on Dec. 1, 1931, amounted to 5,272.4 million rubles.

Cash and gold holdings, about 850 million rubles, were less than 12 per cent of the notes, currency notes, and deposits, amounting to over 7300 million rubles.

For comparison the balance sheet for May 1932 is given, showing amazing increase in current accounts and deposits, a condition which in other countries would be called inflation:

BALANCE SHEET OF THE STATE BANK OF THE U.S.S.R.[6]

May 1, 1932
(in million rubles)

Assets		*Liabilities*	
		Capital	400.0
Cash	165.4	Reserve fund	302.3
Gold, precious metals, foreign currency, and correspondent accounts in foreign currency	729.6	Notes in circulation *	2,739.8
		Currency note account of Commissariat for Finance	2,641.6
		Treasury monies for allocation of loans	274.4
Bonds of the Long-Term Credit Bank for Industry and Electrification	5,501.9	Current accounts, single current accounts, and deposits	8,135.8
Short-term debtors	8,533.7	Treasury monies for long-term agricultural loans	1,821.4
Long-term agricultural loans	2,094.5	Offices, branches, and agencies	975.5
Special loans on Treasury account	208.7	Commission and interest	572.7
Other assets	2,253.1	Other liabilities	1,623.4
Total	19,486.9	Total	19,486.9

* The total volume of currency in actual circulation on April 1, 1932, amounted to 5,240.7 million rubles and on May 1, 1932—5,543.9 million rubles.

Cash and gold holdings about 895 million rubles were about 6.6 per cent of the notes, currency notes, and deposits amounting to over 13,517 million rubles.

STATEMENT OF THE NOTE ISSUE DEPARTMENT OF THE STATE BANK OF THE U.S.S.R.

(in thousand chervonetz—1 chervonetz = 10 rubles)

Assets	*December 1, 1931*	*April 1, 1932*	*May 1, 1932*
Gold in coins & bars	61,259	64,050	64,318
Other precious metals in coins & bars	2,224	2,282	2,144
Foreign currency	4,605	4,559	3,239
Drafts in foreign currencies	163	164	101
Collateral for short term assets	200,251	198,445	211,698
Total	268,500	269,500	281,500

STATEMENT OF THE NOTE ISSUE DEPARTMENT OF THE STATE BANK OF THE U.S.S.R.—*Continued*

(in thousand chervonetz—1 chervonetz = 10 rubles)

Liabilities	*December 1, 1931*	*April 1, 1932*	*May 1, 1932*
Bank notes transferred to the State Bank	267,321	267,577	273,978
Balance to which notes may still be issued	1,179	1,923	7,522
Total	268,500	269,500	281,500

The growth of the issue of chervonetz notes and the corresponding growth of the cash and metal cover are shown in the table below: [5]

MONTHLY CHANGES IN NOTE ISSUE, FIRM COVER AND RATIO

Date	*Bank Notes Issued Thousand Chervonetz*	*Firm Cover Thousand Chervonetz*	*Ratio Per cent*
Oct. 1, 1927	102,657	26,895	26.2
Oct. 1, 1928	109,010	27,952	25.6
Oct. 1, 1929	146,628	36,919	25.2
Nov. 1, "	156,586	39,558	25.3
Dec. 1, "	157,540	39,739	25.2
Jan. 1, 1930	153,697	38,816	25.2
Feb. 1, "	150,027	38,374	25.5
March 1, "	153,580	38,895	25.3
Apr. 1, "	155,598	39,144	25.2
May 1, "	164,629	41,375	25.1
June 1, "	170,087	42,770	25.1
July 1, "	186,037	47,820	25.7
Aug. 1, "	210,860	53,932	25.6
Sept. 1, "	217,692	56,085	25.7
Oct. 1, "	214,565	55,787	26.0

It is interesting to note that the cover of gold, cash, etc., was raised proportionately with the issue of chervonetz notes, thus complying with the terms of the decree.

The currency in circulation rose as follows:

CURRENCY IN ACTUAL CIRCULATION
(in million rubles)

Date	Bank Notes	Treasury Notes	Coin	Total	Firm Cover in Rubles	Per cent Cover
Oct. 1, 1923	207.4	——	——	282.0 *	——	——
Oct. 1, 1924	346.5	205.3	75.4	627.2	——	——
Oct. 1, 1925	652.0	340.6	150.3	1,142.9	——	——
Oct. 1, 1926	780.6	400.7	161.8	1,343.1	——	——
Oct. 1, 1927	989.8	461.0	177.5	1,628.3	268.9	16.8
Oct. 1, 1928	1,063.4	710.8	196.6	1,970.8	279.5	14.2
Oct. 1, 1929	1,428.2	983.4	230.6	2,642.2	369.2	14.0
Nov. 1, 1929	1,527.0	1,067.7	238.9	2,833.6	395.6	13.9
Dec. 1, 1929	1,538.3	1,091.5	242.8	2,872.6	397.4	13.8
Jan. 1, 1930	1,501.0	1,028.2	243.8	2,773.0	388.2	14.0
July 1, 1930	1,843.2	1,349.3	262.1	3,454.6	478.2	13.9
Oct. 1, 1930	2,130.3	1,859.1	274.5	4,263.3	557.9	13.1
Jan. 1, 1931	2,080.4	1,946.3	275.3	4,302.0	561.0	13.0
July 1, 1931	2,199.9	2,012.9	286.2	4,499.0	585.6	13.0
Dec. 1, 1931	2,673.2	2,452.4	——	——	672.8	——
Apr. 1, 1932	2,675.8	2,454.8	322.6	5,453.2	706.2	12.9
May 1, 1932	2,739.8	2,641.6	——	——	698.0	——
June 1, 1932	2,766.8	2,687.9	331.8	5,786.5	704.0	12.2
One year's increase to—						
Oct. 1, 1928	73.6	249.8				
Oct. 1, 1929	364.8	272.6				
Oct. 1, 1930	702.1	875.7				

* Includes 74,400,000 rubles of old currency notes (value in chervonetz rubles).

Excluding the deposit liabilities, therefore, the banking ratio fluctuates between 13 and 14 per cent. If the deposits are included the ratio would fall considerably lower. This low ratio indicates inflation. The fact that the rate of increase in bank notes and in Treasury notes grows more rapidly from year to year is evidence that the inflation is running its usual course, as exemplified in the history of the belligerent countries during the war. In the fiscal year ended October 1, 1928, bank notes increased only 73 million rubles, in the next year 364 million rubles, and in the following year 702 millions, a rise of almost 1000 per cent in the rate of increase in two years. The increase in circulation of Treasury notes, without any direct cover, was even more rapid. The volume approached the maximum limit of 100 per cent of the secured chervonetz notes.

The law requires that the State Bank notes and the Treasury notes should be accepted on a par, but neither can be exchanged for gold or foreign currency.

D. Inflation

The economic phenomena of the World War are still fresh in the memory of this generation. The traveler in Europe during the troublous years immediately following the war still has recollections of the havoc of currency inflation. The tourist in Russia today has a similar experience. True, inflation is disguised. As was the case in several of the belligerent countries, quotations are pegged, transactions in foreign exchange are restricted. In fact there is no free market. Foreign currency may be exchanged to rubles, but rubles cannot be exchanged to foreign currency. Normally, inflated currency means rising prices, but as formerly in the belligerent countries, by price fixing and by ration tickets prices are maintained at artificially low levels for limited quantities, insufficient for human comfort. And open market prices are higher than the fixed prices.

1. Ratio of Gold to Notes. By the law of 1924 "fiat" money having no gold backing could be issued up to 50 per cent of the amount of the chervonetz notes, which had to have a minimum cover of 25 per cent. In other words, every 25 rubles of gold could support the equivalent of 100 rubles in bank notes plus another 50 rubles in Treasury notes. The 150 rubles of notes would then have a gold cover of 16 per cent. In August, 1928 a decree authorized the issuance of Treasury notes up to a limit of 75 per cent of the banknote issues. In other words, 25 rubles in gold could not support 175 rubles in paper, or on a ratio of 14 per cent. Finally, in September 1930, the limit was raised to 100 per cent, and thus the coverage was reduced to 12½ per cent. This ratio excludes deposits, against which there is no gold reserve. If the sound banking practice prevalent throughout the rest of the world were to prevail, and a gold reserve set up against deposit liabilities, the ratio of gold to bank notes, currency notes, aand deposits combined would be between 8 and 9 per cent. In countries whose notes are freely exchangeable for gold, the ratio varies from 40 to 80 per cent of note and deposit liabilities, or at least five times the Soviet ratio. It is small wonder then that gold and paper are not freely interchangeable.

When this difference was pointed out to the statistician of the State Bank, he replied that it was a capitalist notion that deposits had to be covered by a gold reserve. In a capitalist system a bank never knew when deposits would be withdrawn, and it had to be ready to pay out gold on demand. But under the Soviet system the central bank was part of the planning department, and the Bank knew in advance when and how much money would be needed by the trusts under the Five-Year Plan. Therefore there never was any emergency need for meeting demands for funds. Everything was provided for in advance and therefore the gold reserve did not have to be as large.

Another defense of the low Soviet ratio was given by Professor Katzenellenbaum, who stated that since the purchasing power of the pre-war ruble was twice that of the present ruble, the present circulation should really be cut in two to find the equivalent pre-war circulation, and on the basis of purchasing power there was no inflation.

2. Evidences of Inflation. In addition to the low ratio of gold to notes and deposits there are other evidences of inflation. Anti-Bolshevik sources report that duplicate notes of one, three, and five rubles are issued with identical serial numbers. As shown above the rise in bank notes outstanding has indeed been very rapid, and as in the case of all inflation, the rate of increase has become increasingly rapid.

Price increases as compared with other countries are cited by the Bureau of Research on Russian Economic Conditions.[7]

> The rise in prices on industrial goods which became marked in 1929–30 in the U.S.S.R. is very significant. The divergence of prices existing between Russia and other countries can be seen from the following table, worked out by Soviet economists; and published officially in Moscow, in 1929, in the second edition (Vol. 2, p. 416) of *The Five-Year Plan:*

	1913	*1928*
Russia and U.S.S.R.	100	100
United States	59	43
Germany	55	42
Great Britain	62	39
France	67	37

> Thus, the world prices for industrial products, which in 1913 were about 60 per cent of the Russian prices, amounted in 1928 to only about 40 per cent. If the world prices continue to fall whilst in the U.S.S.R. they soar or even remain stationary, the dangerous difference in the national productivity of labor will become still more marked. [See pp. 204 and 211 for Soviet error in interpretation.]

All the inflation phenomena of war-time Europe are to be observed in Russia today. Hard money is being hoarded. The government, instead of deflating the currency, punishes the hoarders. Again, the peasants, as in war-time Austria, prefer to hold on to their produce rather than take paper. Periodically a so-called silver crisis appears, and silver vanishes. One of the amusing, but distracting, experiences of the writer in the summer of 1930 was to watch passengers trying to induce conductors on the Moscow street cars to change a paper ruble for kopeks. There was much loud discussion and argument, and the disgruntled passengers got a free ride. Subsequently street-car tokens, of paper, were sold at 12 rides for a paper ruble, obviating the need for making small change in metallic currency.

Perhaps the most striking phenomenon of inflation is the "bootleg" exchange. Foreigners in Moscow are accosted by Muscovites with offers to exchange dollars for rubles at varying high rates above the official, approximately two for one. The ruble in Berlin was selling privately at 8 to 12 to the dollar in the summer of 1930. Recently a Paris banking house officially offered Russian rubles at the rate of about 10 for a dollar. On the southern and eastern frontiers and in Turkey, Persia, and China the ruble is sold at still lower rates. And finally the Russian Government itself recognized the depreciation of the ruble in the agreement with Japan on its payment to the Soviets for the fishing concession at Saghalin Island on the coast of Siberia. The Bank of Korea had been buying rubles at about one-third of the gold value of 50 cents. The Soviet Ambassador in Tokio asked for payment on the basis of 40 per cent of gold parity, but the Japanese offered to pay in paper rubles, on the basis of about 27.5 per cent of parity. The difference was finally settled by arbitration between the Japanese Foreign Minister and the Soviet representative on the basis of .325 yen (about 16.25 cents) for a ruble. At par one Japanese yen equals 49.8 cents and one Russian ruble equals 51.4 cents.[8] The actual quotation of the ruble in Japan about that time was ten sen (about five cents).[9] A British banker who visited Russia in August 1932 stated in a memorandum, privately circulated, that on the "Black Bourse" "transactions were effected at around 100 rubles per £1 British"; that "the internal purchasing power of the ruble was declining heavily," and real wages were declining.

Even within Russia, the depreciation of the ruble is admitted by the government. In the summer of 1932, according to press reports, rubles were exchanged not at gold parity or 2 to the dollar, but up to 36 to the dollar. At one of the "Torgsin" stores purchases were made in foreign currency and on a balance which had to be met and for which there were only paper rubles available, the store demanded payment at the rate of 16 rubles for one gold ruble, or the equivalent of 32 to the dollar. The coffee house of the Hotel Metropole, a government-owned institution, sold a portion of pastry either at 15 cents or 6½ rubles. This exchange would make 2.31 cents a ruble or 43.3 rubles to the dollar. Tourists in Russia in the summer of 1932 reported similar high rates of exchange in the alternative dollar or ruble prices of food in the hotels, all government-owned.[9a]

Because of the distrust of the currency, the peasants have resorted to barter, as did the peasants in the warring countries. They will refuse to take paper for their produce but will take cigarettes, shoes, shirts, etc. In the summer of 1930 one lamp wick was exchangeable for 1½ poods of oats (1 pood = 36 pounds), and one pair of shoes (worth about $2 in the United States or at Russian prices about $50) for 16 bushels of wheat, equivalent at world prices to about $10.

3. Causes of Inflation. The causes of inflation are inherent in the Five-Year Plan. The rapid tempo of industrialization leads inevitably to inflation. The state pays out millions of rubles for the building of plants over a period of two to three years, and in the meantime these plants produce no goods. They are financed by the issuance of paper money. The faster the tempo of industrialization, the faster the increase in circulation. Currency is increasing faster than the output of consumers' goods, and for this reason purchasing power in terms of consumers' goods is declining.

Another important cause is the failure to reduce costs. According to the Five-Year Plan costs were to be reduced by 12 per cent in the second fiscal year but the actual reduction was only 6 per cent. Each one per cent is said to equal about 100 million rubles, so that a 6 per cent deficiency is equivalent to about 600 million rubles, of which about 500 millions were supplied by the printing of paper money.

Still another reason for currency inflation was the fall in commodity prices throughout the world. As a result the Soviets had to export a larger physical volume of raw materials in order to import machinery, which did not decline as greatly in value as did their products. Again, the heavy exports of grain left less for home consumption, likewise raising prices.

4. Denial of Inflation. Even sound economists, like Professor Katzenellenbaum, denied to the writer that Russia was suffering from inflation. The increase in note circulation and the increase in credit was said to be due not to inflation, but rather to the prosperity of the country, manifested in the great

increase in industrial capacity. Likewise, the statistician of the Gosbank, the state bank of issue, denied the assertion of other Soviet officials that the high cost of construction per ton of steel, or the high cost of power-house construction per million kilowatt hours, compared to American costs, was an indication of inflation. Construction costs of Magnitogorsk, the steel center, he said, seemed high because costs in Russia included the building of homes, electric power stations, railroads, etc., all of which are furnished by separate corporations under the capitalist system, whereas here the state built them all, and the costs of the accessory plants should not really be capitalized per ton of steel capacity. Again, at Dnieprostroy, the electric power plant, the costs of construction were high because they included other operations as, irrigation, navigation, etc.

The statistician likewise said that the increased output of goods was the cause of the increase in currency circulation. The country is producing more steel, more oil, and more wheat, and therefore requires more currency to finance the larger output.

Occasionally a Soviet sympathizer will admit inflation, as noted above, but not when discussing the Bank. Rather, in trying to prove that prices in Russia are not as high as they seem when rubles are converted into dollars at parity, the Soviet sympathizers will say, "It is altogether misleading to translate the Russian ruble quotations into foreign currency. The ruble does not represent 50 cents in buying capacity." [10]

The Economic Survey of the State Bank similarly refutes the charge of inflation. Foreign economists say that the country is threatened by inflation because the volume of currency in circulation increased by 1.5 billion rubles during the preceding fiscal year. *The Economic Survey,* however, offers an explanation.

> Such pessimistic theories lose sight of the difference between the Soviet and the capitalist economic systems. Our gross industrial production for the past year increased 25 per cent and the output of heavy industry increased 40 per cent. Capital investments in the socialized economy increased 84 per cent. The original issuance of currency was caused by the rapid economic development of the country.[11]

It is indeed true, these authorities admit, that most of the goods are capital goods, construction or producers' goods. There is still a shortage of consumers' goods, and for this reason the prices of consumers' goods are high, but this shortage is temporary only.

Another refutation comes from G. Grinko, Commissar for Finance, in his report to the third session of the Central Executive Committee of the Soviet Union.[12]

> They (the economists) cannot get rid of their capitalist conceptions and cannot understand that their outcry against inflation misses its aim in a socialist economy where the distribution of the national resources is in the hands of a centralized economic system subjected to a plan. . . .
>
> Is there any ground for talk of inflation when prices of manufactured goods remain stable for the majority of consumers? How can one speak about inflation when the regulated prices on agricultural produce are unchanged?

Grinko stressed the fact that there would be no issue of any currency in 1931 in spite of the fact that a large increase of industrial construction was planned. In fact his Unified Financial Plan showed that there would be an estimated surplus of two billion rubles.[13]

5. Disguise of Inflation. None of the exchange markets of the world quotes Russian rubles, and in Russia they can be bought only surreptitiously. Travelers are not permitted to bring rubles into the country. They can legally obtain ruble currency only at the border or at the banks in exchange for their own currency at a fixed rate. The tourist is asked to declare all the foreign currency he brings into the country and subsequently at his departure to declare the amount of foreign currency he is taking out of the country. The difference must be represented by slips from the State Bank or its branches, showing that the foreign currency spent was exchanged for Soviet rubles at the legally fixed rate. The tourist's minimum daily living expense is figured at 10 rubles. The exchange slip reads, "It is advisable to preserve this receipt to be produced in case of the desire to re-exchange the unspent ruble balance into foreign currency. This re-exchange is effected within the limits and on the basis of the existing currency regulations." A humorous item in the regulation reads, "It is therefore inadvisable to trust the statements of malicious persons regarding difficulties in *converting foreign money into Soviet currency*." [14] At all the frontier offices of the U.S.S.R. there are exchange bureaus of the State Bank that freely effect conversion of foreign currency into Soviet currency at official rates. Thus the exchange of rubles is completely under control. It is only by such rigid control that the depreciation of the ruble can be disguised.

The rise in prices which would naturally follow inflation of the currency is disguised through an elaborate system of governmental control of prices and rationing of quantities. However, while the regulated market hides the inflation, the free market removes the disguise. In the open market, prices soar in a disconcertingly unrestrained manner. But even in the regulated market the very inadequacy of supplies reveals how poor is the disguise of inflation. Governmental control, government ration cards, curtailed consumption, are as much evidences of inflation as are rising prices. In fact, prices have little significance unless they are free.

6. Results of Inflation. The results of inflation appear in the various aspects of economic life. On the one hand there is little incentive to save. Goods are not available for purchase. Saving and the accumulation of wealth are contrary to the spirit of communism, and large bank balances may bring about investigation by the vigilant political police.

As a result of inflation peasants hoard hard money. The cities have subscribed almost their entire quota of the government "Five-Year-Plan-in-Four" loan, but the villagers have subscribed less than one-third. Silver money is hidden away, and a great shortage results. In Germany and France during the war the shortage of hard money was relieved by the use of postage stamps, trolley car tickets, and other equivalents of small change, and hard money was selling at a premium over paper money. In Soviet Russia the hoarding of silver is regarded as a social offense, and the guilty are subject to the penalty of being shot.

Several kinds of markets have developed. There is a government market, at which limited quantities of rationed goods may be obtained at low prices upon presentation of workers' cards. Here the prices are fixed, but the goods are scarce. Then, there are free public markets. Private traders will sell goods without limit as to quantity at prices many times higher than those of the government stores. The goods are available and there are no queues. There is no time lost in waiting; the higher price covers the waiting time. In addition there is an intermediate market in the state stores. To overcome the shortage of goods supplied on ration cards, and to drive out the small trader, the government set up 25 "open shops" in Moscow, in which purchasers may buy without limit as to quantity or as to price. While the stores were bare, the worker could not spend his modest wage and the state could not bring money into circulation. The new stores sold clothing, shoes, and food at two or three times the regulated price. Beer at one ruble a stein and wine at three rubles a bottle were bought eagerly. The government has also introduced installment selling, whereby the purchaser makes advance partial payment and the goods are delivered later.[15] However, former aristocrats, priests, and kulaks, may not shop in these stores. The prices prevailing, taking rubles at about 2 per dollar, the official rate, are higher than the government prices and lower than the open-market prices. The following prices may be compared with those given on page 191:

Butter	$5 a pound
Cheese	$6 a pound
Smoked sausage	$6 a pound
Ham	$4.50 a pound
Potatoes	25¢ a pound
Smoked fish	$5 a pound
Head of cabbage	$1 each
Apples	$1 a pound

On May 11, 1931, the government raised prices 50 per cent on food, liquor, and basic commodities. This measure was regarded as part of a program to deflate the currency by bringing it out of hoards into circulation. Commissar Grinko stated also that there would be no further increase in note circulation.

In 1932, the price of food was increased a second time indicating further inflation. As shown above, the following price increase of about 50 per cent went into effect on September 1st.

Item	*Unit*	*Old Price* (*rubles*)	*New Price* (*rubles*)
Eggs	10 pieces	1.00	3.50
Sour cream	kilo	3.00	4.50
Meat	"	1.45	2.12

The increase was almost inevitable because the Soviet note circulation rose from 5.4 billion rubles on July 1 to 6.8 billion rubles on September 1, an increase in two months exceeding that of the entire preceding twelve months.[15a]

Occasionally deflation occurs, particularly in connection with seasonal movement of agricultural products. During October and November 1930, for example, the currency note issue was reduced 400 million rubles.

7. Dumping. The depreciation of the currency stimulates exports. In Germany, during the period of inflation, foreigners rushed in to buy and the

German population had to suffer from underconsumption. Likewise in Russia commodities are thrown on the world markets for what they will bring, and the Russian population cannot afford to buy. In Montevideo, for example, the Soviet Trade Agency offered Russian gasoline at the equivalent of about 9⅓ cents a gallon, and lumber at a price equivalent to $20 per thousand feet as against a market quotation of $28.[16]

American engineers and business men in Russia try to prove that this dumping is not due to inflation of currency. They say that the government gets its raw materials for nothing and pays no rent, and labor is underpaid. This point of view was presented by M. Litvinov in his address in Geneva on May 21, 1931:

> We do not, of course, deny that special conditions of agriculture and foreign trade in the Soviet Union allow the sale of agricultural products at lower prices than can be offered by other countries. These conditions, thanks to the nationalization of land, are the absence of rent, lease, and mortgage, which are such a drain on agriculture in other lands, absorbing sometimes 70 per cent of the cost of production, and the elimination of private profits, exchange speculation, and middlemen.

This argument, however, is specious. Raw materials cost money to extract from the ground, interest and rent are charges which, though not visible, still persist, and labor must be paid enough to provide the minimum needs of even a low standard of living. Dumping abroad is not the result of low cost of production; it is the result of inflated currency. Furthermore, the lack of credit makes it essential that the few available commodities be sold at whatever price they will bring on the world markets in order to pay for greatly desired machinery.

Commissar Grinko denied that there was any "dumping" or that the Soviet government sold its products at a loss. Quite the contrary, he said that his analysis of the income from the state enterprises of the Soviet Union proves that they were being operated at a high rate of profit.[17]

8. Opposition to Inflation. That inflation is progressive has been recognized by the responsible heads in the government. There is a continuous struggle between the Supreme Council of National Economy, which plans for an ever-increasing production requiring ever-increasing note issues on the one hand, and on the other hand the officials of the Bank, who are trying to keep the increase of currency within bounds and to check inflation. The former Commissar of Finance, Briukhanov, who assisted in the development of the Five-Year Plan, and the head of the State Bank, Pyatakov, both were

opposed to expanding the currency, even though the requirements of industry were increasing. Rumor has it that the removal of both was due to this opposition.

9. Cure for Inflation. The cure for inflation is either to increase the output of consumers' goods, to decrease the currency outstanding or to reduce the cost of production. Any deflation that occurs must be something more than reductions such as that mentioned, a drop of 400 million rubles in the fall of 1930, which, as noted was probably in part, at least, a seasonal diminution after the harvest. Such seasonal declines in currency characterize agricultural countries. The Soviets expect to flood the country with goods and thus restore the relationship between goods and money.

Even though the pledge is kept that the currency issue will not be increased, there will still be inflation. There is a discrepancy between the volume of goods and the volume of currency. Under a rationing system, goods are not available and currency is redundant. To reduce this discrepancy either consumers' goods must be increased or the excess cash must be absorbed by means of public loans.[18]

E. Banking in Relation to the Five-Year Plan

The increasing output of producers' goods required by the Five-Year Plan has increased the financial requirements of the country. Funds for expansion are obtained from taxes, from the profits of the Bank, from the profits of industry, which are considered as budgetary receipts, and finally from an increase of the note circulation. If the financial requirements of industry seem too large to the banking authorities, they may be cut down, or in case of dispute officials of the Bank and the industry arbitrate their differences at the Gosplan or State Planning Department.

In capitalist countries the price of a commodity is determined by supply and demand, but in Soviet Russia the supply is planned and the demand is curtailed by rationing. Prices are therefore not free and are not of first importance. Furthermore, because prices are fixed the banker does not play as important a part in Russia as in a country where economic forces play freely.

One of the objects of the Five-Year Plan was to reduce prices. Prices fell throughout the world in 1930 and the plan to reduce Russian prices to the world level was made more difficult. But without a reduction in the price of consumers' goods the buying power of agricultural producers must remain small. Price inflation is exaggerated by the Five-Year Plan. Consumers' goods are not produced in sufficient quantities and therefore prices rise. The emphasis is on the production of farm products, raw materials, and producers' goods, and these are dumped at such low prices as will move great quantities. The dumping of forest and farm products and minerals and ores intensifies the maladjustment between prices of producers' goods and consumers' goods. To reduce prices the technical heads of industry attempt to introduce efficiency methods to effect a saving in raw materials and to increase the output per man.

F. Reform of Credit

The credit reform of 1930 is similar to the war experience of the belligerent countries. When the currency note circulation rose very rapidly, several of the great powers, both during and after the war, attempted to introduce checks and a clearing system to eliminate the passing of currency from hand to hand. In other words, instead of having a note liability of the bank of issue, they thought that a deposit liability would constitute less of an inflation. This curious differentiation between the two liabilities is similar to the principles which obtained in England prior to the Bank Act of 1844. There also a gold reserve was set up against notes but not against deposits, with the result that in times of panic, when the deposits were withdrawn in gold, an unfavorable situation developed into a crisis.

1. Aims and Methods. Under the scheme prevailing in Soviet Russia until 1930 a seller of merchandise would discount his paper at the central bank. In this way the bank was often faced with unexpected claims. Under the recent credit reform, the bank finances not the seller but the buyer. In other words, under the Five-Year Plan a fixed output is sought. The Bank approves the production schedule, and is prepared to advance the credit required under the plan. As a result commercial paper is eliminated. The Bank becomes a sort of clearing house. All requirements for credit are centered there. Such a reform, it is hoped, will result in a decrease in circulation. Possibly this was an important object in view, as a means of disguising the inflation which would then be reflected chiefly in deposits rather than in note circulation. By reducing the need for borrowing in advance, even deposits should decline, since almost every bank loan automatically increased deposits. The officials of the Bank and the Soviet economists hail this step as the abandonment of the capitalist banking system and the creation of a new and original socialist conception with wide implications.

The trusts, the great corporations, are forbidden by law to give bills in payment. Payments between trusts are made through the central bank as a bookkeeping item, somewhat similar to inter-company transactions of a holding company or to the gold settlement fund between the Federal Reserve banks in our country, or to the Giro-Verkehr in Germany.*

With the introduction of the New Economic Policy the sale of goods was transacted by means of bills of exchange. These bills were discounted at the Bank, whose chief operations consisted in loans and discounts. This system is similar to the practice prevailing in other countries. As Russia became rapidly industrialized, inflation resulted. The practice suitable for capitalist systems proved unsuitable for a socialist system. Therefore, on January 30, 1930, the Credit Reform Act was passed. The unrestricted granting of credit by the state trusts interfered with the planning of credit. As the seller presented bills for discount at the Bank, the financial burden of the buyer was transferred to the Bank. This system proved troublesome and was abolished. Instead, the Bank advanced credit directly to the purchaser. The seller did not appear in the transaction. Commercial credit was replaced by bank credit. Such a credit system, the Soviet officials say, is better adapted to an era of socialism and communism, and tends more effectively to direct the credit resources of the Bank into the channels planned for.

Under the new system state organizations are prohibited from extending credit to each other. Credit follows industry, and both are regulated under the state plan. If a development planned for does not take place, then no credit is advanced. On the other hand, if some development takes place that is not provided for in the Plan, the discrepancy is noted at the Bank. Thus the Bank correlates financing and industry. The stream of goods and of credit will be parallel. The method involves not currency circulation, but bookkeeping items or current accounts, through which the Bank's clients are debited or credited. The Bank thus becomes a central clearing house for short-term credit of state institutions.

2. Planned Credit and Planned Production.[19] In the opinion of Soviet economists, the distinction between the Soviet credit system and the capitalist credit system is in the feature of planning. In the capitalist world, credit management is intended to regulate production, but in the Soviet system the entire economic life is regulated, and with it also the credit system. In the capitalist world credit is adapted to other economic factors. In the Soviet

* The system is described in the *Economic Survey*, the official publication of the State Bank, in the issues of March, July, and November, 1930 (Vol. V, nos. 4, 12, and 19).

world, credit controls production, the production plan is based on the credit resources, and the credit plan constitutes actual instructions for the production of goods. The mere fact that the credit plan does not work perfectly does not invalidate its importance, in the opinion of Soviet economists.

3. TECHNIQUE. The credit plan is divided into two sections, covering revenue and expenditures.[20]

REVENUE

1. Proceeds of the sale of commodities
2. Taxes and duties including—
   Taxes
   State insurance
   Local taxes and duties
3. Proceeds of state loans
4. Trade unions
5. Transport
6. Communication
7. Miscellaneous

EXPENDITURES

1. Factory and office payrolls
2. Salaries of handicraftsmen
3. Procurements (purchases) of agricultural produce
4. Timber felling
5. Loans to agriculture (advances on contracts)
6. Social insurance
7. State insurance
8. Service of state loans
9. Transport
10. Communication
11. Miscellaneous

The principal source of revenue is the proceeds of the sale of commodities, mainly by the consumers' co-operatives. The principal expenditures are for payrolls, purchase of agricultural produce, advances on contracts, insurance payments, and the service of state loans.

All the state and co-operative enterprises have an account with either the State Bank or its branches, and submit their credit plan along with the industrial or commercial plan for the quarter. They also present a plan of receipts and disbursements in cash, for the current quarter. On the basis of these estimates of the numerous customers of the banks, as revised by the local offices of the State Bank, each of the regional offices of the State Bank prepares a regional plan of cash payments. Thereupon the State Bank prepares a combined plan for the entire Union and submits it for approval together with the quarterly credit plan to the proper governmental authorities. After the plan has been approved, the State Bank returns it to the regional offices, and they in turn to their district branches, who submit the plan of cash payments for every customer.

As a result of this centralization of credit the trend has been toward a single clearing house or a single bank. This idea was developed by Lenin, and the Sixteenth Congress of the All-Union Communist Party invoked his forecast to justify the reform. In the words of Stalin: "Thus the State Bank will be transformed into a general state accounting apparatus for production and distribution. Secondly, large amounts of currency will be released from circulation, thus strengthening the chervonetz." [21]

4. Results. When the plan is functioning, every client of the State Bank will become part of a cycle of accounting. The new credit reform should simplify the accounting system of the Soviet Union. It should increase check payments which were practically unknown until the decree of June 1929, which legalized the issue of "non-cash accounts" in financial transactions within the Soviet Union. A campaign to popularize this method of payment is still being carried on particularly in the rural districts, where the new method is little understood and, therefore, suspected. Another result of the credit reform is to reduce the cash requirements and therefore the net currency circulation.[22] In the so-called special quarter, October to December 1930, the actual reduction in net circulation was ascribed to the new credit reform, which eliminated the use of money within the "socialistic sector." Cash payments were required only in settlement between the "socialistic sector" and the "private sector" of business.[20]

5. Difficulties. Any such far-reaching reform was bound to lead to difficulties, and difficulties did crop out everywhere. The chief one was that credits were granted to the several state organizations in accordance with their plan and not in accordance with the actual production. This resulted in relaxing responsibilities and in increasing expenditures. Again, the State Bank automatically credited the shipper of merchandise, regardless of whether the purchaser approved the shipment or whether he had money at the bank. As a result shippers became careless with respect to the quantity of merchandise, its quality, or the time of delivery. Furthermore, the buyers were careless about their finances, since the Bank made payments against their account, even if it was overdrawn. Furthermore, the Bank would credit profits to the producer on the basis of the cost price estimated in the plan. Therefore there was no incentive to reduce production costs or to maintain a system of cost accounting. Apparently the State Bank had undertaken too large a task in attempting to plan and regulate production and credit for the entire country.[23]

A few concrete examples of the difficulties are given herewith: The workers at the Molotov factory of the Non-Ferrous Metals Trust received no pay because the plant was having financial difficulties at the Bank, even though the Bank and the plant were both located in Moscow.[24] Another difficulty was the absence of the directors and managers from this factory as was also the case in the Rostov plant while they waited in the offices of the State Bank trying to get money to run their businesses. Again, the inefficient working of the system caused finished products to pile up sometimes with the shipper and sometimes with the customer. The State Sewing Machine Trust in Kharkov, which controls the bicycle factory Velozavod, actually had a credit balance of 500,000 rubles to pay for goods purchased, but the State Bank could find no such credit in their account. As a result the workmen received no wages, payments were not made for goods purchased, and operations of the plant were interrupted by the credit reform.[24]

The Moscow plant of the Rubber Trust, Caoutchouc, accumulated a huge inventory of rubber products, because the customers presumably had no credit at the Bank. The workers in the Caoutchouc plant maintained that the Moscow offices of the State Bank were responsible for their difficulties.[25]

6. Remedies. To overcome these difficulties a decree was issued in January 1931 modifying the Credit Reform Act. The principle still was maintained concerning "the supply of goods and rendering of various services without the use of commercial credit," that enterprises could not issue bills of exchange to each other or grant credits in the form of open accounts and that operations must all be conducted through the State Bank. Modification of the Credit Reform Act permitted the State Bank to grant advances secured by merchandise in case of difficulties in transportation. This is due to the fact that owing to inadequate transport facilities large inventories accumulated with the producers and thus strained their financial credit. Such advances against accumulated inventories should not exceed 75 per cent of the value of the goods. Another modification was that the minimum amount of bills to be cleared through the State Bank was to be one hundred rubles, to avoid cluttering the accounts with small sums.[26] Further the State Bank would no longer pay indiscriminately, but would limit payments to the seller to the extent that the buyer had credit available, and then only if the buyer ordered and approved the merchandise as to quality, quantity, and the meeting of sundry terms of the contract.

In March 1931, a supplementary decree was issued, under the title, "Measures to Revise the System of Credits and to Introduce Economic Accounting." Under the new decree the State Bank became the central institution for keeping account of the production and distribution of goods. It was to provide a daily check concerning the execution of the production plans, merchandise sales, and accumulated inventories. The bank was thus to insure that the principles of strict accounting would prevail in business enterprises.[27]

To improve the operation of the Credit Reform Act, the Council of Labor and Defense decreed that payment should be made to trusts and factories only in proportion as they had completed their work, that money advanced for construction might not be used for operating expenses, and that money must be used only for the purpose agreed upon when the credit was granted.[28]

To the western mind, the attempt to regulate the entire economic life of the country through a single bank seems staggering. The establishment of a clearing house for all the economic operations of a large country introduces an element of centralization which seems bound to lead to inefficiency.

CHAPTER XI

THE BUDGET

A. Unique Character of the Budget

The Soviet budget differs from the budgets of other governments. The latter deal only with government receipts and expenditures. The income and expenses of private corporations are regarded as private tabulations utterly unrelated to government affairs. But in Soviet Russia the budget of the state includes besides all the receipts and expenditures which usually go into the budget of other states, the additional revenues and expenses of the businesses run by the state, such as railroads, mines, factories, etc. True, in the United States the revenues and expenditures of the Post Office are included in the government budget, and in some Continental countries receipts and expenditures of the railroads and state-owned public utilities are likewise included. But in Soviet Russia the budget is more inclusive and represents a large part of the national income.

In the fiscal year ended September 1928, approximately 17 per cent of the total national income was saved and diverted for the uses of the state, and in the fiscal year ended September 1929 almost 30 per cent. Naturally this involved very heavy taxes. According to Russian economists, the Russian peasant was taxed about 10 per cent of his income during the fiscal year 1926, and the city laborer about 12 per cent. This high rate increased still further in 1927 and 1928, when the burden of taxation exceeded the pre-war level. But the national income in 1927 was 9 per cent, and in 1928 was 21 per cent, above 1913.

The budget grows continuously. The increasing activity of the state and the launching of the Five-Year Plan have caused the rise, in part.[1]

The steep rise in the budget total in 1931 was due partly to the wider scope of the budget, partly to the depreciation of the ruble, partly to the increased

Fiscal Year	*Budget (billion rubles)*
1923	1.47
1924	2.28
1925	2.95
1926	3.98
1927	5.71
1928	6.95
1929	8.03
1930	12.52
1931	20.45
1932 (planned)	27.43

scale of industrialization, and partly to the large loans raised to meet the budget. Of course, the 31-billion-ruble total of the unified financial plan included the receipts of industry, railroads, etc.[2]

The actual Soviet budgets for the fiscal years 1927–31 are given in the accompanying tables.*

SOVIET BUDGET, 1926–27 TO 1928–29 [3]
(in millions of rubles)

REVENUE	*1926–27*	*1927–28*	*1928–29*
I. Direct taxation			
1. Single agricultural tax	358	354	430
2. Turnover (sales) tax	886	901	1,173
3. Income tax	192	231	283
4. Miscellaneous taxes	16	23	21
Total	1,452	1,509	1,907
II. Indirect taxation			
1. Excise taxes	1,109	1,366	1,663
2. Customs duties	189	259	254
Total	1,298	1,625	1,917
III. Stamp and miscellaneous duties	90	120	134
Total revenue from taxation	2,841	3,255	3,960
IV. State property and enterprises			
1. Posts and Telegraphs	156	173	198

* Official statistics in Soviet Russia are not as carefully checked as those, for example, in the United States. A few discrepancies appear between the different sets of figures presented in different publications. Those given herewith, taken from accepted sources, are as nearly correct as any, and the differences between them and other budget figures are not of major importance.

SOVIET BUDGET, 1926–27 TO 1928–29—*Continued*

(in millions of rubles)

Revenue	*1926–27*	*1927–28*	*1928–29*
2. Transportation	1,684	1,928	2,189
3. Industry	199	258	270
4. Commerce	38	34	32
5. Banks	68	86	108
6. Forestry	221	246	304
7. Miscellaneous state property and concessions	67	94	98
Total revenue from state property and enterprises	2,434	2,819	3,199
V. State loans	319	727	703
VI. Miscellaneous income	104	97	137
VII. Surplus from previous budget	16	52	113
Grand total	5,713	6,950	8,112
Expenditures			
I. Financing of national economy			
1. Industry	456	654	922
2. Agriculture *	159	229	435
3. Electrification	103	136	184
4. Forestry	32	40	46
5. Water economy (rivers and canals)	32	32	37
6. Payments for social insurance	58	63	62
7. Measures for promotion of trade	67	158	187
8. Co-operatives	27	13	11
9. Municipal economy and housing	43	110	73
10. Construction of new railways	36	69	127
11. Miscellaneous	48	57	91
Total	1,061	1,561	2,175
II. Transportation and communications			
1. Railways (exclusive of new construction)	1,506	1,666	1,749
2. Water transport	67	94	132
3. Posts, telegraphs, telephones, and radio	146	166	188
4. Miscellaneous	146	193	186
Total	1,867	2,120	2,256

SOVIET BUDGET 1926–27 TO 1928–29—*Continued*
(in millions of rubles)

REVENUES	*1926–27*	*1927–28*	*1928–29*
III. Social and cultural activities			
1. Scientific research work	40	55	88
2. Education and art	220	250	330
3. Labor protection and social insurance	154	183	182
4. Miscellaneous	44	49	44
Total	458	537	644
IV. Government administrative expenditures			
1. General administrative expenditures	107	95	84
2. Miscellaneous	174	152	154
Total	281	247	238
V. Army and navy	651	765	875
VI. Special corps	40	49	55
VII. Debt service	101	299	293
VIII. Funds turned over to local budgets	927	918	1,078
IX. Expenditures of autonomous republics of R.S.F.S.R.	73	83	95
X. Various reserve funds	199	165	152
Grand Total	5,662	6,747	7,864

NOTE: Owing to the omission of six figures, the totals do not exactly equal the sum of the constituent items.

* Includes seven sub-classes, as follows: (a) state farms; (b) machinery and tractor stations; (c) experimental research work; (d) land organization; (e) migration and colonization; (f) agricultural banks; (g) other agricultural expenditures. The growth in several of these sub-classes has been stupendous. Between the fiscal years 1927 and 1930 the item "state farms" rose from 5 million to 517 million rubles; "experimental research work" from 72 million to 126 million rubles; and "agricultural banks" from 38 million to 148 million rubles.

SOVIET BUDGET 1929–30 AND 1930–31

(in millions of rubles)

	1929–30 (estimate)	1930–31 (plan)
REVENUE		
A. Revenue from taxation		
1. Single agricultural tax	359	500
2. Business turnover (sales) tax	6,280	9,393
3. Trade and industry tax	133	180
4. Income tax	283	300
5. Customs duties and other revenues	328	300
6. Special for cultural needs	—	150
7. Other taxes and duties	17	20
Total	7,400	10,843
B. Revenue from state and co-operative property and enterprises		
1. Industry under Supreme Economic Council	1,350	1,559
2. Electric power plants	13	48
3. State farms	28	58
4. Internal and foreign trade	77	350
5. Other trading organizations	102	107
6. Banks	141	181
7. Consumers' co-operatives	121	537
8. Producers', agricultural, housing, etc. co-operatives	36	47
9. State insurance funds	78	23
10. Special commodity funds	283	600
11. Other revenues	223	164
12. Miscellaneous	310	—
Total	2,762	3,674
C. State loans (including revenue of 400,000,000 rubles from savings banks)	1,032	1,700
D. Revenue from other sources		
1. Transportation	3,325	4,811
2. Communications	336	480
3. Repayment of loans advanced for agricultural purposes from 1929–30 budget	—	17
4. Revenue from local budgets	—	249
Total	3,661	5,557
Total revenues	14,855	21,774

SOVIET BUDGET 1929–30 AND 1930–31—*Continued*

(in millions of rubles)

	1929–30 (estimate)	*1930–31 (plan)*
EXPENDITURES		
A. Financing of national economy		
1. Industry	2,477	5,306
2. Electrification	290	768
3. Agriculture	1,536	2,378
4. Trade	893	1,412
5. Transportation	3,370	4,624
6. Civil aviation	27	150
7. Road construction, from budget of federated republics	—	34
8. Communications	321	556
9. Municipal and other buildings	53	31
10. Miscellaneous	133	85
Total	9,100	15,344
B. Social and cultural expenditures		
1. Education	735	1,104
2. Health conservation	51	80
3. Labor protection and social welfare	41	46
4. Administrative expenses for social and cultural work	8	9
Total	835	1,239
C. Army, navy, and special militia	1,322	1,390
D. Administration	200	230
E. Reserve funds		
1. Reserve fund of the Council of People's Commissars	296	380
2. State grain reserve fund	173	—
3. Other funds	21	26
Total	490	406
F. Expenditures for federal loans	401	395
G. Social insurance	33	35
H. Local budgets	1,757	1,315
I. State insurance	31	20
Total	14,169	20,374

SOVIET BUDGET 1929–30 AND 1930–31—*Continued*

(in millions of rubles)

	1929–30 (estimate)	*1930–31 (plan)*
J. Miscellaneous deductions	7	100
	14,162	20,274
K. State reserve fund	533	1,500
Total expenditures	14,695	21,774

The totals of revenues and expenditures in the budget for the fiscal year 1932 and the final figures for the fiscal year 1931 are given in the following table:

SOVIET BUDGET, 1931 AND 1932 [4]

REVENUES		*Execution in 1931* *Million rubles*		*Per cent of Total*		*Planned for 1932* *Million rubles*		*Per cent of Total*
I. Payments of the socialist sector		15,871		77.6		21,763		79.4
II. Funds provided by the population including—		2,868		14.0		4,890		17.8
(a) Taxes	1,008		4.9		1,400		5.1	
(b) National loans	1,581		7.7		2,750		10.0	
III. Miscellaneous revenues		1,715		8.4		776		2.8
Total		20,454		100.0		27,429		100.0
EXPENDITURES								
I. Financing of national economy including—		15,304		74.8		20,061		74.5
Industry	6,265		30.6		8,107		30.1	
Agriculture	2,447		12.0		3,480		12.9	
Railroad transport	2,144		10.5		2,487		9.2	
Food, industry, and trade	1,751		8.6		2,802		10.4	
II. Social and cultural needs *		1,234		6.0		1,527		5.7
III. National defense		1,132		5.5		1,278		4.7
IV. Administration		380		1.9		583		2.2
V. Reserve fund		610		3.0		840		3.1
VI. Service of loans		379		1.9		1,000		3.7

SOVIET BUDGET, 1931 AND 1932—*Continued*

Expenditures	Execution in 1931 Million rubles	Execution in 1931 Per cent of Total	Planned for 1932 Million rubles	Planned for 1932 Per cent of Total
VII. Financing of local budgets	1,231	6.0	1,429	5.3
VIII. Miscellaneous expenditures	184	0.9	211	0.8
Total	20,454	100.0	26,929	100.0
Reserve	——	——	500	——
Grand total	20,454	——	27,429	——

* The main part of these expenses are financed through the local budget. The state budget supports only universities, outstanding museums, theaters, sanatoriums, etc. The financing of high schools and public schools, local dispensaries and hospitals, is covered by the local budget.

For the calendar year 1932 the All-Union Central Executive Committee ratified the state budget calling for receipts of 27,541.9 million rubles and expenditures of 500 million rubles less, the latter amount going into a state reserve fund. The largest item of receipts was the turnover or sales tax, estimated to bring in 15 billion rubles, compared with only 15 million rubles for the income tax and 600 millions from the unified agricultural tax. Total taxation was to produce 16,753.6 million rubles. Receipts from state industry, transport, etc., were estimated at 6320.9 million rubles, and the rest was to be provided by loans. Expenditures for the national economy were placed at 20,078.6 million rubles.[5]

B. Unified Financial Plan

The Unified Financial Plan includes the state budget, and in addition the local budgets, the credit system, the savings banks, social insurance funds, and the "socialized sector" of industry and agriculture, namely, the state and co-operative enterprises and the trade unions. It represents receipts and disbursements for the entire country, excepting only the diminishing part of the national economy still in private hands and the current expenses of industry and transportation.

The Unified Financial Plan for 1931, presented by Commissar Grinko,[6] totaled almost 32 billion rubles or about two-thirds of the entire national income of about 49 billion rubles.[7] According to the Five-Year Plan, the financial plan for 1933 was expected to embrace only one-half of the total national income. The growth of the Unified Financial Plan was as follows:

Fiscal Year	*Million Rubles*
1928	10,000
1929	13,000
1930	22,000
1931	31,750

According to Mr. Grinko the annual increase of the national income in pre-war Russia averaged about 2 to 3 per cent. But in the Soviet Union the national income in 1929 increased by 11.5 per cent, in 1930 by 20 per cent, and in 1931 by 39 per cent.[8] Part of the rise seems due to inflation.

The United Financial Plan for 1931, as submitted by Commissar of Finance Grinko at a meeting of the Central Executive Committee on January 5, 1931, is as follows:

BALANCE SHEET OF THE UNIFIED FINANCIAL PLAN, 1931 [9]

REVENUES		*Million rubles*
I. Revenue from the socialized sector of the national economy:		
1. Industry	4,076	
2. Electric power plants	140	
3. Agriculture	1,094	
4. Timber	70	
5. Municipal enterprises	773	
6. State trade	1,480	
7. Consumers' co-operatives	779	
8. Transportation	3,381	
9. Communications	136	
10. Credit institutions	932	
11. Economic organs of the Commissariat for Finance	61	
12. Special funds of departments and institutions supported by state and local budgets	106	
13. Miscellaneous	365	
Total		13,393
II. Revenue from taxation:		
1. General state	10,843	
2. Local	435	
Total		11,278
III. Revenue from insurance organizations:		
1. Social insurance	2,174	
2. State insurance	490	
Total		2,664

BALANCE SHEET OF THE UNIFIED FINANCIAL PLAN, 1931—*Continued*

REVENUES		*Million rubles*
IV. Revenue from individual citizens:		
1. Loans	1,300	
2. Voluntary contributions	400	
3. Co-operative deposits and dues	921	
4. Savings banks	400	
5. Bonds of Tractor Center	160	
6. Repayment of loans advanced by the All-Union co-operative Credit Bank	700	
Total		3,881
V. Revenue from trade unions		400
VI. Miscellaneous revenue		302
Total revenues		31,918
EXPENDITURES		
I. Financing national economy:		
1. Industry	7,991	
2. Electrification	865	
3. Agriculture	4,833	
4. Municipal and housing construction	815	
5. Housing co-operation	100	
6. State trade	2,183	
7. Consumers' co-operatives	525	
8. Transportation	3,310	
9. Civil aviation	150	
10. Communications	260	
11. Economic organs of the Commissariat for Finance	30	
12. Miscellaneous	37	
Total		21,099
II. Financing social and cultural enterprises:		
1. Education	3,516	
2. Health	1,189	
3. Labor protection and social welfare	1,012	
4. Administrative expenses	68	
Total		5,785
III. Commissariat for War and Navy		1,310
IV. Administration		696

BALANCE SHEET OF THE UNIFIED FINANCIAL PLAN, 1931—*Continued*

Expenditures		*Million rubles*
V.	Reserve funds	430
VI.	Loan payments	382
VII.	State insurance	286
VIII.	Miscellaneous expenditures	430
	Total expenditures	30,418
	State reserve fund	1,500
	Grand total	31,918

With the progress of socialization, the funds absorbed by the socialized sector grew both absolutely and as a percentage of the national income. The national income of the U.S.S.R. in the fiscal year 1930 was approximately four billion rubles larger than the previous year, while the United Financial Plan involved investments of six billion rubles more. The Unified Financial Plan absorbed 53 per cent of the national income during the fiscal year 1930, as compared with 41 per cent in 1929.

THE UNIFIED FINANCIAL PLAN OF SOCIALIZED ECONOMY FOR THE FISCAL YEARS ENDING SEPTEMBER 30, 1929 AND 1930 [10]

A. Revenue

	1929		*1930*	
	Million rubles	*Per cent of Total*	*Million rubles*	*Per cent of Total*
State Economy—				
Federal budget	6,202.0	50.8	9,475.0	52.0
Local budgets and self-taxation	1,055.5	8.7	1,343.0	7.4
Banking system (own resources)	1,513.0	12.4	1,894.0	10.4
Social insurance	916.0	7.5	1,045.0	5.7
State insurance	234.2	1.9	349.0	1.9
Funds of economic enterprises	942.6	7.7	1,739.0	9.6
Miscellaneous	429.7	3.5	933.0	5.1
Total	11,293.0	92.5	16,778.0	92.1
Co-operatives	533.4	4.4	1,000.0	5.5
Trade unions	376.0	3.1	444.0	2.4
Grand total	12,202.4	100.0	18,222.0	100.0

REVENUE DISTRIBUTION BY ULTIMATE SOURCES OF INCOME

	1928–29		*1929–30*	
	Million rubles	*Per cent of Total*	*Million rubles*	*Per cent of Total*
Profits of economic enterprises	3,797.0	31.2	6,663.4	36.6
Taxes	4,205.6	34.5	5,667.6	31.2
Attracted funds (borrowings, etc.)	1,625.6	13.3	2,590.0	14.2
Insurance funds	1,360.0	11.1	1,657.0	9.0
Currency issue	200.0	1.6	425.0	2.3
Miscellaneous	1,014.2	8.3	1,219.0	6.7
Total	12,202.4	100.0	18,222.0	100.0

B. Expenditures

	1928–29		*1929–30*	
	Million rubles	*Per cent of Total*	*Million rubles*	*Per cent of Total*
Administration and defense	1,637.4	13.4	1,864.0	10.2
Financing national economy	6,646.1	54.5	11,119.5	61.0
Industry	2,555.4	20.9	4,062.3	22.3
Agriculture *	936.7	7.7	1,583.5	8.7
Transportation	1,141.3	9.4	1,727.2	9.5
Miscellaneous	2,012.7	16.5	3,746.5	20.5
Social and cultural needs	3,034.7	24.9	4,152.2	22.8
Miscellaneous	884.2	7.2	1,086.3	6.0
Total	12,202.4	100.0	18,222.0	100.0

* In addition, 450 million rubles were invested in 1928–29 from the funds of the population and of economic enterprises. The corresponding investments for 1929–30 were estimated at about 1,095,000,000 rubles.

More than 42 per cent of the receipts of the Unified Financial Plan for 1931 come from profits of the socialized sector, industry, transportation, and trade under state or co-operative control; 35 per cent from taxation, of which four-fifths come from the socialized sector; and about 12 per cent from the public in the form of income taxes and state loans.

The percentage of the national income of the Soviet Union planned to be taken to finance the national economy is very high and is rising, as shown herewith. If social welfare, cultural purposes, and government functions are included the percentages are even higher.[11]

Fiscal Year	*Percentage of National Income Taken for— Economic Purposes*	*Economic, Cultural, and Governmental Purposes*
1928	22	38
1929	25	42
1930	27	43
1931	28	45
1932	31	49
1933	34	53

These percentages, like the Five-Year Plan itself, have minimum and "optimum" variants. Even though the figures may not tally with those compiled at other times and for other purposes, the following table is interesting as showing what a large and growing percentage of the national income is taken for the financial plan under the minimum variant: [12]

Fiscal Year	*National Income*	*Unified Financial Plan*	*Percentage*
	Billion rubles	*Billion rubles*	
1928	24.8	9.5	38.1
1929	27.5	11.4	41.8
1930	30.8	13.4	43.3
1931	33.8	15.2	44.9
1932	37.6	17.3	45.7
1933	40.7	19.5	48.0
Total	195.2	86.3	44.2

C. Expenditures and Revenues

The budget indicates the huge scale on which industry is being developed. Funds are taken from various sources and redistributed in the discretion of a small group, in accordance with the Plan. In Russia the state collects income from the various sources and reallocates it. In the capitalist world thousands of individuals voluntarily invest in stocks and bonds of industry in accordance with the apparent safety or possibility of profit. In Russia new industries are established by existing and related industries. In other words the Electrical Trust may develop a mica plant or the Automobile Trust may develop a glass plant. Part of the profits of every trust are used for expansion of its own activities, and part goes into the budget and is reallocated to industries that may be utterly unrelated to it.

The resources of the budget, as was true in the warring countries, are derived partly from inflation, partly from state loans, partly from indirect taxes, and partly from income and profits taxes. However, unlike the example of the warring countries, foreign capital is utilized relatively little. That funds are derived from inflation is indicated by the rapidly increasing issue of currency notes as shown in the chapter on "Banking." State loans, which are virtually conscription of capital, or forced loans, even though the force be only moral rather than legal, constitute a growing source of income. The industrial profits of trusts and co-operatives are also utilized.

The "socialized sector" of business produces the largest percentage of the total budget, about 42 per cent in 1931. However, only part of the profit of state industry goes to the state budget, part of it being reserved for the extension of industry and social welfare. The second largest source of income is taxation, and under taxation the largest item is the sales tax, or the tax on the turnover of business. But Russia is poor and primitive and the sales tax is most expedient, if not most ethical. When the Soviets are faced with a crisis, they discard their radical doctrines and follow the practical and sensible policy. Similarly, the United States may as an emergency means of balancing its budget resort to a sales tax, until the depression lifts and incomes rise again. Excise duties are next in importance.

Almost 80 per cent of the indirect taxes are on so-called "consumer" goods, salt, tea, sugar, coffee, matches, and vodka. Strange indeed that a régime which regards itself as socialistic or communistic should tax the table of the poor so heavily! As shown above, the salt tax was the basis of the popular uprising resulting in the French Revolution. The salt tax was recently also the basis of an uprising in India led by Ghandi. The tax on tea led up to the American Revolution.

D. Tax Schedules

The following details of the sources of income were obtained from the Commissariat of Finance. The personnel at the Bureau of the Budget seemed to be well trained in the principles of taxation, as applied both in Soviet Russia and in other countries.

1. Agricultural Taxes. The single agricultural tax replaced the numerous

local taxes and the tax in kind to which the peasants were liable.[13] This tax applies to the individual peasant, to the agricultural co-operatives, and to the state farms. It is levied on the income from farm land, cattle breeding, and home industry. Payment of the single agricultural tax relieves the assessed from any other central or local taxation.

Generally the basis of taxation is the amount of land and live stock. It is assumed that a certain area will yield a given income, and the tax is levied on this basis. For example, in the Russian Republic proper, the annual taxable income is fixed at 46 rubles per dessiatin (equivalent at par to $23.70 per 2.7 acres); in the Ukraine at 58 rubles; in the Central Asiatic Republics at 108 rubles up. The assessed income from live stock, horses, mules, and camels ranges from 13 to 26 rubles, depending on the region. The taxable income from crops is based in some localities on the area sown and in others on the area plowed, according to the decision of the district Soviet Executive Committee. Such variation in the taxable basis, in the discretion of local political executives, makes possible much injustice.

The tax varies with the class of the peasant. The kulaks, or rich peasants, about three per cent of the peasantry, pay 30 per cent of the total tax. About 35 per cent of the private farms are so small that they pay no tax, because the peasants are too poor. If the kulaks are eliminated receipts from agricultural taxes will undoubtedly decline, but taxes from other sources, as collective farms, should offset the loss.

The highest tax is on the kulak and the lowest tax on the poor peasant. The legal definition of a kulak is a peasant who systematically employs hired labor, who possesses power-driven machinery such as a flour mill or a wool-combing machine, who hires out such machinery or contracts to do work on other farms, who rents out living quarters, who leases land for commercial purposes, or who receives unearned income of any kind.[14] The regional Soviet Executive Committee may change the interpretation according to local conditions.[15] That is, this committee may decide that a man is a kulak and thus increase his tax burden. The principle of the tax is not merely to raise revenue but to force agriculture toward socialism. For example, the tax rate on collective farms is lower than on individual farms. It is not graduated, and therefore places no restriction on increasing the size and income of the collective farm. By thus reducing the burden on the peasant who joins the collective farm, the movement for collective farming is stimulated. The individual peasant has the right to deduct 20 rubles for each member of the household and the remainder is taxed at the following rates:

Rate per cent	*Annual Taxable Income in rubles*
4%	First 25
7%	26–100
Up to 30%	600 and over

Kulaks, however, pay more. No deduction is allowable for any member of the household. The rate begins at 20 per cent for the first 500 rubles and rises to 70 per cent for incomes of 6000 rubles (about $3000 at par) and over. On collective farms the tax is 4 per cent on the annual income for communes, or the radical co-operatives and 5 per cent for the other types. If an accounting system is installed, the rate is lower, only 2 per cent for communes and 3 per cent for the other collectives. The tax on state farms is based on the average rate in the district.

The minimum income which is exempt from tax on individual farms ranges from 110 rubles for households of one or two members to 150 rubles for households of five or more members. If there are twelve or more children, 20 per cent of the tax is refunded. If there is an actual deficit, no tax is paid even though the above taxable basis calls for payment. On collective farms the income exempt from taxation is 30 rubles per member, or if books are kept the exempt income is 60 rubles. In communes or radical co-operatives, composed mainly of poor peasants, even though the gross income exceeds the taxable minimum, the tax may be reduced 50 per cent if there is a net deficit.

The tax policy is also manipulated to bring land into cultivation. Newly plowed land is exempt for two years. Taxes are reduced 15 per cent if crop rotation is applied for the first time. Land devoted to growth of industrial crops, sugar beets, castor oil, soya bean, etc., is exempt from taxation. Land devoted to cotton, flax, and hemp is assessed only one-half the rate of other plowed or sown land.[16]

2. Industrial or Sales Tax. By decree of the Central Executive Committee and the Council of People's Commissars, August 10, 1928, an industrial tax, a tax on the annual sales or turnover, is levied on all industry and trading companies, including co-operatives. The rates vary with the percentage of the turnover from 1.6 per cent to 14.8 per cent for state and co-operative enterprises and from 2.15 per cent to 17.15 per cent for private enterprises. Some undertakings, such as public utilities, belonging to city or state, drug stores belonging to the state or to the co-operatives, scientific and technical organizations, are exempt from the industrial or sales tax.

Under a new tax reform, a unified method of taxation or single tax superseded all the forty-eight varieties of taxes and assessment.[17] According to the budget for 1931 more than 86 per cent of the entire tax revenue for the year was derived from the tax on sales. Obviously the sales tax is the basis of the tax system. Eliminating revenues from transportation and communications, because they are offset by the corresponding expenditures, the sales tax furnished about 53 per cent of the national revenue of the Soviet Union in 1931. The sales tax reduces personal consumption and diverts these savings into the construction of capital goods, plants for industry, power plants, and state and collective farms. The old sales tax imposed low rates on necessities and higher rates on luxuries. For example the rates were: coal, 1.6 per cent; grain, 2 per cent; automobiles, 6 per cent; optical goods, 7 per cent; cosmetics, 11 per cent. The single unified sales tax revised these scales.

Taxes on private industry yield about 10 per cent of the total tax on industry, and the state industries and co-operatives yield the balance. About 40 per cent of the total taxes are retained for local purposes.

3. PROFITS AND INCOME TAXES. Every individual, except the peasants and persons whose income has fallen below a certain minimum which varies in different parts of the Union, pays profits or income taxes, be he laborer, artisan, or trader. The income tax is based on three schedules and two sub-schedules of workers. Schedule I covers workers, employees, and pensioners. Schedule IA includes members of the producers' co-operatives, journalists, actors, etc. Persons engaged in small industries not employing hired workers come under Schedule II. Under Schedule IIA are those who carry on small industries employing not more than three hired workers. Schedule III includes all persons who derive their income from ownership of industrial or trading enterprises, money investments, dividends, etc. The basic rates for the lowest and highest brackets under each category as revised by decree of September 2, 1930, follow:[20]

Income in Rubles	*Basic Tax*	*Additional Tax*	
SCHEDULE I. (Workers and employees)			
Monthly Income			
Up to 85	0.75%		......
85 to 100	0.64 rubles	1.25% above	85 rubles
100 to 150	0.83 rubles	1.6 % above	100 rubles
......			
2,000 and above	442.53 rubles	37.5 % above	2000 rubles

Income in Rubles	*Basic Tax*	*Additional Tax*
SCHEDULE IA. (Journalists, actors, etc.)		
Annual Income		
Up to 1000	0.9 %	......
1000 to 1200	9 rubles	1.25% above 1000 rubles
1200 to 1800	11.5 rubles	1.75% above 1200 rubles
......		
20,000 to 24,000	3,995 rubles	36.5 % above 20,000 rubles
24,000 and above	5,455 rubles	37.5 % above 24,000 rubles
SCHEDULE II. (Home industries, handicrafts)		
Annual Income		
Up to 600	1.5 %	......
600 to 900	2.25%	......
900 to 1000	3.75%	......
......		
24,000 and above	11,619 rubles	75 % above 24,000 rubles
SCHEDULE IIA. (Artisans with not more than three workers)		
Annual Income		
Up to 1000	4 %	......
1000 to 1200	40 rubles	6 % above 1000 rubles
1200 to 1800	52 rubles	9 % above 1200 rubles
......		
24,000 and above	12,880 rubles	81 % above 24,000 rubles
SCHEDULE III. (Income from industrial and trading enterprises, dividends, etc.)		
Annual Income		
Up to 1000	4.8 %	......
1000 to 1200	54 rubles	8 % above 1000 rubles
......		
10,000 to 12,000	3,585 rubles	65.5 % above 10,000 rubles
......		
16,000 to 20,000	7,835 rubles	77 % above 16,000 rubles
20,000 to 24,000	10,915 rubles	80 % above 20,000 rubles
24,000 and above	14,115 rubles	86.5 % above 24,000 rubles

In addition all state enterprises, co-operative organizations and joint-stock companies owned by the state or co-operatives pay 20 per cent of their income as a tax. However, such amounts should not exceed the corresponding amounts payable under Schedule III.[19]

The tax is discriminatory. It is less for the manual laborer, increases for the independent artisan and professional man, and is highest of all on the private trader, and the bourgeois. Of the 12 million urban laborers in Russia, about 1,200,000 pay taxes. The tax is collected at the source.

How the discrimination affects the various classes is shown in the receipts as follows:

Class	*Total Taxes*
Workers	40,000,000 rubles
Artisans	60,000,000 rubles
Bourgeois	100,000,000 rubles

To raise money for building workers' homes in 1931 the government levied a special income tax. The schedules are as follows:

Monthly Income	*Tax*
75 rubles	12 to 40 rubles
250 rubles	30 to 135 rubles
300 rubles up	36 to 180 rubles

This special income tax to provide housing applies to everybody except agricultural workers or members of the army and navy, policemen, students, pensioners, and persons who have received honors or decorations. Otherwise the new tax applied to the schedules as defined above.[21]

4. Excess-Profits Tax. In addition to an income tax, there is an excess-profits tax. It applies to individual incomes in excess of 2000 to 3000 rubles. Public companies earning more than "normal profits" are subject to the tax. Such normal profits are fixed yearly by the Finance Department and are published before December 1 each year. The rate of tax varies from 24 per cent to 40 per cent on income from personal work and 6 per cent to 50 per cent on business profits.[22]

This tax is levied on private traders if they charge open-market prices, but if they charge only the government prices, they pay no tax. This is in practice an impossible condition, because the private trader cannot obtain goods at the low fixed prices of the government. Besides, it is better business for him to charge what the traffic will bear and pay the tax, because even if he charges five to six times the government prices and pays the 50 per cent tax he will still retain a net profit. The state trusts, however, also pay profits taxes at the rate of 20 per cent as noted above. The rate is fixed, not graduated.

5. Excise Taxes. Excise taxes are very heavy. They produced in the fiscal year 1928, 2300 million rubles, or approximately 20 per cent of the total budget. Excise duties apply to tobacco, sugar, petroleum products, alcoholic beverages, perfumery, cosmetics, tea, matches, rubber goods, etc.[23] The

tobacco tax is very high. A decree of February 7, 1930, taxed yellow smoking tobacco \$8.80 per pound (converting rubles at par), cigarettes \$7.18 per thousand, and cigars \$15 per thousand. The tax on liquor produced nearly 70 per cent of the total excise tax, or 1.5 billion rubles. The tax practically constitutes the high cost of liquor. A liter of vodka, for instance, sells for 3.50 rubles, and the cost is allocated as follows: the tax, 3 rubles, the bottle 10 kopeks, and the liquor 40 kopeks.

6. Customs Duties. Import duties produced about 400 million rubles, or, about 4 per cent of the total budget in 1928. But the imports of consumers' goods consist chiefly of tea, as the importation of goods like clothing, leather, etc. is prohibited. There are considerable imports of iron and steel products, machinery, electrical goods, copper, lead, tin, zinc, cotton, wool, chemicals, and rubber.

7. Real-Estate Taxes. There are taxes on churches and church property. The rate is the same as on private buildings, and amounts to one-eighth to one-half of one per cent of the total valuation per annum. Taxes on factories and similar buildings are lower.

8. Inheritance Taxes. The inheritance tax runs quite high although it is difficult to conceive, under the Soviet scheme, of the accumulation of enough property to be subject to the maximum tax. The Soviet law recognizes the right of inheritance regardless of the amounts involved, but it is confined to direct descendants, such as children, grandchildren, etc., surviving wife or husband, and indigent persons incapable of self-support who had been dependent upon the deceased for a period of one year or more before his death. However, inheritances as well as gifts (*inter vivos*) are subject to taxation, if the amount exceeds 1000 rubles. The inheritance tax rates for various brackets are as follows:

Amount of Inheritance	*For Proprietors in Trade and Industry, for Landlords, Rentiers, etc.*		*All Others*	
Rubles	*On Lower Limit*	*Plus Tax on Balance*	*On Lower Limit*	*Plus Tax on Balance*
1,000	5 % only		1 % only	....
2,000	5 %	10%	1 %	5%
....				
10,000	11 %	20%	5.4%	10%
.....				
100,000	22.1%	40%	18.5%	40%
......				
500,000	55.4%	90%	47.7%	90%

E. International Comparisons of Taxation

Despite differences of theory, the fiscal policies of the Soviet Union and the western countries are similar. The graduated income tax is used in both systems. The minimum amount of taxable income in Soviet Russia is not the lowest in the world nor is the corresponding rate in Russia the highest in the world. Several capitalist countries give smaller exemptions and tax more heavily at the bottom of the scale.

The minimum taxed income in Russia is 500 rubles (about $250 at par), for members of the least-favored class, such as traders. For members of the most-favored class, as manual workers, the tax applies to incomes above 900 rubles (about $450 at par). In France the lower limit is 10,000 francs (about $400), in Great Britain 150 pounds (about $730 at par), in Germany 720 marks ($180), and in the United States $1500 for single persons. The minimum tax rate for Russia is 0.7 per cent, for Great Britain 22½ per cent, for Germany 10 per cent, for France 1⅓ per cent, and for the United States 4 per cent.

The most notable differences appear in the graduation of the tax. In the Soviet Union the maximum rate is highest and applies to relatively smaller incomes than in the other countries. The tax is more confiscatory. In Russia the maximum rate of 54 per cent on incomes of traders and 30 per cent on those of laborers, journalists, etc., applies to incomes of 24,000 rubles or more (about $12,000 at par). In Germany the maximum rate of 40 per cent applies to incomes of about $20,000 or over. In France the maximum rate of 33⅓ per cent applies to incomes of about $22,000 or over. In the United States the maximum rate of 8 per cent normal and 55 per cent surtax applies to incomes over $1,000,000, and in Great Britain the upper limit of 41½ per cent is reached at incomes of $250,000.

The Soviet Union in its taxation of incomes discriminates in favor of "earned incomes" as against "unearned incomes," as do also Great Britain and other capitalist countries. The maximum rates in Russia are only slightly more confiscatory than in Germany. Here is an excellent illustration of the theory of convergence of the two systems. Russia copied from the western countries a socialistic tax system. Both systems portend similar rising trends for countries not yet so highly socialized.

A similar principle applies to confiscation of large estates by inheritance taxes. In Soviet Russia the lower limit of inheritance taxes applies to estates of 1000 rubles (about $500 at par). This compares with 100 pounds (general limit) in Great Britain (about $487 at par); 15,000 francs, or about $600, in France (for lineal descendants); 500 to 5000 marks (about $125 to $1250) in Germany, depending on relationship of legatee; and $100,000 (federal) in the United States. The rate on the lowest bracket is 1 per cent (for laborers) to 5 per cent (for traders) in Russia; 1 per cent in Great Britain and the United States; 1.2 to 30 per cent in France, and 2 to 14 per cent in Germany.

But the maximum rate, which is almost confiscatory, is reached on small estates in Russia—inheritances over 500,000 rubles ($250,000 at par) pay a tax of 90 per cent. In the United States the maximum rate of 20 per cent applies to estates over $10,000,000. In Great Britain the maximum rate is 50 per cent, applying to estates of 2,000,000 pounds (about $9,500,000 at par) and over. In France the maximum rate is reached at 50,000,000 francs (about $2,000,000). It amounts to 10.8 per cent for father, son, etc., 58.8 per cent for nephew, uncle, etc., and 70.8 per cent for strangers. In Germany the maximum rate is reached at 10,000,000 marks (about $2,500,000). For wife or children the rate is 15 per cent, with higher rates, up to 60 per cent, for other classes of legatees.

The Soviet inheritance taxes virtually confiscate estates at the death of the owner. But France and Germany are only slightly less confiscatory. Two successive transfers of an estate would whittle it down to a small fraction of its original amount. Here again social forces in both systems are converging toward a common goal.

F. Tax Reform [24]

The multiplicity of taxes proved cumbersome, and a sweeping reform was adopted in September 1930. The system thitherto prevailing was suited to a varied group of private industries which flourished under the New Economic Policy. But as industry came under the control of the state and the co-operatives, and as the Five-Year Plan developed, tax reform became practicable. Furthermore, taxes were reformed in order to avoid checking the growth of certain lines of industry and trade. Taxation has therefore been simplified. The two main sources are the sales tax and the profits tax. Instead of a series of sales taxes on the same article at various stages of manufacture, resulting in a high and excessive total tax, a single sales tax was levied at the point of final production, replacing 53 types of taxes, excises and duties, such as the trade license tax, excise tax, freight tax, stamp tax, etc., which were added to the price paid by the consumer.

An integrated trust will have to pay only a single sales tax, and its various factories will not be taxed at all. The simplification of the sales tax should help to keep retail prices down. The tax reform became simple after the introduction of the credit reform. Prior to the reform, profits were collected by the state through various sources, through the income tax, through that part of the profits of industry reserved for the Treasury, and by other means. Since the tax reform all these sources have been merged into one. If a trust buys goods, the State Bank does the financing, charging the buyer on the books of the Bank, crediting the seller for part of the proceeds, and crediting the state budget with the tax. Thus the taxes of the state are collected by the central bank at the time of the sale.

Co-operative industries will continue to pay a tax on income. They sell at their own discretion, and after the income tax is paid their profits are not subject to requisition by the state. Such private industry as may still be left will continue to pay the old taxes—income tax, trade-license tax, excess-profits tax, and special taxes. However, even here taxation has been simplified. The number of taxes has been reduced from sixty-four to twenty-eight.

G. Effects of Taxation

The burden of taxation is heavy. True, the people cannot use their money to buy commodities when few commodities are to be had. Consumption of the essentials of life is curtailed. But of the income still remaining, much is taken by the state. Again, forced borrowing is really an additional form of taxation. When the worker is asked to contribute 4 per cent of his yearly salary to subscribe to state loans, he dare not refuse because of the pressure of opinion in the factory.

As a result of taxation the resources of the country are developed along lines required by the Plan. The resources are redistributed; they are taken from consumption and put into new plants. As the plants grow and payments become due for machinery within one, two, or three years, and as additional machinery is installed requiring spot payments, particularly cash, the burden on the state will increase, and the burden of taxation is likely to become swiftly heavier owing to the rapid increase of industrial development.

Taxation in Soviet Russia represents a series of compromises with capitalism. In a country which aimed to establish equal incomes for all, one finds provisions for taxing incomes which range as high as 500,000 rubles per annum and tax provisions applying to workers' wages as high as 24,000 rubles, almost 2000 rubles per month as compared with the theoretical maximum of 300 rubles per month for members of the Communist Party. The floating of loans by the state represents a compromise with capitalism. People are now even encouraged to accumulate wealth, and the state agrees to sanction it by paying interest to them. Apparently in taxation, as in various other departments of administration, the Soviet authorities had the good sense to abandon their theories when they collided with the realities of life. Their aim seems more recently to have changed from developing their doctrine to industrializing Russia, and when the two aims conflict they take the practical road. They favor economic efficiency as against political theory.

H. Loans

1. Foreign Loans. Foreign loans to the Soviet Union have not been granted by investors, but foreign manufacturers have granted short-term credits for industry.

2. Long-Term Credits. There are no investment bankers in Russia, and therefore there are no offerings of industrial, utility, or railroad shares. The state owns all the shares of the state industries, and there are no offerings of bonds of industry. Bonds are issued by the government, which in turn makes loans to individual state-owned industries. The quotations, however, are for the government loan, not for the industrial sub-loan.

There are several types of long-term banks, such as the Bank for Industry and Electrification, the Bank for Town Building and Public Works, and the Bank for Agriculture. None of these institutions borrows direct from the public; they borrow from the state and the state borrows from the public. The Treasury extends to industry through these banks a long-term credit, a loan to be repaid in five to ten years at a low rate of interest, say 4 to 5 per cent, although the state pays 8, 10, and 12 per cent. These loans are not gifts, they are expected to be amortized and repaid.

3. Domestic Loans. a. Incentives. Floating of domestic loans is difficult. The citizens of Soviet Russia are reluctant to appear well dressed, or in other ways to show that they have any money. It is not only bad taste but it may bring the citizen into disrepute and conflict with his government. For this reason people hesitate to deposit money freely in the savings banks or to lend it to the government. As an example of the troubles which they may encounter, it is reported that one workman with several grown-up sons took their joint savings to the Bank to invest it; he was seized by the secret police, who inquired how he came to have so much money.

Capital requires safety, otherwise it will hide. Accumulation cannot proceed under conditions of political uncertainty. One of the difficulties in post-war Europe was that political instability led to inflation because hard money, gold and silver, was hoarded. When currency stability was restored and political conditions improved, great floods of money returned to the banks where it would earn interest. The case of France is notable in this regard. From one of the weakest countries financially in 1924 it has become today one of the strongest. And if the members of a society will not save because there is no incentive to do so, they will not accumulate a surplus for social expansion. They will consume all that they produce or hide a part.

The very principle of borrowing on a large scale and the principle of saving by the individual for investment purposes are essentially capitalist notions. And the whole spirit of the Soviets is opposed to these principles. Yet the government must find new sources of funds, after it has taxed the people to the limit of sufferance. The loans are called loans, but they are virtually conscriptions of capital. At the great factories which the traveler visits he will see propaganda posters, such as were common throughout the belligerent countries during the war, warning of the invasion of the enemy and appealing for funds to fight the enemy or to preserve or advance a patriotic cause. He will also see lists which show, in red and black, to what extent shops and workers are reaching their subscription quotas.

To stimulate subscriptions, all sorts of attractive features are presented, such as high premiums on redemption, or gambling chances on bonds being called at fanciful lottery figures. And because there are few other chances of making a fortune, the gambling instinct pours funds into the lottery loans. One of the many interesting sights in Moscow is the great crowds of people standing until well past midnight before the public bulletin boards, seeking with absorbing interest to find out if their lottery numbers had been called.

The loans have been distributed chiefly among the masses of workingmen. However, bonds are not sold by individual subscription as in the western world, but in a typical Russian way through collective subscriptions. The factory as a unit subscribes for the bonds and the allotments are distributed to the workingmen. The percentage of subscriptions rose steadily with the different loans:

	Percentage of Total Number of Workers	*Percentage of Payroll*
First industrial loan	60	16
Second industrial loan	83	60
Third industrial loan	84	82

In the villages, however, where group subscriptions are more difficult, the loans have not been well taken. In fact the well-to-do peasants and their sympathizers are opposed to the campaigns for the sale of bonds. In some cases peasants who were supporting the bond campaigns were killed and their homes were burned. The opposition was reported to have spread rumors that the loans were to be used for financing a war with China, etc. To induce the peasants to subscribe the government officials maintained that the bonds could be disposed of after subscription but in fact they are practically unsalable.[25]

b. Growth of the Debt. The national debt of the Soviet Union grew rapidly from about 366 million rubles in 1925 to 2950 million rubles in 1930. The growth of the state debt is shown as follows:

GROWTH OF STATE DEBT OF SOVIET UNION *

(in million rubles)

	Oct. 1 1925	*Oct. 1 1926*	*Oct. 1 1927*	*Oct. 1 1928*	*Oct. 1 1929*
First 6% Lottery Loan, 1922	98.9	100.0	100.0	100.0	80.5
Second Lottery Loan, 1924	69.4	51.2	37.4	18.2	2.9
5% Short-Term Loan, 1925	10.0	0.1	—	—	—
First Peasants' Loan, 1924	46.2	0.9	0.5	0.3	0.2
Second Peasants' Loan, 1925	—	82.0	95.6	—	—
Third Peasants' Loan, 1927	—	—	—	3.9	4.3
10% Reconstruction Loan	—	245.6	192.6	124.2	65.6
First 8% Internal Gold Loan, 1924	64.7	71.5	63.3	33.1	—
Second 8% Internal Gold Loan, 1926	—	32.8	95.8	89.2	—
Third 8% Internal Gold Loan, 1927	—	—	51.7	189.8	491.1
Fourth 8% Internal Gold Loan, 1928	—	—	—	1.7	—
12% Internal Loan, 1927	—	—	40.1	187.7	199.4
Internal Lottery Loan, 1926	—	—	28.2	24.6	17.9
10% Internal Lottery Loan, 1927	—	—	99.9	99.6	99.1
First Industrialization Loan, 1927	—	—	16.4	197.0	164.6
Agricultural Development Internal Lottery Loan, 1928	—	—	—	135.3	123.6
Treasury Bills	77.5	78.6	103.7	87.0	52.5
Second Industrialization Loan, 1928	—	—	—	60.5	465.8
11% Internal Loan, 1928	—	—	—	70.0	270.8
Internal Loan, 1929	—	—	—	—	36.4
Third Industrialization Loan, 1929	—	—	—	—	520.3
Total	366.7 †	662.7	933.7 †	1422.1	2595.0

* Other lists give figures which vary somewhat from this compilation. On October 1, 1930, according to the *Statisticheski Spravochnik*, 1932, (pp. 598–9) the total state debt was 2686.8 million rubles and on January 1, 1931, it was 3011.8 million rubles.

† Includes other small loans.

It is interesting to note that the old issues outstanding declined and apparently were taken up by new loans. This general program of financing is similar to the program of war borrowing of Russia, Germany, and Austria. New loans in increased amounts were used to retire the old loans. The amount subscribed has been rising continually, as follows:

Name of Loan	*Total Issue (Million rubles)*
First Industrial Loan	200
Second Industrial Loan	507
Third Industrial Loan	941
First loan, "Five-Year-Plan-in-Four" Loan	1047
Second loan, "Loan of the Third or Decisive Year"	2030
Third loan, "Loan of the Fourth, or Completing Year"	3200

The number of subscribers for each loan increased. The issue of the "Third or Decisive Year Loan" came from 33 million subscribers, according to official Soviet sources.[26]

c. Terms and New Issues. The loans run for long periods, but they do have a maturity date and most bear interest. They are used for industrial purposes. The appeal on posters is "Subscribe to the Loan and Help Overtake and Surpass the Capitalist Countries," or "Subscribe to the Loan and Achieve the Five-Year Plan in Four," with innumerable variations on the theme of serving the home cause or worsting the universal enemy.

Interest charges are relatively high because of the great demand for capital and the limited supply, both domestic and foreign. Some loans bear no interest—for instance, the State Lottery Loan of 1926 and also of 1929, and parts of the Second and Third Industrialization loans, payments being in lump sums determined by lot.

On the initiative of workers at factories in Moscow, Leningrad, and other cities, the question of the further development of state credit was discussed. A proposal was submitted that the government reduce the number and variety of loans in circulation by issuing a single consolidated loan. The work of the credit institutions was complicated by the fact that the loans were numerous in number and diverse in form, some being interest-bearing loans and some lottery loans and some partly both. There were varying dates of lottery drawings, of interest, of notice to bond holders, which complicated the mechanics of the loans.

As a result, the Council of People's Commissars on February 21, 1930, ordered the issue of the "Pyatiletka-in-Four-Years" loan. Its main features were as follows. It was to be issued in the fiscal years 1931–32. Bonds of old issues held by workers might be, or rather, had to be converted into the new loan. The rate of interest was not to be less than the rate on the Third Industrialization Loan. To force conversion, the government prohibited the purchase or pledging of the old loans which were to be converted. "This measure will not materially affect the financial position of the workers for, when investing their savings in these loans they knew beforehand and agreed that they were to be long-term investments." [27]

To force the conversion of the old loans into the new "Pyatiletka-in-Four-Years" loan, the Commissariat of Finance ordered that all obligations of the preceding four loans were to be converted not later than January 1, 1931. Bonds which were not converted would receive no interest and no lottery premiums but only the face value of the old bonds, and after January 1934, the bonds would be invalid. Where the old bonds constituted collateral for loans the holders must redeem them in cash, otherwise the pledged bonds would be converted automatically into the new issue.[28]

The bond holders enter into a contract with each other whereby all the workers in a factory agree to deposit their bonds in some credit institution. The workers thus incur a moral obligation to leave their bonds on deposit for the life of the issue and withdraw them only in case of extreme need. The bond holder regards himself as aiding in the socialization of industry and therefore invests his funds not merely for personal gain but for public good.

"Under the terms of the new issue, the new consolidated loan, holders are prohibited from selling the bonds except in case of dire need, sickness, or misfortune. In such cases bonds may be purchased by the credit institutions according to special regulations governing such cases, provided the transaction is approved by the State Credit Aid Societies to be found in every factory.[27]

The "Pyatiletka-in-Four-Years" bonds were placed chiefly among the workers. These brought over 48 per cent of the amount allotted to that class of the population. On the other hand the peasants took only 2.2 per cent of the bonds allotted for sale in the villages. However, subscription for bonds does not mean the actual purchase. Of the total tentative subscriptions to these bonds reported only a small fraction "were actually subscribed for in a formal way." [29]

In the middle of 1930, loans were floated for special designated purposes. Loans were issued to finance the construction of particular factories designated in the bond. There were tractor loans, automobile loans, and bicycle loans. The bicycle loan was intended for a wide public, who would be interested in the cheapest form of rapid transportation. The price of each bond was 660 rubles to be paid in instalments. The loan consisted of four series, and the holders of the bonds of the first series were scheduled to receive bicycles in April 1931, the second series in August 1931, the third series in April 1932, and the fourth series in August 1932. This is a form of instalment selling, with payments made in advance for the construction of the factory which was to deliver a finished product.[30]

During 1931 a continuation of the "Pyatiletka-in-Four-Years" loan was offered. The new loan was called the "Third-Decisive-Year" loan. While the first section of the Pyatiletka loan amounted to one billion rubles, the second issue or "Third Decisive Year" loan was expected to bring about 2 billion rubles.

The workers and peasants were asked to help to lay the cornerstone of the socialist development of the Soviet Union. The loan has a maturity of ten years. It is divided into two parts, the lottery section, which bears no interest and the coupon section which bears interest at the rate of 10 per cent per annum. The denominations are as low as 25 rubles. A special drive was made to attract subscriptions in the rural districts, where past loans received little support. Peasants were expected to contribute 20 rubles as against 70 rubles for workers. Subscriptions by the workers were paid by deductions from monthly wages.[31]

On June 9, 1932, the Central Executive Committee of the Communist Party, and the Council of Commissars, announced in all the Moscow papers the new state loan, called the "Fourth or Conclusive Year of the Five-Year Plan Loan." This loan is the third issue of the so-called *"Pyatiletka"* bonds, or "the Five-Year Plan in Four Years," and is the sixth large loan issued for constructive purposes. The new loan matures on December 1, 1942. It is divided into two groups, one section having a lottery certificate offering prizes of 100 rubles to 3000 rubles at four annual drawings, and another bearing 10 per cent interest annually. The loan was voluntary theoretically, but as in the case of the drives to sell war bonds in all countries, subscriptions were obtained under social pressure. The government expected every worker to subscribe three weeks of his wages to the loans, that is, about 6 per cent of his annual income. In some cases where subscription was made by groups, as in factories, subscriptions equivalent to one month's wages or even two months' wages were not unusual. The total amount of the issue is 3.2 billion rubles. The usual ballyhoo attending such social efforts was raised. The newspaper *Pravda* wrote: "We need huge sums to complete the Five-Year Plan. No one will give them to us. We must raise them ourselves. It is necessary to convince the most backward workers of the importance of this loan. Get out into the remotest village with the news."

d. Quotations and Yields. Theoretically the loans are marketable, but the seller finds genuine difficulty in selling. Although there are free quotations, there are no free markets. A seller must prove that there is either sickness or distress in his family before the state will re-buy the bond, and the state is the sole purchaser. One list of quotations follows:

STOCK EXCHANGE QUOTATIONS OF STATE LOANS [32]

	Par value rubles	*Per Cent of Par Value* *November 30, 1930*	*July 10, 1932*
First 6% Loan, 1922	5	99.70	97.20
Internal Loan, 1926	100	134.80	.....
10% Internal Loan, 1927	25	103.16	103.80
First 6% Industrialization Loan, 1927	25	100.00	.....
Second Industrial Loan, 1928			
Interest-bearing bonds	25	100.00	.....
Non-interest-bearing bonds	25	100.00	.....
Third Industrialization Loan, 1929			
Interest-bearing bonds	50	106.00	.....
Non-interest-bearing bonds	50	100.00	.....
Internal Loan, 1929	100	102.35	.....
9% Internal Loan, 1930	50	103.48	.....
Municipal Loan Moscow Soviet, 1929	25	101.16	.....
12% Internal Loan, 1927	100	106.00	101.35
Second 8% Internal Loan, 1926	100	97.90	.....
Third 8% Internal Loan, 1927	100	97.90	102.90
Fourth 8% Internal Loan, 1927	100	101.90	102.90
11% Internal Loan, 1928	100	102.75	104.00
Agricultural Improvement Loan, 1928	10	105.00	.....
9% Internal Loan of the People's Commissariat for Ways and Communication	100	97.20	95.45
Five-Year-Plan-in-Four Loan			
Interest-bearing bonds	50	.....	103.70
Non-interest-bearing bonds	50	.....	100.00
Third-Decisive-Year Loan			
Interest-bearing bonds	50	.....	106.20
Non-interest-bearing bonds	50	.....	100.00

It is difficult for the capitalist mind to understand why a 6 per cent, 8 per cent, 9 per cent, 10 per cent, 11 per cent, and 12 per cent issue should be sold at so nearly the same percentage of parity. In perplexity the author wrote to one of the representatives of the Soviet Union in the United States. The answer was not very enlightening:

> There is a small fluctuation in the price quoted on the various internal loan issues depending somewhat on the variation in demand. Most of the internal bond issues, besides being interest-bearing, have lottery features. The relation between the amounts allotted for prizes and for interest in the various issues varies. Thus a bond bearing interest of 6 per cent might actually be in as great demand as one yielding a higher rate of interest due to the fact that the lottery prizes are greater in the former. There have been a few state loans which pay no interest at all, all the payments to the holders being paid in the form of prizes. The variations in the demand for the various loan issues probably depends on whether a coupon has just been paid or is due for payment in the near future, or whether a lottery drawing will be held in the near future.

Apparently there is no real market, in the "capitalist" sense.

4. Savings Banks. The savings banks are also a resource for the budget. The government encourages deposits in savings banks. The rise in the activities of the savings banks is shown herewith:[33]

	Oct. 1, 1924	*Oct. 1, 1928*	*Oct. 1, 1929*	*June 1, 1930*	*Oct. 1, 1930*
Number of savings banks	5,284	16,924	20,068	23,357	.....
Number of depositors (thousands)	430	3,788	7,630	10,485	12,904
Depositors per bank	81	223	381	450	.....
Balance of deposits (million rubles)	8.7	336	507	600	753
Deposits per bank	1,620	20,000	25,300	25,600	.....
Savings per depositor	22	78	67	67	.....

These totals indicate a rapid increase in the number of depositors. The savings per depositor, however, have been declining continuously in recent years. The number of savings banks is now three times as great as in 1913. In 1924 the chain of savings banks grew rapidly in order to serve the masses. Because of the sparse population the banking net had to cover a very wide area, and the rapid growth in the number of banks may have resulted in adding many small depositors and thus have contributed to the decline in savings per depositor. The annual increase in deposits has been rising recently and is more rapid now than before the war, if one disregards the declining purchasing power of the ruble.

Period	*Average Annual Increase Million rubles*
Pre-war:	
1894–1903	57.5
1904–1913	82.5
Post-war:	
1925	24.8
1926	57.0
1927	96.5
1928	148.8
1929	171.0

In 1913 the average savings per depositor amounted to 180 rubles as compared with about 87 rubles on October 1, 1928. The savings per depositor in pre-war Russia were larger than in France and Great Britain because in Russia the well-to-do saved, and in the other countries the masses saved. The decline per depositor in Soviet Russia as compared with pre-war Russia is due to the fact that social insurance obviates the need for individual savings. Society saves for the whole group, therefore each individual does not have to save for himself.

The savings banks invest their money in state bonds which bring a return as high as 12 per cent. The cash in the tills of the banks is usually small. The savings banks are also a clearing house for payment of small sums by the masses, thus popularizing the idea of payment by check transfers.

PART FOUR

INTERPRETATION AND APPRAISAL

—Rather bear those ills we have
Than fly to others that we know not of.

—Hamlet

If to do were as easy as to know what were good to do, chapels had been churches and poor men's cottages princes' palaces.

—Merchant of Venice

CHAPTER XII

AIMS

The Soviet experiment is too young to permit a final appraisal. However, some successes and failures have already been registered which bid fair to stand for the long term. Some policies can be judged as successful or unsuccessful, as short-term developments. Again, some of the results represent clear gains, long range and permanent, such as the adoption of social insurance, the reduction of illiteracy, and freedom for minority national, racial, and cultural groups. There are also some clear losses—individual initiative has been suppressed, the advantages of competition have been lost. These in part seem to be long-range and apparently permanent losses. On the other hand, certain features of social life which are the very breath of our nostrils in the west, such as individual freedom, may be short-term losses of the Soviet. But by and large most of the results are in the doubtful area and it is difficult, even for the short term, to appraise and predict. To maintain an impartial attitude in a situation so large and with so many conflicting intellectual and emotional interests is difficult. However, errors cannot be condoned and progress cannot be denied.

Some classification is necessary in this appraisal, and to help in an understanding, it has been classified into aims, methods, and results, and each of these subjects is considered with respect to economic, political, social, and spiritual aspects.

A. Background

1. Similarity to Historic Religious Ideals. The aims of the Soviets are the aims of idealists. The social philosophy of Karl Marx was of a piece with the visions of the great religious leaders throughout history. The Soviet aims contain many elements that are part of the social legislation of the Bible—

ownership of land by the community, its inalienability, opposition to a régime of hereditary rulers, expressed in the Book of Samuel. The Soviet ideal is described in the Book of Isaiah:[1] "Is not this the fast I have chosen? To undo the bands of the yoke and to let the oppressed go free? Is it not to deal thy bread to the hungry and that thou bring the poor and the cast-out to thy house?"

There is spiritual idealism in Soviet aims, which make the renunciation of the great religious books all the more striking. The ideals of the Bible have become working aims with the Soviets. Without any precedent and without any model, the Soviet leaders' goal is the creation of a new earth, aye, and even a new heaven, for man. The aims are long-range. They regard little the present generation and strive for the well-being of the future generations. This is a new conception of the hereafter. And as the truly religious believer of past generations bore with resignation the evils of this life in the hope of a reward in a future life, so the present generations of Russians are being asked to bear patiently their present ills for the sake of the future bliss of themselves or their children.

2. Similarity to French Revolution. In some of its aims, the Russian Revolution was a repetition of the French Revolution—revolt against a tyrannical, hereditary royalty, and then distribution of the land. To this extent the history of France after the revolution may provide some clue to the probable future of Russia. However, it may be that the Soviet upheaval is a new type of revolution, coming in a régime of economic capitalism. Certainly the French Revolution had no such wide-spread objectives, economic, political, and social, as the Soviets. To this extent the course of the Russian Revolution will be more difficult to prognosticate. History alone can provide the answer.

3. Criteria of Social Progress. In determining whether the aims of the Soviet represent social progress, one must view them in the light of the conditions in Russia before the revolution, and in the light of current conditions in the rest of Europe. The science of sociology has provided a basis for the measurement of social progress, and it would be interesting to test the aims of the revolution by these standards. The many standards that have been set up by thinkers of the past may be reduced to a basic one, the socialization of the individual, or to two, control of the physical environment for the benefit of society, and the self-control of man in relation to his fellows. Or, in slightly amplified form, progress may be measured by the extent of—

(1) The extension of human knowledge and the application of science and art to the well-being of society,
(2) The utilization of insurance and mutual aid to eliminate extreme suffering,
(3) The exercise of freedom of thought and of expression and the tolerance of minority views,
(4) The improvement in the principles of conduct and the establishment of justice,
(5) The abolition of hereditary or other unearned privileges, and the establishment of opportunity for self-development,
(6) The destruction of inequality between nations and between citizens of a nation,
(7) The respect for law and the stability of government,
(8) Decision by compromise instead of by combat, or the substitution of rational persuasion for force,
(9) The widening of the social unit,
(10) The belief in the Infinite as the ultimate inspiration to just and rational social conduct.[2]

The mere statement of these norms of progress reveals that Soviet policies in several instances mark not progress, but retrogression.

4. Maladjustments of Economics and Politics. The Soviet aims are the aims of all reform, namely to bring politics and economics in line. It is the lag of one behind the other that creates social tension. There is one striking difference, however. In the western world individual initiative makes for rapid economic progress. Social inertia makes for slower political progress. Tension arises when political change lags too far behind economic advance. The industrial revolution in England was a spontaneous development resulting from the invention of the steam engine, power machinery, and the locomotive. But labor legislation protecting women and children lagged behind it for more than a generation, and in the meantime they suffered the extreme evils of early capitalism. As Mr. Hoover has pointed out:

> In the crude historic processes of adaptation, government always lags behind social development. The industrial system developed, and only generations later were factory laws enacted. The great corporations of today grew, and only years later were effective anti-monopoly measures adopted. The lag between the development of social functions and the creation of governmental machinery to deal with them is the period of acute unrest and agitation. . . . But progress, in making up the handicap, though slow, has been certain.[3]

However, social tension in Russia arises not because political and social change lags behind economic change, but quite the reverse. Advanced and radical political and social theories have been set up and the attempt is being made to bring into line with these doctrines not merely economics but even human nature. High ideals have been set, for which our economic régime and human nature are as yet unprepared.

B. Economic Aims

In the economic field Soviet aims are rather mundane. The Soviet's ideal is one of economic abundance. Just as the Israelites in the desert, feeding on a monotonous diet of manna which in their imagination might partake of the substance and flavor of any desired food, dreamed of a promised land flowing with milk and honey, so the Russians, eating black bread and cabbage as a constant diet, dream of an abundance of good things to eat. As the hungry little Match Girl in Hans Christian Andersen's tale dreams of a Christmas dinner, which in its richness and variety almost compensates for the absence of any real or prospective dinner, so the economic abundance held out as the Soviet aim is the dream of a starving people.

The aim heralded on banners throughout the streets of Moscow and in various factories is "to overtake and surpass capitalism." Through the Five-Year Plan the Russians believe they can attain within a brief period an economic development equivalent to that reached by capitalist nations only after generations. In fact the industrialization of Russia is the one *idée fixe* which the Soviets have not abandoned in spite of numerous strategic retreats and reversals of policy in the past fifteen years. The constant aim is to develop the resources of the country for the common good. In this process of development, however, it is the intention to avoid exploitation of labor, but to treat labor, particularly manual labor, as the new nobility.

Again money is to be abolished as a useless category under communism and an obsolete remnant of capitalism, and with it the social gradations and stratification and the psychological servility that accompany a money régime. In order to abolish the evil of money the Soviets abolished money and banks. Unfortunately, they did not realize that the social evils of money were an accompaniment or by-product of certain indispensable and useful social functions performed by money and the banks. And after a few years this aim was abandoned. Another original aim was the abolition of profit, which was regarded as a source of exploitation of the working class. Here again the evil of a régime of profits was stressed and its utility overlooked. The pressure of actual life, however, also forced the abandonment of this aim. Profits again became a vigorous aim of Soviet officials. Profits of large industries went to the state; individual peasants and artisans were encouraged to make profits in order to increase the supply of their products. Now there has been another reversal and the profit motive is again in disfavor. Thus do new theory and old custom play battledore and shuttlecock.

C. Political Aims

In the field of politics the aim was to transfer power to the masses. The Soviet was to be a proletarian state. The dictatorship was to be one of the proletariat. Liberty was the watchword, liberty of the 160 odd nationalities in the Soviet Union, and liberty of the divers cultures of Russia. Hereditary rule was to be abolished. There was to be no dominion of politics by capitalists and by exploiters, who would bend the political system to the perpetuation of their own privileges. In the factory the régime of industrial democracy was to hold sway. These ideals were popular slogans. They caught the imagination of the masses of Russia, and enlisted popular support for the new régime. Yet liberty of the individual cannot be the aim of a régime which is based on the extension of social control, such as communism or state capitalism.

D. Social Aims

The social aims impinge upon the realm of religious idealism. The parables of Jesus would form the basis for the social aims of the Soviets. Social ideals are those of service, rather than of parasitism—not how much you can get out of society but how much you can contribute to it. The Communist Party members work harder and get less in money than do the non-member workers. To serve the masses—that is the function of state. Social co-operation and mutual helpfulness is to be a dominant note.

Western civilization, with its freedom of initiative, stimulates great achievements of the superman. But the Soviets' aim is to distribute more of society's goods to the average man. In western society the incompetent is a burden on philanthropy. The Soviets aim to give even the incompetent adequate social and medical care, education, recreation, and protection in old age. Social justice is the watchword of the Soviet aims. Instead of relying on individual initiative for the accumulation of an individual surplus against the crises of life—childbirth, sickness, unemployment, accident, and death—a social insurance reserve is established, on which the unfortunate individual can draw.

A higher standard of social ethics is sought. In addition to reducing the possibility of the accumulation of money, the social value of such accumulation is lessened. If society takes care of the life crises of the individual, much of the incentive to steal and to cheat is gone. And to enforce this aim the penal code of Russia, which is relatively mild, visits the extreme penalty, death, on violation of public ethics rather than violation of private ethics. The aim is to abolish classes and the exploitation of classes. Such in substance are the social aims and ideals of the Soviets.

E. Spiritual Aims

The spiritual aims of the Soviets are shot through with the yearnings and aspirations of the prophets of all time. The lofty hopes, the aspirations, the promises, have the ring of religious messages of the past. The ideals of the Hebrew prophets of humbling the haughty and exalting the lowly are rephrased in the communist song, "Arise, ye damned of the Earth." The ideal of the prophets of beating swords into plowshares and spears into pruning hooks are rephrased in the communist aim of ultimate universal peace and the abolition of war. Micah's ideal of doing justice and loving mercy forecast the ideals which the Soviets espouse. The abolition of superstition is similar to the Biblical injunction against the consulting of soothsayers and sorcerers. The monks' vows of poverty and asceticism reappear in the Soviet ideals of self-denial and simplicity. The monastic rule of obedience to a cause greater than the individual is the keynote of the Soviet program. The Essenes and St. Francis of Assisi would be at home in Soviet Russia in this respect. New social motives of co-operation and social service are part of the fabric of communistic doctrine.

Universal compulsory education is an attempt to enable the masses to appreciate the fine intangibles of life, which the Soviets share with other ethical systems of living. The unshackling of the individual from fear, freedom in domestic relations, and the release of human energies repressed by a rigid and archaic system of divorce, are ideals of communism. Absolute equality of women, a modern conception, is part of the Soviet doctrine.

The citing of these aims does not imply that they have been realized. Ideals are the unattainables of life.

CHAPTER XIII

METHODS

A. Some General Observations

Whereas capitalism is merely a symbol of a mode of living, communism in Russia actually represents an organized social will. Therefore one would be justified in expecting it to have a sounder method. However lofty the Soviet ideal, its method is inefficient. There is a strange contrast between high goals and incompetent procedure. Apparently the men that dream dreams are not the ones that execute plans.

1. Ideals vs. Methods. Marx was a secluded philosopher rather than a leader in practical affairs. He took little part in concrete British labor problems during his exile in England. Similarly, Lenin though brilliant, creative and daring, was a theorist who had little experience in fields other than political propaganda. The Soviet leaders may be long on ideals, but they are short on technique. They hold out panaceas to cure all the ills of the whole world and they proceed by reckless methods which discredit even the ideals. The world is a complicated organism. No simple formula can rectify those continuing maladjustments, whose very existence is a sign of growth and struggle and of life.

2. Experimental Attitude and "New Economic Policies." Soviet methods are characterized by their experimental attitude. Ever new economic policies are being tested. Tradition is swept aside. Like a keen speculator who sells out all his securities at times, in order to get a fresh viewpoint and not be tied by sentimental associations to particular holdings, the Soviets have "liquidated" all tradition and have started afresh. Every institution and every method is weighed anew. The Soviet leaders have great daring. They have attempted solutions of basic social and economic problems. This experimental attitude and the willingness to test new methods have made them

pioneers in many fields as in the mass mechanization of agriculture, the socialization of industry, and economic planning, to cite but a few.

An experimental attitude requires an open mind, and in the past fifteen years of trial Soviet policy has been reversed when its results appeared harmful or dangerous.

3. Defects in Method. Because of the daring, even recklessness, with which new experiments were undertaken, enormous mistakes were made. But as the errors were realized, rapid reversals of policy followed. The Soviet leaders may be doctrinaires, but they are realists. They do not hesitate to discard their methods when events prove them to be unworkable. The new or successful method sometimes runs counter to the original aim.

High social idealism is often ranged in strange contrast alongside anti-social methods, as for example, the forcible collectivizing of peasants and the practice of compelling them to sell wheat under the world price. Again, the very haste of method sometimes leads to waste. Social adaptation requires time. Compromises on method often lead to strange inconsistencies and paradoxes, which are characteristic of Russian Soviet life. High ideals and ruthless methods are noticeable on all sides. Communist professions alongside of capitalist practices are constantly seen, for example, in factory administration.

4. Communist vs. Capitalist Method. To make the economic machine work the Soviets have adopted capitalist methods, such as the use of money, banks, piece rates, subscriptions to government loans, etc. The labels may be communist but the content is capitalist. In this land of paradoxes, one of the most amazing is the contrast between the policies of expropriation and confiscation of property on the one hand, and on the other the right of inheritance of private property.

Russia affords a study in contrasts in the approach and method of the two systems. Under the capitalist system the first objective is to produce goods at the lowest cost. The evils in the system of distributing the profits then lead to a struggle between the workers and the owners. Under a democratic, parliamentary form of government the method of distribution of profits is open to continuous, if slow, adjustment. The communist idea is first to attack the evils by devising a new social and political program, regardless of whether the new methods will produce as much of the goods as society needs and regardless of the suffering inflicted on the community.

Under the capitalist régime the European socialists, whatever their party label, have relied on an evolutionary procedure. The time factor is important in social adjustment.

In the race between idealism and efficiency a more satisfactory result will be obtained through the method of slow change. An efficient economic machine can be revamped in the interest of greater idealism or social justice. Concretely, a distributing mechanism, like Sears, Roebuck & Co. or the Great Atlantic & Pacific Tea Company, serves society more efficiently than anything that the Soviet régime or any co-operative society has yet devised. It should be easier to modify the distribution of the profits, if desirable, in such efficient corporations rather than to introduce efficiency into the Russian co-operative companies. If in the generations to come some common ground between the communist and capitalist régimes may be found, it will be reached through the adoption by communism of capitalist methods or the infusion of a social viewpoint into the capitalist system.

B. Economic Method

1. Expropriation. Expropriation of property was the basis of Soviet method. In other words, the old factories, built under the capitalist régime, furnished the foundation for the communist experiment. Communism in Soviet Russia is the heir of capitalism in Tsarist Russia. Much of the success that the communist régime has achieved is due to the plant and facilities created under a system of private ownership. Expropriation, or as the Russians euphemistically call it, nationalization, is not new. In the past property has been taken even by capitalist governments without compensation. The abolition of slavery in the United States was a form of expropriation of property as contrasted with the British policy of compensating the slave owners. European countries have taken property of their colonial natives, for instance, the Belgians in the Congo. Prohibition in the United States was a form of expropriation of the property of many thousands of stockholders in distilleries and breweries. Default by foreign governments is a form of expropriation. But all these examples do not alter the fact that the seizure of private property, even on a national scale, is still a form of theft, or justify the Soviet theory that the state has a right to take what it pleases and that the state can do no wrong.

2. Management. Soviet management of industry reveals lamentable incompetence. True, many of the difficulties are not essentially communist but rather are distinctly Russian, and these difficulties would have been ex-

perienced even under a capitalist attempt at rapid industrialization. But many of them also are intrinsically communist. The centralization of management in trusts creates a large bureaucracy. Such centralization, be it in Soviet Russia or wartime Europe and America, must result in slow cumbersome methods, much red tape, high cost of management, and poor quality of product.

Large, incompetent staffs waste much or all of that part of the product of industry which would go into profits. The attempt to nationalize all industry quickly and simultaneously has retarded the efficient industrial development of the country, for it created a sudden draft on managerial personnel of a very high order. Furthermore, the lack of raw materials, inadequate transportation, poor technique, lack of a trained labor supply, have complicated the problems of management. In the attempt to remedy these defects there has been a speeding up of labor. Russia aims at the capitalist achievement of higher wages, lower costs, and larger profits (to the state) which has characterized, for example, American industry for several decades.

3. Labor. Labor has been mobilized almost in military fashion. If there is a shortage of railroad workers or of farm laborers for the spring sowing they are drafted regardless of their willingness to take on the assigned tasks. The individual workman has in a measure lost his right to choose the nature or place of his work. Not the wishes of the individual, but the needs of the state is the deciding factor.

On the other hand, for the sake of efficiency, the methods of capitalism have been adopted; piece work and the bonus system have been installed. However, in addition there is the social motive, the appeal to advance the Soviet cause, in the form of socialist competition among factories or among groups of workers.

The right of the supreme factory authority to discharge workers has been introduced, and the original influence of workers' councils in the management has been reduced and almost eliminated. This is not merely a compromise with capitalism. It is a retrogression, because in capitalist countries the trade unions safeguard the worker against the abuse of the right to discharge.

4. The Five-Year Plan. The purposeful development of the nation's resources is not essentially a communist idea. The belligerent countries including Tsarist Russia developed central planning of industry during the war. But as a peacetime measure, is there any group with the wisdom and vision to plan completely the economic life of 160 million people? The results of

the early years of the Plan prove the weakness of the method. In some lines the Plan has almost been attained, while in others progress is seriously lagging. At various points there are so-called "gross miscalculations and errors" of plan. Some projects have been abandoned, such as the tile factory, and in other cases only the important phases have been fostered and the balance suspended. The Stalingrad tractor plant was reduced to making motors for tractors. The cost of the Plan in suffering has been so great that already there are plans for slowing down the rate of development. The attempt to build huge industrial plants without providing an adequate transportation system reflects the weakness of the general method. In fact, the Five-Year Plan involves a vicious circle. The attempt to industrialize the country quickly involves a huge expenditure on plant and equipment. This involves underconsumption of food and clothing, the "dumping" of wheat, antagonizing the world, the development of a war psychosis in Russia, therefore the need for preparation for war, and the renewed belief in the need for industrialization.

5. Trade. In domestic trade the method of selling at low fixed prices and rationing supplies seems futile. The time wasted by the innumerable queues in the cities is a social cost which must be added to the price. It is a strange anomaly for a country suffering from a shortage of labor to have millions of people wasting hours daily in buying the necessities of life.

Again, "dumping" as a method of obtaining credits abroad represents a social loss. Because the Soviets have not settled the old Russian debt, they have no credit abroad. The increased cost of the machinery imported, and the loss on goods "dumped" abroad would be enough to pay a substantial instalment on the repudiated debt. Such payment would restore Russian credit and make it unnecessary to "dump" merchandise. "Dumping" as a method of obtaining credits may have to increase as the plans already under way are completed and new ones are projected. On the other hand, "dumping" may cease as the new plants approach completion, but this is not an immediate prospect. The Soviets defend "dumping" by the argument that the capitalist countries had their natural resources appropriated by private interests and therefore the Soviets can afford to give up a small fraction of their resources in the national interest. However, if goods are sold so far below cost of production, based on the world level of wages, the workers must be exploited.

6. The Budget. Russia must raise funds for expanding its industries out of its own resources, because it is said the capitalist world is warring on the Soviets.

But is that true? Is it not rather because the Soviets have repudiated the Russian bonds held by investors throughout the world and these individuals are not willing to lend money again? Even if the bankers should be willing to float a loan to Russia, would investors buy such securities? Credit is a matter of confidence and faith, and the Soviet policies are not calculated to increase the confidence of the investors of the world. For this reason the funds that young countries normally obtain from the older capitalist countries must be obtained out of Russia's own resources.

What are these resources? Chiefly tax funds. Originally even these were lacking. In the period of "war communism" taxes were to cease, because "money no longer functions as a means of payment." [1] Then under the New Economic Policy money was restored and capitalist methods of taxation were introduced, including income and profits taxes. The sales tax is the chief source of tax revenue. Apparently in a crisis the Soviets are realists and discard cherished doctrines. Another source of national income is savings for investment. But since all social measures were aimed at deterring the accumulation of capital and the development of a bourgeoisie and rentier class, funds available for investment were meager. Subsequently saving and capital accumulation were encouraged.

In the field of finance as well as in the field of industry communist aims have defeated communist methods. To accomplish communist aims, capitalist methods have been utilized.

7. Economic Zigzags. Soviet method was based on expediency. The course therefore was zigzag. For a period of three years, 1918 to 1920, pure communism prevailed. Upon coming into control the Soviets nationalized land, houses, and all enterprise. Banks were abolished and money was no longer an instrument of exchange. The state was to supply all the needs of the population. The results were disastrous. Production practically ceased. The system of distribution broke down. Food rotted. "Bootleg" trade in the necessities of life developed. Cities became depopulated because of the migration to the land. The catastrophe resulted in a reversal of policy in March 1921. The Nep was introduced. Lenin confessed the failure of the communist régime. A reversal of policy was the prudent and realistic acceptance of defeat. The bankrupt policy was thereafter politely called "war communism."

In October 1921, private trade was again restored. Goods began to come out of hiding, and moved in response to the law of supply and demand. The status of money was restored and banks were reopened. In 1928 private trade was again outlawed. Privation resulted. In 1932 private trade was not only tolerated but encouraged by decrees. Again, goods appeared. In other words, necessity dictated Soviet policy.

8. Service vs. Profits. The Soviet policy was based on the principle that the aim of production is service to the community. The capitalist principle is production for profit subject to rules of cost accounting. The Soviet principle has been abandoned. The strict accounting methods of industrial corporations in capitalist countries prevail in great detail in the Soviet trusts and have been completely accepted.

9. Determinants of Soviet Method. When the Soviet system works, it is largely through the adoption of capitalist methods. When communist methods are applied, the system breaks down. The reversals of policy are testimony to this effect. The Soviets have not only compromised but have adopted completely the methods of capitalism with respect to the use of money, the operation of banks, system of wage payments, profits as the goal, the taxation of sales, income, and profits, the desirability of savings and public subscription to government loans. They have gone even further than capitalist countries in incorporating gambling or lottery features as a stimulus to public subscriptions to loans. Communism has copied the technique of capitalism. It is grafting the tried and successful methods of an orderly world on to radical doctrines. The communists were successful in destroying the old civilization, but they have not proved themselves competent to build a new one.

Incompetent as communism may be, its ideals and aspirations have already affected the capitalist countries. Despite its cruelty and its failures, its mere existence is setting the pace or bogey for the western world. The fear of communism during the depression throughout the world has led to the adoption of measures of social alleviation and the application of socialist principles to ward off extreme distress from the least fortunate classes in society.

C. Political Method

1. Diffusion of Power. The political methods are in striking contrast to the political ideals of the Soviet. The short-lived parliamentary régime of Kerensky planned to diffuse power throughout the population, but the Soviet revolt resulted in a diametrically opposite political method. Under the Soviet régime a small group assumed the power which under the Tsarist régime had likewise been held by a small group. The power that the Kerensky régime had attempted to turn over to the people was again taken from the people.

The history of man is the history of the diffusion of power. In the Middle Ages the popes originally were recognized as all-powerful, the vicars of God, and therefore kings were to be subservient. The kings challenged the claim. Some succeeded in setting up claims to derive their power directly from God. Power was thus split up. The divine right of kings was challenged by the slightly less powerful nobles. Power was then taken from the king and distributed among the nobility. In the parliamentary struggle of the following 700 years, suffrage was extended to an ever-increasing number of people. The property qualification was finally abolished, and with the adoption of woman suffrage the final goal of political history was achieved. Political power was finally diffused universally and was recognized as coming not from above, from pope, king, or nobles who claimed it by divine right but from below, from the people themselves. In depriving the masses of the source of power, the Soviet method is a retrogression.

2. Restriction of Suffrage. In contrast with the multi-party system of parliamentary liberalism, the Communist Party is single. It is the only party. It must be kept "monolithic" so-called. From it there can be no defection. The members of the opposite party are regarded as enemies and traitors and must be crushed. They cannot live, move, or have their being in Russia. They cannot work within the country and they cannot move out of the country. Such methods of fanaticism and intolerance are characteristic of a militant church, not of a parliamentary state. The Bolsheviks claimed to have—

> —won over to them the majority of the population . . . but even in the days of their greatest popularity they very wisely avoided putting it to the test by allowing the whole population to have free elections. . . . In the towns there was a representative for every 25,000 voters, and in the country for every 120,000 inhabitants. . . . Thus the town proletarians were given a vote between two and three times more effective than that of the peasants. . . . They do not even select delegates for the election of a deputy. The deputies to the All-Russian Congress are elected by the Soviets of the large towns on the one hand, and by the Soviet Congresses of the provinces on the other. The Provincial Congresses are likewise appointed by the Soviets of the large towns (who therefore receive a double indirect vote in the election of the All-Russian Soviet) and by the Regional Soviets. Soviets of the smaller towns and of the districts (*volost*) in turn elect the latter. Finally the Volost Soviets are elected by the village Soviets. . . . The proportion of members of the Communist Party in this same year was 8 per cent in the village Soviets, 20 per cent in the Volost Soviets, 58 per cent in the Regional Soviets, and 68 per cent in the Provincial Soviets. Non-Communists, attached to no party, were a disappearing quantity in the All-Russian Con-

gress. . . . Henceforth, there could be no candidates and delegates other than Communists or those tolerated by the Communist Party, not even mere oppositional speakers. . . . The organization of the suffrage is now only continued in order to make the workers believe that they are the ruling class in the Soviet system.[2]

The kulaks were expelled from the villages and were deprived of their franchises and their civil rights. According to a decree of the Central Executive Committee,[3] kulaks could have their rights restored within five years if they proved themselves honest workers and discontinued their opposition to the policy of collectivization. The essence of democracy is the right to differ and to register that difference by means of the vote. Suffrage is not restricted to those who agree with the administration. Have the Russian workers and peasants ever had an opportunity of expressing their opinion at any time within the past fifteen years? Policies have been framed by a dictatorship and those who dissented have been punished.

D. Social Method

1. Russia Unripe. The Soviets are trying to develop a socialist régime in a country which is utterly unprepared for it. Of the 150 million people in Russia in 1914 less than 20 per cent were living in towns and over 80 per cent on farms. A country in such a state is not ready for industrialization or for socialization—it is not ripe industrially or socially. Therefore a huge industrial development is not a logical or organic growth but a superimposed notion. Russia is attempting at one bound to run the entire gamut from a primitive and primarily agricultural society to the most advanced industrial and socialized community. True, the essence of Russian method is to ignore history. However, all pioneering societies have ignored it. They have made history. But it is unlikely that the methods now being employed to achieve this forced growth will succeed.

2. Time Standards: Evolution vs. Revolution. The time standard of the individual is the year. The time standard of a nation or of society is the generation. Large as was Lenin's vision, and daring as were his policies, his impatience at the rate of development of Russia indicated the lack of a social conception of time standards. The haste reveals a short-sighted view. It represents the attempt to reach perfection in the development of a nation within the lifetime of one generation of its people. The zeal of the leaders may be laudable, but their time standards are lamentable. The time standards of

the Soviets are contrary to the experience of history or of industrial evolution, and to the teachings of sociology. Some phases of American life have become socialized, but the change took a generation to accomplish.

From 1885 to 1932 the American railroads became almost completely socialized. Prior to the former year they had a right to fix their own traffic rates and wage scales, the right to borrow money, and the right to keep resulting profits. By a series of legislative enactments they have been deprived of these property rights. They no longer have the right, without government consent, to fix traffic rates or wage scales, or to say under what terms they shall borrow money. And if after all this regulation by the Interstate Commerce Commission there should be any profits, the stockholders have a legal right to only part. The balance is recapturable by the government. The vestiges of property rights left to the security holder are the right to a curtailment of dividends, the right to pay assessments, and the right to become insolvent. These do not require any government consent. Not within five years but in about fifty years, this profound abridgment of property rights has taken place in the railroad field. The process was a gradual encroachment through legislative enactment by the community upon the property rights of the railroad owners.[3a]

The difference in the method is the difference between evolution and revolution. The very speed of change contemplated by the Soviets makes mistakes costly and even dangerous. Social change is largely a matter of mental adjustments. To have attempted the above change in the status of the American railroads within five years would have been regarded as revolutionary and would have created a profound social upheaval. Within fifty years the change was so imperceptible as hardly to be noticed.

3. Human Nature as a Limitation. The limits imposed upon the rate of reform depend not merely on the longer time standards of society, but also on the element of human nature. Though co-operation was practiced before the war, the old society in Russia was based on motives which had been operative for countless generations—namely, the sense of possession and the desire for personal satisfaction. Is it possible to eradicate these completely? Or is it not more likely that, as society develops, the social motives will eventually become more pronounced and the two sets of motives, individual and social, will through social heredity shift in value? However, such psychological changes are not a matter of government decree, but rather a matter of slow education and social practice over a period of years.

4. A Growing Civilization vs. an Invented Scheme. The method of social

development in the past has generally been that of growth and slow change. Growth is organic and complex. But the communist doctrine has simplified society into two classes, the exploiters and the exploited. Unfortunately life is not so simple. There are many classes in a complex society, and any individual in it may be a member of numerous classes. In fact a wage earner who owns stock in his own company is a member, theoretically, of both the exploiting and the exploited classes. If a wage earner owns stock in another company, the Marxian doctrine would consider him as being the exploited in his own shop and the exploiter in the other. The numerous other classifications of distributors, advisers, etc., are eliminated. Again, in a democratic society the individual may and does constantly move from one class to another.

In an evolving society the rich and the poor are not rigid classes. Fortunes made in the wagon business, in the jobbing business, and in the packing business have disappeared overnight and descendants of multi-millionaires have been shifted to the ranks of the workers. Fortunes have been lost in the traction industry. Great fortunes of the seventies were made in the railroad business, of the eighties in the oil business, of the nineties in the steel business, of the 1900's in the automobile, mail-order, and chain-store businesses, and of the second decade of the twentieth century in the chemical business. And in the present decade fortunes may be made in some new industry.

A growing society makes and unmakes fortunes. It likewise creates its successor stage. The hunting stage gave way to the pastoral, the pastoral to the agricultural, the agricultural to the artisan, the artisan to the industrial, the industrial to the socialist stage. Sticking the label of socialism on a society which has not evolved into it will not create a socialized society. England, Germany, and the older industrial countries of Europe have gradually evolved various socialized devices, such as workers' insurance, graduated income taxes, steep inheritance taxes, and various measures designed to redistribute the accumulated wealth of the country and to save the lowest class from extreme suffering. Socialism will be an outgrowth of capitalism. It can hardly be "planted" on a country. Communism was a stage in primitive societies. It is still prevalent among the tribes of Africa and Australia. The colony of Virginia in the United States began as a communist settlement. Captain John Smith's rule antedated by 300 years the Soviet rules. He enacted as a law of the colony the preachment of Paul: "Who does not work, neither shall he eat."

According to Karl Kautsky, pupil of Marx and Engels, the Marxists, including Lenin, until the revolution of 1917—

> —were convinced that the revolution which they were expecting in Russia could do nothing but open up the way for a complete development of capitalism, and that only when the latter attained a high degree of development would a socialist community be possible. Thus the countries of industrialized western Europe would have to precede the countries of eastern Europe on the road toward socialism. . . . Unforeseen circumstances delivered the complete control of the state into the hands of Lenin, who until then had been an outlawed refugee having to hide whenever he went to Russia. This dazzling turn of fortune went to his head and made him reverse his former theoretical convictions. He suddenly became of the opinion that the extremely small, backward stratum of the industrial workers of Russia was capable of plunging at once into socialism and organizing a socialist state.[4]

Admittedly, Russia will not have to follow exactly the course of its predecessors in the path of social evolution. The rate of progress in society is not always even and it is now accelerated. Therefore, it is quite conceivable that the development of Russia may be more rapid than that of the countries which pioneered ahead of it. The Soviet Revolution is not to be regarded as a final step. Life is struggle. No one revolution will bring the millennium, but a series of evolutionary stages, all the result of struggle, will mark the steps toward a better social scheme. As society develops, new goals and new ideals come into view, and the adjustment of the structure of society to new aims is a continuous process.

E. Spiritual Method

1. Idealism and Self-Denial. After the visitor leaves Russia he observes the scene in its perspective and notes its heroic aspects. The experiment is conceived on a colossal scale. It is motivated by unparalleled courage. Seemingly impossible tasks are attempted. The very errors, which are so numerous, are on a grand scale. As a result of these gigantic errors, want is unparalleled. The leaders in their conceptions and the people in their acceptance of the burdens and difficulties seem cast in the mold of warriors and martyrs.

Even where privation is not acute, the Soviet aims involve a spiritual method of living. An austere mode of life flows from the Soviet aims. Self-denial is practiced, but not, as in the case of monasticism, in pursuit of superhuman ideals, but rather for the sake of social good. The individual is supposed to improve his status, not as in the west by establishing a personal reserve fund, but rather through advancing the good of the whole group. To raise oneself above the group is regarded as anti-social.

2. Fanaticism, Intolerance, and Violence. What seems most lacking in the Soviet method is belief in slow growth. Sublime faith and patient hope, spiritual notes, are absent. The atmosphere is rather characterized by restless energy and a pressing impatience for quick results. It seems like a form of hypomania on a national scale. In the individual the symptoms of hypomania are unqualified self-confidence, emotional exaltation, occasional hallucinations, and delusions of persecution and these are all very noticeable in Russia.[5]

Hatred and oppression are characteristic of Soviet procedure. Hatred has been focused on the kulaks, and has taken the form of confiscation of property, deprivation of rights, exile from their homes, and forced labor in distant parts. Just as under the mediæval church the Jews, the class that then bore the hatred of society, had to wear a yellow badge, so in Soviet Russia, the hated kulak must register with the police and obtain a permit before migrating. Kulak children over 14 must publish a statement in the press renouncing their parents, in order to be freed from the stigma.

When the minority differs with the majority, in a régime like that of the Soviets, there is no freedom of discussion or freedom of belief. The nonconformists are heretics. As with the dogmatism of a militant church there is no tolerance for dissenters. Disbelievers are enemies. They must either recant or suffer exile or death. The acid qualities of fanaticism, intolerance, and violence are characteristic of an emerging faith, rather than of a mature or decadent system.

3. Self-Criticism, Confession, Recantation, and Penance. The question that greets the traveler returning from Russia is; "Can you see what you wish to see or only what they show you?" The answer is that not only do the Russians not hide their faults and weaknesses, but they advertise them. Self-criticism is a popular means of blowing off steam. Any one of the hundred and sixty odd million people in Russia can write a "letter to the editor" and criticize everything except communist principles or the leading officials of the Kremlin. The traditionally destructive faculties of the Russians find full scope here.

This self-criticism may be the frankness of pioneer peoples, which the Russians share with Americans or Australians, a frankness which is different from the subtlety or indirection of older civilizations, like the French, for instance. On the other hand, this country-wide campaign of self-criticism may be a sort of national ballyhoo to cheer the working teams, or a form of national scolding, or perhaps a national wringing of the hands at the failures round about. Or it may be a sublimation of the sense of failure to achieve. But whatever else it is, self-criticism, like confession at a prayer meeting, is a shriving which is good for the soul.

Confession, recantation, and penance are essentially mediæval theological conceptions which have reappeared in the new religion of communism. On June 22, 1633, Galileo, under the threat of torture and at the express command of Pope Urban VIII, recanted publicly as follows: "I, Galileo, being in my seventieth year, a prisoner and on my knees, and before Your Eminences . . . abjure, curse, and detest the error and the heresy of the movement of the earth." [6] On November 25, 1929, in agnostic Russia, a similar episode was witnessed. Tomsky, Rykov and Bukharin, threatened with expulsion from the Political Bureau in much the same terms confessed that their opposition had been an error, and that they were ready to fight all dissent from the orthodoxy of the party:

> During the last year and a half there were between us and the majority of the Central Committee of the All-Russian Communist Party differences of opinion on a number of political and tactical questions. Our views were expressed in a number of documents and speeches at plenary and other sessions of the Central Committee and the party itself.
>
> We regard it as our duty to state that in this controversy the party and its Central Committee have proven right, while our views, as expressed in certain documents, have proved in error. We confess these errors and we shall, on our part, endeavor, together with the entire party, to struggle with all our might against all deviation from the general party line. . . .
>
> (*Signed*)
>
> M. Tomsky
> N. Bukharin
> A. T. Rykov
>
> Moscow
> *November 25, 1929*

4. A New Chauvinism. To maintain the spirit of self-confidence and of national superiority, the Soviets make the same appeal as Kaiser Wilhelm in pre-war Germany, or Mussolini in post-war Italy. The enemy without is depicted as ever ready to attack. The object seems to be to consolidate the nation within for defense. War against a nation results in unifying and energizing it. Therefore the device seems to be to raise the specter of war in order to unify and energize the people. And war includes not only military invasion, but also opposition to the Soviet idea by anti-communist Russians.

5. Distributive Justice. The Soviet program is part of a method of redistributing rights and privileges among classes. No class is to thrive at the

expense of another class that suffers. In this reasoning the Soviets think of particular social classes in a single generation. But the problem can also be regarded in terms of time factors. Has any generation the right to ask for happiness at the expense of another? If future descendants of Russians are to enjoy great happiness, is it right to expect the present generation to undergo extreme privation? In the ethics of distributive justice what are the rights to happiness of this generation as against its successors? [7] As the late G. Stanley Hall well said, "Each generation has the duty of passing on the torch of life burning a little more brightly than when it was received." Indeed, the obligation of providing for the future rests upon each generation. The wasting of natural resources is a wanton act, depriving a generation which is not yet here to protect its rights. It is a form of exploitation. However, the martyrdom of the Russians of today in the hope of a better, yet uncertain future for their children is equally wanton. It is likewise a form of exploitation. And as that lovable Irish wit, "Mr. Dooley," said, "Sure, and what has posterity ever done for us?"

CHAPTER XIV

RESULTS

A. General Results

It is difficult to appraise the Soviet achievements at this close range. How accurate a picture would one have obtained of the future of the American republic at the time of the "critical period" in American history, or what appraisal could one have made of the results of the French Revolution at the time of Napoleon? The results of 1932 put a different light on any appraisal of the Russian Revolution that one might have made in 1926. And any appraisal made in 1932 may be altered by the influence of manifold forces that may appear before 1937. Furthermore, the results must be judged in the light, not of modern western civilization, but rather of pre-war Russia, with its preponderantly agricultural population, illiterate, superstitious, emancipated from serfdom, yet not wholly free, and exposed ruthlessly to all the physical woes of mankind.

The new contrasts with the old. Hospitals, schools, libraries, are opened in feverish haste in a world in which they were formerly conspicuously lacking. The masses are being taught. The landed estates were seized by the peasants who increased their holdings, which were then reaggregated in great collectives. Private industry has been replaced by state industry. Commerce and finance are likewise state controlled. The social classes have been inverted. The proletariat are the new élite. The "white-collar" workers and the professional classes have lost their privileged status. Priests and merchants have become the new disinherited.

B. Contrasts Between Aims and Results

1. Economic Contrasts. Without attempting to minimize the marvelous record of achievement of the Soviets, under very difficult conditions, some

of them of their own creation, it is interesting to note the striking contrast between their lofty aims and their actual achievements.

Materially, the Soviet aim is abundance of goods; the result hitherto has been privation and want. The aim is to abolish profit and to produce for service; the result hitherto has been to exploit labor for the profit of the state trusts. The aim is to abolish price as a source of profit, money as a form of profit, and banks as capitalist institutions. After a period of economic chaos, all three were restored, price as a mechanism of distribution, money as a medium of exchange, and banks as agencies of credit. The aim is to distribute the social surplus among the masses; the result has been to waste much of the social surplus by bureaucracy. The masses have not been served, but rather an incompetent and inefficient class of administrators. The aim is equal distribution; the result has been that nobody has much of anything. Real wages in rich Russia are less than in many poor capitalist countries. Only the huge resources make possible such incompetence. In a less rich country such as Switzerland the economic machinery would have broken down. The aim has been and is to overtake and surpass the older industrial countries, and in this respect it is too early to appraise the result of the Soviet attempt. Ultimately it may be successful.

2. Political Contrasts. The political aim is liberty; the result hitherto has been terrorism. The aim is political equality; the result has been the loss of the rights of the individual. There is no protection for the individual in Russia, such as the American Bill of Rights sets forth. The aim is fraternity; the result hitherto has been violence. The ultimate aim is democracy; the result has been tyranny. The aim is popular government; the result has been an oligarchy. The aim is a machinery for democratic succession; the result has been self-perpetuation of a small group.

3. Social Contrasts. The aim is labor as a new nobility; the result hitherto has been a new serfdom and the drafting of labor. The aim is an industrial democracy; the result has been a benevolent tyranny. The aim is worker representation; the result has been centralized, arbitrary authority and sweated labor. The aim is to serve the masses; the result has been exploitation of the peasantry for the benefit of the industrial worker. The aim is to develop new social motives; the result has been to lose the old valuable individual incentives. Personal initiative is a social good, and small individual strivings can be made to further the common good. The aim is to abolish all classes; the result has been to create new ones. Society became stratified along new lines. The old underdogs were replaced by new under-

dogs. The aim is to abolish exploitation; the result has been to foster new exploitation. The "white-collar" workers, the traders, artisans, farmers, are the exploited under the new régime. The aim is to ruin the "exploiters"; the result hitherto has been to bring woe as well to the "exploited."

4. Spiritual Contrasts. The aim is a lofty idealism; the result has been a debasing cruelty, as in the treatment of the remnants of the privileged classes. The aim is to abolish money as a source of evil; the result has been to develop new sources of evil, nepotism, spying, and "heresy" hunting. The aim is to benefit future generations; the result has been to inflict cruelty and suffering on the present generation. In life, as in a railroad journey, it is important not only to arrive at one's destination but to enjoy the trip. The aim is universal education; the result has been widespread propaganda.

Enlightened and sympathetic travelers are having an educative influence on Russia for the masses are filled with stories of capitalist evils. In a conversation with the writer in a railroad coach going from Moscow to Leningrad, four young engineers refused to believe that the United States had any free state universities, or that poor bright boys could obtain scholarships in our "capitalist" country. After much discussion they still thought the matter impossible and regarded the statement of the writer as anti-Soviet propaganda.

The aim is to abolish religion; the result has been worship of the dynamo. The idealization of material things, the devastating enthusiasm for factories and machines, shows a distortion of spiritual values. Abolition of chairs of philosophy and of pure science in the universities is a reflection of the new materialism. The aim is public ethics; the result has been personal self-aggrandizement in many cases. The stealing of public moneys is punishable by death; but the stealing of public power is a legitimate road to political ambition.

C. Economic Results

Communist Russia is not communist. It is capitalist. The extremes meet. The state has become the owner, exploiter, and profiteer. Soviet Russia seems to be an atavism, a throwback to a more primitive type. Conscription of labor for special work is similar to the now obsolete scheme of labor by forced or indentured servants. Conscription of labor is opposed to the fundamental right of labor, namely, freedom of contract. The 10-hour day invoked at times in order "to overtake and surpass capitalist countries" represents a form of labor sweating. Other capitalist devices are visible on every hand.

Profit is the test of industry. Interest on capital advanced to industry is charged by the State Bank. Piece work and the income tax in the new régime are revivals of the successful experience of the old.

1. Property Rights. Private property was abolished with respect to ownership of the means of production, for the state is the sole producer. The individual may not produce for private gain. Even purely personal property, such as clothing and household goods, which is theoretically still inviolate, has been subjected to illegal seizure when in the hands of the enemies of the state. For example, the kulaks when transported to distant parts were not allowed to take their personal belongings. Not only was private profit abolished but also the right to enjoy private property.

2. Agriculture. The nationalization of land and machinery has interfered with the industrial recovery of Russia. It has added a vast complex of new problems to an already difficult task of economic reconstruction. As for example, the case cited above, when after depleting the herds of the country by forcible collectivization agricultural Soviet Russia has had to import from capitalist industrial Germany live stock to remedy the ravages of socialization.

The Russian policy of expropriation differed from the policy, say, of Czechoslovakia and other Succession States, where the land was not confiscated, but was purchased by the state with payment to the land owners in long-term bonds, bearing low interest rates. Although the present discounted value of such payments is not large, the procedure was technically legal. The partition of the estates in Russia resulted in the granting of the land to the peasants. But it was never intended that they should keep it, for it was "recaptured" by the state. In fact, they had few of the rights that go with property, such as the unrestricted right to sell. One of the permanent results of the revolution is that these estates will probably never revert to the landlords who held title before the revolution. Though the old landlords are gone, it is the government now that requisitions the surplus of the peasant and causes the low agricultural output. When the serfs were freed in 1861, the land they received was held communally, but operated individually. Now the tractor, which can be applied only to large holdings, serves to consolidate or freeze the situation and prevent the return of the system of small holdings.

Both in history and in communist doctrine the individual peasant has been a hindrance to the progress of socialization. The progress made thus far in state farms and in collective farming is one of the more important accomplishments of the Soviets. It introduced a profound change in the lives of a majority of the Russian peasants. It raised their standard of living, increased their efficiency, and to an extent changed their very psychology.

3. INDUSTRY. The policy of industrialization is in a measure independent of communism. The success or failure in industrializing Russia has no bearing on the success or failure of communism as an experiment. Today Russia is being industrialized under a system of profits. The government is the capitalist, the sole stockholder. The technique is capitalist and the incentives are largely capitalist. The communist formula, "From each according to his means and to each according to his needs," has no place in this system. The marketing problem is simple. There is no need for merchandising efforts; shortages are universal. Goods are always inadequate, and therefore the skill and ability to produce good merchandise at low cost is not tested, as in the western capitalist system. The centralization of management leads to bureaucracy, and bureaucracy leads to red tape and high prices. Under a system of state capitalism, Russian goods are higher in price and poorer in quality. Before the war, Russian rails lasted more than forty years. At present the Soviet steel trust is unwilling to guarantee rails for five years according to Commissar of Transportation, Y. E. Rudzutak. Centralization of industrial management raises not merely the cost of producing goods but the cost of constructing plants. In both cases it delays the completion of jobs.

Management is lacking. Justice Brandeis years ago presented the thesis that mere size does not make for efficiency, and that some of the very large American corporations might be less efficient than smaller organizations that were sufficiently large to permit economies, but not so large as to make it difficult to find managers.[1] The decline of the Armour Company as compared with Swift or Cudahy resulted from the inability to find a successor with the managerial ability of the elder Armour. Managers cannot be developed as rapidly in Russia as plants can be built. The defective quality of the machines and the lack of experience of labor can be cured only slowly, and no amount of drastic penalties imposed on incompetent managers will increase the capabilities of the remainder. Such success as Russia's industrial program has achieved is partly a tribute to the American engineers. They do equally well in the United States, in Uruguay or in Russia. In plant management, the democratic control of industry has been practically abandoned. Soviet Russia has now adopted capitalist methods. Production has been speeded up. As in capitalist countries, the aim is a continuous lowering of prices, accompanied by a continuous raising of wages. The accounting system is predicated on making profits, but the ownership of all industry by the state makes accounting complicated, to say the least. In the transformation of iron ore, say, into the finished automobile, individual companies in a capitalist country compete, set prices, and thus determine profits. But without competition, and with the sole producer, the state, controlling industry from iron ore to finished machinery, it is more difficult to allocate profit to any particular stage, and to determine the efficiency of production.

4. Labor. Among the favorable results claimed by the Soviet officials is that while the rest of the world is suffering from severe depression Russia has no unemployed. The manual laborer constitutes the new aristocracy. The Soviet officials use this position of attributed superiority as an inducement to secure the co-operation of labor. Not merely are preferences in food and clothing, but cultural opportunities in painting, music, and literature granted to the workman. On the other hand, he is subject to almost military conscription. Labor is speeded up by methods of mass production, and the new plants at Stalingrad and elsewhere are to be operated on that basis, although mass production had been once condemned as exploitation of labor.

Labor has no voice in management. The councils of workmen set up at the beginning of the Soviet régime proved incompetent and irresponsible and were subsequently ignored. Shop discipline had to be improved. Policies are now determined entirely by the management, which has complete authority. Furthermore, in the effort to show profits the heads of several trusts reduce wages, and it is difficult for the workmen to strike as they might under a scheme of private production.

The status of labor is somewhat similar under the system of state capitalism in Russia to that in a capitalist corporation. In both cases a large industrial machine is run for profit. However, in Russia, profits return to the community directly, but in the western world indirectly through income taxes on corporations and individuals. Under a capitalist system, however, labor organizations are free. They may protest against their private employers, whereas in Soviet Russia all workmen come under the class of state employees. It is as difficult for them to strike, as it would be, say, for the post office employees in the United States. The trade unions become subordinated to the state. Too great opposition may result in the charge of counter-revolutionary activities.

The standard of living is probably really lower than before the war for the general average of labor. The statistical gain is certainly less than in other countries. Such advance as may have taken place has been achieved not because of communism but rather because of the introduction of western methods, as for example the mechanization of agriculture. Capitalist methods are harnessed to socialist or communist aims.

5. TRADE. In domestic trade, the result of communist methods has been to cause suffering. Under the Nep, goods were available. Consumer demand was satisfied. When the Nep was abolished and the state took over internal trade, the result was a universal shortage of merchandise. Goods were not available and the population suffered. Then when trade was unshackled in 1932, shortages were relieved. Freedom of trade resulted in satisfaction. Communism resulted in deprivation. Price fixing curtailed the profits of the private trader, but it also checked the distribution of merchandise. Goods disappeared and the low prices fixed had no significance. In order to induce the farmers to sell their products, goods had to be sent from the towns to the rural districts. However, after the harvest the government shifted the flow of merchandise back to the towns.

Official efforts at socialization included not only industry and agriculture, but also internal trade. The state became a merchant. The individual artisan became a socialized factory worker and the individual peasant a worker on a collective government grain farm. The small tradesman became an employee of the state or co-operative trade organization. The cost of selling rose greatly and efficiency declined. Distribution was so inefficient that it raised the price of consumers' goods greatly above the pre-war level, but the price of farm products did not rise equally above the pre-war level. This maladjustment was known as the "scissors," which caught the peasants in two ways. It gave rise to the theory of exploitation of the peasant by the laborer, of the country by the towns, of the agricultural capitalists by the industrial communists.

Not merely trade in commodities but trade in services were socialized. The services of tailors, shoemakers, etc., were taken out of the hands of the individual capitalist and placed in the hands of state trusts or co-operatives. There are syndicates for performing all these services. In a way they are similar to recent developments in big cities of the United States, where shoe-repairing, valet service, etc., are offered in chain establishments. However, the development in the United States has resulted either in lower cost or in standardization of service, but the growth of socialization in Moscow, for example, has resulted in great delays. It takes several weeks to have shoes repaired unless the job is given to the ubiquitous itinerant cobbler who works on the sidewalks of Moscow, while the customer waits. As a result of the delay and inefficiency of state trade, a public demand created a new class of private traders, who were tolerated by the government as a necessary evil. Speculators employed clerks to stand in queues and buy goods in small quantities at the fixed price, which were then resold in larger quantities at higher prices, to people who were willing to pay for the prompter service. Finally in the summer of 1932 the artisan, cobbler, tailor, and tinsmith could again produce and sell for a private profit. Even the patient Russian, who has little sense of the value of time, often refuses to wait, even for vodka.

6. Foreign Trade. In international trade the economic result was striking. In order to prosecute the Five-Year Plan the authorities purchased hundreds of millions of dollars' worth of machinery, chiefly from America. However, due to lack of credit these machinery imports were paid for by the export of raw materials and agricultural products. Ultimate successful operation of the plants at Stalingrad, Kharkov, Cheliabinsk, etc., should lessen greatly the importation of tractors from foreign countries.

In the field of manufactured goods, Russia has not become an important exporter and is unlikely to be for many years. The domestic demand is too great. And even though the Soviets ignore costs of production, the quality of their finished goods is too inferior for western consumption. This was true even under the old régime.

7. Money and Credit. As stated above, money was officially abolished as part of the program of communism. Economic chaos resulted, and money was restored. At the same time the levying of taxes was first abolished and then restored. The official recognition of private profit is evident in graduated supertaxes on incomes and profits.

Banks were abolished and subsequently not only restored but greatly extended in scope of operations and in number even in remote rural areas. The debt, both domestic and foreign, was repudiated. Therefore the Soviets have little credit. The lack of credit has involved the population in great sacrifices and has hampered the industrial development. Now they re-acknowledge the debt, but the terms are not acceptable to the old creditors. The state has made large investments in industrial projects. These are not yet productive. To the extent that they divert funds from importation of consumers' goods, these investments have imposed on the masses as much privation as did the money invested or wasted in munitions factories during the World War. In neither case were consumers' goods produced, and consumers suffered accordingly.

8. PRIVATE CAPITALISM VS. STATE CAPITALISM. a. Distribution of the Surplus. Private capitalism may suffer from maldistribution of profits. But the Soviet system suffers from inadequate distribution of merchandise. Soviet wheat is shipped abroad, and the Russian masses eat black bread. The communists say that in the western world the workers hand over the surplus to the capitalists. But in the Soviet state the surplus does not go to the capitalist, but is wasted in incompetent administration and in paying bureaucratic staffs. In neither case does the surplus go to the workers. In the Soviet state the manual laborers are being exploited in the interests of bureaucracy and "Red" officialdom, propaganda in China, etc. The Soviet worker is expected to submit to physical want and to underconsumption on behalf of a campaign of education of foreigners in Soviet political theories. True, much of the money spent by the western world in peddling various brands of denominational theology to the "heathen" Chinese might better be used for constructive social purposes at home.

b. Wages. Although private capitalism has been largely abolished in the Soviet Union, real wages there probably are lower than in the western world. The abolition of the private capitalist has probably not yet enriched labor. The elimination of private profit has not raised the standard of living of the masses notably or even at all. The efficiency of private capitalism is pitted against the incompetence of nationalized industry though Russian industry before the war was likewise inefficient. From the point of view of the laborer, his chief interest is, which system gives him the highest wage. He is less interested in the equality of the distribution, if in securing that equality he himself receives less.*

Not merely in Russia, but in other countries is there a similar contrast. The employees of the state in the United States receive lower wages than the employees of private corporations. The government runs the postal service, and private companies run the railroads. The salaries of the railroad workers on the whole are far larger than the salaries of the postal employees, who are among the most underpaid employees in the country.

Theoretically, all members of the Communist Party are still limited equally

* Compare Bowley, Arthur L., *The Division of the Products of Industry.* Oxford: University Press, 1919, pp. 57–58.

to the small pay of 300 rubles per month, though a raise was proposed in July 1932. But rewards proportionate to ability and responsibility are made, not in money but in an equivalent, in the class of car used, from Rolls-Royces down to Chevrolets and Fords, in the type of homes available, the privileges of travel, quality of medical attention, vacation accommodations, and social status. There is a striking contrast between the theory of equal pay and the actual practice.

c. Comparison with Other European Countries. Yugov points out, in spite of the overthrow of a despotic government, the division of landholdings and the abundance of natural resources, the Soviets have not made as great progress as Germany, which was hampered by the reparations burden and is limited in its natural resources. His point of view is that wages and the standard of living in the Soviet Union have lagged behind other countries which changed from monarchies to democracies, namely, Germany, Austria, and Czechoslovakia, and this in spite of the fact that Tsarist Russia, with its unprogressive and corrupt leadership, showed in the two decades before the war a greater increase in the national income than did Great Britain, France, or Austria, due partly, of course, to the relatively lower starting point of industrial development.

d. Comparison with Other Young Countries. The industrial and agricultural production of Soviet Russia grew far less from 1913 to 1930 than did that of Canada, Australia, or the Argentine. On the average Russia has not yet correspondingly increased her industrial output, except in a few items, such as petroleum. In items which would require substantial foreign financing, as the development of the non-ferrous metal mines, and in consumers' goods the production is far less.

COMPARATIVE PROGRESS OF SOVIET UNION AND OTHER COUNTRIES [a]

Wheat Production

(millions of bushels)

	1909/10–1913/14 Average	*1928/29*	*Per cent Change*
U.S.S.R. (Russia)	757.3	795.2	+ 5.0
Argentina	147.1	349.0	+137.3
Australia	90.5	159.6	+ 76.4
Canada	197.1	566.7	+187.5

COMPARATIVE PROGRESS OF SOVIET UNION AND OTHER COUNTRIES—*Continued*

Wool Production

(millions of pounds)

	1909 to 1913 Average	*1929*	*Per cent Change*
U.S.S.R. (Russia)	[b] 330	397	+20.3
United States	314	363	+15.6
Union of South Africa	[c] 158	[c] 302	+91.1
Australia	728	925	+27.1
New Zealand	180	255	+41.7

Coal and Lignite Production

(thousands of short tons)

	1913	*1929*	*Per cent Change*
U.S.S.R. (Russia)	37,273	37,901	+ 1.7
British India	18,153	24,802	+36.6
Japan and Taiwan [d]	24,072	39,683	+64.9

Pig Iron Production

(thousands of long tons)

	1913	*1929*	*Per cent Change*
U.S.S.R. (Russia)	4,563	4,000	— 12.3
Belgium	2,445	4,035	+ 65.0
Japan	236	1,500	+535.6
British India	204	1,350	+561.8

Crude Petroleum Production

(millions of barrels of 42 U. S. gallons)

	1913	*1929*	*Per cent Change*
U.S.S.R. (Russia)	62.8	103.0	+ 64.0
Rumania	13.6	34.9	+ 156.6
Persia	1.9	45.3	+2284.2
Netherland East Indies	11.2	37.9	+ 238.4
Venezuela	0.0	137.0	—
Colombia	0.0	20.4	—

COMPARATIVE PROGRESS OF SOVIET UNION AND OTHER COUNTRIES—*Continued*

Cotton Spindles [e]

(thousands)

	1914	*1929*	*Per cent Change*
U.S.S.R. (Russia)	9,160	7,465	— 18.5
Brazil	1,250	2,750	+120.0
India	6,500	8,704	+ 33.9
Japan	2,750	6,530	+137.5
China	1,000	3,620	+262.0

Railroad Mileage

(thousands of miles)

	1913	*1928*	*Per cent Change*
U.S.S.R. (Russia)	36.3	48.2	+32.8
Argentina	20.8	24.4	+17.3
Australia	17.6	25.8	+46.6
Canada	29.3	41.0	+39.9

Telephones

(thousands of instruments)

	1913	*1928*	*Per cent Change*
U.S.S.R. (Russia)	[f] 336.5	300.0	— 10.8
Canada	463.7	1,334.5	+187.8
Argentina	74.3	245.3	+230.1
Sweden	159.3	472.2	+196.4
Finland	40.0	113.8	+184.5
Netherlands East Indies	[f] 16.4	45.2	+175.6
Japan (proper)	[f] 219.6	811.3	+269.4
Australia	132.7	476.7	+259.2

International Trade

(millions of dollars)

	IMPORTS			EXPORTS		
	1913	*1929*	*Per cent Change*	*1913*	*1929*	*Per cent Change*
U.S.S.R. (Russia)	707.1	430.7	— 39.1	782.3	452.0	— 42.1
Canada	659.1	1,299.0	+ 97.1	460.5	1,208.2	+162.4
Cuba	140.1	213.7	+ 52.5	164.6	272.4	+ 65.5

COMPARATIVE PROGRESS OF SOVIET UNION AND OTHER COUNTRIES—*Continued*

International Trade (millions of dollars)—*Continued*

	IMPORTS			EXPORTS		
	1913	*1929*	*Per cent Change*	*1913*	*1929*	*Per cent Change*
Argentina	492.5	821.1	+ 66.7	515.2	952.6	+ 84.9
India	584.5	900.0	+ 71.1	797.1	1,191.0	+ 49.4
China	428.0	820.0	+ 91.6	306.2	660.0	+115.5
Australia	388.1	708.1	+ 82.5	382.4	661.5	+ 73.0
New Zealand	105.4	237.2	+125.0	111.9	270.5	+141.7
Union of South Africa	187.5	384.6	+105.1	324.4	476.2	+ 46.8

[a] Figures on wheat production taken from 1931 *Yearbook, U. S. Department of Agriculture.* Other figures are from the *Commerce Yearkbook, U. S. Department of Commerce,* 1930.
[b] 1916.
[c] Estimates.
[d] Including not more than 3 per cent lignite.
[e] Data for 1914 are for active spindles; for 1929 for both active and idle; all years ended July 31. No adjustment for pre-war figures to post-war boundaries has been made.
[f] 1915.

e. Capitalist Devices in Soviet Russia. The Soviet régime is the heir of the preceding capitalist régime. To an extent it is living on the resources of the capitalist régime, including industrial plants, workmen's homes, farms, and, in general, plant and equipment. The huge empire as a whole furnished a starting point for the Soviet experiment.

The actual development of the resources of the Soviets from the revolution up to date, is largely an achievement of capitalism, rather than of communism. Engineers trained in capitalist countries were drafted to do the major tasks. The purposeful policy of the Soviet Union, of planning production, is not essentially a communist notion except in its application to the complete economic life of the nation. As noted above, before the war Germany had planned its economic life for a generation ahead. Differential freight rates were utilized to facilitate export trade. Subsidies and bounties were given for increasing exports.* The system of cartels and of planning production for consumption within a particular industry was known not only in Germany, but internationally throughout Europe.

The whole economic structure of the Soviet Union is shot through with capitalist devices, some of which were originally abolished and had to be reinstated in the interest of efficiency: profits, as the goal of industry, a

* This development is discussed in detail by Henri Hauser in his *Les Méthodes Allemandes d'Expansion Économique.*

system of accounting designed to reveal profits, budgets for the trusts, income taxes on profits of companies and individuals, etc. The adoption of these capitalist devices and mechanisms was practically forced on Soviet Russia, because they did work and the communist methods did not. And, therefore, if the present régime succeeds, it will prove not that communism works, but that capitalist methods work, not only under private capitalism, but also under state capitalism.

f. Socialized Devices in the United States. Even the United States, with its adherence to principles of individual initiative, has developed a socialist trend, though very gradually. Graduated income taxes and graduated inheritance taxes were regarded as radical a generation ago and are now an accepted part of the fiscal scheme. The former leads to a more even distribution of income, and the other to more even distribution of wealth. As shown above the regulation of the railroads has changed them from forms of private property with few restrictions into the most completely socialized form of property in the United States, with few vestiges of private property rights. The regulation of utilities is now under way. Accident insurance, old-age insurance, and maternity relief have now become part of the social welfare laws in many states. Unemployment insurance, which has already made some progress in many large corporations, is being increasingly discussed as a measure of social reform. Under a very conservative administration at Washington, the government embarked upon some of the most socialistic enterprises ever adopted in any country.

Socialism is making piece-meal progress in the capitalist world. Its development is not painful to any class. The time factor is determined by organized public opinion, which moves only very slowly and only gradually becomes accustomed to change. Legislation for which the public mind is not educated induces political disturbance.

The difference between private capitalism, as exemplified in the United States, and state capitalism, as exemplified in Russia, is that with the former the changes are slow and with the latter violent. With the former each step is tested before the next is taken, so that no great error is committed or harm done, while the latter puts into effect bold and daring plans, commits costly mistakes, imposes great suffering, and then faces right about.

For example, the Swope Plan for the stabilization of American industry, presented by Gerard Swope, president of the General Electric Company, represents very mild and cautious steps as compared with the Soviet plans. Some of its chief provisions are: unemployment insurance when workers cannot be assured of regular and continuous employment; action by organized industry to provide protection for workers rather than action by either state or federal government; full information to stockholders through standardized forms of reports; removal from the minds of workers of apprehension regarding lack of continuous employment, support of their surviving dependents in case of their death, and provision for old age, through co-ordinating production and consumption and thus regularizing employment; preservation of individual originality, initiative, and enterprise, and protection of the interests of the public, preferably through the agency of the federal government.

It is possible that the trend toward humanization of industry which has characterized several large American corporations, and which is reflected in such proposals as the Swope Plan may have been accelerated by the growth of socialism in Europe and the rapid development of state capitalism in Russia.

The capitalist world is moving under the influence of forces of evolution in economic as well as in social affairs. Old industries die and new industries are born. When the "gas" engine was invented, the carriage industry died and the automobile industry was born. The risks of private industry are borne by the private individuals that own it. The risks of developing a new industry are borne by the daring speculators that stake their money. In 1932 the shares of railroads a century old sold at the lowest levels in a century. On the hundredth anniversary of Morse's invention of the telegraph, Western Union shares fell to the lowest prices in many decades. In twenty years the pioneers in the automobile industry, under the influence of competition and under capitalism, have given the world an example of great service to the consumer. The dollar probably buys greater values in automobiles than in most other articles of consumption, chiefly because the industry is one of the most competitive. The inefficient producers are being eliminated and consolidations like General Motors and Chrysler are emerging.

Probably the capitalist world will continue to move gradually and by evolutionary means in the direction of socialization and eventually even approach the communist ideals. In America, for example, industry is moving toward large-scale production just as if the state had encouraged the organization of industrial syndicates or trusts. For instance, in the field of electrical equipment there are only two important companies, General Electric and Westinghouse. In the field of can manufacturing there are also only two, American Can Company and Continental Can Company. In mail-order distribution there are only two important companies, Sears Roebuck & Company and Montgomery Ward & Company. In automobiles, General Motors, Ford, and Chrysler, and perhaps a few others cover practically the entire field, and alone could supply the nation's needs. In several industries there is only one important producer such as Eastman Kodak Company, Aluminum Company of America, Otis Elevator Company and American Radiator Company. Each would correspond to a state trust in the Soviet Union. In other words, industry in the United States under the stress of competition and in the search for efficiency, has been aggregated into very large units. Eventually, after some generations these corporations will probably become socialized. The early steps of this process are even now apparent—profit sharing and stock ownership by employees, pension plans and unemployment relief within the corporation, development of managers from the ranks of the industry, contributions in their several communities for the public good, etc. In other words, the search for efficiency is leading to socialization of capitalism.

g. Soviet Crises. The Soviets point to the depression in the capitalist world and to the boom in Russia as final proof that their system is superior. But this particular conjuncture is purely accidental. The Soviets have not abolished crises. In the western world there are crises of overproduction and of falling prices. But call it crisis or not, the Soviets are suffering from a painful underconsumption and a lack of goods. The mere fact that there is no general unemployment is no proof of the absence of a crisis. The direction in which production is moving in Russia is not toward satisfaction of human needs, which is after all the prime aim of the economic system, but rather toward a long-range plan of development of the raw-material resources of the country. In this process continuous minor crises arise in various industries. Raw material is short and the plants must stop. Labor is unavailable and must be conscripted from other industries. Crises are not essentially related to capitalism. They are maladjustments which arise when industry and agriculture are conducted on a large scale. The question of avoiding crises or keeping in equilibrium all the elements of production is little related to the question as to who gets the profits, whether it be the state, as in Russia, or the stockholders, as in the rest of the world. The inability to estimate the requirements of an unknown group of consumers is the principal cause of crises. The form in which industry is organized has little bearing on the existence or elimination of crises.

Because Soviet Russia has not developed gradually, but is trying to change in one leap from a primitive agricultural country to a highly mechanized industrial community, crises are likely to be even more frequent than in the more slowly developing capitalist countries. The argument by some sympathizers with the Soviet régime that there are defects in our system is quite beside the point. Admittedly, there are, but the defects of our system are not a vindication of the Soviets, for they are suffering from still greater evils.

D. Political Results

1. Undemocratic Régime. Democracy in the western sense does not exist in Russia. The Soviets represent not the great mass of the workers and the peasants, as the world is told, but rather a small bureaucracy. The dictatorship of the proletariat is really the dictatorship of the dictatorship. However, the small group that dominates Russia does not exploit public office for private ends, but regards itself as the trustee for a people, supposedly not yet ready for self-government, a sort of mandatory. This oligarchy, however, has the saving grace that it is not hereditary, but honestly and sincerely aims to benefit the people, ultimately if not immediately.

There is no machinery for registering the will of the masses. If the authorities in control are influenced by popular sentiment, it is not through any direct expression, as the ballot, but rather through the confidential observations of the secret police. The decrease in the rate of collectivization was due to the fact that the peasants objected to it by consuming their cattle and by shooting the government agents. The people have also expressed themselves positively by an enthusiastic co-operation in the Five-Year Plan, and by a flood of letters to the press in criticism of incompetence and mismanagement. However, criticism is permitted only as to method, not as to principles. Major policies are not decided by the masses; they are decided by the small group in control of the party. Expression of the popular will by methods of violence is historic in Russia. The people have had neither training nor experience in self-government.

Yet under the old régime there was a persistent and bitter struggle for freedom. The goal was clear and was similar to the American and English bills of rights—freedom of speech, freedom of the press, and freedom from search and seizure. Today such a struggle for freedom is regarded as counter-revolutionary. Though the present régime undoubtedly has in mind the long-range interest of the masses, yet in the determination of policies, the masses have little voice or control as might be expressed in the form of elections under a parliamentary scheme.

The character of the control of the party has changed. The original Bolsheviks were internationalists and intellectuals. But they have been outmaneuvered by the new rulers, who are neither but are chiefly local leaders who rose from the ranks and are expert at tactics and strategy of politics. Therefore, they look to Lenin as a prophet, quote him, almost in theologian fashion, and attempt to interpret the words of the dead leader and to imagine what he might have done in the current crisis.

2. MINORITY RETAINS POWER. In Russia a minority rules. In a republic the masses can register their protests through recognized and established machinery and oust the party in control. In a dictatorship such change is impossible. There is no possibility of replacing leaders gradually and legally. As a result the Soviets have worked themselves into the position of a mountain climber who has reached a peak from which he cannot easily descend. All opposition and dissent is crushed. The left deviationists, such as the Trotsky group, are expelled, and the right deviationists, such as the Rykov and Bukharin group, are suppressed. How undemocratic the régime is! As in all dictatorships it requires powerful forces, a powerful army, secret police, arrests, murders, executions, exile, and other penalties to keep fundamental dissent from expressing itself. The instability of the current régime may be measured by the amount of force which must be imposed to crush latent dissent. The minority retains power largely because of the weariness of the masses. As Leon Trotsky stated:

> The years of the revolutionary earthquake and the civil war left the masses in a desperate need of rest. The workers, oppressed with need and hunger, wanted a revival of economic life at any price. In the presence of a considerable unemployment the removal of a worker from a factory for Oppositional views was a fearful weapon in the hands of the Stalin faction. Political interests fell away. The workers were ready to give the bureaucracy the broadest powers, if only it would restore order, offer an opportunity to revive the factories, and furnish provisions and raw material from the country.
>
> In this reaction of weariness, quite inevitable after every great revolutionary tension, lies the chief cause of the consolidation of the bureaucratic régime and the growth of that personal power of Stalin in which the new bureaucracy has found its personification.[1a]

Parliamentary capitalism may have its defects, but at least there is generally greater freedom of the individual, and an established machinery for expression of mass opinions.

In Soviet Russia power is centralized not in the masses, nor even in a small committee, but rather in an inner group of this committee, and this inner group is dominated by one man, Joseph Stalin. Who is sufficiently wise and just to deserve to exercise so great a power?

Is this centralized and arbitrary control permanent, or is it merely a transition stage? Is it a phase in the passing of the Russian people from Tsardom to democracy? If so, how can the transition be effected? The pressing political problem is to work out a machinery for handing power back where it belongs, to the rank and file of the population. The current state of affairs cannot be permanent. If a legal machinery of transition is not developed, the transition will take place by violence. Ultimately dictatorships maintained by force have been ended by force. If there is no machinery of adjustment, the system can change only by collapse.

3. Suppression of Freedom and Personal Rights. Even more so than under the Tsarist régime, there is no freedom of speech, of the press, or of academic thought. Such precious rights of the individual as in England were wrested from kings and nobles over a period of 700 years are utterly non-existent. The rights protecting the individual against the state, such as the assurance of a fair trial, are unknown. The individual has not the protection of habeas corpus. Arrest, trial, conviction, and sentence are without the safeguards prevailing in the western world.

In 1919, Lenin stated in his pamphlet, *The Dictatorship of the Proletariat and the Renegade Kautsky:* "The dictatorship is a rule founded directly upon force, and is bound by no laws! . . ." The speech in which Lenin announced the New Economic Policy on March 11, 1921, closed with the words: "The Socialists must nevertheless be kept in prison." [2]

At the Communist Party Day in Moscow in 1930, N. Krylenko, then Public Prosecutor, declared quite frankly: "Soviet laws are nothing but the injunctions of the party." [3]

These are not the characteristics of any democratic or popular political régime; they are the vestigial institutions inherited from Tsardom. The very notion of individual liberty is unknown; it is a product of the western world. Liberalism in political views of university teachers is non-existent. The courageous have been silenced, dismissed, exiled, imprisoned, or killed. There is no liberalism in the sense of a critical minority, which exposes the policy of the majority to public opinion. There is no public opinion save that which the state-controlled press echoes, and which the censorship may tolerate. There are no privately owned newspapers for the expression of independent opinion, so essential for the maintenance of political equilibrium. One Bolshevik seriously stated that since there is only one truth, it was not necessary to have two views expressed—a view of the case which recalls George Bernard Shaw's facetious question to a Soviet official at a Moscow race track: "Do you have more than one horse in the race?"

The individual is submerged as a matter of long-time policy, as he was submerged in the western countries during the World War. Terror and violence are tolerated, because the proletariat is supposed to rule. The freedom of the laboring class is suppressed because there is no private capital. In the machinery of government the evils of ward politics flourish—small loyalties to party, favoritism, inefficiency but not graft. Denunciation of personal enemies on the ground of counter-revolution is not uncommon.

4. DEFECTS OF DICTATORSHIPS. A dictatorship has the advantage of prompt change of policy. But the very speed of reversal of policy may be a disadvantage. Economic life cannot progress under conditions of rapid reversal of policy from communism to capitalism, back to communism, and again back to a new economic policy which is now beginning to manifest itself. As Lord Balfour stated in his *Fragment on Progress:* "Progress is not a form of indestructible energy which, if suppressed here, breaks out there, if refused embodiment in one shape, needs show itself in another. It is a plant of tender habit, difficult to propagate, not difficult to destroy, that refuses to flourish except in a soil which is not to be found everywhere nor at all times." [4] Prevailing winds often make trees grow in a certain direction. They accommodate themselves. But when violent winds blow alternately from opposite directions the tree will break. And it is the violent reversal of policy that is breaking up organized life in Russia.

Even though the dictatorship in Soviet Russia is conscientiously and sincerely striving to confer upon the masses the benefits that it conceives as desirable, yet the dictatorship regards its goals as more important than the general good, as the masses themselves see it. It sets itself up as having superior knowledge and judgment as to the needs and ideals of the people. It is thus a commentary on the soundness of the conception, judgment, and wishes of the people, which is the very essence of popular government. Such a view is unfortunate for the government and dangerous to the governing class.

The defects of dictatorship may be inferred from the words of President Hoover, in his address on our system of government at King's Mountain Battlefield, October 7, 1930:

> Our political system was a revolt from dictatorship, whether by individuals or classes. It was founded upon the conception that freedom was inalienable, and

that liberty and freedom should rest upon law, and that law should spring from the expressed wisdom of the representatives of the majority of the people themselves. . . . Yet of vastly more importance than the machinery of government was the charter of the rights of men which it guaranteed. Under them we hold that all men are created equal, that they are equal before the law, and that they should be safeguarded in liberty and, as we express it latterly, in equality of opportunity to every individual, that he may achieve for himself and for the community the best to which his character, his ability, and his ambition entitle him. . . .

5. Freedom for Nationalities. Undoubtedly the leading contribution of the Soviets is cultural and political autonomy for all the nationalities in the Soviet Union. True, Switzerland has been a laboratory model of this ideal for several hundred years. But a huge territory like the Soviet Union reveals the possibility of peaceful co-operation between peoples of different languages, cultures, and habits, which may be a model for Europe and the whole world. The war has left a heritage of ill-will and hatred between the majority and the minorities in each state, and the progress of the Soviet Union toward this goal may blaze a trail for the new European states to follow.

Before the war minor nationalities were forcibly assimilated or Russianized. The official language was always Russian in the courts and in public affairs. But under the Soviet régime newspapers are being published in 62 languages and dialects. The critics of the Soviets, however, insist that, as before, there is no diffusion of power or authority, that the Kremlin dominates the outermost minor nationality. Just as a conquering power sends it own soldiers to control the vanquished territory, so Moscow sends its communist administrators and Communist Party agents from Moscow.

Another benefit which is claimed for Soviet policy is that the Soviets have held the vast empire intact. But the fact is that the Soviet empire is held intact, not because of the Soviet idea but in spite of it. Much pressure is used to suppress opposition to Soviet principles. If the present method of government and suppression of individual liberty were to be permanent, then the maintenance of such an immense area under Soviet control would have infinite possibilities of evil. On the other hand the gradual introduction of the ideas of popular government and individual liberty may make the Soviet Union a model of civilization, with vast potentialities for good.

6. Internal Peace and Order. Again it has been asserted that the people must endorse the government because the country is quiet and at peace. But the peace and quiet is not spontaneous or voluntary. The same might have

been said of the Russian government under the Tsar. Then also there seemed to be domestic peace and quiet because powerful forces operated to keep the masses under control. True, under the Tsar a small, selfish, unprogressive, hereditary monarchy exploited the masses and fomented the murder of its innocent subjects. It was evil in its intention. In this regard the present régime is in direct contrast. In both cases, however, there is little freedom for the individual. There is pressure by a minority to keep the masses in line.

E. Social Results

The social-welfare program of the Soviet is an important contribution to the well-being of the population. But the program of insurance against the inevitable crises of life was copied from the capitalist countries. Lloyd George in 1911 said that if he wanted to see progressive social legislation in operation he would go to Germany. In the third decade of the present century Russia is apparently going to Germany for her model of insurance against accident, sickness, unemployment, old age and death.

1. Favorable Factors. a. New Attitude toward Money. A clear social gain is the changed attitude toward money and toward the accumulation of wealth. In the western world generally the individual bends his energies to the accumulation of a fortune for himself. In Soviet Russia the accumulation of much wealth is not permitted, therefore human energies are diverted to other objectives.

b. Social Equality. Another important gain is the removal of prejudice against races and colored peoples. This equality is not theoretical; there is no color line in Russia: they do have white, yellow and brown peoples. Manifestation of race prejudice is a punishable offense. Equality of nationalities and of cultural minorities is a striking characteristic of the Soviet régime.

c. Abolition of Hereditary Privilege. Hereditary privilege has been abolished. Each individual must make his own career. He cannot inherit wealth, social position, or privilege except in a limited way. Even though the new aristocracy consists of the manual laborers who have privileges in educational opportunities and in travel, yet even these privileges are not hereditary. Retention of position in this class depends upon continued labor and service to the community. Professor Calvin Hoover stresses this aspect strongly:

> The creation of a system of life which has displaced the money standard of measurement must be registered as a distinct contribution to human welfare. In Soviet Russia, men do not devote their time to money-making activities, in order to ape the standards of living of the wealthy leisure class. The servility

> induced by the desire to obtain monetary rewards has almost disappeared. Tipping is an alien element in the Soviet system. Private wealth hardly exists in Soviet Russia. There is no class which has a special position on account of wealth ownership. Power, influence and authority are not accorded to fools, incompetents and mediocrities, merely because of their wealth.[5]

d. Improved Domestic Relations. Not the least of the clear social gains of the Soviet system are the more liberal divorce laws. Divorce is not made contingent upon the archaic system of perjury prevalent in the western world. On the other hand, the abuse of the divorce privilege is checked. Repeated divorce is regarded as anti-social conduct.

It is interesting to note, however, in vindication of the marriage system prevailing in the western world, that after a short period of extreme liberality in domestic relations, the pendulum seems to have swung in the other direction and the Soviets, after trying their radical doctrines, have come back to a simple and austere life in matters of personal conduct.

2. Unfavorable Factors. a. New Submerged Classes. Not only have classes not been abolished but new and more classes have been created. Under the old régime there were in agriculture two classes, the landlords and the peasants. Now the peasants are further divided into "rich" peasants, "middle" peasants, poor peasants, and landless workers. In industry there are the office workers and the manual laborers, and the manual laborers are further divided into skilled and unskilled, all with different caste privileges. While the new nobility consists of the poor and landless peasants and the unskilled manual laborers, the other classes grade off through the tolerated classes to the new underdogs. The latter include the numerous official groups of social pariahs, the kulaks, and the *lishentzi,* including private traders, ex-noblemen, priests, lawyers, etc. These are the new proletariat. The favored groups have preference in food, medical facilities, and travel probably because their loyalty is required for the maintenance of the régime. Because of the favored status of the working class, many prospective students first become manual laborers in order to obtain admission to the universities. On the other hand the status of the laborer is so much superior to that of most professional classes that many prefer to remain laborers rather than follow an intellectual career. Such a scheme is obviously anti-social. Its duration can be only temporary.

b. Individualism Suppressed. Social forces have been given great scope at the expense of individualism. Individual initiative as a driving force is curtailed. The individual is supposed to seek the good of his class rather than of himself. Loyalty to the family is regarded as a remnant of bourgeois traditions;

loyalty should go to all of society. The building up of a home is discouraged. These energies are supposed to go to the furtherance of the Five-Year Plan. What often passes as communism is really repression of the individual and restriction of his initiative.

The "party theorists" in Soviet Russia concoct theories to prove that communism is the ideal form of social organization. But the philosophers of the western world have been no less ready to construct theories to justify the principles of individualism. The effectiveness of individualism in building up a civilization which functioned fairly well led to several theories to justify it philosophically. The economists proved that competition of individuals created western civilization, therefore the government should not check the free play of these forces. In other words, the struggle of individuals resulted in benefit to the community. The philosophy of individualism was developed by economists, sociologists, and political thinkers. It received added support from the biological theory that competing individuals created the struggle for existence that resulted in the survival of the fittest. Therefore, restrictions or regulations by society interfere with the natural progress of man. The biologists said: "What survives works," and the pragmatists said: "What works is true." Much as the critics of capitalism may ridicule this theory, communism itself must meet the test of competition with other systems and of survival. If it does not work, it is not true.

c. Violent Reversals of Policy. Because the entire Soviet experiment depends on pioneering in new fields, the approach must always be through the experimental attitude—through trial and error. A series of reversals of policy is the result. For example, in the agricultural program, at first the peasants were told to take the land from the landlords, and then the government reassembled the land in large collectives. First, huge state farms were established, then they were reduced to a more manageable size. At first the officials forced agricultural co-operation ruthlessly, and then when trouble arose Stalin denounced the policy and ordered that all entry into the co-operatives be voluntary. Again at first the government prohibited the slaughter of cattle, and then, when food became scarce, the government reversed itself and not only authorized, but encouraged the private breeding and private slaughter of cattle, relying on the motive of private profit to stimulate production. At first the government took over all the crops, over and above a fixed amount, estimated at what the peasant needed, and then, as a result of the famine, reversed itself and took only a fixed amount and let the peasant keep the rest. Subsequently, the government paid for this fixed amount at an official low price, but when production was curtailed, it relied on the old motive of individual profit, reducing the quotas purchased at fixed prices and not only permitting but encouraging the sale of the balance on the open market at a price dictated by competition. As stated above Trotsky showed how the Stalin faction reversed itself a number of times in the policy of rapid industrialization.[1] First, Stalin was opposed to rapid industrialization. After ousting its proponents, he accelerated the speed and a new opposition resulted, which would slow down the speed of industrialization, because of the shortage of consumers' goods and because of the general want and distress. This opposition was squelched, but a second reversal of policy was inaugurated, which retarded the heavy industries and accelerated the light industries.

These zigzags in policy were not always voluntary, or the result of political insight or statesmanlike vision. Most of the reverses were forced upon the Soviets by stubborn realities.

> The civil war and economic ruin had brought about such misery that many of the Bolsheviks themselves lost faith in their leaders and became incensed against them. . . . This led to a general strike in Petrograd and Moscow at the end of February 1921 and, in conjunction with this, a rising of the nucleus of the Bolshevik troops, to whom they owed their victory most, viz., the sailors who revolted in Kronstadt (near Petrograd). . . . The communists felt that the monopoly of their party in the state was threatened. The danger became serious when the sailors took up the cause of liberty for the workers and peasants. They did not send delegates to the government, but acted as Lenin and Trotsky had taught them to do; they took up arms. . . . The crushing of the Kronstadt revolt after much bloodshed was certainly successful, but the warning did not fall upon deaf ears. The only means of making any impression on the Bolsheviks had, up till then, been by actual or threatened revolts. . . . In reply to the revolt, Lenin announced the "New Economic Policy" (Nep). This loosened the reins of the dictatorship both in the towns and in the country as far as production of, and trading in, goods was concerned. From now on, the "communism" which had been in force for three years, and in the name of which hundreds of thousands of people had gone to the prisons, concentration camps, the dungeons of the Cheka, and thence to death, was no longer described as "a work of social construction" but as War Communism, a painful necessity, the forced result of the civil war.[6]

Lenin, a man of heroic mold and large vision, thereupon stated at the Tenth Congress of the Communist Party in the same month as the revolt: "Life has shown us our mistake. Our attempt at the transition to communism sustained a defeat more serious than ever before." This is a clear thinker's courageous confession of error forced by the low industrial output and agrarian opposition. However much the leaders might try to gloss it over by calling it a strategic retreat, the new economic policy, the Nep, was an admission of failure.

Another reversal of policy forced by armed resistance of the masses occurred in the spring of 1930. The ruthless collectivization of the farms and the attempt to eliminate the kulak had to be suspended. The peasants resisted, but troops were sent to suppress the revolt. However, many of the officers came from kulak families; in fact upon their return to their homes many soldiers found their parents sent to distant parts. It is even said that the troops refused to obey orders to shoot the resisting peasants. The advocates of a speedy collectivization realized the error of their policy. Not by ballots but by armed resistance was the Kremlin led to reverse its policy. Stalin unexpectedly appeared as a defender of the peasants who had been mistreated by the agents of collectivization. His article, "Dizziness from Success" [7] was a signal of retreat from the policy of hasty and compulsory collectivization.

As an element of a method, a willingness to reverse a policy is essential to a program of experimentation. But the experimental attitude is not valid everywhere. You may try everything once—except death. The killing of cattle during the enforced collectivization of live stock may require a decade to rectify. Such reversals of policy can be traced throughout the entire economic scheme, in wages, in industrial management, in governmental loans. Saving by the individual was originally discountenanced, and later encouraged because of the financial needs of the Soviet budget. In an uncharted field and lacking a pattern to work on, Soviet policy must necessarily be hand-to-mouth. On a great scale such reversals of policy are inefficient and costly. They have an unsettling effect on progress and on the loyalties of the various classes in the community. Even the credo changes, until the faithful no longer know whether they are believers or heretics.

d. Lowered Standard of Living. Visitors who have returned repeatedly to Russia say that consumers were worse off in 1931 than in the years 1925 to 1930. Under the Nep the department stores had stocks for sale of such goods as shoes, shirts, and clothing. Now the stores are bare. Food was available and although under the system of private trade prices were high, the quality was good. Now food is available only in limited quantities, and the quality is inferior, though the fixed prices are reasonable. The abolition of the New Economic Policy and the vigorous prosecution of the Five-Year Plan have greatly depressed the standard of living, so that even the minimum standards are not attained in some parts of the Union. As for comparison with foreign countries, the condition of the laborer, say in post-war Argentina or Canada, is undoubtedly superior to that of the laborer in Russia.

According to an American newspaper correspondent in Moscow, a Russian youngster, son of an engineer, told his playmates about the things he had seen in America. What impressed him most was that the stores were filled with all sorts of merchandise, that there were no empty shelves, and that purchasers did not have to present a ration ticket or wait in line to buy.

3. New Names for Old Evils. a. Exploitation Continues. The so-called exploitation of labor by private capital has been abolished, but new exploiters have appeared on the scene. They are now the Soviet managers and the bureaucrats in industry. These managers are often ruthless and will cut wages in order to show profits. The peasant is now being exploited by the towns. His grains are taken from him at low fixed prices, and other commodities are exchanged therefor at high prices. The exploitation by the large land owners is gone, but the government requisitions are even a more ruthless form of exploitation. The profits formerly taken by the owners of industry, or the so-called exploiters, are now absorbed by incompetent bureaucrats. The exploited classes in both cases are still the same. The standard of living of the workman cannot be said to have improved. The sins charged to the capitalist system have persisted under a new guise. The rebels have destroyed old injustices but have substituted new injustices.

b. Reappearance of Capitalism. The revolution destroyed the old capitalism. But a new capitalism arose because of class differences among the peasants. The competent and the incompetent, the prudent and the reckless, the thrifty and the wasteful, fell into two new classes, the "newly rich" peasants, the kulaks, and those who sold or leased their land and hired themselves out as landless laborers. So long as human capacities vary, the economic status of individuals will vary.

Furthermore, capitalism was never really eliminated. Private capitalism has been replaced by state capitalism. Even though the names are socialist, the institutions in Soviet Russia are capitalist.

4. Sudden Changes vs. Gradual Development. In the history of civilization or even pre-history, social evolution has generally been a gradual process. The old gradually merges into the new. From the hunting stage thousands of years ago to modern mass production, the change was imperceptible. Similarly the form of social organization varied from communist, as in the

hunting stage, to individualist as in the pastoral stage. The artisan was an individualist, but the industrial worker under mass production became socialized. Machinery makes him one of the interdependent specialists in production. Because sound social growth usually is gradual, the sudden changes in Russia seem premature. As a result, crises arise. Statesmanship and social vision justify a slower rate of change.

5. CONTRASTS WITH CAPITALISM. The Soviet social system differs from others in its attitude toward the exceptional individual and toward the average. A society which gives free scope to individual initiative and stimulates individual effort by large rewards is designed for the small fraction, or what the intelligence test might call the supernormal. Such a system elicits talent and genius and gives it free scope. The Soviet system is designed for the masses. It is less concerned with developing the genius than with helping the mediocre and sub-average. Our society is designed to raise the superior individual to great heights; Soviet society is designed to prevent the inferior from falling to great depths. Is it possible to develop a society in which the best of both systems can be preserved? Can Russia permit the genius to develop and thus serve the masses? Can our society pay more attention to sub-average men? In some respects Germany seems to have reached the happy medium among the nations. She has thus far been the leader in social welfare, without at the same time imposing a repressive hand upon the superman, in whatever class he may be found.

Our society calls for equality of opportunity and personal freedom. The Soviet régime calls for restriction of individual freedom and a large measure of social control. In the words of Nicholas Murray Butler:

> Liberalism builds upon equal opportunity for each individual and looks to such control and guidance of social and economic forces as will make this equality of opportunity a reality, and not a mere formula. Communism on the other hand accepts an economic system (capitalism) to which it takes violent exception as the basis for the erection of a class state with a class government.[8]

Equality of opportunity broadens the base on which the social structure may be reared. In Great Britain, for instance, the base of the pyramid has been narrow; the ruling class politically and industrially has come from a small fraction of the population. In the United States on the other hand the base is broad; the heads of big business, our leading scientists, and men high in politics usually rise from the ranks, as President Hoover pointed out in his address at King's Mountain. Neither the system of Soviet Russia nor any other will be able to show greater equality of opportunity than now prevails in some of the younger, so-called capitalist countries, the United States, Canada, Australia, etc.

Common ground will probably be reached by the Soviets' abandonment of some of their unworkable theories and the western world's moving toward Soviet ideals.

F. Spiritual Results

1. Gains. a. Changing Human Nature. After the French Revolution the release from the repressions of the old régime gave the French people a new character. Likewise since the destruction of the Tsarist régime a new psychology has developed among the Russians.

The lethargic Slavic peasant is to become an energetic industrial worker. Human energies repressed under the Tsar have been released under the Soviets. The hobbling effect of tradition under the Tsar has been replaced by a mobility and receptiveness to change, which is the basis of future progress. The gospel of work is becoming popular in Russia. The very character of the people is changing. Though the Five-Year Plan may fail in its material aspect, it should succeed in its psychological aspects, inspiring the nation to intense activity. It is because the people are by nature so inert and so slow to respond, that propaganda which is wearying to the westerner is necessary and acceptable to the Russians. They need continuous repetition to drive home the program of changing human nature. Like the cigarette advertisements in the United States, which repeat their simple monotonous message day after day and thus succeed in changing the habits of many American people, so the slogans, banners, and propaganda that assail Russian eyes everywhere every day are designed to change their habits and nature.

The messages are varied. The chief message is subordination of the wishes of the individual to the needs of the community, the message of duty to the state, as against personal satisfaction. Entertainment for its own sake is an unworthy aim. Prohibition is preached as a social good. The conduct held up to Soviet workers is the altruistic life in the service of the state.

b. Wealth vs. Power. The struggle of the individual for wealth has been suppressed in Soviet Russia. The energies of men now seek new outlets and there is a struggle for power. All the wiles, devices, and subterfuges which characterize the acquisition of wealth are now pressed into service in the search for power. Under the so-called capitalist system wealth is a source of power, influence, and social standing, but in the Soviet system power is sought indirectly, through political promotion. Sycophancy and nepotism are utilized to curry favor with the political leaders. Power has shifted from the men of wealth to men of political position. Even though the members of the Communist Party are limited in nominal wages, the total compensation of higher officials, most of whom are members of the Communist Party, is not limited, but is increased and graduated by an abundance of goods and services which are placed at the disposal of the various classes in the hierarchy of officialdom.

Replacement of material values by spiritual values marks a psychological advance for the race. The removal of the incentive for personal gain, and the public discountenancing of personal display have eliminated the incentive for public graft and private cheating. If money has so little value, why steal it?

c. Enthusiasm and Ideals. Capitalism is efficient; it gives the individual satisfaction. But it has no spiritual appeal. On the other hand, communism has proven inefficient, but it gives intangible satisfactions. Service to the community generates enthusiasm. This idealism may be a passing phase, incidental to the creating of a new order. It is too early to say that it is permanent. But it is an interesting fact that the widow of Lenin is engaged in active and useful work. Exiled presidents of Latin American republics retire to foreign countries with fortunes at their disposal, but Trotsky is living without means in Turkey, and has to write for a living.

An idealism pervades the Russians at present. They are trying to erect a social structure that will be a model for the world to follow. A strong feeling of service to mankind runs through their aims and policies.

d. Abolition of Illiteracy. The purposeful and intense attempt to raise the cultural level of the masses is a distinct spiritual gain. In connection with the All-Russian Congress on Universal Education, in Moscow, February 19, 1931, *Izvestia* stated that—

> The "liquidation of illiteracy" is going forward very rapidly in the Soviet Union. In 1913 it was estimated that at most 27 per cent of the population of Tsarist Russia was literate, while in 1930 about 62 per cent of the people of the U.S.S.R. were literate. If the program is successfully carried through, the literacy among the Soviet population will be raised to 75 per cent during 1931, which surpasses the goal set by the cultural Five-Year Plan for 1933, providing that between eighteen and nineteen million persons should be accommodated in the *likbez* courses [for the liquidation of illiteracy].

In the streets of Moscow, in the factories, in the dining rooms, everywhere, there is the appeal to the masses, "Learn to read and write." Slogans herald the progress in liquidating illiteracy and hold out the hopes for its complete elimination. By the middle of August 1931, there were more than 55 million children (or more than 97 per cent of the total) enrolled in the four-year course.[9] Newspaper circulation in Russia is tremendous. *Pravda* has a circulation of more than 1.5 millions, *Izvestia* of more than a million, and the *Peasants' Gazette,* a farmers' tri-weekly, has a circulation of more than 2.5 millions. Altogether there are about 257 newspapers in the large towns, and 1100 in the small towns, and a very much larger number of factory house organs. The total circulation of newspapers is estimated to be more than 35 times greater than before the war. The national minorities have more than 500 newspapers, printed in 67 different languages and dialects.[10]

Here the foundations are being laid for some ultimate kind of democracy ultimately. It is questionable whether in the present state of illiteracy in Russia the people could exercise popular control as effectively as in Germany. The zeal for popular education is one of the indications that the present oligarchy means to prepare the people for ultimate control; indeed such control is inevitable, when the educational program is complete.

e. Abolition of Superstition. The crass superstition in which the Greek Orthodox clergy kept the peasantry steeped has been abolished. In the antireligious museum in Moscow one sees wax models of the impoverished peasants bringing to the well-fed and well-clothed priest at Easter time their offerings of poultry, geese, etc. He in turn would wave a few stalks of wheat over the fields and curse the bugs and pests for the peasants, that they might have a good harvest. It is difficult for the followers of a modern, enlightened faith to conceive the depths of superstition and sorcery to which the priests permitted the mujiks to fall. One of the icons in Moscow had two outlets in the eyes, through which, according to the Soviet guide, the priests squirted drops of water with a rubber ball, and these "tears" were reported to have been sold to the devout believers. The Church apparently used the superstitions of the people as a means for intrenching the Tsarist régime.

With the fall of Tsardom superstition has been swept away. Life is viewed more realistically. In the Revolutionary Museum, next to the model of the priest cursing the insect pests and abjuring them to depart, and blessing the seed, is another model of peasants fertilizing the soil, plowing with tractors and applying insect powder.

2. Losses. a. Materialistic Philosophy. In brushing away the structure of superstition some of the deepest spiritual truths have been displaced. The air of Russia is permeated with a gross materialistic philosophy. The revo-

lutionists rejected the worship of a Divine Being, and the whole nation is worshiping dynamos and machines. One has but to watch the workmen patting the machines as if they were alive, or to listen to enthusiastic Bolsheviks seeking salvation through machinery. They have discarded the old superstitions and have adopted new ones.

This materialistic outlook on life is reflected in the very names of their children. The Pilgrims called their girls Faith, Hope, Charity, Patience, Mercy, Comfort, Prudence, etc., but the Bolsheviks give their children mechanical names. Chamberlain [11] quotes among girls' names, Elektrifikátzia, Barrikáda, and one baby girl was called Diamata, which is the Soviet abbreviation for dialectic materialism. The dynamo has become the iron calf, which the "generation of the wilderness" in Russia is now worshiping.

The change in the spiritual attitude in Russia is symbolized in one fact. The engineer has replaced the priest. The Five-Year Plan has become both catechism and creed. The shortage of material comforts has made Russians idealize the material things of life, for the human mind idealizes the things it lacks. They interpret spiritual values in mechanical terms. They idealize machinery.

b. Lust for Power. The lust for power has been intensified. Under the system of capitalism power is obtained through money; in Soviet Russia it is obtained through office. And the evils of capitalism crop out. Office is held by loyal communists and former revolutionary propagandists. Therefore, incompetents also hold power. Servility to money, which characterizes the capitalist régime, is replaced by servility to a higher office. Chicanery in acquiring wealth in the capitalist world is replaced by chicanery in acquiring office in the communist world. Log rolling and small politics, as satirized on the Soviet stage, are the by-product of this striving for power. The clever manner in which the present Soviet leaders have gradually eliminated their rivals for power is worthy of a Croker or a Murphy in Tammany Hall.

The quest for power and for admiration of the multitude may be an expression of a sense of inferiority. Stalin has permitted the naming after him of three cities, numerous villages, collective farms, factories, etc. Factories have also been named in occasional cases, though less lavishly than in the case of Stalin, after other members of the Politbureau. If communism requires the homely virtues, an ascetic way of life, poverty, obedience, and simplicity, the extravagant expression of power does not seem in keeping with it.

Stalin is accused of making himself dictator, but he justifies his strong single-handed control of affairs on the grounds of the needs of the country. In this he conforms to the historic type. Even the Tsarist régime and all the tyrannies that preceded it identified their own interests with the welfare of the masses. They constructed a theory to justify their maintaining absolute power.

Power is sought not merely by individuals but by classes. The manual laborers, the *rabochiye,* seek power at the expense of the other classes of workers. There is as much log-rolling, lobbying, and pork-barrel politics on behalf of classes in Russia as there is on behalf of geographical sections in other countries.

c. Suppression of Individuality. Since individual freedom and initiative is suppressed, there is little urge to achieve, little urge to grow. Since the individual cannot hope to build anything for himself, personal ambition declines. Since he has little voice in how he shall live or what he shall eat, he becomes an obedient servant to the state. His will bows to the collective will. Independence of judgment has little opportunity for expression. Life is not a great adventure, it is a supine resignation. The individual cannot hope to do things; he therefore expects to have things done for him. Yet the old Adam rises in the bosoms of the Russians at times, as evidenced by the great interest in the lottery loans.

To the extent that the individual is denied reward for additional effort whether in factory or farm he can only work less intently, less boldly, less daringly. The unfavorable spiritual effect upon the community is inevitable.

Bordering Central Park in New York are a series of new tall towers built in the boom years by men who took great risks. Today most of the builders and erstwhile owners are either bankrupt or living in greatly reduced circumstances. One of them has a temporary salaried position with the bank attempting to liquidate his assets. The catastrophe in the western world has probably wiped out fortunes almost to as great an extent as the Bolshevik revolution. In fact by a strange coincidence, one Russian entrepreneur lost a fortune twice. He began as a small oil merchant in the Baku District and rose to become a multi-millionaire in St. Petersburg, owner of a large bank, mines, forests, sugar factories, and docks and harbor works in the port of St. Petersburg. The Bolshevik revolution wiped out all but that small fraction of his wealth which was invested abroad. He came to New York in 1919 and in the next ten years had built up another fortune, which the present catastrophe also wiped out. Communism as a leveling force was no more disastrous to wealth than the present world crisis of capitalism.

Under both systems, a redistribution of wealth takes place, but in the western world the opportunities for the entrepreneur still remain open. The principle of risk-taking by the individual still prevails. In Soviet Russia no individual takes any risks. The state takes the risks and up to date has proven itself less competent than individuals in developing backward countries and has demonstrated its capacity for making mistakes on a scale so huge as would bankrupt private capital. The elimination of the initiative of the individual is bound to prove a loss to society.

d. Propaganda. To convince the masses and to keep them convinced a veritable stream of propaganda and misinformation is fed to the public. On matters of common knowledge in the western world the Soviet masses are kept in complete ignorance. The capitalist world is always painted in dark colors; the Bolshevik world is always glorified. Every minor unfavorable incident in the capitalist world is magnified through the moving pictures. The theater, instead of being devoted to art, is in the main an agency for popularizing the Five-Year Plan. A play the writer happened to see in Moscow was concerned with a committee of inspectors who visited a plant, and a vaudeville performance at the Hermitage Theater was devoted to the wiles and worries of the manager of a collective store, to the disapproval of the display of finery by girls, and to similar items of Soviet propaganda. A moving picture film showed the military drill of the Soviet Army, a drinking scene in the night life of Berlin and other views disparaging capitalism. In the broadcasting of propaganda, every manner of approach is made to the public attention. To the visitor the atmosphere eventually becomes suffocating and he longs for a respite and a bit of truth, freshness, and reality.

e. Force, Fear, and Violence. Perhaps the most serious spiritual loss under the Soviet régime is the prevalence of force and fear. In strange contrast to the lofty ideals are the ruthless measures which are used to realize them. Suspicion, distrust, hatred, force, terrorism, violence, these are degrading characteristics of Russian spiritual life. This may not be essentially communist; it may be a hangover from the tradition and habits of the Tsarist régime. But regardless of its origin, it is in strange contrast to the high pretensions of the Soviet régime.

People in Russia seem to have an uneasy feeling that they are under surveillance. They give that impression constantly. This holds not only for native Russians, who timidly hint at strange sorts of happenings. Foreigners are more frank. One newspaper correspondent in Moscow with strong anti-Soviet prejudices, and now no longer in Russia, refused to discuss Soviet affairs in the lobby of the Grand Hotel in Moscow, for fear of being shadowed. He suggested he could talk more freely in the writer's room. On entering, the correspondent noticed the telephone instrument, of the Ericsson movable box type. He pushed the large box to the outside window sill and closed the French windows saying, "Most of these boxes are dictaphones, and it is prudent to be suspicious. This hotel is filled with secret police." Allowing even for his anti-Soviet bias and his desire to place the Soviet régime in an unfavorable light, one could not help being impressed by his fears. The writer had no personal unpleasant experience, of any kind. Despite his frank criticism of Soviet economic methods, he was unmolested during the entire trip and had no difficulties at the border, even though he had in his possession a number of books, probably on the *Index Expurgatorius* of the Soviets, such as Paul Scheffer's *Sieben Jahre Sowjetunion* (Italian), then a best seller in Berlin bookshops, and Istrati's *Russland Nackt.*

Trotsky, one of the most extreme advocates of force in the heyday of his power, complains of the repression of his followers by the group now in control.[1]

Early in 1928 mass raids against the Opposition were carried out—expulsions, arrests, banishments. During that same year a new five-year plan was carried into action, following upon all essential questions the platform of the Left Opposition. This about-face was so sharp that the bureaucracy came into direct opposition to everything that it had defended during the first four years after Lenin's death. The accusation of super-industrialism lost all meaning, and active repressions against Left Opposition still more so.

But here the interest of the new ruling stratum in its own self-preservation stepped to the front. If the Opposition was right in its judgments and proposals, so much the worse for the Opposition. If yesterday's arguments against it are worthless, we must have new ones—and in order to justify repressions we must have extraordinarily bitter ones. It is just in this sphere, however, that Stalin is especially gifted.

It was not enough, however, to bring forward fantastic accusations; it was necessary that people should believe them, or at least be afraid to object. In its struggle for self-preservation the Stalin bureaucracy was, therefore, compelled to begin by suppressing all criticism. Along this line, accordingly, the Opposition opened its most fervent struggle—a struggle for a democratic régime in the party, in the trade unions, in the Soviets.

Tens of thousands of so-called "Trotskyists" were excluded from the party. More than 10,000 were subjected to various forms of criminal repression. Several were shot. Many tens of thousands of fighting revolutionists of the first draft were retained in the party only because they turned away and kept their mouths shut. Thus in the course of these years not only the membership of the ruling stratum has completely changed, but also the inner régime of the Bolshevist Party.

The shattering of the Opposition has become at the same time a shattering of the party of Lenin. This shattering has been promoted by deep although transitory causes.

Communism as a social philosophy is associated with co-operation, faith, love, kindness, good will, understanding, and rational moral suasion. But none of these traits is evident in communism at work. There is no liberty. Imprisonment, exile, and death are penalties imposed without legal protection for the accused. The shooting of the scientists in September 1930, without a trial, outraged the opinion of the world. The punishment of technicians because the Five-Year Plan does not work smoothly is a condemnation alike of the competence and the conscience of the Soviet régime.

Communism has come to be associated inevitably with terror and violence. "In Soviet Russia there is not alone bitterness, but more. Communism has not brought peace to Russia but a sword."[12] Again:

> The three outstanding evils of communism are a dictatorship with its constant danger of tyranny, the policy of world revolution by violence and destruction, and the attitude of bigotry and intolerance. . . . Under the alchemy of communism they are to sow dictatorship and reap liberty, to sow hatred and reap love, to sow violence and destruction and reap lasting peace and brotherhood ever afterward. This policy of world revolution involves complete reliance on force and the distrust of moral suasion and the principle of consent. It involves contempt for all patient, evolutionary, constitutional, and educational means.[13]

3. Moot Questions. Civilization, as we know it, is the external expression of human nature. Society is what it is because individual instincts are what they are. So long as human beings are dominated by instincts of anger, sex, love of power, parental affection, sense of property, etc., so long will our society by and large remain what it is. Slow changes in human behavior and in social tradition will bring about corresponding changes in social institutions. For this reason many of the new institutions devised by the Soviets are likely to fail. The educational process cannot be compressed into a Five-Year Plan. Over a period of several generations the world as a whole will move toward the ideals of the Soviets, and it will do so not by the fiat of any congress, but rather through slow educational processes and the development of new ideals of social living.

The ease and abundance enjoyed by the few under the Tsarist régime led to its degeneration and downfall. It died with no hope or expectation of any return. It had outlived its day. The privation of the present generation is deplorable, and it is a question whether any government has the right to impose it for the sake of potential benefit to a future generation. But suffering seems inseparable from life and growth. Every new birth is attended by suffering.

Russia is in the pangs of labor. The suffering of the masses may spiritualize them in spite of their rejection of religion, and probably a new and cleaner religion will arise on the wreck of the old.

G. Conclusions

To speak of conclusions in a country like Soviet Russia, a society in transition, is indeed difficult. All that one can say at the present stage is that some of the aims have been realized, at least in part, and some have failed. One may conclude that, while the Soviet régime is an advance over the Tsarist régime, it fails to measure up to its own standards, or to those of most capitalist countries. The scene is changing rapidly, and Russia is still evolving. Results cannot yet be truly assessed.

It was Krassin who remarked, with keen social insight, that any new social order must at the beginning compare unfavorably with the order it is displacing. The new order is an experiment, the old order is a finished product. After a period of trial and experiment the new order may prove the better.

1. Qualified Success. One may well apply to Russia Samuel Johnson's remark that it is not wonderful that the bear dances well, but that he dances at all. The Soviets set for themselves some very high aims. But with a primitive country, devastated by war more than that of any other great power, with a population largely illiterate, a personnel inadequate, untrained, and inexperienced, and antiquated industrial equipment, it is little wonder that the results are yet so meager. What a contrast between such high aspirations and such inadequate means of realizing them! As these handicaps are removed by education and the passing of time, the results should improve.

The social gains of revolution have been neither entirely lost, nor entirely retained. The social pendulum swings from reaction to radicalism. Some of the benefits of the French Revolution were transmitted throughout Europe. On the other hand some important gains of that revolution were lost, even to France itself.

By agile rationalization the leaders were able to delude themselves and convince the masses that the adoption of capitalism was a step toward communism. "The free exchange of goods," said Lenin, "may temporarily strengthen the petty bourgoisie and individual peasants, but in far greater degree it strengthens the proletariat." Stalin stated similarly that Nep meant a victory of the socialized elements over the capitalists. This capacity for explaining a retreat from communism as a step toward communism smacks of mediæval casuistry. Apparently, regardless of all the vacillation of policy from communism to capitalism and back again to communism, the only aim that was consistently maintained was the aim to industrialize Russia, whatever be the system, communism, state socialism, or even private capitalism.

2. SUCCESSES OF COMMUNISM. Undoubtedly the greatest success of communism is the social value of the experiment, *per se*. Not merely what it achieved, but even what it failed to achieve, is a contribution to social theory and social experience. The world is richer for the experiment. Variation in the political world is necessary. Out of it arises competition and struggle and survival of the fit. If the Russians are willing to try out the experiment in Soviet Russia, and not elsewhere, the world should be willing to watch its progress, certainly not to oppose it. It will be manifest to the world once and for all that communism was tested and did not work in the present state of civilization. The experiments, successes, and even the failures are a valuable addition to the experience of the human race.

The social experiment goes forward by stages. Following the failure of pure communism came state socialism as applied to agriculture, industry, and trade. In agriculture its success seems more likely than in trade and industry. In fact in industry the prize venture, the Stalingrad tractor plant, seems likely to prove a huge failure for some years. It is based on principles of mass production which can only work in a highly organized society with an efficient personnel. The social value of these great experiments is undeniable. Some observers, like Calvin Hoover, have said that the Soviets have proved that a socialist state can exist and that it is impossible to deny this fact. However, this is a large and unwarranted conclusion. All that one can say is that for fifteen years a socialist state has not fallen into chaos. That it has existed is true, but only at the cost of great sacrifice by the population. It has not proved that it can survive permanently nor has it proved that it can provide satisfaction to the masses equal or superior to private capitalism. The maximum proof it has provided is that it has not broken down in fifteen years of trial. Further one cannot say yet.

The very failures of the Soviets are of value. They vindicate the success of capitalist processes. For example, the attempt to eliminate individual reward for effort by paying equal wages broke down. To restore production, piece work and rewards for efficiency had to be utilized. Again, the communist notion of division of authority in factory management proved a failure, and the Soviets have reaffirmed their belief in strong, centralized, and responsible authority. And so on through the long list of communist failures and the adoption of capitalist methods as cited elsewhere.

Some sentimental Americans writing on Russia have pointed out the defects of our system as proof of the excellence of the Soviet system. This is an irrational argument. The Soviet system has not proven superior to ours.

Everywhere one meets native Russians trying to flee the country but not people voluntarily seeking to live and stay in Russia, in spite of widespread unemployment in the capitalist world. By means of large salaries the Soviets are trying to attract such foreign labor as is absolutely indispensable. Furthermore, Soviet engineers sent abroad have deserted in order to remain in capitalist countries, and in a few cases Russian engineers sent abroad to study have committed suicide rather than go back. This is in striking contrast to the flood of immigration which swamped America during the period of the opening of our west.

3. Failures of Communism. The failures of the communist régime are seen in its imitation of capitalism. Imitation is the compliment that failure pays to success. Obviously Lenin was a theorist without experience. No one really had any idea whether communism would work, perhaps not even himself. The Bolsheviks not only hitched their wagon to a star but actually proceeded to drive it thither.

Regarded from the point of view of biological evolution, the fauna and flora that have remained to this day have survival value under present conditions of climate and temperature. And so in the social world institutions that have persisted throughout many generations likewise have survival value. In the process of evolution some institutions die, such as feudalism, human slavery, etc. But it is unlikely that any change will develop a totally new world. And because existing institutions work moderately well, the Russians, confused by the failure of their doctrinaire régime, are beating an orderly and successful retreat toward the scheme that has worked elsewhere.

The world has proved too organic for a formula, too complex for a panacea. Evolutionary socialism has proved sounder than revolutionary communism. The former builds on the past, it moves slowly, it does not make a *volte face* or a strategic retreat continuously as the communists have had to do. It imposes no widespread privation on the masses. In the biological laboratories experiments are performed without much thought for the guinea pigs, because the ultimate application to human beings is the end in view. But in Soviet Russia human beings are the subjects of an experiment and they are in want. The area involved is almost as large as was affected by the World War, and as for the population, it affects a larger number than were affected by the Thirty Years' War.

A striking commentary on the failure of communism is made by Karl Kautsky, the venerable German socialist, who knew Karl Marx personally. Kautsky, advocate of evolutionary socialism, would be classed with moderates. He speaks frankly as a Menshevik, or as a constitutional or parliamentary socialist. The Kerensky revolution of 1917 aimed to give the land to the peasants, to free the mujik from landlordism. It democratized the army, destroyed the old reactionary government, and established freedom of speech, of the press, and of assembly. It laid the foundations of industrial democracy, and established the beginning of self-government. The Bolsheviks utilized this freedom to destroy the republican régime. They set up a dictatorship based on force. According to Karl Kautsky, Lenin's attempt, by means of terrorism, to build in a brief period in primitive Russia the most advanced social system, is a mark of recklessness, based on ignorance and lack of vision. Collectivization is really mass expropriation and enslavement of the peasantry, and is really counter-revolutionary. Similarly, in industry the trade unions were replaced by organizations servile to the bureaucracy, and under one pretext or another labor was drafted, longer hours were introduced, and labor standards were lowered. Briefly, the Bolsheviks destroyed liberty, deceived the working class, reintroduced serfdom in agriculture, and have become the new feudal lords. The spirit of tolerance and kindliness which characterized the liberal régime has been replaced by a spirit of force and terrorism against the so-called enemies of the Soviets. The attitude toward the non-laboring classes is characterized by sadism and a spirit of brutality and revenge. Kautsky regards the Bolshevik rule not as progress but as reaction from the brief republican interlude, just as the Napoleonic régime was the reaction from the republicanism of revolutionary France.[14]

4. Capitalism vs. Communism. George Theunis, former premier of Belgium, speaking to the International Chamber of Commerce at Washington in May 1931, contrasted capitalism and communism:

> The two systems are in open conflict. On the one hand, there is the present western system, which, through the long and patient work of the centuries, has brought about a prosperity and well-being theretofore unknown. It is sufficient to have a superficial acquaintance with the United States to realize how far all the social strata have benefited from that civilization through a considerable improvement in their standard of living.
>
> This economic system is based on private initiative, on the development of the individual, and on the maintenance of personal liberty in the greatest possible measure. . . .
>
> On the other hand, the system which is proposed by the Soviets as the ideal

system reduces the individual to the rôle of an inert organ, a part of a vast machine which crushes him by its formidable strength.

The total suppression of personal liberty, the absolute subjection to anonymous orders—such are the characteristics of this régime. All classes, from the peasant to the workman, are reduced to a state of complete slavery, under the absolutism of an all-powerful, heartless, and pitiless bureaucracy.

The two systems may be tested with respect to their capacity for economic production, the better distribution of the social surplus, the greater freedom of the individual, the greater security against the crises of life, and greater opportunity for self-realization of the individual. As the inadequacy of money as the source of happiness becomes more generally realized, the urge to acquire wealth, even if not by anti-social means, will diminish. By lessening the gulf between the richest and the poorest, envy and covetousness will diminish. Undoubtedly communism, in spite of its failures, is having a profound effect on the western world. It is unlikely that as an efficient machine communism will ever be a threat to capitalism. But it may be a challenge or a stimulus. To threaten capitalism, communism must actually succeed, and it is not likely to do so. To stimulate, however, communism must merely strive toward an ideal. Then, even if it fails, it will at least point the way.

Hitherto private property, individual initiative, and freedom of opportunity were the basis of economic advance. These aspects characterize the early stage of an evolving community. As society becomes more organized, more complicated, and more co-ordinated, new economic methods and a new intellectual approach must be devised. As the world becomes more unified, more international co-operation is necessary in the production of wheat, copper, rubber, sugar, etc. The problem of the capitalist world is whether this can be done without the compulsion that characterizes Soviet Russia.

As the capitalist world matures economically it tends to become socialized. The individual is restrained, and the large private corporations tend to assume a quasi-public character. In the spring of 1930, when President Hoover attempted to check the depression, he called upon the large private corporations, the railroads and the utilities, to perform a public service, to keep up their maintenance programs and to continue their expansion. Disregarding the private interests of the shareholders, the officials of these corporations complied with the wish of the President in behalf of the public interest. Again, the President adopted the policy of maintaining wages and requested the presidents of large corporations not to reduce wages. Here again they subordinated the interests of their stockholders to the interests of the public.

Dividends were cut before wages were reduced. For example, though a 10 per cent cut in the wages of the United States Steel Corporation would be equivalent to earnings of $5.00 per share, the corporation maintained the wage scale of 1929 throughout all of 1930 and a large part of 1931.

The large private corporation assumes another characteristic of the public corporation in that pioneering is checked. For example, in the United States, the new processes in the steel industry were developed not by the United States Steel Corporation but by the small companies. The American Rolling Mills Company developed the continuous process for rolling steel. Ludlum Steel Company and Central Alloy Steel Company developed the stainless steel process, and several new processes for making pipe were developed by the Republic Iron & Steel Company, the U. S. Pipe & Foundry Company and other smaller corporations. At best, the gradual socialization of private capital will not prove an unmixed blessing.

5. Test of a Civilization. The test of the two systems, communism and capitalism, is: "Which can serve the masses better?" We do know that as a result of competition the cost to the consumer has been reduced very greatly. Our packers make 5 mills or less per dollar of sales, and then only through the very efficient utilization of by-products. Our chain grocers make 2 per cent on sales. It is a question whether any system will be able to show examples of more efficient administration. And if, as a result of incompetence or lack of incentive to the constructive individual, the communist régime cannot produce and distribute as efficiently, of what advantage will it be to the individual? How much should he be asked to pay for political theories of the Kremlin? What price communism?

However, capitalism must take steps to improve the economic condition of its least fortunate class. Capitalism represents a great disparity between the poorest and the richest, while on the other hand communism is a great leveling agent, although so far the leveling has been downward.

How much of an incentive is required to elicit the best efforts of the individual? The income tax returns for the year 1928 in the United States, as published by the Treasury Department, showed that the highest 10 per cent of the taxpayers earned 33 per cent of the total income, and thus received per capita 4.4 times as much as the remaining 90 per cent. If the income were distributed equally the 90 per cent of the taxpayers would get 23 per cent more of the total income. However, with individual initiative suppressed, the per capita income might be less absolutely though more relatively. Clearly, in providing incentives it is necessary to strike a certain balance. If the rewards are too little, no effort will be put forth. If the rewards are very great, the result may be exploitation of the community. The slow process of change is reflected in the increasing percentage of total realized income which is distributed in wages. According to the Report on Recent Economic Changes [15] employees in the United States in 1913 received 53 per cent of the total income and 59 per cent in 1925. In the latter year rents, interest, dividends, all were proportionately lower than in 1913.

Judged by the tests of progress mentioned the results in Soviet Russia indicate some genuine progress. Human knowledge has increased. Science and art are being increasingly applied to advance the welfare of man. Insurance and mutual aid are used to eliminate extreme suffering. Hereditary and other unearned privilege is being abolished. On the other hand other important tests tell of failure. There is no freedom of thought and of expression, no tolerance of minority views. There is no opportunity for the individual's self-development. Inequality between the citizens of the nation is increased rather than eliminated. Respect for law is diminishing, as the fear of government increases. The establishment of justice has been hindered, particularly with reference to the outlawed classes. Principles of conduct have not improved, with respect to others than the members of the favored class. Substitution of rational persuasion for force has not been achieved.

Striking a balance, one may say that the benevolent oligarchy which now rules Russia has failed on more tests of civilization than it has succeeded. As a whole, it is a vast improvement over the Tsarist régime. But it does not begin to measure up to the possibilities that inhere in a responsible republican régime, such as Russia was developing under the leadership of the constitutional party, and such as Russia ultimately must attain, when the present régime evolves in response to the freely expressed wishes of the population.

CHAPTER XV

FORECASTS

A. Limitations and Difficulties

To make categoric forecasts on Russia is impossible, as there are many limitations and difficulties. It is too early to make any final predictions. Russia is evolving and the possibilities are too varied to permit of precise prediction. In making forecasts, perspective is important. What is the goal of the Five-Year Plan? What is the condition from which this development began? It was not that of America of 1930 but rather that of Russia emerging from a semi-feudal state.

1. Rapidly Changing Factors. In a mechanical system, as in astronomy, the observer can make a forecast, because he knows either that conditions are not variable, or that the variations are under control and confined to certain scientific limits. But in the economic and social world not all the factors are known. For example, the extent of the decline in commodity prices throughout the world was an unpredictable factor. When the price of wheat dropped from $1.50 to 60 cents per bushel the Five-Year Plan was seriously affected. Similar unpredictable factors may qualify other forecasts. The scene changes almost from month to month and it is difficult to see more than a few months ahead. Long-range predictions have almost as little validity as crystal-gazing or fortune-telling. In fact the very aims change, and naturally the methods and results must change. Life consists of flying goals, some of which approach while others recede.

Again, the rate of social change conforms to a law similar in character to the law of gravitation,[1] that is change is accelerated with time. For example, the first invasion of property rights of the railroads in the United States met with great resistance, and took much time. But in the four years from 1916 to 1920 the concept of private property as applied to the railroads was whittled down much more rapidly than in the preceding 30 years. After public opinion becomes adjusted to the idea of a new tendency, social change is accelerated. It may be that the world at large will become accustomed to some of the Soviet ideas and the current resistance to them will yield in certain directions.

How can one predict the industrial effects of hastily constructing huge plants without the simultaneous training of personnel to run them? Or how can one predict the rate of depreciation of the currency, which if much accelerated would have a very profound adverse effect on the situation economically, politically, and socially? How can one predict the reaction of the masses to the failure to relieve the shortage of consumers' goods at the end of the first Five-Year Plan? Or how is it possible to predict at what point Slavic patience will break and precipitate social disorder? How can any one tell whether there is any minority sufficiently strong and capable of taking hold, should the present régime lose its control?

2. Delimitations of the Forecast. In forecasts concerning social forces, therefore, conclusions must be confined within certain limitations. In history no revolution or social movement has maintained all its pristine ideals. Christianity, the Reformation, the American Revolution, the French Revolution, the labor movement, all have lost some of their original ideals and their fresh approach to the problems of life. They became mature and less adaptable, institutionalized and crusted. The Russian Revolution will probably travel the same road. In its infancy it is filled with possibilities. In its adolescence it will have to approach problems of reality, and make adjustments to them. In its maturity it will become organized and finally set in its mold. On the other hand, every social movement retains some of its gains. Rarely are they all lost.

3. Human Factor. Predictions as to the movements of heavenly bodies can be made because they are inert, unconscious, and not self-moving. In society the human factor is exactly the reverse. For example, before 1914 political conditions throughout Europe seemed to be whirling the human race into the vortex of war, but there were possibilities for several men in high places to speak out to prevent the war. Again, in 1927, in the United States, it was the deliberate action of the Federal Reserve Board in easing money rates to check the flow of gold into the United States which resulted in the inflation of 1927–29. In Russia it was the political maneuvering between Stalin and Trotsky which resulted in the abandonment of the New Economic Policy and caused the new and intensive drive toward socialization. Trotsky

was veering to the extreme left. As shown elsewhere Stalin ousted him and then adopted his program. Now Rykov is pressing toward the right and pleading for a slower tempo. His personal influence alone could vitiate any forecast that an observer might now make.

Another unknown factor is the reaction of the Russian people. Patient as they are, they moved with terrific momentum in overthrowing the Tsarist régime. Who can tell what their reaction will be if at the end of the Five-Year Plan they find themselves still without adequate food, clothing, and shelter? How long will an idealism for the new order last on a long unfilled stomach? Already the public mind in Russia is being prepared for some additional Five-Year Plans, after the present plan shall have ended in 1932. Apparently new enthusiasm is to be manufactured to inspire an imponderable vote of confidence in the present régime.

Not least among the factors affecting any forecast is the peaceful compromise between the leaders to avert a break. Stalin ousted Trotsky and numerous other leaders, but more recently he has been reported to be looking with more favor toward Rykov, Bukharin, and their group. Compromise means less of a clear-cut policy.

4. Experience of the Race. In the western world, where the forces of history and evolution are working themselves out, one can make some prediction as to general trends. There is enough history to furnish the cue. Given any part of a curve in a circle or a parabola one can project the curve farther. But in Soviet Russia not enough history is available to permit a forward projection. In the case of a historic and continuous régime prediction is simpler than in a system based on untried doctrines and simplified formulas. It is uncertain to what extent the Soviets will adhere to their doctrines. Thus far they have veered, vacillated, and beaten strategic retreats. It is difficult to forecast whether they will continue their wholesale adoption of capitalist methods.

For the long range the experience of the race does provide a clue, namely: that advances of the race have generally been achieved by conflict. Except in very rare cases no ruling group, neither kings, nobles, nor ecclesiastics, has yielded power voluntarily. The racial tendency has been toward taking power from the few and distributing it to the many, whether this power be represented by the control of wealth, the control of government, or the control of men in other ways. The widening of the base of suffrage is merely one phase of this larger development. The experience of history would therefore indicate that the present oligarchy in Russia will go the way of all oligarchies, and that power will ultimately be returned to the great masses of the people, who will by universal suffrage determine their own destinies.

5. Time Factor. Some of the forecasts which the Russians themselves have made will probably come true. They will undoubtedly not come true within the expected time limit. The time factor is of great importance. Will Russia follow the economic history of America, Canada, Australia, the Argentine, and other young countries of the world? If so then the slogan of the Russians will have to be changed from "The Five-Year Plan in Four" to "The Five-Decade Plan in Five Decades." Civilization develops more slowly than the visions of the social prophet. The Five-Year Plan is part of a long program which will last many times five years. Will it be possible to continue to impose sacrifices over this inevitable length of time? Human endurance is not unlimited. Excessive heat, cold, or pain, can be endured only for limited periods, assuming even a great capacity for suffering. The Tsar ruled Russia with an iron hand, but the people were illiterate. Will the Soviets be able to rule a literate people, gaining in political education?

B. Economic Forecasts

Part of the Soviet program has been realized. Part of it has failed. There are some open questions which cannot yet be answered.

1. Favorable Forecasts. a. Abolition of Private Property and Development of State Capitalism. Very likely the institution of private property, as it now exists in the western world, will never wholly return to Russia. A new generation of Russians is rising which did not know the old concept and a return to it would be revolutionary to them. A young Russian asked an American resident if it was true that in America one man can own a factory and have thousands of workmen, or own houses and receive rents, or live without working. This state of mind is increasingly general. There is no mass impetus to bring about a restoration of private capitalism. Probably the individuals that would try to reacquire their former private property from the state would meet powerful opposition. In the words of Trotsky, "Things may take a backward turn. But the great things we have achieved will remain, the abolition of private ownership above all. The handing back of millions of acres to a couple of thousand idlers has become impossible." [2]

The state owns not merely the public-utility systems, but also the large industries, such as mining, iron, and steel, chemicals and textiles. It is difficult to conceive of the state relinquishing control. But it is not difficult to conceive of a breakdown of the state management, followed by private operation of all these state-owned industries with the state sharing in the profits.

The development of large co-operatives for the production of food, large co-operatives of consumers, agricultural co-operatives to buy fertilizer, machinery, and seed, and to sell the agricultural products co-operatively, credit co-operatives for the borrowing of long-term and short-term money, all of these economic developments, which are not new entirely, are probably permanent.

According to Kautsky, when a constitutional parliamentary régime emerges—

> —we must demand that the new Nep, like the old one of Lenin, but in a greater degree, must work in a way which will recognize the economic freedom gained, and permit free enterprises of capitalist, co-operative or communal nature to flourish side by side with state undertakings. Should the former work with more success, more cheaply, or deliver better products, pay better wages, etc., then the state undertakings should be given up, but not before it is proved. . . . The victorious democracy will have every reason to retain the state character of the natural monopolies, such, for instance, as the railways, the forests, the mines, and other mineral resources like petroleum. . . . Under these circumstances it is quite possible that even beyond the sphere of the natural monopoly there will be a good many branches of production in which nationalized production, after complete transformation to an economic democracy, will continue.[3]

b. Mechanization and Socialization of Agriculture. When the government requisitioned the grain supplies of the individual peasant, he resisted. Production declined. Thereupon the government proceeded to develop large-scale farming either on state lands or in the collectives. This involved mechanization. Actual progress has been made in this field, so much so that Stalin stated: "The Soviet Union will soon be the greatest agricultural nation in the world."[4] Of the many superlative forecasts made by Russians about Russia this one seems reasonably likely of realization. Furthermore, if Russia does become the world's leading agricultural producer, it may ultimately also become an important producer of agricultural machinery. Furthermore, mechanized farming involves the disappearance of the small individual holding. A tractor, combine, or harvester used by a group of peasants in a collective virtually compels the members to remain within the collective.

The mechanization of agriculture made socialization in the villages inevitable. To that extent it strengthened the socialization of industry. Had private capitalism remained in agriculture it would have constituted a continuous threat to state capitalism in industry. Thus far fair progress has been made in socializing both agriculture and industry.

The future courses of socialism in industry and in agriculture are interdependent. At present the peasants are exploited for the benefit of the towns. If the state farms and the collective farms do not succeed and if the individual peasant reverts to the small private holding, he may dictate the industrial policy. The peasantry will demand consumers' goods in return for their grain. The state will then not be able to continue the policy of developing the heavy industries and neglecting the consumers' goods industries. The latter are less standardized and less fitted for state operation. Development of the consumers' goods industries will swing the country toward private capitalism, leaving the major heavy industries and the railroad and utility systems under state control.

c. Industrialization of the Country. Regardless of whether socialism or capitalism be the form of the industrial development of Russia, one forecast may safely be made. Russia will become industrialized, if not in five years then in several times five years. This is the inevitable process of civilization. Countries rich in raw materials are developed, usually by foreigners, as was the case when private capital opened up Asia, Africa, and South America. Foreign capitalists fifty years ago derived the benefits of developing the United States. But ultimately, local industries grew, using these raw materials, as in Argentina and India.

The industrialization of Russia will proceed along the lines of historic precedent. With the growth of industrialization will come the development of technical methods, the increase of mechanization, the development of engineering and technical education, and success in striving for efficiency. These are definitely predictable prospects. The time factor is unpredictable. It will undoubtedly, however, be longer than the Russians think, perhaps a generation or two. The speed of development is likely to be less than under the system of competitive private capitalism. It is unlikely that under state capitalism any such progress will be made as was recorded in the American automobile industry from 1910 to 1930, either in lowering costs or in raising the quality of the product. On the other hand without the tradition of individual freedom that prevailed in America, and with the tradition of community ownership even under the Tsar, some new forms of industrial development are likely to arise.

d. More Equal Distribution of Wealth. Unequal distribution of wealth leads to social stratification. The economic and political views of those who possess great wealth are different from and usually opposed to the views of those who have nothing. A nation in which there is greater equality of wealth has greater political stability and greater internal harmony. Even in Russia today, when everybody has nothing, there is little likelihood of a social overturn, because there is no hereditary class against whom to revolt. Everybody is making sacrifices. However, such equal distribution of wealth means a low level for all. It involves the elimination of the difference of property and freedom, that adds to the interest of western civilization and constitutes one of the goals of striving for the individual. It means no private automobiles, no private city or country homes, no domestic servants, no made-to-order clothing, no retirement for study, writing, or other creative work, or for play and travel. Everybody will have a fairly equal amount, but little. Uniform and simple standards of food, clothing and shelter, transportation, recreation, etc. will prevail. Coney Island and Woolworth are ideals of the Soviets today. It is a question, however, whether the new upper strata of able people that are now arising out of the leveled masses will readily yield the comforts and rewards for their ability and effort to the less competent, to support whom at a level beyond their own capacities and productivity the general standard of living has to be dragged down. In any event the discrepancy between the higher and the lower standards of living will undoubtedly be less in Soviet Russia than in the capitalist world. The new ideals disapprove the exaggerated expression of social superiority. Ostentation and conspicuous waste will not be fashionable. This process of course is not unique to Russia. In other countries too there is a continuous democratization of the economic rewards of life.

2. Ufavorable Forecasts. A crisp summary of the Soviet program would be as follows—to the extent that the régime has been successful the method has been capitalist; to the extent that the method has remained pure communist it has failed. The Soviets, in using capitalist methods, the weapons of the enemy, have still retained anti-capitalist aims and motives. Profits are sought. But they go to the state, not to any individual or group.

a. Capitalism as a Refuge. Pure communism was tried in the early days of the Soviet régime. Communism failed and private capitalism, through an underground system of trade, came to the rescue. Will communism work any better in the future? According to the Soviets the return to capitalism was not an end in itself, but a transition stage in the evolution toward an ultimate socialism. Farbman states:

> The revolutionary impetus in the country seemed to have spent its force. Evolution and not revolution appeared to be the order of the day. The Russian Communist Party itself seemed to be ready to assume the position of a grand old party

> of stalwart guardians of evolutionary tradition rather than a party of revolutionary change.[5]

The goal of communism of production for service was abandoned, and the goal of state capitalism of production for profits was instituted and will probably remain. Payment according to need, rather than according to production was abandoned. The capitalist principle of piece work, or payment in proportion to output, was adopted. The state turned profiteer. However, under private capitalism profits arise from competition and the survival of the low-cost producers. The distribution of this surplus is the object of struggle between the various elements in society. With the American railroads, for example, the profits have been whittled away in the last generation by increasing local and federal taxes, by rising wages paid to highly organized union labor, by rate reductions granted to persistent and aggressive shippers or to impecunious farmers crying for state aid. But our railroads are probably the most efficient in the world. The competitive system at least provides good service and also a surplus about the distribution of which to quarrel.

Under state capitalism the stimulus of competition is lacking and there is an army of public servants who eat up the surplus. Under a system of private capitalism the surplus is regarded as a potential addition to the share of the workers in the distribution of national income. A profiteering state cannot compete in international trade without debasing the standard of living of the workers. This is true in Russia now. It is unlikely to remain true in the future if there is free migration between countries. For then Russian workers will migrate from a system of state capitalism and low standards of living to a system of private capitalism with higher standards of living. The stimulus of competition for free labor and the competition, as to price and quality, of the products in the open market should gradually force more efficient production under state capitalism in Soviet Russia. The present Russian system seems incompatible with such free movement of trade or labor.

The Stalingrad Tractor Plant, even by Soviet admission, has thus far proved a failure. "For some months," says Molotov, "the Stalingrad works have not been fulfilling their production program. It has been shown that we are better able to build new great works than to organize their production afterwards."[6] The alternative now is to bungle along under Soviet management, or perhaps to hire foreign managers and foreign staffs to operate the plants, as was the case in the British gold mines in Transvaal or the Belgian copper mines in Katanga, which were operated at first with the aid of American mining engineers who were subsequently released. Or the Soviets might even lease the property to a foreign firm for a limited term of years. A company like the International Harvester Company could probably operate the plant on a basis profitable both to itself and to the Soviet state. At the expiration of the term of the lease the state would probably have an efficient unit with a trained and adequate Russian personnel. The system could then revert to state capitalism. But pure communism in the industrial régime in any reasonable period of time is unlikely to be restored.

However, foreign capital may be unwilling to enter, without guaranties, and these may lead to basic political changes internally. As Kautsky said:

> The Bolsheviks would certainly have granted concessions to foreign capital in order to attract a steady stream of it into Russia, for they became more and more in need of it as their own industries collapsed. They were, however, unwilling and unable to renounce their despotic rule without bringing their own domination to an end. Without security of property, however, there can be no accumulation and investment of capital.[7]

b. A New Nep to the Rescue. The quarrel between Stalin and Trotsky resulted in the abolition of the Nep. Then followed the new nationalization in agriculture, in industry and in trade. This step indicated that the Nep never was really regarded by Soviet apologists as a surrender to capitalism, but merely as a strategic retreat in the advance toward socialism. The abolition of the Nep was virtually a new revolution. New hardships arose. A new class, the kulaks, the "rich" farmers and the "Nepmen," the new private traders, had to be expropriated, just as were the landlords and the owners of factories in 1917. And again as under "war-communism," the stores became empty after a period of successful private distribution of goods during the Nep. Again people suffered, though perhaps somewhat less than under the earlier period of communism.

A new Nep developed called the "State Nep." New stores were opened in the spring of 1931.[8] Here food and commodities were sold above the artificially low prices applicable to the rationed amounts. These prices, however, were lower than the prices in the open market of the few remaining private traders, who were subject to many restrictions. It is true that in the summer of 1932 Soviet policy moved in the direction of private trade for profit in agricultural produce and in consumers' goods, not as a relinquishment of Soviet doctrine, but as a new strategic retreat. But the new policy was short-lived and presently private trading in food was again abolished. These reversals are symptoms of deep struggle between cherished theory and relentless facts.

Twice in ten years the system of private trade was supplanted by a new system, first communism and then state capitalism, and twice private trade was brought to the rescue. Eventually a system of state control of trade in consumers' goods may work, but it is unlikely to do so for some time to come. However, a system of consumers' co-operative societies can work, provided it has that freedom in buying which the competitive system makes possible, and provided it has the stimulus of competition from private trade. It is even probable that the future development of internal trade in Russia will not be confined to any one system but that the three systems may compete in serving society—state-controlled trade, consumers' co-operatives, and private trade, which would supply the stimulus of competition, the factor of elasticity and would insure the distribution of goods.

c. New Native Personnel for New Plants. The industrial future hinges not upon the new plants that were built by foreigners, but upon the existence of a trained native staff to run them. Of the approximately 160 million people in Russia less than one-fifth are in the towns. The country is not prepared for the final stage of industrialism, and the mere building of new plants does not make it so. There is no industrial tradition. Colonel Cooper, who is a sympathetic observer of Soviet Russia and knows the industrial situation at first hand, said, "It will take more than a generation to train workers to a point where they can produce efficiently for their own market, without considering the outside world." [9]

As a part of the program of training an industrial army the element of capitalism, requiring rewards for individual effort, is utilized. The first tractor that ran off the conveyor on June 16, 1930, at Stalingrad was really made by hand and merely run over the conveyor. At Stalingrad the present production is only a fraction of the total capacity of 100,000. Regardless of how ambitious the Soviet industrial program is or how many plants are erected, a safe prediction is that they will not be run efficiently or at capacity for many years. Mass production on the huge scale that the Soviets have attempted implies co-ordination of other large units, supplying raw materials and making accessory parts, to say nothing of adequate transportation. These conditions do not exist in Russia.

d. Shortage of Consumers' Goods. The shortage of consumers' goods is due partly to poor distribution and to the curtailment of "small-time" or home production by peasants and artisans, as a result of the pressure for socialization both in industry and in agriculture.

The shortage of consumers' goods is likely to continue for several years unless the tempo of the Five-Year Plan is reduced. As the newly established industries increase in number, their construction will divert more labor from the consumers' goods industries, require more imports of machinery and thus further curtail the necessary imports of consumers' goods. The draft of the heavy industries on the national income should postpone for some time the production of sufficient consumers' goods to relieve the current underconsumption, and therefore defer raising the standard of living toward the level of other countries. One contingency which may remedy this situation is such great success in the agricultural program as will make it possible for the exports of grain to pay not merely for the imports for the heavy industries but also for consumers' goods. This contingency is not very likely, as prices will decline, to offset rising production and export. When the construction program is completed or slackened in tempo, the standard of living could rise.

e. Financial Situation Grows Serious. The pressure to sell petroleum, wheat, manganese, lumber, etc., at sacrifice prices is an indication of the financial difficulties of the Soviets. The idea that Russia is trying to create a world revolution by lowering prices is untenable. Lower prices are rather a direct result of the decline in the finances of the Soviets. The shift of business in the spring of 1931 from America to Germany was contingent upon getting a credit in Germany, because American firms demand cash or early payment. The credit then opened by Germany for Russia equals a large part of the total imports from America during the previous year for which cash or short credit had to be found.

There is another indication of the increasingly adverse financial situation. In private trade, when a debtor's payments become increasingly slow, it is a sign of growing financial difficulty. The same observation applies to the Soviets. They have been gradually prolonging the time of payment. In 1928 credits ran from 9 to 12 months, in 1930 for 18 months, and in 1931 for 24 to 48 months. In 1932 German credits were reduced to 21 months and British credits to 12 months. Two-year terms for fertilizer and other quickly consumable goods are unsound.

Another indication of the financial stringency is the fact that the Soviets demand cash for their exports. It has even been reported that Woolworth's in London have been selling electric light bulbs bearing German trade marks and bought in Russia at bargain prices. One explanation given is that the Soviets were buying German lamps on long-term credits at high prices and thereupon selling them in London at bargain prices in order to get cash. In other words, they were using the German electric companies as their bankers at penalty rates. The merchandise merely was an incident in the transaction. Soviet representatives in the United States have denied this report. From other private sources come similar reports that Russia has been buying on credit of one year or more, at 30 per cent above the world market and selling for cash at or under the market, or in other words, paying 30 per cent per annum for money. Such a state of affairs cannot continue very long. These indicators of financial difficulty are crucial.

f. Crises Not Abolished. Stalin and other Soviet spokesmen point out that Russia is now unique. Its industries are growing by leaps and bounds. It is not suffering from unemployment, whereas other countries are in the throes of depression. Stalin addressing the All-Union Conference of Industrial Executives stated that the communist system had proved "the only one in which the economic crisis such as laid low capitalist countries was an impossibility." [10] However, the Soviet point of view ignores the fact that even in capitalist countries during the early stages of development, such as the United States, Argentina and Australia, there was often great activity while the older countries of Europe were in depression. Willard L. Thorp and Wesley C. Mitchell, in their *Business Annals,* show divergent cyclical trends for England and the United States since 1790 and for 15 other countries for shorter periods.[11] The phases of the cycle lag behind and do not occur simultaneously in all countries. Countries that are in close relation with the rest of the world, move through a cycle in fair unison, but as in the case of China before the war and Russia at present, the booms and depressions did not synchronize with those of other countries.

Furthermore, Soviet Russia is not in free and active economic intercourse with the rest of the world. It is in some respects a sealed chamber. Therefore forces which influence the outside world leave it unaffected. At present Russia is expanding at a rapid rate. It is trying to accomplish a five-decade task in five years. Therefore employment is universal. But what is the outlook when the inevitable lull in the expansion program comes? Russia will probably be gripped by as profound a crisis as struck all the younger countries after their periods of great expansion, as America in the middle seventies succeeding the opening of the west and Argentina in the early nineties after the great expansion under Baring's financing.

When the author predicted that the present boom in Russia would end in a profound depression (incidentally, he was neither shot nor arrested) the various Soviet officials disputed the prophecy with the remark that there was too much work yet to be done in Russia. However, they overlooked the fact that the United States in 1800 had just as much work to do, and yet has suffered profound depressions practically every 20 years since the beginning of the last century. These depressions were due to the very fact that there was so much work to be done, and that growth was so rapid. A depression results from the maladjustment of the several economic factors. It is unlikely that the Russians will be able to keep these factors on an even front. They have not yet done so and no other more highly developed nation has.

The Soviet system of state capitalism has not yet been tested in a depression. That depression is inevitable in the next few years. When it comes, it will bring in its train profound repercussions not merely economic, but also probably political.

3. Foreign Aspects. a. "Overtaking and Surpassing the Capitalist Countries." The history of the economic rise of young countries is a history of foreign investment. There is no case on record of any young country financing its own development as Russia is trying to do. Pre-war Russia itself was developed and financed by foreign investors. It is therefore likely that the historic pattern will be followed by Soviet Russia. If she relies on her own resources, either the people must underconsume, or development will be slow, because the surplus of the country will be inadequate to finance the economic expansion. And capital will only enter Russia on terms which will inspire the confidence of the investor. In other words, the program of industrialization of Russia means a compromise with capitalist principles, so far as foreign investment is concerned. The foreigner investing voluntarily will ask for security and guarantees as to the safety of principal and interest, which the conscripted domestic investor cannot ask.

b. Are the Soviets a Menace? The opponents of the Soviets proclaim that capitalism is helping the Soviets to build up a system which will in the end destroy capitalism. They say that Soviet competition is dangerous because costs are disregarded, that the chief object of the Soviets is the throttling of the capitalist system. However, as Soviet Russia comes into closer contact with the capitalist world, her own welfare will be tied up with it. The worldwide depression may not have engulfed Russia but it has affected her adversely and seriously. The drop in the price of wheat has made it necessary for her to increase her exports and to curtail supplies to her own population in order to pay for machinery. Economically the world and Russia are interdependent. Russia has not yet the equipment to compete industrially with the outside world. She will be an effective competitor only in those fields where nature does the work. The sun shines as brightly in Russia as elsewhere, and Russian wheat will undoubtedly resume its pre-war importance as an important item of Russian exports.

With reference to any extensive exports of manufactured goods soon Russia's prospect is very slim. She will not be a significant factor in this field for years. Even before the war the quality of Russian manufactures was inferior to that of western Europe and her costs were higher. With the huge and rapid industrial development now under way it is unlikely that for many years the quality will be even up to the pre-war standard of the relatively small industry then existing. Certainly costs of manufacturing will remain high for years, until the management problems in the new huge plants are solved.

The second Five-Year Plan will stress the development of consumers' goods, and will reduce the rate of industrialization. Therefore, imports from abroad will be less necessary, and as a result, offsetting exports to provide the credits will be less necessary. In national economics, it always holds true that as the twig is bent so the tree will grow. It is probable that the principal exports of Russia over the decades to come will be smaller than in the case of countries which borrowed heavily abroad, like Argentina, which must export to provide interest and amortization on foreign loans.

According to one of the leaders of the German Federation of Labor, the position of Russia as a competitor with the other nations depends upon the rate of technical education of the Russian workers.

> Ten or twenty years may be only a brief span as time goes, but it will suffice to rear a generation of skilled Soviet proletarians with whom the workman of the western states will be expected to compete. With millions of artisans accustomed to lower standards of living, and wage conditions which even ten years hence may still be synonymous with conscripted labor, Soviet industry is bound to play havoc in the labor markets of the more civilized States.[12]

So long as the Russian workman and Russian management are inefficient, the much lower standard of living there is not a menace to the standard of the western workman. As the Russian laborer becomes more skilled, the Bolshevik theory is that his standard of living will be raised. Should his output equal that of the western worker and his standard of living not rise, the Soviet economic system may be able to drag western standards of labor to lower levels.

c. Stimulus to International Trade. In the last two years the raw-material industries have made substantial progress at a rising rate. The heavy industries will probably continue their growth for a while, though at probably a less rapid rate, both relatively and absolutely. The population will probably be unable to stand the strain that the present rate imposes, and therefore importation of consumers' goods by Soviet Russia should stimulate the industries of other countries. The standard of living in Russia is so low that it will take many years before the home needs are satisfied and before there will be a surplus for export. Unlike the foreign market, the home market will be willing, indeed will have no choice, but to take inferior domestic manufactures at higher cost, particularly since foreign trade is a monopoly of the government, which can embargo foreign merchandise. Foreign trade, therefore, probably will continue on the basis of exchange of Russian raw materials for foreign goods, at first foreign machinery and later foreign consumers' goods. Eventually, probably after several decades, Russia will become more efficient. Quality will improve. Costs will come down. She will then become competitive with the countries in an advanced stage of industrialization.

As Russia develops industrially she will rely increasingly on foreign capital, like other young countries. For the twenty years before the war capital flowed into Russia at the average rate of about 100 million dollars per annum, of which 60 million dollars was for the state, 25 million dollars for industry, and 15 million dollars for municipalities and guaranteed loans.[13] Pre-war investments amounted to over 3.5 billion dollars, and were found in rails, utilities, mines, oils, and miscellaneous industries, such as the manufacture of agricultural machinery, elevators, sewing machines, etc. Should normal relations be restored with the outside world, Russia will probably become a great field for foreign investments, just as America was for several decades.

Kautsky believes that "the victory of democracy in Russia would not only open this market to the industry of the world, it would also swiftly extend it to tremendous dimensions." [14]

The aim of the Soviet leaders is to raise the standard of living in Russia. It will be years before this aim is realized, but when it is, it will have a stimulating effect on world trade in much the same way as the industrialization of Germany stimulated England's trade and the development of Canada greatly increased trade with the United States. It is unlikely that the standard of living in Soviet Russia will for years equal that, say of the United States or even of Germany. If it ultimately should, it would result in an immigration of foreign labor and thus tend to raise the status of the workmen in other countries. This would be tangible propaganda for the Soviets.

4. Open Questions. a. Communism vs. Capitalism. It is unlikely that any future high standard of living in Russia will result in a revolution in other countries, as some observers predict. The social and economic systems of the world will probably gradually evolve under the now almost world-wide system of parliamentary government and universal suffrage. Economic and social reforms in one country are copied in other countries, but it is unlikely that the capitalist system, with its freedom of individual initiative, will ever be completely replaced. Or as Professor E. R. A. Seligman stated:

> In the future capitalism will be regulated and subject to control in the interest of the community. The trend toward social legislation is bound to continue. . . . Taxes on income and inheritances will be considerably higher and the burden placed on those who can afford it. . . . But intellectual freedom must be the basis of social progress.[15]

Will our system of capitalism, with an abundance of goods, freedom of individual initiative and opportunity for the individual, survive? Or will communism, producing less goods but leveling the upper classes down to the status of the lowest, give the masses greater satisfaction? It is a question of material values as against psychological values.

Do the developments up to date justify the following forecast made by one observer? Is it not too soon to draw any such conclusion?

> There can no longer be any reasonable expectation that the Soviet Union will revert to "capitalism." A country which rivals America in natural resources, in combined potentialities of industrial and agricultural development, has definitely broken with the traditional economic system and has set about the task of organizing its economic life on socialist lines. As Kuybyshev said, the race between the "capitalist" and "socialist" economic systems has begun.[16]

b. Russian Nationalism vs. Labor's Internationalism. Will the international fellowship of labor, which the communists now espouse, lead them to share their raw materials with the other workers of the world? Or will a form of Russian nationalism arise which will result in chauvinist policies with respect to tariffs, investments, labor standards, emigration, etc.? In other words, will the ideal of being missionaries to the laboring world fade away into the age-old selfish personal motives? With the halo of revolution about them the workers throughout Russia tell American visitors: "We are the vanguard of the liberated workers, and our duty is to emancipate labor elsewhere." When Russia becomes settled, and the interests of foreign and Russian workers conflict, will this sense of fellowship still be maintained?

Soviet Russia, which had been condemning financial imperialism, is following in the footsteps of the capitalistic countries. Even in this early stage,

Soviet Russia is making foreign investments. It opened a credit for Turkey and plans to install Soviet machinery in Turkish factories and is providing Soviet engineers for this task.[17] Soviet Russia is making investments in Turkey as capitalistic France has done. Similarly, Soviet Russia will be perfectly willing to join the imperialists in taking long-term loans from England, France, and the United States. There has been much idealization of economic conditions, which have been forced upon them.

c. Russian Labor and Industrial Efficiency. The question is raised, "Will the Russian laborer ever become as efficient as the laborer in the western world?" Foreign engineers, with experience in Russia, comment unfavorably on the sense of discipline of the Russian worker. They say there is something inherent in his attitude which makes him less amenable to factory discipline. However, this is probably not a biological trait, but rather a form of social behavior. The American changed from a pioneer in the wilderness to a farmer and then became a highly efficient industrial worker. The Slavic immigrant working in the mines and factories of the United States becomes as efficient as his fellow workers. He acquires the social and industrial behavior of his milieu. Eventually the same mental adjustment will follow in Russia over a lapse of time.

What is true of the individual will also probably be true of the nation. In fifty years the Japanese have become highly efficient industrial workers and technicians. The Germans at the beginning of the nineteenth century were a nation of poets and philosophers; their national heroes were Fichte and Schelling, Hegel and Schlegel. Within two generations they were transformed into a people of technicians and scientists, as the long roster of present-day heroes and leaders indicates. In two generations Germany also realized its program of "overtaking and surpassing" the other industrial countries. A similar prospect is in store for Russia. Her mystical and superstitious peasants are being transformed into energetic mill hands. The Russian laborer is a man of good physique and good mind, adaptable and thorough, but lacking in the tradition of industrialism. To develop this will take much more than five years. But eventually after several decades the Russian worker will probably be as competent as the worker of other industrial countries.

C. Political Forecast

An attempt at forecasting in politics is more difficult than in economics. There are no basic factors here, such as competition, production costs, or labor incentives, which provide the framework within which future development may take place. Politics is more dependent upon strong men, upon personal influence, and upon political machinery. But allowing for the vaguer guiding principles some attempt at political forecasting may be made, on the basis of political experience in Russia and elsewhere.

Prognostication must take account of many variable factors, such as the internal politics of Russia, how long the people will be willing to submit, the foreign policy, and the attitude of other governments. In case of an impasse war may save the face of the leaders, although this device of kings is hardly likely to be tried by the Soviets. Peace at any price has been their policy and is likely to continue to be. How long will it be possible to exile the able men of the opposition, thus weakening the personnel of the régime of the "ins" and strengthening the influence of the "outs"? It was this stupid policy of the Tsarist régime that caused its downfall. It exiled its intelligent and vigorous personalities, so that they became an active, organized opposition outside of Russia. In republican governments, the minority leaders are not exiled. They work within the frame of the existing laws but against the administration and in favor of continuous change.

1. FACTORS FAVORING PRESENT RÉGIME. a. No Return of the Monarchy. The Soviet Revolution is hardly likely to follow the model of the French Revolution in its political aspects. The return of the Bourbons is hardly likely to furnish an historic analogy for the return of the Romanovs, because of progress in the political democratization of Europe and the absence of strong monarchic influence such as prevailed in the last century. The Tsarist régime in Russia would seem definitely to have passed. The emperors of Russia and of Austria and the king of Prussia helped to restore the Bourbons; but now all these governments are republics. The few remaining important kings of Europe are constitutional monarchs and devoid of power.

May one predict the permanence of the present régime? For the time being the leaders are powerfully intrenched, and their overthrow is unlikely. They have control of the army, which is well fed and well clothed, and is the favored element of the population. The tourist is amazed at the striking contrast between the spick-and-span costumes of the soldiers and the drab and forlorn clothing of the rest of the population.

b. Control of the Press, Army and Secret Police. Again, the secret police or intelligence service attempts to gauge the political pressure of the population and to determine the rebellion point. Without votes to express the will of the masses, the G.P.U. is expected to furnish the Kremlin with a cross-section of public opinion. Economic and political policies have been changed, sometimes even reversed, as a result of such reports. Such pliability of the ruling régime may avoid popular resentment leading to an overturn. Up to the danger point the G.P.U. suppresses opposition by terror. On the other hand by control of education and of the press the Soviet régime has created a large body of opinion among the young people who never knew the old régime and who accept the new régime enthusiastically as their own.

c. Against Whom to Revolt? The old system was overthrown, partly because of the great discrepancy between the status of the highest and the lowest classes. The stimulus to revolt was present, but a terrorism worse than that which prevails in Russia today maintained the ruling class in power against the forces of liberation which were continually at work. But at present practically everybody is in want; the gap between the highest and lowest classes is very small. The upper classes, the Soviet officials and the members of the party probably have not much more material goods than they had under the Tsarist régime. There is really no hereditary class against whom the resentment of the masses can be directed. No rebels can make the charge of exploitation. The charges that can be made are of incompetence, lack of experience, political experimentation and recklessness, but the effects of these must go very far before a revolt can be stimulated. For some time, therefore, no great political change in the system is likely.

d. Illiteracy and Lack of Political Tradition. Rule by a minority is likely to continue for some time, because of the lack of the requirements for complete self-government, namely, a tradition of political freedom, a free press and the prerequisite, high literacy. Psychologically the people are prepared for self-government; they have rejected all authority; they are ready and willing to govern themselves. But the machinery of creating public opinion requires free discussion, general reading, and a political minority, vigorous and critical. The disadvantage of a lack of literacy may be and is being overcome. The press is controlled entirely by the government. Criticism of details is permitted, but no dissenting opinion on fundamentals is tolerated. The public, therefore, does not know what is wrong, to say nothing of being offered an alternative remedy. If the present régime were foresighted and interested in making a gradual transition to free government, it might remedy these deficiencies. But the principle that they invoked against the old régime still holds. Like the Tsarist régime, the Soviets will wish to retain control, because like other human beings the leaders enjoy the aggrandizement of the ego resulting from the exercise of power. For some time, therefore, it may reasonably be expected that the current political régime will try to maintain control and to check the forces making for political democracy and parliamentary government.

e. Freedom of Minor Nationalities. The rights accorded to minority peoples in Soviet Russia are probably a permanent political advance. The failure to grant rights to the various nationalities would probably have resulted in separatist movements and disintegration of the Soviet Union. In fact a cynic may say that granting freedom to racial and cultural minorities was probably forced upon the Soviets, because there was no political instrument available to continue the oppression of the minorities. However, not merely is freedom of nationalities likely to continue in Soviet Russia, but this is probably the outstanding original contribution of the Soviet Revolution to the political and cultural advance of Europe and of the world. A Europe modeled along similar lines would certainly represent a great step forward. The Soviet régime has realized one of the great aims of the war, more honored in the breach than in the observance, namely freedom of minorities. Economic unity and the absence of tariff barriers as realized within the vast domains of the Soviets, coupled with the freedom of minor nationalities, if adopted on the rest of the continent may afford the solution for many of Europe's problems.

Europe organized politically on the Soviet model would constitute a large free-trade area with liberty for cultural, racial, and national minorities, a new unity which might lead to a great increase in economic productivity. In spite of all the unfortunate and unhappy aspects of the Soviet régime, this one tremendous contribution cannot be overlooked. In the perspective of history this may be left as the one distinctive advance in civilization first actually embodied in practice on a large scale in Soviet Russia. Indeed the Russian Revolution will have achieved for the freedom of nationalities what the French Revolution achieved for the freedom of the individual.

2. Factors Inimical to Current Régime. As a long-range forecast one should be able to say very definitely that the present régime is not permanent. It has some very serious flaws. It is unstable. It does not express the popular will. The opposition is crushed and there is no machinery for succession. In the past all oligarchies, whether benevolent or tyrannical, have fallen. The Russian oligarchy is likely eventually to share the same fate. Free and popular government, arising out of the popular will is the inevitable political goal toward which civilization is tending, and Russia will hardly prove an exception.

a. Political Instability. To the dispassionate observer the outstanding characteristic of the present dictatorship is its instability. A small group is in complete and arbitrary control. This group resembles in many respects the old Tsarist régime, whose eventual downfall was certain and predictable. The forces of repression which enable this minority to continue in power cannot operate permanently. The stability of the present leadership and its future are contingent upon its wisdom. Have the leaders the political foresight gradually to effect a democratization, or will they, like all their predecessors, hold on until a popular uprising throws them out?

Not only is the régime and its personnel unstable, but political communism as such is unstable. An American called into consultation by the Russians stated to the writer in the summer of 1930: "Communism will not last another five years. The leaders are afraid to reverse their policies now, as the public will not understand. The process of conversion will be a slow one, and a theory will have to be developed to tell the public why the change had to be made." Some new doctrine of a strategic retreat will have to be evolved to show the public why the departure from communism really constitutes a step toward communism. But the theorists in Russia are very agile and the public apparently gullible. This combination of traits in politicians and in voters is not unique in Russia. It merely exaggerates a universal characteristic. The forces of oppression are bound to bring about some overturn.

b. Revolt Latent. Revolt seems to be an essential element of Soviet theory. In fact Trotsky had the notion of continuous revolt as a means of keeping society vigorous, just, and in equilibrium. The great fear was of settling down and becoming rigid and unadaptable. Revolt is latent in Soviet Russia today, and is likely to break out as soon as the tremendous pressure now keeping it down is released. It actually flared up in 1921, but was suppressed. Kautsky described the revolt as follows:

> The continuation of the Terror, of the violent despotism exercised by the communists over the whole working population, seemed insufferable. On February 27, 1921 [during the sailors' revolt in Kronstadt and the general strike in Moscow and Petrograd], a proclamation running as follows was circulated amongst the strikers:
>
> "A radical change in the whole policy of the government is necessary, and, above all, the workers and peasants must have liberty. They do not wish to submit to the rule of the Bolsheviks, but desire to determine their own destinies.
>
> "You must demand the following insistently and in an organized way: The setting free of all imprisoned socialists and workers outside all parties; the raising of the state of siege; freedom of speech and of the press; freedom of all the

working classes to hold meetings; free elections in the works committees, in the unions, and in the Soviets. Organize meetings, pass resolutions, send your delegations to the government, see that your will is carried out." [18]

c. Popular Basis of Revolt. The scarcity of goods and pyhsical suffering are so widespread that if an expression of popular opinion were possible today, the vote would be overwhelmingly against the present régime. This "vote" was made powerfully evident in the resistance to agricultural collectivization, which expressed itself over a period of months in forty deaths per day, assassinations of government agents and murders of peasants.

It is true that there is no rich and powerful class of "exploiters" against whom to revolt. But there are several basic conditions for revolt. First, emigration is impossible. The discontented just cannot get out of the country. They have no alternative except to vent their feelings at home. Then there is no minority party which makes possible continuous and gradual change. As a result, when a change does come, it must be abrupt. Again, people of 35 years or older, were adolescent or mature before the war. They can remember the relative abundance of consumers' goods in the Tsarist days, in contrast to the current universal lack of them. Hunger and deprivation are the allies of revolt. People refuse to suffer indefinitely. Starvation constitutes the nether limit of tolerance, regardless of the fact that practically everybody is equally affected and regardless of a previous history of generations of want. The masses are less interested in Soviet doctrines than in satisfying their minimum physical needs. They can remember that only a few years ago, under the New Economic Policy, food and clothing were relatively abundant. They know also that under the recent "left" move food has become scarce and clothing almost unavailable. The régime which thus deprives the masses faces the consequences of popular resentment.

d. Politicians Ousted and in Exile. When the writer commented generally in Russia on the suppression of the minority party, the universal defense of Soviet supporters was: "Russia is engaged in a great war with capitalism and, therefore, as in all warring countries, only a single party is possible." The consequences of such a policy are dangerous. As critics the minority serve to keep the government in equilibrium. Without such a balance even a cautious oligarchy which tries to sense popular sentiment, may swing too far in one direction and eventually be overturned.

The original group of communists that led the revolution are diminishing in number. Fewer able people are left within the party, and more able people are outside the party, and the result is almost as inevitable as in a "couple of forces" in mechanics. Of the original group that dominated the communist party, Stalin "broke" every one and he alone is left. As this danger of ousting rivals and concentrating power increases progressively, it is probable that the historic precedent of the French Revolution will again apply. Then, the successive leaders that assumed power by the subjugation of rivals eventually were removed. In the French Revolution they were killed. In the Russian Revolution they were merely exiled or demoted.

The elimination of able associates is a distinctly disintegrating factor. Stalin's illness or death would leave the régime in control of those second-rate men, whom he does not fear, who are loyal to him but not strong enough to challenge him. This weakness characterizes no form of popular or bipartisan government.

e. Contrast Between Present Status and Future Hopes. The future hope is for democracy, but the current régime is an oligarchy. The future hope is for dictatorship of the proletariat, but the present government is a dictatorship of the dictatorship. The future hope is for rule by the majority, but the present status is rule by minority. The future hope is for a communist society, but the present status is a capitalist society with the state as its only stockholder.

Will the future hopes be realized? It will require either a continuous compromise or a revolution. Continuous compromise assumes a stable and adaptable political machinery. This the Soviets lack. Revolution requires wide-spread discontent and a small group in power. This the Soviet now has. The British political changes have been by evolution, through centuries of experience since the Magna Charta. Not merely in economic experience but in political experience the Russians are far behind. Hence the discrepancy in both instances between their aspirations and the means for achieving them. However, people emerging from bondage cannot have a tradition of liberty or be prepared for self-government. They can learn only if given a chance. The method must be trial and error, cautious experimentation and the adoption of methods that will work.

The political future of Russia depends upon the conflict between the welfare of the people and the love of power of the men in control. Most régimes attempt to identify these two conflicting elements. Even the tyrannical Tsar asserted and doubtless really believed that his selfish interests coincided with the good of the people. He looked upon the people as his children, and had them regard him as the Little Father. Is Stalin making the same mistake?

3. Open Questions. On some matters it is impossible to prognosticate. Yet

a few alternatives suggest themselves. Only time will tell which alternatives will be realized.

a. Strategy of Politicians. Policies do not make themselves; they are the expression of the conflict of human wills. Russia is now following an extreme left policy, which was not predictable. In fact, until the abandonment of the Nep, the trend of the Russian Revolution might have been predicted on the basis of the history of the French Revolution. In the early years of the Napoleonic régime the French Revolution began to settle down to such an extent that it seemed as if the revolution had come to an end and that the *status quo ante* was being restored.

However, in Russia, when the elements of capitalism were slowly emerging after the failure of communism, a personal political quarrel, as noted above, accelerated events. Stalin's struggle with Trotsky resulted in a whole nation of 160,000,000 people being moved in the direction of a radical policy. This will probably fail within the next few years. The great plants built by foreign technicians in a country unprepared for them, will probably not work. Again recently Rykov urged a move to the right, in order to save the program of industrial development. In this, he also was suppressed. Stalin ousted him from the premiership, but may adopt his policy. And so the personal differences among the leaders will result in zigzagging policies.

b. Foreign War and Revolutions Abroad. The political future of the Soviets would be seriously affected by an upset in international affairs. Their deliberate policy is peace. In any event the policy of peace makes possible consolidation at home. The Soviets are unlikely to pursue any war of offense. It is equally unlikely that the war-fatigued European nations will attack Russia, in spite of the hallucinations to the contrary which continually crop up in the Russian press. Any war of offense is likely to lead to the disintegration of the Soviet régime. Any war of defense is likely to lead to its strengthening.

On the other hand, radical revolutions abroad would probably have the aid and sympathy of the Soviets, for such revolutions in other countries would probably strengthen the Soviet régime. However the post-war recuperation has proceeded relatively smoothly, and no communist uprising has yet occurred. World revolution is still a Soviet delusion. The Soviets hardly realize that their own revolution was the result of Tsarist oppression, and cannot be transplanted. Revolutions spring forth if the soil is fertile and the seed is planted. The settling down of Europe leaves Russia in political and economic isolation. Russia's internal problems are so great that she has neither energy nor funds left for either foreign wars or foreign revolutions. Apparently the Soviet régime cannot look for much support in the future either to a war of defense or communist uprisings in other countries.

c. Chaos. A possibility, although not a predictable probability, is that Russia will fall into chaos, as did Mexico for over a decade after the fall of Diaz. If the Five-Year Plan fails to produce the necessities of life or relieve the suffering, and if the ruling group becomes enfeebled and the opposition strengthened by elimination from the Central Committee of men of ability, there is danger of a breakdown. It is possible that the latent discontent with the centralized government may even result in the splitting off of a number of lesser states, as has already been the case with Lithuania, Latvia, and Esthonia. Perhaps the European powers would even favor such a situation because it would lessen the danger and continuous threat of Bolshevism in so large an area. The huge empire has been kept intact largely through the strong, centralized, despotic régime of the Tsars and through an equally strong and centralized régime of a benevolent oligarchy. A weakening of the central government might result in chaos for an indeterminate interval until some new strong group arose. The Soviet régime deserves some credit at least for keeping this vast empire quiet and in order.

d. Constitutional Parliamentary Régime. However, in Moscow the rights, and in the other capitals of Europe, the constitutional socialists, tell the observer that the present order is not stable and that the only hope rests in the diffusion of power among the masses. Soviet opponents say that the right wing is ready now to take control and to lead the country to a democratic rule.[19] They say that discontent is latent, that ultimately autocratic power must be overturned, that stable equilibrium will be reached only when the voice of the masses is effective, that democratic machinery must be created, that when the electorate is again free revolution will become impossible, because there will be adequate means for the expression of the popular will. The present oligarchy, regarded as similar to the Napoleonic stage of the French Revolution, must likewise be succeeded by the republican stage. The dictatorship of the left in Russia, as well as the Tsarist dictatorships of the right, must follow the course of all dictatorships, as it has recently in Spain and as it threatens in Italy. Parliamentary system and party government must ultimately emerge, and political opposition must not only be not suppressed, as in Russia, or even merely tolerated; it must be encouraged, so as to be politically trained and ready to assume power whenever the electorate so votes.

Over a longer period, the emergence of a democratic state in Russia is inevitable. The groupings are already there. It requires merely the release of the forces of oppression to call them into being. The history of mankind is a history of the struggle for freedom, and no régime or group of men can, except for short periods, interfere with this universal urge for liberty, for which men have given everything.

Kautsky believes there is no prospect of a gradual democratization of present Russia. Only a mass revolt can facilitate the return of the social democracy of the Kerensky revolution. He predicts "that this insane experiment can only end in a terrible collapse. Not even the greatest genius can prevent it. As bankruptcy approaches, daring increases. As the impoverishment of the masses increases, new plans become even more gigantic."[20]

e. Karl Kautsky's Forecast. What are the possible forms of a new revolution in Russia? According to Kautsky, the manifesto of the Labor Socialist Internationale expresses the hope that whether the Bolsheviks are Communists or not members of any party they will "join the Socialists," and give "freedom to the peoples of the Soviet Union and thus lead them peacefully toward full democracy." He further says:

> If we do not merely listen to wishes, but give our ear to previous experience and to the nature of things, then we are obliged to say that this kind of solution is the most unlikely one of all. . . . To transform an autocracy into a democracy has never yet been peaceably achieved. . . . The expectation of converting communism to democracy is not seriously to be considered. . . .
>
> [Though] the demand for the democratization of the Soviets may be one of the starting points leading to the end of the communist rule [experience showed that] it required a powerful revolt in the spring of 1921 to cause Lenin to grant concessions [the Nep], and it was no less than the beginnings of such a revolt which, in the spring of 1930, induced Stalin to moderate his pace [of forcible collectivization in agriculture]. . . . Among the factors which will affect the characteristics of the coming movement of Russia, the attitude of the Communist Party will of course be one of the most important. It is quite possible that in this situation it will be split up, before it is completely annihilated. . . . [Like the former autocracy, the communists will meet liberal opposition with two main plans], the one seeks to soften the elements of the opposition by concession and lenience, the other seeks to intimidate them by increased severity. . . . If, for the last twelve years the dictatorship has sought to destroy thoroughly every starting point for a possible opposition, it has thereby so disorganized and compromised itself, caused so many disagreements, occasioned such instability, that perhaps no very great impetus is required to make it lose the ground under its feet. . . . What dimensions and what conquering strength a revolt of the peasant population in Russia can attain in such circumstances has already been proved by the revolt of Stenka Razin, a rebellious Cossack, who in 1668 gathered around him a robber band of more than a thousand men,

with whom he waged a formal war, and whose military conquests soon brought crowds of peasants and proletarians to his camp.

Yet even the workers and peasants cannot alone found a state without intellectuals. . . . If the proletarians have the insight to unite themselves with intellectuals and peasants in the fight for democracy, that is to say, above all for universal equal suffrage and a parliamentary republic, with complete freedom for all its inhabitants, then we may think that Russia is approaching happier times.[21]

f. Leon Trotsky's Forecast.[22]

The system of opinions which the Stalin bureaucracy imposes has come into more and more serious conflict with the traditions of the party.

The bitter character of the present campaign against "Trotskyists" has inspired the Russian emigrant press to new prophecies of the coming downfall of the Soviet power. . . . This is not, after all, surprising; not only does the Stalin bureaucracy stubbornly identify itself with the Soviet régime, but its enemies also, in search for comfortable illusions, become victims of the same political aberration.

As a matter of fact, there is not the slightest foundation for this talk of the approaching long-awaited "end." The development of the productive forces of the Soviet Union is the most colossal phenomenon of contemporary history. The gigantic advantage of a planned leadership has been demonstrated with a force which nothing can ever refute. The near-sightedness and zigzagging of the Stalin bureaucracy only the more clearly emphasizes the power of the methods themselves. Only the maniacs of the restoration can imagine that the toiling masses of Russia want to turn back to the conditions of backward Russian capitalism.

But it is no less an error to imagine that the economic successes in strengthening the new industrial régime have also automatically reinforced the political position of Stalin and his faction. Up to a certain moment it was so. But at present a process of exactly the opposite kind is developing. A people who have achieved a mighty revolution may temporarily, in difficult circumstances, hand over the guidance of their destinies to a bureaucracy. But they are not able to renounce politics for long.

It would be blindness not to see that the very strengthening of the economic situation of the country sets the toiling masses in more and more hostile opposition to the omnipotence of a bureaucracy. The workers, not without justification, attribute to themselves the achieved successes, and follow the bureaucracy with more and more critical eyes. For the masses see from below not only the successes and the possibilities flowing from them, but also the crude mistakes of the leaders and their continuous tendency to shift the responsibility for these mistakes from themselves to their agents. In raising the pride of the workers the successes have also raised their political demands.

The lessons of the economic zigzags have taken deep root in the consciousness of the population and greatly undermined even the prestige of Stalin. The inference comes of itself: "It seems as though the Opposition was right!" The oppositional thought, although not showing itself at the surface, has long been laying down hidden roads.

A critical period is now opening. The workers desire not only to obey but to decide. They intend to change many things. It is more than ever demanded of them, however, that they merely ratify decisions adopted without them. The workers are discontented—not with the Soviet régime, but with the fact that a bureaucracy is replacing the Soviets. In various workers' locals the "Trotskyists" are lifting their heads, sometimes very courageously. They are being expelled. This has opened a new chapter in the life of the ruling party. Critical voices can no longer be silenced.

Whereas the former party crises reflected directly the difficulties and contradictions of the development of the Soviet republic under bureaucratic leadership, what comes to view in the present period is the contradiction in the position of the Stalin faction, and above all of Stalin himself.

The campaign against "Trotskyism" now developing signalizes the twilight of the omnipotence of the Stalin bureaucracy. But therewith it foretells, not the fall of the Bolshevist power, but on the contrary a new rise of the Soviet régime—not only its industry, but its politics and culture. That tendency, to which the author belongs, is firmly confident of finding its place in the gigantic work to come.

D. Social Forecasts

1. Prospective Gains. a. Decrease in Infant Mortality. Perhaps the most concrete statistical index of better public hygiene is the decrease in infant mortality. A comparison of present and pre-war figures follows:

BIRTH AND DEATH RATE AND INFANT MORTALITY

(per thousand)

	1912–13	*1928–29*	*1930*
Birth rate	33.0	22.0	22.2
Death rate	24.5	12.7	13.0
Net increase	8.5	9.3	9.2
Infant mortality per thousand births	287	127	124

Hygiene and sanitation have improved so greatly that a rising trend of population is predicted. The net increase is far higher than the average for Europe. Moscow statisticians expect the population of the Soviet Union to double by 1960, rising from 160 to 300 million people.

b. Rising Standard of Living. The future higher average standard of living will probably be still below that attained under private capitalism in other young countries, like Canada. On the other hand, the lowest level of the Soviet standard of living should undoubtedly be higher than it was in Russia under the Tsars, but probably not above the lowest standard of living in a country like Germany, operating under private capitalism and enjoying wise social legislation. The Soviet standard of living will be a herd standard based on mass consumption at a low level of uniformity. Russia is now discovering the benefits of standardized industrial production but is still laggard in standardized consumption. The masses now lack consumers' goods but hope the Plan will soon provide them. Standardized and cheap articles of consumption will make possible simple standards of living in food, clothing, shelter, transportation, and recreation—a sort of glorified ant-heap. To enable people to live happily under such conditions, ideals of the simple life are inculcated. Spartan and Puritan ideals will enable the Russian masses to live happily at low levels. For individuals with initiative and ability, whether in the industrial, agricultural, or professional classes, such standards will be lower than those attainable under the capitalist system, but to the incompetents, the morons, the "almosts," it may represent a standard higher than they can attain by their own efforts. They will have cast their burdens on the state and will trust to its constant care. Social insurance will probably be further extended to lessen the ills and woes of life. Undoubtedly some concession will eventually have to be made in raising the upper limit of the standard of living. Perhaps Lord Balfour's cynical remark in his note to Chicherin, that Bolshevism was able to make rich men poor, but was unable to make poor men rich, may hold less true as the Soviet industrial and social technique improves. Riches will not be set up as a goal of life, but perhaps some compromise between the leveling forces that Bolshevism now exercises and the urge that actuates superaverage individuals, may arise to relieve the drab sameness of present Soviet Russia on the one hand and on the other hand to eliminate those extreme examples of maldistribution of wealth and income which characterize other countries. The standard of living of the masses may not have been raised absolutely, but, in a sense, it has been raised relatively, and perhaps that in itself makes them somewhat happier. People will not mind the lack of cake so much if nobody has it. The elimination of the causes of envy may increase the happiness of the masses, for happiness is largely subjective.

c. Marriage and Divorce. Greater tolerance and liberalism in marriage relations will probably continue. The removal of the shackles of an outworn code of domestic relations is probably permanent. The freedom of spirit and the elimination of suffering which the system in some other countries involves, is a gain probably never to be surrendered.

2. Prospective Reaction. a. Marriage and Divorce. Yet marriage and divorce, which had been on a rather free basis are gradually, under the pressure of actual living, approaching more the western standards. Many divorces and marriages for any individual will continue to be regarded as anti-social be-

havior, and while marriage will probably not acquire the status of a sacrament, a prudential ethics will probably lead to the adoption of a relationship somewhat approaching that worked out in the liberal countries of the western world. Economic considerations alone will tend to check multiple divorces, for no individual under the new régime can ever be rich enough to support a number of households. At present the shortage of living quarters in the cities makes it preferable for couples to remain childless. As living quarters become more available and the rearing of children becomes less difficult, divorces should become less frequent.

Shaw's play, *Getting Married,* testing various substitutes for marriage, indicates a process which has been going on in Soviet Russia. Monogamic marriage seems to be the latest stage of social evolution which fits the present industrial society and as an institution should continue. Even now the divorce rate is lower in Moscow than in Chicago.

b. New Bourgeoisie. The attempt to eliminate a bourgeois class, even at the low standard of living now prevalent in Russia, has failed and a new bourgeoisie has emerged. It consists of the official classes, state employees, members of the party, members of various trade unions, and highly skilled labor. As the Bolshevik revolutionists get older, the surging fire of youth should settle, they should seek comfort, perhaps become smug, and develop the very traits for which they so much despised the old bourgeois class. The bourgeois mind seems psychologically inevitable, with the advancing years, the growth of a family, and the cessation of the acute phase of the revolutionary struggle.

c. Abolition of Classes. Old classes have been abolished, but Soviet society does not consist of a single working class, the proletariat. A host of new classes has arisen, as is inevitable under any system of social organization with its complications and gradations. As shown above, there is a new group of exploiters and exploited, a new group of leaders and followers. The degradation of the intelligentsia cannot continue. No society can long survive which puts a penalty on brain and a premium on brawn. As John Fiske stated fifty years ago, the step in evolution from monkey to man was more significant than the entire gamut of evolution from amœba to monkey. When brain replaced brawn as the means of survival, the beginning of civilization was laid, and no revolution, Soviet or other, is likely to reverse this evolutionary process.

d. Status of Labor. Labor has returned to the status occupied under private capitalism. Once again the workman is a cog in a large machine. Authority

is again centralized in the management. The worker's share in industry is as little as under private capitalism, in fact far less than in progressive corporations in the United States. The dawn of a new era has faded into the light of common day for the workman. Communistic sharing of wages by members of teams in the machine shop has largely disappeared. Each laborer works to get the maximum wages for himself and his family. The incompetent workman is left to shift for himself. The instinctive feeling of retaining the reward for one's effort has reasserted itself and is likely to remain.
e. Return of Old Motives. Individualism has little place in the Soviet scheme, and yet it was one or two outstanding figures that made the Soviet revolution possible. Great men, as individuals, have made history, and there is little doubt that under a future Soviet order the scope of the individual will be enlarged and the checks imposed by the community upon the individual will be diminished. Personal liberty will return, and with it the right of free speech, free assembly, and free press. Terrorism by an organized minority, powerful as it is today, will undoubtedly yield to the love of liberty, which is precious to men. The current extreme hatred between classes, which dominates the Soviet social scheme, is likely to yield further to tolerance and co-operation. The new social motives will effect a compromise with the old individual motives, which have made history to this day. The social contributions of individualism have not been unfruitful. It was the individual's search for profit that made possible large-scale production, cheap goods, mass consumption, and the democratization of the material good of life.
3. Soviet Influence on Foreign Countries. No such basic and violent change as the Soviet revolution is likely to leave other countries unaffected. The effects will be produced not by the words of paid propagandists sent abroad, but by the unconscious adoption by the rest of the world of those benefits and achievements in Russia which survive the test of time. Reckless of the results on the population and discarding tradition, the Soviets have embarked on great experiments which may furnish some lessons to other countries. At present Russia is a vast experimental laboratory in economics, politics, and sociology, and a critical if not hostile world is the observer.

The Soviet experiment has probably stimulated the efforts in other countries to ameliorate the cruel effects of the current depression. Skeptics will deny this and say the social trend is toward greater humanitarianism. However, the profit motive, though important and basic to our social structure, has been tempered by ideals of the common welfare. This is concretely illustrated in the widespread hope for resisting a reduction in wages, expressed by government officials and heads of some large corporations. In various ways the right of the unemployed workers to an increasing share of the social surplus is recognized in all countries.

The Soviet experiment has affected not only our economic policy, but our social philosophy. As Nicholas Murray Butler stated, liberalism must produce a new social concept to challenge the Soviets.[23] Western civilization will probably be molded as profoundly by that part of Russian experience which survives as Europe has been affected by the surviving and successful reforms of the French Revolution. But such effect on the rest of the world is not likely to take the form of revolution. Revolutions are the result of indigenous conditions. They are not importable. The effect on the western world will grow largely as a result of unconscious imitation and the diffusion of ideas. The stimulus to social change in other countries will probably arise from the votes and opinion of the intellectual proletariat, the underpaid professional classes, engineers, and teachers, who today are probably getting as little under capitalist society as they could under a well-managed socialist society. It will not come from the overpaid, highly unionized workers as in the building trades, to whom other workers pay tribute in the form of high rents.

4. Open Questions. a. How Will Russia Affect Other Countries? Shall not the world let Soviet Russia test out the experiment at home on a tractable, patient people inured to suffering, that such benefits as may emerge can accrue to other countries? Imitation is a means of spreading progress. Great Britain and Russia copied social insurance from Germany, and the United States copied the central banking system from Europe. The co-operative societies in Denmark have been the basis for co-operatives everywhere. Imitation of the successful phases of the Soviet experiment will be the means of adding to world progress.

Not only will the Soviet experiment affect the social organization in other countries but it may affect the flow of migration. Until now many of the foreign communities that continued their national life in Soviet Russia have fled the country.

An entire community of Swedes living in Russia for generations were repatriated a few years ago. Recently the German Government repatriated several hundred German colonists, residents in Russia for generations who fled to Prussia, after their property in Russia was confiscated. In Harbin there are over 1500 descendants of German immigrants into Russia of two centuries ago. These small Russian communities, descendants of foreign settlers, had survived the Tsarist régime but fled before the severities imposed by Soviet reform. On the other hand, the number of foreigners migrating into Russia is practically nil. In spite of worldwide unemployment, both high wages and extraordinary privileges are needed to attract the specialists into the country to render services indispensable under the Five-Year Plan. When the Soviet régime enjoys some measure of success, the tide of immigration should turn, and such a turn in the tide may be the means of improving conditions in other countries.

Undoubtedly, the ferment that is going on in Russia will not leave the world of ideas unaffected. As Walter Duranty pointed out in an interesting survey of the American situation upon his return after six years' absence, the people of the United States look with more sympathy upon ideas that were formerly regarded as visionary or Bolshevik; namely, the right of labor to share in the profit of capital and the planning of the national economy.[24] The development in Soviet Russia will "bring about not revolution, but evolution, not socialism, but a modification of capitalism. When the change is completed, it may be found that the Bolsheviki unwittingly, one might also say against their will, have contributed in no small measure to the development of American society."

In an address before the Union League Club of Chicago, on June 10, 1932, Col. Henry W. Anderson, counsel of the Baltimore & Ohio Railroad, challenged the justice and validity of the prevailing social and economic system and called for a fundamental adjustment to eliminate the inequalities of wealth. The solution for the United States and other industrially developed countries lay midway between the despotism of Soviet Russia and the "anarchic economic individualism of the United States." He predicted the need of "the abandoning of the present extreme competitive order and the substitution of a co-operative society in which industry would be under government regulation, directed toward protecting the rights of the individual and the community against exploitation. The Sherman and Clayton Anti-Trust Acts would have to be revised to permit more co-operation in industry, buttressed by such laws as would protect the community against encroachment by large combinations."

b. Can Religion and the Family Disappear? The entire Soviet scheme is in a state of transition, and many future conditions are in the making. Economically, politically, and educationally the Russian people are unprepared for many of the radical changes that have been made, and it is very likely that, as in the case of the French Revolution, many advances will be lost temporarily, and many of the rash experiments will fail. Can a society dispense entirely with some form of organized spiritual life? Will an intense realism suit the cravings of a certain type of mind for those subtle, intangible ideals which have added beauty to life and a philosophic sense of kinship with the Source of life, symbol to man of justice and of mercy? Can the family become so tenuous and weak as to make place for a larger social group, or will not the family remain permanently as a unit of the social structure?

What is the danger of social chaos if the current régime breaks down? Or can it slowly shear itself of power, as no régime before it has ever done, in order to effect a slow transition toward the next stage of civilization? Communism in Soviet Russia challenges thinking and discussion in the rest of the world. Its influence is too vast to permit it to be ignored. It may get a more sympathetic hearing, when it publicly renounces all attempts at violence both at home and abroad and proceeds in the high spirit which pervades many aspects of the experiment.

c. The Classless State—the Communists' "Kingdom of Heaven." Even the most partisan Bolsheviks realize that the present régime is merely a stage in the development toward a socialized society. In the words of Lenin, "Only in communist society, when capitalists have disappeared, where there are no longer any classes, does the state disappear, and can one speak of freedom."

A refutation of this idea for many years was democratic Germany, which left relative freedom to the "Nazis" and to the Communists, freedom of the press, freedom of assembly, and freedom of speech, even though both sought to overturn the existing state. The decree of March 28, 1931, issued under Article 48 of the Constitution of the German Republic, authorized the temporary suspension of these rights during the emergency then existing. Yet the German press criticized the "suspension of constitutional rights." However, all violators retained full legal rights in court, and punishment was mild—imprisonment, or suspension of publication for three months.[25] And when the Reich government required the Prussian papers to publish its opposition to the plebiscite of Sunday, August 9, 1931, it left them free to criticize the policy editorially—and the Nazi and Communist organs denounced it in parallel columns as "an unheard-of infringement of the freedom of the press."[26]

At the distant day of Lenin's dream, similar to the prophetic vision of the kingdom of God, the state presumably will disappear because it will no longer be necessary to legislate or to enforce laws.

Eventually the Soviet prophets foresee a day of peace, when classes will disappear and when there will be no conflict. Is not this the dream of the tired warriors? Bukharin believes "the bourgeoisie will fuse with the proletariat, the workers' state will cease to be, classes will disappear and society will become communist." This is a picture of the communist heaven, of the eventual day of cessation of struggle, when all will be at peace. How similar this is to the vision of Isaiah! "With righteousness shall he judge the poor, and decide with equity for the meek of the land; . . . And the wolf shall dwell with the lamb, and the leopard shall lie down with the kid. . . . They shall not hurt nor destroy in all my holy mountain; For the earth shall be full of the knowledge of the Lord, as the waters cover the sea."

Probably for a long time both Soviet Russia and the so-called capitalist system will exist side by side, as competing modes of social organization. The capitalist principle of competition and survival of the fittest may be invoked in behalf of communist Russia. Let the two exist, compete, and struggle for survival. All the social forces whose operations are revealed in history indicate that so-called capitalist society will probably emerge the victor. Evolution rather than revolution will triumph. Communism will influence capitalist society by its ideals, and capitalism will influence communism by its technique. Eventually they will meet on some common ground. For even the communists now realize that the World War did not mark the end of the capitalist system. It works and despite its weaknesses serves society better than any system developed thus far.

E. Spiritual Prospects

1. Prospective Gains. Some of the spiritual gains achieved by the Soviets bid fair to last. The abolition of illiteracy and the introduction of universal compulsory education is probably a permanent gain. The lessening influence of money in social affairs will probably remain in large part. The spiritual appeal of communist ideals will probably continue to inspire mankind. The changes in human nature, as effected by changes of social heredity, customs, habits, and institutions, will probably continue at an accelerating pace. Tradition will in future be less of a hampering influence on progress. There will probably be a smaller gap between the disinherited and the successful.

Strange as it may seem, the communist spiritual ideals, words so hateful to the Soviet spokesmen, are akin to those of the Puritans in some respects. They both stress the sterner aspects of life: duty rather than happiness, service to the community rather than satisfaction of the individual, simplicity rather than display. Not least, they share the one fanatic quality of imposing their theory of life on other people by force. "The Communist Party demands from its members faith and works, temperance and soberness. Its ideal is devotion to duty, instead of devotion to financial success. It disapproves of selfish vanities such as lipstick and silk stockings. Beauty and art for art's sake are regarded as the works of the devil. More and more it is a rule that literature, painting, the drama, and music shall teach lessons and contribute to the cause. Dancing and drink in public places are banned. Smart dress is frowned upon. The communists, like the Puritans, are bent on reducing every one to the same level of drab, useful, dutiful, painstaking ugliness. And like the Puritans the communists lay great stress on discipline, obedience, self-denial and public service." [27]

2. Prospective Losses. The losses in the future are likely to be many. Fanaticism, ruthlessness, struggle for power, suppression of the individual are likely to continue as a tradition. In the future there is likely to develop a fatigue and a disillusionment, whose consequences it would be difficult to forecast.

a. Propaganda and Bias. Lacking free and spontaneous organs of public opinion, the press, the drama, the novel, all public information becomes propaganda. The state owns the newspapers. It controls the press and the theater. Truth has little chance, except as it appears in innuendo. Part of the bias which is the basis of the current propaganda reflects the reaction from the extreme pressure of the Tsarist régime. Will the young people, who never suffered under the Tsar, be moved by these violent emotions, or will they not be more seekers after objective truth?

b. Fanaticism and Ruthlessness. The difficult goals of the Five-Year Plan have developed traits among the Russian people of impatience for results and fanaticism, which are necessary to overcome difficulties and to steel the masses against suffering and hardship. Ruthlessness and fanaticism will probably continue so long as the present aims persist. When the important tasks are not promptly achieved, individuals are blamed. Recently 138,000 government employees were subjected to a "cleansing" process, in order to stir up further enthusiasm for the Plan and to punish incompetence in a bureaucracy which seemed to be inevitable under Soviet rule. Incompetence, bureaucracy, and red tape are likely to continue under the present scheme of excessive centralization.

c. Struggle for Power. Admittedly the capitalist system may be still suffering from an excessive concentration of wealth in few hands, but the Soviet system is suffering from an excessive concentration of power. This is likely to continue so long as the present oligarchic government remains. A republican régime should result in a diffusing of power, decentralization of authority, and therefore less incompetence, suspicion, fear, and repression, which are essential to retain power in a few hands.

d. Individualism. The leveling process will leave its mark on the ambitions of the people. For when the individual can rise but little above a dead level of uniformity, striving will diminish. Already, with the state assuming the burden of insurance against the accidents of life, there is less incentive to accumulate a personal surplus. Will the peasant in the future relinquish his desire to be his own master and to be independent? Will he fall in with the industrial scheme as applied to agriculture, with day wages, subordination, and a socialized job? Throughout the world the peasantry is strongly individualistic. Will the Russian peasant ultimately prove an exception?

e. Fatigue and Disillusionment. The atmosphere of Russia today is the atmosphere of war. The strain of the Five-Year Plan is terrific, not merely on the masses who must dispense with essential goods, but upon the small group responsible for the execution of the Plan. Crisis after crisis arises, which demands tremendous intellectual application and emotional energy. The apathetic Slav temperament, continuously restimulated, is finally developing a certain protective immunity, a callousness and indifference, which in turn calls for more intense propaganda and more ruthless driving. The nation-wide appeal for sacrifice and superhuman exertion cannot be permanent. The fever and the excitement are abnormal. It is a manic condition. The consequences of this excessive expenditure of energy is inevitable. Just as a manic patient finally slides into fatigue and even into melancholia, so the prospect for Soviet Russia is for a temporary exhaustion of the energies of even as strong and vigorous a people as the Russians.

Should the Five-Year Plan fail—and it is quite likely that it will in many respects—should the consumer find goods just as scarce after 1932, the leaders will then realize along what a fearful road they have led their people. The masses, anticipating abundance and freedom, will have only a prospect of another Five-Year Plan, of more underconsumption and new restrictions. A painful disillusionment awaits the Russian people in the next few years. What its social consequences will be it is difficult to forecast. Probably before any sharp break occurs, the leaders will reduce the tempo of the Plan, or even abandon some of the large factories that cannot be operated efficiently, and use Russian exports to buy not machinery or capital goods, but food and clothing to assuage the discontent and resentment of the masses.

Will such a disillusionment result in the breakdown of the party that recklessly attempted such an impossible task? Will there be a revolt against the Soviets, or will the consequence merely be a lowering of the morale of a people that can suffer and yet not revolt?

3. Open Questions. a. Americanism in Russia. The goal of the Russian leaders is to emulate American industrial technique. This they are unlikely to accomplish for many years. American life today is the result of peculiar antecedent forces, the tradition of pioneering, the wresting of land from the wilderness, the advance on a geographical frontier, activities that called forth courage, initiative, and resourcefulness. Furthermore, the American spirit today is the result of fusion of many strains. The emigrants that left Europe were selected from the hardy, adventurous type. They found new problems awaiting them which called for a spirit of daring. Russia lacks these two characteristics of America. There is no geographical frontier to conquer, and there is no selective emigration of adventuresome spirits. At best emigration to Russia is never likely to become as large as was that to the United States. And for this reason a vigorous civilization is less likely to grow out of Soviet Russia than in the United States. It is unlikely that the specifically American tradition can be transplanted there.

However, there may be no geographical frontier in the sense that there is no wilderness to be wrested from primitive inhabitants like the Indians, but there is an economic frontier in Russia. There are large untouched resources which call for development. New industries will have to be built, and grappling with the problems involved may develop a new type of Russian character, the industrial genius, serving the community, which may be likewise a heritage of later generations. Again there is a social frontier in Russia; new institutions are emerging. And then there is a spiritual frontier; men are striving toward ideals such as have been felt throughout all history and in all climes. These Utopias were actually tinkered with in small colonies, but in Russia, for the first time they are being tested on a large scale.

b. New Psychology and New Motives. There are some spiritual aspects of Russian life concerning which it is difficult even to attempt a prediction. The structure of the new society is dependent upon a new spirit. The attempt within a few years to effect profound changes in the attitude toward life of 160,000,000 people is without parallel. Will it be possible to change the slow-tempered Slav into an efficient, alert factory workman, except after decades of experiment? Will it be possible to change an inherently conservative peasant into a semi-altruistic and co-operative worker in a grain factory? Will it be possible permanently to effect a change in the attitude of the people toward their property, their fellows and the state? Can the mental attitude be maintained which courageously embarks on new experiments and which is essential for the carrying out of the Soviet program? Or will the Russian Revolution follow the way of other revolutions of history? Will zeal be replaced by indifference, and the experimental, adventurous attitude toward life by one of comfort, smugness and satisfaction?

As the individual worker on piece rates earns high wages and accumulates savings, as the government now requests, and as he becomes the owner of government bonds, will he be willing to risk as much in experimentation as he did before he became a small capitalist? Will the missionary attitude continue in the next generation? In the Putilov Iron Works in Leningrad, the author met two workers. One was an old workman of about sixty who had been active in the revolution, a radical under the Tsarist régime. He said that he preferred to have but one shirt and remain in Russia, not for chauvinist reasons, but to help create a model commonwealth to show to the workingmen of the world. The other, a young foreman about thirty, who had just come back from America, said that he preferred to live in America under the capitalist régime, own an automobile, and have many shirts. He was not interested in teaching the workmen of the world. Will the Soviet Revolution, like Christianity, lose its pristine ideals, become institutionalized and set, and fall into the hands of vested interests?

Civilization is merely the external expression of the human mind. Can a new civilization be built without changing the human mind? And can the human mind change its fundamental attitude toward parental affection, property rights, individualistic urge and achievement, desire for possession, love of power, desire to accumulate a personal reserve and to rise above the average? Time alone can answer. It has not been done before.

c. Reaction. It took about a hundred years of persecution and skillful radical leadership to effect the overturn of the Tsarist rule. How much suffering will be required to arouse a people who, when stirred, become powerful in action? The same forces that upset the monarchy—suffering by the masses and a planned revolutionary technique—may upset the present oligarchy. As Duranty points out: "After Cromwell's death the English people, weary of Puritan rigor and its attempt to change their mode of life, swung back without bloodshed to a monarchic system so thoroughly, that the reign of Charles II became a by-word of privilege, luxury, and naughty conduct as a reaction from Puritanism." [28] History may similarly repeat itself in Russia.

d. Interaction of Capitalism and Communism. As the contacts of the Soviets with the capitalist world increase, both through the engineers they send abroad and the western visitors to Russia, the sobering effect of western life on Soviet Russia is inevitable. The western world now enjoys a higher standard of living, and as a result Russian methods and institutions will probably veer gradually toward western ideas, particularly with reference to utilizing the fruits of individualism.

On the other hand, not in the standards of living but rather in the ideals of protecting the unfortunates of society, the western world will probably learn from Russia. That which constitutes the problem of philanthropy and private charity in the western world is in Soviet Russia the concern of the state. The western world, capitalism, will unconsciously copy Soviet ideas. The ultimate free dissemination of foreign literature in Russia must lead to modification of the Soviet program. The justification for American participation in Russian affairs is the moderating influence it probably will have on Russian ideas and policies.

According to Maxim Litvinov, Soviet Foreign Commissar, in an address to the European Union Commission of the League of Nations, May 18, 1931:

> The Soviet and capitalist systems are struggling and will continue to struggle against each other by the very fact of their existence and development. The question is whether this struggle and development will be allowed to follow a natural process or whether both systems will have recourse to mutually hostile measures.

e. Psychological Maturity. The Russians are emerging from a state of national infancy to adolescence. The life history of the nation repeats the life history of the individual. Maturity has been defined as the point at which declining ambitions meet rising capacities. As the Russians trim down their extravagant ideas and as they simultaneously acquire experience in life, they will probably finally settle into a social system that is practical enough to work and ideal enough to suit their aspirations.

Joseph Wood Krutch, in his book, *The Modern Temper,* points to the degeneration of western civilization and predicts the emergence of a strong, crude people to take on its burdens. When the Roman Empire fell the barbarians took up the burden. And therefore, he implies, as western civilization becomes effete, Russian civilization may step to the helm. The law of life is the law of birth, maturity, and decay. New industries spring up, show rising profits, become competitive, show declining profits, and finally decay. Similar laws apply to civilizations. Undoubtedly Russia is on the rise;

western civilization is well advanced; it may be that some of the fresh views of Soviet Russia may infuse new elements of strength into western life.

Beginnings are always interesting—the beginning of life, beginning of marriage, beginning of a career. Russia is beginning a new civilization, and the attention of the world is riveted on her. Great possibilities inhere in the experiment, despite the cynics and the skeptics and the heresy hunters. For the vast struggle and the great suffering cannot be entirely in vain. Growth is accompanied by pain. And life is born out of suffering. Russia is in labor. A new life and a new social growth will probably come out of the travail.

PART FIVE

WANTED—AN AMERICAN POLICY TOWARD RUSSIA

The flighty purpose never is o'ertook
Unless the deed go with it.

—*Macbeth*

CHAPTER XVI

THE ISSUES

America's policy toward Russia is difficult to understand. It is a mixture of curiously inconsistent components. It seems more of a muddling affair than a clearly thought-out program. On the one hand we permit American engineers and American corporations to build up the industries of Russia, and on the other we refuse to recognize the Soviets for several reasons, not the least of which is that they profess to intend to destroy the capitalist system. A consistent policy might follow one of two lines: either formulate or participate in a world policy to isolate and crush the Soviets, or else recognize them and help in the economic restoration of the country. The latter policy would be based on the theory that the experiment should be permitted, either to test the superiority of one of the two types of society—communist and capitalist—or to demonstrate to the world that communism will fail as a method of organizing the economic life of a country. Its failure under such conditions would leave no excuse to the Soviet leaders. On the other hand, should they fail under the present policy, they may well say that communism could not work because of the opposition of capitalist society.

Recognition of Russia, subject to important conditions, would probably involve a slow readjustment toward capitalism and a "strategic retreat" from communism, accompanied by suitable plausible explanations to the Russian masses. A continuance of the present muddling policy of the entire world toward Russia will probably result in another decade of economic dislocation of the world, to say nothing of the suffering of 160,000,000 Russians who are helpless to change their status. A policy toward Russia should embrace the question of propaganda, the question of foreign debts and new credits, and a consistent policy on recognition.*

A. Propaganda

Communist propaganda was based on certain theories and had definite aims. It manifested itself in several countries. But its results were meager.

* For an excellent history of American-Russian relations see Schuman, Frederick L., *American Policy Toward Russia Since 1917*. New York: International Publishers, 1928.

Propaganda was then abandoned as an immediate policy, although ultimately the aim of the Soviet leaders still seems to be world revolution.

1. THEORY AND AIM—WORLD REVOLUTION. When the Soviet régime was established, on November 7, 1917, the leaders regarded it merely as the first step in a world revolution. An eye-witness of those turbulent days describes the impatient telephoning of Lenin twelve times within an hour as to whether the expected revolutionary outbreak in Berlin or Hamburg had already occurred.[1] The theory was that Russia could not be an island of communism in a sea of capitalism. Untroubled as yet by the pressing administrative problems which subsequently arose, they made world revolution a matter of major interest and the preservation of the Russian Revolution one of minor interest. The revolutionary program for America which the communists adopted sounds crazy to the American. The plan was to arouse the negroes, to foment war in Latin America against the United States, and to unite the "peasants" and workers of the United States in revolution. Other countries were to be attacked under divers programs. Great Britain was to be weakened by a communist revolt in India. An uprising in China directed by the Soviets was to spread the ruin of capitalism. This communist policy, however, was left to the Communist Party and the Third Internationale, which did the plotting and the fomenting of revolt, while the Soviet government itself maintained a scrupulously proper attitude toward other governments.

2. COMMUNIST INTERNATIONALE. a. Aims of the Communist Internationale. The aim of the Communist Internationale (abbreviated as "Comintern") is frankly to destroy capitalism everywhere. Its aim is world revolution. The constitution of the Third Internationale describes its aims—"to unite the communist parties into one proletarian party, to fight for the establishment of the dictatorship of the proletariat, to create a world union of socialist Soviet republics, to destroy all classes, and to achieve socialism, the first stage of communist society." At the 1928 meeting of the Communist Internationale these aims were restated.

Pravda, an official organ, states the aims of the Communist Party frankly as follows: "Our ultimate aim is world communism. Our fighting program is for world revolution and the establishment of a world dictatorship of the proletariat. Everywhere class war must take place. Our program openly throws down the challenge to the bourgeois world."

b. Comintern vs. the Soviet Government. The Comintern was formed in March 1919, but a year and a half after the establishment of the Soviet dictatorship. In the program of world revolution the Soviet government has found it desirable to be inactive officially, but the Communist Party is very aggressive in its advocacy of world revolt. This separation of the two is more fictitious than real, because, although the Soviet government is neutral, its policies are framed by the Communist Party. In fact Stalin is Secretary General of the party and as such dominates the policies of the Soviet government, much as Charles Francis Murphy, noted boss of Tammany Hall, dominated the policies of New York City, though he held no office in city government. The Comintern is merely the Soviet government in disguise.

At times, however, there are differences between the official policy of the government and the program of the party. For example, the Soviet government signified its adherence to the Kellogg pact, but the Comintern criticized it. The Soviet government in its trade relations has become friendly with Italy, but the Comintern is opposed to Fascism. These differences of policy are regarded by Soviet sympathizers as indicating a clear cleavage between the party and the government. But if so, the cleavage merely reflects the fact that the government must make concessions to practical politics, whereas the Communist Party can revel in social theories.

c. Independence of Communist Party and the Soviet Government. The government itself claims that the party is a private organization and does not officially represent it. This separation is convenient and makes it possible for the party to continue its revolutionary propaganda without exposing the government to the unfavorable international consequences. In defense of such a separation Soviet sympathizers point to an analogous separateness in other countries. For example, the British Labor Party, which twice controlled the British government, is a member of the Second Internationale. But the British government and the Second Internationale are utterly unrelated. Again, Mikoyan stated [2] that they were in possession of proof that members of the Second Internationale attempted to organize a rebellion in Russian Georgia, yet no protest was made to the government of Belgium, requesting that the Second Internationale be enjoined from maintaining its offices in Belgium and that members of the Belgian government be prohibited from membership in the Second Internationale. According to Soviet sympathizers the Soviet government does not subsidize the Comintern.

3. Evidences of Revolutionary Propaganda. The effort to foment revolt abroad has stirred the protest of statesmen in various countries. In 1921, Lord Curzon protested against Soviet propaganda, and in 1923 he threatened

to break off diplomatic relations. He accused the Russian ministers in Persia and Afghanistan of "stirring up anti-British sentiment in violation of the terms of the agreement."

The British general strike in 1926 was said to have been financed in part from funds sent by the trade unions in Moscow. The anti-British sentiment among the Chinese nationalists, who were advised by Russian communists, finally led to the raid on the Arcos and a breach of diplomatic relations. These relations, terminated in May 1927, were resumed in May 1929, on the promise to cease agitation in India, although the Soviet officials denied such activity on their part. In October 1930, Foreign Minister Arthur Henderson protested to the Soviet ambassador that his government was not observing the promise that there must be no hostile Russian propaganda in Great Britain, and the ambassador assured him that the Soviet government was trying to keep the agreement, but could not control the activities of the Third Internationale.

In Germany, on the other hand, there were a series of communist intrigues in the Ruhr. The object apparently was to stir up revolution in Germany. Germany protested to Moscow against the activities of Russian agents in Germany, and on May Day in 1929 the Soviet War Commissar, in a public address in Moscow in the presence of the German ambassador, stated that the German proletariat would make an attempt at world revolution on that day.

With reference to the American Communist Party, *Pravda* gave instructions "to develop communism in the factories, to mobilize the working masses for revolution, to bore from within the organized Federation of Labor, to bring the proletarian workers into the Communist Party." [3]

Similarly, during the Spanish Revolution the official organ *Pravda* published "instructions" to Spain to turn communist. According to *Pravda,* the Spanish Revolution is now similar to the pre-Kerensky phase of the Russian Revolution. They, the Bolsheviks, believe that revolutions cannot be created, yet when one does break out it can be directed toward a communist goal. Therefore, *Pravda* appeals to the Communist Party in Spain to organize the peasants, workers, soldiers, and sailors under a program of direct action for nationalization and expropriation and establishment of a Soviet republic.[4] This incitement to revolt is in striking contrast with the attitude of the Soviet press toward the critical situation in Germany in the spring of 1931 and the summer of 1932. The difference may be that the Soviet had machinery orders in Germany and none in Spain, and they were realists enough to subordinate communist doctrine to business sense.

4. Denial of Propaganda. That the Soviets are indulging in propaganda has been denied in various quarters. Stalin told Walter Duranty, "All this talk of propaganda is ridiculous. Constitutions and systems are changed by internal causes, not by talks or books. In the old days the Tsars blamed the French or German socialists for importing socialism into Russia, forgetting that the conditions of life and not socialist propaganda determine the course of events. Now they are making the same mistake in the United States when they say we are re-exporting socialism to Europe."[5] In a similar vein Karl Radek stated: "Revolutions are not carried in suitcases. They cannot be imported, they grow." Radek's views were repeated by two United States senators. Senator Cutting stated that, if revolution should ever come to our country, it will have no relation to foreign propaganda, but will be due to our failure to meet our own problems. Senator Wheeler stated similarly that the conditions upon which communism thrives are long hours, poor wages, and undesirable working conditions, and not soap-box oratory.

A British White Paper, entitled *Documents Listing the Hostile Activities of the Soviet Government,* reveals nothing to support the accusation implied in the title. It was termed by Ramsay Macdonald "a tragi-comic melodrama."[6]

5. Failure of Propaganda. After fifteen years of agitation the Communist Party has not only failed to achieve the world revolution, but has precipitated universal opposition to the Soviet government and has thereby added to the economic problems that are troubling Russia. In view of the pressing difficulties of the Soviets the Comintern is decreasing in importance.

a. In America. Communism has made no headway in America. In fact it is insignificant. The number of communist voters in the United States in 1928 was about 48,000, less than one-twentith of one per cent of the population, and at the end of 1930 William Z. Foster, testifying before the Fish Committee, estimated that the Communist Party had about 12,000 dues-paying members as against 40,000 in 1920. America has not proved fertile soil for the propaganda of the Comintern. The standards of living are high, and the opportunity open to the poor to improve their status is not favorable to the growth of a doctrine which has grown out of long oppression.

b. In Germany. On the other hand, the Communist Party in Germany is strong. In the elections of 1930 the Communists obtained more than 4,500,000 votes and actually elected 76 representatives to the Reichstag. This vote represented almost 8 per cent of the population. In July 1932, they polled 5,300,000 votes and elected 89 representatives. Yet Germany does not complain about Soviet propaganda. Both Russia and Germany feel themselves the "victims of Versailles," which serves as a common bond to unite them.

c. In Great Britain. In Great Britain the Communist Party is small, numbering about 5000. It is not a very active or important element in politics. According to a Labor member of Parliament from Manchester, Joseph Toole, who visited Russia, the aim of Soviet propaganda to extend the revolution throughout the world "would more properly be laid in a lunatic asylum." The Soviet system would not suit Great Britain.[7]

6. ABANDONMENT OF FOREIGN PROPAGANDA. a. Concentrating on Home Problems. Russia has so many problems of her own that she has no time to meddle with the problems of others. The bristling difficulties that beset the Five-Year Plan on all sides are keeping Soviet energies riveted at home. As a result the Sun Yat Sen University in Moscow, a training school for Chinese communists, has been closed. The Stalin University for the Training of Foreigners in Communism has likewise closed its doors. Home problems are so pressing that, if the world revolution should occur, the Five-Year Plan would be upset. In fact a world revolution now would be a calamity for Russia.

The plan for world revolution was favored by Trotsky. But as soon as the Five-Year Plan got under way, Stalin opposed such a program. In fact as between saving the Russian Revolution and starting revolutions in other countries, the Soviets are sufficiently nationalistic to try to attend to their domestic realities rather than to extend their political fantasies abroad. To succeed in Russia the Five-Year Plan requires not world revolution but world peace. Therefore peace has become the keynote of Soviet foreign policy and communist parties abroad have become a nuisance to the Kremlin. Apparently the Soviets have trimmed down their aims to the limitations imposed by the practical problems that confront them.

b. Revolutions Not Transferable. It is becoming increasingly clear to the Soviet officials that revolutions are historic phenomena that grow out of preceding conditions. They believe that economic rivalries of the capitalist nations, and not communist propaganda, make world revolution inevitable. As Chicherin wrote to Secretary of State Colby: "The Soviet government clearly understands that the revolutionary movement of the working masses in every country is their own affair. Communism cannot be imposed by force. The fight for communism in every country must be carried on by its working masses themselves." Whether this conviction is the result of an historic insight, or was rudely imposed upon the Soviets by necessity, makes little difference. They realize that they cannot build up Russia economically and at the same time attempt to destroy social systems elsewhere.

c. Non-Intervention as a Policy. In various diplomatic communications and documents the Soviet government has agreed to refrain from interfering with the internal affairs of other countries. As Chicherin wrote to Colby: "If the Russian Government binds itself to abstain from spreading communist literature, all its representatives abroad are enjoined scrupulously to observe the pledge." The elementary needs of the peoples of Russia and of other countries demand normal relations. The first condition of such relations is mutual good faith and non-intervention on both sides. The Soviets point out that in 1923, when political conditions in Germany were very unstable, the Soviet Government was unwilling to aid German communists for fear it would hurt the Russian diplomatic position. This is contrary to the statement made by Paul Scheffer [8] that an economic and military plan was made to stir up revolution when the French marched into the Ruhr in 1923. During the period of the Chinese Revolution from 1924 to 1927, Soviet sympathizers say that Stalin was opposed to the establishment of a Soviet régime in China.

During the financial crisis in Germany in the early summer of 1931, when the Communists and the Hitlerites were struggling to overthrow the moderate government of Bruening, and again in the critical summer of 1932 both *Pravda* and *Izvestia* were strangely silent. The Soviet press made no attempt to stimulate an uprising in Germany. There were several reasons. The Soviet government had large orders in Germany, and was chafing at the prospect of late deliveries. Furthermore, it was necessary that Germany should receive financial aid from other countries in order to be able to extend it to Russia. A communist uprising in Germany would therefore endanger the Bolshevik government in Russia. In fact, an upset in Europe would be a calamity to Russia; it would delay the industrial upbuilding of the country and would ruin the markets for Russian exports. The founding of the Third Internationale was due in part to the desire of the Soviets to have nests of communist sympathizers in case of a world war against Russia, but with the fading prospects of another Russian invasion by the western world and with the growing strength of the Soviet Union this device became less necessary. This may be an additional reason why the Moscow press has remained silent in the face of the possibility of an overturn in Germany.

d. High Cost of Propaganda. In view of Russia's great difficulties in obtaining foreign exchange for the importation of machinery and in view of the exportation of foodstuffs out of Russia even though the population is underfed, it seems unlikely that the Russians can even afford the luxury of spending money for propaganda. Bread at home is a greater necessity than propaganda abroad. The *valuta* that is wasted for stimulating propaganda abroad can be used more effectively for preventing revolution at home by an underfed population. Furthermore, considering the number of communists abroad, the cost per vote is very high. It is an inefficient use of Soviet funds. In fact it is reported that the Comintern itself finds difficulty in obtaining foreign exchange in view of the competing requirement for foreign money to pay for imported machinery.

The scope of operations is revealed in the 1930 budget of the Comintern.[9] At the Eleventh Plenary Session of the Executive Committee of the Communist Internationale, the budget was submitted for approval. It showed a total membership throughout the world of 2,518,000. Contributions throughout the world totaled $956,000, or approximately 40 cents per member. Of the aggregate receipts $321,000, or over one-third, was devoted to administrative expenses, presumably chiefly jobs for the faithful. About $641,000 was spent for party newspapers and propaganda work throughout the world. This total has been surpassed by the campaign expenditures of a single candidate for Senator in the United States, or those of a mayoralty election in one of the larger American cities. The small amount of contributions per member and the restricted range of operations is indicated in the unimportance of proceedings at this session. For example, the Executive Committee debated the admittance, as separate sections of the Comintern, of the Communist Parties of Iceland and of Cyprus.

7. Immediate Policy. a. Propaganda by Achievements. The threats and boasts concerning world revolution, taken from the addresses of the Soviet leaders and from the press, are very much like the chauvinist appeals made in other countries. For example an address by Mussolini a year ago, as printed in the Italian papers, contained much inflammatory material which was not included in the translation prepared for foreign countries. It was only the unfavorable reaction in Europe of the original version that fixed attention on the deleted chauvinistic bombast. Similarly, a good deal of the Soviet propaganda is buncombe, intended for home consumption and to maintain popular enthusiasm, in spite of the widespread want. Soviet deeds and Soviet words of propaganda are far from identical.

The Russian attitude now is that the best propaganda would be the success of the Five-Year Plan and the Soviet program of industrialization, or the failure of capitalist economics. The idea of propaganda by deeds instead of words was stressed by Stalin. "If you say we are sending back to the west the practical experience of creating a socialist society you are right. How do we do it? We show visiting foreigners that socialist production is possible, is growing, and will succeed. Whether they like it or not, socialist economics will develop and exist for them to study. That is propaganda, too." [10]

b. Russia Dependent on Capitalist World. The industrial program requires Russia to trade with the capitalist world, to import machinery and to export grain and raw materials. Therefore Russia's program depends upon an accommodation to the capitalist world. Russian state industry and state agriculture are therefore dependent upon the existence of a stable capitalist order and upon imports and exports. It is apparently inconsistent with Soviet theories, but it is evident that the building of socialism at home requires the avoidance of revolution abroad. For some time, therefore, the propaganda for world revolution is likely to be negligible, not merely on the part of the Soviet government but also on the part of the Communist Party.

8. ULTIMATE POLICY. a. Official Statements. In spite of the fact that Russia is now concentrating all her efforts on succeeding in her industrial program, which would in itself be the best communist propaganda, the plan of world revolution has not been definitely abandoned. Even Soviet sympathizers, who refute the world's charge of propaganda, admit that ultimate world revolution is still on the long-range program of the Soviet leaders. In fact, Stalin told the First Conference of the All-Union Communist Industrial Executives: "We have a duty to our fellows abroad. The job we are doing, if it succeeds, will overturn the whole world and the whole working class who regard us as their vanguard, their shock brigade, in the battle against capitalism." [11] This is merely a repetition of a similar statement made in 1927 on the tenth anniversary of the October Revolution: "The October Revolution is a revolution of the working class. . . . It is the center of the revolutionary movement which will take advantage of the situation which will inevitably be produced by capitalist rivalries. The era of capitalism's ruin has begun." Even though this sounds suspiciously like the blatant chauvinism of the Kaiser before the war, or the stupid boasting of dictators in other European countries, there is probably an express intention in the Stalin statement.

When the proletariat of the capitalist countries disappointed Lenin and his associates by failing to revolt in October 1917, the plan for world revolution was changed. The first step was to build up a strong Russian Soviet Union, which, when economically developed, would be an effective instrument for world revolt.

b. Psychological Explanations. A psychological analysis of the self-imposed mission of world revolution is interesting. This militant purpose may merely be a psychological compensation for present weakness. The notion that the Russians will be the leaders in the world revolution is an illusion of superiority, to compensate them for their present inferiority, economic and cultural. And not least, how else can popular enthusiasm be kept at fever heat, necessary for the accomplishment of the Five-Year Plan, except by flattering the masses with the idea that they are the vanguard of the world's progress, an exalting thought which, when truly believed, has accomplished miracles among the believers of the great religions in the past?

9. American Reaction. a. Propaganda Not Harmful. Mr. Ivy Lee, speaking at Williamstown, Massachusetts, in 1930, stated that American workmen had too much common sense to pay any attention to the Soviet agitators. The Bolsheviks had no need of distributing their literature secretly, for their most violent utterances were printed openly in the American papers. Again, the usual feeling seems to be that America does not constitute fertile soil for a Soviet uprising, and the fears of Bolshevik-hunters indicate their lack of faith in American institutions. Mr. Thomas Campbell, the American agricultural expert retained by the Soviet government, stated repeatedly that Russian propaganda cannot affect American workmen because of the high standard of living here. He may be overlooking the fact, however, that America, even if invulnerable, may not enjoy Soviet propaganda. Even a man with a bullet-proof-vest does not enjoy being sniped at—even with blank cartridges.

b. Other Anti-American Propaganda. Soviet sympathizers in the United States say that anti-American propaganda exists in various parts of the world. The Argentines resent our interpretation of the Monroe Doctrine and do not hesitate to say so in their newspapers. Directly after the enactment of the Hawley-Smoot tariff law, a wave of anti-American sentiment swept over Europe and tariff schedules were raised to discriminate against American exports. However, Soviet defenders overlooked the fact that such propaganda is not intended like Soviet propaganda to upset American institutions, but rather to effect a change in American policy. On the other hand, Soviet propaganda is not particularly anti-American. It is anti-capitalist. America is not particularly singled out. In propaganda, at least, we enjoy most-favored-nation treatment.

c. America's Anti-Russian Propaganda. Soviet sympathizers defend Russian propaganda with the statement that America has done much more to overthrow the Soviet government than the Soviets have done to uproot American institutions. These sympathizers refer specifically to the expulsion of Russians from the United States, the protests against Russian convict labor, the threats of embargoes, and the failure to recognize Russia. They should remember however, that these measures were not initiated by the United States aggressively, but merely as a defense against Soviet policies. After fifteen years of continuous threats to overthrow established governments, the Soviets should not be surprised that these governments take strong measures to protect themselves. As part of their plea for recognition the Soviets offered a clause pledging mutual non-interference in domestic affairs—that is, the Soviet Union and the United States would each agree not to engage in propaganda in the other's territory. Such a clause may be taken as an admission that the Russians did try to interfere in American affairs, because America certainly made no effort at capitalist propaganda in Russia.

B. Debt and Foreign Property

The attitude of the Soviets on the question of the foreign debt is amazing. The observer in Russia is impressed with the large vision and grand conceptions which underlie the economic and social policies. And yet the Soviet leaders seem to overlook the one large and outstanding fact in their foreign trade. The failure to meet the requirements of the creditor countries has impaired Soviet credit abroad. Russian borrowing power is limited, therefore they pay as much as 30 per cent more for their imports. Lacking credit they must force exports at whatever price the world will pay for large quantities of distress merchandise of a few items. On both exports and imports, therefore, the Soviets suffer a substantial loss. Lack of foreign credit has resulted also in inflation. These three losses probably exceed the annual interest on the entire foreign debt now in default.

Another broad aspect of the public-debt question is the fact that the outstanding foreign debt in default of about 7 billion dollars is probably less than 1 per cent of the undiscovered national wealth of the country. The area of the Soviet Union is more than two and a half times that of the United States. Its natural resources are known to be vast. The sum of 7 billion dollars is small in comparison with the new wealth which can be created by recognizing the debt without too great delay and too many reservations, to say nothing of the intangible value of lifting 160 million people from their pitifully low level of existence. Again, the Soviets in their various statements imply that the Tsarist debt was contracted primarily for the purpose of suppressing the liberal movement. The fact is that only a small percentage of it was for the general purposes of the government and by far the largest part was used for productive purposes, for railroads, utilities, and industries. If the foreign capitalists had not furnished the funds the Soviets today would have had to obtain new funds to acquire these economic assets.

1. Soviet Argument for Repudiation. The policy of the Soviet government on Russia's debt is shortsighted, to say the least, in striking contrast with the large vision manifested in other aspects of the Soviet economic life.

a. Amount Involved. The national debt of Russia began to grow in the middle of the last century. When the serfs were freed, the government bought the land from the landlords and financed the operation by borrowing money abroad. But a large and continuous demand for foreign funds arose from the development of the railroad system. Of a total debt outstanding before the war of 8.8 billion rubles about 3 billion rubles were spent for railroad construction.[12]

About one-half the total debt was foreign. In the decade prior to the war the debt increased by 33 per cent, due chiefly to the growing industrialization of the country. The percentage of foreign debt increased from 30 per cent in 1895 to almost 50 per cent in 1914. In the two decades prior to the war the foreign debt increased by 2500 million rubles but the domestic debt by only 500 million rubles.

THE RUSSIAN PRE-WAR STATE DEBT [13]

(in millions of rubles)

Jan. 1 of—	*Total Debt*	*Domestic*	*Foreign*	*Per cent Foreign to Total*
1895	5,775	4,042	1,733	30
1904	6,651	3,592	3,059	46
1914	8,811	4,582	4,229	48
Increase 1895–1914	3,036	540	2,496	82

In addition to these increases, in the twenty years before the war foreign investments in Russian industrials increased about 1000 million rubles and in municipal loans and guaranteed loans about 600 million rubles. The total increase from 1895 to 1914 in the foreign indebtedness for all purposes was thus 4100 million rubles. During the war Russia's foreign debt increased by 7600 million rubles, making a total increase from 1895 to 1918 of 11,700 million rubles. In 1895 the foreign debt amounted to about 1800 million rubles, so that the total foreign debt of Russia at the end of the war amounted to over 13,500 million rubles. This debt was distributed as follows:

EXTENT AND DISTRIBUTION OF RUSSIAN FOREIGN DEBTS [14]

(in millions of rubles)

Pre-war state debt	3,850
Guaranteed loans	870
Municipal loans	422
Industrial investments	2,000
Total pre-war debt	7,142
War loans, deducting gold exports and repayments	6,681
Total	13,823

The largest creditors of Russia were Great Britain and France. The latter owned most of the pre-war debt and Great Britain held most of the war debt.

PERCENTAGE OF DISTRIBUTION OF RUSSIA'S FOREIGN DEBT [15]

	Pre-War debt		*War debt*
	Government	*Industrial*	
Great Britain	14	23	70
France	80	33	19
Germany	—	20	—
Belgium	—	14	—
United States	—	5	7
Others	6	5	4
	100	100	100

b. Original Attitude. For years prior to the revolution, the Russian radicals threatened the bankers of the world that in case of a revolution they would repudiate the foreign obligations of the Russian Empire. This may have been merely a gesture to frighten capital from making new loans to Russia and thus to aid the cause of the revolutionists. The Bolsheviks now regard these early threats as legally binding. A few months after the October Revolution the Bolsheviks officially decreed that all the Russian foreign obligations were thereby repudiated.*

* Text of the Soviet Decree on the Annulment of Foreign Debts, January 21, 1918 (translated from the *Gazette of the Temporary Workmen-Peasants Government,* January 28, 1918.)

1. All national loans concluded by the governments of Russian landowners and Russian

This act has been heralded by the Soviet leaders as a benefit to the Russian masses. In depicting the advantages that the Soviet régime brought to the Russian people, emancipation from the foreign capitalists is advertised in the lobbies of museums and other public places. At the entrance to one of the former palaces, the writer saw large statistical charts in colors showing the amount of the foreign investment in Russian government bonds, in industries, etc. and the saving for the Russian masses effected by repudiation. The annual interest charge is also calculated, showing how much of a tax burden has been lifted from the shoulders of the Russian people.

The man in the street in Moscow is convinced that the debts to these foreign capitalists should never be paid, and even several of the directors of the state trusts share the same conviction. One director in a plant erected by foreign capital before the war stated to the writer that even debts incurred for productive purposes should not be recognized. On the other hand, several of the more far-seeing trust directors realized that Russia would be helped in her economic program by acknowledging and paying the foreign debt. Mr. Spundi, Assistant Commissar of Railroads, stated very clearly to the writer that the Soviets tried in 1924 and again in 1930 to reach some understanding with Great Britain on the question of the debt as a prerequisite for hastening the upbuilding of the country and to relieve the pressure under which the people were laboring.

The Soviet propagandists are willing that Russia dispense with foreign capital rather than pay the old debts. The more recent doctrine that Russia must pay her debts in order to live in a capitalist world apparently has not yet trickled through from the Soviet leaders to the trust directors and to the masses.

c. Historic Justification for Repudiation. In defense of their policy of repudiation, the Soviets have marshaled an array of historic precedents. In the memorandum of May 11, 1922, submitted to the Genoa Conference, they went back to the policy of the French Republic after the Revolution. The Russian memorandum stated that "the French Convention proclaimed, on

---

bourgeoisie enumerated in specially published lists are annulled (annihilated) from December 1, 1917. The December coupons of these loans are not subject to payment.

2. In the same manner are annulled all guarantees given by the said governments on loans for different undertakings and institutions.

3. Unconditionally and without exceptions, all foreign loans are annulled. . . .

These commissions have the right to annul in entirety savings not gained by toil, even if these savings do not exceed five thousand (5000) rubles.

(Signed) President of the Central Executive Committee
Y. Sverdlov

December 22, 1792, that 'The sovereignty of people is not bound by the treaties of tyrants.' In accordance with this declaration revolutionary France repudiated her national debt." Then, coming down to more recent history the Russian memorandum stated that "more than one of the states represented at the conference at Genoa have in the past repudiated their debts . . . more than one state has confiscated . . . the property of foreigners . . . without having been subjected to the ostracism of which Soviet Russia has been the victim."

The Soviets further tried to find an American precedent for their repudiation, and they cited the Fourteenth Amendment to our Constitution. The second clause cited by the Soviet note reads: "Neither the United States nor any state shall assume or pay any debt or obligation incurred in aid of insurrection or rebellion against the United States . . . but all such debts, obligations, and claims shall be held illegal and void." According to the Soviet point of view, many of these debts were due to foreigners and therefore they say the United States Constitution "hallows the doctrine of debt repudiation." Soviet spokesmen, however, overlook this fundamental difference. The Fourteenth Amendment was intended to prevent any future rebellion against the established government of the United States, and the debts of any rebels are therefore not to be recognized. But this point will not help the Soviets. It is not a question of recognizing the debt of any rebels. The question is, shall the debt of the old Russian Government which had been established for generations be recognized by a new, succeeding government? And for this purpose perhaps one can use the same amendment which the Soviets invoked in behalf of their theory of repudiation. The first sentence of Section 4 of the Fourteenth Amendment, which apparently was overlooked by the Soviet advocates, reads as follows: "The validity of the public debt of the United States authorized by law, including debts incurred . . . for suppressing insurrection or rebellion, shall not be questioned." In other words, this very amendment would require the Soviets to pay not merely the debts incurred by the previous government for productive purposes but also debts incurred for suppressing rebellion. It is unfortunate that such deliberate misuse of quotations should be invoked on behalf of the Soviets' unjustifiable breach of international faith and violation of public credit. Indeed, under the second clause of the Fourteenth Amendment, the Soviet debts could be voided by any succeeding stable régime.

d. Adverse Results. Because of the repudiation of their international debts and the confiscation of foreign private property the world not merely refused to make any new short-term loans to Russia excepting at rates of 25 to 30 per cent per annum, which measures the loss of confidence in Russian credit, but long-term loans are still utterly unavailable. Manufacturers may take a short-term risk against their profits, but private investors are unwilling to take any risk. Furthermore, repudiation and the lame attempts to justify it have aroused the united opposition of all investors and of all governments.

2. Offer to Pay. a. Basis—Expediency, Not Ethics. From January 1918 to May 1922, Russia experienced famine and great suffering. The consequences of the Bolsheviks' doctrinaire policy were visted upon them. Being realists, the Soviets came to the Genoa Conference and admitted that as a matter of expediency, they would pay their debts, as other governments must. But they retained a bit of their Bolshevik incorrigibility, and said that they really believed as a matter of doctrine they did not have to pay their debts, but did so only under compulsion. To permit themselves to feel like correct revolutionists, they relied on the precedents of the French Revolution—even revolutionists have traditions and precedents—and cited the fact that the French compromised by paying one-third of the debt on grounds of expediency, such as now move the Russians. They stated formally that their government "declared itself ready to accept the liability for payment of the public debts."

b. Reversal of Policy. This was not the first time that the Russians had reversed their policy on the public debt. The original decree repudiating their foreign debt was effective January 1, 1918. In February 1918, under military pressure, the Bolsheviks signed the Treaty of Brest-Litovsk, undertaking to recognize their financial obligations. They actually paid the equivalent of $60,000,000 to Germany in September 1918. Under the same treaty they also reversed their policy on confiscation of private property.

Without military pressure, and entirely of its own accord, the Bolshevik Government notified the Peace Conference at Versailles in February 1919 that it was willing to recognize its financial obligations to its creditors in the Entente countries, and in March 1919 Lenin offered to recognize the responsibility for the financial obligations of the former Russian Empire.[16]

c. Prerequisites to a Settlement. These offers to pay were not unconditional. They were not the voluntary offering of a debtor who realizes that he has had "value received." The Soviets needed new money, and the only way they could get it was to pay the old debts. So the first Soviet condition was that Russia should get new loans. The new money needed for the industrial program would become part of a debt settlement. The Russian offer was that they would pay a high rate of interest on the new loans, part of which would be used to meet the interest and sinking fund on the old loans. This principle was actually embodied in the British negotiations in 1924 and the French negotiations in 1926. Furthermore, to reduce the amount of their debt they wished to offset counterclaims for the Allied campaign against the Bolsheviks.[17]

d. A Compromise. The Russian offer to pay was not merely conditioned by these two prerequisites, but payment was not intended to be in any large amount. At the Sixteenth Congress of the Communist Party, held in Moscow June 27, 1930, Stalin stated:

> We are prepared to pay a *small part* of the pre-war debts in return for credits, regarding these payments as supplementary interest on the credits. If they ask for more than this, we will not give it, because we refuse to accept obligations contracted by the Tsarist government. They talk about international law. What international law justified Rumania grabbing Bessarabia and the American, French, British, and Japanese invasion of Russian territory?

In other words, Stalin, addressing his own followers, suggests a face-saving compromise. The Soviets realize that they must get new money, as all younger countries of history have had to do, in order to develop their resources. But to get new money the old debt must be paid. However, because of communist doctrine he must speak differently to his party followers than he would privately at an international conference.

Partial repudiation is not new. The French, Italians, and Belgians are paying only a small fraction of the principal of their war debt to the United States Government. And the history of national bankruptcy contains numerous cases of the reduction of the principal, such as the conversion of a gold debt to a paper one, the reduction of the rate of interest, the deferment of payment of principal, and high taxation on the interest, which constitutes virtual arbitrary reduction.*

3. Debt Negotiations. a. Cannes, Genoa and The Hague Offers. The conditions under which the powers of the world were willing to grant credit to Russia were defined at conferences at Cannes, Genoa, and The Hague. The Genoa Conference memorandum of May 1922 confirmed the Cannes resolution whereby the Russian Government must recognize all the public obligations of the Imperial Government, the Provisional Government, and the

---

* For further data, see Friedman, Elisha M., *International Finance and Its Reorganization*, Chapter XIV, "National Bankruptcies in the Nineteenth Century," pp. 522–38. New York: E. P. Dutton & Co., 1921.

Soviet Government. Under the resolutions of The Hague Conference in July 1922 the Soviet Government must recognize the obligations due to private investors abroad contracted by past or present Russian governments, provinces, municipalities, or utility enterprises. Further, the Soviet Government must in addition restore to their former foreign owners all investments which had been confiscated or nationalized or make compensation for them, where restoration was no longer possible. On the other hand, the Allies agreed to make no claims on account of war debts, and to give Russia the benefit of any general arrangement concluded for the liquidation of the war debts.

Litvinov, Assistant Commissar of Foreign Affairs, again offered to pay the debt on the condition that new credits be extended to Russia, but The Hague Conference ignored the proposal. He thereupon stated that he would inquire whether the Russian Government would consent to recognize the old debts to foreign citizens, even if credits would not be granted. He also offered persons whose property was confiscated the opportunity to bid for concessions. The Hague Conference adjourned before a reply was received.

The Soviets' reply to the Genoa Conference Memorandum was an interesting display of the Soviet mentality. First, they spent much effort to prove that they were entitled to new credits, even if they did not pay their old debts, and they cited chapter, verse, and line from history and from the recent experience of the creditor powers to prove that they (the Soviets) did not have to pay. However, in order to arrive at an agreement with the powers they agreed to the terms of the Genoa Memorandum subject to the proviso that the creditor governments would pay for the damage due to the Allied intervention.

The resolutions of the Hague Conference on recognition of the Russian debt indicate that although the Soviet Government agreed to recognize the pre-war debts, yet it had not revoked the several decrees repudiating them. The sub-commission on credit went further and said that Russia should not use acknowledgment of its debt as a bargaining point in order to get new credit, but that first she must restore confidence in her financial integrity and that Europe would then co-operate with her.

GENOA CONFERENCE MEMORANDUM, MAY 2, 1922 [18]

CLAUSE II.

(1) In conformity with the Cannes resolution, the Russian Soviet Government recognizes all public debts and obligations which have been contracted or

guaranteed by the Imperial Russian Government or the Russian Provisional Government or by the Soviet Government itself towards foreign Powers.

Being desirous of facilitating the immediate reconstruction of Russia and the rehabilitation of her credit, the creditor powers are willing to make no claim upon Russia at present, either as to capital or interest, for the repayment of the advances made to the Russian Governments during the war.

(2) The Allies can admit no liability for the claims against them set up by the Russian Soviet Government for loss and damage suffered during the revolution in Russia since the war.

(3) When an arrangement is concluded between the Allied and Associated Powers for the liquidation or rearrangement of war debts, the Allied Governments concerned will submit to their parliaments measures for reducing or modifying the amount due by the Russian Soviet Government on similar lines and with due regard to the economic and financial condition of Russia; but these measures will be conditional on the renunciation by Russia of the claims mentioned in paragraph 2. . . .

Clause IV.

In conformity with the general principle admitted by all governments, the Russian Soviet Government recognizes its obligations to fulfill the financial engagements which it or its predecessors, that is to say, the Imperial Russian Government or the Russian Provisional Government, have contracted vis-à-vis foreign nationals.

Clause V.

The Russian Soviet Government undertakes to recognize, or to cause to be recognized, the financial engagements of all authorities in Russia, provincial or local, as well as all public utility enterprises in Russia contracted before this date vis-à-vis the nationals of other Powers.

Clause VI.

The Russian Soviet Government agrees to conclude an arrangement within twelve months of the coming into force of this clause with the representatives of foreign holders of bonds and bills issued or guaranteed by the Russian Soviet Government or its predecessors, for insuring the restarting of the service of the loans and the payment of the bills. . . .

The said arrangement shall apply as far as possible to all foreign holders without distinction of nationality.

In case a collective agreement cannot be reached, the benefit of an arrangement concluded with any particular group may be claimed by all other foreign holders.

Clause VII.

In order to encourage the restarting of foreign economic activity in Russia and to permit foreign states to furnish to Russia the aid indicated above in the introduction and thereby to facilitate the restoration of the country, the Russian Soviet Government accepts the following arrangement with respect to private property:

Without prejudice to its freedom, as recognized in the Cannes resolution, to regulate its system of ownership, internal economy, and government, and to choose for itself the system which it prefers in this respect, the Russian Soviet

Government recognizes its obligation, in accordance with the said resolution, to restore or compensate all foreign interests for loss or damage caused to them when property has been confiscated or withheld.

In cases in which the previous owner is not enabled to resume possession of his former rights, the Russian Soviet Government will make an offer of compensation.

RUSSIAN REPLY TO GENOA CONFERENCE MEMORANDUM, MAY 11, 1922 [18]

The problems of the future [new credits], which interest every one, have been subordinated to the interests of the past [old debts], which affect only certain groups of foreigners. The assertion that a recognition of the debts of former Russian Governments and the claims of private individuals is a condition essential to the co-operation of foreign capital in resuscitating the credit of New Russia is contradicted by the fact that many foreign capitalists have already given their collaboration to Russia without waiting for a settlement of the question of debts. . . .

The repudiation of the debts and obligations contracted by the former régime, can in no wise indicate in advance the attitude of Soviet Russia, the child of the revolution, toward those who would come with their capital and technical knowledge to help in its reconstruction. . . .

It is worthy of remark that more than one of the states represented at the Conference of Genoa have in the past repudiated debts and obligations contracted by it; more than one state has confiscated and sequestrated the property of foreigners or of its own nationals without having been subjected on that account to the ostracism of which Soviet Russia has been the victim. . . .

The Russian delegation feels obliged to recall that principle of law according to which revolutions which are a violent rupture with the past carry with them new juridical relations in the foreign and domestic affairs of states. Governments and systems that spring from revolution are not bound to respect the obligations of fallen governments. The French Convention, of which France declares herself to be the legitimate successor, proclaimed on the 22nd December, 1792, that "the sovereignty of peoples is not bound by the treaties of tyrants." In accordance with this declaration, revolutionary France not only tore up the political treaties of the former régime with foreign countries, but also repudiated her national debt. She consented to pay only one-third of that debt, and that from motives of political expedience. This was the *tiers consolidé,* the interest on which did not begin to be regularly paid until the commencement of the nineteenth century.

This practice, which has been elevated to the rank of a doctrine by eminent legal authorities, has been followed almost universally by governments born of a revolution or a war of liberation. . . .

On the other hand, the governments of the victorious states did not hesitate during the (Great) War, and especially on the conclusion of the treaties of peace to seize the property of the nationals of the vanquished states situated upon their territory and even upon foreign territory.

In conformity with these precedents, Russia cannot be obliged to assume any responsibility whatever toward foreign Powers and their nationals for the cancellation of public debts and for the nationalization of private porperty. . . .

Revolution, assimilated like all great popular movements, being akin to *force majeure,* does not confer any title to indemnity upon those who have suffered from it. When foreign nationals, supported by their governments, demanded from the Tsarist government the repayment of the losses caused to them by the revolutionary events of 1905 and 1906, the government rejected their demands, basing its refusal upon the fact that not having accorded damages to its own subjects for similar losses, it could not place foreigners in a privileged position.

Thus, from the point of view of law, Russia is in no wise obliged to pay the debts of the past, to restore property, or to compensate their former owners, nor is she obliged to pay indemnities for other damages suffered by foreign nationals, whether as a result of legislation adopted by Russia in the exercise of her sovereignty, or as a result of the revolutionary events. Nevertheless, in a spirit of conciliation and in order to arrive at an understanding with all the Powers, Russia has accepted under the reserve of reciprocity the principle . . . that is, the obligation resting on every government to pay compensation for damages caused by its acts or its negligence. . . .

The foreign Powers who organized the armed intervention in Russia [should] cease to hold toward Russia the language of a victor to the vanquished, Russia not having been conquered. The only language which could have led to a common agreement was that which states adopt toward each other when negotiating upon a footing of equality. . . .

The Russian delegation observes that the great obstacle which has, up to the present time, impeded the labors of the conference, is the fact that the idea of reciprocity expressed above is not yet sufficiently shared by all the Powers. . . .

Reports and Resolution of the Hague Conference, July, 1922 [18]

D. Recognition of the Debt—In the letter in which M. Chicherin, on October 28, 1921, asked for assistance from the Powers for the economic reconstruction of Russia, it was explicitly stated that the Russian Government was ready to recognize "obligations to other states and their nationals arising from state loans concluded by the Tsarist Government in 1914, with the express proviso that special conditions should be agreed to and facilities given, which would render it possible for this undertaking to be fulfilled." . . .

The Cannes resolution of January 6, 1922, laid it down that this recognition was an essential condition for the re-establishment of that sense of security which was indispensable for the co-operation of foreign capital.

Taking its stand on the facts of the case, the non-Russian subcommission came to the conclusion that no steps had been taken to revoke the decree of December 28, 1917, which was followed up by the decree of January 21, 1918, nor the decree of September 16, 1920, which suspended the right to receive compensation for the cancellation of state debts.

Report of the Subcommission on Credits of the Hague Conference, July, 1922 [18]

If it be true, as we all have acknowledged, that there is an economic solidarity between Russia and the remainder of Europe; that on one hand it is to the interest of Europe that Russia should once more participate in the economic European system, and that on the other hand Russia requires the help of

Europe in order to accelerate its own revival, then we should all recognize that we have got beyond the conception that the acknowledgment of obligations on the part of Russia is a matter for bargain against credits, and that future negotiations will have to be inspired by the principles of solidarity and of reciprocal interest.

Only if this conception shall prevail will an agreement be possible, because in that case Russia will spontaneously re-establish the conditions of confidence which she considers today a matter of bargaining, and Europe will offer willingly her co-operation to Russia within the limits of her powers such as they may be.

b. German Negotiations. The Brest-Litovsk negotiations of February 1918 between Imperial Germany and Bolshevist Russia were replaced by the Rapallo Treaty signed in April 1922 between Republican Germany and Soviet Russia. Under this treaty both governments cancelled all claims and debts on the condition that the Russian Government did not actually pay the similar claims of other states. This clause is significant. It was probably inserted as a result of German pressure, but its acceptance by the Soviets implies a possible future willingness to pay their debts to other countries, and constitutes now a difficulty in settling financial claims of Great Britain and France.

c. British Negotiations. The Soviet Government negotiated with Great Britain several times. On the first occasion in July 1920, it officially notified Lloyd George, then premier, of its intention to recognize its debt to Great Britain. When the Labor government came into power in 1924 a treaty covering the debt was discussed between the Soviet Government and the British Government. The British Government agreed to guarantee a loan to the Soviet Government, and on its part the Soviet Government agreed to make partial payment to British holders on such pre-war bonds of the Russian Government and Russian municipalities as were payable in foreign currency. Payment for private foreign property confiscated by the Soviets was to be handled by a Mixed Commission. This treaty was signed by Ramsay Macdonald and Arthur Ponsonby for Great Britain, and by Christian Rakovsky for the Soviet government. A subsequent treaty, to determine the details of the loan to be advanced by Great Britain and the payments to be made by Russia, was in course of negotiation when the Labor government fell.

Since 1930 negotiations were reported to be in progress in Great Britain, and a sub-committee was to have been established to consider claims arising from foreign intervention in Russia. The British did not accept the principle of responsibility for losses caused during the invasion. In the negotiations of

1924 this question had not even been reached. The Russian counter-claims, as compiled by a Russian commission that worked for several years, were said to be equivalent to about 10 billion dollars, and the Russians assessed the British share at about 5 billion dollars. The British private claims against Russia amount to about 1 billion dollars, and the war loans of the British government to the Russian government amount to about 3.5 billion dollars. Apparently, what the Russians are trying to do is to make the counter-claims for intervention large enough to offset their total foreign debt. These reported negotiations have never been officially confirmed, but the London Stock Exchange quotations on pre-war Russian bonds usually fluctuate with the negotiations.

d. French Negotiations. The governments of France and Russia began similar negotiations in February 1926. The Soviet ambassador in Paris, Rakovsky, submitted a concrete offer of 61 annuities, of 60 million francs, equal to approximately 2.4 million dollars, each. In return the Soviets asked for a credit of 3 billion francs, approximately 120 million dollars, to be taken within six years. While the French rejected the principle that the payment of the old debt could be made conditional upon new loans, the French delegate, de Monzie, agreed to consider the request for new loans independently. The settlement was prevented by a newspaper campaign against the Russian negotiator, Rakovsky, the ambassador at Paris, which resulted in his recall.

e. War Debts. The claims for war loans to Russia have not been pressed as vigorously as the pre-war loans to Russia for productive purposes. Russian war loans amount to almost 7 billion rubles, or about 3.5 billion dollars. In the 1924 negotiations with Great Britain and in the French negotiations, the question of debts incurred during the war received little attention. On the other hand, neither Italy nor Japan ever raised the question of their war loans to Russia. This attitude toward these war loans is part of a general European policy of cancellation of war debts as outlined in the Balfour note, whereunder England, in effect, agreed to cancel all her war debts to the extent that America canceled the British war debt to the United States. The basis for this policy is that, on balance, America's war debtors are more solvent than Europe's war debtors.

4. Russian Policy toward the United States. a. Counter-claims. As an offset to the debt of Russia to the United States the Soviets make certain counter-claims. They maintain that the American army, in conjunction with the Allied armies, during the military intervention, destroyed property which

the Russians assess in the billions. The Soviets again look to the precedent of the Civil War and again are illogical. At that time a privateer, the *Alabama,* acting on behalf of Great Britain, aided the seceding southern states. A court of arbitration granted the United States 15 million dollars as compensation. But the analogy adduced by the Bolsheviks does not hold. In the Civil War, aid was given to the seceding states against the established and constituted American Government, which was victorious. Great Britain had to pay for helping an uprising. This was not the case in the Allied intervention. There is a legal as well as an ethical difference between the Russian situation and the Civil War precedent.

b. Russian Overtures. In the following section on recognition the history of the Russian overtures to make payment on the debt is given. Suffice it to say here that within a few months after the decree of repudiation, the Soviet Government publicly offered to make settlement with its creditors on the old debt. Later on, in 1925, Chicherin stated that the Soviet Government made a proposal to settle all questions in dispute with the United States, including the loan granted to the Kerensky government. Similarly, in 1926, Litvinov stated that the Soviet Government was willing to start immediate negotiations on the debt, including the recognition of the Kerensky loan. Stalin continued along the same lines in 1930.[19] In an interview with Walter Duranty he stated:

> America knows where we stand from Litvinov's declarations. We have done what we could, but we won't hang on their necks. We still are willing to get the debt question settled by the payment of an extra percentage on credits or a loan and to resume normal relations as we have done with the rest of the great powers. They know we can pay . . . and do pay our debts and fulfill our pledges. An extra percentage—that is a mere trifle, and debt settlement with America—that is easy.

c. American Private Property in Russia. Under the Brest-Litovsk Treaty, German nationals were to be indemnified for property taken. As a result, all foreign property in Russia was transferred to German nationals. Thereupon the government nationalized all property on June 28, 1918. American property was made the exception.[20] In fact, theoretically, American property was never nationalized. Practically, the Russians did take it over on the excuse that the plants were idle. Technically American property in Russia is to be treated differently from other foreign property. The amount involved in claims for foreign properties is relatively small. Financially, it is the least difficult of the problems involved in the relations between the United States and Russia. The Soviet officials repeatedly stated that the Soviet Government is willing to compensate the owners on a reasonable basis. The general principle involved is that foreigners whose properties were taken would receive in return concessions, the profits on which would cover the losses incurred in the confiscation of their properties. As a matter of fact, the claims of the General Electric Company were actually adjusted with the knowledge of the State Department.

5. United States' Policy toward Russia. a. American Claims. President Coolidge made American recognition dependent, among other things, upon compensation to Americans for property seized. The Russian loan floated by the National City Bank amounted to about $86,000,000, and the loans extended to the Kerensky government amounted to about $187,000,000, a total of $273,000,000, excluding interest. In addition, private property of Americans confiscated by the Russian Government ranged upward of $100,000,000.

b. National City Bank Negotiations. The claims of the National City Bank were almost settled in 1927. Negotiations began in New York and were continued in Paris. President Mitchell of the National City Bank made it clear that a settlement of the debt was to be made on its own merits, and quite independent of any conditions that the bank extend new credits to Russia or issue a new public loan. He did say that a settlement might make possible such financial assistance. The Mitchell memorandum attempted to transfer the debt from the government to the State Bank, and the Bank was to have paid a small percentage on the par value of the bonds outstanding. After studying the Mitchell memorandum, the Soviet officials made an offer as follows: The American bonds were to be deposited and held under option with an agency to be designated by the American committee. The option price was to be the present value of a 3 per cent bond due in 1988, but discounted on an 8 per cent basis. Such terms greatly shrank the "present value" of the obligation. The agency was to buy 2 per cent of the obligations annually after the first 10-year period. For this option the Russians were to pay 2 per cent of the par value of the bonds during the first decade and 3 per cent for the next 10-year period. Simultaneously, and as a condition of this settlement, the Russians asked for new credits, in contravention of the terms suggested by Mr. Mitchell that settlement of the old debt and new loans were to be the subject of independent negotiations. He did repeat, however, that settlement of the old debt would facilitate the extension of new credits. In reply, Ambassador Christian Rakovsky asked for a credit of 75 million dollars. This request terminated the negotiations.

c. Conditions of the Rapallo Treaty. Under the terms of the Rapallo Treaty, Germany enjoyed most-favored-nation treatment, and if the Soviets recognized their old debts to the United States and received new credits therefor, they would have to make similar terms with the German Government. For this reason the Soviet Government is in a difficult position. During the negotiations between the Soviets and other governments, Germany stressed the most-favored-nation treatment of the Rapallo Treaty. By offering to pay supplementary interest charges on new loans in lieu of repaying old loans, the Soviets can claim technically that they are not recognizing old debts and thus, it becomes easier for the Soviet Government to live up to the requirements of the Rapallo Treaty.

C. Loans and Credits

International loans to Russia would be of world-wide benefit. Such loans would lessen the pressure of Russian exports, regarded as dumping by the injured competitors. It would stimulate world trade, give Russia a westward orientation, and tend toward a less radical policy there. The questions of safety of the loan and guarantees are difficult, but not insuperable, problems.

1. International Benefits of Loans to Russia. a. Cessation of Dumping. Because Russia lacks international credit she must force her exports. In a few important commodities, this depresses prices under world costs. A loan would diminish this insistent selling and thus lessen the pressure on the world's market. In fact, extension of credit might be contingent on the limitation of exports and of cutting of prices. Russia needs for her home population much of the grain, eggs, butter, and fruit which she is throwing on foreign markets. The amazing paradox of this decade is the dumping by Russia of agricultural products on unwilling foreign markets, while at home underfed people wait in lines for food, either rationed in limited quantities or selling at profiteering prices in the open markets. No one country has an exact balance of exports and imports. Invisible items such as loans, tourist expenditures, etc. absorb the difference. And Russia needs such loans to finance a debit balance in international payments, characteristic of young countries, and thus avoid dumping of exports.

b. Stimulation of World Trade. Because Russia has no credit, the Soviet

Government must pay huge premiums above world prices or pay fantastic interest rates of 20 to 30 per cent per annum. Thereby international trade is hindered, not helped. Expansion of credit would stimulate world trade. Thomas D. Campbell, American agricultural adviser to the Soviet Government, told the writer that there are in Russia today potentially 2 billion dollars' worth of orders for American goods, enough to stimulate American industry out of depression. Most of these orders would naturally come to America because of the topographical and climatic similarity of the two countries. Again, on his return to the United States Ralph Budd, President of the Great Northern Railway and consulting engineer to the Soviet Government, stated that because of the similarity of railroad conditions American railroad engineers are best suited to direct the reconstruction of Russian railroads, and American railroad equipment companies are likely to benefit by reason of the similarity in types of equipment required.

With adequate credit Soviet imports from the United States could very greatly increase. This would stimulate the more rapid industrialization of Russia and raise the standard of living of its people, and this in turn would still further stimulate imports from other countries and world trade generally.

The vast area of Russia, her very backward condition, and the desire of the Soviet leaders to industrialize the country rapidly should provide a stimulus to the export trade of other countries for a decade or more. International aid in reconstructing Russia would be of great help in making effective the purchasing power of 160,000,000 Russians in the markets of the world.

c. Westward Orientation. Practically cut off from the rest of the world from 1917 to 1921, Soviet Russia was able to indulge in the communist phantasy. The New Economic Policy put the country into touch again with the western world. As her contacts with the western world multiplied, Soviet Russia applied so-called capitalist methods increasingly. Such contacts have been an influence away from communist theory and toward practical methods. An international loan to Russia would have a sobering influence, and it would give Russia westward orientation. It would increase the influence of the capitalist countries, in so far as they desire to be helpful, and Russia eventually would come into a working harmony and understanding with the west, the lack of which has caused much misunderstanding and suspicion on both sides.

2. Safety of Loans. a. Economic Capacity to Pay. For almost fifteen years the Soviet government has met its obligations. One of the American firms holding a fur concession in Russia stated that Russia was a safer risk than many American customers in New York City. The Soviets have

lived up to their contracts. The huge resources of Russia, the productive capacity of her people, are an indication of her economic ability to meet her obligations.

b. Moral Risk. As for the will to pay, that is present. The negotiations with the British and the French indicate this willingness. The moral risk should be small. For half a decade the Russians have suffered and have saved enough to furnish the principal for the reconstruction of the country. How much easier it would be to raise merely the interest charges on such principal. The Russian people could pay the interest on their debt and still be happy and prosperous. A default thereon would bring on them again the burden they are now carrying. With adequate economic resources to pay and with a demonstrated capacity of the people to undergo privation for future social good, the risks should be small.

c. Soviet Short-Term Loans. The maintenance of Russian credit is vital to the whole scheme of industrialization. If Russian credit fails, the Five-Year Plan is seriously crippled. For this reason alone all debts due in the next few years are likely to be met promptly as in the past. Default on a current debt will curtail all future credit. For this reason it is reasonable to expect that loans maturing within nine, twelve, or even eighteen months are very likely to be safe. The risks beyond this point involve political and social uncertainties.

d. Risks in Long-Term Loans. Loans running for a period of years are much less secure. They involve a great many unknown factors—for example, how long will the present government last? Will any succeeding government honor debts of the current government? Will there be a repudiation of the loans of the existing régime by any future less radical régime? It seems reasonable that if the newly established Soviet Government repudiates or drastically curtails the foreign obligations of the long-established Tsarist government, there is likely to be more justification for any new régime taking the same attitude toward a possibly short-lived Soviet Government. Or granting even that the current régime will last for a considerable time, what guaranty is there that the present government itself may not repudiate its debts, when there is no longer urgency to pay them to get further credit? In fact, even the high officials of the government say that the war on capitalism has been deferred but not abandoned. What better way to make effective war on capitalism than by refusal to pay debts to the capitalist states?

3. Security and Guarantees. a. Security Inadequate. It is hardly likely that

Russia will be able to get international credit without effective guarantees. The interlude of pure communism deterred saving and checked the accumulation of capital. More recently, not only has this policy been abandoned but it has been strikingly reversed. The government is begging the people to save and buy bonds, just as any capitalist government might. But there have been stories of subscriptions to government bonds that were so large that the sources of income of the subscribers were investigated. The lack of home capital, therefore, makes Russia more dependent on foreign capital, and foreign capital is timid. It requires security and guarantees to attract it into Russia or any other country. Young and developing countries of the world have offered pledges and guarantees and Russia's credit today, viewed in the large, is on a par with some of the young countries of South America, which pledge revenues from customs, sale monopolies, tobacco, coffee, etc.

b. Safeguards for Investors. It is not what the foreign governments wish or think, but rather what the private investor demands, that will determine whether Russia is to receive money. Even if Russia were recognized by all the governments in the world, and even if short-term credits were granted by all the banks in the world, the private investor would be unlikely to risk his savings in Russia, unless he was sure that the principal and interest would be paid. It will not be entirely impossible to sell an unsecured loan, but the rate of interest would have to be exceedingly high, perhaps 10 to 12 per cent or more. But if Russia can guarantee safety of principal and interest under suitable pledges, funds should be available and at more reasonable rates of interest.

c. A "Young Plan" for Russia. Assuming that Russia will ultimately receive recognition by the United States, she should be able to get funds by giving adequate guarantees, yet without compromising her political or economic independence. As a parallel, before the floating of the German reparations loan in 1924, German internal bonds payable in reichsmarks or in gold were selling to yield 10 per cent or higher. After the reparations loan was floated, in which the charges on the loan were a first lien on reparations payments, these German internal bonds rose in price or declined in yield substantially. Similar guarantees of safety by Russia would make money cheaper and more abundant for her internally. The Russians say that they are willing to submit to any terms, short of a Young Plan. But the investors say they will not lend on terms less secure than such a plan provides. The Soviets say they would regard such a plan as enslavement by the capitalists. But the investors would regard anything less as giving hostages to the enemies of capitalism.

Can a compromise be found? Russian officials have publicly stated that the problem is not beyond solution. Germany, Austria, Poland, and other countries of Europe have submitted to the supervision of an adviser or a comptroller installed to represent the international investors. None of these countries so far has found these burdens severe. In fact the American solicitude for Russia is even greater than that of the Russian Government itself. America has not yet recognized the Rumanian seizure of Bessarabia, and was late in recognizing the independence of the three border states, Esthonia, Latvia, and Lithuania. She has no territorial ambitions in regard to Russia, and it is unlikely that an American administrator in Russia would be any less impartial than, say, S. Parker Gilbert, whose work in Germany as Agent General for Reparations was highly praised by the Germans themselves. It is not what the Soviets are willing to do, but rather on what terms the investors will lend them money. The money is available. It is for the Russians to decide, whether they are willing to pay lower interest rates and give guaranties, or to continue in the crude present method of paying 30 per cent per annum without guaranties.

D. Russian Foreign Policy

This section does not aim to cover the whole field of Russian foreign policy, but only such phases as are relevant to the large question of American policy toward Russia.

1. Maintaining the War Atmosphere. a. Solidifying Home Sentiment. The Soviet War Department and the press continually hold out the danger of invasion by the capitalist world. This is part of the general program of keeping the country keyed up in a spirit of enmity toward the capitalist world, whose military designs on Russia exist only in the minds of the Soviet propagandists. The war scares seem to be aimed simply at solidifying sentiment at home. This policy is similar to that of Mussolini's truculent speeches, although the adverse effect on the Italian bonds listed on the world exchanges has compelled him to modify his military threats. In pre-war days the saber-rattling of the Kaiser and his references to the circle of enemies around Germany were intended to raise patriotism within Germany to fever heat. Apparently Soviet Russia and pre-war imperialist Germany use the same ruses and subterfuges for exciting patriotism.

b. International Conferences as Threats to Russia. In Russia every international conference is heralded as primarily an anti-Soviet threat. In the spring of 1931 M. Briand's pan-European plan was regarded by the Soviet newspapers as a capitalist threat against Russia. By attempting to foster a European union, Briand was supposed to be forming an anti-Soviet alliance. As a result the Soviets hoped for Italian and German opposition to the plan.

Characteristic of their attitude is the editorial exclamation in *Pravda:* "Let them make their preparations against us . . . but the Soviet delegation will be present to hear. The Soviet Union does not fear the discussion." *Izvestia* similarly says: "In 1917 Europe gave birth to the proletarian revolution, which grew quickly in thirteen years and became a mighty proletarian state. Unlucky capitalist Europe tried to stifle the babe in its infancy but failed, and now it is too late." [21]

Again, when Great Britain tried to reduce the naval competition between France and Italy, the Soviet papers spoke of bringing France and Italy together in an entente against Russia. Or when the British tried to ease French pressure on Germany, the Soviets said that Germany was being brought into an anti-Soviet combination and was to agree to remain neutral in the event of a Russian-Polish war—a war which is a nightmare to the Soviets.[22]

The meeting of the International Chamber of Commerce at Washington called forth new anxiety in the *Industrial Gazette,* lest the Chamber of Commerce lay the foundation for a united capitalist action against the Soviet menace.[23]

The academic trial at which a group of engineers and professors publicly confessed their plotting with foreigners is a reflection of this Soviet fear of the foreigner. The trial seemed to have been a grand show. The names of the foreigners were mentioned at first, but when some of these people were proved to have been dead for a great many years, no more such names were mentioned. The confessions of these professors were given nation-wide publicity through radio, and when the trial was over, punishment was nominal. The fear of the Russians may be part of their foreign policy, but it is morbid, it is a hypochondria.

c. War Psychosis. The whole country is suffering from a war psychosis. The objectives of this war fever are: first, to realize communism, and second: to industrialize the country. The enemy is capitalism and the bourgeois class. The campaign is the Five-Year Plan. The methods are a ruthless handling of the population, and the waste and inefficiencies of war are an essential part of these methods. The thing is not lightly to be condemned. It is an interesting social phenomenon. Great social forces are apparently in action. The people, who have suffered under the heel of oppression for centuries, are now the victims of a psychosis. The world's kindness, rather than its cruelty, is likely to be a healing influence. The cruel practices in the sanatoria for the mentally ill of generations ago are now being replaced by gentler methods. Russia needs understanding and sympathy, until she regains her equilibrium economically and psychologically.

2. DUMPING AS A POLITICAL POLICY. a. Fear of Permanent Dumping Unwarranted. The present heavy volume of exports in the few items of which Russia has an abundance is regarded in some quarters as part of a permanent policy of the Soviets. Moreover, it is thought that, after the goal of the Five-Year Plan is reached, such dumping will even be exaggerated. The country is so backward, however, that to raise the standard of living, construct roads, railroads, factories, power plants, etc., will require all the domestic production for years. Again, the growing population, now about 160,000,000, is likely to require most of the output of the factories. Further, even the Soviet sympathizers in Russia will admit that the standard of living is low, but the great gain which they stress is not the rise in the actual standard of living but the growing wish for a higher standard of living. The peasants want to wear shoes and the peasant women want to wear better clothing, and it is such wishes that must precede the rise in the general standard.

The fear of permanent dumping is idle. In spite of all the propaganda about the success of the Five-Year Plan, Russia's foreign trade is far below the pre-war level. Even in wheat, concerning which the world complains so bitterly, Russian exports in 1930 were less than one-third of the Russian exports of 1913. Yet before the war the Russians were not accused of dumping. Dumping is not a political policy in Russia; it is merely an economic readjustment. While Russia was cut off from the world by war and later by communism, the other nations increased their exports of goods in which Russia was an important factor, such as platinum and wheat, and when Russia re-entered the market the other countries resented her attempt to regain her pre-war position. The precipitous drop in the price of platinum was not the result of Russian dumping, but of the unwillingness of the other platinum producers to give Russia what she thought was a reasonable quota of the world trade. However, in several fields of trade, such as oil, Russia was very much pleased to enter into negotiations with other countries, in order to raise the export price. She has likewise joined the conference to curtail the exports and raise the price of sugar and of wheat.

The Soviet Government likewise indicated its willingness to participate in an international conference on the co-ordination of production and consumption of petroleum. The fact that it did not come to an understanding in 1932 with the other producing countries does not lessen the force of the contention that Russia is not interested in cutting prices in international trade or in dumping. There is still a possibility and a hope of her participation in an international oil agreement.

A vigorous and logical defense against the charge of dumping was presented by Viacheslav Molotov, Chairman of the Council of People's Commissars, at the Sixth Congress of Soviets at Moscow on March 8, 1931.

> In 1913 Russia's share in the world's exports was altogether about 3.5 per cent, which was rather little. Well, we have not reached that level yet. For in 1930 our share of world's exports was only 1.9 per cent. . . . In both Europe and America industries, even though they make products which our country does not export at all but imports from them, are caught in the common crisis. Indeed, can the depression of the steel industry be seriously ascribed to the effect of "Soviet dumping"? The U.S.S.R. does not export, but it imports metal. Or, can "Soviet dumping" explain the crisis of machine construction in America and Europe? The crisis in that industry is growing, whereas the Soviet Union increases year by year the importation of equipment from Europe as well as from America. Or, does "Soviet dumping" account for the catastrophic curtailment of automobile production? Does it not sound ridiculous at a time when we have to import large quantities of automobiles from abroad? [24]

Dumping intentionally would be folly even for the Soviets. As a result of the fall of prices throughout the world, Russia has had to increase greatly the quantity of her exports in 1930 to obtain the same amount of money as she did in 1929.

b. World's Reaction to Dumping. The so-called dumping policy of Russia met with responses from two groups of countries. The young countries, producers of food and raw materials, protested against the exports of competing Russian raw materials. Canada in February 1930 embargoed imports of Soviet coal, asbestos, lumber, and furs. Rumania and New Zealand protested against the dumping of Soviet grain, lumber, and oil. On the other hand the old industrial countries, Great Britain, Germany, Italy, which lack raw materials, not only do not complain of Russian dumping, but are glad to get the raw materials at such low prices. Eventually some international co-operation is likely to regulate exports, and to pro-rate allotments, so as to keep world prices above the cost of production. In such an international conference the problem will be not so much the conflict between Russia and the other competitive producers of raw materials, but rather that between the young countries producing raw materials on the one hand and the old countries consuming raw materials on the other.

c. Soviet Reprisals. The Soviets have not remained passive in the face of embargoes against their exports. Against the Canadian embargo they retaliated by prohibiting Canadian imports into Russia, and the use of Canadian ships. When Austria embargoed imports of eggs from Russia, the latter threatened to withdraw orders for machinery. This caused a hurried cancellation of the embargo. In fact the trade discrimination against Russia has become so general, that the Soviets took protective measures. By decree Soviet representatives abroad were ordered to allot orders for goods and cargo space in favor of countries which did not embargo Soviet goods and to divert business from those that did. The boycott by Belgium elicited a sharp reprisal. The centralization of the entire foreign trade in the hands of the government makes it possible for the Soviets to wage a trade war on any front.

When the threat against Soviet dumping and the charges of forced labor were circulated in France, Great Britain, and the United States, the Soviets replied by inviting a large delegation of German industrialists to make a survey. It has been a policy of the Soviets to set off one power against the other. Orders are shifted from country to country, as measures of defense against trade aggression. Duranty reports that "information from Berlin and London has induced American firms to refuse Soviet orders which later were accepted by German or British firms."[25] The diversion of business from American firms is due also to the shorter terms of credit granted by the United States. Soviet reprisals are based not only on commercial grounds but occasionally on political grounds. After the recall of the Russian ambassador from Great Britain, when the Labor Government fell, orders were transferred from Great Britain to other countries.

3. Exploiting Political Enmities and Antagonisms. Russian foreign policy is based on the old European notion of the balance of power, which, as practiced in the beginning of the century, led to the World War, and which in recent years has divided Europe into two mutually offsetting groups of powers. Russia is utilizing the antagonism between Germany and Poland, over the "Polish Corridor," between France and Italy over naval armament, and other controversial situations. If Russia wishes to drive a bargain with France or England, her friendliness for Germany suddenly becomes very apparent. The diversion of business from country to country was used as

a club to secure recognition, and the recent rivalry between the great powers who were competing for Russian business was a favorable factor in obtaining good terms of trade or even in eliciting invitations to international conferences at Geneva.

During the early period of protests by the American Government on Japanese aggression in Manchuria, the Moscow paper *Izvestia* carried news reports about the intention of the United States to recognize the Soviet Union in order to establish an equilibrium of forces in the Far East. The Moscow press became much more favorable in its comments on America. The general feeling in Moscow is that a Soviet-American *rapport* would act as a brake upon the Japanese militarists. Furthermore, Russia, "earnestly desires to prevent a war, because it is engaged in the great work of peaceful construction which it is desirable not to interrupt."

4. "Victims of Versailles." Germany and Russia are mutually sympathetic, despite the protests of many German industrialists of the danger of Bolshevism to Germany. This feeling is based on a mutual sympathy of the two "victims of Versailles." Russia regards Germany as the balance wheel of her strategy. In 1930 for the first time the Soviet Government developed a world policy based on opposition to the Treaty of Versailles. France, the chief beneficiary of the Versailles peace, regards with apprehension this *rapprochement* between Germany and Russia. No doubt Russia will continue to exploit the friendship for Germany in order to wring advantages from the other European powers. To Germany on the other hand the overtures of Russia are a bargaining point in her dealings with France and England. At all events, Russia is a growing factor in the international political situation.

5. A Policy of Peace. Despite the blusterings of her propagandists, Russia is sincerely wedded to a policy of peace. She has nothing to gain by war. The Soviets have enough territory, enough resources, and also—enough problems. Her politics, therefore, have always been in favor of disarmament, as in 1928, when she made the bold and stark proposal, not of reduction but of the abandonment of all military and naval forces throughout the world. Her subsequent less drastic proposals were still far in excess of what the other powers were willing to surrender. With the nations on her eastern frontiers, Afghanistan, Persia, and Turkey, she has treaties providing for the amicable adjustment of disputes. Similar treaties were concluded with Germany and Lithuania. Early in 1932 a non-aggression pact was signed with Finland and similar treaties were negotiated with France and Poland. So much are

the Soviets pacific in their policy, that they have gone almost to the extreme in the policy of peace at any price.

The Polish-Soviet non-aggression treaty, signed July 25, 1932, was negotiated in spite of the opposition of Rumania, which had hoped to be offered a similar treaty. However, the Soviet Government does not yet recognize the seizure of Bessarabia by Rumania, and the Bucharest government contented itself with the comforting thought that under the Briand-Kellogg pact, ratified by Russia, she renounces war as an instrument of policy.

The anti-Soviet spokesmen say that the present policy of pacifism is temporary, that the Soviets are now trying to "lull the bourgeois countries into a sense of security," and that the policy of peace now is to be followed by a policy of war later. But, this may be a capitalist illusion as to the Soviets' future intentions, just as the threat of war now is a Soviet illusion as to present capitalist intentions. As a matter of fact, Russian policy may be based either on a sincere conviction of the ultimate good of a pacific policy or on the very practical considerations that Russia was defeated in every war in the west and that emerging Japan administered a severe beating to her in the east. The Soviet policy of peace is likely to continue on grounds either of principle or of prudence despite the continuous threats of world revolution. These are merely salve to the conscience of the Soviets, whose departure from communist principles and adherence to capitalist principles as a result of the pressure of real life are increasing in practice. They look toward illusions for compensation.

CHAPTER XVII

SHALL WE RECOGNIZE RUSSIA?

A. Non-Recognition

The American policy of non-recognition needs to be examined with respect to its aims, the reasons for non-recognition as given by American statesmen, publicists, and others, the effects of non-recognition, and its long-range significance.

1. Aims of Non-Recognition. That the nations of the world did not recognize the Soviet Government shortly after the October Revolution is understandable. Here was a new phenomenon. The extreme left wing of political doctrine had driven out the republican or moderate régime that had succeeded the Tsar. It boastfully threatened the fall of all other governments, and indeed the critically unstable condition of Europe in the years immediately succeeding the peace of Versailles constituted fertile ground for the stirring up of revolt. However, world revolution did not ensue.

After the destruction of the old régime, the Soviet Government had to settle down to administrative problems of feeding and clothing the people and of restoring stable social conditions. This was a difficult task. It called for all the energy and ability that could be mustered. Even the enthusiastic sympathizers of the Soviets cannot yet say they have succeeded. The aim of fomenting world revolution was displaced by the aim of making the Russian Revolution a success. The Soviets got down to work.

Non-recognition and isolation by the outside world failed to displace the Soviets. Nation after nation recognized them. Whatever value lay in America's policy of non-recognition in conjunction with the other governments has been diminished if not eliminated by the lone continuance of America in that policy. Non-recognition as a means of terminating Soviet rule has failed, and American policy alone is hardly likely to succeed in bringing about its downfall.

2. Reasons for Non-Recognition. The reasons for American non-recognition have been given by American statesmen at various times. The opposition to recognition is based on the principle of legitimacy rather than on the *de facto* principle, as will be seen in the section to follow.

a. Elihu Root. Elihu Root opposed recognition for the following reason:

> Each government accepts the implied assurance of the other that it will maintain true friendship, true respect, and true observance of the obligation of good neighborhood . . . but the fundamental doctrine of the men who govern Russia is that it is their mission in the world to overturn and destroy the governments of the civilized nations. The act of recognition would be a lie, and a false pretense of accepting the obligations of the rulers of Russia to observe friendship to the government and people of the United States.

b. Secretary of State Bainbridge Colby. Secretary Colby on August 10, 1920 issued the first and probably the strongest note, vigorously supporting the American policy of non-recognition.

> That the present rulers of Russia do not rule by the will or the consent of any considerable proportion of the Russian people is an incontestable fact. . . . At the moment when the work of creating a popular representative government, based upon universal suffrage, was nearing completion, the Bolsheviki, although in number an inconsiderable minority of the people, by force and cunning seized the powers and machinery of government, and have continued to use them with savage oppression to maintain themselves in power. . . . It is not possible for the government of the United States to recognize the present rulers of Russia as a government with which the relations common to friendly governments can be maintained. . . . Indeed, the responsible spokesmen of this power and its official agencies have declared that it is their understanding that the very existence of Bolshevism in Russia, the maintenance of their own rule, depends upon the occurrence of revolutions in all other great civilized nations, including the United States, which will overthrow and destroy their governments and set up Bolshevist rule in their stead. . . . The responsible leaders of the régime have frequently and openly boasted that they are willing to sign agreements and undertakings with foreign powers, while not having the slightest intention of observing such undertakings or carrying out such agreements.[1]

Since the date of this note the Soviets have been recognized by twenty-four powers, and up to date have not only signed agreements and undertakings, but have carried them out.

c. Secretary of State Charles E. Hughes. In March 1921, Litvinov made a plea for the establishment of trade relations between the Soviets and the United States. Secretary of State Hughes replied:

> It is idle to expect resumption of trade until the economic bases of production are securely established. Production is conditioned upon the safety of life, the recognition of firm guarantees of private property, the sanctity of contract,

and the rights of free labor. If fundamental changes are contemplated . . . this government will be glad to have convincing evidence of the consummation of such changes. . . . Until this evidence is supplied this government is unable to perceive that there is any proper basis for considering trade relations.

In the Stafford Little lecture at Princeton in 1928, Mr. Hughes justified the policy of non-recognition:

> Recognition by our government of the Soviet régime in Russia was refused on the ground that the international obligations of the Russian state had been repudiated, that American property held in Russia under valid titles had been confiscated without the prospect of indemnification, and that those in control of the régime at Moscow were intent upon doing all within their power, by insidious propaganda and the promotion of strife, to destroy or embarrass existing governments throughout the world.[2]

In a letter of July 19, 1923, to Mr. Samuel Gompers, President of the American Federation of Labor, Mr. Hughes said:

> Recognition . . . implies obligations . . . which include protection of the persons and property of the citizens of one country lawfully pursuing their business in the territory of the other, and abstention of hostile propaganda by one country in the territory of the other.

d. Secretary of State Frank B. Kellogg. In a statement entitled "Foreign Relations" issued by the Republican National Committee in 1928, Secretary of State Kellogg reiterated America's attitude:

> It is the conviction of the government of the United States that relations on a basis usual between friendly nations cannot be established with a governmental entity which is the agency of a group who hold it as their mission to bring about the overthrow of the existing political, economic, and social order throughout the world and who regulate their conduct towards other nations accordingly.
>
> The experience of various European governments which have recognized and entered into relations with the Soviet régime have demonstrated conclusively the wisdom of the policy to which the government of the United States has consistently adhered. Recognition of the Soviet régime has not brought about any cessation of interference by the Bolshevik leaders in the internal affairs of any recognizing country, nor has it led to the acceptance by them of other fundamental obligations of international intercourse. No state has been able to obtain the payment of debts contracted by Russia under preceding governments or the indemnification of its citizens for confiscated property. Indeed, there is every reason to believe that the granting of recognition and the holding of discussions have served only to encourage the present rulers of Russia in their policy of repudiation and confiscation.

e. Solicitor G. H. Hackworth, Department of State. Mr. G. H. Hackworth, Solicitor of the State Department, stated the official attitude of that department in 1931, in an address before the American Society of International

Law defending the American policy of non-recognition. Apparently he was trying to justify such non-recognition, even though the United States had recently promptly recognized governments resulting from revolutions in Argentina, Bolivia, Brazil, Panama, and Peru. American recognition of these new governments in Latin America was granted as soon as they demonstrated that they were in control of the administrative machinery of the state, and that there was not active resistance to their rule:

> If any feature of our policy on recognition deserves greater emphasis than others it would seem to be the requirement that a new government, before it can claim the right to recognition, should show evidence of ability and willingness to perform its international obligations. If it is unable to perform such obligation, it has not reached that degree of stability which other powers are entitled to expect before entering into international relations with it. If, on the other hand, it is able but is unwilling to perform its obligations, it has failed to adopt that standard of international conduct, which is supposed to characterize the relations between States.
>
> We have consistently refused to recognize the present régime in Russia because, among other things, of its failure to assume responsibility for its international obligations.
>
> It will be seen from the statements by Secretary Hughes that this government has considered that the present régime in Russia is deficient in its observance of the fundamental conditions of international intercourse in three respects, namely:
>
> (1) Its failure to accord to the persons and property of foreigners within its jurisdiction that degree of respect and protection required by international law.
>
> (2) Its failure to respect the international obligations of preceding governments.
>
> (3) Its failure to respect the right of other nations to develop their institutions and to conduct their internal affairs without interference or control by other states.

It would seem that the standards set up for the recognition of the above new Latin-American governments would apply equally as well to Russia. As regards the three other requirements stated, repeated offers have been made by the Soviet Government to pay the debts of the Tsarist and Kerensky governments, to settle the claims of Americans whose property was confiscated, and to refrain from propaganda.

f. Foreign Opposition to American Recognition of the Soviets. Paul Scheffer, formerly Moscow correspondent of the *Berliner Tageblatt* and erstwhile friend of the Soviets, introduces a new note into the discussion of non-recognition. Even though his own government, Germany, recognizes the Soviet Government, and even though all the arguments he presents apply with equal or greater validity to countries other than the United States, yet he would have America alone persist in her policy of non-recognition. He makes the assertion that recognition by America, "the greatest capitalist state" would greatly strengthen the Soviets and would imply American acceptance of Soviet principles. An American loan to Russia would be used against the United States. It would lead to more intrigue and to world revolt and to the ultimate downfall of capitalism. Recognition by America would, in Scheffer's opinion, vindicate Stalin and his ruthless policies and vindicate Soviet Russia to the communists of Europe and stimulate revolution there. In his own words:

> Under these circumstances recognition by America could only provoke Communist Russia to greater aggressiveness and enterprise in its attacks on the bourgeois European countries and their colonial points of weakness; in other words, upon those very European governments (also commercially important to America) which maintain official relations with Moscow.[3]

If these arguments are valid, why have these very governments actually recognized Russia? Mr. Scheffer believes that after Russia's recent policy, recognition today by America would be less justifiable than it was when Germany first extended recognition. Furthermore, since they have recognized her, why have these threatened revolts not materialized?

> The fate of the Russian people, today delivered over to a group of violent dictators, can thus be affected to a very material degree by America's decision to give or withhold positive approval of Stalin's measures. In Russia itself that is the principal significance which would be attached to American recognition.[3]

If this argument is sound, why should America alone bear the burden and the responsibility? If non-recognition is desirable for America why is it not equally desirable for the neighboring countries of Europe?

g. Other Arguments. John Spargo says that this is the first case in history where a government asked for recognition as a friendly power for the purpose of overturning the recognizing country.[4] Patriotic societies and trade organizations, in industries which compete with Russian exports, have marshaled the several justifications for non-recognition. One interesting and plausible reason was presented by an American who had been living in Russia for some time, namely, that recognition by America had value only so long as it was withheld. Once it was granted, the Soviets would probably treat America with the same slight regard with which she treats the other powers that have already recognized her. On the other hand, Americans in Russia who favor recognition say that the opposition by foreigners to America's recognition of Russia is merely a subterfuge to enable their own countries to increase their trade at America's expense.

3. Acts of Non-Recognition. America has forcefully expressed her opposition to recognition of Soviet Russia, and originally refused to join international conferences, when the Russian delegates were invited, as at The Hague and at Genoa. Again, when the United States invited other powers to the Washington Conference for the Limitation of Armaments, no invitation was extended to Russia. This is contrary to precedent. The United States in the past did participate in conferences with governments which refused to discharge their international obligations for the very purpose of inducing them to do so, as in the case of Mexico. Indeed, every effort made by the Soviets until 1931 has been either ignored or rejected.

4. Effects of Non-Recognition. a. Futility of Non-Recognition. The attitude of the American Government has failed and will probably continue to fail. As stated by an outstanding international lawyer, Mr. Paul D. Cravath:

> It is a question whether the attitude of our government in respect of recognition would have an appreciable influence on the ultimate fate of the Soviet Government.[5]

Senator Borah points out emphatically the futility of the American policy of non-recognition:

> Certainly we are not accomplishing it by the course which we are pursuing now. Six years have passed, and no debt has been recognized, so far as permanent recognition is concerned, nor settled. No claims have been adjusted, and the contention is that propaganda is more rife at this time than it has been at any time.[6]

Whatever may have been the aim of non-recognition of Russia by other countries, the result has been futile. Non-recognition by the United States has not resulted in the downfall of the Soviet régime. Allied intervention, in conjunction with a strong anti-Soviet element in Russia, failed to accomplish any result, even though Russia was then disorganized as a result of the World War and the revolution. Today there is greater stability, there is no active opposition on which foreign governments can depend for aid, and the régime seems to have full control. The American policy of non-recognition recalls the Negro spiritual, that "Joshua blew a blast before Jericho and the walls came tumbling down." That non-recognition is a futile policy is evident in the history of our Latin-American neighbors. In the words of John Bassett Moore, "A frown or a scowl on the face of the United States is not a cure for revolution."

b. Danger of Non-Recognition. Non-recognition is now futile. It may ultimately be a source of irritation, if not of danger. Misunderstandings can arise more easily. It increases Russian capacity for mischief.

5. Non-Recognition as a Permanent Policy. a. Isolation by the United States Alone. Non-recognition by the United States alone is illogical. Can the United States alone isolate a country having one-sixth of the world's surface and one-tenth of the world's population? Can the United States alone effectively embargo Russian goods? Whatever may be the merits of the general principle of non-recognition, the maintenance of that policy by America alone greatly reduces its value, although America could play an effective part in a world policy of isolation.

b. World Isolation. The Soviets have raised a problem both for themselves and the world. Some people regard the Soviet leaders as international bad boys. But the historian and the sociologist see in the Russian Revolution a reaction from the unspeakable oppression under the Tsar. Soviet Russia is a problem for the entire war. How will isolation help to solve it? Before the war, Russia had a place in the economic and political scheme. Permanent isolation can only perpetuate the economic upset of the world, which was precipitated by the world. The economic depression from which the world is now suffering is an illustration of the interdependence of nations, of the need of the world for Russia as well as the need of Russia for the world. A great people cannot be isolated permanently.

Is the American policy to be that of Bourbonism, never learning anything? From the end of the war until the Dawes Plan the policy of the Allies toward Germany was actuated, not by common sense, but by violent emotion. They attempted to isolate the relatively small territory of Germany. It took six years for the Allies to realize that despite their strong armies on the Rhine, it was a crazy policy. Hard facts ultimately reconciled them to the idea that Germany had to be reckoned with, and in 1931, thirteen years after the war, French bankers actually made a loan to Germany with the German railroads as security. Is Hegel's dictum, "The lesson of history is that we learn nothing from history," to be again proven? The American policy toward Russia is similar to the world's chauvinist attitude toward Germany.

As John Bassett Moore has put it: "Misunderstanding is something of which no nation can have a monopoly. The perception of this fact should induce us to be circumspect, tolerant, even charitable in our judgments." [7] Intransigence and self-righteousness have little place in dealing with others. The British idea of intelligent compromise is the more satisfactory method.

The war came in 1914, because nations did not know how to compromise their differences. The Tsarist régime fell because the rulers did not know how to compromise. British policy, both at home and abroad, has been reasonably successful because at crucial moments suitable compromises were made on what seemed to be essential principles and questions of national honor. Perhaps ultimately we may learn this lesson and take seriously the repeated pleas of the Soviets for recognition, and their willingness to discuss all questions at issue, debts to the United States, private property of American citizens, as well as their willingness to refrain from propaganda. Such a step on our part would lead to some realizable goal. The policy of non-recognition leads nowhere.

B. Recognition

The outstanding question at issue between the United States and Russia is that of recognition. Russia has been recognized by most of the other great powers. Certain acts of the United States have implied recognition. According to the American policy on recognition for 120 years since 1793, Russia would have been recognized. What have been the obstacles? And what are the justifications and benefits of recognition? These are some of the aspects of the general problem.

1. Some General Principles. The legal aspects of the general question of recognition constitute too large a subject to be fully discussed here. As applied to Soviet Russia the reader will find an interesting discussion of them in an article "Pros and Cons of Soviet Recognition," by the international lawyer Paul D. Cravath, in the quarterly *Foreign Affairs*.[8] The diplomatic aspects of recognition in general, and particularly with respect to Latin American affairs, is treated in the same issue in an article by Lawrence Dennis, formerly of the State Department, on "Revolution, Recognition, and Intervention." [9]

"Recognition may be either expressly granted or implied from the acts of the recognizing state." [10] The methods of recognition are several:

> Recognition may be accorded by merely carrying on such negotiations or entering into such relations as exist only between independent states. Diplomatic intercourse and treaty negotiations may be carried on in such a way as to result in recognition. Finally a new state or government may be recognized by the dispatch of an accredited representative to it, by the reception of accredited diplomatic agents from the new state or the granting of an exequatur to a consul.[11]

Mere communication does not in itself constitute an act of recognition. President Coolidge in his message to Congress on December 9, 1923, referred to the wish of America "to go to the economic and moral rescue of Russia." On December 16, Chicherin, the Commissar for Foreign Affairs, replied direct to the President. He said: "After reading your message to Congress, the Soviet Government informs you of its complete readiness to discuss with your government all problems mentioned in your message." On December 18, Secretary of State Hughes replied to this note indirectly, through the American Legation in Riga, saying: "There would seem to be at this time no reason for negotiations." Apparently, exchange of messages does not expressly or impliedly mean recognition. An extended treatment of acts falling short of recognition is given below in this chapter.

2. Acts of Recognition. a. By Other Powers. Since the Soviet Government had the appearance of being a fairly permanent one, recognition by the powers soon followed its establishment. The first to recognize Soviet Russia were her nearest neighbors, Esthonia and Finland in 1920, Poland in 1921, and Germany in 1922. Today the Soviet Government has been recognized by more than twenty-four countries. By 1924 it was recognized by Great Britain, France, Italy, Norway, Sweden, Denmark, Austria, and Greece. By 1931 the countries in Europe that had not recognized Soviet Russia were Holland, Belgium, Switzerland, Spain, Portugal, Czechoslovakia, Rumania, Bulgaria, and Yugoslavia. Since then Czechoslovakia has had a trade but not a diplomatic representation. There was a brief interruption of diplomatic relations with Soviet Russia on the part of Great Britain and France, but they were resumed.

The twenty-four governments that now recognize Soviet Russia do not necessarily approve of communist principles nor the policies of the Soviet Government. Recognition by these countries was merely a device to put the inevitable trade relationship on a legal and official basis.

b. By United States. *i. Co-signatory of the Kellogg-Briand Pact.* In spite of the fact that America did not formally recognize Soviet Russia we impliedly recognize her, according to some authorities. As John Bassett Moore stated, "recognition may be implied as well as expressed." [12] Recognition of Soviet Russia by the United States is implied in the fact that the Kellogg Pact was signed by the Soviet Government with the knowledge and consent of the United States. Accordingly, "we necessarily recognize the Soviet Government by this act." He says further that America's policy approaches the limit of human incoherence, "when it agrees with Soviet Russia that differences shall not be settled by war, and then denies to Russia the recognition which will enable it to settle its differences by diplomacy."

ii. Mediation in the Russian-Chinese Dispute. The second act of implied recognition was the note of December 2, 1929. On July 10, 1929, the government of Manchuria seized the Chinese-Eastern Railway, which had hitherto been regarded as Soviet property. Shortly thereafter the United States, under the terms of the Kellogg-Briand Pact, urged that the Soviet and Chinese governments adjust their differences under the provisions of that pact. This the Soviet and Chinese Governments agreed to do. This Soviet willingness to comply with the American wish received the favorable comment of ex-Secretary of State Kellogg, after whom the pact was named. After some hostilities between China and Soviet Russia, and the apparent settlement of their differences, Secretary Stimson again, on December 2, 1929, indicated that the signatories of the Kellogg Pact must fulfill their obligations. Litvinov, the Commissar of Foreign Affairs, resented America's intervention with the statement that no single state may exercise the function of protector of the Kellogg-Briand Pact, and that "the Soviet Government cannot forbear expressing amazement at the government of the United States, which by its own will has no official relation with the Soviet, yet deems it possible to apply to it with advice and counsel." The action of the United States in the Sino-Soviet dispute constitutes implied recognition. If the Soviet Government had followed up this situation, it virtually could have forced the United States into the position of either making this implied recognition an express one, or of reversing its policy of interceding.

c. Decision by Courts. British and American courts have decided that in extending recognition to a new state or a new government, the political department of the government is supreme, and that these court cases have no bearing.[13] An unofficial exception to these decisions is the case of Sokoloff v. National City Bank (page 196 N. Y. Supp., 1922, pages 355 and 359).[14]

Judge Ford makes a distinction:

> While this court may not recognize the Soviet Government as sovereign, and therefore possessing power to confiscate property or debts, as must be done in respect of a foreign state which has been recognized either *de facto* or *de jure,* it does not follow that we must assume a state of anarchy in Russia. True, by legal fiction, for some purposes which appertain more particularly to the other, the "political" branches of the government than to the judiciary, we must continue to assume that the old Imperial Government is the only sovereign government in Russia.
>
> Indeed we know as a matter of common knowledge that there is a govern-

ment there which has been functioning in some fashion for five years or more, and that it is not the Imperial Government of the Tsars.

3. History of American Policy on Recognition. The American policy on recognition from 1793 until 1913, excepting Civil War times, followed the *de facto* theory of recognition, that is, any government which was able to maintain itself in power was recognized. Wilson initiated a new policy, namely that only a government legitimately established would be recognized. This has led to several absurd situations, and now under Stimson the doctrine of legitimacy is being abandoned and the previous doctrine of *de facto* recognition is being restored. A series of revolutions in the Latin-American countries was the immediate occasion for this reversal of policy.

a. Recognition *De Facto*. *i. Moore's Interpretation of the Recognition of the French Republic.* On March 12, 1793, Secretary of State Thomas Jefferson, writing to Gouverneur Morris, United States Minister to France, stated:

> We surely cannot deny to any nation that right whereon our own government is founded—that every one may govern itself according to whatever form it pleases, and change these forms at its own will; and that it may transact its business with foreign nations through whatever organ it thinks proper, whether king, convention, assembly, committee, president, or anything else it may choose. The will of the nation is the only thing essential to be regarded.[15]

On May 19, 1793, after a brief consideration, the United States Government recognized the revolutionary government of France. Answering the critics of this policy, Washington stated that, while the French people were traveling over a bloody road, it was the only road over which they could travel away from Bourbonism and to a sound democracy.

The sentiment of Washington is no less significant, as applied to the Russian people in their march away from Tsarist tyranny.

> When Genet was received as minister, the Reign of Terror in France was in full swing. The government of Louis XVI, our friend in our struggle for independence, had been overthrown, and Louis had himself been beheaded; the Goddess of Reason had been enthroned, and the streets echoed with hoarse cries for hanging at the lamp posts the prelates of the dethroned church; the guillotine had been installed, and heads were daily rolling into the basket; the Place de la Concorde was encrimsoned with blood, and the Jacobite government was conducting abroad what Edmund Burke called an anarchic propagandism. In these things there must have been much to offend the sensibilities of our sober rulers at Philadelphia and much to excite their strong disapprobation.[16]

That *de facto* recognition does not imply approval by the United States of the policies of the new government is indicated in subsequent history. Shortly after the recognition by the United States of the French revolutionary government, the new minister from France, Edmond Genet, arrived at Charleston, S. C. En route to Philadelphia he made several revolutionary addresses, unauthorized by his government and not in harmony with the policy of the United States. After some warning Genet ceased his revolutionary propaganda, and when he resumed it and violated the American policy of neutrality in the war between England and France, President Washington asked for his recall, which followed.

From 1793 to 1913 the United States followed the policy enunciated by Secretary of State Jefferson to the Minister to France, Gouverneur Morris, except for a period during and after the Civil War, when the new governments resulting from revolution were not recognized, because it would reflect on the wish of the United States that the seceding southern states should not be recognized. This attitude, however, ceased at the end of the Civil War and has not since been resumed.

ii. Policy Until Civil War.[17] President Jefferson readily accorded recognition to Napoleon in 1804.[18] On the other hand Madison readily recognized the French monarchy in 1814. Monroe formally recognized the republics of Latin America following the revolution against Spain, as follows: Colombia in 1822, Mexico in 1823, Buenos Aires in 1823, Chile in 1823, and the Central American States in 1824.

The *de facto* policy of the government was again stated in recognizing the French Republic set up following the revolution of 1848. Mr. Buchanan writing to Mr. Rush stated:

> In its intercourse with foreign nations the government of the United States has from its origin, always recognized *de facto* governments. We recognize the right of all nations to create and reform their political institutions according to their own will. We do not go behind the existing government to involve ourselves in the question of legitimacy. It is sufficient for us to know that a government exists capable of maintaining itself; and then its recognition on our part inevitably follows.[19]

In a message of May 15, 1856, President Pierce stated that the United States had successively recognized, within the course of a few months, five revolutionary governments in Mexico. Again the American policy of *de facto* recognition was reiterated:

> We do not go behind the fact of a foreign government, exercising actual power, to investigate the question of legitimacy; we do not inquire into the causes which lead to a change of governments. To us it is indifferent whether a successful revolution has been aided by foreign intervention or not; whether insurrection

has overthrown an existing government and another has been established in its place, according to pre-existing form; or in a manner adopted for the occasion by those whom we may find in the actual possession of power. . . . All these matters we leave to the people and public authorities of the particular country to determine; and their determination, whether it be by positive action or by ascertained acquiescence, is to us sufficient warrant of the legitimacy of the new government.[20]

iii. Policy from the Civil War Until 1900.[21] As a result of the Civil War the American policy on recognition changed. In order to prevent the European powers from recognizing the Confederacy, the Federal Government was less ready to recognize new states. Although recognition was granted when the new government had proved its independence, it was not to be granted as a means of fostering or aiding revolution.

Seward introduced a new note, namely, the public acceptance of a constitution. In his note of March 8, 1866, Seward wrote to General Horey, United States Minister to Peru, after a dictatorship had been set up by military force, and after the government had been recognized by all the other important governments except the United States.

> The policy of the United States is settled upon the principle that revolutions in republican states ought not to be accepted until the people have adopted them by organic law with the solemnities which would seem sufficient to guarantee their stability and permanency. This is the result of reflection upon national trials of our own.[22]

When the government in Peru changed again Seward dispatched another note to the American ministry, in which he reiterated the principle that the new government must be accepted by the people and gave as his reason the protest of the Federal Government against recognition of the Confederacy by foreign governments.

> What we wait for in this case is the legal evidence that the existing administration has been deliberately accepted by the people of Peru. . . . All that we do require is when a change of administration has been made, not by peaceful constitutional process, but by force, that then the new administration shall be sanctioned by the formal acquiescence and acceptance of the people.
>
> We insist upon this because the adoption of a different principle in regard to foreign states would necessarily tend to impair the constitutional vigor of our own government, and thus favor disorganization, disintegration, and anarchy throughout the American continent. In our own late political convulsion, we protested to all the world against any recognition of the insurgents as a political body by the foreign nations, and we denied the right of any such nation to recognize a government here independent of our constitutional republic until such new government should be not only successful in arms, but should also be proclaimed by the people of the United States.[23]

This slight trend toward a policy of legitimacy was also stated in the dispatch of Secretary Evarts in 1879. Even though England, France, Germany, Italy, Spain, and Brazil had recognized the provisional government of Venezuela, Secretary Evarts decided to defer formal intercourse until—

> such a step will not only rest on the popular will of Venezuela, but will also be beneficial to the relations between the United States and that country. Good faith in the observance of international obligations is the first essential toward the maintenance of such relations.

After the revolution in Colombia in 1890, American Minister Egan received the following instructions:

> The rule of the United States is to defer recognition of another executive in its place until it shall appear that it is in possession of the machinery of the state, administering government with the assent of the people thereof, and that it is in a position to fulfill all the international obligations and responsibilities incumbent upon a sovereign state under treaties and international law.[24]

Again four days after the revolution in Chile in 1891 the American Minister, Mr. Egan, received instructions to recognize the new government if it was accepted by the people.[24]

iv. Policy Since 1900. With the beginning of the twentieth century and the extension abroad of American economic interests, another note developed in the American policy—namely, the question whether the new government met its international obligations. Where American interest was slight, we were not very insistent upon this aspect, but where it was extensive this phase of recognition policy was stressed. For example, when King Alexander of Servia was assassinated in 1903 and King Peter was proclaimed his successor, the American Minister took steps toward formal recognition rather promptly. A *de facto* government existed and there were no American interests at stake. But in Latin America, formal recognition was not extended until the new government expressed its willingness to assume its financial obligations and to fulfill its financial responsibilities. For example our State Department authorized the chargé d'affaires at Mexico City, on May 27, 1921, to present a treaty of amity and commerce "to regulate and promote commercial intercourse between the two countries and to remove all causes of difference between them." But certain conditions were stipulated, such as assurances that the Mexican Government would not apply retroactively the Carranza agrarian decree of January 6, 1915, or Article 27 of the Constitution of 1917, and that property and rights taken from the Americans by the Mexican Government since 1910 would be restored.[25]

In this case not only was it stipulated that a *de facto* government exist, and that it enjoy popular approval, but that in addition American rights remain unabridged. In fact the third element was made a prerequisite of recognition. In the words of Secretary Hughes' statement of June 7, 1921:

> Whenever Mexico is ready to give assurance that she will perform her fundamental obligation in the protection both of persons and of rights of property validly acquired, there will be no obstacles to the most advantageous relations between the two peoples. The question of recognition is a subordinate one, but there will be no difficulty as to this, for if General Obregon is ready to negotiate a proper treaty, it is drawn so as to be negotiated with him and the making of the treaty in proper form will accomplish the recognition of the government that makes it.[26]

The acceptance of recognition under such conditions was regarded by President Obregon of Mexico as an impairment of "its national dignity and sovereignty."[27] For almost two years the United States maintained this attitude, but Mexico was too proud to limit her sovereignty even to attain the goal of recognition by the United States. In the meantime, however, the Mexican Government proceeded along the lines indicated by Secretary Hughes.

On March 31, 1923, the Foreign Minister of Mexico stated that the Mexican Government had "accomplished acts of such importance that the problem of diplomatic relations between the two governments" might be settled. Thereupon President Harding appointed two commissioners in May 1923 to discuss the matters in dispute, and on August 31, 1923, the Mexican Government was recognized. In accordance with the suggestion of Secretary Hughes and the Mexican Foreign Minister, two claims commissions were created to handle the details. The attitude of the United States Government toward Mexico was based, not upon the stability of the government or on the consent of the people, but on the willingness of the new government to respect existing American rights.

This attitude toward Mexico is in many respects similar to the attitude of our State Department toward the Soviet Union. However, the régime of Kerensky and Milyukov was subjected to no such severe conditions. In spite of the foreign policy adopted during the Civil War of not recognizing a government for the purpose of aiding the revolutionists, the State Department issued an announcement on March 20, 1917, "that officials here believe that it would be a most appropriate act for the American Government to be the first to welcome the new Russian democratic government into the society of governments, especially as the Petrograd revolutionary authorities have abolished all class, religious, and national limitations, doing away with inequalities of every kind and guaranteeing universal suffrage." The Minister of Foreign Affairs, M. Milyukov, the very next day, March 21, 1917, cabled that Russia would "continue to respect the financial undertakings made by the fallen régime," and on the following day, March 22, 1917, the United States Government recognized the new Russian Government. It actually was the first to do so.[28]

The United States Government also recognized Esthonia, Latvia, and Lithuania, because these governments had existed for some period of time and maintained a stable régime, although America at first refused to recognize them on the grounds that the chaos in Russia was not to be made the occasion for its geographical disintegration.

v. Stimson's Statement of Policy. Secretary of State Stimson, in an address before the Council of Foreign Relations, February 6, 1931, and subsequently printed and distributed publicly by the State Department, gave a summary of American policy on recognition. His address was concerned primarily with the problem of recognition of the newly formed Latin-American republics originating in the recent revolutions. Yet it was concerned with issues so vital to the Russian problem that, following it, the audience inquired as to whether Russia's status was implied under the cover of the Latin-American discussion, and whether the Secretary's address was not preparing the public mind for a resumption of the historic American policy and the abandonment of the Wilsonian recognition doctrine of legitimacy. He said:

> The practice of this country as to the recognition of new governments has been substantially uniform from the days of the administration of Secretary of State Jefferson in 1792 to the days of Secretary of State Bryan in 1913. . . . This general policy, as thus observed, was to base the act of recognition not upon the question of the constitutional legitimacy of the new government but upon its *de facto* capacity to fulfill its obligations as a member of the family of nations. This country recognized the right of other nations to regulate their own internal affairs of government and disclaimed any attempt to base its recognition upon the correctness of their constitutional action.[29]

Continuing, Mr. Stimson indicated that the considerations underlying America's policy of recognition were stated by Mr. Alva A. Adee, long the trusted Assistant Secretary of State of this government, as follows:

> Ever since the American Revolution, entrance upon diplomatic intercourse with foreign states has been *de facto,* dependent upon the existence of three conditions of fact: the control of the administrative machinery of the state; the gen-

eral acquiescence of its people; and the ability and willingness of their government to discharge international and conventional obligations. The form of government has not been a conditional factor in such recognition; in other words, the *de jure* element of legitimacy of title has been left aside.[30]

vi. Hughes Interpretation. Adherence to the *de facto* doctrine of recognition was clearly stated by Charles Evans Hughes, twice Secretary of State and now Chief Justice of the United States Supreme Court: "We are not concerned with the question of the legitimacy of a government. . . . We recognize the right of revolution and do not attempt to determine the internal concerns of other states." He quotes Buchanan, who as Secretary of State said:

The United States Government has from its origin always recognized *de facto* governments. We recognize the right of all nations to create and reform their political institutions according to their own will and pleasure. We do not go behind the existing government to involve ourselves in the question of legitimacy. It is sufficient for us to know that a government exists, capable of maintaining itself; and then its recognition on our part inevitably follows.[31]

This interpretation by Mr. Hughes as a private citizen[32] was made in 1928, in connection with the Latin-American countries, but its significance is just as great and its validity just as binding in connection with Russia. Yet Mr. Hughes, in 1923, acting officially as Secretary of State, utterly ignored this principle in connection with the Russian plea for recognition.

vii. Cravath Interpretation. Mr. Paul D. Cravath's clear legal statement on *de facto* recognition is of great interest:

Our government was the first of the Great Powers to support the *de facto* theory of recognition, as contrasted with the legitimacy theory. The American State Department has consistently adhered to the *de facto* theory for more than a century. . . . The theory and practice of our State Department were admirably summarized in a memorandum of Mr. A. A. Adee, Assistant Secretary of State, on March 28, 1913, as follows:

"It will, I think, simplify the matter to keep in mind the distinction between the recognition necessary to the conduct of international business between two countries and the recognition of the form of government professed by a foreign country. . . . The form of government has not been a conditional factor in such recognition; in other words, the *de jure* element of legitimacy of title has been left aside, probably because liable to involve dynastic or constitutional questions hardly within our competency to adjudicate, especially so when the organic form of government has been changed, as by revolution, from a monarchy to a commonwealth or vice versa. The general practice in such cases has been to satisfy ourselves that the change was effective and to enter into relation with the authority in *de facto* possession."

Our government has frequently established cordial diplomatic relations with governments that were notoriously autocratic and vicious. Usually the sole test that our government seeks to apply is whether the new government is sufficiently entrenched in power effectively to govern within its own borders and to perform its international obligations. After that test has been met, our government in the recognition of governments in the eastern hemisphere does not usually concern itself with the morals or motives of the government seeking recognition. . . . The recognition of a newly established government by the United States Government does not remotely carry with it the implication that the aims and practices of the new government meet with our approval or inspire our admiration.[33]

viii. Similarity to British Policy. The *de facto* theory of recognition is a practical one. After the revolution in Brazil, the State Department, on November 8, 1930, instructed Ambassador Morgan that the United States Government would be happy to continue with the new government the same friendly relations as with its predecessors. Two days later the Prime Minister of Great Britain clinched the action of his government by a highly significant and sagacious speech in which he used these words:

South America has gone through revolution after revolution. They are all friends of ours. It is not our business to inquire into their internal conditions, and we recognize government after government, so soon as that government has shown signs that it has come to stay for a reasonable time.[34]

ix. Implications of the De Facto *Theory.* The historic policy of the United States was prompt recognition of any *de facto* government soon after the violent overthrow of its predecessor. This was merely a formality. The American diplomatic representatives were promptly authorized to recognize the new government as soon as they considered it in effective control of the country, as evidenced by the fact that the people paid taxes, rendered military service, and obeyed the new government.[35]

The American policy has been that it is possible to trade with another people without forcing on them our own standards of government. The *de facto* policy merely means that the new government is in control. It does not mean that the recognizing government approves of the new. Washington recognized the French Republic in spite of its bloody deeds. The United States Government recognized the old Tsarist régime in spite of its oppression and the murder of its citizens for political activity. We recognized polygamists, slave states, cannibals, and pirates without even faintly implying that we approved of their policy. Pirates were recognized, in the case of the Barbary States in 1793. Polygamists were recognized in the cases of the Barbary States, and also Turkey, Persia, Egypt, and Samoa. Furthermore, polygamy is legitimate today in Persia, Egypt, and in practically all of the eastern governments recognized by the United States. Cannibals were recognized as in the accession of Malietoa of Samoa (January 20, 1880) then known as the Sandwich Islands, whose inhabitants were known as notorious cannibals since their discovery in 1772 by Captain Cook.[36]

b. Doctrine of Legitimacy. The historic policy of the United States of recognizing revolutionary governments that conformed with the simple *de facto* requirements, was discarded in 1913.

i. Wilson's Departure. With the advent of President Wilson's administration this policy of over a century was most radically reversed in respect to the Republic of Mexico, and, by a public declaration on March 11, 1913, it was announced that—

> Co-operation (with our sister republics of Central and South America) is possible only when supported at every turn by the orderly processes of just government based upon law, not upon arbitrary or irregular force. We hold, as I am sure that all thoughtful leaders of republican government everywhere hold, that just government rests always upon the consent of the governed, and that there can be no freedom without order based upon law and upon the public conscience and approval. We shall look to make these principles the basis of mutual intercourse, respect, and helpfulness between our sister republics and ourselves.[37]

An equally significant part of this state paper was omitted from Mr. Stimson's address mentioned above, as follows:

> We shall lend our influence of every kind to the realization of these principles in fact and practice, knowing that disorder, personal intrigues, and defiance of constitutional rights weaken and discredit government and injure none so much as the people who are unfortunate enough to have their common life and their common affairs so tainted and disturbed. We can have no sympathy with those who seek to seize the power of government to advance their own personal interests or ambition. We are the friends of peace, but we know that there can be no lasting or stable peace in such circumstances. As friends, therefore, we shall prefer those who act in the interest of peace and honor, who protect private rights, and respect the restraints of constitutional provision.[38]

ii. Implications of the Legitimacy Doctrine. The implications of the legitimacy doctrine are widespread. Judge Moore states them clearly as follows:

> This declaration [of Mr. Wilson] constituted a radical and subversive departure from our previous policy and practice, and also from the established practice and policy of all other governments, in the following particulars:
>
> 1. In declaring that co-operation with other governments was possible only so far as it was supported by the observance in their own affairs of orderly processes, free from the exercise of arbitrary or irregular force.
>
> 2. That it was our purpose to make these principles the basis of mutual intercourse, respect and helpfulness between our sister republics and ourselves.

3. That we should "lend our influence of every kind" to the realization of those principles in fact and in practice by the other governments of the hemisphere.

4. That there could be "no lasting or stable peace" between us and those who sought to seize the power of government "to advance their own personal interests or ambition."

5. That we should "prefer" in our friendships those who acted in the interest of peace and honor, and who respected the restraints of constitutional provisions.

It is to be observed that there was no intimation that we should leave it to our sister republics to determine whether they were behaving in an orderly way and respecting the restraints of their constitutions. On the contrary, there was a clear implication that we should determine this question for ourselves.[39]

Lawrence Dennis also shows the practical difficulties:

The revolutionary disturbances must be followed by months of the uncertain vicissitudes of a constitutional convention, political maneuvers, campaigning, and finally by general elections held by the provisional government—all before the country can settle down to normal political life. . . .

Now, if one is not an academic idealist or a doctrinaire, one must appreciate that few things can be worse just after a successful revolution than to say: "No Washington, Franklin, or Hamilton of the revolution may head the new government; no new government may immediately consolidate its position by *de jure* recognition." [40]

In the last few decades the American policy on recognition developed two tendencies, first the attempt to secure the assent of the new government to a number of the demands of the United States as a sort of condition precedent, and second a tendency to revive—

the defunct legitimacy doctrine of the extinct Holy Alliance with its old regal robes replaced by the more up-to-date garments of republican constitutionality. . . . Up to near the end of the nineteenth century the second of these conditions, the disposition to fulfill international obligations, was never mentioned in communications of the State Department. It was taken for granted. Expressed interest in this condition seems to be in direct ratio to the amount of American investments in the country.[41]

As an example, in the interval from November 1921 to March 1923, the United States demanded the acceptance by Mexico of a treaty embodying the American views of what Mexico ought to do. Mexico refused to sign. By conciliation on both sides a compromise was effected and Mexico was recognized. To quote Dennis:

This may be shrewd trading for private individuals, but from the point of view of international law and good relations between nations, it is difficult to imagine a more regrettable procedure. The fairness of the claims has nothing to do with the propriety of making their satisfaction the price of recognition. International law, diplomacy, and arbitration exist for the purpose of defining rights and settling claims between nations.[42]

iii. Results of the Legitimacy Doctrine. The implication of the legitimacy doctrine is interference and even military intervention in other countries. And just as America interfered in the affairs of Mexico with a military expedition in 1913 in the maintenance of the legitimacy doctrine, so the participation in the Allied intervention in Russia is the consequence of the same policy.

Whenever the American representative mentions to the head of a *de facto* government a number of things which the United States desires, and intimates that compliance with these wishes might help along recognition, the United States is using *Machtpolitik* or economic imperialism in a very overt manner. The United States is a nearly invincible world power. The new government with which such tactics are employed is always weak and badly in need of recognition. We may gain a point by this sort of trading, but it is dearly bought in good will, as our relations with Mexico, for instance, eloquently testify. It cannot be shown that the use of recognition and non-recognition as instruments of an American policy of interference with the internal political processes of Mexico and Central America has contributed to peace or stability in those countries.[43]

c. Abandonment of the Doctrine of Legitimacy. *i. Objections to the Doctrine.* The doctrine of legitimacy involves some serious difficulties. It justifies a *Machtpolitik* on the part of the United States. Further, it leads to a pernicious corollary, armed intervention. Moore points out further objections:

Not only does our recent departure keep us in an attitude of intervention in the domestic affairs of other countries, but it has indoctrinated our people in the preposterous and mischievous supposition that the recognition of a government implies approval of its constitution, its economic system, its attitude towards religion, and its general course of conduct. Not only is this supposition contrary to elementary principles of international law, which assure to each independent state the right to regulate its domestic affairs, but it is flagrantly at variance with the facts. It is, for instance, inconceivable that the government of the United States has at any time approved all the governments with which it held diplomatic relations. Even at the lowest ebb of our fortunes, I believe we should have resented such an imputation.

Yet another fallacy which has come to prevail is the supposition that recognition and the establishment of diplomatic relations imply the relinquishment of claims. Nothing could be more contrary to the truth. . . . When our government abandons the departures that have marked the past fifteen years [from the *de facto* policy of recognition], we probably shall see less of the spectacular good-will missions to Latin America which seem to have become a permanent and necessary part of our recent policies [of the doctrine of legitimacy].[44]

Dennis in *Foreign Affairs,* says:

> Once nations get away from the objective criteria of the sound *de factoism* of international law and old American policy, into the specious metaphysics of any system of legitimacy, be it constitutional or monarchical, irreconcilable differences of opinion will inevitably arise, making national honor, rather than reason and political expediency, the ultimate arbiter of policy. . . . The legitimacy doctrine is feasible only when applied to weak countries, easy of subjugation. It is a sort of *Machtpolitik*. It is not good international law. Unlike good law, it cannot be applied to large as well as to small, to strong as well as to weak. In nations like Russia or China, no matter what happens or how greatly foreign interests are menaced or injured, there can be no serious question of a foreign intervention to put things right. . . . The second development, or the masquerade of the reactionary Holy Alliance legitimacy doctrine in the garments of republican constitutionalism, is one of the most interesting features of American policy since 1913.[45]

ii. Restatement of Policy. Under Mr. Stimson, the legitimacy doctrine of recognition has been rejected and the foreign policy of the United States has returned to the *de facto* doctrine of recognition which was effective continuously since the founding of the republic except for the lapse during the Wilson administration. Mr. Stimson says further:

> In his sympathy for the development of free constitutional institutions among the people of our Latin-American neighbors, Mr. Wilson did not differ from the feelings of the great mass of his countrymen in the United States, including Mr. Jefferson and Mr. Adams, but he differed from the practice of his predecessors in seeking actively to propagate these institutions in a foreign country by the direct influence of this government and to do this against the desire of the authorities and people of Mexico.
>
> The present administration has refused to follow the policy of Mr. Wilson and has followed consistently the former practice of this government since the days of Jefferson. As soon as it was reported to us, through our diplomatic representatives, that the new governments in Bolivia, Peru, Argentina, Brazil, and Panama were in control of the administrative machinery of the state, with the apparent general acquiescence of their people, and that they were willing and apparently able to discharge their international and conventional obligations, they were recognized by our government. And, in view of the economic depression, with the consequent need for prompt measures of financial stabilization, we did this with as little delay as possible, in order to give those sorely pressed countries the quickest possible opportunities for recovering their economic poise.[46]

Even though the United States bears a special relation to the Central American and other Latin American republics, these principles cannot be restricted. They have universal validity.

A later statement of the *de facto* principle was by Solicitor G. H. Hackworth of the State Department:

> During the post-war period the policy of this government with respect to recognition of new governments has followed closely the principles laid down by Jefferson. In the recent changes in Argentina, Peru, Bolivia, Brazil, and Panama, Secretary Stimson recognized the new governments as soon as he was assured (1) that they were in control of the administrative ministry of the state, (2) that there was no active resistance to their rule, and (3) that they were willing and apparently able to fulfill their international obligations.[47]

The Hackworth statement is a restatement of the Draft Convention, prepared by the Pan-American Juristical Conference at Rio de Janeiro in 1927, to the effect that "every abnormally constituted government may be recognized, if it is capable of maintaining order and tranquillity and is disposed to fulfill the international obligations of the nation."

iii. Summary of American Policies on Recognition. The policy of the United States on recognition has undergone an evolution. At the beginning of our history we were the first to recognize new governments. Our own republican government was established as a result of a revolution and our foreign policy was then dedicated to the ideal of republican propaganda. This policy was also the basis of the Monroe Doctrine. American policy then was one of *de facto* recognition. There was no requirement of assurance of stability. Our own government was very young, and by European monarchies it was regarded for some time as of doubtful stability. American interests abroad at that time were negligible and, therefore, our recognition policy did not require the guarantee of financial obligations and respect for American rights.

Popular approval subsequently came to be a requirement during and after the Civil War because the Confederate States sought recognition in Europe. The requirement that a new government be set up by constitutional means introduced a legitimist note, which was exaggerated during the administration of President Wilson. Within the last few decades and particularly more recently the financial interests of the United States came to be an important consideration in determining our policy on recognition.

iv. Application to Russia. Apparently the foreign policy of the United States has been reversed in its application to Latin America. The recognition in rapid succession of the revolutionary governments in Latin America, and the withdrawal of troops from Nicaragua are in line with the statement of Secretary of State Stimson concerning the reversal of policy and the abandonment of the doctrine of legitimacy. Is this a forerunner of the abandonment of the policy with respect to Russia? Shall we there follow the same policy as in Latin America? The Soviet Government is permanent, there is no resistance to its rule, the inhabitants pay taxes and render military service. Shall we there also no longer insist that the people elect their officials by constitutional means?

> It is undoubtedly a noble dream, that of ridding Latin-American republics of disorders, but as it can be recognized only by removing the causes, it is not the business of foreign countries. The policy of practical idealism and enlightened self-interest is to encourage the American republics in ways approved by international law to work out their own salvation without armed intervention. . . . We should be tolerant of their shortcomings and patient with their slow progress, remembering that long decades of uninterrupted civil war and several great revolutions are part of the political experience out of which the present political institutions of the English-speaking peoples have flowered.[48]

Substitute the words "Soviet Russia" for "Latin-American republics" and there emerge the outlines of a rational and legal policy toward that country.

However, the State Department makes a distinction between the Latin-American countries and Russia. Mr. Cole states the case clearly:

> No government, even though it came into power through a revolution, which has been in control for ten years and which is now more firmly planted than ever, could hardly fail to show sufficient evidences of present and future stability as not to merit recognition on that ground alone. The ability of the Russian Government to meet its international undertakings, if we may take the ability of other governments that have been recognized as a proper criterion upon which to base judgment, can hardly be impugned. The willingness of the Soviet régime to fulfill its international responsibilities has justly been questioned in the past, but it may well be asked whether the State Department has not been overscrupulous in applying this criterion during the last few years. Russian representatives have expressed the willingness of their government to acknowledge, after recognition has been tendered by the United States, the amount of her indebtedness which may be agreed upon through diplomatic channels. The United States has persistently demanded an acknowledgment of the amount of indebtedness which the State Department maintains is due our country *before* recognition will even be considered. And this attitude in the face of the agreement finally reached with the Mexican Government in 1923! By virtue of the attendant circumstances, we are justified in assuming that the objections to recognition on the part of the Department of State are based primarily upon American objections to the principles upon which the Soviet Government is based and to the principles which it wishes to propagate. If this assumption be correct, the United States is applying that very instrument, recognition, which has been used to help spread republicanism to prevent another state from propagating a government founded upon principles repugnant to us.[49]

4. History of American Policy toward Russia. a. Kerensky Government. The Provisional Government, under Kerensky and Milyukov, assumed control on March 12, 1917. The Tsar abdicated three days later. The United States Government recognized the new régime on March 20, eight days after

the new government assumed power, and five days after the old régime fell. The new régime apparently was not permanent, in fact its representatives informed Ambassador Francis that, if American recognition was not promptly forthcoming, it might fall. Apparently the rules for recognition were suspended in this instance. The American Government recognized the Kerensky régime after it had been in power for eight days, but refuses to recognize the Soviet régime after it has been in power for fifteen years.

b. Prinkipo Island Conference. Soon after the arrival in Europe of President Wilson in December 1918, Litvinov cabled inviting him to come to an understanding with the Soviet Government. Thereupon President Wilson sent a representative to confer with Litvinov in Stockholm. It was orginally proposed to invite all the Russian governments, Bolshevik and anti-Bolshevik, to the peace conference, but owing to strong opposition by the diplomats at Versailles it was decided to hold a separate Russian conference on Prinkipo Island in February 1919. Invitations were sent to the border states and to the anti-Bolshevik factions, but not to the Bolsheviks. Nevertheless, the Bolsheviks assumed that they ought to attend and "accepted." In their "acceptance" they actually stated:

> The Soviet Government does not refuse to recognize its financial obligations to its creditors, who are subjects of the Entente powers. But in view of the financial difficulties of the Russian Soviet Republic and its insufficient foreign credits the Soviet Republic proposes to guarantee the payment of interest on its loans in raw materials. . . . The Russian Soviet Government is ready to include in the general agreement with the Entente powers the obligation not to interfere in their internal affairs.

Owing to the refusal of the anti-Bolsheviks to attend, the Prinkipo Island Conference was abandoned. In the meantime, President Wilson sent William Bullitt to Lenin. He conferred with Lenin and the other Soviet leaders. The Soviet Government proposed a conference and agreed to recognize the financial obligations of the former Russian Empire. The American peace commissioners, Lansing, Bliss, and White, as well as Colonel House, thought that the Soviet proposals could form the basis of possible negotiations with Russia, but President Wilson ignored the matter, and his associates on the Peace Commission were without power to take any action.

c. Colby Note of 1920. In August 1920, Bainbridge Colby, Secretary of State under Wilson, summarized the American attitude of non-recognition toward Russia which stands to this day. In brief this was a refusal to recognize the Bolshevik régime or to approve of the dismemberment of Russia. The attitude of the American Government was stated by Mr. Colby, reviewing our friendly attitude toward the efforts of the Russian people to reconstruct their national life upon the basis of popular self-government; in fact the government of the United States was first to recognize the Provisional Government preceding the Bolshevik régime. According to Secretary Colby our attitude was "based on the negation of every principle of honor and faith by the Soviets." The Soviets would not keep any agreement and therefore it would be useless to negotiate any agreement with them. The Third Internationale aimed at world revolution, and the Soviet embassies would be the centers of propaganda. He also appealed for fair treatment of Soviet Russia, so as to prevent the Soviet officials from becoming martyrs in the eyes of the Russian people.

d. Martens' Reply. In reply to Secretary Colby's note Ludwig C. A. K. Martens, unrecognized Soviet appointee as ambassador to the United States, said: "The domestic affairs of the Russian people are no concern of the United States, and we do not desire to enter into any controversy with American officials upon matters concerning which they are so lamentably ill informed." Furthermore, Martens rejected the legitimacy doctrine of recognition and maintained that recognition of a government does not imply approval of its policies. The Soviet and the capitalist governments are not asked mutually to approve each others' institutions. Chicherin also replied to the Colby note with a blanket denial that the Soviet Government rested on brute force, that it ruled without the consent of the people, and that its diplomats were agents of Soviet propaganda. Furthermore, the Soviet Government believed that the working masses in each country must effect their own revolution.

Later, in 1920, important concessions were offered for petroleum, coal, and timber, of a value of several billion dollars, to an American group, provided the United States recognized Russia. The Soviets tried to use the possible antagonism between Japan and the United States as a leverage to force America's hand, without avail.

e. Litvinov Appeal. In March 1921, Assistant Commissar for Foreign Affairs Litvinov urged the resumption of business relations between the United States and Russia. Secretary of Commerce Hoover replied that under the Soviet system "there can be no real return to production and that Russia will have no considerable commodities to export and consequently no great ability to obtain imports." At about the same time Secretary of State Hughes stated that, without the safety of life, the guarantee of private property, the sanctity of contract, and the rights of free labor, Soviet Russia could not be productive, and therefore he could not perceive that there was any basis for considering trade relations.

f. Houghton Inquiry. Under the influence of business men and members of Congress, the administration yielded somewhat. In the autumn of 1922 the State Department instructed Ambassador Houghton at Berlin to inquire concerning the attitude of the Soviet Government, if the United States decided to send to Russia a commission of experts to study and report on the situation. Ambassador Houghton held conversations with the Commissars of Trade and Foreign Affairs, Krassin and Chicherin. The Soviet Government agreed to the American suggestion on the condition that a similar Soviet commission go to the United States. Thereupon the American State Department declared that the matter was considered terminated. The "cocky" answer to the well-intentioned inquiry by the United States has done much to prejudice the Soviet case in the United States.

g. Coolidge Message. President Coolidge, in his message to Congress in December 1923 made another overture to Russia:

> Whenever there appears any disposition to compensate our citizens who were despoiled, and to recognize the debt contracted with our government, not by the Tsar, but by the newly formed Republic of Russia; whenever the active spirit of enmity to our institutions is abated; whenever there appear works meet for repentance, our country ought to be the first to go to the economic and moral rescue of Russia.

Thereupon Mr. Chicherin, Commissar for Foreign Affairs, readily assented on behalf of the Soviet Government to open negotiations subject to the principle of mutual non-intervention in internal affairs. "The Soviet Government is fully prepared to do all in its power, so far as the dignity and the interests of its country permit, to bring about the desired renewal of friendship with the United States of America." Secretary of State Hughes sent a drastic reply. On December 18, 1823, he instructed the American Consul at Reval to transmit to the local diplomatic agent of the Soviet Government the following note:

> If the Soviet authorities are ready to restore the confiscated property of American citizens or make effective compensations, they can do so. If the Soviet authorities are ready to repeal their decree repudiating Russia's obligations to this country they can do so. It requires no conference or negotiations to accomplish these results which can and should be achieved at Moscow as evidence of good faith. . . . Most serious is the continued propaganda to overthrow the institutions of this country. This government can enter into no negotiations until these efforts directed from Moscow are abandoned.

h. Other Soviet Proposals. In December 1925, Foreign Commissar Chicherin stated in Moscow that the Soviet Government had proposed to settle all questions, including the loan granted to Kerensky. Again, in 1926, Litvinov, Acting Foreign Commissar, speaking before the Central Executive Committee of the Soviet, stated that—

> From official and semi-official sources, we have heard repeatedly that the American Government's condition for the resumption of relations with us is the recognition on our part of the loan contracted by the Provisional Government of Kerensky, the American Government being prepared to consider favorably our just counter-claims. Such a formulation of the question would not create any difficulties in the case of direct negotiations. On its part, the Soviet Government has declared repeatedly that it is ready to start immediate negotiations with the American Government, and I am repeating it at present from this platform.

i. Kellogg-Briand Pact and Chinese-Eastern Railway Dispute. In 1928, when the Kellogg-Briand Peace Pact was signed, the German Government wished to have Soviet Russia included as a signatory. The American attitude was that after the treaty had been signed by the fifteen original parties, Soviet Russia might then also be permitted to sign. Apparently the American delegates did not wish to meet the Russian delegates formally, nor did they wish an expression of opinion of the Soviet representatives on the Pact. According to the rules of international law, the signature of the Soviet Government of the Kellogg-Briand Pact implied recognition. Secretary Kellogg held the other view, that signature to a multi-lateral treaty is not recognition, particularly if there is no intention to recognize. The Soviets, however, did not wish implied or unintentional recognition and, therefore, in the address giving adherence to the Kellogg-Briand Pact Litvinov made another plea for resumption of diplomatic relations with the United States.

The American intervention in the Sino-Soviet difficulty over the Chinese-Eastern Railway constituted another possibility for a closer rapprochement between the United States and Soviet Russia. Skillfully handled, the Stimson note inviting Russia and China to refrain from war and to utilize the machinery of the Kellogg-Briand Pact, could have been made the basis for an approach to recognition, but the Soviet spokesman did not utilize the opportunity.

j. Russian Territorial Integrity. The one policy of friendship toward Russia which is characteristic of the American attitude from the revolution up to date, is the American refusal to approve the disintegration of Russia. In its reply of October 15, 1919, to the Lithuanian National Council, and in its refusal at first to recognize the Baltic states, Esthonia and Latvia as well as

Lithuania, as independent governments, the United States formulated its policy against the dismemberment of the Russian territory. It was only after the Soviet Government itself recognized the Baltic states that the United States also did, even though we did not recognize the right of the Soviet Government to speak on behalf of the Russian people. At the Washington conference of 1921–22, the United States argued for the maintenance of Russian rights in the Far East. Again, the United States never recognized the annexation of Bessarabia by Rumania, because Soviet Russia never recognized it.

On March 24, 1920, the American State Department maintained that no final decision should be made in the Near East without the consent of Russia.[50] Carrying out the idea of maintaining the *status quo ante,* the American Government still recognizes consuls and other officials of the Tsarist régime. The Consul General for Russia, appointed in March 1913, is still recognized by this government as the Russian Consul General at New York, and the financial attaché of the Russian Embassy of the Kerensky régime is still recognized by the American Government. This attaché is formally in charge of the property of the Russian Government in the United States.

k. Congressional Resolutions. Innumerable resolutions have been introduced in both the House of Representatives and the Senate in the past few years, advocating the recognition of Russia. In the spring of 1932 Senator Robinson of Arkansas, Democratic floor leader, and Representative Sabath of Illinois, simultaneously introduced resolutions urging recognition. Senator Johnson of California endorsed these resolutions as wise and statesman-like because orders from Russia would provide employment for American workers. Senator Borah of Idaho and Representative Rainey of Illinois, Democratic floor leader, have been consistent advocates of recognition of Russia by the United States. However, the attitude of the United States has remained unchanged since the days of President Wilson, and State Department officials refuse even to reiterate the principles which underlie the American policy of non-recognition.

5. Justifications of Recognition. The justifications of recognition are commercial and political. Recognition of Russia by the United States should be followed by an increase of commercial relations and mutual knowledge and understanding resulting from travel.

a. Commercial Gains. Russia's trade with the United States has grown very rapidly. It is now sixth in the volume of our trade. In 1913 Russian imports of American industrial and electrical equipment amounted to 1.8 million dollars, and in 1928–29 to over 34 million dollars. The large number of American engineers and technicians in Russia will probably result in increasingly large orders for machinery, textile and other, and equipment for agriculture, power houses, and railroads. In a year of depression the United States exported to Russia more than 100 million dollars' worth of commodities, chiefly machinery.

Under the Five-Year Plan Russian trade is likely to grow substantially and become increasingly important. Colonel Cooper estimated that United States exports to Russia could grow to one billion dollars annually under mutually favorable conditions, and in a paper at a meeting of the International Chamber of Commerce in Washington, May 5, 1931, predicted total imports into Russia from all countries at over 3 billion dollars.

In September 1930, Senator Wheeler, on his return from a trip through Russia, stated that Russia was the greatest potential market in the world for American goods, and that recognition would increase trade, but would not mean endorsement of Soviet policy or political support. Similarly, Mr. Thomas B. Campbell, agricultural adviser to the Russian Government, stated that Russia, with a population of over 160,000,000 people, and undeveloped areas as large as North America, was a better industrial prospect than South America, where competition was keen, or Europe, which was already using American methods of mass production.[51]

Russian raw materials and American manufactured goods are supplementary. As Soviet Russia becomes industrialized, the trade of the world will be stimulated just as the industrial development of Germany and Canada stimulated trade with the neighboring countries.

Recognition was withheld by the United States because of the official statement that Soviet Russia was an economic vacuum, and that there could be no production and therefore no foreign trade. The large volume of trade with the United States which has since developed removes this argument for non-recognition.

b. Financial Gains. Recognition of Russia would be conditioned upon payment of the old debts and restoration of confiscated American private property. If Soviet credit were thus restored, Russia should constitute a good economic risk and make possible increasing credits, both short-term and long-term. In turn these credits would facilitate increasing trade and help relieve some of the economic maladjustments, which are now regarded as a cause of the world depression. Increase of trade with Russia could lead to increasing employment in the United States and other countries and the restoration of international financial stability.

c. Settlement of Differences. The differences at issue between the United States and Russia, such as "dumping," could be handled more effectively if there were normal diplomatic relations between the two countries. The differences with Mexico on debts and confiscated property were effectively dealt with because of the prior recognition of Mexico. Non-recognition hinders, rather than helps, the settlement of differences.

d. Protection of American Interests. At present there are about one thousand American engineers in Russia. In addition many thousands of Americans visit Russia annually. At this time these are without political protection. Americans going to Russia travel under a visa of the Soviet consul attached to a mutually friendly country, such as Germany. As stated by Mr. Cravath: "When our government in 1923 encouraged American merchants and manufacturers to engage in trade with Russia, it owed them the duty of protecting this trade by the usual diplomatic machinery." Or in the words of Senator Borah: "It is better to deal with 150,000,000 people through the ordinary and normal channels than through the abnormal and extraordinary methods we are using today. Establishing normal relations with Soviet Russia is not an endorsement of communist theories and methods." [52]

e. Greater Influence in Russia. Because, unlike the important European governments, the United States has not recognized Russia, its influence there is diminished. It cannot join the other important countries in treating with Russia, and some Soviet writers believe that this is an offsetting benefit of American non-recognition. The United States is "the only one of the great powers which has deliberately excluded itself from exercising any influence through the usual diplomatic channels in the development of the most populous nation in Europe whose return to stability is essential for the peace and stability of the civilized world." [53]

Even an ardent opponent of American recognition of Soviet Russia, Paul Scheffer, admits one benefit of recognition:

> If America insisted upon the same freedom of movement for her representatives in Russia that agents of the Soviet régime enjoy in America . . . Moscow would find it difficult to give the nationals of other countries worse treatment than that accorded Americans. To this extent all would profit. . . . And many Europeans who do business in Russia would welcome American recognition.[54]

6. Objections to Recognition Answered. a. Prestige and Propaganda. Certain opponents of Russian recognition, such as Mr. Scheffer, believe that

recognition by the United States would tend to strengthen the Soviet Government, because the United States, regarded as the great exponent of capitalism, finally capitulated. Though American business would be stimulated by recognition, Soviet prestige at home would also be strengthened thereby. However, this argument does not hold. American recognition would be dependent upon important conditions, the fulfillment of which would in itself indicate Soviet willingness to conform to the demands of the capitalist world. The stock argument against recognition by the United States is that Soviet propaganda will increase. But this argument is also not valid. Russia's neighbors who have extended recognition have not had this experience. Furthermore, as Mr. Cravath points out:

> It may well be that, when recognition has removed the principal cause of irritation in Russia against the United States, the communist leaders will deem it to their interest to terminate their subversive activities in this country, which they must have found by experience to be futile in promoting the cause of communism within our borders.[55]

The propaganda argument against recognition may work to Russia's disadvantage, as was incidentally stated by Mr. Scheffer in his argument against recognition. "From the very outset the Red leaders were aware of the danger of contact with western capitalism. They were much quicker to grasp the threat that capitalism held for them than was the bourgeois west to understand the dangers inherent in contact with the Soviet Union." [56] Apparently recognition by the United States might be just as effective as anti-communist propaganda in Soviet Russia, as is anti-capitalist propaganda in the United States.

b. Historical Precedents. Propaganda has not in the past been a cause of non-recognition. The Monroe Doctrine, which was officially anti-royalist propaganda, was not the reason for the severance of diplomatic relations between the United States and foreign monarchies. The United States welcomed the Hungarian rebel, Louis Kossuth, who received financial and moral support in the United States, and yet it did not disturb the diplomatic relations with Austria. England and Switzerland have long been the asylums for political revolutionaries of other countries. In the Revolutionary Museum at Moscow there are originals of revolutionary proclamations covering several decades and setting forth the anti-Tsarist resolutions of London meetings of Russian socialists. Apparently London was the focus for international agitation against the Tsarist government, and yet this fact did not constitute any reason for a breach of diplomatic relations. England is the traditional home of liberals and revolutionaries, and yet other governments have not for that reason severed political relations with her. The Sinn Fein agitation was fomented and financed in America, but the cordial diplomatic relations with Great Britain were not thereby disturbed. These historical precedents seem to indicate that propaganda is not a reason for severance of diplomatic relations.

c. Settlement before Recognition. The settlement of debts and of claims of American citizens should be no argument against recognition. The fundamental principle of international arbitration is that differences can be adjusted between two states that mutually recognize each other. Mr. Borah defends the principle that settlement of outstanding differences between the United States and Russia can be better achieved after recognition rather than before. In fact he takes Mr. Hughes's very drastic rebuff to Soviet Russia and reverses it in terms of Mexican recognition in order to show the weakness of this argument against recognition.

> We had not repudiated any debt to Mexico; we had not incurred any obligation, as we contended. Mexico had destroyed American property and had destroyed the lives of American citizens. We did not say to Mexico: "Pay for the lives of these citizens, pay for their property, satisfy the debt which you owe us, and then we will recognize you." We said to Mexico: "Although human life has been sacrificed and millions of dollars' worth of property destroyed, we will appoint a committee on claims to adjust these matters with you." [57]

This argument of Senator Borah becomes doubly effective in view of the mutual adherence by both Soviet Russia and the United States to the Kellogg-Briand Pact.

7. Inevitable Course. The policy of non-recognition obviously cannot be permanent. It is merely a temporary stage. Ultimately the United States will recognize Russia.

a. Failure of Non-Recognition. There are few historic parallels for the failure of a government to be recognized after fifteen years of continued existence. Non-recognition by the United States has not solved the outstanding problems of debt and confiscation of property, and continuance of this policy by the United States is unlikely to bring a solution any nearer.

The failure of recognition of Soviet Russia by the United States must be regarded from the point of view of long-range friendship or enmity. Whatever may be the political evolution of Soviet Russia, our present policy of non-recognition postulates the fall of the present régime or its succession by a very conservative one. These two contingencies seem questionable. The failure to recognize Russia has not received the unanimous support of Americans in high office, such as Senators Borah, Wheeler, and Cutting, or of distinguished students of international law, such as John Bassett Moore and Paul D. Cravath, to say nothing of a host of business men who favor recognition not merely on selfish grounds but because of insight into the international economic situation.

Some indication of a change in American policy of recognition of Russia seems to be pending. As noted above, officials of the State Department have recently pronounced the return to the *de facto* theory of recognition which prevailed since the founding of our government, in connection with the Latin-American republics, and the rejection of the legitimacy theory of recognition initiated by President Wilson. The recognition within nine months of two successive governments in Peru and the prompt recognition of the revolutionary governments in the other Latin-American republics may have weakened the legal basis for the policy of non-recognition of Russia.

b. Differences Justiciable. Mr. Hughes' statement that there was no need for negotiation is unique and has not applied in any previous similar case, as in Mexico and in the inter-Allied debts. In fact, negotiation is necessary before the terms and method of payment can be decided upon. Further, our own states, before the Civil War, had repudiated debts to foreign bondholders, and yet such a lack of security for foreign property was not held as a reason for non-recognition of the United States. As Mr. Cravath put it:

> Enough has been said to show that it would be impossible to reach an agreement upon the reciprocal claims between the American and Soviet Governments without an extended inquiry. Even if there be ground for hope that an agreement might ultimately be reached, is it wise diplomacy to insist upon a definitive agreement as a condition of recognition? Would it not be wiser to pursue the course that was adopted by the United States Government in dealing with somewhat similar problems in its relations with the present revolutionary government in Mexico, which had assumed an attitude toward American property rights not dissimilar in principle to that of the Soviet Government? Instead of insisting upon a definitive settlement of the American claims as a condition of recognition, the United States Government sent a diplomatic mission to Mexico to ascertain by negotiation with the Mexican Government whether there could be found a promising basis for the ultimate recognition and determination of those claims. Upon receiving a satisfactory report from its mission, the American Government entered into diplomatic relations with the revolutionary government in Mexico and after prolonged negotiations the American ambassador brought about a settlement of most of the questions at issue between the two nations. Would not a similar course in dealing with the Soviet Government be more likely to be effective than our continued insistence on unconditional recognition of the American claims as a prerequisite to recognition? [58]

Even though recognition may be conditional, the adjudication of differences is a step following rather than preceding recognition.

c. Strategy of Recognition. President Wilson's policy was to avoid strengthening the prestige of the Soviet Government by foreign antagonism. His proposal for a conference on Prinkipo Island and for the mission to Russia were part of a policy of fair dealing, whose intent was to prevent the consolidation of home sentiment against a supposed enemy abroad. Now such a policy could be tried again. Recognition could be made subject to certain conditions. The acceptance of these conditions by the Soviet Government would make available international credit and make possible the importation of more consumers' goods and thus tend to relieve the suffering and distress of the masses in Russia. The acceptance of these terms would indicate that the Soviet Government realized the friendly nature of the American offer. Again, recognition by the United States would lessen the intellectual and educational isolation of Russia. There would be a free circulation of ideas and the probability of a swing toward a policy of moderation and freedom.

d. Acts Falling Short of Recognition.[59] Recognition of a government is not necessarily implied from the fact of holding written or oral communication with it. Special agents are employed for communicating with new states, since sending a minister to a new state necessarily implies recognition. Recognition of a new government requires the formal presentation of credentials. Until then communications are merely unofficial. Moore cites the case of Venezuela:

> This government [United States] has a clear right to have its properly appointed agents residing at Venezuela, although the authorities with which it has heretofore treated have been subverted more or less completely, and to communicate with the new authorities upon international matters affecting either the government of the United State or its citizens. . . . He [the agent of the United States] is entitled to be heard as the representative of the United States, without a previous recognition of the existing authorities, in place of those which have been either more or less effectually supplanted.[60]

Correspondingly a new diplomatic representative from the new government in Venezuela was told that his credentials could not yet be presented, but that he might "enjoy any privileges and immunities incident to his official character which were usually extended to diplomatic agents of friendly powers under similar circumstances." [61]

When a chargé d'affaires of the deposed Venezuelan Government informed the State Department that chargés d'affaires and consuls would continue to serve under the new government, he was told that until formal recognition, the United States would conduct diplomatic business with him as if no change had occurred in the home government.[62]

Moore again cites the case of Salvador. After a revolution, Seward wrote:

> In the meantime [until the re-establishment of government in Salvador] there being no person in the United States claiming to represent Salvador, all communications Mr. Yrissari [who had submitted credentials as minister of the new government] may have occasion to make to this government will be received unofficially and have respectful attention. You [the Minister to Salvador] will unofficially communicate this information to the provisional president, and until you shall receive further instructions, will not claim to be officially and formally recognized by him.[63]

Again, in the case of Mexico, because of disorders on the Rio Grande frontier, recognition was withheld from the newly installed Diaz government. Diplomatic correspondence was nevertheless carried on through the usual channels on all matters arising between the two countries.[64]

An extreme case, strangely contradictory to the present American attitude toward Russia, is cited by Moore. In July 1865, Mr. Louis de Arrayo published in a New York newspaper a decree of the Maximilian government, not recognized by the United States, stating that invoices and manifests of merchandise to Mexican ports would have to be legalized by consuls of the Empire, and that the agents appointed by the Juarez administration were to discontinue their functions. At this time the United States was recognizing the Juarez government. Seward, however, admitted "that the party in arms against the government is . . . in possession of some, at least, of the ports of Mexico," and could prescribe the terms upon which commerce could be carried on with those ports. While the insurgents' commercial agent—

> can perform no consular act relating to the affairs of his countrymen in the United States—to prohibit him from attesting invoices and manifests, under the circumstances referred to, would be tantamount to an interdiction of trade between the United States—

and the Mexican ports not in possession of the Juarez government.[65] In other words, though not recognizing Maximilian, the United States permitted his representative to publish an official announcement and granted that régime the right to attest shipping documents.

Where there is no stable retention of public power, the minister to Nicaragua was instructed in 1893 to—

remain in intercourse with the authorities in control of the seat of the government, looking to them for the protection of the interests of American citizens.*

To avert embarrassments in dealing with evenly balanced factions, alternating in power or succeeding thereto in the changes of civil contest, the minister's tact should be exercised to confine his relations with the ascendant authority to questions affecting the public interests of the United States and the security of American life and property in Nicaragua, thus giving to his intercourse a provisional and *de facto* character, without sympathetic leaning on either side, and without prejudice to the fullest liberty on the part of the United States to declare formal recognition of the government which shall eventually establish itself on a firm basis and effectively administer the affairs of the state and insure orderly respect for its acts by the people of the nation.[66]

Apparently, the present policy of the United States in refusing to appoint or receive unofficial representatives in any informal relationship short of recognition is utterly at variance with historic precedent in American diplomatic policy.

e. Terms of "Conditional Recognition." Recognition of Russia should not be unconditional. There is little to be gained by that. France and England are still waiting for a settlement of Russia's debt to their nationals. Conditional recognition would remove many of the objections offered by the opponents of recognition.

Recognition could be extended by the United States only after the mutual agreement in principle on terms by the two parties. If recognition be unconditional and precede negotiation of mutually satisfactory terms, then in case of disagreement the only available remedy would be a breach of diplomatic relations—at best a futile gesture, as the experience of Great Britain indicated. After recognition is granted, it is impossible to withdraw it.

The relation once established is perpetual, conditioned only by the existence of the states which participate therein. Hence it cannot be changed by the act of any state concerned. Even in the event of a state's going to war with another, this does not deny the perpetuity of the relationship, but on the contrary serves only to strengthen it.[67]

Recognition of the Soviet Union by France and Great Britain was unconditional, and when diplomatic relations between the Soviet Government and Great Britain were broken, recognition still remained.[68] This is in accord with a British interpretation that even though diplomatic relation is severed, recognition cannot be withdrawn. As Mr. Arthur Henderson, then Secretary of State for Foreign Affairs, said:

* Baty in 31 Y.L.J. 469 severely criticizes this standard, which he says would make any swashbuckler who happened to seize the capital the authority over the entire country, for the purposes of the American minister.

I have since been in contact with the legal adviser to my department. His Majesty's Government in the United Kingdom accorded *de jure* recognition to the government of Soviet Russia in 1924. From that time the government of Soviet Russia was entitled to be recognized as the government of a state, and is still so recognized by His Majesty's Government. It follows that the reciprocal rights and duties which international law recognizes as incumbent on states in their relations with one another continue to subsist between this country and Russia. What the rupture of 1927 did was to suspend the normal machinery of diplomatic relations. It is that machinery which now requires to be re-established.[69]

With reference to conditional recognition, there are two opposed views. One of the leading American authorities on international law is strongly opposed to the idea. In a letter to the author he says:[70]

One of the governments may say prior to formal recognition, that if it does not get what it wants, it will withdraw its minister. Of course it might make such a proposal, but what would the other governments say? How much progress would individuals make in their ordinary daily business if they should essay to proceed in that way? As a rule neither side could say at the outset what it would be willing to take in the end, because neither knows what the other may in the end be willing to take or to concede.

He cites an example from the beginning of American history in support of his view:

When the revolutionary government of France was recognized by the United States in 1793, two members of Washington's Cabinet proposed that the reception of the new French Minister should be qualified by a prior declaration that the United States reserved the question whether the treaties made with the old government of France were not to be deemed temporarily and provisionally suspended. This proposal Washington rejected.

A similar view is held by Goebel. On the question of conditional recognition he says:

Excluding the element of the independent expression of will of the new state, it [conditional recognition] reduces the process to one of complete constitutive force, and makes of it an instrument for enforcing the demands of the recognizant state. This is . . . a total repudiation of the fundamental nature of the process. . . . Because recognition of governments, though a mere formality, is generally considered to be a necessity, foreign powers by making recognition of new governments conditional, frequently extort from new *de facto* organizations concessions which they otherwise would not obtain. This policy gives to an almost meaningless process constitutive force which it does not and should not possess and which is inconsistent with the facts of international existence. . . . It may be noted that on what is generally supposed to have been the greatest occasion of its use, the recognition of the Balkan states by the Treaty of Berlin of 1878, the condition was a condition of guaranty and not a condition of recognition.[71]

However, opinion on this subject is by no means unanimous. An equally outstanding authority believes that "either conditional or unconditional recognition may be accorded." [72] As precedents for conditional recognition, one may cite two cases, one dealing with the Papal States, and one with the recognition of Brazil, November 17, 1889, when the provisional government was recognized on the condition that it respect all prior contracts and international obligations.[73] The recognition of Mexico by the United States in 1923 was accorded only after the conditions, set forth previously by the United States, had been accepted by the Mexican Government. Apparently conditional recognition is not a new concept and with the growth of interdependence and international co-operation, it is likely to acquire increasing significance.

Among the terms would be recognition of the debts of the Tsarist and Provisional Governments. Many of these debts were incurred not for the balancing of the budget, but for purely productive purposes, such as the building of railroads, electric light and power plants, harbor works, grain elevators, and other public works. Property confiscated would have to be returned. New loans would then become available on the same terms as other young and newly formed governments receive loans, namely, control by an independent agent of the receipts and expenditures of the government. A Young Plan for Russia would make it possible for bankers to appeal to private investors to risk their money in Russia. Without some such control it would be futile to expect any loans. The bankers do not give their own money; they merely offer the securities to investors. These individuals seek first safety of principal.

The appointment of an Agent General for the collection of the service of the loan might be regarded as a surrender to capitalism. However Germany, Poland, Hungary, and other countries were willing to accept such financial advisers. Soviet officials believe that even these objections can be met. Certainly a government which so successfully influences its own public opinion could explain the acceptance of a foreign financial adviser as a "strategic retreat." The acceptance of the Nep was a far greater surrender to capitalism, and yet it was explained away.

The United States Government could then continue its policy of being friends with the Russian people, as it proved itself to be when it furnished relief during the famine, and refused to recognize the seizure by Rumania of Bessarabia and originally refused to recognize Esthonia, Lithuania, and Latvia until the Soviets themselves did.

f. Historic Parallels. Strangely, America and England have swapped policies toward revolutionary governments. When Great Britain delayed recognizing the Republic of France, Fox, speaking in Parliament, admitted that after twelve years of non-recognition Great Britain was compelled to follow the lead of other countries in ultimately recognizing the new republic. For this reason, as the late Lord Asquith stated in Parliament, England did not refuse recognition to revolutionary Russia, as she did 140 years before refuse to recognize revolutionary France. On the other hand, the United States Government was prompt to recognize revolutionary France in 1793, but we have been as dilatory in recognizing Russia recently, as Great Britain was in 1793 in recognizing revolutionary France. Great Britain seemed to have profited by her history, while we have neither followed George Washington's precedent, nor profited by Great Britain's experience with revolutionary France.

8. Is Recognition by the United States Necessary? a. Recognition Does Not Create a State—the Estrada Doctrine. There is a school in international law which greatly minimizes the importance of the formal act of recognition. When a state or government comes into being, the mere fact that it is not recognized does not alter the fact that it exists. Existence is a fact as much as two plus two equals four. Of the latter statement there is no conditional admission. Non-recognition does not change the facts.

A stricter interpretation of recognition has been invented by the great powers for use as a club on the small powers. The old notion of recognition implies that when a new government comes into being it requires a capacity to act from the other powers. The Mexican Government rejected such a view.

The Estrada Doctrine of Recognition was embodied in the declaration of Señor Don Genaro Estrada, Secretary of Foreign Relations of Mexico, published in the press on September 27, 1930, relating to the express recognition of governments.[73a]

He stated that Mexico in particular had suffered from the consequences of the present practice of recognition whereby foreign governments assumed the prerogative of passing on the legitimacy or illegitimacy of governments, thus subordinating national authority to foreign opinion. This recognition practice was largely of post-war development and of particular application to the Latin-American Republics.

> After a very careful study of the subject, the Government of Mexico has transmitted instructions to its Ministers or Chargés d'Affaires in the countries affected by the recent political crises, informing them that the Mexican Govern-

ment is issuing no declarations in the sense of grants of recognition, since that nation considers that such a course is an insulting practice and one which, in addition to the fact that it offends the sovereignty of other nations, implies that judgment of some sort may be passed upon the internal affairs of those nations by other governments, inasmuch as the latter assume, in effect, an attitude of criticism, when they decide, favorably or unfavorably, as to the legal qualifications of foreign régimes.

Therefore, the Government of Mexico confines itself to the maintenance or withdrawal, as it may deem advisable, of its diplomatic agents, and to the continued acceptance, also when it may deem advisable, of such similar accredited diplomatic agents as the respective nations may have in Mexico; and in so doing it does not pronounce judgment, either precipitately or *a posteriori,* regarding the right of foreign nations to accept, maintain, or replace their governments or authorities.

In a discussion of the Estrada Doctrine [73b] Professor Philip C. Jessup cites the following as an example of its application:

A successful revolution takes place in State X. While other states may be considering recognizing or not recognizing the new *de facto* government, Mexico will merely continue its diplomatic representation without expressing any opinion as to recognition, *vel non.* If some circumstance, other than the mere change of government, gives umbrage to Mexico, the Mexican diplomat will be withdrawn.

The existing method of recognition of governments which came into power by revolution or *coup d'etat* is unsatisfactory, as is evidenced by the reactions of governments to the epidemic of revolutions in Latin America in 1931. This method has also been criticized by Taft in the Tinoco arbitration and by Baty, cited below. Theoretically there is much to be said in favor of the Estrada Doctrine, since governments *de facto* are necessarily *de jure,* and the doctrine admits this reality. The doctrine moreover assumes, and properly so, that diplomatic representatives should be considered as accredited to the state and not to the government.*

Basically the Estrada Doctrine contemplates abolishing the distinction between a change in government by peaceful balloting and a change by revolution or *coup d'etat.* As, in the former, diplomatic relations remain unbroken, so with the latter. Since even the most well-meaning of the strong states may

* Professor Jessup says further: "Practically, however, not all difficulties are removed. With whom shall foreign diplomats deal in circumstances like these: Local officials are in control of the capital and revolutionists are in *de facto* control of the rest of the country; or money payments by a foreign nation fall due when there is a revolution in the creditor country? In both of these situations, the Estrada Doctrine gives no better guide than the present recognition policy as to which group to deal with. The same criticism applies to a situation such as gave rise to the Tinoco arbitration, i. e.; obligation of a government to assume the debts of a prior *de facto* regime. This problem is not solved by doing away with the existing recognition policy."

err in its judgment of what is best for a small neighbor, extending recognition to or withholding it from a *de facto* government for reasons other than its factual control of its country is not conducive to the smooth working of international affairs.

On the other hand, there is no compulsion on the part of any power to recognize a new state or government. It does not have to extend recognition, even though certain conditions have been fulfilled by the new power requesting recognition. Therefore, there is no compelling reason why the United States must recognize Russia. On the other hand, the failure of the United States to do so does not make the Russian state or its government disappear. Judge John Bassett Moore in general stresses the theory that the existence of a new government is a fact and that recognition does not affect that fact in any way. This point of view is of importance in any legal treatment of the question of the American recognition of Russia.

Baty, in an article on "So-Called *De Facto* Recognition," develops this point further.[74]

> "*De facto* recognition" is a misnomer. The only question in international law is whether there is, in any given tract of country, an authority in fact obeyed in that area and not threatened by any real efforts at subjugation by a sovereign to which it has hitherto been subject. If such supremacy exists, there is a state. Supremacy is a question of fact, and is the sole fact governments pass on in extending recognition. A state exists without recognition and recognition does not create the state. Nevertheless, it is the best evidence of the existence of the state. Since statehood is a fact, recognition cannot be conditioned, since it is impossible to recognize a fact conditionally. To say that an authority has the characteristics of a state subject to its proving them, or subject to its conduct's being satisfactory in other respects, is a contradiction of terms. . . . When a revolutionary group conclusively seizes power, it constitutes the government. This is popularly called "*de facto* government." But the recognition extended to such a government is not *de facto* recognition (as distinct from full recognition) because the government, though popularly called *de facto,* is in truth supreme and, therefore, in international law, *de jure*. Recognition, if granted, must therefore be full.*

Baty proceeds to disapprove Wilson's attaching, as a condition to recognizing Carranza's government in Mexico, the requirement that a constituent assembly be summoned to confirm Carranza's presidency. He attributes this to an unwarranted extension of Jefferson's doctrine that the United States cannot, consistently with their own political history, decline to recognize the legitimacy of a government "formed by the will of the nation substantially declared." There is no substantial difference between this assertion and the

* "So far as we are concerned," wrote Van Buren in 1829, "that which is the government *de facto* is equally so *de jure*." Cited Moore's *Digest of International Law*, Vol. 1, p. 137.

requirement of supremacy. It has been interpreted to mean, however, that the will of the nation must be ascertained by a vote of a "constituent assembly."

Baty also criticizes Seward, who, after admitting to unofficial relations the representatives of a revolutionary and as yet unrecognized authority of Salvador, stated that "while this government [United States] does not intend or desire to question the rightfulness or stability of the government now provisionally existing in Salvador . . . it does not find itself at liberty to make a formal recognition of that provisional government."[75] Seward in other words admitted the supremacy of the government, but refused to recognize it (1864).

Baty's contention that acknowledgment of supremacy, with no other considerations, requires recognition, is borne out in several cases. In 1868 Seward recognized a revolutionary Costa Rican Government without waiting for a call of a national convention. In 1899 Castro's seizure of power in Venezuela by a violent revolution was recognized without reference to popular vote. The same principle was applied in Bolivia in 1866.

b. Taft Decision in Costa Rica Arbitration (1923). Ex-President Taft, in a decision as arbitrator in a dispute between Costa Rica and Great Britain, developed the liberal construction of the doctrine of recognition laid down by Moore and also followed by Baty. The Royal Bank of Canada had made advances to a revolutionary régime in 1917, which the succeeding government refused to acknowledge. The revolutionary régime had not been recognized by the United States, and therefore not by England, then our associate in the World War. Nevertheless, Mr. Taft decided that even though the revolutionary government was not recognized, yet it existed and the succeeding government had to honor the debts of the revolutionary régime. (This decision is significant in view of outstanding debts of Soviet Russia.) Recognition was not a privilege conferred upon new governments, but merely an admission of what is. The fact that a government continues to retain control and to exercise the functions of government in itself constitutes proof of its existence. President Taft quoted Moore:[76]

> Changes in the government or the internal policy of a state do not as a rule affect its position in international law. . . . Though the government changes, the nation remains, with rights and obligations unimpaired. . . .
>
> The principle of continuity of states has important results. The state is bound by engagements entered into by governments that have ceased to exist; the restored government is generally liable for the acts of the usurper. . . .
>
> The origin and organization of government are questions generally of in-

ternal discussion and decision. Foreign powers deal with the existing *de facto* government, when sufficiently established to give reasonable assurance of its permanence and of the acquiescence of those who constitute the state in its ability to maintain itself, and discharge its internal duties and its external obligations.

President Taft then quoted Borchard:[77]

A general government *de facto* having completely taken the place of the regularly constituted authorities in the state binds the nation. . . . So far as its international obligations are concerned, it represents the state. It succeeds to the debts of the regular government it has displaced, and transmits its own obligations to succeeding titular governments. Its loans and contracts bind the state and the state is responsible for the governmental acts of the *de facto* authorities. In general, its treaties are valid obligations of the state. . . . An exception to these rules has occasionally been noted in the practice of some of the states of Latin America, which declare null and void the acts of a usurping *de facto* intermediary government, when the regular government it has displaced succeeds in restoring its control. Nevertheless, acts validly undertaken in the name of the state, and having an international character, cannot lightly be repudiated and foreign governments generally insist on their binding force.*

Mr. Taft as arbitrator held from the evidence that President Tinoco, the insurgent, carried on his government effectively and peacefully and that it was an actual sovereign government. The fact that it was not recognized does not outweigh other evidence, according to international law, that the Tinoco government was of a *de facto* character. The mere fact that a government does not conform to a previously adopted constitution does not prevent it from being a *de facto* government. The sole test is whether it has established itself in such a way that all within its influence recognize its control. The above decision by ex-President Taft removes much of the legal significance of the formal act of recognition. The question, therefore, of Russian recognition must depend upon economic rather than legal considerations.

---

* For similar views, Mr. Taft referred to:
Chancellor Kent, *Commentaries* (14th ed.) Vol. I, p. 25.
Wheaton, *International Law* (Philippson's 5th English edition), p. 37.
Hall, *International Law* (6th ed., J. B. Attay, 1909), pp. 20, 21.
Woolsey, *Introduction to the Study of International Law* (1873 ed.), pp. 32, 52, 53, 171, 172.

CHAPTER XVIII

CONCLUSIONS

The American policy toward Russia has proved inconsistent and does not seem to have led to fruitful results. A new attitude would seem necessary. The co-existence of capitalism and communism should be a possibility. Those who deny that the two systems can exist side by side agree with Trotsky's thesis that communism in Russia can thrive only in a communist world. The isolation of Russia is now too late as a policy. Co-operation with her seems inevitable. A world conference on Russia could clarify many moot points.

A. Our Policy Inconsistent

The attitude of the United States Government and that of American business men do not seem to be in accord. When our government consented that American business men could do business in Russia, it virtually meant that the American Government was willing that American citizens should help in the industrialization of the Soviets. But the American Government was opposed to the political system under which this took place. The development of the industrial interests of Americans in Russia must ultimately conflict with the present policy of our government.

Every bushel of wheat produced in Russia under their low standards of living is competitive with the wheat produced in the United States. By refusing to recognize Russia, which would make loans possible, we virtually force Russia to obtain money through the only other means, namely forced exports. A world policy of refusing to make loans to Russia should therefore have as its consistent counterpart an embargo on Russian exports.

B. A New Attitude

Not vengeance on the Soviets but the best interests of the world should be the basis of a new attitude toward Russia.

1. Misunderstanding. The policy of the nations toward Russia has been dominated by fear, hatred, and misunderstanding. Yet international hatreds have never yielded profits. The presentation of Russia as an ogre that will ultimately destroy civilization is part of a campaign of misunderstanding. The prospect of a giant industrial régime that threatens the peace of other countries is a bar to a rational policy toward Russia. As Judge Moore pointed out, in view of general international misunderstanding, nations should be tolerant and charitable in their judgments.[1]

The "Red"-hunting zealots in the United States and elsewhere might well have applied their righteous indignation toward the Tsarist régime and thus perhaps have influenced liberal reform, which would have obviated a revolution. The Soviet régime is the consequence of oppression by an unyielding despotism, whereby a people were maddened to revolt. The Soviet leaders cannot be regarded as bandits or wicked men; they are the leaders in the fight for liberty of an oppressed people. The obvious and protested excesses of the revolution are merely the reaction from the equally obvious but unprotested excesses of the tyranny. As stated above the mild oppression in Spain produced a moderate revolution. The ruthless oppression of the Tsar provoked a violent revolution. Apparently, action and reaction are equal, as in the physical world. Rebels are not pirates or bandits. As Dennis points out:

> The fundamental error in our . . . policy lies in a misapprehension of the true nature of political revolution. Jefferson and the fathers of the American Republic were too near to the American and French Revolutions and too critical in their political thinking to suffer from any such misapprehension. Revolutions, like bodily pain or fever, are not diseases, but symptoms. They are nature's way of calling attention to, and reacting protectively against, something wrong in the body. Sound therapy aims at the eradication of causes, not of symptoms. Without symptoms we should not know when we are sick.[2]

2. Franco-German Precedent. The policy of hatred was recently tried and found wanting. Germany was the "boche" or "hun" to the Allies. It took thirteen years, from 1918 to 1931, for the French to change from an intransigeant enemy to an objective creditor. The policy of hatred toward Germany reacted harmfully on both France and England. A policy of hatred toward Russia is similarly likely to bear bitter fruit. Germany was eventually brought into co-operation with the other great powers and it is inevitable that Russia likewise will be brought within the family of nations. The world is an economic unit.

The Allies tried to isolate Germany from 1919 until the Dawes Loan of

1924. The world, and particularly the United States, is evidently going through the same antagonistic gestures toward Russia that were so futile when applied to Germany.

3. Need for Good Will. A solution of the Franco-German dispute was preceded by a psychological change, and a spirit of good will on the part of far-seeing statesmen in both countries. The Loucheur-Rathenau negotiations were objective. They represented the perspective and approach of two business men. The policy of the world, and particularly of America, toward Russia needs a similar new basis. If the analogy of a mental malady applies to Russia, then modern therapy should be utilized. Cruelty and violence have given place to sympathy and understanding in the treatment of mental maladies. The world must help Russia solve her problem or she will drag down all the nations.

C. Co-existence of Communism and Capitalism

1. American View. The two capitalist principles of *laissez faire* and competition may be invoked on behalf of communism. Let communism attempt to work out its solution of the social problem. Let it compete with capitalism, and then let the world judge as to the results. Colonel Cooper, speaking before the Institute for International Politics at Williamstown, Massachusetts, August 1, 1930, stated that communism and capitalism would compete for world supremacy. The United States was developing its resources under the system of private ownership, and Russia under communist ownership, and the future history of the world will depend on the outcome of this competition. Colonel Cooper held out the two possible policies. Shall the United States say: "We fear your competition and will therefore try to hinder you," or shall they say: "We accept the challenge and are willing to help your experiment in every reasonable way"? Because he was convinced that the capitalist method of production was superior, Colonel Cooper pleaded for tolerance to Russia in her experiment with communism, as a road to Utopia.

Again, in a paper before the International Chamber of Commerce at Washington, May 6, 1931, Colonel Cooper felt that in a friendly competition between private capitalism and the state capitalism of Soviet Russia there would be decisive demonstration of the superiority of private capitalism. If such a free encounter is permitted, and if state capitalism should fail, as it probably will, then the question is settled for all time. However, if the nations of the world hamper its growth, the proponents of state capitalism will always be able to say: "It would have worked, if it had not been hampered." Private capitalism will succeed rather than communism, not because it is capitalism or because it is old, but because it is an organic growth rather than an invented scheme.

2. Russian View. The possibility of communism and private capitalism existing side by side is the accepted doctrine of Soviet Russia today. Marx believed that a proletarian revolution could not survive in one country. He was thinking in terms of the small and highly industrialized states of Europe. But the Soviet doctrine is that the country constituting a large fraction of the earth's habitable area, abundantly endowed with natural resources, and economically independent, is virtually a small world, a veritable union of socialist states.

Trotsky believed that the world could not exist half-communist and half-capitalist, and therefore he believed in the world revolution. In a pamphlet prepared for American readers he amplified this point.

> The impossibility of constructing a self-sufficient socialist economy in a single country revives . . . basic contradictions . . . at every new stage on an even greater scale and with an ever greater depth. . . . The complete . . . way out of the . . . contradictions will be found by the U.S.S.R. in a victorious revolution of the world proletariat and only there. . . . The dictatorship of the proletariat in the U.S.S.R. would inevitably have to suffer destruction if the capitalist régime in the rest of the world would prove to be capable of maintaining itself for another long historical epoch.[3]

But Stalin stated to Duranty that capitalism and communism can co-exist. They have not fought for ten years. "We do not want to fight and some of their people do not either."

At the Economic Conference at Geneva, on May 18, 1931, Mr. Litvinov stated that the main idea of his pact was to assure the peaceful co-existence of the communist and capitalist systems. He furthermore pledged that the Soviet Union would adhere to the principle of "the peaceful co-existence of the two systems." However, he qualified this to mean "for a given duration and at a given stage." This qualification was probably, like speeches of Mussolini or the ex-Kaiser, meant for home consumption.

D. Isolation or Co-operation?

1. Russia a World Problem. The relationship toward Russia is not an American problem, nor a French, German, or British problem. As an international problem it calls for international treatment. Russia's debt is international, and some issues were offered simultaneously in several cur-

rencies. In fact, the reservations of the Rapallo Treaty implied an international settlement. The underfeeding of Russians who are not consuming the goods which the world has produced in surplus is a world problem and calls for international consideration. The underpayment of Russian labor in inflated rubles which makes it possible to underbid the world's labor is also a world problem. The forcing of exports in order to obtain credit abroad is an international evil and not merely one for the competing countries. A rising standard of living in Russia would be a benefit for the producing nations of the world. All countries constitute an international economic unit.

Because Russia is a world problem and has been treated as a local problem, because it involves international questions but has been considered as a national question, no solution has yet been found. A solution is unlikely until the international character of the problem is recognized and met by international treatment, despite diplomatic difficulties.

2. Changing Orientation. The policy of the Soviet is changing. In domestic affairs the trend, while still socialist in aim, is leaning toward capitalist methods, as in piece work, sales taxes, and the other indications mentioned above. In international affairs the trend of the Soviet government is toward political and economic peace, despite much sabre-rattling and whistling to keep up the military spirit. They have expressed their willingness to cooperate with the Chadbourne Plan for the curtailment of sugar production and for negotiating the terms of the international wheat quotas, asking only that their pre-war status be maintained.

Despite these startling changes in Soviet policy, our government has maintained its policy of non-recognition. The Soviets are attempting to adjust their system peaceably to that of the rest of the world. Upon the capitalist nations, who should be able more objectively to place the Soviet régime in its historical setting, falls the burden of making suitable adjustments. The Soviets are too subjective about their revolution, still too fanatic, too emotional.

The American policy of non-recognition may have had justification during the past ten years, but its justification is weakening with the change of events.

3. Policy of Isolation. From some quarters has come a revival of the *cordon sanitare,* with which the Allied powers once tried to encircle Russia. The opponents of Soviet Russia have proposed an international conference for the isolation of Russia commercially as well as politically. Although complete isolation is impossible now, many commercial interests believe in a

world union to impose uniform conditions on credits and in trade. Such a uniform front in dealing with Russia will make it possible to eliminate Russia's setting off competing countries against each other to their disadvantage.

a. Consequences of Isolation. But such a policy of isolation would tend to consolidate the sentiment within Russia against the foreigner. It would increase the prestige of the rulers with the masses in Russia. It would increase misunderstanding and prevent co-operation along peaceable lines. It would limit Russia's capacity for good and increase her capacity for harm to the other nations. It would check the policy of industrialization, but on the other hand it would not check trade dislocation resulting from forced sales of lumber, grain, and other raw materials in countries not parties to the policy of isolation. The menace of Soviet competition in the world's markets would then become more serious.

The exports of Russian wheat to countries not parties to the plan of isolation would further dislocate agriculture in Canada, Australia, Argentina, and the United States, and shipments of Russian lumber would ruin the industries of Canada, Poland, and Finland. A still further decline in the standard of living in Russia would aggravate the world crisis, because it would tend to depress the wages of competing workers in agriculture and forestry in other countries.

b. Difficulties of Isolation. The policy of isolation advocated by the foreign enemies of the Soviets cannot be enforced at this late date. One or a few countries not participating in such an anti-Soviet conference could vitiate the expected benefits, and such a non-participating country would enjoy certain advantages. There are enough cross-currents in European politics to make it impossible to form a united front to hurt Russia; in fact the large German credit to Soviet Russia, is evidence that a united front against the Soviets is impossible. One or more great powers would probably refuse to join in such a pact.

The difficulties of an anti-Russian bloc became generally patent during the Ottawa Conference in 1932 when Great Britain and the dominions clashed fundamentally on the question of an embargo on Russian goods. The dominions and Argentina, competing in the export markets with the Soviets, have different interests from Great Britain, Italy, or Germany, purchasers of Russian raw materials and sellers of industrial products to Russia. Even within the United States there is a conflict. The Steel Corporation and the International Paper Company favor the importation of high-grade Russian manganese and high-grade spruce pulp, respectively, but the small manganese producers and the scattered lumber interests favor an embargo against a powerful competitor.

4. Policy of Co-operation. A united world would be in a position to make an honest offer for the amicable adjustment of outstanding differences on debts and other international difficulties. Should such an honest offer not be honestly met, the powers would then be in a position by united action to enforce their terms.

a. Political Benefits. Referring to the antagonism between the American colonies, Benjamin Franklin, advocating the union of the colonies, said: "We must hang together, or we shall hang separately." The phrase was applied to a small war and in the days of slow communication and slow transportation. But the sentiment holds equally true in an era of world economics and world politics. As H. G. Wells stated in a discussion of Russia, "We must live as world citizens or perish." [4] In the opinon of British and American statesmen, without Russia it is difficult to have peace or disarmament in Europe or Asia. Unless Russia is brought within the family of nations Europe cannot disarm.

International agreement with Russia should aid in relieving the serious economic depression and the resulting political maladjustments. Recognition of Russia by the United States and a policy of helpful co-operation may lead toward economic relief from the burdens of armament and make for industrial development rather than international suspicion. The world followed the leadership of the old Tsarist tyranny in the development of The Hague court. Should it be less willing to follow a lesser tyranny along the paths of peace?

b. Economic Benefits. *i. World Economic Interrelationship.* The economic interrelationships of the nations of the world have been dislocated by the World War, but their interdependence remains. The pre-war economic system is not functioning. Over 160,000,000 people are underfed and underclothed, and the rest of the world suffers as a result. Russia cannot be economically ignored either as a producer or as a consumer. Soviet Russia needs the world and the world needs Soviet Russia. Their interdependence is mutual. Trade will bring understanding. As for the United States, it has more points of agreement with Russia than of disagreement. Neither country wishes additional territory. Neither has any imperialist designs. Neither wishes to exploit other nations commercially. Other economic aims of the two countries are similar. In physical features the two countries have similarities. The policy of world co-operation with Russia, and particularly American co-operation, is likely to lead to progress. Refusal to co-operate is more likely to prolong the economic chaos in which the world now struggles.

World co-operation with Russia will lead to an orderly economic development. The standard of living in Russia will be raised, which will result in a great increase of trade with the rest of the world. There is a five years' shortage of consumers' goods in Russia, the satisfaction of which could relieve much unemployment of the producing countries of the world. The world-wide decline of commodity prices due to lack of buying is an anomaly, when Russia is eager to buy, eager to raise the standards of living, if only the world will help her obtain the credit. The Soviet economic plan calls for a program of industrial development over the next twenty-five years. A burst of world prosperity should follow the industrialization of Russia, as was the case when Germany and Japan underwent a similar development.

Foreign Commissar Litvinov at Geneva, on May 18, 1931, presented the case for international co-operation with Russia:

> We are not totally unconcerned by the world crisis. . . . The interests of the Soviet Union are affected thereby. . . . The decline in the price of raw materials during the last few years, taken into conjunction with the practically unaltered level of the prices of manufactured goods, reacts, of course, detrimentally upon the economic life of the Soviet Union. Thus the immediate connection between the world crisis and the interests of the Soviet Union is evident. . . .
>
> Economic crises existed before the Soviet state came into being and, this being so, we are entitled to assert that the present crisis would have been more acute and widespread if Tsarist or bourgeois Russia, that is to say, a political-economic organism similar to that of the rest of the world, were in the place of the Soviet Union, for it would undoubtedly have been drawn into the general crisis, and brought its whole weight to bear upon it. Statesmen especially concerned to stave off social upheavals in other countries would have yet another care, and would perhaps be forced to call special international conferences to find means for averting social upheavals arising out of the crisis in Russia. . . .
>
> There can be no sort of doubt that Soviet orders, increasing from year to year, constitute a mitigating factor in the crisis. It [should be] borne in mind that 53.5 per cent of the total tractor exports of the United States went to the U.S.S.R. in 1930, that in the same year the U.S.S.R. received about 12 per cent of the textile machinery exports of Great Britain. . . .
>
> Before going any further I should like to remind you that Soviet exports in the majority of cases are far from having attained the pre-war level.
>
> Wheat exports of Tsarist Russia, for instance, amounted to 25 per cent of world exports, whereas even in 1930, the Soviet Union exported not more than 20 per cent of the wheat on the world market. Soviet manganese exports were only 35 per cent of world exports, as against 51 per cent from Tsarist Russia. The flax exports of Tsarist Russia composed 53 per cent of all flax on the market, that of the Soviet Union being only 42 per cent. Tsarist Russia exported 78 thousand tons of butter as against 10 thousand from the Soviet Union. . . .

> Not much imagination is required to realize that in depriving Europe of a market so important and rapidly expanding as the Soviet Union, in depriving whole branches of industry of orders and thus increasing unemployment, the world crisis will be intensified and not lessened. . . . The reconstruction going on in the country, the carrying out of the Five-Year Plan, do not and will not lead to the curtailment of the Soviet Union's foreign trade. The more our national economy develops, the stronger it becomes, the greater will be its demands with their almost infinite potentialities. . . . Is not this sufficient proof that business considerations and economic interests of the capitalist countries (precisely during the present crisis) demand not conflict, but the extension and consolidation of relations with the Soviet Union, and that anti-Soviet campaigns have nothing to do with the crisis, but merely pursue either political or narrow competitive aims? . . .
>
> It is time to realize that the Soviet Union is a fact that has got to be reckoned with, that the Soviet Union cannot be made to disappear by the incantations, abuse, and the resolutions of certain groups and individuals, still clinging to their dreams of somehow getting rid of it by magic. If the countries here represented decided at a world conference meeting at Geneva exactly four years ago, to pass a resolution on the possibility of the peaceful co-existence of the two systems at a given historical stage, how much more reasonable to recognize and loyally carry out this resolution now, when the Soviet Union is still stronger, when it has shown in the last few years the immense scope of all its branches of economic construction. . . .
>
> This pact of non-aggression will at least serve as evidence of the readiness of the Soviet Union to adhere as before to the principle of the peaceful co-existence of the two systems at the given stage of history, and of its having no aggressive intentions, whether of a political or economic nature, against any other nations.[5]

ii. Benefits to Russia. A policy of co-operation could help to re-establish Russian credit. The high prices paid by Russia for her imports and the low prices realized on her exports are really an index of Russia's low credit. On the one billion dollars of foreign trade of Russia, she loses from 20 to 40 per cent in the high prices she must pay for machinery bought on long-term credit. In turn, on the manganese, platinum, lumber, and wheat which she exports there are also substantial losses due to the need for cutting prices. These losses combined probably amount to 300 million dollars per annum. This sum is enough to pay interest on a 10-billion-dollar debt. In other words, Russia is paying the equivalent of interest on her 10-billion-dollar debt but receives no benefit therefrom. In fact she even incurs the ill will of the raw-material countries with which she competes, and with the older manufacturing and financing countries she still lacks credit. Payment of such a sum, 300 million dollars, directly as interest on the pre-war debts, rather than in disguise, would make it possible to mitigate the suffering of the Russian masses. They would not have to deny themselves bread, in order that the Soviet government might be able to buy machinery from abroad on poor credit.

E. World Conference on Russia

1. Politics Lags behind Economics. The world is an international economic unit but not yet an international political unit, and for this reason civilization suffers greatly. Wheat and machinery produced in the various parts of the world compete, and then tariff-makers help to dislocate trade. Since the war international co-operation has made it possible to develop political institutions as agencies to meet international needs. The several conferences on disarmament, on immigration, on labor standards, on drugs and narcotics, on white slavery, on gold movements, the Bank for International Settlements, all indicate the development of an international-mindedness. To these efforts Russia has been sympathetic. The Soviets have shown their willingness to co-operate by joining the international sugar, oil, and wheat conferences.

2. Geneva Conference of 1931. The League of Nations invited the Soviet Government to participate in an international conference on the world economic crisis. The invitation was unconditional. The conference was marked by a striking spirit of friendship between representatives of the Soviet Government and those of the capitalist countries. Foreign Commissar Litvinov, representing the Soviet Union, made a proposal to the Pan-European Commission for an economic peace, the text of which follows:

> Representatives of the undersigned European countries, recognizing that:
>
> (a) The mitigation of the crisis which has overtaken the national economy of most countries requires, in addition to abstention from war as a means for solution of international conflicts, the most complete cessation of all forms of economic aggression, both avowed and concealed, by any countries or groups of countries against any other countries or groups of countries;
>
> (b) The cessation of economic aggression is an essential condition for peaceful co-operation of states in the sphere of economics, irrespective of their political-economic systems;
>
> (c) The cessation of economic aggression would help to put an end to the present atmosphere of distrust, uncertainty, and alarm weighing heavily upon the economic position;
>
> And hoping that all other countries, inspired by their example, will join this protocol, have decided to recommend that their governments sign the following protocol:
>
> First: The contracting parties once more solemnly confirm the principle proclaimed at the international economic conference of 1927 of peaceful co-existence of countries, irrespective of their social, political, and economic systems.
>
> Second: In accordance with clause two, the parties undertake not to adopt in their relations with each other any discrimination whatsoever, and regard adop-

tion in any of their countries of a special attitude militating against the interests of one or any of the countries subscribing to this protocol as incompatible with its principles.

This protocol is to become effective when any parties deposit their ratifications with the president of the commission, M. Briand.[6]

The proposal took the conference by surprise, but it manifested the co-operative spirit of the Soviets. The representatives of France and Poland gave a warm reception to the Soviet principles. M. Briand even hoped that the results would constitute in the economic domain a pact of non-aggression, such as those concluded in the political domain.

The Soviet proposal for international co-operation belies the oft-repeated statement of anti-Soviet spokesmen that Russia fears to participate in an international conference of the powers and would rather negotiate separately with each and thus play off one against the other. Admittedly such a conference will probably not be an unqualified success. The powers have differing interests in Russian affairs, as for example Italy and Argentina concerning Russian wheat; Finland and Belgium concerning Russian lumber; France and Japan concerning Russian pre-war debts; or Mexico and the United States concerning war debts and confiscated property.

Yet the very existence of such opposed interests should insure fairness in dealing with Russia. But pessimists say the results will be valueless, and cite the futility of the concert of powers in dealing with the Sick Man of Europe for fifty years before the war.

3. A Program for a World Conference on Russia. Subject to Soviet acceptance of the conditions for recognition, namely, settlement of the problem of debt and of confiscated private property, a world conference on Russia should be ready to consider questions of the production and export of raw materials, labor standards, foreign loans and credits, the stabilization of production and disarmament. At a meeting of the International Chamber of Commerce in Washington, May 5, 1931, Colonel Cooper of the Russian-American Chamber of Commerce thought that co-operation with Russia for relief from the world depression, and economic study of the Soviet Union by an international committee of industrial and financial leaders of the world, would be desirable. The Soviet Government would welcome such a study and any conference that might follow.

Recognition of Russia and co-operation with her would probably have the same result that the election had on the Labor Party in England. It became conservative. Speeches can be radical, when they do not entail the responsibility of action. Dreams of world revolution are feasible at a distance. The concrete problems of economics and politics have a sobering influence. "Contact with reality and with the limitation of facts is a stern form of education," as Nicholas Murray Butler phrased it. It is time to talk of embargo of Russian goods and economic isolation after Russia indicates her unwillingness to co-operate with the capitalist nations along sound international lines.

APPENDIX

References to Sources

OFFICIAL NEWSPAPERS PUBLISHED IN MOSCOW

Izvestia (News)
Pravda (Truth)
Ekonom. Zhisn. Ekonomicheskaya Zhisn (Economic Life).
Za Ind. Za Industrializatsiu (Toward Industrialization).
Trud. (Labor)
Duranty. References so marked apply to dispatches from Mr. Walter Duranty, Moscow correspondent of the *New York Times.*

YEAR BOOKS.

Soviet Union Yearbook. Gives data for the Soviet Union corresponding to that found in *The Statesman's Yearbook* for all countries. Compiled by Santalov and Segal, and published annually by George Allen and Unwin, Ltd., London, in English. In the present list all references apply to the Yearbook for 1930 unless otherwise specified.
Economic Handbook. Economic Handbook of the Soviet Union. Unless otherwise specified, all references are to the Handbook for 1931. Issued by The American-Russian Chamber of Commerce, New York.

PERIODICALS.

Economic Review. Economic Review of the Soviet Union. A semi-monthly periodical, published in English by the Amtorg Trading Corporation, New York.
Soviet Union Review. A monthly periodical, published in English, Soviet Information Bureau, Washington, D. C.
Economic Survey of the State Bank of the U.S.S.R. Official monthly, published in Moscow, also in an English edition.

Chapter I. Perspectives

1. Hakluyt, Richard, *The Principal Navigations, Voyages, Traffiques, and Discoveries of the English Nation.* 1589. Masefield edition. London: Dent, 1927. Vol. I, pp. 261 and 284.
2. Moscow wireless from Duranty to *N. Y. Times,* Nov. 1, 1931.
3. *N. Y. Times,* Feb. 10, 1932.
4. Macdonald, J. Ramsay. *The Socialist Movement.* New York: Henry Holt & Co. 1913. Pp. 122 ff.
5. Hobhouse, Leonard T. *Social Evolution and Political Theory.* New York: Columbia University Press, 1913. P. 139.
6. *N. Y. Times,* June 18, 1931, p. 1, col. 4.
7. Dr. A. D. Weeks, Dean of the School of Education, North Dakota Agricultural College, "Mental Differences and Future Society," in *Scientific Monthly,* February, 1931.

8. Address at the Lincoln birthplace farm, Hodgenville, Ky., Sept. 4, 1916.
9. *Pravda,* Aug. 21, 1930.

CHAPTER II. AN HISTORICAL ANALOGY—THE FRENCH REVOLUTION

1. See also Hobhouse, Leonard T., *Social Evolution and Political Theory.* N. Y., Columbia University Press, 1913. Chap. VI, The Growth of the State, pp. 136–147; also his *Liberalism* (Holt), p. 15.

1[a]. Macdonald, J. Ramsay, ibid., p. 18.
2. Schapiro, J. S. *Modern Times in Europe.* New York: Houghton, Mifflin & Co. 1930. Part II, "The French Revolution."
3. Schapiro, ibid., p. 100.
4. Schapiro, ibid., p. 96.
5. Chamberlin, W. H. *Soviet Russia.* Boston: Little, Brown and Co. 1930. P. 213.
6. Kautsky, Karl. *Bolshevism at a Deadlock.* New York: Rand School Press. 1931. Pp. 128, 129, 135–36, 138.
7. Gottschalk, L. R. *Era of the French Revolution.* New York: Houghton, Mifflin & Co. 1929. P. 105.
8. Gottschalk, ibid., p. 224. P. Gaxotte's *French Revolution* is also helpful to readers on Soviet Russia.

CHAPTER III. THE SOVIET MIND

1. *N. Y. Times,* April 25, 1931.
2. *N. Y. Times,* July 14, 1931.
3. *Izvestia,* Feb. 5, 1931.
4. Duranty dispatch, *N. Y. Times,* Dec. 3, 1930.
5. *N. Y. Times,* May 8, 1932.
6. Joseph Shaplen, *N. Y. Times,* Dec. 28, 1930.
7. Dennis, Lawrence. "Revolution, Recognition and Intervention," article in *Foreign Affairs,* January, 1931. Vol. IX, No. 2, p. 204.

CHAPTER IV. THE FIVE-YEAR PLAN

1. Ballod, Karl. *The Future State.* This is a study in Socialist economics. The author was born in Lithuania in 1864, studied and taught statistics in Germany, and since 1928 has been at the University of Riga.
2. Address before the Central Executive Committee, Jan. 4, 1931, quoted in *Soviet Union Review,* February, 1931, p. 31.
3. Yugoff, A. *Economic Trends in Soviet Russia.* New York: Richard R. Smith, Inc. 1930. P. 23.
4. *Economic Handbook,* pp. 68 and 143. *Commerce Year Book,* U. S. Dept. of Commerce, 1926. Vol. II, p. 472.
5. Ohl, P. *Foreign Capital in Russia.* Petrograd: Institute of Economic Research, 1922; quoted by Yugoff, ibid., p. 24.

   Pasvolsky and Moulton. *Russian Debts and Russian Reconstruction.* New York: McGraw-Hill. 1924. Pp. 21 and 182.
6. Farbman, Michael. *Pyatiletka, Russia's Five-Year Plan.* New York: New Republic, Inc. 1931. Pp. 12 ff.
7. Trotsky, Leon. *N. Y. Times,* May 8, 1932.
8. *Pravda,* Sept. 12, 1931.
9. Knickerbocker, H. R. *The Red Trade Menace.* New York: Dodd, Mead and Co. 1930. P. 79.
10. Resolution of the Fifth Congress of Soviets, Moscow, May 28, 1929; Bulletin No. 22 of the *Decisions of the Congress,* pp. 9–14, quoted in Chamberlin, ibid., p. 167.
11. Chamberlin, W. H. *The Soviet Planned Economic Order.* Boston: World Peace Foundation, 1931, p. 14.
12. *The Soviet Union Looks Ahead,* issued by the State Planning Commission of the U.S.S.R. New York: Liveright. 1930. Note of editor who prepared English translation, p. 223.
13. Farbman, M., ibid., p. 53.
14. *The Five-Year Plan.* (In Russian.) Moscow; 1929. Vol. I, p. 130.
15. *The Soviet Union Looks Ahead.* Table X, pp. 266–67.
16. *The Soviet Union Looks Ahead.* Table III, pp. 250–52.
17. *Economic Handbook,* pp. 142–45.

17[a]. *Economic Review,* Jan. 15, 1932, p. 32.
18. Farbman, M., ibid., pp. 18 and 19. Figures of final estimate taken from *The Soviet Union Looks Ahead,* p. 266.
19. *Izvestia,* Nov. 10, 1930, quoted in Chamberlin, ibid., p. 37.
20. *Economic Review,* Jan. 1, 1931, Vol. VI, No. 1, pp. 8–9.
21. *Pravda,* Dec. 7, 1929.
22. *The Soviet Union Looks Ahead,* p. 223.
23. *The Soviet Union Looks Ahead,* p. 266.
24. *Economic Handbook,* p. 11.
25. *The Soviet Union Looks Ahead,* p. 23.
26. Address delivered Dec. 16, 1930. Printed in the *Economic Review of the Soviet Union,* Jan. 15, 1931, Vol. VI, No. 2, p. 41.
27. *Za Ind.,* Dec. 10, 1929.
28. *Soviet Union Review,* May, 1931. Vol. IX, No. 5, p. 99.
29. Duranty, wireless from Moscow, *N. Y. Times,* May 20, 1931.
30. United Press dispatch from Moscow, in *N. Y. Herald-Tribune,* Aug. 2, 1931.
31. *Yearbook of U. S. Dept. of Agriculture,* 1931. Washington: Government Printing Office. Pp. 843, 861, 931.
32. *Pyatiletni Plan: Narodno-Khozyaistvennovo Strotelstva U.S.S.R. The Five-Year Plan of National Economic Construction of the Soviet Union,* Vol. 1, pp. 9–13, quoted in *Soviet Planned Economic Order,* by Chamberlin, pp. 176–80.
33. *Pyatiletni Plan,* ibid., quoted by Chamberlin, pp. 176–80.
34. *Economic Handbook,* pp. 12–13.
35. *Economic Handbook,* p. 9.
36. *Rabochaya Moskva,* Sept. 4, 1930. See also *Soviet Planned Economic Order,* ibid., pp. 191–193.
37. *Za Ind.,* Oct. 17, 1931.
38. *Pravda,* Mar. 24 and 28, 1931.
39. Summary of industrial accomplishments, *Za Ind.,* April 13 and 16, 1930.
40. *Pravda,* Mar. 24 and 28, 1931.
41. *Za Ind.,* Sept. 30, 1930 and Oct. 4, 1930.
42. *Pravda,* Mar. 24 and 28, 1931.
43. *Za Ind.,* Mar. 8, 1931.
44. *Za Ind.,* Aug. 13, 27, 29, 1930, and *Izvestia,* Aug. 6 and Sept. 2, 1930.
45. *Pravda,* April 10, 19, 1931.
46. *Current History,* January, 1931, pp. 487–88.
47. *Economic Review,* May 15, 1931. Vol. VI, No. 10.
48. Berlin wireless, *N. Y. Times,* Nov. 21, 1930.
49. *Ekonom. Zhisn,* Aug. 9, 1930.
50. Moscow dispatch in *N. Y. Times,* June 27, 1931.
51. *Rabochaya Moskva,* Sept. 4, 1930, quoted in Chamberlin, ibid., p. 185.
52. *Izvestia,* June 12, 1931; *Pravda,* June 30, 1931.
53. Cross, S. S., *Harvard Business Review,* January, 1931.
53[a]. Bureau of Research on Russian Economic Conditions, University of Birmingham, England. Memorandum No. 1, *Remarks on the Five-Year Plan,* May 1931, p. 7.
54. Moscow dispatch in *N. Y. Herald-Tribune,* Sept. 26, 1931.
55. Duranty dispatch from Moscow, *N. Y. Times,* May 27, 1931.
56. *Soviet Planned Economic Order,* ibid., pp. 153 ff.
57. *Economic Handbook,* pp. 18, 21, 24, and 42.
58. *Soviet Union Review,* April, 1931, Vol. IX, No. 4, pp. 74–80. Last six items of table from *Econom. Zhisn,* Mar. 12, 1931.
59. *Planovoye Khoziatistvo,* Nov. 12, 1931, pp. 14 and 340.
59[a]. *New York Times,* Sept. 12; *New York Post,* Sept. 8, 16; *New York Herald-Tribune,* Sept. 18, 28; *New York Sun,* Sept. 21, 1932.
60. *Za Ind.,* July 18, 1930.
61. *Rabochaya Moskva,* Sept. 4, 1930, quoted in Chamberlin, ibid., pp. 181–85.
62. *Ekonom. Zhisn,* Jan. 22, 1932.
63. *Economic Handbook,* 1931, pp. 18, 21, 24, 29, 31, 42, 142.
64. *Soviet Planned Economic Order,* Chamberlin, ibid., pp. 39–41.
65. See also Chamberlin, ibid., pp. 150 ff.
66. Dispatch from Moscow, *N. Y. Times,* Aug. 7, 1931.

67. Bron, S. G. *Soviet Economic Development and American Business,* ibid., pp. 4–5.
67[a]. Bureau of Research, Memorandum No. 5, May, 1932, p. 5, footnote 3.
68. *Soviet Union Review,* April, 1931. Vol. IX, No. 4, pp. 74–80.
69. *Pravda,* Oct. 2, 1930.
70. *Pravda,* Oct. 2, 1931.
71. *The Soviet Union Looks Ahead,* ibid., p. 9.
72. *Bulletin of Timber Exports.* (In Russian.) No. 1, 1931, p. 11.
73. *Economic Handbook,* p. 18.
74. *Economic Handbook,* p. 142. *Statisticheski Spravochnik S.S.S.R. za 1928 god.* (In Russian.) Pp. 302–05 (for the years 1918–22). *The Five-Year Plan,* Vol. II, Part 2, (in Russian) (for Five-Year Plan figures). *Economic Review,* May 15, 1932, p. 239.
75. *Economic Handbook,* p. 20.
76. *Economic Handbook,* p. 21.
77. *Economic Review,* June 1, 1930, p. 223; Aug. 1, 1930, p. 307; Oct. 15, 1930, p. 419; Feb. 1, 1931, p. 66; March 1, 1931, p. 119; April 1, 1931, p. 187; June 1, 1931, p. 263.
78. *Petroleum World,* February, 1931, p. 161.
79. Same sources as in Note 74, above.
80. *Economic Handbook,* p. 24.
81. *Economic Handbook,* pp. 27 ff.
82. *Economic Review,* Jan. 1, 1931. Vol. VI, No. 1, pp. 8–9.
83. *Economic Handbook,* pp. 36–38, 42.
84. *Izvestia,* June 25, 1930.
85. *Izvestia,* June 23, 1930.
86. *Izvestia,* May 8, 1932.
87. *Economic Handbook,* pp. 31–33.
88. Moscow wireless to *N. Y. Times,* Jan. 19, 1932.
88[a]. *Za Ind.,* July 3, 1932; *Ek. Zhisn,* Aug. 6, 1932.
88[b]. *N. Y. Herald-Tribune,* Moscow dispatch, Aug. 13, 1932, and Nizhni Novgorod dispatch, Sept. 23, 1932.
89. *Economic Handbook,* pp. 34–35.
90. *Economic Handbook,* pp. 51–54.
91. *Economic Review,* June 1, 1931, p. 251.
92. *Economic Handbook,* p. 55.
93. *Ekonom. Zhisn,* April 1, 1931.
94. *Economic Review,* May 15, 1931. Vol. VI, No. 10, p. 237.
95. *Economic Handbook,* p. 142.
96. *Pravda,* Oct. 2, 1930.
97. *Economic Review,* May 15, 1931. Vol. VI, No. 10, p. 238.
98. *Pravda,* May 25, 1931.
99. *Za Ind.,* April 13 and 16, 1930.
100. *Izvestia,* June 14 and 16, 1931.
101. *Pravda,* Oct. 2, 1930.
102. Duranty dispatch to *N. Y. Times.* Dec. 28, 1931. *Economic Review,* May 15, 1932, p. 239.
103. *Economic Review,* Aug. 1, 1931. Vol. VI, No. 15, p. 352.
104. *Za Ind.,* Mar. 8, 1931, and *Izvestia,* Mar. 7, 1931.
105. *Za Ind.,* Jan. 3 and 4, 1931.
106. *Za Ind.,* Feb. 14, 1930.
107. *Pravda,* May 24, 1931.
108. *Pravda,* Oct. 2, 1930.
108[a]. *Izvestia and Ek. Zhisn,* July 28, 1932.
109. *Za Ind.,* April 13 and 16, 1930.
110. *Control Figures,* 1929–30, p. 430. (In Russian.)
111. *Pravda,* Oct. 2, 1930.
112. *Pravda,* Sept. 12, 1930.
113. *Za Ind.,* Feb. 7 and 12, 1931.
114. *Pravda,* April 10, 14, 1931 and *Za Ind.,* April 13–16, 1930.
115. *Za Ind.,* April 13–16, 1930.
115[a]. Bureau of Research on Russian Economic Conditions, Memorandum No. 5, May, 1932, p. 3.
116. *Za Ind.,* Feb. 7 and 12, 1931.
116[a]. Bureau of Research, Memorandum No. 5, May, 1932, p. 3.

117. Fischer, Louis, in *The Nation,* Nov. 25, 1931. Reprinted in his *Machines and Men in Russia* New York: Harrison Smith, 1932.
118. *Ekonom. Zhisn,* Jan. 22, 1932; *Pravda,* Feb. 4, 1932.
118[a]. *Za Ind.,* Mar. 2, 1931.
118[b]. Bureau of Research, Memorandum No. 1, *Remarks on the Five-Year Plan,* May, 1931, p. 12.
119. Mitchell, Wesley C. *Business Cycles.* New York: National Bureau of Economic Research, 1930. P. 173.
120. Soviet Blueprints, *N. Y. Times,* May 3, 1931.
120[a]. Bureau of Research, Memorandum No. 5, May, 1932, p. 8.

Chapter V. Agriculture

1. *Economic Handbook,* p. 57.
2. Quoted in Kautsky, ibid., p. 132. See also Illustrated *History of the Russian Revolution of 1917.* Berlin: Willi Munzenberg, 1928. P. 561.
3. *Ekonom. Zhisn,* Mar. 20 and 22, 1930; and *Pravda,* Mar. 21, 23, and 24, 1930.
4. *Izvestia,* April 19, 1930.
5. *Izvestia,* July 10, 1930.
6. *Izvestia,* April 19, 1930.
7. Official statement signed by Stalin and Molotov, dated Jan. 24, 1931.
8. *Soviet Union Review,* Vol. IX, No. 4, April, 1931, p. 84; *Economic Review,* Vol. VI, No. 8, April 15, 1931, pp. 176, 177.
9. *Economic Review,* June 15, 1930. Vol. V, No. 12, pp. 249–52.
10. *Izvestia,* April 3, 1930; also quoted in Chamberlin, *Soviet Planned Economic Order,* Appendix X, pp. 222–23.
11. *Izvestia,* April 19, 1930.
12. *Soviet Union Review,* April, 1931, Vol. IX, No. 4, pp. 80–83.
13. *Soviet Union Review,* May, 1931. Vol. IX, No. 5, p. 106.
14. From *A Selection of Documents Relative to the Labour Legislation in Force in the Union of Soviet Socialist Republics.* London: His Majesty's Stationery Office, Russia No. 1 (1931) Cmd. 3775, p. 115. Quoted also in Chamberlin, ibid. See also the *Soviet Union Review,* April, 1930.
15. *The Five-Year Plan,* Vol. 2, Part 1. P. 337.
16. *Pravda,* June 27, 1931.
17. Report of V. M. Molotov, Chairman of the Council of People's Commissars, and report of Y. A. Yakovley, Commissar for Agriculture, at the Sixth Congress of Soviets, March 8 to 17, 1931; also Molotov, V. M., *The Success of the Five-Year Plan,* p. 45; Kuybyshev, V., *Planned Economy,* December, 1930, p. 18; *Economic Review,* April 15, 1931, Vol. VI, No. 8, pp. 176, 177, and July 15, 1931, p. 334; *Soviet Union Review,* April, 1931, Vol. IX, No. 4, pp. 80–83.
18. *Economic Handbook,* pp. 60–62. *Economic Review,* May 15, 1932.
19. *Economic Review,* Aug. 1931. Vol. VI, No. 15, p. 345.
20. *Economic Handbook,* pp. 58–60.
21. *Economic Review,* April 15, 1931. Vol. VI, No. 8, pp. 176, 177.
22. *Economic Review,* April 1, 1930. Vol. V, No. 7, p. 123.
23. *Izvestia,* Mar. 15, 1930. Quoted in Chamberlin, *Soviet Planned Economic Order.*
24. *Izvestia,* April 19, 1930.
25. *Pravda,* May 22, June 2, 5, 1932; *Izvestia,* May 27, 29, 1932; *Ekonom. Zhisn,* June 6, 11, 14, 1932.
26. Moscow dispatch to the *N. Y. Herald-Tribune,* June 12, 1932.
27. *Economic Handbook,* pp. 62–63.
28. *Economic Review,* April 15, 1931. Vol. VI, No. 8, p. 177.
29. *Soviet Union Review,* April, 1931. Vol. IX, No. 4, pp. 80–83.
30. *Soviet Union Review,* April, 1931, pp. 80–83.
31. *The Five-Year Plan,* Vol. II, Part 1, p. 337.
32. *Economic Review,* May 15, 1932. Vol. VII, No. 10, p. 240.
33. Kuybyshev, V., *Planned Economy,* December, 1930, p. 18.
34. *Izvestia,* April 19, 1930.
35. *Izvestia,* June 10, 1930.
36. *Izvestia,* April 22, 1931; *N. Y. Times,* April 23, 1931.

37. *Ekonom. Zhisn,* Nov. 21, 1930.
38. *Pravda,* Aug. 31, 1930.
39. *Ekonom. Zhisn,* Nov. 21, 1930.
40. *Pravda,* Mar. 27, 28, 1932.
40[a]. *N. Y. Times,* Moscow dispatches, Aug. 10, 11, and Sept. 25, 1932; *Wall Street Journal,* Paris dispatches, Aug. 18 and 20, 1932.
40[b]. *N. Y. Times,* Moscow dispatch, Sept. 25, 1932.
41. *Economic Handbook,* pp. 58–60.
42. National City Bank Bulletin, June, 1931. Figures taken from *Yearbook, U. S. Department of Agriculture, 1931;* production figures, pp. 590–91, export figures, p. 599.
43. Address to the Sixth Congress of Soviets on March 8, 1931. *Soviet Union Review,* April, 1931, pp. 80–83.
44. *Economic Review,* April 15, 1931, pp. 176–77.
44[a]. *N. Y. Times,* Moscow dispatches, Aug. 14, 23, and Sept. 1, 1932; *Herald-Tribune,* Sept. 18, 1932; *Wall Street Journal,* Washington dispatch, Sept. 29, 1932.
44[b]. Bureau of Research, Memorandum No. 5, May, 1932, p. 4.
45. *Soviet Union Review,* April, 1931, pp. 80–83.
46. *Economic Handbook,* pp. 64, 65.
47. Bron, S. G., *Soviet Economic Development and American Business.* New York: Liveright, 1930. Pp. 4, 5.
48. Jean Walker, quoted in *N. Y. Times,* Nov. 4, 1931.
49. *Soviet Union Review,* May, 1931. Vol. IX, No. 5, p. 107.
50. Chamberlin, W. H. "The Bolshevist Revolution in a New Phase," in *Current History,* May, 1930.

CHAPTER VI. LABOR

1. Zagorsky, Simon. *Wages and Regulation of Conditions of Labour in the U.S.S.R.* Geneva: International Labor Office, 1930. Also London: P. S. King & Son, and Boston: World Peace Foundation. Pp. 108 ff.
2. Duranty dispatch from Moscow, *N. Y. Times,* June 3, 1931.
3. *Soviet Union Yearbook,* p. 450.
4. *Izvestia,* Jan. 4, 1931.
5. *N. Y. Times,* July 2, 1931.
6. *Izvestia,* Dec. 20, 1930; also *Documents Relative to Labor Lesgislation* (see note 13, chap. V, above), p. 174.
7. *Ekonom. Zhisn,* May 27, 1931; *N. Y. Herald-Tribune,* June 14, 1931.
8. Moscow Associated Press dispatch, May 10, 1931.
9. Cable dispatch, *N. Y. Times,* June 11, 1931.
10. Associated Press dispatch from Moscow, July 7, 1931.
11. *Economic Review,* Jan. 15, 1931, Vol. VI, No. 2, p. 36.
12. Duranty cable dispatch from Moscow, *N. Y. Times,* Feb. 17, 1931.
13. Bourke-White, Margaret, *N. Y. Times Magazine,* Mar. 27, 1932.
14. *Economic Handbook,* pp. 132–36. Cf. Soviet Union Year Book.
15. Resolution of the Central Executive Committee. *Pravda,* Dec. 22, 1930.
16. Budish, J. M. and Shipman, S. S. *Soviet Foreign Trade.* New York: Liveright, 1931.
16[a]. As given in Bureau of Research, Memorandum No. 6, *Wages of Industrial Workers in the U.S.S.R.,* July, 1932, p. 16.
17. *Trud v SSSR; Spravochnik* (Labor Handbook), 1926–30.
18. *Trud and Spravochnik.* Quoted in *Documents Relative to Labor Legislation,* ibid., pp. 185–88.
19. *Documents Relative to Labor Legislation,* ibid., p. 98. (Under collection of "Laws of the Soviet Union," 1930, No. 63, chap. 586.)
20. *Documents Relative to Labor Legislation,* ibid., p. 29.
21. *Ekonom. Zhisn,* Mar. 2, 1919.
22. *Ekonom. Zhisn,* No. 213, 1919, quoted in Zagorsky, ibid., 103–04.
23. *Ekonom. Zhisn,* Mar. 5, 1919.
24. *N-Ski;* Second Congress of Trade Unions, Moscow, 1919, p. 112.
25. Zagorsky, ibid., pp. 151–54.
26. *Vestnik Truda,* 1925, No. 7, and *Ekonomicheskoye Obozreniye,* 1925, No. 12, and 1929, No. 3, quoted in Zagorsky, ibid., p. 107.
27. Saveliev, M. *Guiding Principles of the Communist Party of U.S.S.R. in Economic Policy*

during a Period of Ten Years. Moscow: 1928, p. 260. Quoted in Zagorsky, ibid., p. 104 ff.

28. Zagorsky, ibid., pp. 104–06.
29. Report to the Sixth Trade Union Congress, Moscow, 1924, p. 183. Quoted in Zagorsky, ibid., pp. 111–13.
30. *Trud,* Oct. 7, 1923. Cf. also Circular of the General Council of Trade Unions, No. 582, Trud, Nov. 7, 1923, and B. Livschitz, "The Question of Wage Scales" in *Vestnik Truda,* No. 3, 1923.
31. Report to the Sixth Trade Union Congress, quoted in Zagorsky, p. 114.
32. Report of the Seventh Trade Union Congress, quoted in Zagorsky, p. 116.
33. Zagorsky, ibid., p. 117.
34. S. Heinmann, in *Ekonomicheskoye Obozreniye,* 1929, No. 10, quoted in Zagorsky, ibid., p. 124.
35. *Statistika Truda* and *Ekonomicheskoye Obozreniye,* March, 1929, quoted in Zagorsky, ibid., p. 175. The figures refer to the month of March each year.
36. *Problems of Labor in Progress,* publication of the Soviet Commissariat for Labor, pp. 59–61, quoted in Chamberlin, ibid., pp. 53–55.
37. *Soviet Union Review,* June, 1931, Vol. IX, No. 6, pp. 135–36.
38. Published in *Statisticheskoye Obozreniye,* April, 1930, a monthly publication of the Central Statistical Department of the U.S.S.R., quoted in *Documents Relative to Labor Legislation,* ibid., pp. 185–87.
39. *Trud v SSSSR,* ibid., quoted in *Documents Relative to Labor Legislation,* pp. 186–88.
40. *Monthly Statistical Bulletin of the Supreme Economic Council,* October, 1925; Stat. Oboz., 1928, No. 1; 1929, No. 3 and No. 12; quoted in Zagorsky, pp. 187–88.
41. S. Nekrassov, "Social Charges in Industry," in *Statisticheskoye Obozreniye,* 1928, No. 1, quoted in Zagorsky, p. 189.
42. Address at Sixteenth Congress of Communist Party, June 29, 1930.
43. *Trud,* March 26, April 6, 9, and 24, quoted in Zagorsky, ibid., p. 189.
44. Order of the Commissariat of Labor, quoted in Zagorsky, ibid., p. 81.
45. *Izvestia,* Aug. 15, 1929.
46. *Soviet Union Yearbook,* p. 454.
47. *Economic Handbook,* pp. 134–36.
48. *Economic Handbook,* pp. 132–36; *Soviet Union Yearbook,* 1930, pp. 462–78.
49. *Economic Handbook,* pp. 132–36.
50. *Soviet Union Yearbook,* pp. 449–50, 478.
51. *Economic Review,* June 1, 1931. Vol. VI, No. 11, p. 245.
52. Prokopovich, S. N. *The New Economic Policy: Ekonomichesky Viestnik,* p. 47, Berlin, 1923; quoted in Pasvolsky and Moulton, *Russian Debts, etc.,* p. 103.
53. Knickerbocker, H. R. *The Red Trade Menace.* New York: Dodd, Mead and Co., 1930, p. 129.
54. *Wages and Regulations on Conditions of Labor in the U.S.S.R.,* p. 208.
55. *Economic Survey of the State Bank of the U.S.S.R.,* May, 1930, Vol. V, No. 8–9.
56. *Soviet Union Yearbook,* pp. 267–69.
57. *Economic Review,* Jan. 15, 1930. Vol. V, No. 2, p. 38.
58. *Economic Review,* July 1, 1930. Vol. V, No. 13, pp. 285–86.
59. *Economic Review,* July 1, 1930. Vol. V, No. 13, pp. 285–86.
60. Fischer, Louis, in *The Nation,* July 22, 1931. Also his *Machines and Men in Russia.* Ibid.
61. *Izvestia,* June 22, 1931.
62. Address at the Seventh Annual Convention of the American Cotton Shippers Association at New Orleans, April 24, 1931, quoted in the *Economic Review,* May 15, 1931. Vol. VI, No. 10, p. 221.
63. Moscow dispatch, *N. Y. Times,* June 1, 1931.
64. *Za Ind.,* Aug. 15, 1930.

64[a]. Moscow dispatch, *The Sun,* September 7, 1932; *Pravda,* July 13, 29, and 30, 1932.

65. Zagorsky, ibid., p. 207.
66. Zagorsky, ibid., pp. 203–207.
67. Hoover, Calvin, *The Economic Life of Soviet Russia.* New York: Macmillan, 1931, pp. 253–55.
68. Chamberlin, W. H. *Soviet Planned Economic Order,* pp. 56–59.
69. *Cost of Living in the United States,* 1924. U. S. Department of Labor, Bureau of Vital Statistics, Bulletin No. 357, May, 1924.

69[a]. *N. Y. Times* dispatch, August 16, September 3, 1932.

70. *Cost of Living in the United States,* ibid., May, 1924.
70a. Moscow dispatch, N. Y. *Sun,* September 7, 1932.
71. Moscow cable to *N. Y. Times,* May 13, 1931.
72. Moscow dispatch to *N. Y. Times,* May 17, 1931.
73. Moscow dispatch, June 24, 1932.
74. Chamberlin, ibid., p. 142.
74a. Bureau of Research, Memorandum No. 6, July, 1932.
75. Fischer, Louis, in *The Nation,* Jan. 6, 1932. Reprinted in his *Machines and Men in Russia,* ibid.
76. Address delivered at the Sixteenth Congress of the Communist Party, June 29, 1930. *Economic Review,* Aug. 1, 1930, Vol. V, No. 14–15, p. 316.
77. *Soviet Union Review,* June, 1931, Vol. 9, No. 6, pp. 135–36.
78. Zagorsky, ibid., (A) p. 182, (B) p. 183, quoting A. Rabinovitch, "The Labor Problem in the U.S.S.R.," in *Ekon. Oboz.,* 1927, No. 10.
78a. Bureau of Research, Memorandum No. 5, May, 1932, p. 7; Memorandum No. 6, July, 1932, pp. 14, 22–24.
79. Zagorsky, ibid., p. 184.
79a. *N. Y. Times,* August 16, 1932; *Wall Street Journal,* Sept. 20, 1932.
80. G. T. Grinko, op. cit., p. 129; also *Soviet Foreign Trade,* ibid., p. 215.
81. *International Labor Review,* October, 1930, Vol XXII, No. 4, pp. 546–51.
82. Quoted in *Soviet Foreign Trade,* ibid., p. 217.
83. *Economic Review,* April 1, 1931, p. 149.
83a. G. Strumilin, *Zarabotnaya Plata i proizvodilelnost trudam,* 1923, pp. 58, 59.
84. Tolstopiatov, "Factory Discipline and Absenteeism," *Voprosy Truda,* 1929, No. 1; "Factory Discipline Must be Strengthened," *Voprosy Truda,* 1929, No. 8; quoted in Zagorsky, ibid., p. 18.
85. Zagorsky, ibid., pp. 16–17.
86. *Pravda,* May 7, 8, 9, and 19, 1931; *Za Ind.,* May 4 and 8, 1931.
87. *Izvestia,* July 12, 1930.
88. *Za Ind.,* Feb. 14, 1930.
89. *Za Ind.,* July 9, 1930.
90. *Pravda,* April 30 and May 4, 1931.
91. *Izvestia,* Sept. 7, 1929, quoted in Zagorsky, ibid., pp. 25, 26.
92. *Torgovo-Promyshennaya Gazetta,* Feb. 2, 1929, quoted in Zagorsky, ibid., pp. 23–24.
93. Decree No. 8/371 of June 3, 1931, quoted in *Bulleten Finansovovo i Khoziastvennovo Zakonodatelstva* No. 17, June 17, 1931, and *N. Y. Times,* June 5, 1931.
94. *Izvestia,* N.K.T., 1929, No. 37, quoted in Zagorsky, ibid., pp. 27–29.
95. Zagorsky, ibid., pp. 14–15 and 31–32.
96. *Bulletin of Financial and Economic Legislation,* No. 3, January 27, 1930, p. 51, quoted in *Documents Relative to Labor Legislation,* ibid., p. 145.
97. Moscow dispatch, in *N. Y. Times,* May 23, 1931.
98. *Economic Review,* Aug. 1, 1931, p. 339.
99. *Izvestia,* Aug. 18, 1930; *Za Ind.,* Sept. 7, 1930.
100. Duranty cable from Moscow, *N. Y. Times,* Aug. 14, 1930.
101. *Na Planovom Fronte,* No. 21–22, November, 1930.
101a. *Wall Street Journal,* Paris dispatch, September 20, 1932.
102. *Izvestia,* Aug. 17, 1930.
103. *Za. Ind.,* Sept. 27, 1930.
104. *Pravda,* May 25, 1931.
105. *Izvestia,* Aug. 18, 1930; *Za Ind.,* Sept. 7, 1930.
106. *Soviet Union Review,* July and August, 1931. Vol. IX, No. 7–8, pp. 146–53.
107. *Za Ind.,* Sept. 27, 1930.
108. *Za Ind.,* Feb. 14, 1930.
109. Joseph Stalin, Conference of Industrial Managers held in Moscow, June 23, 1931. *Izvestia,* July 5, 1931; *Soviet Union Review,* July–Aug., 1931, Vol. IX, Nos. 7, 8, pp. 146–53.
110. *Economic Review,* Jan. 15, 1931.
111. *Pravda,* Oct. 22, 1930.
112. *Economic Review,* Jan. 15, 1931.
113. *Izvestia,* Dec. 17, 1930.
114. *Wages and Conditions of Labor in the U.S.S.R.,* Zagorsky, ibid., pp. 8–10.

115. Lewisohn, Sam A., "Russia, the Industrial Laboratory." *Political Science Quarterly,* March, 1931, Vol. XLVI; 1. Pp. 41–50.
116. Zagorsky, ibid., p. 127.
116[a]. *Wall Street Journal,* Paris dispatch, September 20, 1932.
117. *Izvestia,* Feb. 15, 1930.
118. *Pravda,* Jan. 10, 1931; also *N. Y. Times,* May 18, 1931.
119. *Pravda,* Sept. 19, 1930; *Izvestia,* Oct. 6, 1930.
120. *Izvestia,* Nov. 11, 1930.
121. *Pravda,* Oct. 22, 1930.
122. *Economic Review,* Jan. 15, 1931.
123. *Pravda,* Jan. 19, 1931; *Za Ind.,* Jan. 18, 1931.
124. *Bulletin of Financial and Economic Legislation,* No. 26, 1929, quoted in *Documents Relative to Labor Legislation,* ibid., p. 141.
125. *Collection of Laws of the R.S.F.S.R.,* 1930, No. 9, chap. 107. Quoted in "Russia No. 1 (1931)" Cmd. 3775.
126. *Bulletin of Financial and Economic Legislation,* No. 27, July 5, 1929.
127. Decree of Oct. 5, 1929, published in *Bulletin of Financial and Economic Legislation,* No. 42, Oct. 18, 1929, p. 40.
128. *Pravda,* Aug. 22, 1930.
129. *Izvestia,* April 26, 1931.
130. 1922 edition, with amendments up to April 20, 1930.
130[a]. Bureau of Research, Memorandum No. 2, *Compulsory Labor in the U.S.S.R.,* May, 1931.
131. Lewisohn, Sam A., ibid.

Chapter VII. Industry

1. *Izvestia,* April 13, 1931.
2. Bron, S. G., *Soviet Economic Development and American Business,* pp. 64–65.
3. *Economic Review,* Oct. 1, 1930. Vol. V, No. 18–19, p. 394.
4. Levine, Isaac Don. *Red Smoke.* New York: Robert M. McBride & Co., 1932. Chap. II, pp. 22–31, and Chap. IV, pp. 43–55.
4[a]. Smith, George Otis, *The Strategy of Minerals.* New York: Appleton, 1919, p. 75.
5. Levine, ibid., p. 48.
6. Yugoff, ibid., pp. 24–25 and *Russia in Transition,* p. 503.
7. *Economic Handbook,* pp. 15 ff.
8. *Izvestia,* Feb. 5, 1931; also *N. Y. Times,* Feb. 6, 1931.
8[a]. Bureau of Research on Russian Economic Conditions, Memorandum No. 1, *Remarks on the Five-Year Plan,* May, 1931, p. 8.
9. *Ekonom. Zhisn,* March 10, 1931.
10. *Soviet Union Looks Ahead,* ibid., pp. 117 ff.
11. *Za Ind.,* Feb. 10, 1931.
12. Address to the Economic Conference of Industrial Managers, Moscow, June 23, 1931. *Izvestia,* July 5, 1931; *Soviet Union Review,* July and Aug., 1931, pp. 146–53; pamphlet by Joseph Stalin, "The New Russian Policy," Jonathan, Cape and Co., N. Y., 1931.
13. Duranty dispatch from Moscow, *N. Y. Times,* Aug. 13, 14, 1931.
14. Grady, W. H., in *N. Y. Evening Post,* July 8, 1931.
15. Wireless from Moscow, *N. Y. Times,* July 11, 1931.
16. Moscow dispatch, *N. Y. Times,* Aug. 4, 1931.
17. *Za Ind.,* Aug. 3, 1931.
18. Duranty dispatch from Moscow, *N. Y. Times,* Aug. 4, 1931.
18[a]. *N. Y. Times,* December 11, 1931.
18[b]. Bureau of Research, Memorandum No. 4, *The Balance of Payments and the Foreign Debt of the U.S.S.R.,* February, 1932, p. 12.
19. *Za Ind.,* Dec. 8, 18, 26, and 28, 1929.
20. Moscow dispatch to *N. Y. Times,* Jan. 26, 1931.
21. *Za Ind.,* July 5, 1930.
22. Associated Press dispatch from Moscow, May 28, 1932.
23. *Za Ind.,* March 27, 1930.
24. *Izvestia,* July 19, 1930.

25. *Za Ind.*, Aug. 22, 1930.
26. Duranty wireless from Moscow, *N. Y. Times*, Aug. 18, 1931.
27. Ferlin, Charles R., dispatch from Moscow, *N. Y. Sun*, June 12, 1931.
28. Moscow dispatch *N. Y. Times*, June 2, 1931.
29. Paris dispatch to the *Wall Street Journal*, Mar. 31, 1932.
30. U. S. Department of Commerce, Nov. 29, 1930.
31. *Za Ind.*, Sept. 27, 1930.
32. Moscow dispatch to *N. Y. Times*, Jan. 31, 1931.
33. *Ekonom. Zhisn*, April 1, 1931.
34. Circular of the Supreme Economic Council, Oct. 23, 1929.
35. Circular of the Supreme Economic Council and of the General Council of Trade Unions, Sept. 28, 1930. Vassiliev, N., "The Campaign of the Collective Agreements for 1929–30," in *Voprosy Truda*, 1930, No. 3 quoted in Zagorsky, ibid., pp. 128–29.
36. *Pravda*, May 7, 8, 9, and 10, 1931; *Za Ind.*, May 4 and 8, 1931.
37. *Za Ind.*, July 19, 1931.
38. *Pravda*, July 4, 1931; *Za Ind.*, July 6, 1931.
39. *Izvestia*, July 5, 1931; *Soviet Union Review*, July–Aug., 1931. Vol. IX, No. 7–8, 146–53.
40. *Ekonom. Zhisn*, Dec. 29, 1929.
41. *Za Ind.*, Aug. 17, 1931; also *N. Y. Times*, Aug. 18, 1931.
42. *Pravda*, May 7, 8, 9, 1931; *Za Ind.*, May 4 and 8, 1931.
43. *Za Ind.*, Sept. 19, 20, 23, 1930.
44. *Ekonom. Zhisn*, April 3, 1931.
45. *Za Ind.*, May 15, 1932.
46. Moscow dispatch *N. Y. Times*, Feb. 17, 1931.
47. *Pravda*, May 7, 8, 9, and 19, 1931; *Za Ind.*, May 4 and 8, 1931.
48. *Pravda*, April 30 and May 4, 1931.
49. *Za Ind.*, Mar. 8, 1931; *Izvestia*, Mar. 7, 1931.
50. *Ekonom. Zhisn*, Sept. 10, 1930.
51. *Za Ind.*, Sept. 19, and following dates, 1930.
52. *Za Ind.*, Jan. 3, 4, 1931.
53. *Ekonom. Zhisn*, April 3, 1931.
54. *Za Ind.*, Oct. 8, 1930.
55. *Za Ind.*, Sept. 27, 1930; *Izvestia*, June 14, 1931.
56. *Pravda*, July 4, 1931; *Za Ind.*, July 6, 1931.
57. *Za Ind.*, Jan. 7 and May 24, 1931.
58. *Za Ind.*, May 20, 1932; *Izvestia*, May 23, 1932.
59. *Pravda*, April 7, 1932.
60. *Pravda*, May 24, 1932.
61. *Pravda*, June 12, 13, 14, 1932.
62. *Za Ind.*, April 17, 1932.
63. *Za Ind.*, May 21, 1932.
64. *Za Ind.*, May 23, June 4; Associated Press dispatches from Moscow, April 18 and May 18, 1932; Moscow dispatch to *N. Y. Times*, June 23, 1932; *Pravda*, June 3, 1932.
65. *Izvestia*, Mar. 19, 1930.
66. Duranty dispatch from Moscow, *N. Y. Times*, May 6, 1931.
67. Moscow dispatch to *N. Y. Times*, Sept. 29, 1931.
68. Moscow cable to *N. Y. Times*, July 9, 1931.
69. *Pravda*, May 7, 8, 9, and 19, 1931; *Za Ind.*, May 4, 1931.
70. Moscow cable to the *Herald-Tribune*, April 26, 1932.
71. Associated Press dispatch from Moscow, June 21, 1932.
72. Duranty dispatch from Moscow, *N. Y. Times*, May 26, 1931.
73. *Izvestia*, Feb. 2, 4, 1930; *Za Ind.*, Feb. 6 and 7, 1930; *Ekonom. Zhisn*, Feb. 4 and 11, 1930.
74. *Za Ind.*, Sept. 19, 20, and 23, 1930.
75. Moscow dispatch *N. Y. Times*, June 5, 1931.
76. *Rabochaya Moskva*, May 10, quoted in Duranty dispatch *N. Y. Times*, May 11, 1931.
77. *Izvestia*, July 10, 1931.
78 *Za Ind.*, Jan. 24, Feb. 6 and 7, 1930; *Izvestia*, Feb. 2 and 4, 1930.
79. *Pravda*, May 7, 8, 9, and 19, 1931; *Za Ind.*, May 4, 8, 1931; *Ekonom. Zhisn*, April 8, 1931.
80. *Pravda*, May 7, 8, 9, and 19, 1931; *Za Ind.*, May 4 and 8, 1931.
81. Translated from "The Five-Year Plan" by Isaac Don Levine, in *Red Smoke*, p. 92.
82. Chamberlin, *Soviet Russia*, ibid., p. 148; Yugoff, ibid., pp. 26 and 287.

83. Moscow dispatch *N. Y. Times,* July 9, 1931.
84. *N. Y. Times,* Sept. 6, 1931.
85. *Soviet Union Yearbook,* pp. 452–53.
86. *Za Ind.,* Oct. 17, 1930.
87. *Za Ind.,* Oct. 17, 1930.
88. *Pravda,* May 25, 1931.
89. *Izvestia,* Feb. 2 and 4, 1930; *Ekonom. Zhisn,* Feb. 4 and 11, 1930; *Za Ind.,* Jan. 24, Feb. 6 and 7, 1930.
90. *Za Ind.,* July 9, 1930.
91. *Za Ind.,* Feb. 14, 1930.
92. *Za Ind.,* Mar. 8, 1931; *Izvestia,* Mar. 7, 1931.
93. *Ekonom. Zhisn,* April 8, 1931.
94. *Ekonom. Zhisn,* Dec. 11 and 24, 1929.
95. *Za Ind.,* July 9, 1930.
96. *Za Ind.,* Mar. 8, 1931; *Izvestia,* Mar. 7, 1931.
97. *Economic Review,* April 1, 1931. Vol. VI, No. 7, p. 149.
98. *Barrons,* Aug. 24, 1931.
99. *Za Ind.,* July 9, 1930.
100. *Pravda,* July 30 and 31, 1930.
101. *Pravda,* April 10 and 19, 1931.
102. *Za Ind.,* Sept. 19, 20, and 23, 1930.
103. *Izvestia,* Feb. 14, 1931.
104. *Za Ind.,* May 23, 1931.
105. *Pravda,* May 21, 1931.
106. *Za Ind.,* Nov. 4, 1930.
107. *Za Ind.,* July 9, 1930.
108. *Za Ind.,* Oct. 10, 1930.
109. *Za Ind.,* July 9, 1930.
110. *Izvestia,* Feb. 2, 4, 1930; *Za Ind.,* Jan. 24 and Feb. 6, 7, 1930; *Ekonom. Zhisn,* Feb. 4 and 11, 1930.
111. *Za Ind.,* Oct. 12, 1930.
112. *Izvestia,* July 5, 1931; *Soviet Union Review,* July and August, 1931, pp. 146–53.
113. *Ekonom. Zhisn,* April 1, 1931.
114. *Outline of Industry during 1927–28.* Moscow: State Publishing Company. p. 92.
115. *Soviet Union Review,* June, 1931. Vol. IX, No. 6, p. 140.
116. *Izvestia,* July 5, 1931; *Soviet Union Review,* July and August, 1931, pp. 146–53.

Chapter VIII. Transportation

1. *Economic Review,* Jan. 1, 1932.
2. *Economic Handbook,* p. 71.
3. *Soviet Union Yearbook,* p. 229. Figures for 1930 and 1931 from *Economic Review,* Jan. 1, 1932.
4. *Economic Handbook,* p. 70.
5. *Soviet Union Yearbook,* p. 227. Figures for 1930–32 from *Economic Handbook,* p. 68.
6. *Economic Review,* Jan. 1, 1932.
6[a]. *Wall Street Journal,* Paris dispatch, Sept. 8, 1932.
7. *Economic Handbook,* p. 68.
7[a]. *Wall Street Journal,* Paris dispatch, Sept. 8, 1932.
8. *Soviet Union Yearbook,* 1930, p. 229.
9. *Economic Review,* Feb. 1, 1932.
10. *Economic Handbook,* p. 70.
11. Levine, Isaac Don, *Red Smoke.* New York: McBride, 1932, p. 107.
12. Duranty, *N. Y. Times,* Oct. 7, 1930.
13. Levine, Isaac Don, ibid., p. 107.
14. Ellery Walker, *Herald-Tribune,* Jan. 10, 1932.
15. *Ekonom. Zhisn,* Mar. 3, 1931.
16. *Ekonom. Zhisn,* Aug. 9, 1930.
17. *Pravda,* Mar. 11, 25, 1932.
18. *Za Ind.,* Oct. 5, 1931.
19. *Soviet Union Review,* December, 1931, p. 250.

19[a]. *N. Y. Times,* Aug. 26, 1932.
20. *Economic Handbook,* p. 72.
21. *Economic Handbook,* p. 76.
22. *Economic Handbook,* p. 77.
23. *Economic Handbook,* p. 73.

Chapter IX. Trade—Foreign and Domestic

1. *Economic Handbook,* p. 109.
1[a]. Bureau of Research, Memorandum No. 4, *The Balance of Payments and the Foreign Debt of the U.S.S.R.,* February, 1932, pp. 3, 5.
1[b]. Ibid., p. 13.
2. Report from the Ottawa Conference, July 29, 1932.
2[a]. Bureau of Research, Memorandum No. 4, February, 1932, p. 10.
3. Article by Basil W. Delgass, formerly vice-president of Amtorg Trading Co., in the *Magazine of Wall Street,* Feb. 6, 1932.
4. *Economic Review,* July 15, 1932.
5. Cable from Frankfort-on-the-Main to *N. Y. Journal of Commerce,* July 30, 1932.
6. Paris dispatch, April 20, 1932.
6[a]. Bureau of Research, Memorandum No. 4, February, 1932, pp. 20–21.
7. The Whaley-Eaton Letter, March 22, 1932.
7[a]. Bureau of Research, Memorandum No. 4, February, 1932, pp. 15, 16.
8. *Soviet Union Yearbook,* p. 261.
9. Control figures for 1929–30. (In Russian) p. 22.
10. *Soviet Union Yearbook,* p. 262.
11. *Pravda,* Feb. 19, 1931.
12. *Soviet Union Yearbook,* section on "Internal Trade."
13. *Ekonom. Zhisn,* Mar. 15, 1930.
14. Associated Press dispatch from Moscow, June 17, 1932.
14[a]. *N. Y. Times,* August 26; *Sun,* September 21; *Herald-Tribune,* September 23, 1932.

Chapter X. Banking

1. Address to Central Executive Committee of U.S.S.R., Jan. 5, 1931.
2. Katzenellenbaum, S. S. "The Banking System in Russia," chapter in *Foreign Banking Systems.* Edited by H. P. Willis and B. H. Beckhart, New York: Henry Holt and Co., 1929.
3. *Soviet Union Yearbook,* pp. 425–26.
4. *Soviet Union Yearbook,* pp. 430–38. See also article on Prombank by the president, N. G. Tumanov, in *Economic Survey of State Bank,* Feb., 1932, Vol. VII, No. 2–3, pp. 1–5.
5. *Economic Survey, State Bank,* December, 1931. Vol. VI, No. 12.
6. *Economic Survey, State Bank,* April–May, 1932, Vol. VII, No. 4–5.
7. Bureau of Research, Memorandum No. 1, May, 1931, p. 8.
8. *Daily Investment News,* April 28, 1931.
9. Tokio dispatch to *N. Y. Times,* quoting the Tokio *Asahi.*
9[a]. Moscow dispatch, N. Y. *Herald-Tribune,* August 14; Paris dispatch, *Wall Street Journal,* September 16, 1932.
10. Fischer, Louis, in *The Nation* (New York), July 22, 1931.
11. *Economic Survey, State Bank,* December, 1930, Vol. V, No. 20.
12. *Economic Survey, State Bank,* January, 1931.
13. Report to the Central Executive Committee of the U.S.S.R., Jan. 5, 1931. *Izvestia,* Jan. 9, 1931; *Economic Survey,* Feb. 1, 1931, pp. 51–53.
14. Regulation No. 9, from the *Summary of Currency Regulations,* issued to travelers on their entry into the country.
15. Moscow dispatches in *N. Y. Times,* May 12 and June 11, 1931.
15[a]. Moscow dispatches in *N. Y. Times,* Sept. 3, 6, 1932.
16. Montevideo cable in *N. Y. Times,* Aug. 7, 1931.
17. Address to the Central Executive Committee of the U.S.S.R., Jan. 6, 1931. *Izvestia,* Jan. 9, 1931; *Economic Review,* Feb. 1, 1931, pp. 51–53.
18. Duranty cable, *N. Y. Times,* Aug. 7, 1931.

19. *Economic Survey, State Bank,* November and December, 1930. Vol. V. Nos. 19 and 20.
20. *Economic Survey, State Bank,* December, 1930. Vol. V, No. 20.
21. *Economic Survey, State Bank,* July, 1930. Vol. V. No. 12–13, pp. 1–3.
22. *Economic Review,* May 1, 1930, p. 174.
23. *Economic Review,* June 15, 1931. Vol. VI, No. 12, p. 268.
24. *Za Ind.,* May 27, 1931.
25. *Za Ind.,* May 20, 1931.
26. *Economic Survey, State Bank,* January, 1931. Vol. VI, No. 1.
27. *Economic Review,* June 15, 1931. Vol. VI, No. 12, p. 268.
28. *Izvestia,* June 16, 1931.

Chapter XI. The Budget

1. *Economic Handbook,* p. 87. Figure for unified financial plan, 1931, from *Economic Review,* Feb. 1931, p. 51.
2. *Economic Handbook,* p. 87.
3. Figures for the first three years are taken from the *Economic Review,* May 1, 1930 (Vol. V, No. 9, p. 178) and for the last two years from the same publication for April 1, 1931 (Vol. VI, No. 7, p. 147). A comparison of the estimated and actual budgets for 1928–29 will be found in the issue for Jan. 15, 1930 (Vol. V, No. 2, p. 33).
4. *Economic Survey, State Bank,* January, 1932, Vol. VII, No. 1, pp. 5 and 7.
5. Duranty dispatch from Moscow, in *N. Y. Times,* Dec. 30, 1931.
6. Report presented at the Central Executive Committee of the Soviet Union, Jan. 5, 1931. *Izvestia,* Jan. 9, 1931.
7. *Economic Review,* Feb. 1, 1931. Vol. VI, No. 3, pp. 51–53.
8. Report of G. T. Grinko, at Third Session of the Central Executive Committee. Quoted in *Economic Survey, State Bank,* January, 1931. Vol. VI, No. 1.
9. *Economic Review,* Feb. 1, 1931. Vol. VI, No. 3, p. 51. *Izvestia,* Jan. 12, 1931. Chamberlin, *Soviet Planned Economic Order,* pp. 234–37.
10. *Economic Review,* March 15, 1930. Vol. V, No. 6, pp. 98, 99.
11. *The Soviet Union Looks Ahead,* p. 169.
12. *The Five-Year Plan,* Vol. II, part 2, pp. 323, 325.
13. Decree of the Central Executive Committee and the Council of People's Commissars, Feb. 20, 1929.
14. *Economic Review,* June 15, 1930. Vol. V, No. 12.
15. *Izvestia,* Feb. 25, 1930.
16. *Izvestia,* Feb. 5, 1930.
17. G. T. Grinko, address of Jan. 5, 1931. *Izvestia,* Jan. 9, 1931; *Economic Review,* Feb. 1, 1931, Vol. VI, No. 3, pp. 51–53.
18. Decree of the Central Executive Committee and Council of People's Commissars, Sept. 27 and Oct. 28, 1929.
19. Decree of the Central Executive Committee and Council of People's Commissars, Dec. 16, 1929.
20. *Izvestia,* Sept. 11, 1930.
21. Associated Press dispatch from Moscow, May 25, 1931.
22. Decree of the Central Executive Committee and Council of People's Commissars, May 18, 1927.
23. *Soviet Union Yearbook,* 1930, p. 408.
24. *Economic Survey, State Bank,* September, 1930. Vol. V, No. 16–17, pp. 6–10.
25. *Ekonom. Zhisn,* June 26, 1930.
26. *Za Ind.,* June 10, 1932.
27. *Economic Survey, State Bank,* March 1, 1930. Vol. V, No. 4.
28. *Pravda,* Feb. 20 and 21, 1930; *Izvestia,* Feb. 26, 1930; *Ekonom. Zhisn,* Feb. 20 and March 11, 1930; *Za Ind.,* March 1 and 13, 1930.
29. *Izvestia,* Aug. 8, 1930.
30. *Ekonom. Zhisn,* June 24, 1930.
31. Moscow dispatches, in *N. Y. Times,* June 11, Aug. 7, 1931.
32. *Economic Survey, State Bank,* November, 1930. Vol. V, No. 19.
33. *Economic Survey, State Bank,* July, 1930. Vol. V, No. 12–13, pp. 3–6.

Chapter XII. Aims

1. LVIII, 5–7.
2. Friedman, Elisha M. Ed. *America and the New Era.* New York: E. P. Dutton & Co., 1920. See Todd, A. J., *Theories of Social Progress,* New York: Macmillan, 1918.
3. In foreword to *America and the New Era,* op. cit.

Chapter XIII. Methods

1. Yugoff, ibid., p. 31.
2. Kautsky, Karl. *Bolshevism at a Deadlock.* New York: Rand School Press, 1931. Pp. 114–18.
3. Associated Press dispatch, July 4, 1931.
3[a]. Strauss, Frederick, "The Railroads," in *Century Magazine,* March, 1928.
4. Kautsky, ibid., p. 17.
5. White, William A. *Outline of Psychiatry.* Washington: Nervous and Mental Disease Pub. Co., 1919. Pp. 117–21.
6. White, Andrew D. *History of the Warfare of Science with Theology.* New York: Appleton. Vol. I, p. 142.
7. See Fite, Warner, "Individualism in the New Social Order," Chap. VI in *America and the New Era,* Elisha M. Friedman, ed. New York: E. P. Dutton & Co., 1920.

Chapter XIV. Results

1. Brandeis, Louis D. *Other People's Money,* New York: Stokes, 1914, p. 188.
1[a]. *N. Y. Times,* May 8, 1932.
2. Dan, Th., quoted in Kautsky, ibid., pp. 123 and 135.
3. Kautsky, ibid., p. 120.
4. Essays and Addresses, pp. 243–44.
5. *Royal Economic Journal,* September, 1930. Vol. XL, 159, p. 440, reprinted in his book, p. 340.
6. Dan, Th., quoted in Kautsky, ibid., pp. 129–32.
7. *Pravda,* Mar. 2, 1930.
8. Address, "The One and the Many," at Southampton, N. Y., Aug. 31, 1930.
9. Duranty dispatch in *N. Y. Times,* Aug. 15, 1931.
10. Duranty dispatch in *N. Y. Times,* May 6, 1931.
11. *Soviet Russia,* p. 330.
12. *Harvard Economic Review,* "Soviet Russia," p. 332.
13. Eddy, Sherwood. *The Challenge of Russia.* New York: Farrar and Rinehart, 1931. P. 200.
14. Kautsky, ibid., pp. 93–94.
15. Vol. II, p. 769.

Chapter XV. Forecasts

1. Todd, Arthur James. *Theories of Social Progress.* New York: Macmillan, 1926. P. 112.
2. Quoted by Emil Ludwig, *Nineteenth Century Magazine,* October, 1930.
3. Kautsky, ibid., pp. 177–78.
4. Associated Press dispatch from Moscow, Feb. 8, 1931.
5. Farbman, M., ibid., p. 4.
6. *The Success of the Five-Year Plan.* New York: International Publishers, 1931. P. 58.
7. Kautsky, ibid., p. 133.
8. Duranty, Moscow dispatch in *N. Y. Times,* April 3, 1931.
9. *N. Y. Times,* Dec. 7, 1930.
10. *Izvestia,* Feb. 5, 1931; Associated Press dispatch, Feb. 5, 1931.
11. Chart No. 6, pp. 94, 95, *Conspectus of Business Cycles in Various Countries.*
12. Guido Enderis, Berlin cable to *N. Y. Times,* May 22, 1931.
13. Pasvolsky and Moulton. *Russian Debts and Russian Reconstruction.* New York: McGraw-Hill, 1924. Pp. 17–21.
14. Kautsky, ibid., p. 182.
15. *N. Y. Times,* May 25, 1931.
16. Chamberlin, W. H. *The Soviet Planned Economic Order.* Boston: World Peace Foundation, 1931. Pp. 163–164.

17. Dispatch from Istanbul, Aug. 4, 1932, in *N. Y. Times.*
17[a]. Miller, H. A. *Races, Nations, and Classes,* Philadelphia: Lippincott; 1924. An illuminating study of group conflict.
18. Kautsky, ibid., p. 130.
19. Kautsky, ibid., pp. 151 ff.
20. Kautsky, ibid., pp. 151–56. See also abstract by Joseph Shaplen, *N. Y. Times,* Nov. 30, 1930.
21. Kautsky, ibid., pp. 124, 143, 144, 146, 148, 151 and 153.
22. *N. Y. Times,* May 8, 1932.
23. Address at Southampton, L. I., Aug. 31, 1930.
24. *N. Y. Times,* July 31, 1932, sec. 2, p. 1.
25. Berlin dispatch, *N. Y. Times,* March 29, 1931.
26. *N. Y. Times,* Aug. 7, 8, 1931.
27. Duranty, Moscow dispatch in *N. Y. Times,* Feb. 14, 1931.
28. *N. Y. Times,* Feb. 14, 1931.

Chapter XVI. The Issues

1. Ledoc, K. J., "Shattering Soviet Idols," *Current History, N. Y. Times,* May, 1931. P. 198.
2. Arnot, R. P. *Soviet Russia and Her Neighbors.* Quoted by Fischer in *Why Recognize Russia?* p. 267.
3. *N. Y. Times,* July 7, 1930.
4. Duranty, Moscow wireless to *N. Y. Times,* May 15, 1931.
5. Duranty, *N. Y. Times,* Dec. 1, 1930.
6. *Document Listing the Hostile Activities of the Soviet Government and the Third Internationale against Great Britain.* London, 1927. Cmd. 2874. Comment of Ramsay Macdonald and other members of the Cabinet appeared in the London newspapers. May 25, 1927, *Daily Express.*
7. *N. Y. Times,* Aug. 27, 1930.
8. *Foreign Affairs,* October, 1930.
9. Duranty, wireless from Moscow to *N. Y. Times,* April 25, 1931.
10. *N. Y. Times,* Dec. 1, 1930.
11. Moscow dispatch to *N. Y. Times,* Feb. 6, 1931.
12. Pasvolsky, G. A., "The Russian National Debt," *The Russian Economist,* Sept.–Oct., London, 1920, p. 40. Quoted in Pasvolsky and Moulton, *Russian Debts and Russian Reconstruction,* McGraw-Hill, 1924. Pp. 15–17.
13. Ohl, Prof. P. V. *Foreign Capital in Russia.* (In Russian.) Petrograd: Institute of Economic Research, 1922. Quoted in Pasvolsky and Moulton, ibid., p. 17.
14. Pasvolsky and Moulton, ibid., pp. 20–21.
15. Pasvolsky and Moulton, ibid., pp. 16 and 182.
16. Fischer, Louis, *The Soviet in World Affairs.* New York: Cape and Smith, 1930. Pp. 167 and 172.
17. *Pravda,* June 29, 1930.
18. *British Parliamentary Papers,* Cmd. 1667, 1724. Quoted in Pasvolsky and Moulton, ibid., pp. 199–205, 209–220, 221–228, 231.
19. *N. Y. Times,* Dec. 1, 1930.
20. Fischer, Louis, *Why Recognize Russia?* p. 250.
21. Duranty cable from Moscow, *N. Y. Times,* Feb. 8, 1931.
22. Duranty cable from Moscow, *N. Y. Times,* Mar. 5, 1931.
23. Duranty, *N. Y. Times,* May 5, 1931.
24. *Soviet Union Review,* April, 1931. Vol. IX, No. 4, pp. 74–80.
25. *N. Y. Times,* April 26, 1931.

Chapter XVII: Shall We Recognize Russia?

1. *International Conciliation,* No. 155, pp. 5–11.
2. "Our Relations to the Nations of the Western Hemisphere," Charles E. Hughes, Princeton, 1928.
3. *Foreign Affairs,* October, 1930. Pp. 39, 40.
4. *Current History, N. Y. Times,* September, 1930, pp. 1072–79.
5. *Foreign Affairs,* January, 1931, p. 275.

6. Quoted by Fischer, *Why Recognize Russia?* p. 178.
7. Moore, John Basset. Address before the Bar Association of the City of New York, "Candor and Common Sense," Dec. 4, 1930.
8. *Foreign Affairs,* January, 1931, pp. 266–67.
9. *Foreign Affairs,* January, 1931, pp. 266–67 and 204–22. See also Moore, John Basset, *Digest of International Law,* 1906, Vol. I, pp. 72 *et seq.* and 206 *et seq.;* Houghton, W. D., *De Facto Governments,* 1929; Potter, Pittman B., "Nature of American Foreign Policy," *American Journal of International Law,* 53, 55, 61, 71, 1927.
10. Wilson, G. G. *Handbook of International Law.* 2nd ed. P. 21.
11. Berdahl, Clarence H., "The Power of Recognition," in *American Journal of International Law,* Vol. XIV, p. 519.
12. Address before the Bar Association of the City of New York, Dec. 4, 1930.
13. Hervey, John G. The *Legal Effects of Recognition in International Law.* Philadelphia: University of Pennsylvania Press, 1928. Pp. 115 *et seq* and 150 *et seq.*
14. Quoted in Hervey, ibid., pp. 78–81.
15. *Jefferson to Pinckney,* Jefferson's Works, Vol. III, p. 500. Quoted in the address of John Basset Moore previously cited.
16. Moore, John Basset. Address before the Bar Association of the City of New York, ibid., p. 28.
17. Cole, Taylor. *Recognition Policy of the United States.* Univ. of Louisiana Press, 1928. Pp. 23–27.
18. Moore, *Digest,* ibid., Vol. I, p. 122.
19. Moore, *Digest,* ibid., Vol. I, p. 124.
20. Moore, *Digest,* ibid., Vol. I, p. 142.
21. Cole, ibid., pp. 28 *et seq.*
22. *Seward's Diplomatic Correspondence,* 1866, Vol. 2, p. 617.
23. *Seward's Diplomatic Correspondence,* ibid., p. 863.
24. Moore, *Digest,* ibid., Vol. I, p. 139, 162.
25. Cole, ibid., p. 74.
26. *Current History,* Vol. 14, p. 710.
27. *Cole,* ibid., pp. 74 *et seq.*
28. *Foreign Relations of the United States,* 1917, p. 1211. (Official State Dept. publication.) quoted by Cole, ibid., pp. 62–63.
29. Stimson, Henry L. "The United States and Other American Republics." Address before the Council on Foreign Relations, New York City, Feb. 6, 1931.
30. *Foreign Relations of the United States,* 1913, p. 100.
31. Quoted from Moore's *Digest of International Law,* Vol. I, p. 124.
32. Hughes, Charles E., "Our Relations to the Nations of the Western Hemisphere," Princeton, 1928, p. 38.
33. *Foreign Affairs,* January, 1931, pp. 266–67.
34. Moore, "Candor and Common Sense," ibid., p. 21.
35. Dennis, Lawrence, in *Foreign Affairs,* January, 1931.
36. Moore, *Digest,* ibid., Vol. 1, p. 183.
37. *Foreign Relations of the United States,* 1913. P. 7.
38. Moore, "Candor and Common Sense," ibid., p. 23.
39. Moore, ibid., pp. 24–25.
40. Dennis, Lawrence, in *Foreign Affairs,* January, 1931, p. 212.
41. Dennis, ibid., p. 206.
42. Dennis, ibid., p. 207.
43. Dennis, ibid., p. 208.
44. Moore, ibid., pp. 26 and 30.
45. Dennis, ibid., pp. 208, 214, 216.
46. Stimson, Henry L., address before the Council on Foreign Relations, Feb. 6, 1931.
47. Address before the American Society of International Law, Washington, April 24, 1931.
48. Dennis, ibid., p. 215.
49. Cole, ibid., p. 89.
50. *Current History, N. Y. Times,* September, 1930. Vol. XXXII, No. 6, pp. 1065–78.
51. Address at the School of Business of Columbia University, New York, April 27, 1931.
52. Address in the U. S. Senate, Mar. 2, 1931.
53. Cravath, ibid., p. 275.
54. Scheffer, Paul, "American Recognition of Russia," in *Foreign Affairs,* October, 1930, p. 41.
55. Cravath, ibid., p. 274.

56. Scheffer, ibid., p. 36.
57. Quoted by Fischer, ibid., p. 179.
58. Cravath, ibid., p. 273.
59. Moore's *Digest of International Law,* Vol. I, p. 235.
60. Mr. Seward, Secretary of State, to Mr. Culver, Mar. 9, 1863, M.S. Inst. Venez., I 266.
61. Seward to Culver, Oct. 21, 1863. M.S. Inst. Venez., I 288.
62. Wm. Hay, Secretary of State, to Mr. Loomis, Minister to Venezuela, Nov. 18, 1899. For. Rel. 1899, 809.
63. Mr. Seward, Secretary of State, to Mr. Partridge, Minister to Salvador, Jan. 2, 1864. M.S. Inst. American States, Salvador XVI, 399.
64. Annual Message of President Hayes, Dec. 3, 1877.
65. Mr. Seward, Secretary of State, to Mr. Romero, Mexican Minister, Aug. 9, 1865. Dip. Cor. 1865, III 486–488.
66. Mr. Gresham, Secretary of State, to Mr. Baker, Minister to Nicaragua, Aug. 15, 1893. For. Rel. 1893, 212.
67. Goebel, Julius, *The Theory of Recognition,* p. 63.
68. Moore, *Digest,* ibid., Vol. I, pp. 206 *et seq.* Also Hudson, Manley O., ibid., and Wilson, G. G., ibid., p. 21.
69. *Parliamentary Debates,* House of Commons, Official Report, Fifth Series, Vol. 229, p. 465, July 5, 1929.
70. In a letter to the author, which the writer requested should be kept confidential.
71. Goebel, Julius. *Theory of Recognition,* ibid., pp. 65–67.
72. Hyde, C. C. *International Law,* Vol. I, pp. 58–59; Cole, ibid., p. 3.
73. Moore, *Digest,* ibid., Vol. I, pp. 129–30, 160 *et seq.*
73[a]. *American Journal of International Law,* October, 1931. Vol. 25, Supplement, p. 203.
73[b]. Ibid., October, 1931, p. 719.
74. *Yale Law Journal,* 31, 469, March, 1922.
75. Cited by Moore, *Digest,* Vol. I, p. 231.
76. *American Journal of International Law,* Vol. 18, pp. 147, 249.
77. *American Journal of International Law,* Vol. 18.

Chapter XVIII. Conclusions

1. Moore, Address before N. Y. Bar Association, ibid., p. 27.
2. Dennis, Lawrence, in *Foreign Affairs,* January, 1931, p. 215.
3. *N. Y. Evening Post,* July 22, 1931.
4. *N. Y. Evening Post,* July 14, 1931.
5. *Soviet Union Review,* June, 1931, Vol. IX, No. 6, p. 123.
6. Associated Press cable from Geneva, May 18, 1931.

Weights and Measures

Russian

1 pood = 36 pounds avoirdupois
1 vedro = 2.7 gallons
1 verst = 0.66 miles
1 dessiatine = 2.7 acres
1 zolotnik = 65.83 grains
1 dolya = 0.68 grains

Metric

1 liter = 1.0567 quarts
1 kilogram = 2.2046 pounds
1 centner = 220.46 pounds
1 metric ton = 2,204.6 pounds
1 meter = 39.37 inches
1 kilometer = 0.621 miles
1 square meter = 10.764 square feet
1 hectare = 2.471 acres
1 square kilometer = 0.3856 square miles

Currency

1 kopek = .01 of a ruble
1 (gold) ruble at par = 51.46 cents U. S. currency
1 chervonetz = 10 gold rubles, at par $5.146

INDEX OF PERSONS

SUBJECT INDEX

See Index to Persons for complete list of references to persons

For Product Safety Concerns and Information please contact our EU representative GPSR@taylorandfrancis.com Taylor & Francis Verlag GmbH, Kaufingerstraße 24, 80331 München, Germany